Discovering Computer Science

Chapman & Hall/CRC
Textbooks in Computing

Series Editors
John Impagliazzo
Andrew McGettrick

Pascal Hitzler, Markus Krötzsch, and Sebastian Rudolph, Foundations of Semantic Web Technologies

Henrik Bærbak Christensen, Flexible, Reliable Software: Using Patterns and Agile Development

John S. Conery, Explorations in Computing: An Introduction to Computer Science

Lisa C. Kaczmarczyk, Computers and Society: Computing for Good

Mark Johnson, A Concise Introduction to Programming in Python

Paul Anderson, Web 2.0 and Beyond: Principles and Technologies

Henry Walker, The Tao of Computing, Second Edition

Ted Herman, A Functional Start to Computing with Python

Mark Johnson, A Concise Introduction to Data Structures Using Java

David D. Riley and Kenny A. Hunt, Computational Thinking for the Modern Problem Solver

Bill Manaris and Andrew R. Brown, Making Music with Computers: Creative Programming in Python

John S. Conery, Explorations in Computing: An Introduction to Computer Science and Python Programming

Jessen Havill, Discovering Computer Science: Interdisciplinary Problems, Principles, and Python Programming

Efrem G. Mallach, Information Systems: What Every Business Student Needs to Know

Iztok Fajfar, Start Programming Using HTML, CSS, and JavaScript

Mark C. Lewis and Lisa L. Lacher, Introduction to Programming and Problem-Solving Using Scala, Second Edition

Aharon Yadin, Computer Systems Architecture

Mark C. Lewis and Lisa L. Lacher, Object-Orientation, Abstraction, and Data Structures Using Scala, Second Edition

Henry M. Walker, Teaching Computing: A Practitioner's Perspective

Efrem G. Mallach, Information Systems:What Every Business Student Needs to Know, Second Edition

Jessen Havill, Discovering Computer Science: Interdisciplinary Problems, Principles, and Python Programming, Second Edition

For more information about this series please visit:

https://www.crcpress.com/Chapman--HallCRC-Textbooks-in-Computing/book-series/CANDHTEXCO
MSER?page=2&order=pubdate&size=12&view=list&status=published,forthcoming

Discovering Computer Science
Interdisciplinary Problems, Principles, and Python Programming
Second Edition

Jessen Havill

CRC Press
Taylor & Francis Group
Boca Raton London New York

CRC Press is an imprint of the
Taylor & Francis Group, an **informa** business

A CHAPMAN & HALL BOOK

Second edition published 2021
by CRC Press
2 Park Square, Milton Park, Abingdon, Oxon, OX14 4RN

and by CRC Press
6000 Broken Sound Parkway NW, Suite 300, Boca Raton, FL 33487-2742

British Library Cataloguing-in-Publication Data
A catalogue record for this book is available from the British Library

---

Library of Congress Cataloging-in-Publication Data

Names: Havill, Jessen, author.
Title: Discovering computer science : interdisciplinary problems, principles, and Python programming / Jessen Havill.
Description: Second edition. | Boca Raton : CRC Press, 2021. | Series: Chapman & Hall/CRC press textbooks in computing | Includes bibliographical references and index.
Identifiers: LCCN 2020030144 | ISBN 9780367472498 (paperback) | ISBN 9780367613358 (hardback) | ISBN 9781003037149 (ebook)
Subjects: LCSH: Computer science--Textbooks. | Python (Computer program language)--Textbooks.
Classification: LCC QA76 .H3735 2021 | DDC 005.13/3--dc23
LC record available at https://lccn.loc.gov/2020030144

ISBN: 9780367613358 (hbk)
ISBN: 9780367472498 (pbk)
ISBN: 9781003037149 (ebk)

Typeset in Computer Modern font
by Cenveo Publisher Services

Contents

---

*Sections with *** in lieu of a page number are available on the book website.

Preface

I N my view, an introductory computer science course should strive to accomplish three things. First, it should demonstrate to students how computing has become a powerful mode of inquiry, and a vehicle of discovery, in a wide variety of disciplines. This orientation is also inviting to students of the natural and social sciences, and the humanities, who increasingly benefit from an introduction to computational thinking, beyond the limited "black box" recipes often found in manuals and "Computing for X" books. Second, the course should engage students in computational problem solving, and lead them to discover the power of abstraction, efficiency, and data organization in the design of their solutions. Third, the course should teach students how to implement their solutions as computer programs. In learning how to program, students more deeply learn the core principles, and experience the thrill of seeing their solutions come to life.

Unlike most introductory computer science textbooks, which are organized around programming language constructs, I deliberately lead with interdisciplinary problems and techniques. This orientation is more interesting to a more diverse audience, and more accurately reflects the role of programming in problem solving and discovery. A computational discovery does not, of course, originate in a programming language feature in search of an application. Rather, it starts with a compelling problem which is modeled and solved algorithmically, by leveraging abstraction and prior experience with similar problems. Only then is the solution implemented as a program.

Like most introductory computer science textbooks, I introduce programming skills in an incremental fashion, and include many opportunities for students to practice them. The topics in this book are arranged to ease students into computational thinking, and encourage them to incrementally build on prior knowledge. Each chapter focuses on a general class of problems that is tackled by new algorithmic techniques and programming language features. My hope is that students will leave the course, not only with strong programming skills, but with a set of problem solving strategies and simulation techniques that they can apply in their future work, whether or not they take another computer science course.

I use Python to introduce computer programming for two reasons. First, Python's intuitive syntax allows students to focus on interesting problems and powerful principles, without unnecessary distractions. Learning how to think algorithmically is hard enough without also having to struggle with a non-intuitive syntax. Second, the expressiveness of Python (in particular, low-overhead lists and dictionaries) expands tremendously the range of accessible problems in the introductory course.

Teaching with Python over the last fifteen years has been a revelation; introductory computer science has become fun again.

Changes in the second edition

In this comprehensive, cover-to-cover update, some sections were entirely rewritten while others saw only minor revisions. Here are the highlights:

Problem solving   The new first chapter, *How to Solve It*, sets the stage by focusing on Polya's elegant four-step problem solving process, adapted to a computational framework. I introduce informal pseudocode, functional decomposition, hand-execution with informal trace tables, and testing, practices that are now carried on throughout the book. The introduction to Python (formally Chapter 2) is integrated into this framework. Chapter 7, *Designing Programs*, from the first edition has been eliminated, with that material spread out more naturally among Chapters 1, 5, and 6 in the second edition.

Chapter 2, *Visualizing Abstraction* (based on the previous Chapter 3), elaborates on the themes in Chapter 1, and their implementations in Python, introducing turtle graphics, functions, and loops. The new Chapter 3, *Inside a Computer* (based on the previous Sections 1.4 and 2.5), takes students on a brief excursion into the simple principles underlying how computers work.

Online materials   To reduce the size of the printed book, we have moved some sections and all of the projects online. These sections are marked in the table of contents with ***. Online materials are still indexed in the main book for convenience.

Exercises   I've added exercises to most sections, bringing the total to about 750. Solutions to exercises marked with an asterisk are available online for both students and self-learners.

Digital humanities   The interdisciplinary problems in the first edition were focused primarily in the natural and social sciences. In this edition, especially in Chapters 1, 6, and 7, we have added new material on text analysis techniques commonly used in the "digital humanities."

Object-oriented design   Chapter 12 begins with a new section to introduce object-oriented design in a more concrete way through the development of an agent-based simulation of a viral epidemic. The following sections flesh out more details on how to implement polymorphic operators and collection classes.

Book website

Online materials for this book are available at

https://www.discoveringCS.net.

Here you will find

- additional "optional" sections, marked with an asterisk in the main text,
- over thirty interdisciplinary programming projects,
- solutions to selected exercises,
- programs and data files referenced in the text, exercises, and projects, and
- pointers for further exploration and links to additional documentation.

To students

Active learning   Learning how to solve computational problems and implement them as computer programs requires daily practice. Like an athlete, you will get out of shape and fall behind quickly if you skip it. There are no shortcuts. Your instructor is there to help, but he or she cannot do the work for you.

With this in mind, it is important that you type in and try the examples throughout the text, and then go beyond them. Be curious! There are numbered "Reflection" questions throughout the book that ask you to stop and think about, or apply, something that you just read. Often, the question is answered in the book immediately thereafter, so that you can check your understanding, but peeking ahead will rob you of an important opportunity.

Further discovery   There are many opportunities to delve into topics more deeply. "Tangent" boxes scattered throughout the text briefly introduce related, but more technical or applied, topics. For the most part, these are not strictly required to understand what comes next, but I encourage you to read them anyway. In the "Summary and Further Discovery" section of each chapter, you can find both a high-level summary of the chapter and additional pointers to explore chapter topics in more depth.

Exercises and projects   At the end of most sections are several programming exercises that ask you to further apply concepts from that section. Often, the exercises assume that you have already worked through all of the examples in that section. Solutions to the starred exercises are available on the book website. There are also more involved projects available on the book website that challenge you to solve a variety of interdisciplinary problems.

No prerequisites   The book assumes no prior knowledge of computer science. However, it does assume a modest comfort with high school algebra. In optional sections, trigonometry is occasionally mentioned, as is the idea of convergence to a limit, but these are not relevant to understanding the main topics in the book.

Have fun!   Programming and problem solving should be a fun, creative activity. I hope that this book sparks your curiosity and love of learning, and that you enjoy the journey as much as I have enjoyed writing this book.

To instructors

This book is appropriate for a traditional CS1 course for majors, a CS0 course for non-majors (at a slower pace and omitting more material), or a targeted introductory computing course for students in the natural sciences, social sciences, or humanities.

The approach is gentle and holistic, introducing programming concepts in the context of interdisciplinary problems. We start with problem-solving, featuring pseudocode and hand-execution with trace tables, and carry these techniques forward, especially in the first half of the book.

Problem focus   Most chapters begin with an interesting problem, and new concepts and programming techniques are introduced in the context of solving it. As new techniques are introduced, students are frequently challenged to re-solve old problems in different ways. They are also encouraged to reuse their previous functions as components in later programs.

Reflection questions, exercises, and projects   "Reflection" questions are embedded in every section to encourage active reading. These may also be assigned as "reading questions" before class. The end-of-section exercises are appropriate for regular home-work, and some more complex ones may form the basis of longer-term assignments. The book website also hosts a few dozen interdisciplinary projects that students may work on independently or in pairs over a longer time frame. I believe that projects like these are crucial for students to develop both problem solving skills and an appreciation for the many fascinating applications of computer science.

Additional instructor resources   All of the reflection questions and exercises are available to instructors as Jupyter notebooks. Solutions to all exercises and projects are also available. Please visit the publisher's website to request access.

Python coverage   This book is not intended to be a Python manual. Some features of the language were intentionally omitted because they would have muddled the core problem solving focus or are not commonly found in other languages that students may see in future CS courses (e.g., simultaneous swap, chained comparisons, `zip`, `enumerate` in `for` loops).

Topic coverage   There is more in this book than can be covered in a single semester, giving instructors the opportunity to tailor the content to their particular situation

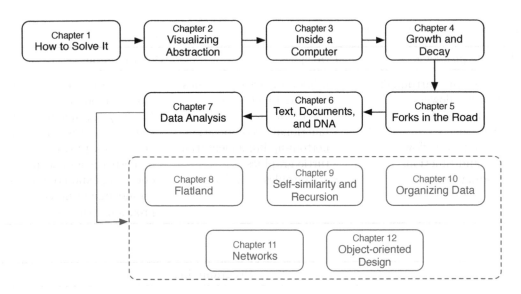

Figure 1 An overview of chapter dependencies.

and interests. As illustrated in Figure 1, Chapters 1–7 form the core of the book, and should be covered sequentially. The remaining chapters can be covered, partially or entirely, at your discretion, although I would expect that most instructors will cover at least parts of Chapters 8–10, and 12 if the course covers object-oriented design. Chapter 11 introduces social network graphs and small-world and scale-free networks as additional powerful applications of dictionaries, and may come any time after Chapter 7. Sections marked with an asterisk are optional, in the sense that they are not assumed for future sections in that chapter. When exercises and projects depend on optional sections, they are also marked with an asterisk, and the dependency is stated at the beginning of the project.

Chapter outlines The following tables provide brief overviews of what is available in each chapter. Each table's three columns, reflecting the three parts of the book's subtitle, provide three lenses through which to view the chapter.

1 How to Solve It

Sample problems	Principles	Programming
• reading level	• problems, input/output	• `int`, `float`, `str` types
• counting syllables, words	• functional abstraction	• arithmetic
• sphere volume	• functional decomposition	• assignment
• digital music	• top-down design	• variable names
• search engines	• bottom-up implementation	• calling built-in functions
• GPS devices	• algorithms and programs	• using strings
• phone trees	• pseudocode	• string operators
• wind chill	• names as references	• `print` and `input`
• compounding interest	• trace tables	
• Mad Libs	• constant- vs. linear-time	

2 Visualizing Abstraction

Sample problems	Principles	Programming
• visualizing earthquakes • drawing flowers • random walks • ideal gas • groundwater flow • demand functions • reading level	• using abstract data types • creating functional abstractions • functional decomposition • bottom-up implementation • turtle graphics • trace tables with loops	• using classes and objects • `turtle` module • `for` loops (`range` and lists) • using and writing functions • `return` vs. `print` • namespaces and scope • docstrings and comments • self-documenting code • program structure

3 Inside a Computer

Principles	Programming
• computer organization • machine language • binary representations • computer arithmetic • finite precision, error propagation • Boolean logic, truth tables, logic gates • Turing machines, finite state machines	• `int` and `float` types • arithmetic errors • true vs. floor division

4 Growth and Decay

Sample problems	Principles	Programming
• population models • network value • demand and profit • loans and investing • bacterial growth • radiocarbon dating • epidemics (SIR, SIS) • diffusion models	• accumulators • list accumulators • data visualization • conditional iteration • classes of growth • continuous models • accuracy vs. time • numerical approximation	• `for` loops, `range` • format strings • `matplotlib.pyplot` • appending to lists • `while` loops

5 Forks in the Road

Sample problems	Principles	Programming
• random walks • Monte Carlo simulation • guessing games • polling and sampling • particle escape	• random number generators • simulating probabilities • flag variables • using distributions • DeMorgan's laws • defensive programming • pre- and post-conditions • unit testing	• `random` module • `if/elif/else` • comparison operators • Boolean operators • short circuit evaluation • predicate functions • `assert`, `isinstance` • catching exceptions • histograms • `while` loops

6 Text, Documents, and DNA

Sample problems	Principles	Programming
• text analysis	• functional decomposition	• `str` class and methods
• word frequency trends	• unit testing	• iterating over strings, lists
• checksums	• ASCII, Unicode	• indexing and slicing
• concordances	• linear-time algorithms	• iterating over indices
• dot plots, plagiarism	• time complexity	• creating a module
• congressional votes	• linear search	• text files and the web
• genomics	• string accumulators	• `break`
		• nested loops

7 Data Analysis

Sample problems	Principles	Programming
• word, bigram frequencies	• histograms	• `list` class
• smoothing data	• hash tables	• indexing and slicing
• 100-year floods	• tabular data files	• list operators and methods
• traveling salesman	• efficient algorithm design	• reading CSV files
• meteorite sites	• linear regression	• modifying lists in place
• zebra migration	• k-means clustering	• list parameters
• tumor diagnosis	• heuristics	• tuples
• supply and demand		• list comprehensions
• voting methods		• dictionaries

8 Flatland

Sample problems	Principles	Programming
• earthquake data	• 2-D data	• lists of lists
• Game of Life	• cellular automata	• nested loops
• image filters	• digital images	• 2-D data in a dictionary
• racial segregation	• color models	
• ferromagnetism		
• dendrites		
• epidemics		
• tumor growth		

9 Self-similarity and Recursion

Sample problems	Principles	Programming
• fractals	• self-similarity	• writing recursive functions
• cracking passwords	• recursion	• divide and conquer
• Tower of Hanoi	• linear search	• backtracking
• maximizing profit	• recurrence relations	
• navigating a maze	• divide and conquer	
• Lindenmayer systems	• depth-first search	
• gerrymandering	• grammars	
• percolation		

10   Organizing Data

Sample problems	Principles	Programming
• spell check • querying data sets	• binary search • quadratic-time sorting • parallel lists • merge sort • recurrence relations • intractability, P=NP?	• nested loops • writing recursive functions

11   Networks

Sample problems	Principles	Programming
• social media, web graphs • diffusion of ideas • epidemics • Oracle of Bacon	• graphs • adjacency list, matrix • breadth-first search • queues • shortest paths • depth-first search • small-world networks • scale-free networks • uniform random graphs	• dictionaries

12   Object-oriented Design

Sample problems	Principles	Programming
• epidemic simulation • data sets • genomic sequences • rational numbers • flocking behavior • slime mold aggregation	• abstract data types • encapsulation • polymorphism • data structures • stacks • hash tables • agent-based simulation • swarm intelligence	• object-oriented design • writing classes • special methods • overriding operators • modules

Software assumptions

To follow along in this book and complete the exercises, you will need to have installed Python 3.6 or later on your computer, and have access to IDLE or another programming environment. The book also assumes that you have installed the `matplotlib.pyplot` and `numpy` modules. The easiest way to get this software is to install the free open source Anaconda distribution from `http://www.anaconda.com`.

Errata

While I (and my students) have ferreted out many errors, readers will inevitably find more. You can find an up-to-date list of errata on the book website. If you find an error in the text or have another suggestion, please let me know at `havill@denison.edu`.

Acknowledgments

In addition to those who provided their support and expertise for the first edition, I wish to thank Janet Davis (Whitman College), Jim Deverick (The College of William and Mary), David Goodwin (Denison University), and Ashwin Lall (Denison University) for their valuable feedback on drafts of the second edition.

I would also like to thank Dee Ghiloni, Mary Lucas-Miller, and Tony Silveira for their steadfast support, Mike Brady and my Data Analytics colleagues for reminding me how much fun it can be to learn new things, and the Book Group for reminding me to not take life too seriously. A Bowen Fellowship awarded by Denison University gave me the time needed to complete this project.

Finally, my family has once again provided me with seemingly infinite patience and love during this intensive period of writing. I am an extraordinarily lucky husband and father.

About the author

Jessen Havill is a Professor of Computer Science at Denison University. He has been teaching courses across the computer science curriculum for almost thirty years, and was awarded the College's highest teaching honor, the Charles A. Brickman Teaching Excellence Award, in 2013. Although his primary expertise is in the development and analysis of online algorithms, Dr. Havill has spent many years collaborating with colleagues across the curriculum to develop interdisciplinary academic opportunities for students. From 2016–2019, he became the founding Director of Denison University's interdisciplinary Data Analytics program. Dr. Havill earned his bachelor's degree from Bucknell University and his Ph.D. in computer science from The College of William and Mary.

CHAPTER 1

How to Solve It

We need to do away with the myth that computer science is about computers. Computer science is no more about computers than astronomy is about telescopes, biology is about microscopes or chemistry is about beakers and test tubes. Science is not about tools, it is about how we use them and what we find out when we do.

Michael R. Fellows and Ian Parberry
Computing Research News (1993)

It has often been said that a person does not really understand something until after teaching it to someone else. Actually a person does not really understand something until after teaching it to a computer, i.e., expressing it as an algorithm.

Donald E. Knuth
American Scientist (1973)

COMPUTERS now touch almost every facet of our daily lives, whether we are consciously aware of them or not. Computers have changed the way we learn, communicate, shop, travel, receive healthcare, and entertain ourselves. They are embedded in virtually everything, from major feats of engineering like airplanes, spaceships, and factories to everyday items like microwaves, cameras, and tooth-brushes. In addition, all of our critical infrastructure—utilities, transportation, finance, communication, healthcare, law enforcement—relies upon computers.

Since computers are the most versatile tools ever invented, it should come as no surprise that they are also employed throughout academia in the pursuit of new knowledge. Social scientists use computational models to better understand social networks, epidemics, population dynamics, markets, and auctions. Humanists use computational tools to gain insight into literary trends, authorship of ancient texts, and the macroscopic significance of historical records. Artists are increasingly incorporating digital technologies into their compositions and performances. Natural

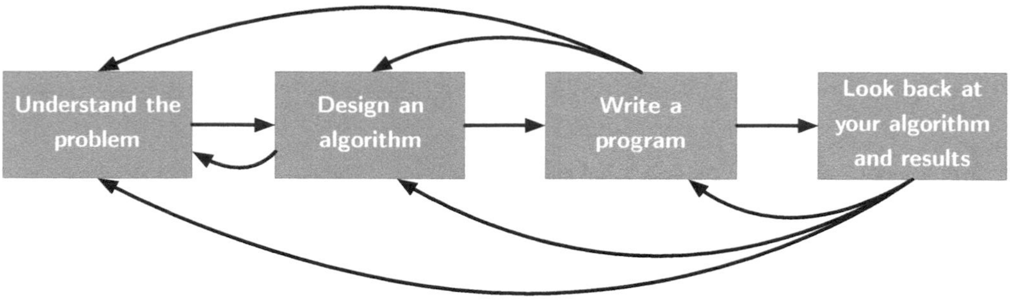

Figure 1.1 A simplified view of the problem solving process.

scientists use computers to collect and analyze immense quantities of data to make discoveries in environmental science, genomics, particle physics, neuroscience, pharmacology, and medicine.

But computers are neither productive nor consequential on their own. All of the computers now driving civilization, for good or ill, were taught by humans. Computers are amplifiers of human ingenuity. Without us, they are just dumb machines.

The goal of this book is to empower *you* to teach computers to solve problems and make discoveries. Computational problem solving is a process that you will find both familiar and new. We all solve problems every day and employ a variety of strategies in doing so. Some of these strategies, like breaking big problems into smaller, more manageable ones, are also fundamental to solving problems with a computer. Where computational problem solving is different stems from computers' lack of intellect and intuition. Computers will only do what you tell them to and nothing more. They cannot tolerate ambiguity or intuit your intentions. Computational problem solving, by necessity, must be more precise and intentional than you may be used to. The payoff though, paraphrasing Donald Knuth[1], is that teaching a computer to do something can also dramatically deepen our understanding of that thing.

The problem solving process that we will outline in this chapter is inspired by *How to Solve It*, a short book written by mathematician George Polya [50] in 1945. Polya's problem solving framework, having withstood the test of time, consists of four steps:

1. *First, understand the problem. What is the unknown? What are the data? What is the condition?*

2. *Second, devise a plan to solve the problem.*

3. *Third, carry out your plan, checking each step.*

4. *Fourth, look back. Check the result. Can you derive the result differently?*

These four steps, with some modifications, can be applied just as well to computational problem solving, as illustrated in Figure 1.1. In the first step, we make

---

[1]You can learn more about Donald Knuth at the end of this chapter.

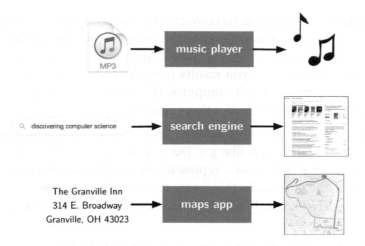

Figure 1.2 Some examples of computational problems.

sure that we understand the problem to be solved. In the second step, we devise an *algorithm*, a sequence of steps to solve the problem. In the third step, we translate our algorithm into a correct *program* that can be carried out by a computer. We will be using a programming language called Python throughout this book to write programs. Finally, in the fourth step, we look back on our results and ask whether we can improve them or the algorithm that derived them. Notice that this process is often not linear. Work on one step can refine our understanding of a previous step and nudge us backward, not unlike the process of writing a paper.

This chapter serves as a framework for your learning throughout the rest of the book. Each subsequent chapter will flesh out aspects of these steps and make them more concrete by focusing on new types of computational problems and the techniques used to solve them.

1.1 UNDERSTAND THE PROBLEM

First, understand the problem. What is the unknown? What are the data? What is the condition?

In computer science, we think of a **problem** as a relationship between some initial information, an **input**, and some desired result, the **output**. To solve the problem, we need to teach a computer how to transform the input into the output. The steps that the computer takes to do this are called a **computation**. In Polya's language, the "data" are the inputs, the "unknown" is the output, and the "condition" is the relationship between the two.

Figure 1.2 illustrates three common computational problems. In each, an input enters on the left and a corresponding output exits on the right. In between, a computation transforms the input into the correct output. When you listen to a song, your music player performs a computation to convert a digital sound file (input) into a sound pattern that can be reproduced by your headphones (output). When you submit a web search request (input), your computer, and many others across the Internet, perform computations to get you results (outputs). And when you use an app on your phone to get directions, it computes the directions (output) based on your current position and desired destination (inputs).

Inputs and outputs are probably familiar to you from high school algebra. When you were given an expression like $y = 18x + 31$ or $f(x) = 18x + 31$, you may have thought about the variable x as a representation of the input and y, or $f(x)$, as a representation of the output. In this example, when the input is $x = 2$, the output is $y = 67$, or $f(x) = 67$. The arithmetic that turns x into y is a very simple (and boring) example of a computation.

> **Reflection 1.1** *What kinds of problems are you interested in? What are their inputs and outputs? Are the inputs and outputs, as you have defined them, sufficient to define the problems completely?*

A first problem: computing reading level

Suppose you are a teacher who wants to evaluate whether some text is at an appropriate grade level for your class. In other words, you want to solve the problem illustrated below.

The input and output for this problem seem straightforward. But they actually aren't; once you start thinking carefully about the problem, you realize there are many questions that need to be answered. For example, are there any restrictions or special conditions associated with the input? What kinds of texts are we talking about? Should the solution work equally well for children's books, newspaper articles, scientific papers, and technical manuals? For what language(s) should the solution work? In what electronic format do the texts need to be? Is there a minimum or maximum length requirement for the text? It is important to formulate these kinds of questions and seek any needed clarifications right away; it is much better to do so immediately than to wait until you have spent a lot of time working on the wrong problem!

The same sorts of questions should be asked about the output. How is a reading level represented? Is it an integer value corresponding to a school year? Or can it be a fraction? To what educational system should the grade levels correspond? Are their minimum and/or maximum allowed values? Once you have answers to your questions, it is a good idea to re-explain the problem back to the poser, either orally or in writing. The feedback you get from this exercise might identify additional points of misunderstanding. You might also draw a picture and work out some examples by hand to make sure you understand all of the requirements and subtleties involved.

We will answer these questions by clarifying that the solution should work for any English language text, available as a plain text file like those on Project Gutenberg.[2] The output will be a number like 4.2, indicating that the text is appropriate for a student who has completed 2/10 of fourth grade in the U.S. educational system. Negative reading level values will not make sense in this system, but any positive number will be acceptable if we interpret the number to mean the number of years of education required to understand the text.

Functional abstraction

A problem at this stage, before we know how to solve it, is an example of a ***functional abstraction***.

> *A functional abstraction describes how to use a tool or technology without necessarily providing any knowledge about how it works.*

In other words, a functional abstraction is a "black box" that we know how to use effectively, without necessarily understand what is happening inside the box to produce the output. In the case of the reading level problem, now that we have a better handle on the specifics, if we had a black box that computed the reading level, we would know how to use it, even without understanding *how* the output was computed. Similarly, to use each of the technologies illustrated in Figure 1.2 we do not need to understand *how* the underlying computation transforms the input to the output.

We exist in a world of functional abstractions that we usually take for granted. We even think about our own bodies in terms of abstractions. Move your fingers. Did you need to understand how your brain triggered your nervous and musculoskeletal systems to make that happen? As far as most of us are concerned, a car is also an abstraction. To drive a car, do you need to know how turning the steering wheel turns the car or pushing the accelerator makes it go faster? We understand *what* should happen when we do these things, but not necessarily *how* they happen. Without abstractions, we would be paralyzed by an avalanche of minutiae.

> **Reflection 1.2** *Imagine that it was necessary to understand how your phone works in order to use it. Or a car. Or a computer. How would this affect your ability to use these technologies?*

New technologies and automation have introduced new functional abstractions into everyday life. Our food supply is a compelling example of this. Only a few hundred years ago, our ancestors knew exactly where their food came from. Inputs of hard work and suitable weather produced outputs of grain and livestock to sustain a family. In modern times, we input money and get packaged food; the origins of our food have become much more abstract.

---

[2]Project Gutenberg (http://www.gutenberg.org) is a library of freely available classic literature with expired U.S. copyrights. The books are available in a variety of formats, but we will be interested in those in a plain text format like the version of *Walden* by Henry David Thoreau at http://www.gutenberg.org/files/205/205-0.txt.

Reflection 1.3 *Think about a common functional abstraction that you use regularly, such as your phone or a credit card. How has this functional abstraction changed over time? Can you think of instances in which better functional abstractions have enhanced our ability to use a technology?*

Functional abstraction is a very important idea in computer science. In the next section, we will demonstrate how more complex problems are solved by breaking them into smaller functional abstractions that we can solve and then recombine into a solution for the original problem.

Exercises

1.1.1. What is a problem in your life that you have to solve regularly? Define the input and output of the problem well enough for someone else to propose an algorithm to solve it. Here is an example.

> Problem: scan pages in a book
> Inputs: a book and page numbers to scan
> Output: one PDF file containing all of the pages, one physical page per page in the file, full color, text recognized

1.1.2. What information is missing from each of the inputs and/or outputs of the following problem definitions? In each case, assume that you know how to complete the task given enough information about the input and output.

(a)* Problem: Make brownies
  Inputs: butter, sugar, eggs, vanilla, cocoa powder, flour, salt, baking powder
  Output: brownies

(b) Problem: Dig a hole
  Inputs: a shovel
  Output: a hole (of course)

(c) Problem: Plant a vegetable garden
  Inputs: seeds
  Output: a planted garden plot

1.1.3. Describe three examples from your everyday life in which an abstraction is beneficial. Explain the benefits of each abstraction versus what life would be like without it.

1.2 DESIGN AN ALGORITHM

Second, devise a plan to solve the problem.

To compute reading level, we will use the well-known *Flesch-Kincaid grade level score*, which approximates the grade level of a text using the formula

$$0.39 \times \text{average words per sentence} + 11.8 \times \text{average syllables per word} - 15.59.$$

Reflection 1.4 *To better understand how the Flesch-Kincaid grade level formula works, apply it to the first epigraph (Fellows and Parberry) at the beginning of this chapter. What does the formula output as the grade level of this quote?*

The 3 sentences in the quote contain 14, 24, and 20 words, respectively, so the average number of words per sentence is $(14 + 24 + 20)/3 \approx 19.33$. There are 90 total syllables in the quote's 58 words, so the average number of syllables per word is $90/58 \approx 1.55$. Plugging these values into the formula, we get

$$0.39 \times 19.33 + 11.8 \times 1.55 - 15.59 \approx 10.24.$$

So the formula says that the quote is at about a tenth grade reading level.

You may be surprised to hear that this formula does not provide nearly enough detail for a computer to carry it out. *You* can figure out how to find the average number of words per sentence and the average number of syllables per word, but a computer definitely cannot without a lot more help. Instead, this formula is more appropriately thought of as a more detailed description of what the output "reading level" means.

To teach a computer how to apply the Flesch-Kincaid formula to any text, we need to replace the black box with a detailed sequence of steps that transforms the input (text) into the correct output (reading level). This sequence of steps is called an **algorithm**. An algorithm is how we teach a computer how to solve a problem.

Take it from the top

To make designing an algorithm more manageable, we can decompose it into simpler **subproblems**. A subproblem is an easier problem that, once solved, will make solving the original problem more straightforward.

Reflection 1.5 *Look at the Flesch-Kincaid formula again. What are the two subproblems we need to solve before we can apply the formula?*

As we saw when we applied the formula, we need to determine two things about the text: the average number of words per sentence and the average number of syllables per word. So these are two subproblems of the overall problem, together with the actual calculation of the Flesch-Kincaid grade level score. We can represent this as follows.

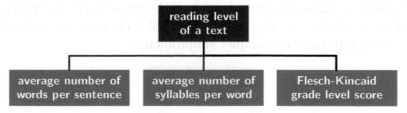

This diagram shows us that there are three subproblems involved in solving the reading level problem. If we had functional abstractions, "black boxes," for these three subproblems, then we could easily solve the reading level problem by getting the

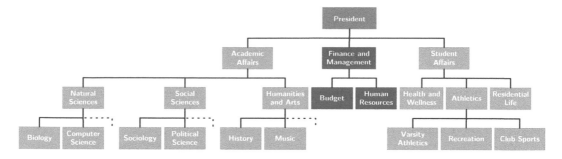

Figure 1.3   A simplified organizational chart of a hypothetical college.

required values from the two leftmost subproblems and then plugging their outputs into the third subproblem. This technique is called ***top-down design*** because it involves starting from the top, the problem to be solved, and then breaking it down into smaller pieces. The final result of this process is called a ***functional decomposition***.

Top-down design and functional decomposition are commonly used to make all sorts of things more manageable. For example, suppose you are the president of a college. Because you cannot effectively manage every detail of such a large organization, you hire a vice president to oversee each of three divisions, as illustrated in Figure 1.3. You expect each vice president to keep you informed about the general activity and performance of their division, but insulate you from the day-to-day details. In this arrangement, each division becomes a functional abstraction to you; you know what each division does, but not necessarily how it does it, freeing you to focus on more important organization-level activity. Each vice president may utilize a similar arrangement within their division. Indeed, organizations are often subdivided many times until the number of employees in a unit is small enough to be overseen by a single manager.

Similarly, each of the subproblems in a functional decomposition might be further broken down, until we arrive at subproblems that are straightforward to solve.

> **Reflection 1.6** *Can the left subproblem in the reading level problem, "average number of words per sentence," be computed directly? Or can it be decomposed further? (Think about how you computed the reading level in Reflection 1.2.)*

We saw above that the average number of words per sentence is equal to the total number of words divided by the total number of sentences, so we can decompose this subproblem into two even simpler subproblems:

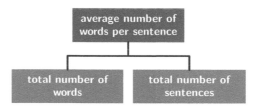

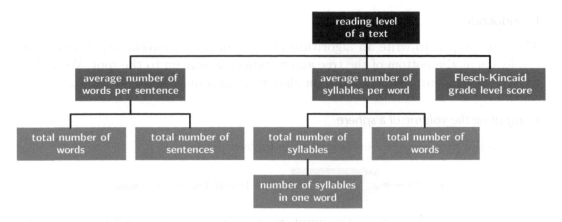

Figure 1.4 Functional decomposition of the reading level problem.

Similarly, we can also decompose the problem of computing the average number of syllables per word into two subproblems:

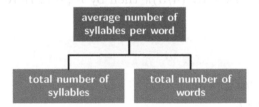

Taken altogether, we are now left with three relatively simple subproblems to solve: (a) counting the total number of words, (b) counting the total number of sentences, and (c) counting the total number of syllables.

Reflection 1.7 *Can computing the total numbers of words, sentences, or syllables be broken down further?*

Counting the total numbers of words and sentences seems pretty straightforward. But finding the total number of syllables is not as simple because even finding the number of syllables in one word is not trivial for a computer, especially with all of the oddities of the English language. Thus it makes sense to further decompose finding the *total* number of syllables into the subproblem of finding the number of syllables in just *one* word.

A diagram of the final functional decomposition is shown in Figure 1.4. These kinds of diagrams are called **trees** because they resemble an upside down tree with the *root* at the top and branches spreading out below. Nodes at the bottom of the tree are called *leaves*.

Pseudocode

The next step is to write an algorithm for each of the subproblems, starting with the leaves at the bottom of the tree and working our way up to the root. We will get to this shortly, but first let's write an algorithm for a more straightforward problem.

Computing the volume of a sphere

This simple problem can be visualized as follows.

To compute the output from the input, we can simply use the well-known formula $V = (4/3)\pi r^3$. Although this is much closer to an algorithm than the Flesch-Kincaid formula, it still does not explicitly specify a sequence of steps; there are several alternative sequences that one could follow to carry it out.[3] For example, we could cube r first, then multiply that result by the rest of the terms, or we could cube r last, or we could multiply r by $(4/3)\pi$ then by r^2, etc. Here is one algorithm that follows the formula:

Algorithm SPHERE VOLUME

Input: the radius r of the sphere
1. Multiply $r \times r \times r$.
2. Multiply the previous result by π.
3. Multiply the previous result by 4.
4. Divide the previous result by 3.

Output: the final result, which is the volume of the sphere

At the top of the algorithm, we note the input and at the bottom we note the output. In between, the individual lines are called **statements**. Carrying out the sequence of statements in an algorithm is called **executing** or **running** the algorithm.

The informal style in which this algorithm is written is known as **pseudocode**, to differentiate it from *code*, which is another name for a computer program. In common usage, the prefix *pseudo* often has a negative connotation, as in *pseudo-intellectual* or *pseudoscience*, but here it simply connotes a relaxed manner of writing algorithms that is meant to be read by a human rather than a computer. The flexibility afforded by pseudocode allows us to more clearly focus on how to solve the problem at hand without becoming distracted by the more demanding requirements of a programming language. Once we have refined the algorithm adequately and convinced ourselves that it is correct, we can translate it into a formal program. We'll talk more about that in the next section.

---

[3]In Python, we can actually use this formula more or less directly, but to facilitate this simple example, we'll pretend otherwise for now.

Here is a different algorithm that also computes the volume of a sphere. We are calling this algorithm a "draft" because, like other kinds of writing, algorithms also require rounds of revisions. We will revise this algorithm two more times.

Algorithm SPHERE VOLUME 2 — DRAFT 1

Input: the radius r of the sphere
1   Divide 4 by 3.
2   Multiply the previous result by π.
3   Repeat the following three times: multiply the previous result by r.
Output: the final result, which is the volume of the sphere

To better understand what an algorithm is doing, we can execute it on an example, using a **trace table**. In a trace table, we *trace* through each step of the algorithm and keep track of what is happening. The following trace table shows the execution of our draft SPHERE VOLUME 2 algorithm with input value $r = 10$.

Trace input: $r = 10$

Step	Line	Result	Notes
1	1	$1.\bar{3}$	$4 \div 3 = 1.\bar{3}$
2	2	$4.18\bar{6}$	multiplying the previous result ($1.\bar{3}$) by π
3	3	$41.8\bar{6}$	multiplying the previous result ($4.18\bar{6}$) by 10
4	3	$418.\bar{6}$	multiplying the previous result ($41.8\bar{6}$) by 10
5	3	$4,186.\bar{6}$	multiplying the previous result ($418.\bar{6}$) by 10

Output: $4,186.\bar{6}$

The four columns keep track of the number of steps executed by the algorithm, the line number in the algorithm being executed, the result after that line is executed, and notes explaining what is happening in that line.

The first two steps are pretty self-explanatory. Then, because line 3 of the algorithm instructs us to repeat something three times, line 3 is executed 3 times in the trace table. A statement that repeats like this is called a **loop**. When algorithms contain loops, the number of steps is not necessarily the same as the number of lines.

Because we will eventually want to translate our pseudocode algorithms into *actual* code, it will be important to adhere to some important principles that will make this translation easier. First, we must strive to eliminate any **ambiguity** from our algorithms. In other words, the steps in an algorithm must never require creative interpretation by a human being. As we will see in Section 3.1, computers are, at their core, only able to perform very simple instructions like arithmetic and comparing two numbers, and are incapable of creative inference. Second, the steps of an algorithm must be **executable** by a computer. In other words, they must correlate to things a computer can actually do. The definition of *executable* will become clearer as we learn more about programming.

These two requirements are not really unique to computer algorithms. For example, we hope that new surgical techniques are unambiguously presented with references to actual anatomy and real surgical tools. Likewise, when an architect designs a building, they must use only available materials and be precise about their placement. And when an author writes a novel, they must write to their audience, using appropriate language and culturally familiar references.

By these standards, both of the previous algorithms are less than ideal in at least two ways. First, references to the "previous result" are not precise and will not get us very far in more complex algorithms where multiple intermediate values need to be remembered. This kind of imprecision can easily lead to problematic ambiguity in our algorithms. Second, in none of the steps did we explicitly state that we needed to remember a result to be used later. When you executed the algorithms, you could infer this necessity, but this is an example of the kind of ambiguity that we need to avoid when writing algorithms for a computer.

To remedy these issues, algorithms use **variables** to give names to values that need to be remembered later. To make our algorithms understandable to a human reader, we will use descriptive variable names, unlike the single letter x and y variables that are common in mathematics. In our pseudocode algorithms, we will indicate variables in italics and **assign** a value to a variable with the notation

$$variable \leftarrow value$$

The left-facing arrow indicates that the value on the right is being assigned to the variable on the left. For example, *eggs* ← 12 would assign the value 12 to the variable named *eggs*. Using variables, the Sphere Volume 2 algorithm can be rewritten as follows.

Algorithm Sphere Volume 2 — Draft 2

Input: the radius *r* of the sphere
1 | *volume* ← 4 ÷ 3
2 | *volume* ← previous value of *volume* × π
3 | repeat the following three times:
4 | *volume* ← previous value of *volume* × *r*
Output: the value of *volume*

In this version, we have also formatted the loop a little bit differently, indenting the statement that is being repeated on a separate line (line 4). The statements that are executed repeatedly by a loop are called the **body** of the loop. So line 4 is the body of the loop that starts on line 3. The following trace table, again with input value *r* = 10, illustrates how the revised algorithm works.

Trace input: $r = 10$

Step	Line	volume	Notes
1	1	$1.\bar{3}$	$volume \leftarrow 4 \div 3 = 1.\bar{3}$
2	2	$4.18\bar{6}$	$volume \leftarrow$ previous $volume \times \pi = 1.\bar{3} \times 3.14 = 4.18\bar{6}$
3	3	"	volume unaffected; execute line 4 three times
4	4	$41.8\bar{6}$	$volume \leftarrow$ previous $volume \times r = 4.18\bar{6} \times 10 = 41.8\bar{6}$
5	4	$418.\bar{6}$	$volume \leftarrow$ previous $volume \times r = 41.8\bar{6} \times 10 = 418.\bar{6}$
6	4	$4{,}186.\bar{6}$	$volume \leftarrow$ previous $volume \times r = 418.\bar{6} \times 10 = 4{,}186.\bar{6}$

Output: $volume = 4{,}186.\bar{6}$

Notice that we have replaced the generic "Result" column with a column that keeps track of the value of the introduced variable, which we named *volume* because it will eventually be assigned the volume of the sphere. The first line of the trace table shows that the variable named *volume* is assigned the result of dividing 4 by 3. In line 2, the value of *volume*, which is now $1.\bar{3}$, is multiplied by π (which we truncate to 3.14), and the result, which is $4.18\bar{6}$, is assigned to *volume*. Notice how much less ambiguous this is, compared to a reference to a "previous result." Also note that this assignment has *overwritten* the previous value of *volume*. Next, line 3 does not do anything on its own; it just instructs us to repeat line 4 three times. (The "ditto" marks indicate no change to *volume*.) Each execution of line 4 multiplies the value of *volume* by 10, and overwrites the value of *volume* with this result. At the end, *volume* corresponds to the value $4{,}186.\bar{6}$, which is output by the algorithm.

Reflection 1.8 *Trace through the algorithm again with input value $r = 5$. Create a new trace table to show your progress. (The final answer should be $523.\bar{3}$.)*

Let's make one more refinement to our algorithm. In line 2 (and similarly in line 4), the algorithm refers to the "previous value of" *volume* on the righthand side of the assignment:

$$volume \leftarrow \text{previous value of } volume \times \pi$$

We included this language for clarity, but it is not actually necessary; the statement can be abbreviated to

$$volume \leftarrow volume \times \pi \, .$$

In any assignment statement, the righthand side after the arrow must be evaluated first, *before* the result of this evaluation is assigned to the variable on the lefthand side. Therefore, when *volume* is referenced on the righthand side of this assignment, it *must* refer to the previous value of *volume*, assigned in the previous line, as illustrated below.

$$\underbrace{volume}_{\substack{\uparrow \\ \text{next value} \\ (4.18\bar{6})}} \leftarrow \overbrace{volume}^{\substack{\text{first step}}} \times \pi$$

second step   first step

volume ← volume × π

next value   previous value
$(4.18\bar{6})$ $(1.\bar{3})$

With this revision, the algorithm now looks like this:

Algorithm SPHERE VOLUME 2 — FINAL

Input: the radius *r* of the sphere
1 | *volume* ← 4 ÷ 3
2 | *volume* ← *volume* × π
3 | repeat the following three times:
4 | *volume* ← *volume* × *r*
Output: *volume*

A trace table for this algorithm looks exactly like the previous one.

Implement from the bottom

We are now prepared to return our attention to the reading level problem. Based on our decomposition tree in Figure 1.4, there are two ways that we can proceed. Our first option is to start at the top of the tree and work our way down. For this to work, we would need to assume that algorithms for the three main subproblems already exist. Although it is possible to work this way, it is trickier because we cannot test whether anything is working correctly until we have written algorithms for everything in the tree.

Instead, we will start at the bottom of the decomposition tree and work our way up, in what we call a ***bottom-up implementation***. The subproblems that are leaves of the tree are not dependent on any other subproblems, so we can design algorithms for these first, make sure they work, and then call upon them in algorithms for subproblems one level higher. If we continue this process until we reach the root of the tree, we will have a complete algorithm. Let's start with an algorithm for the "Flesch-Kincaid grade level score" subproblem, which takes as inputs the average number of words per sentence and the average number of syllables per word, and outputs the grade level of the text according to the Flesch-Kincaid formula.

In pseudocode, we can write this algorithm as follows:

Algorithm FLESCH KINCAID

Input: *average words, average syllables*
1 | *reading level* ← 0.39 × *average words* + 11.8 × *average syllables* − 15.59
Output: *reading level*

This one-line algorithm simply uses its two input values to compute the grade level, assigns this value to the variable named *reading level*, and then outputs this value.

Let's next write an algorithm to compute the number of syllables in a word. This algorithm will take a single word as input and output the number of syllables.

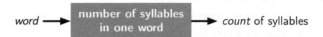

word ⟶ **number of syllables in one word** ⟶ *count* of syllables

Reflection 1.9 *How do you count the number of syllables in a word? Do you think your method can be "taught" to a computer?*

As you might imagine, a computer cannot use the "clapping method" or something similar to compute the number of syllables in a word. Instead, a syllable-counting algorithm will need to "look at" the letters in the word and follow some rules based on those letters. Since the number of syllables in a word is defined to be the number of distinct vowel sounds, a first approximation would be to simply count the number of vowels in the word.

Algorithm SYLLABLE COUNT — DRAFT 1

Input: a *word*

1 | *count* ← the number of vowels in *word*

Output: *count*

Reflection 1.10 *What does it mean for an algorithm to be correct? Is this algorithm correct? If it is not, why not?*

An algorithm is **correct** if it gives the correct output for *every* possible input. This algorithm is obviously too simplistic to be correct. For example, the algorithm will over-count the number of syllables in words containing diphthongs, such as *rain* and *loan*, and in words ending with a silent *e*.

Reflection 1.11 *There is also some ambiguity in this one-line syllable-counting algorithm. Do you see what it is?*

The ambiguity arises from the definition of a vowel in the English language. The letters *a*, *e*, *i*, *o*, and *u* are always vowels but sometimes so is *y*. So our algorithm needs to clarify this. Incorporating these insights (and ignoring *y* as a vowel) leads to the following enhanced algorithm.

Algorithm SYLLABLE COUNT — DRAFT 2

Input: a *word*
1	*count* ← the number of vowels (*a, e, i, o, u*) in *word*
2	repeat for each pair of adjacent *letters* in *word*:
3	if the *letters* are both vowels, then subtract 1 from *count*
4	if *word* ends in *e*, then subtract 1 from *count*

Output: *count*

Notice two new kinds of pseudocode statements in this algorithm. First, line 2, is a different kind of loop. Imagine yourself looking carefully for adjacent vowels in a very long word like *consanguineous.* You would probably scan along the word visually or with your finger, from left to right, repeatedly checking pairs of adjacent letters. This is also what lines 2 and 3 are doing; for each pair of adjacent letters you look at, check if they are both vowels and subtract one from the *count* if they are. Another name for the repetitive process carried out by a loop is **iteration**; implicit in line 2 is a process of *iterating over* the letters of the word.

Lines 3 and 4 both illustrate the second new type of statement, called a **conditional statement**, or sometimes an **if-then statement**. Simple conditional statements like this are self-explanatory: if the condition after the *if* is true, do the thing after *then*. We will work with more sophisticated conditional statements in Chapter 5.

Let's use a trace table to show the execution of this algorithm on the word "ancient."

Trace input: *word* = `"ancient"`

Step	Line	*count*	*letters*	Notes
1	1	3	—	there are three vowels in `"ancient"`
2	2	"	`"an"`	first pair of adjacent letters in `"ancient"` is `"an"`
3	3	"	"	`"an"` are not both vowels; no change to *count*
4	2	"	`"nc"`	next pair of adjacent letters is `"nc"`
5	3	"	"	`"nc"` are not both vowels; no change to *count*
6	2	"	`"ci"`	next pair of adjacent letters is `"ci"`
7	3	"	"	`"ci"` are not both vowels; no change to *count*
8	2	"	`"ie"`	next pair of adjacent letters is `"ie"`
9	3	2	"	`"ie"` are both vowels; subtract 1 from *count*
10	2	"	`"en"`	next pair of adjacent letters is `"en"`
11	3	"	"	`"en"` are not both vowels; no change to *count*
12	2	"	`"nt"`	next pair of adjacent letters is `"nt"`
13	3	"	"	`"nt"` are not both vowels; no change to *count*
14	4	"	"	`"ancient"` does not end in e; no change to *count*

Output: *count* = 2

The horizontal lines in the trace table make it easier to see the individual iterations of the loop. In the first step, we count the number of vowels in the input and assign *count* to this value. In step 2, we begin the loop by considering the first pair of adjacent letters in the input, **"an"**. In step 3, we check if these are both vowels. Since they are not, we leave *count* alone. In step 4, we repeat the loop by executing line 2 again with the next pair of adjacent letters, **"nc"**. In step 5, we repeat line 3 which, again, has no effect on the *count*. In the third iteration, in lines 6–7, the same thing happens. In the fourth iteration of the loop, starting in step 8, we do find a pair of adjacent letters that are both vowels, so we subtract one from *count*. The loop continues until we run out of letters from the input. Finally, in step 14, we execute line 4, which finds that the input does not end in *e*, so *count* remains 2.

Reflection 1.12 *Use trace tables to also execute the algorithm on the words "create" and "syllable." Do you get the correct numbers of syllables?*

From these examples, you can see that our algorithm is still not correct. Indeed, designing a computer algorithm that correctly counts syllables for every word in the English language is virtually impossible; there are just too many exceptions! But we can certainly get closer than we are now. We will leave it as an exercise for you to draft further improvements.

To continue our bottom-up implementation of the reading level algorithm, we will use the Syllable Count algorithm to solve the "total number of syllables" problem. The idea of the Total Syllable Count algorithm is simple: for each word in the text, call upon the Syllable Count algorithm for the number of syllables in that word, and add this number to a running sum of the total number of syllables.

Algorithm Total Syllable Count

Input: a *text*

1 | *total count* ← 0
2 | repeat for each *word* in the *text*:
3 | *number* ← Syllable Count (*word*)
4 | *total count* ← *total count* + *number*

Output: *total count*

In line 1 of the algorithm, we initialize the *total count* of syllables to zero. Line 2 is a loop that iterates over all of the words in the text. For every *word*, we execute lines 3 and 4, indented to indicate that these comprise the body of the loop. In line 3, we call upon the Syllable Count algorithm to get the number of syllables in the *word* that is being considered in that iteration. Syllable Count (*word*) is shorthand for "execute the Syllable Count algorithm with input *word*," where *word* is the variable name representing the word that is being examined in each iteration of the loop. The output of the Syllable Count algorithm is then assigned to the variable named *number*. So altogether, line 3 is shorthand for

"Execute the SYLLABLE COUNT algorithm, with input *word*, and assign the output to the variable named *number*."

Then in line 4, we add the *number* of syllables in the *word* to the *total count* of syllables.

This is a lot to take in, so let's once again illustrate with a trace table, using the first three words of the United Nations charter as input.

Trace input: *text* = "We the peoples"					
Step	Line	*total count*	*word*	*number*	Notes
1	1	0	—	—	initialize *total count* to zero
2	2	"	"We"	—	do the loop body with *word* ← "We"
3	3	"	"	1	get the number of syllables in "We"
4	4	1	"	"	add *number* to *total count*
5	2	"	"the"	"	do the loop body with *word* ← "the"
6	3	"	"	1	get the number of syllables in "the"
7	4	2	"	"	add *number* to *total count*
8	2	"	"peoples"	"	do the loop body with *word* ← "peoples"
9	3	"	"	2	get the number of syllables in "peoples"
10	4	4	"	"	add *number* to *total count*
Output: *total count* = 4					

In the trace table, horizontal lines identify the three iterations of the loop, one for each word in the *text*. In the first iteration, in step 2, the loop assigns *word* to be "We", as the first word in the *text*. Then, in step 3, *number* is assigned the output of SYLLABLE COUNT ("We"), which means that the SYLLABLE COUNT algorithm is called upon to get the number of syllables in "We" and this value (1) is assigned to the variable *number*. In step 4, the value of *number* is added to the *total count*. Remember that, in an assignment statement, the righthand side is evaluated first, so the statement in line 4 is assigning to *total count* the sum of the previous value of *total count* and *number*, as illustrated below:

$$total\ count \leftarrow total\ count + number$$
$$\uparrow \qquad\qquad \uparrow \qquad\qquad \uparrow$$
next value   previous value   (1)
(1)   (0)

In the second iteration, starting in step 5, the loop assigns *word* to be "the", the SYLLABLE COUNT algorithm is called upon to get the number of syllables in "the" and this value is added to *total count*, bringing its value to 2. Finally, in the third iteration, starting on line 8, the process repeats with *word* assigned to be "peoples", bringing the total number of syllables to 4, which is the output of the algorithm.

To flesh out the entire reading level algorithm, we would continue designing algorithms for subproblems at the bottom of the tree, and work our way up, calling upon algorithms at lower levels from algorithms for levels above. This would continue until we get to the root of the tree.

Suppose, for the moment, that we have worked our way up the decomposition tree and that, in addition to the FLESCH-KINCAID algorithm, algorithms for the other two main subproblems have been written—one that computes the average number of words per sentence and one that computes the average number of syllables per word. Also suppose that we have named these algorithms AVERAGE WORDS PER SENTENCE and AVERAGE SYLLABLES PER WORD, respectively. Then the final reading level algorithm would look like the following.

Algorithm READING LEVEL

Input: a *text*

  1   *average words* ← AVERAGE WORDS PER SENTENCE (*text*)

  2   *average syllables* ← AVERAGE SYLLABLES PER WORD (*text*)

  3   *reading level* ← FLESCH-KINCAID (*average words, average syllables*)

Output: *reading level*

Line 1 of the algorithm is shorthand for

> "Execute the AVERAGE WORDS PER SENTENCE algorithm, with input *text*, and assign the output to the variable named *average words*."

Similarly, line 2 of the algorithm is shorthand for

> "Execute the AVERAGE SYLLABLES PER WORD algorithm, with input *text*, and assign the output to the variable named *average syllables*."

Finally, line 3 calls upon the FLESCH-KINCAID algorithm, with the values of these two variables as input, to compute the Flesch-Kincaid grade level score. The output of this algorithm is then assigned to the variable named *reading level*, which is output by the algorithm.

We invite you to take a stab at writing the remaining algorithms in the exercises.

Exercises

1.2.1.   Decompose each of the following problems into subproblems. Continue the decomposition until you think each subproblem is sufficiently simple to solve. Explain your rationale for stopping the decomposition where you did.

    (a)*   an exercise routine from warmup to cool down

    (b)   your complete laundry routine

    (c)   writing a paper for a class

    (d)   your morning routine

    (e)   planning a multiple course menu

1.2.2.   Suppose you want to find the area of each of the following shaded regions. In each of the diagrams, one square represents one square unit. Decompose each problem into subproblems that make finding the solution easier. (You do not need to actually find the areas.)

(a)* 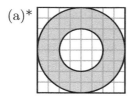   (b) 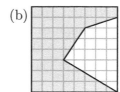   (c)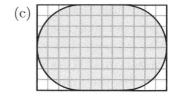

1.2.3.   Look up the organizational chart for your school. Choose one division and explain how the organization of that division supplies a functional abstraction to the office that oversees the division.

1.2.4*   Use a trace table to show how the final SPHERE VOLUME 2 algorithm executes with input $r = 7$.

1.2.5.   Use a trace table to show how the second draft of the SYLLABLE COUNT algorithm executes on the word *algorithm*. Is the result correct?

1.2.6.   The following algorithm computes the surface area of a box.

Algorithm SURFACE AREA OF A BOX

Input: *length, width, height*
1 | *area 1 ← length × width*
2 | *area 2 ← length × height*
3 | *area 3 ← width × height*
4 | *surface ← area 1 + area 2 + area 3*
5 | *surface ← surface × 2*
Output: *surface*

Use a trace table (started below) to show how the algorithm executes with inputs *length* = 4, *width* = 5, and *height* = 2.

Trace input: *length* = 4, *width* = 5, *height* = 2

Step	Line	*area 1*	*area 2*	*area 3*	*surface*	Notes
1	1	20	—	—	—	*area 1 ← length × width*
2	2					
⋮						

Output:

1.2.7*   The following algorithm determines the winner of an election between two candidates, Laura and John. The input is a list votes like [Laura, Laura, John, Laura, ...].

Algorithm COUNT VOTES

Input: *votes*

1	*laura* ← 0
2	*john* ← 0
3	repeat once for each entry in *votes*:
4	if the entry is for Laura, then add 1 to *laura*
5	otherwise, add 1 to *john*
6	if *laura* > *john*, then *winner* ← Laura
7	otherwise, *winner* ← John

Output: *winner*

Use a trace table (started below) to show how the algorithm executes with input *votes* = [John, Laura, Laura, John, Laura].

Trace input: *votes* = [John, Laura, Laura, John, Laura]

Step	Line	*laura*	*john*	*winner*	Notes
1	1	0	—	—	*laura* set to 0
2	2				
⋮					

Output:

1.2.8. There is a subtle mistake in the algorithm in Exercise 1.2.7. Describe and fix it.

1.2.9* Revise the original SPHERE VOLUME algorithm on page 10 so that it also uses a variable instead of referring to the "previous result."

1.2.10. Write yet another algorithm for finding the volume of a sphere.

1.2.11. Write an algorithm to sort a stack of any 5 cards by value in ascending order. In each step, your algorithm may compare or swap the positions of any two cards.

1.2.12. Write an algorithm to walk between two nearby locations, assuming the only legal instructions are "Take *s* steps forward," and "Turn *d* degrees to the left," where *s* and *d* are positive integers.

1.2.13. The term *algorithm* was derived from the name of Muḥammad ibn Mūsā al-Khwārizmī (c. 780–c. 850), a Persian mathematician who introduced both Arabic numerals and algebra to the world. The term *algebra* is derived from the Latin translation of the title of his book, "The Compendious Book on Calculation by Completion and Balancing" [4], which introduced algebra. The following algorithm for a common algebraic operation is from an English translation of this work.

You know that all mercantile transactions of people, such as buying and selling, exchange and hire, comprehend always two notions and four numbers, which are stated by the enquirer; namely, measure and price, and quantity and sum. The number which expresses the measure is inversely proportionate to the number which expresses the sum, and the number of the price inversely proportionate to that of the quantity. Three of these four numbers are always known, one is unknown, and this is implied when the person inquiring says "how much?" and it is the object of the question. The computation in such instances is this, that you try the three given numbers; two of them must necessarily be inversely proportionate the one to the other. Then you multiply these two proportionate numbers by each other, and you divide the product by the third given number, the proportionate of which is unknown. The quotient of this division is the unknown number, which the inquirer asked for; and it is inversely proportionate to the divisor.

Examples.—For the first case: If you are told "ten for six, how much for four?" then ten is the measure; six is the price; the expression how much implies the unknown number of the quantity; and four is the number of the sum. The number of the measure, which is ten, is inversely proportionate to the number of the sum, namely, four. Multiply, therefore, ten by four, that is to say, the two known proportionate numbers by each other; the product is forty. Divide this by the other known number, which is that of the price, namely, six. The quotient is six and two-thirds; it is the unknown number, implied in the words of the question "how much?" it is the quantity, and inversely proportionate to the six, which is the price.

There are four variables identified in the passage: *measure*, *price*, *sum*, and *quantity*. Write an algorithm in pseudocode that answers the "how much?" question posed in the example when the first three quantities are given as input.

1.2.14*   Using the SYLLABLE COUNT algorithm as a guide, write an algorithm named WORD COUNT that approximates the total number of words in a text. Your algorithm should take a text as input and output a count of words. Like the SYLLABLE COUNT algorithm, use a loop to look at each letter in the text and adjust a count as appropriate. As with counting syllables, this problem is fraught with complexity arising from the English language, so your algorithm need not be perfect.

1.2.15.   Write an algorithm named SENTENCE COUNT to count the total number of sentences in a text. Your algorithm should take a text as input and output a count of sentences. The guidance from the previous exercise also applies.

1.2.16*   Using Figure 1.4 and the READING LEVEL algorithm on page 19 as guides, design the AVERAGE WORDS PER SENTENCE algorithm. Call upon your WORD COUNT and SENTENCE COUNT algorithms to do most of the work.

1.2.17.   Using Figure 1.4 and the READING LEVEL algorithm on page 19 as guides, design the AVERAGE SYLLABLES PER WORD algorithm. Call upon your WORD COUNT algorithm and the TOTAL SYLLABLE COUNT algorithm to do most of the work.

1.2.18.   Enhance the SYLLABLE COUNT (VERSION 2) algorithm on page 16 so that it correctly counts the number of syllables in

    (a)   plural words

    (b)   words ending in a consonant plus *le* (e.g., *syllable*)

    (c)   words containing a *y* that acts like a vowel

    (d)   the word *algorithm*

1.3   WRITE A PROGRAM

> *Third, carry out your plan, checking each step.*

The next step in the problem solving process is to "carry out your plan" by translating your algorithm into a ***program*** that a computer can execute. A program must adhere to a set of grammatical rules, called ***syntax***, that are defined by a particular ***programming language***. In this book, we will use a programming language called *Python*. You will find that programming in Python is not too different from writing algorithms in pseudocode, which is why it is a great first language. But Python is not a toy language either; it has become one of the most widely used programming languages in the world, especially in data science, bioinformatics, and digital humanities.

Writing programs (or "programming") is a hands-on activity that allows us to test our algorithms, apply them to real inputs, and harness their results, in tangible and satisfying ways. Learning how to program empowers us to put our algorithms into production. Solving problems and writing programs should also be fun and creative. Guido van Rossum, the inventor of Python understood this when he named Python after the British comedy series "Monty Python's Flying Circus!"

In this section, we will not be able to fully realize our reading level algorithm as a program just yet. Some of the steps that are easy to write as pseudocode, such as breaking a text into individual words, are actually more involved than they look on paper. But we will be able to implement the Flesch-Kincaid algorithm at the bottom of our decomposition tree, and get oriented for what awaits in future chapters. Before long, you will be able to implement everything from the previous section and much more!

Welcome to the circus

As you work through this book, we highly recommend that you do so in front of a computer. The only way to learn how to program is to do it, so every example we provide is meant to be tried by you. Then go beyond the examples, and experiment with your own ideas. Instead of just wondering, "What would happen if I did this?", type it in and see! To get started, launch the application called IDLE that comes with every Python distribution (or another programming environment recommended by your instructor). You should see a window appear with something like this at the top:

```
Python 3.8.4 (v3.8.4:dfa645a65e, Jul 13 2020, 10:45:06)
[Clang 6.0 (clang-600.0.57)] on darwin
Type "help", "copyright", "credits" or "license()" for more information.
>>>
```

The program executing in this window is known as a *Python shell*. The first line tells you which version of Python you are using (in this case, 3.8.4). The programs in this book are based on Python version 3.6 and higher. If you need to install a newer version, you can find one at `http://python.org`. The symbol `>>>` on the fourth line in the IDLE window is called the ***prompt*** because it is prompting you to type in a Python statement. To start, type in `print('Hello world!')` at the prompt and hit return.

```
>>> print('Hello world!')
Hello world!
>>>
```

Congratulations, you have just written your first program! This one-statement program simply prints `Hello world!` on the screen.

Notice that the Python shell responded to your command with a result, and then gave you a new prompt. The shell will continue this "prompt → compute → respond" cycle until we quit (by typing `quit()`). In the "compute" step, as we will see in Section 3.1, the computer does not really understand what we are typing. Instead, each Python statement is transparently translated into ***machine language***, which is the only language a computer actually understands. Then the shell executes the machine language instructions and prints the result. The part of the shell that does this translation is called the ***interpreter***. Python programs can also be executed in "program mode," where the Python interpreter executes an entire program containing multiple statements all at once. We will introduce program mode in the next chapter.

A programming language like Python provides a rich set of abstractions that enable us to solve a wide variety of interesting problems. Your one-line program demonstrates two of these. The sequence of characters in quotes, `'Hello world!'`, is called a *character string* or just a ***string***. Strings, which can be enclosed in either single quotes (`'`) or double quotes (`"`), are how Python represents and stores text, from single characters up to entire books. To display this string, we used the `print` function. ***Functions*** are how functional abstractions are implemented in Python. A function, like the algorithms we developed in the previous section, takes one or more inputs, called ***arguments***, and produces an output, called the ***return value***. We call upon functions to compute things for us with the familiar notation that we used in the previous section to call upon algorithms. The `print` function takes the string `'Hello world!'` as an argument (in parentheses) and prints it to the screen. Alternatively, we could have assigned the string to a ***variable*** and then passed this variable to the `print` function like this:

```
>>> message = 'Hello world!'
>>> print(message)
Hello world!
>>>
```

In our pseudocode algorithms, we used a left-facing arrow to assign values to variables to emphasize that assignment is a two-step, right-to-left process:

1. Evaluate the expression on the righthand side of the assignment operator.

2. Assign the resulting value to the name on the lefthand side of the assignment operator.

	Operators	Description
1.	( )	parentheses
2.	**	exponentiation (power)
3.	+, -	unary positive and negative, e.g., -(4 * 9)
4.	*, /, //, %	multiplication and division
5.	+, -	addition and subtraction

Table 1.1 Arithmetic operator precedence, highest to lowest. Operators with the same precedence are evaluated left to right.

In Python, assignment works exactly the same way, but the **assignment operator** is the equal sign (=) instead of an arrow.

Python can also crunch numbers, of course. Computing the volume of a sphere looks like this:

```
>>> radius = 10
>>> pi = 3.14159
>>> volume = (4 / 3) * pi * radius ** 3
```

We created two new variables above named `radius` and `pi`, and used these variables to compute the volume using the formula $(4/3)\pi r^3$. The /, *, and ** symbols perform division, multiplication, and exponentiation, respectively. The spaces around the operators in the arithmetic expression are optional and ignored by the interpreter. In general, Python does not care if you include spaces in expressions, but you always want to make your programs readable to others, and spaces often help. The interpreter evaluates arithmetic operators in the usual order, summarized in Table 1.1 (i.e., PEMDAS). This precedence may be overridden by parentheses. You can also use parentheses, even when unnecessary, to make expressions easier to understand, as we did above with parentheses around 4 / 3.

Assignment statements do not print any results, but you can display the value of a variable by either typing its name or using `print`.

```
>>> volume
4188.786666666666
>>> print(volume)
4188.786666666666
```

In the shell, both methods do the same thing. (When we start writing programs in the next chapter, using `print` will be necessary.)

Similarly, let's compute the Flesch-Kincaid reading level of a hypothetical text (since we cannot yet analyze a real text) with an average of 16 words per sentence and 1.78 syllables per word, using the formula on page 6.

```
>>> averageWords = 16
>>> averageSyllables = 1.78
>>> readingLevel = 0.39 * averageWords + 11.8 * averageSyllables - 15.59
>>> print(readingLevel)
11.654
```

The `print` function can also take multiple arguments, separated by commas. A space will be inserted between arguments when they are displayed.

```
>>> print('The reading level is', readingLevel, '.')
The reading level is 11.654 .
```

The first and last arguments are strings, and the second argument is the variable we defined above. Notice that there are no quotes around the variable name `readingLevel`.

> **Reflection 1.13** *Why do you think quotation marks are necessary around strings? Try removing them and see what happens.*
>
> ```
> >>> print(The reading level is, readingLevel, .)
> ```

The quotation marks are necessary because otherwise Python has no way to distinguish text from a variable or function name. Without the quotation marks, the Python interpreter will try to make sense of each argument, assuming that each word is a variable or function name, or a reserved word in the Python language. Since this sequence of words does not follow the syntax of the language, and most of these names are not defined, the interpreter will print an error.

Every value in Python has a **type** associated with it. Understanding this is very important when programming because the behaviors of operators and functions often depend upon the type of data they are given. You can see the different types of values assigned to our variables so far by using the `type` function.

```
>>> type(message)
<class 'str'>
>>> type(averageWords)
<class 'int'>
>>> type(averageSyllables)
<class 'float'>
>>> type(readingLevel)
<class 'float'>
```

A *class*, for our purposes at the moment, is a synonym for *type*. (We will talk about classes in more detail in the next chapter.) So this is telling us that the value assigned to `message` is a string (`str`), the value assigned to `averageWords` is an **integer** (`int`), and the value assigned to `averageSyllables` is a **float** (short for *floating point* number). We will have more to say about integers and floats in Section 3.2; for now, suffice to say that any number without a decimal point is an integer and any number with a decimal point is a float. The value assigned to `readingLevel` is also a float because the type of any arithmetic expression involving a float will also be a float. So in the `print` statement above, we actually combined two different types of values: strings and a float. The `print` function transparently converted `readingLevel` to a string before combining it with the other two strings into a longer string to print.

To suppress the extra space that gets inserted before the period in this `print` statement, we can build a string manually using the + operator which, when applied to strings, is called the **concatenation operator**. Concatenation combines strings into longer strings. For example,

```
>>> first = 'Monty'
>>> last = 'Python'
>>> name = first + ' ' + last
>>> print(name)
Monty Python
```

To concatenate `'The reading level is'`, `readingLevel`, and `'.'`, we need to first convert `readingLevel` to a string using the `str` function. The `str` function can take just about any type of value as an argument and it returns the argument represented as a string. For example, try this:

```
>>> readingLevelString = str(readingLevel)
>>> readingLevelString
'11.654'
```

When we use a function like this by passing an argument to it, it is called a **function call**, or a *function invocation*. Calling `str(readingLevel)` returns (i.e., outputs) a string representation of `readingLevel` and assigns this value to the variable `readingLevelString`. Notice the quotes in `'11.654'`, indicating that it is a string rather than a float. The `str` function does not change the value of `readingLevel` though; it remains the same afterwards, as you can confirm:

```
>>> readingLevel
11.654
```

The easiest way to use `str` in the `print` statement is to skip the intermediate variable like this:

```
>>> print('The reading level is ' + str(readingLevel) + '.')
The reading level is 11.654.
```

Reflection 1.14 *Try the previous statement without the* str *function. What happens and why?*

If we do not convert `readingLevel` to a string first, then we are trying to "add" a string to a float, which doesn't make any sense.

Some other useful functions are `float`, `int`, and `round`. The `float` and `int` functions return float and integer versions of their arguments, similar to the way the `str` function returns a string version of its argument.

```
>>> float(3)
3.0
>>> int(-1.618)
-1
```

The `int` function converts its argument to an integer by truncating it, i.e., removing the fractional part to the right of the decimal point. This might be helpful in our reading level computation, since we probably do not really want all of the digits to the right of the decimal point.

```
>>> readingLevel = int(readingLevel)
>>> readingLevel
11
```

Notice that we have overwritten the old value of `readingLevel` with the truncated value. Alternatively, we could have used the `round` function to round the reading level. Function arguments can be more complex than just single constants and variables; they can be anything that evaluates to a value. For example, we could get the rounded reading level like this too:

```
>>> readingLevel = round(0.39*averageWords + 11.8*averageSyllables - 15.59)
>>> readingLevel
12
```

The expression in parentheses is evaluated first, and then the result of the expression is used as the argument to the `round` function.

Not all functions have return values. For example, the `print` function, which simply prints its arguments to the screen, does not. For example, try this:

```
>>> result = print(readingLevel)
12
>>> print(result)
None
```

The variable `result` was assigned whatever the `print` function returned, which is different from what it printed. When we print `result`, we see that it was assigned something called `None`. `None` is a Python keyword that essentially represents "nothing." Any function that does not define a return value itself returns `None` by default. We will see this again shortly when we learn how to define our own functions.

What's in a name?

Let's remind ourselves of a few reasons why variable names are so important.

1. Assigning descriptive names to values can make our algorithms much easier to understand. In the "real world," programming is almost always a collaborative endeavor, so it is important to always write programs that are easy to understand by others. Our goal should be to use sufficient descriptive variable names to create ***self-documenting programs*** that require as little as possible explanation outside the program itself. To see the value of self-documenting programs, just consider if we had written the reading level computation above like this instead:

    ```
    >>> a = 16
    >>> b = 1.78
    >>> c = 0.39 * a + 11.8 * b - 15.59
    ```

    Would you have any idea what these statements did?

2. As we did in our pseudocode algorithms, naming inputs will allow us to generalize algorithms so that, instead of being tied to one particular input,

and	break	elif	for	in	not	True
as	class	else	from	is	or	try
assert	continue	except	global	lambda	pass	while
async	def	False	if	None	raise	with
await	del	finally	import	nonlocal	return	yield

Table 1.2 The 35 Python keywords.

they work for a variety of possible inputs. We will discuss this further in Section 2.5.

3. Names will serve as labels for computed values that we wish to use later, eliminating the need to compute them again at that time.

Variable names in Python can be any sequence of characters drawn from letters, digits, and the underscore (_) character, but they may not start with a digit. And, unlike some of our pseudocode variable names, they may not contain spaces. You also cannot use any of Python's *keywords*, shown in Table 1.2. Keywords are elements of the Python language that have predefined meanings. We will encounter most of these keywords as we progress through this book.

Let's try breaking some of these naming rules to see what happens.

```
>>> average words = 6
         ^
SyntaxError: invalid syntax
```

A *syntax error* indicates a violation of the syntax, or grammar, of the Python language. It is completely *normal* for programmers to encounter syntax errors; it is part of the programming process. With practice, it will often become immediately obvious what you did wrong, you will fix the mistake, and move on. Other times, you will need to look harder to discover the problem but, with practice, these instances too will become easier to diagnose. In this case, the problem is the space we are trying to use in the variable name.

Next, try this one.

```
>>> average-words = 6
SyntaxError: cannot assign to operator
```

This syntax error is referring to the dash/hyphen/minus sign symbol (-) that we have in our name. Python interprets the symbol as the minus operator, which is why it is not allowed in names. Instead, we can use the underscore (_) character (i.e., `average_words`) or vary the capitalization (i.e., `averageWords`) to distinguish the two words in the name.

To develop a more nuanced understanding of what an assignment statement really does, we need to know a little bit about how values are stored. A computer's memory consists of billions of *memory cells*, each of which can store one value. These cells are analogous to post office boxes, each with a unique address. And a variable name is like a "Sticky note"[4] attached to the front of one of those boxes. As we will see in Section 3.2, our programs are also stored in the same memory while they are executing.

The picture below represents the outcome of the three assignment statements in our reading level computation. Each of the three rectangles represents a memory cell, and a variable name (on a sticky note) is attached to each one.

Like a sticky note, a variable name can easily be reassigned to a different value at any time. For example, suppose we change the average number of syllables to 1.625:

```
>>> averageSyllables = 1.625
```

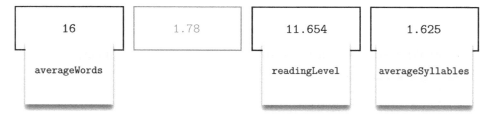

The reassignment caused the averageSyllables sticky note to move to a different memory cell containing the value 1.625. The old value 1.78 may briefly remain in memory without a name attached to it, but since we can no longer access that value without a reference to it, the Python "garbage collection" mechanism will soon free up the memory that it occupies and allow it to be overwritten with something new.

Reflection 1.15 *Did the value of* readingLevel *change when we changed the value of* averageSyllables?

Try it:

```
>>> readingLevel
11.654
```

While the value assigned to averageSyllables has changed, the value assigned to readingLevel has not. This example demonstrates that assignment is a one-time event; Python does not "remember" how the value of readingLevel was computed. Put another way, an assignment is *not* creating an equivalence between a name and a computation. Rather, it performs the computation on the righthand side of the assignment operator only when the assignment happens, and then assigns the result to the name on the lefthand side. That value remains assigned to the name until the

---

[4] "Sticky note" is a registered trademark of the BIC Corporation.

name is explicitly assigned some other value or it ceases to exist. To compute a new value for `readingLevel` based on the new value of `averageSyllables`, we would need to perform the reading level computation again.

```
>>> readingLevel = 0.39 * averageWords + 11.8 * averageSyllables - 15.59
>>> readingLevel
9.825
```

Now the value assigned to `readingLevel` has changed, due to the explicit assignment statement above.

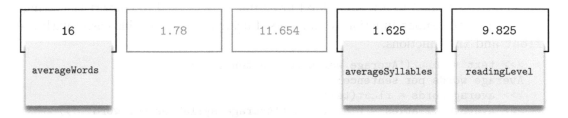

Yet another way to reinforce the nature of assignment is to look at what happens if we add one to `averageWords`:

```
>>> averageWords = averageWords + 1
```

If the equals sign denoted equality, then this statement would not make any sense! However, if we interpret it using the two-step process, it is perfectly reasonable. First, the expression on the righthand side is evaluated, ignoring the lefthand side entirely. Since, at this moment, `averageWords` is 16, the righthand side evaluates to $16 + 1 = 17$. Second, the value 17 is assigned to `averageWords`. So this statement has added 1 to, or *incremented*, the value of `averageWords`.

What if we had not assigned a value to `averageWords` before we tried to increment it? To find out, try this:

```
>>> tryThis = tryThis + 1
NameError: name 'tryThis' is not defined
```

This *name error* occurred because, when the Python interpreter tried to evaluate the righthand side of the assignment, it found that `tryThis` was not assigned a value, i.e., it was not defined. So we need to make sure that we define any variable before we refer to it. This may sound obvious but, in the context of some larger programs later on, it might be easy to forget.

Interactive computing

We can interactively query for string input in our programs with the `input` function. The `input` function takes a string prompt as an argument and returns a string value that is typed in response. For example, the following statement prompts for your name and prints a greeting.

```
>>> name = input('What is your name? ')
What is your name? George
>>> print('Howdy, ' + name + '!')
Howdy, George!
```

The call to the **input** function above prints the string `'What is your name? '` and then waits. After you type something (above, we typed `George`, shown in red) and hit the return key, the text that we typed is returned by the **input** function as a string and assigned to the variable called **name**. The value of **name** is then used in the **print** function.

To adapt this format to a reading level program, we will need to convert the strings returned by the **input** function to numbers. Luckily, we can do this easily with the **float** and **int** functions.

```
>>> text = input('Average words per sentence: ')
Average words per sentence: 4.5
>>> averageWords = float(text)
>>> averageSyllables = float(input('Average syllables per word: '))
Average syllables per word: 2.1
>>> readingLevel = 0.39 * averageWords + 11.8 * averageSyllables - 15.59
>>> print('The reading level is ' + str(round(readingLevel)) + '.')
The reading level is 11.
```

In response to the first prompt above, we typed 4.5. Then the **input** function assigned what we typed to the variable **text** as a string, in this case `'4.5'` (notice the quotes). Then, using the **float** function, the string is converted to the numeric value 4.5 (no quotes) and assigned to the variable **averageWords**. In the second prompt, we combined these two steps by passing the return value of the **input** function in as the argument of **float**. Either way, now that **averageWords** and **averageSyllables** are numerical values, they can be used in the arithmetic expression to compute the reading level. In the last **print** statement, notice how we composed the **str** and **round** functions so that the return value of **round** is being used as the argument to **str**.

> **Reflection 1.16** *Type the statements above again, omitting the* **float** *function:*
>
> ```
> >>> averageWords = input('Average words per sentence: ')
> >>> averageSyllables = input('Average syllables per word: ')
> >>> readingLevel = 0.39 * averageWords + 11.8 * averageSyllables - 15.59
> ```
>
> *What happened? Why?*

Looking ahead

In just this section, we have nearly achieved a full Python implementation of our FLESCH KINCAID algorithm from page 14. What our implementation is missing is the ability to call upon it as a functional abstraction like we did in the READING LEVEL algorithm on page 19:

> *reading level* ← FLESCH-KINCAID (*average words, average syllables*)

Here's a sneak peek at how we will do that in the next chapter:

```
def fleschKincaid(averageWords, averageSyllables):
    return 0.39 * averageWords + 11.8 * averageSyllables - 15.59
```

This defines **fleschKincaid** to be a *function* that takes two arguments as input and returns the corresponding reading level as its output. With this function, we will be able to do things like this:

```
readingLevel = fleschKincaid(16, 1.78)
```

More to come...

Exercises

Use the Python interpreter to answer the following questions. Where appropriate, provide both the answer and the Python expression you used to get it.

1.3.1*   You may have seen a meme that challenges you to find the correct answer for the expression $8 \div 2(2+2)$. Use Python to do this.

1.3.2*   The Library of Congress stores its holdings on 838 miles of shelves. Assuming an average book is one inch thick, how many books would this hold?

1.3.3.   If I gave you a nickel and promised to double the amount you have every hour for the next 24, how much money would you have at the end? What if I only increased the amount by 50% each hour, how much would you have? Use exponentiation to compute these quantities.

1.3.4.   The Library of Congress stores its holdings on 838 miles of shelves. How many round trips is this between Granville, Ohio and Columbus, Ohio?

1.3.5.   What is wrong with each of the following Python names? Suggest a fixed version for each.

    (a)   `word count`

    (b)   `here:there`

    (c)   `'minutes'`

    (d)   `4ever`

    (e)   `#thisisavariable`

1.3.6.   (a)   Assign a variable named **radius** to have the value 10. Using the formula for the area of a circle ($A = \pi r^2$), assign to a new variable named **area** the area of a circle with radius equal to your variable **radius**. (The number 10 should not appear in the formula.)

    (b)   Now change the value of **radius** to 15. What is the value of **area** now? Why?

1.3.7* The formula for computing North American wind chill temperatures, in degrees Celsius, is
$$W = 13.12 + 0.6215\,t + (0.3965\,t - 11.37)\,v^{0.16}$$
where t is the ambient temperature in degrees Celsius and v is the wind speed in km/h.[5]

(a) Compute the wind chill for a temperature of $-3°$ C and wind speed of 13 km/h by assigning this temperature and wind speed to two variables `temperature` and `windChill`, and then assigning the corresponding wind chill to another variable `windChill` using the formula above.

(b) Change the value of `temperature` to 4.0 and then check the value of `windChill`. Why did the value of `windChill` not change? How would you update the value of `windChill` to reflect the change in `temperature`?

1.3.8* Suppose we want to swap the values of two variables named `left` and `right`. Why doesn't the following work? Show a method that does work.
```
left = right
right = left
```

1.3.9. What are the values of `apples` and `oranges` at the end of the following?
```
apples = 12.0
oranges = 2 * apples
apples = 6
```

1.3.10. What is the value of `number` at the end of the following?
```
number = 0
number = number + 1
number = number + 1
number = number + 1
```

1.3.11. In the previous exercise, what happens if you omit the first statement (`number = 0`)? Explain why `number` must be assigned a value before the executing the statement `number = number + 1`.

1.3.12. What are the values of `apples` and `oranges` at the end of the following?
```
apples = 12.0
oranges = 6
oranges = oranges * apples
```

1.3.13. String values can also be manipulated with the `*` operator. Applied to strings, the `*` operator becomes the **repetition operator**, which repeats a string some number of times. The operand on the left side of the repetition operator is a string and the operand on the right side is an integer that indicates the number of times to repeat the string.
```
>>> last * 4
'PythonPythonPythonPython'
>>> print(first + ' ' * 10 + last)
Monty          Python
```

(a) Explain why `18 * 10` and `'18' * 10` give different values.

---

[5] Technically, wind chill is only defined at or below $10°$ C and for wind speeds above 4.8 km/h.

(b) Use the repetition operator to create a string consisting of 20 asterisks separated by spaces.

(c) The special character '\n' (really two characters, but it represents a single character) is called the *newline* character, and causes printing to continue on the next line. To see its effect, try this:

```
>>> print('Hello\nthere')
```

Use the newline character and the repetition operator to create a string that will display a *vertical* line of 20 asterisks when printed.

(d) Combine the techniques from parts (b) and (c) (with some modification) to create a string that will display a 20×20 square of asterisks when printed.

1.3.14* Modify your wind chill computation from Exercise 1.3.7 so that it gives the wind chill rounded to the nearest integer.

1.3.15. Show how you can use the int function to truncate any floating point number to two places to the right of the decimal point. In other words, you want to truncate a number like 3.1415926 to 3.14. Your expression should work with any value of number.

1.3.16* Show how you can use the int function to find the fractional part of any positive floating point number. For example, if the value 3.14 is assigned to number, you want to output 0.14. Your expression should work with any value of number.

1.3.17. Show how to round a floating point number to the nearest tenth in Python.

1.3.18. What happens when you execute the following statements? Explain why.

```
>>> value = print(42)
>>> print(value * 2)
```

1.3.19* Fix the following sequence of statements

```
>>> radius = input('Radius of your circle? ')
>>> area = 3.14159 * radius * radius
>>> print('The area of your circle is ' + area + '.')
```

1.3.20. Write a sequence of statements that

(a) prompt for a person's age,

(b) compute the number of days that person has been alive (assume 365.25 days in a year to account for leap years),

(c) round the number of days to the nearest integer, and then

(d) print the result, nicely formatted.

1.3.21* Repeat Exercise 1.3.14, but this time prompt for the temperature and wind chill using the input function, and print the result formatted like

```
The wind chill is -2 degrees Celsius.
```

1.3.22. The following program implements a Mad Lib.

```
adj1 = input('Adjective: ')
noun1 = input('Noun: ')
noun2 = input('Noun: ')
adj2 = input('Adjective: ')
noun3 = input('Noun: ')

print('How to Throw a Party')
print()
print('If you are looking for a/an', adj1, 'way to')
print('celebrate your love of', noun1 + ', how about a')
print(noun2 + '-themed costume party?  Start by')
print('sending invitations encoded in', adj2, 'format')
print('giving directions to the location of your', noun3 + '.')
```

Write your own Mad Lib program, requiring at least five parts of speech to insert. (You can download the program above from the book website to get you started.)

1.3.23* Write a sequence of statements that accepts three numbers as input, one at a time, and prints the running sum of the numbers after each input. Use only two variables, one for the input number and one for the running sum. Here is an example of what your program should print (omitting the statements you type at the prompt):

```
Number 1: 5.1
The current sum is 5.1.
Number 2: 7
The cu
rrent sum is 12.1.
Number 3: 12.3
The final sum is 24.4.
```

1.4 LOOK BACK

Fourth, look back. Check the result. Can you derive the result differently?

Not all algorithms are *good* algorithms, even if they are correct. And just about any algorithm can be made better. Like writing prose or poetry, writing algorithms and programming involve continual refinement. At every step of the process, we should "look back" on what we have created to see if it can be improved.

Reflection 1.17 *What characteristics might make one algorithm or program better than another?*

Here are some questions we should always ask about our algorithms and programs:

1. Is your program easy to understand?

   Are you using descriptive variable names? Is there anything extraneous that could be omitted? Is there a more elegant way to accomplish the same thing?

2. Does your program work properly?

Is it solving the correct problem? Does it give the correct output for every possible input?

3. How long does your algorithm take? Is it as efficient as it could be?

Is your algorithm doing too much work? Is there a way to streamline it? Does your program use too much memory? Can it be done with less? Our algorithms at this point are too simple to worry about this too much but, as they grow more complex, we will see that efficiency becomes an issue of paramount importance.

4. Are there ethical ramifications to consider?

How will your algorithm or program affect human welfare? Will your algorithm unfairly impact some groups more than others? Are any of your assumptions based on unexamined cultural or racial prejudices? Are there related privacy or intellectual property issues? What is the environmental impact?

These are essential questions to ask at every step of the problem-solving process. Sometimes even determining what problem you should solve requires careful judgment. Similarly, poorly chosen inputs to some problems, e.g., facial recognition and risk assessment algorithms used in the criminal justice system, can have severely damaging effects on entire groups of people. And when designing an algorithm, you may find that ethical considerations are at odds with efficiency; shortcuts and overly simple solutions can lead to damaging results.

Questions such as these are both complex and essential, but largely beyond the scope of this book. Some additional resources well worth exploring are given in Section 1.5.

We will discuss the first point in more detail in the next chapter, as we start to develop more complete programs. We elaborate on the second and third points below.

Testing

It should go without saying that we want our programs to be correct. That is, we want our algorithms to produce the correct output for every possible input, and we want our programs to be faithful to the design of our algorithms. There are techniques that we can use to increase the likelihood that our functions and programs are correct. The first two steps in our problem solving process are a good start: making sure that we thoroughly understand the problem we are trying to solve and spending quality time designing a solution, well before we start typing any code.

However, despite the best planning, errors, or "bugs," will still creep into your programs. To root out bugs from our programs, i.e., *debug* them, we have to test them thoroughly with a variety of carefully chosen inputs. We started to do this when we refined our syllable-counting algorithm in Section 1.2. There are four important categories of inputs that you should be thinking about as we move forward:

1. If there are *disallowed inputs* that don't make sense for the problem and are not guaranteed to work, this should be stated explicitly in the documentation, as we will discuss further in the next section. We will also talk about how to more formally specify and check for these inputs in Section 5.5.

2. Once you have identified the range of legal inputs, test your program with several *common inputs* to make sure that its basic functionality is intact. It is important to test with inputs that are representative of the entire range of possibilities. For example, if your input is a number, try both negative and positive integers and floats.

3. *Boundary cases* are inputs that rests on a boundary of the range of legal inputs. For example, if your allowed inputs are all numbers between 0 and 100, be sure to test both 0 and 100. In many problems, testing boundary cases can identify issues with your algorithm that are easy to overlook.

4. Finally, *corner cases* are any other kind of rare input that might cause the program to break. These are usually the hardest to identify and tend to be quite specific to the problem being solved.

To illustrate, let's look at the simple problem of converting an average course grade between 0 and 100 to a GPA on a standard four-point scale, where 90–100 is a 4, 80–89 is a 3, 70–79 is a 2, 60–69 is a 1, and < 60 is a 0. (For simplicity, we will ignore +/− grades.). As a first stab at an algorithm, we notice that dividing by 10 to get the tens place of the input grade and then subtracting 5 seems to work.

Algorithm CONVERT GRADE — DRAFT

Input: *grade*
  1 | *tens place* ← the digit in the tens place of *grade*
  2 | *GPA* ← *tens place* − 5
Output: *GPA*

In Python, we can implement this algorithm in one line:

```
>>> grade = 87
>>> GPA = int(grade / 10) - 5
>>> GPA
3
```

∎ **Reflection 1.18** *What are the disallowed inputs for this algorithm?*

Assuming that no extra credit is possible, any grade less than zero or greater than 100 should be disallowed. We'll look at how to more formally specify this in the coming chapters. Next, we should try to some common inputs from 0 to 100. To start, trying a grade in each of the five GPA categories makes sense.

| **Reflection 1.19** *Try a grade in each of the five GPA categories. What do you find?*

| **Reflection 1.20** *What boundary cases should you try?*

Did you try grades on the boundaries of the categories (e.g., 60 and 90), grades below 50, and the boundary cases of 0 and 100? Here we have some issues.

```
>>> grade = 42
>>> GPA = int(grade / 10) - 5
>>> GPA
-1
>>> grade = 0
>>> GPA = int(grade / 10) - 5
>>> GPA
-5
>>> grade = 100
>>> GPA = int(grade / 10) - 5
>>> GPA
5
```

To fix these problems, we want to ensure that GPA never falls below zero or exceeds four. We can accomplish this with the `min` and `max` functions, which return the minimum and maximum values among their arguments. To fix the negative GPA issue, we want to return the maximum of GPA and zero.

```
>>> grade = 42
>>> GPA = int(grade / 10) - 5
>>> GPA = max(GPA, 0)
>>> GPA
0
```

To fix a GPA exceeding four, we want to return the minimum of the GPA and 4.

```
>>> grade = 100
>>> GPA = int(grade / 10) - 5
>>> GPA = min(GPA, 4)
>>> GPA
4
```

To fix both problems, we need to combine these solutions:

```
>>> GPA = int(grade / 10) - 5
>>> GPA = max(GPA, 0)
>>> GPA = min(GPA, 4)
```

At this point, you should try all of the test cases again to make sure everything works correctly. We will revisit testing in Section 5.5.

Algorithm efficiency

Now let's look a little more closely at the third question at the beginning of this section:

3. How long does your algorithm take? Is it as efficient as it could be?

To determine how much time an algorithm requires, we could implement it as a program and execute it on a computer. However, this approach presents some problems. First, which programming language do we use? Second, which inputs do we use for our timing experiments? Third, which computer do we use? Once we make these choices, will they give us a complete picture of our algorithm's efficiency? Will they allow us to predict the time required to execute the algorithm on different computers? Will these predictions still be valid ten years from now?

A better way to predict the amount of time required by an algorithm is to count the number of **elementary steps** that are required, independent of any particular computer. An elementary step is one that always requires the same amount of time, regardless of the input. Examples of elementary steps are

- arithmetic operations,
- assignments of values to variables,
- testing a condition involving numbers or a character, and
- examining a character in a string or a number in a list.

Each of these things takes the same amount of time regardless of the numbers being operated upon, the types of values being assigned, or the values being examined. The number of elementary steps required by an algorithm is called the algorithm's **time complexity**. By determining an algorithm's time complexity, we can estimate how long an algorithm will take on any computer, relative to another algorithm for the same problem.

Constant-time algorithms

To make this more concrete, let's count how many elementary steps there are in our final SPHERE VOLUME 2 algorithm on page 14, beginning with line 1:

```
1 |  volume ← 4 ÷ 3
```

Line 1 contains two elementary steps: an arithmetic operation followed by an assignment of the result to a variable. Assignment and arithmetic (with two operands) are elementary steps because they always require the same amount of time regardless of the variable or the operands. Line 2, below, also contains two elementary steps for the same reason.

```
2 |  volume ← volume × π
```

Lines 3–4 consist of a loop that instructs us to perform a similar arithmetic/assignment statement three times:

```
3 |  repeat the following three times:
4 |      volume ← volume × r
```

Line 4 takes two elementary steps by itself, but it is executed three times, so lines 3–4 require a total of six elementary steps. Therefore, all together, this algorithm requires 2 + 2 + 6 = 10 elementary steps.

The most important takeaway from this analysis, however, is that the Sᴘʜᴇʀᴇ Vᴏʟᴜᴍᴇ 2 algorithm requires the same number of elementary steps regardless of what the input is. It executes ten elementary steps whether the input is 10 or 10,000. Therefore, we call it a **constant-time algorithm**.

Linear-time algorithms

Next let's analyze our last Sʏʟʟᴀʙʟᴇ Cᴏᴜɴᴛ algorithm from page 16. The first statement in this algorithm counts the number of vowels in the input *word*:

> 1│ *count* ← the number of vowels (*a, e, i, o, u*) in *word*

Although this may look like one elementary step at first glance, it is not. As we will discuss more in Chapter 6, a computer algorithm cannot just look at a word and instantly tell you how many vowels it has. Instead, it will need to check each letter, one at a time, counting the number of vowels that it sees. In other words, line 1 is equivalent to the following:

> (a)│ *count* ← 0
> (b)│ repeat for each *letter* in *word*:
> (c)│   if *letter* is a vowel (*a, e, i, o, u*), then add 1 to *count*

Writing it in this way makes it more apparent that the number of elementary steps required by line 1 depends on the number of letters in *word*. More specifically, a *word* with n letters will require n iterations of the loop in lines (b)–(c); the longer the *word* is (i.e., the bigger n is), the longer this will take. The body of the loop in line (c) requires at most two elementary steps: one to examine a letter and one to add to *count*. Therefore altogether, including the initialization of *count* to zero in line(a), there are $2n + 1$ elementary steps here.

Lines 2–3 of the algorithm contain a more explicit loop that is very similar to our rewritten version of line 1:

> 2│ repeat for each pair of adjacent *letters* in *word*:
> 3│   if the *letters* are both vowels, then subtract 1 from *count*

The only difference from lines (b)–(c) above is that this loop looks at pairs of letters instead of individual letters and it subtracts from, rather than adds to, *count*. Regardless, once again, the number of elementary steps depends on the length of *word*; if there are n letters in *word*, lines 2–3 repeat $n - 1$ times (because there are $n - 1$ pairs of adjacent letters in a *word* with n letters). You can see this more explicitly in the trace table in page 16. In that case, the input contained $n = 7$ letters and there were $n - 1 = 6$ iterations of the loop. In the body of the loop, there are at most two elementary steps, so the entire loop contains $2(n - 1)$ elementary steps.

Finally, line 4 is much simpler:

> 4│ if *word* ends in *e*, then subtract 1 from *count*

We can safely say that the number of elementary steps in this line does *not* depend on the length of *word*. This conclusion relies on the assumption, which will be

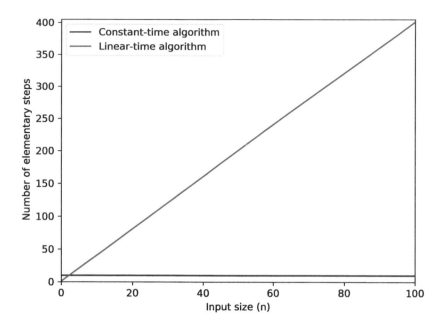

Figure 1.5 A comparison of constant vs. linear time complexity.

verified in Chapter 6, that we can look at the end of any *word* directly, regardless of its length. So we can say that this line requires at most two elementary steps, one to check the last letter in *word* and one to subtract from *count*.

Putting it all together then, the entire algorithm requires about $(2n+1)+2(n-1)+2 = 4n + 1$ elementary steps. As with the sphere-volume algorithm, the exact number is not terribly important. The important thing to notice is that the time complexity of this algorithm is linearly proportional to the length of the input *word*. A linear function is one that contains n but no higher powers of n like n^2 or n^3. We call algorithms with time complexities that are linearly proportional to n, like SYLLABLE COUNT, *linear-time algorithms*.

The real issue underlying time complexity is **scalability**: how quickly the running time grows as the input gets very large. The difference between a constant-time algorithm and a linear-time algorithm is illustrated in Figure 1.5. The blue line represents the time complexity of a constant-time algorithm that always requires ten elementary steps regardless of how large the input becomes. The red line represents the time complexity of a linear-time algorithm that requires $4n + 1$ elementary steps when the input has size n. Notice that the number of elementary steps in the linear-time algorithm grows proportionally to the size of the input. As the input gets larger, the difference between the constant-time algorithm and the linear-time algorithm grows much larger. Therefore, for a particular problem, if we could choose between a constant-time algorithm and a linear-time algorithm, especially if n is

Figure 1.6 Examples of everyday algorithms: a fire alarm, an elevator, and a recipe.

large, we would clearly favor the constant-time algorithm. But even linear-time algorithms are generally considered to be very fast. As will see later, some problems require a lot more time to solve.

A linear-time algorithm is also said to have time complexity $\mathcal{O}(n)$ (pronounced "big oh of n"). The uppercase letter $\mathcal{O}$ is shorthand for "order;" we can also say that a linear-time algorithm has "order of n" time complexity. A constant-time algorithm is said to have $\mathcal{O}(1)$ time complexity. We will study time complexity in more detail in Section 6.7.

Although we have presented "looking back" as the last step in a four-step process, the issues we have discussed here are important to keep in mind in every step. The better your product is at each step, the less work you will have to do later to clean it up. Designing algorithms can be a tricky business and first impressions can sometimes be deceiving. For example, you have already seen that the number of lines in an algorithm is often unrelated to its time complexity. Similarly, techniques that seem to work at first glance may not work for some inputs. As in any worthwhile endeavor, a careful and deliberate approach will pay dividends in the long run.

Exercises

1.4.1. Identify three algorithms from your everyday life and critique them with respect to readability, correctness, and efficiency. Some examples of everyday algorithms are shown in Figure 1.6.

1.4.2. What characteristics, other than the ones we discussed, might make one algorithm better than another?

1.4.3. For each of the following algorithms, demonstrate that it is correct by testing it with at least two common inputs and all boundary inputs you can identify. Say what the algorithm's output is in each case. Also, if there are any inputs that should not be allowed, identify those.

(a)*   your revised Sphere Volume algorithm from Exercise 1.2.9

(b)*   the Count votes algorithm from Exercise 1.2.7

(c)   the Surface area of a box algorithm from Exercise 1.2.6

(d)

Algorithm Maximum value in a list

Input: a list of *numbers*

1 | *maxSoFar* ← first item in *numbers*
2 | repeat for each *item* in *numbers*:
3 | if *item* > *maxSoFar*, then assign *maxSoFar* ← *item*

Output: *maxSoFar*

(e)

Algorithm Distance to lightning strike

Input: elapsed number of *seconds*

1 | *speed of sound* ← 343 m/s
2 | *distance* ← *seconds* × *speed of sound*
3 | *distance* ← *distance* ÷ 1000

Output: *distance*

(f)

Algorithm Raise to the fifth

Input: a *number*

1 | *product* ← 1
2 | repeat 5 times:
3 | *product* ← *product* × *number*

Output: *product*

(g)

Algorithm Count pronouns

Input: a *text*

1 | *countFeminine* ← 0
2 | *countMasculine* ← 0
3 | repeat for each *word* in the *text*:
4 | if the *word* is *she*, then add one to *countFeminine*
5 | if the *word* is *he*, then add one to *countMasculine*
6 | *ratio* ← *countFeminine* ÷ *countMasculine*

Output: *ratio*

1.4.4. For each of the algorithms in the previous exercise, estimate the number of elementary steps and decide whether it is a constant-time or a linear-time algorithm.

1.4.5. Suppose that you have been asked to organize a phone tree for your organization to personally alert everyone with a phone call in the event of an emergency. You have to make the first call, but after that, you can delegate others to make calls as well. Who makes which calls and the order in which they are made constitutes an algorithm. For example, suppose there are only eight people in the organization, and they are named Amelia, Beth, Caroline, Dave, Ernie, Flo, Gretchen, and Homer. Then here is a simple algorithm:

Algorithm ALPHABETICAL PHONE TREE

Input: a list of eight people and their phone numbers
1 | Amelia calls Beth.
2 | Beth calls Caroline.
3 | Caroline calls Dave.
⋮
7 | Gretchen calls Homer.
Output: none (but phone calls were made)

For simplicity, assume that everyone answers the phone right away and every phone call takes the same amount of time.

(a) For the phone tree problem, identify at least two criteria that would make one algorithm better than another. For each criterion, design an algorithm that satisfies it.

(b) In the interest of safety, one criterion for a phone tree would be to ensure that everyone is notified as soon as possible. Design an algorithm that ensures that all eight people are notified in a chain of at most three calls. At the outset, only Amelia is aware of the emergency. (Multiple calls can be made simultaneously.)

(c) Extend the algorithm you designed in the previous question to an arbitrarily large number of people. In general, how many people are called simultaneously during any step $t = 1, 2, 3, \ldots$? First, think about how many calls are made during steps 1, 2, and 3 in your algorithm. Then think about how many calls would be made during time steps 4, 5, and 6. Can you generalize this process to any step t?

1.5 SUMMARY AND FURTHER DISCOVERY

In this chapter, we outlined the four steps in the computational problem solving process. First, we need to understand the problem we are trying to solve, viewed as the relationship between its inputs and the desired output. This may sound obvious, but you would be surprised at how much time is often wasted solving the incorrect problem! Solving some small examples by hand at this point can often help, and illuminate potential pitfalls. At the end of this step, the problem is viewed as a functional abstraction because we understand what an algorithm for it should do, but not yet what the algorithm looks like.

Second, we want to design an algorithm to solve the problem. It helps to use top-down design to decompose the problem into smaller subproblems. Then we can design algorithms for the simplest problems first and work our way up the decomposition tree in a bottom-up fashion. Algorithm design is often the most challenging of the four steps, which is why writing algorithms in pseudocode is so valuable. Pseudocode allows us to think about how to solve the problem without being distracted by the more demanding requirements of a programming language. In our algorithms, we saw four categories of algorithmic statements:

1. assignment statements that assign a value to a variable,
2. arithmetic statements,
3. loops that repeat a set of statements some number of times, and
4. conditional statements that make decisions.

It may surprise you to know that these four types of statements are sufficient to write any algorithm imaginable! So writing algorithms, and programs, in large part amounts to putting this small palette to work in creative ways. As we progress through this book, we will incrementally learn how to use these kinds of statements in myriad combinations to solve a wide variety of problems.

In the third step, we translate the algorithm into a program in Python. We started our introduction to programming by using variables, arithmetic, and simple functions. In the next chapter, you will begin to write your own functions and incorporate them into longer programs. By the end of this book, you will be amazed by the kinds of things you can do!

Fourth, we need to remember to "look back" at our algorithms and programs in a process of continual refinement. Just because a program seems to work on a few simple inputs does not mean that it cannot be improved. We always want to strive for the clearest, most efficient, and fairest solution we can.

Notes for further discovery

The first epigraph at the beginning of this chapter is from an article by computer scientists Michael Fellows and Ian Parberry [16]. A similar quote is often attributed to the late Dutch computer scientist Edsger Dijkstra.

The second epigraph is from the great Donald Knuth [33], Professor Emeritus of The Art of Computer Programming at Stanford University. When he was still in graduate school in the 1960s Dr. Knuth began his life's work, a multi-volume set of books titled, *The Art of Computer Programming* [31]. In 2011, he published the first part of Volume 4, and has plans to write seven volumes total. Although incomplete, this work was cited at the end of 1999 in *American Scientist*'s list of "100 or so Books that Shaped a Century of Science" [42]. Dr. Knuth also invented the typesetting program TEX, which was used to write this book. He is the recipient of many international awards, including the Turing Award, named after Alan Turing, which is considered to be the "Nobel Prize of computer science."

Guido van Rossum is a Dutch computer programmer who invented the Python programming language. IDLE is an acronym for "Integrated DeveLopment Environment," but is also considered to be a tribute to Eric Idle, one of the founders of Monty Python.

The "Hello world!" program is the traditional first program that everyone learns when starting out. See `http://en.wikipedia.org/wiki/Hello_world_program` for an interesting history.

As you continue to learn Python, it will be helpful to add the following documentation site to your "favorites" list: `https://docs.python.org/3/index.html`. There are also a list of links and references for commonly used classes and functions (Appendix A) on the book website.

There are many good resources for learning more about ethics in computing and data science. The ACM Code of Ethics and Professional Conduct (`https://www.acm.org/code-of-ethics`) is the main code followed by computing practitioners around the world. For more in-depth coverage of moral theories and ethics, we recommend *Computer Ethics* by Deborah Johnson [27], *Ethics of Big Data* by Kord Davis [11], and *Ethical and Secure Computing* by Joseph Migga Kizza [30]. *Race after Technology* by Ruha Benjamin [6], *Algorithms of Oppression: How Search Engines Reinforce Racism* by Safiya Umoja Noble [44], and *Weapons of Math Destruction* by Cathy O'Neil [45] delve deeper into the potentially damaging social impacts of computing.

Finally, a note about "big oh" notation. Our use of $\mathcal{O}(n)$ is actually a slight, but common, abuse of notation. Formally, to say that an algorithm has $\mathcal{O}(n)$ time complexity means that its time complexity is asymptotically *at most* linearly proportional to n. In other words, a constant-time algorithm also has $\mathcal{O}(n)$ time complexity! The correct notation is $\Theta(n)$ ("big theta of n"), but "big oh" notation is used so frequently in practice that we chose to also use it, despite some discomfort.

CHAPTER 2

Visualizing Abstraction

We have seen that computer programming is an art, because it applies accumulated knowledge to the world, because it requires skill and ingenuity, and especially because it produces objects of beauty. A programmer who subconsciously views himself as an artist will enjoy what he does and will do it better.

Donald E. Knuth
Turing Award Lecture (1974)

We may say most aptly that the Analytical Engine weaves algebraical patterns just as the Jacquard-loom weaves flowers and leaves.

Ada Lovelace
Notes (1843)

V ISUALIZING large quantities of information can often provide insights that raw data cannot. Compare the following partial list of earthquake epicenters in (longitude, latitude) format with the visualization of these same data in Figure 2.1.

$$(-78.6, 19.3), (144.8, 19.1), (145.9, 43.5), (26.6, 45.7), (39.3, 38.4), (90.8, 26.3), \ldots$$

Simply plotting the points on an appropriate background provides immediate insight into recent seismic activity. A picture really is worth a thousand words, especially when we are faced with a slew of data.

This image was created with **_turtle graphics_**. To draw in turtle graphics, we create an abstraction called a "turtle" in a window and move it with directional commands. As a turtle moves, its "tail" leaves behind a trail, as shown in Figure 2.2. If we lift a turtle's tail up, it can move without leaving a trace. In this chapter, in the course of learning about turtle graphics, we will also explore how abstractions can be created, used, and combined to solve problems.

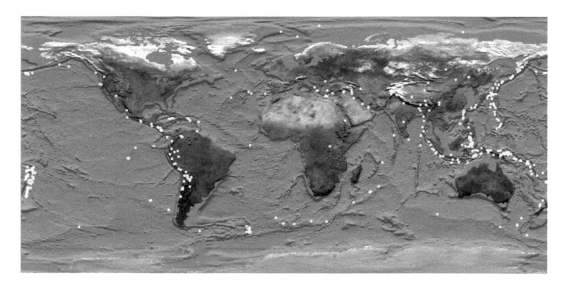

Figure 2.1   One month of magnitude 4.5+ earthquakes plotted.

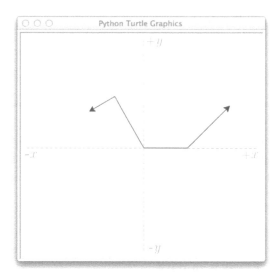

Figure 2.2   A turtle graphics window containing two turtles. The blue turtle moved forward, turned left 45°, and then moved forward again. The red turtle turned left 120°, moved forward, turned left again 90°, and then moved forward again.

2.1 DATA ABSTRACTION

The description of a turtle in turtle graphics is an example of an ***abstract data type*** (ADT). Just as a functional abstraction describes how to use a function or process without specifying how it works, an abstract data type describes how to use a category of *things* without necessarily specifying how they work. An ADT is composed of two parts:

(a) the types of information, called *attributes*, that we need to maintain about the things, and

(b) the *operations* that we are allowed to use to access or modify that information.

In Python, an abstract data type is implemented with a ***class***. In a class, attributes are maintained in a set of ***instance variables*** and the operations that can access these attributes are special functions called ***methods***.

The Python class that implements the Turtle ADT is named `Turtle`. The `Turtle` class contains several instance variables, some of which are listed below.

Instance Variable	Description
position	the turtle's current (x,y) position
heading	the turtle's current heading (in degrees)
color	the turtle's current drawing color
width	the turtle's current pen width
tail position	whether the turtle's tail is up or down

But we will never actually see or manipulate any of these instance variables directly. Instead, we will indirectly access and/or modify their values by calling the `Turtle` methods below.

Method	Argument	Description
forward	distance	move the turtle forward in its current direction
backward	distance	move the turtle opposite to its current direction
right, left	angle	turn the turtle clockwise or counterclockwise
setheading	angle	set the turtle's heading
goto	(x, y)	move the turtle to the given position
up, down	—	put the turtle's tail up or down
pensize	width	set the turtle's pen width
pencolor	color	set the turtle's pen color
position	—	return the turtle's (x,y) position
xcor, ycor	—	return the turtle's x or y coordinate
heading	—	return the turtle's heading

If the method requires an argument as input, that is listed in the second column of the table. The first group of methods move the turtle, the second group change its other attributes, and the third group return information about its attributes. More `Turtle` methods are listed in Appendix A.2.

The `Turtle` class is defined inside a ***module*** named `turtle` (notice the different capitalization). A module is an existing Python program that contains predefined values and functions that you can use. To access the contents of a module, we use the `import` keyword.

```
>>> import turtle
```

After a module has been imported, we can access classes and functions in the module by preceding the name of thing we want with the name of the module, separated by a period (`.`). To confirm the existence of the `Turtle` class, try this:

```
>>> turtle.Turtle
<class 'turtle.Turtle'>
```

Just as a blueprint describes the structure of a house, but is not actually a house, the `Turtle` class describes the structure (i.e., attributes and methods) of a drawing turtle, but is not actually a drawing turtle. Actual turtles in turtle graphics, like those pictured in Figure 2.2, are called turtle ***objects***. An object is also called an *instance* of a class, hence the term *instance variable*. When we create a new turtle object belonging to the `Turtle` class, the turtle object is endowed with its own *independent* values of orientation, position, color, and so on, as described in the class definition. For this reason, there can be more than one turtle object, as illustrated in Figure 2.2.

The distinction between a class and an object can also be loosely described by analogy to animal taxonomy. A species, like a class, describes a category of animals sharing the same general (morphological and/or genetic) characteristics. An actual living organism is an instance of a species, like an object is an instance of a class. For example, the species of Galápagos giant tortoise (*Chelonoidis nigra*) is analogous to a class, while Lonesome George, the famous Galápagos giant tortoise who died in 2012, is analogous to an object of that class. Super Diego, another famous Galápagos giant tortoise, is a member of the same species but, like another object of the same class, is a distinct individual with his own unique attributes.

❙ **Reflection 2.1** *Can you think of another analogy for a class and its associated objects?*

Virtually any consumer product can also be thought of an object belonging to a class of products. For example, a pair of headphones is an object belonging to the class of all headphones with that particular make and model. The ADT or class specification is analogous to the user manual since the user manual tells you how to use the product without necessarily giving any information about how it works or how it is made. A course assignment is also analogous to an ADT because it describes the requirements for the assignment. When a student completes the assignment, she is creating an object that (hopefully) adheres to those requirements.

Turtle graphics

To create a turtle object in Python, we call a function with the class's name, preceded by the name of the module in which the class resides.

```
>>> george = turtle.Turtle()
```

The empty parentheses indicate that we are calling a function with no arguments. The `Turtle()` function returns a reference to a new `Turtle` object, which is then assigned to the name `george`. You should also notice that a window appears on your screen with a little arrow-shaped "turtle" in the center, facing east. The center of the window has coordinates (0,0) and is called the *origin*. In Figure 2.2, the axes are superimposed on the window in light gray to orient you to the coordinate system. We can confirm that `george` is a `Turtle` object by printing the object's value.

```
>>> george
<turtle.Turtle object at 0x100522f10>
```

The odd-looking "0x100522f10" is the address in memory where this `Turtle` object resides. The address is displayed in *hexadecimal*, or base 16, notation. The `0x` at the front is a prefix that indicates hexadecimal; the actual hexadecimal memory address is `100522f10`. If you're curious, see Tangent 3.3 in the next chapter for more about how hexadecimal works.

To call a method belonging to an object, we precede the name of the method with the name of the object, separated by a period. For example, to ask `george` to move forward 200 units, we write

```
>>> george.forward(200)
```

Since the origin has coordinates (0,0) and `george` is initially pointing east (toward positive x values), `george` has moved to position (200,0); the `forward` method silently changed `george`'s hidden position attribute to reflect this, which you can confirm by calling `george`'s `position` method.

```
>>> george.position()
(200.00,0.00)
```

Notice that we did not change the object's position attribute directly. Indeed, we do not even know the name of that attribute because the class definition remains hidden from us. This is by design. By interacting with objects only through their methods, and not tinkering directly with their attributes, we maintain a clear separation between the ADT specification and the underlying implementation. This allows for the possibility that the underlying implementation may change, to make it more efficient, for example, without affecting programs that use it. The formal term for this is ***encapsulation***, something we will discuss in more detail in Chapter 12.

Exercises

2.1.1. Explain the difference between an abstract data type and a Python class.

2.1.2* Design an ADT for a pair of wireless headphones using the same format we used to describe the `Turtle` ADT. Include attributes that describe the state of the headphones at any given time and the operations that you can perform to change or get information about those attributes. You do not need to explain how to perform an operation, just what it does.

2.1.3. Choose an object from your everyday life and design an ADT for it using the format we used to describe the `Turtle` ADT.

2.1.4. Give another analogy for the difference between a class and an object. Explain.

2.1.5. Why do we use methods to change the state of a `Turtle` object instead of directly changing the values of its attributes?

2.1.6* In the Python shell, create a new turtle named `ada` and then turn `ada` 90 degrees clockwise like this:

```
>>> ada.right(90)
```

Use the `heading` method to show how the heading attribute of `ada` changed.

2.1.7. Create a new turtle named `gracie` and then move `gracie` like this:

```
>>> gracie.left(75)
>>> gracie.forward(200)
>>> gracie.right(150)
>>> gracie.forward(200)
>>> gracie.backward(80)
>>> gracie.right(105)
>>> gracie.forward(70)
```

How did these statements change the position and heading attributes of the turtle? Use the `position` and `heading` methods to find out.

2.1.8* Create two `Turtle` objects like this:

```
>>> thing1 = turtle.Turtle()
>>> thing2 = turtle.Turtle()
```

(a) What are the positions and headings of `thing1` and `thing2`? Use the `position` and `heading` methods.

(b) Using the `right` and `forward` methods, cause `thing2` to turn right 30 degrees and then move forward 50 units.

(c) What are the positions and headings of `thing1` and `thing2` now? Explain the values for each turtle and why they are different.

2.1.9. The following statements draw the red turtle in Figure 2.2.

```
>>> redTurtle = turtle.Turtle()
>>> redTurtle.pencolor('red')
>>> redTurtle.left(120)
>>> redTurtle.forward(100)
>>> redTurtle.left(90)
>>> redTurtle.forward(50)
```

Using this as an example and referring to the methods on page 51, create and draw the blue turtle in Figure 2.2 in the same window.

2.1.10. What is the difference between the statements `alice = turtle.Turtle` and `bob = turtle.Turtle()`? Which is the correct way to create a new `Turtle` object?

Figure 2.3 A garden of geometric flowers.

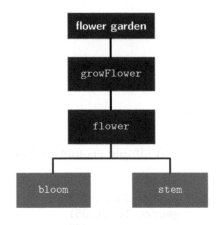

Figure 2.4 Functional decomposition of the flower garden problem.

2.2 DRAWING FLOWERS AND PLOTTING EARTHQUAKES

Before we look at how to plot the earthquakes in Figure 2.1, let's have some fun drawing flowers. Our ultimate goal, which we will complete in the next section, will be to plant a virtual garden of geometric "flowers" like those in Figure 2.3. To do this, we will implement the functional decomposition tree shown in Figure 2.4. An algorithm for the flower garden problem at the root of the tree will repeatedly call upon the **growFlower** algorithm to plant flowers at particular locations. The **growFlower** algorithm will choose the flower's size and color, and then call upon the **flower** algorithm to actually draw the flower. The **flower** algorithm is decomposed into two subproblems: one to draw the flower **bloom** and another to draw the **stem**. In our bottom-up implementation of this design, we will work our way up from the leaves of the tree toward the root, starting with the **bloom** subproblem, which will draw geometric flower bloom in Figure 2.5.

To start the bloom, we can use the line we drew in the last section as the lower horizontal line segment in the figure. Before we draw the next segment, we need to ask **george** to turn left 135 degrees. This line is highlighted below, following the three steps from the last section, in case you need to type them again.

```
>>> import turtle
>>> george = turtle.Turtle()
>>> george.forward(200)
>>> george.left(135)
```

With this method call, we have changed **george**'s hidden heading attribute, which we can confirm by calling the **heading** method.

```
>>> george.heading()
135.0
```

To finish the drawing, we just have to repeat the previous **forward** and **left** calls seven more times! (Hint: see IDLE help for how retrieve previous statements.)

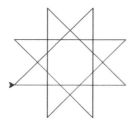

Figure 2.5 A simple geometric flower bloom drawn with turtle graphics.

```
>>> george.forward(200)
>>> george.left(135)
>>> george.forward(200)
>>> george.left(135)
>>> george.forward(200)
>>> george.left(135)
>>> george.forward(200)
>>> george.left(135)
>>> george.forward(200)
>>> george.left(135)
>>> george.forward(200)
>>> george.left(135)
>>> george.forward(200)
>>> george.left(135)
```

That was tedious. But before we look at how to avoid similar tedium in the future, we are going to transition out of the Python shell. This will allow us to save our programs so that we can easily modify them or fix mistakes, and then re-execute them without retyping everything. In IDLE, we can create a new, empty program file by choosing **New Window** from the **File** menu.[1] In the new window, retype (or copy and paste) the work we have done so far, plus the four additional highlighted lines, shown below. (If you copy and paste, be sure to remove the >>> characters.)

```
import turtle

george = turtle.Turtle()
george.hideturtle()
george.speed(6)

george.forward(200)
george.left(135)
george.forward(200)
george.left(135)
george.forward(200)
george.left(135)
george.forward(200)
george.left(135)
```

[1] If you are using a different text editor, the steps are probably very similar.

```
george.forward(200)
george.left(135)
george.forward(200)
george.left(135)
george.forward(200)
george.left(135)
george.forward(200)
george.left(135)

screen = george.getscreen()
screen.exitonclick()
```

The two highlighted statements after the first assignment statement hide `george` and speed up the drawing a bit. (The argument to the `speed` method is a number from 0 to 10, with 1 being slow, 10 being fast, and 0 being fastest.) The second to last statement assigns to the variable `screen` an object of the class `Screen`, which represents the drawing area in which `george` lives. The last statement calls the `Screen` method `exitonclick` which will close the window when we click on it. These last two lines are only necessary if your programming environment closes the turtle graphics window when the program is done. If it does not, you can omit these lines and close the window yourself when you are finished. In the future, we will generally leave these lines out, but feel free to include them in your programs as desired.

When you are done, save your file by selecting Save As. . . from the File menu. The file name of a Python program must always end with the extension `.py`, for example, `george.py`. To execute your new program in IDLE, select Run Module from the Run menu. If IDLE prompts you to save your file again, just click OK. After the program draws the flower, click on the turtle graphics window to dismiss it.

Iteration

Recall from Chapter 1 that we can use *loops* in algorithms to repeat statements multiple times, a process called *iteration*.

Reflection 2.2 *In pseudocode, how could we use a loop to simplify this long sequence of statements?*

Since we have eight identical pairs of calls to the `forward` and `left` methods, we can replace these sixteen drawing statements with a loop that repeats one pair eight times. In pseudocode, this would look something like this:

> repeat the following eight times:
> ```
> george.forward(200)
> george.left(135)
> ```

In Python, we can use a `for` loop, inserted into our program below.

```
1 import turtle

2 george = turtle.Turtle()
3 george.hideturtle()
4 george.speed(6)

5 for count in range(8):
6     george.forward(200)
7     george.left(135)

8 screen = george.getscreen()
9 screen.exitonclick()
```

This `for` loop, in lines 5–7, repeats the indented statements, called the ***body*** of the loop, eight times. After the loop is done, the next non-indented statement on line 8 is executed.

| Reflection 2.3 *What happens if you forget the colon at the end of line 5? (Try it.)*

It is easy to forget the colon. If you do, you will be notified by a syntax error, like the following, that points to the end of the line containing the `for` keyword.

```
for count in range(8)
                     ^
SyntaxError: invalid syntax
```

In the `for` loop syntax, `for` and `in` are Python keywords, and `count` is called the ***index variable***. The name of the index variable can be anything we want, but it should be descriptive of its role in the program. In this case, we chose the name `count` because it is counting the number of line segments that are being drawn. The part after the `in` keyword is a sequence of some kind:

$$\text{for } \underbrace{\text{count}}_{\text{index variable}} \text{ in } \underbrace{\text{range(8)}}_{\text{sequence}}:$$

At the beginning of each iteration of the loop, the next value in the sequence is assigned to the index variable, and then the statements in the body of the loop are executed. In this case, `range(8)` represents the sequence of eight integers from 0 to 7. So this `for` loop is saying

> For each number in the range from 0 to 7, assign the number to `count`, and then execute the body of the loop.

The following trace table shows the execution of the program in more detail. The value of `george` is represented in the trace table by an image of what has been drawn so far in the program.

Trace

Step	Line	george	count	Notes
1–4	1–4		—	initialize george
5	5	"	0	count = 0
6	6		"	george.forward(200)
7	7		"	george.left(135)
8	5	"	1	count = 1
9	6		"	george.forward(200)
10	7		"	george.left(135)
11	5	"	2	count = 2
12	6		"	george.forward(200)
13	7		"	george.left(135)
⋮				
26	5	"	7	count = 7
27	6		"	george.forward(200)
28	7		"	george.left(135)
29	8	"	"	screen = george.getscreen()
30	9	—	"	screen.exitonclick()

After the program initializes the turtle graphics window in lines 1–4, the for loop is reached on line 5. In the first iteration, count is assigned the first value in the range of numbers from 0 to 7. Then the body of the loop in lines 6–7 is executed. Once the body of the loop is complete, we return to line 5 (step 8) to execute the second iteration of the loop. This time, count is assigned 1 and the body of the loop is executed again. This continues for six more iterations since there are six more values in the range from 0 to 7 for count to be assigned. After all eight iterations of the loop are complete, the last two lines in the program are executed.

Tangent 2.1: Defining colors

The most common way to specify an arbitrary color is to specify its red, green, and blue (RGB) components individually. Each of these components is often described by an integer between 0 and 255. (These are the values that can be represented by 8 bits. Together then, a color is specified by 24 bits. If you have heard a reference to "24-bit color," now you know its origin.) Alternatively, each component can be described by a real number between 0 and 1.0. In Python turtle graphics, call `screen.colormode(255)` or `screen.colormode(1.0)`, where `screen` is a turtle's `Screen` object, to choose the desired representation.

A higher value for a particular component represents a brighter color. So, at the extremes, $(0,0,0)$ represents black, and $(255,255,255)$ and $(1.0,1.0,1.0)$ both represent white. Other common colors include $(255,255,0)$ for yellow, $(127,0,127)$ for purple, and $(153,102,51)$ for brown. So, assuming `george` is a `Turtle` object and `screen` has been assigned `george`'s `Screen` object,

```
screen.colormode(255)
george.pencolor((127, 0, 127))
```

would make `george` purple. So would

```
screen.colormode(1.0)
george.pencolor((0.5, 0, 0.5))
```

Reflection 2.4 *Try different values between 1 and 10 in place of 8 in* `range(8)`. *Can you see the connection between the value and the picture?*

Another way to see what is happening in this loop is to print the value of `count` in each iteration. To do this, add `print(count)` to the body of the `for` loop:

```
for count in range(8):
    george.forward(200)
    george.left(135)
    print(count)
```

Now, in each iteration, `george` is drawing a line segment and turning left, and then the current value of `count` is printed. As you run the program, you should notice that the numbers 0 through 7 are printed in the shell as the eight line segments are drawn in the turtle graphics window.

Reflection 2.5 *Try changing* `count` *to some other name. Did changing the name change the behavior of the program? If you changed the name only in the* `for` *loop and not in the* `print` *statement, you will get an error because* `count` *will no longer exist! You need to change it to the same thing in both places because the variable in the* `print` *statement refers to the index variable in the* `for` *loop.*

Adding some color

To finish up the bloom, let's add some color. To set the color that the turtle draws in, we use the `pencolor` method. Insert

```
george.pencolor('red')
```

Figure 2.6 A simple geometric flower bloom, outlined in red and filled in yellow.

before the `for` loop, and run your program again. A color can be specified in one of two ways. First, common colors can be specified with strings such as `'red'`, `'blue'`, and `'yellow'`. Remember that a string must be enclosed in quotes to distinguish it from a variable or function name. A color can also be defined by explicitly specifying its red, green, and blue (RGB) components, as explained in Tangent 2.1.

Finally, we will specify a color with which to fill the "flower" shape. The fill color is set by the `fillcolor` method. The statements that draw the area to be filled must be contained between calls to the `begin_fill` and `end_fill` methods. To color our flower yellow, precede the `for` loop with

```
george.fillcolor('yellow')
george.begin_fill()
```

and follow the `for` loop with

```
george.end_fill()
```

Be sure to *not* indent the call to `george.end_fill()` in the body of the `for` loop since we want that statement to execute just once *after* the loop is finished. Your flower should now look like Figure 2.6, and the complete flower bloom program should look like the following:

```
import turtle

george = turtle.Turtle()
george.hideturtle()
george.speed(6)

george.pencolor('red')
george.fillcolor('yellow')
george.begin_fill()
for count in range(8):
    george.forward(200)
    george.left(135)
george.end_fill()

screen = george.getscreen()
screen.exitonclick()
```

❙ Reflection 2.6 *Can you figure out why the shape was filled this way?*

In the next section, we will put some finishing touches on our flower bloom and flesh out the decomposition tree in Figure 2.4. But first, let's return to the earthquake visualization from Figure 2.1 at the beginning of the chapter.

Data visualization

To create the earthquake visualization, we want to draw a dot at each earthquake location in a list, so our pseudocode algorithm might look like this:

> repeat for each earthquake *location* in a list:
>   draw a dot at the *location*

In Python, drawing a dot is actually a two step process. First, we have to move the turtle to the location and then draw a dot there. The moving part is accomplished by the goto method. For example,

```
george.goto(150, 30)
```

moves george to the coordinates $(150, 30)$ in the turtle graphics window. Once there, we can draw a dot with

```
george.dot()
```

To implement the loop in Python, we will use a for loop that iterates over a list of earthquake locations like (-78.6, 19.3) rather than over a range of numbers. The first value in each ordered pair is the earthquake's longitude and the second value is the latitude. A list of these locations looks like this:

```
quakes = [(-78.6, 19.3), (144.8, 19.1), (145.9, 43.5), (26.6, 45.7)]
```

The variable quakes is being assigned a *list* of ordered pairs.[2] A list in Python is always surrounded by square brackets ([ ]). This list only contains the locations of four earthquakes; the full program with a longer list is available on the book website. To iterate over this list, we use a for loop with the list quakes as the sequence:

for <u>location</u> in <u>quakes</u> :
    index variable   sequence

In the body of the for loop, we will pass the index variable location to the goto method and then draw a dot with the dot method. The full program follows, with some extra pretty formatting. The core plotting statements are highlighted.

---

[2]Each ordered pair is actually called a *tuple* in Python. We will see tuples in more detail in Chapter 7.

```
1 import turtle

2 george = turtle.Turtle()
3 screen = george.getscreen()
4 screen.setup(1024, 512)
5 screen.bgpic('oceanbottom.gif')
6 screen.setworldcoordinates(-180, -90, 180, 90)

7 george.speed(0)
8 george.hideturtle()
9 george.up()
10 george.color('yellow')

11 quakes = [(-78.6, 19.3), (144.8, 19.1), (145.9, 43.5), (26.6, 45.7)]

12 for location in quakes:
13     george.goto(location)
14     george.dot()
```

As with the flower for loop, we can illustrate what is happening in more detail with a trace table. We represent the value of george with an image of what the screen looks like at each point in the program.

Trace

Step	Line	george	location	Notes
1–10	1–10		—	initialize george and the window
11	11	"	—	quakes = a list of ordered pairs
12	12	"	(-78.6, 19.3)	location = (-78.6, 19.3)
13	13		"	george.goto((-78.6, 19.3))
14	14		"	george.dot()
15	12	"	(144.8, 19.1)	location = (144.8, 19.1)
16	13		"	george.goto((144.8, 19.1))
17	14		"	george.dot()
18	12	"	(145.9, 43.5)	location = (145.9, 43.5)
19	13		"	george.goto((145.9, 43.5))
20	14		"	george.dot()
21	12	"	(26.6, 45.7)	location = (26.6, 45.7)
22	13		"	george.goto((26.6, 45.7))
23	14		"	george.dot()

The first ten lines set up the drawing window with a background picture of the earth. The Screen method setworldcoordinates is used to set the coordinate system inside the window to match geographical coordinates: longitude values run from

−180 to 180 and latitude values run from −90 to 90. The first two arguments set the bottom left corner of the window to be (−180, −90) and the last two arguments set the top right corner to be (180, 90). We encourage you to consult Appendix A.3 to learn what the other methods do.

In the first iteration of the `for` loop on line 12, the index variable `location` is assigned the first pair in the list `quakes`, which is `(-78.6, 19.3)`. Next, `george.goto(location)` is executed; since `location` was assigned `(-78.6, 19.3)`, this is equivalent to `george.goto((-78.6, 19.3))`. Then a dot is drawn at that location. Once the first iteration is complete, we return to line 12 for the second iteration, where `location` is assigned the second pair in the list, which is `(144.8, 19.1)`. Lines 13–14 are executed again, which draws a dot at this location. This process continues for two more iterations since there are two more pairs remaining in the list.

Reflection 2.7 *What is the significance of* `george.up()` *in the program? What happens if you omit it?*

You can download `oceanbottom.gif` and this complete program with more earthquake locations from the book website.

Exercises

Write a short program to answer each of the following questions. Submit each as a separate python program file with a `.py` *extension (e.g.,* `picture.py`*).*

2.2.1. Write a program using turtle graphics that draws a national or state flag of your choice. You might want to consult `https://en.wikipedia.org/wiki/Gallery_of_sovereign_state_flags` for ideas and Appendices A.2 and A.3 for additional drawing methods.

2.2.2. Write a program that draws the following three shapes (resembling street signs) using turtle graphics.

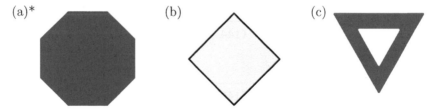

2.2.3. Draw an interesting picture using turtle graphics. Consult Appendices A.2 and A.3 for a list of methods. You might want to draw your picture on graph paper first.

2.2.4. Modify the `for` loop in the flower bloom program so that it draws a flower with 18 line segments, using an angle of 100°.

2.2.5* Write a program that uses a `for` loop to draw a square with side length 200.

2.2.6. Write a program that uses a `for` loop to draw a rectangle with length 200 and width 100.

2.2.7. Write a program that instructs a turtle to repeat the following 180 times: draw forward 200, return to the origin, turns 2 degrees left.

2.2.8* Suppose you have the coordinates of discovered artifacts from a 9 meter × 9 meter plot during an archaeological dig. The coordinates extend from (0,0) in the bottom left corner of the plot to (9,9) in the upper right corner. Write a program that plots a list of these coordinates to detect any patterns in their locations. The list of coordinates is available on the book website.

2.2.9. Write a program that uses turtle graphics to draw a line graph of the world population from 1950 to 2050 (projected). The data is stored in a list of (year, population) pairs, available on the book website. The population is recorded in billions, e.g., 2.5 represents 2.5 billion. Use `setworldcoordinates` to set the bottom left corner of the window to be (1945,0) and the top right corner to be (2055,10). You can draw vertical lines to mark the years in your plot with the following loop:

```
for year in range(1950, 2051, 10):
    george.up()
    george.goto(year, 0)
    george.write(str(year))
    george.down()
    george.goto(year, 10)
```

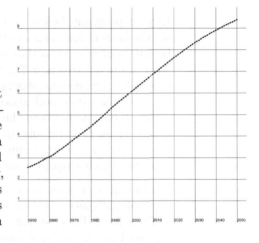

This **range** is equivalent to the list 1950, 1960, ..., 2050. As **year** is assigned to each of these values in the loop, a vertical line is drawn from bottom to top. The **write** method prints the year, converted to a string, at the bottom of each line. Using this as a model, also draw horizontal lines to mark each billion. Your final graph should look like that to the right.

2.2.10. Suppose an ant is moving in a straight line toward its nest three meters away. A hungry fly, exactly one meter above the ant, starts to fly directly toward it at exactly the same speed. Will the fly catch the ant? If not, how close will it come?

We can write a turtle graphics simulation of this scenario by modeling each insect as a turtle. The ant turtle starts at position (0,0) and the fly turtle starts at position (0,1), directly above the ant. At each step, the fly moves one step directly toward the ant and the ant moves one step forward. The length of each step is the distance to the nest divided by the total number of steps that we want the insects to take. The more steps they take, the closer the simulation becomes to a continuous real-life scenario.

Implement this simulation, based on the following pseudocode algorithm.

Algorithm THE ANT AND THE FLY

Input: none

1 | *nest distance* ← 3
2 | *total steps* ← 300
3 | *step length* ← *nest distance* ÷ *total steps*
4 | create the ant at position (0,0)
5 | create the fly and move it to position (0,1)
6 | repeat *total steps* times:
7 | turn the fly toward the ant
8 | move the fly forward *step length*
9 | move the ant forward *step length*

Output: the final distance between the ant and the fly

In your program, before you move any turtles, use `setworldcoordinates` to set the bottom left corner of the window to be (0,0) and the top right corner to be (*nest distance*, 1) so that you can see what is happening much more clearly. Also, there are two new `Turtle` methods that will make your job easier. The methods `towards` and `distance` return the angle and distance, respectively, between the turtle and another turtle. For example, `fly.towards(ant)` will return the angle between the fly turtle and the ant turtle (assuming you have named them `fly` and `ant`, of course). The `distance` method works similarly. At the end of your program, print the final distance between the two insects. Does the result surprise you?

2.2.11. A random walk simulates a particle, or person, randomly moving in a two-dimensional space. At each step, the particle turns in a random direction and walks a fixed distance (e.g., 10 units) in the current direction. If this step is repeated many times, it can simulate Brownian motion or animal foraging behavior.

Write a program that uses turtle graphics to draw a 1000-step random walk. To randomly choose an angle in each step, use

```
angle = random.randrange(360)
```

You will need to import the `random` module to use this function. (We will talk more about random numbers and random walks in Chapter 5.) One particular 1000-step random walk is shown to the right.

2.3 FUNCTIONAL ABSTRACTION

To draw the garden of flowers from Figure 2.3, each with a different color and size, we are going to need to repeat our flower bloom code many times. We could do this by copying the drawing statements and changing method arguments to alter the sizes and colors. However, this strategy is a *very bad idea*. First, it is very time-consuming and error-prone; when you repeatedly copy and paste, it is very easy to make mistakes. Second, it makes your program unnecessarily long and hard to read. Third, it is difficult to correctly make changes. For example, what if you copied enough to draw twenty flowers, and then decided that you wanted to give all of them six petals instead of eight?

Instead, we want to create a self-contained functional abstraction that will draw a flower bloom when called upon to do so. In Python, we do this by creating a new function. Functions are like our pseudocode algorithms in that they can take inputs, produce outputs, and can be called upon by other algorithms to perform tasks. To create a function in Python, we use the **def** keyword, followed by the function name and, for now, empty parentheses (we will come back to those shortly). As with a **for** loop, the **def** line must end with a colon (:).

```
def bloom():
```

The body of the function is then indented relative to the **def** line. The body of our new function will consist of the flower bloom code. Insert this new function into your program from the last section after the **import** statement:

```
import turtle

def bloom():
    george.pencolor('red')
    george.fillcolor('yellow')
    george.begin_fill()
    for count in range(8):
        george.forward(200)
        george.left(135)
    george.end_fill()

george = turtle.Turtle()
george.hideturtle()
george.speed(6)

bloom()

screen = george.getscreen()
screen.exitonclick()
```

The **def** construct *only defines* the new function; it *does not execute* it. We need to *call* the function for it to execute. As we saw earlier, a function call consists of the function name, followed by a list of arguments. Since this function does not have any arguments (yet), and does not return a value, we can call it with

```
bloom()
```

inserted, at the outermost indentation level, where the flower bloom code used to be (as shown above).

Reflection 2.8 *Try running the program with and without the* `bloom()` *function call.* *What happens in each case?*

Before continuing, let's take a moment to look closely at what the program is doing. As illustrated below, execution begins at the top, labeled "start." After that, there are seven labeled steps, explained below.

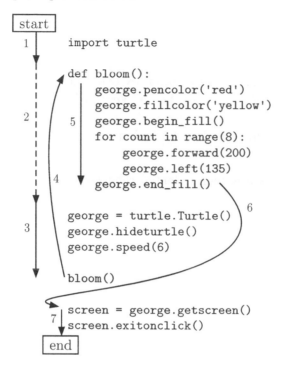

1. Import the **turtle** module.

2. Define the **bloom** function. Note that the function is *not* executed yet; Python is just learning of its existence so that it can be called later.

3. The next three statements *are* executed. They define a new **Turtle** object named **george**, hide the turtle, and speed it up a bit.

4. Next, the **bloom()** function is called, which causes execution to jump up to the beginning of the function.

5. The statements in the function then draw the flower.

6. When the function is complete, execution continues with the statement after the function call.

7. And the program ends.

Function parameters

The `bloom` function is not as useful as it could be because it always draws the same yellow flower with segment length 200. We can generalize the function by accepting the fill color and the segment length as arguments, as depicted below.

$$\text{color, length} \longrightarrow \boxed{\text{bloom}} \longrightarrow \text{None}$$

We do this by adding **parameters** to the function definition. A parameter is the name of an input, like the inputs in our pseudocode algorithms. In the highlighted lines of the new version below, we have defined two parameters in parentheses after the function name to represent the fill color and the segment length, and replaced the old constants `'yellow'` and 200 with the names of these new parameters.

```
import turtle

def bloom(color, length):
    george.pencolor('red')
    george.fillcolor(color)
    george.begin_fill()
    for count in range(8):
        george.forward(length)
        george.left(135)
    george.end_fill()

george = turtle.Turtle()
george.hideturtle()
george.speed(6)

bloom('yellow', 200)

screen = george.getscreen()
screen.exitonclick()
```

To replicate the old behavior, we added two arguments to the function call:

```
bloom('yellow', 200)
```

When this function is called, the value of the first argument `'yellow'` is assigned to the first parameter `color` and the value of the second argument 200 is assigned to the second parameter `length`. Then the body of the function executes. Whenever `color` is referenced, it is replaced with `'yellow'`, and whenever `length` is referenced, it is replaced with 200. (Parameters and arguments are also called *formal parameters* and *actual parameters*, respectively.)

Reflection 2.9 *After making these changes, run the program again. Then try running it a few more times with different arguments passed into the* `bloom` *function call. For example, try* `bloom('orange', 50)` *and* `bloom('purple', 350)`. *What happens if you switch the order of the arguments in one these function calls?*

We are going to make one more change to this function before moving on, motivated by the following question.

Reflection 2.10 *Look at the variable name* `george` *that is used inside the* `bloom` *function. Where is it defined?*

When the `bloom` function executes, the Python interpreter encounters the variable name `george` in the first line, but `george` has not been defined in that function. Realizing this, Python looks for the name `george` outside the function. This behavior is called a ***scoping rule***. The ***scope*** of a variable name is the part of the program where the name is defined, and hence can be used.

The scope of a variable name that is defined inside a function, such as `count` in the `bloom` function, is limited to that function. Such a variable is called a ***local variable***. If we tried to refer to `count` outside of the the `bloom` function, we would get an error. We will look at local variables in more detail in Section 2.6.

A variable name that is defined at the outermost indentation level can be accessed from anywhere in the program, and is called a ***global variable***. In our program, `george` and `screen` are global variable names. It is generally a bad idea to have any global variables at all in a program, a topic that we will further discuss in the next sections. But even aside from that issue, we should be concerned that our function is tied to one specific turtle named `george` that is defined outside our function. It would be much better to make the turtle a parameter to the function, so that we can call it with any turtle we want, as illustrated below:

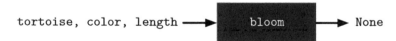

Replacing `george` with a parameter named `tortoise` gives us the following modified function:

```python
def bloom(tortoise, color, length):
    tortoise.pencolor('red')
    tortoise.fillcolor(color)
    tortoise.begin_fill()
    for count in range(8):
        tortoise.forward(length)
        tortoise.left(135)
    tortoise.end_fill()
```

We also need to update the function call by passing `george` as the first argument, to be assigned to the first parameter, `tortoise`.

```python
bloom(george, 'yellow', 200)
```

Now that the bloom is finished, we need to create a function that draws a stem. Our stem-drawing function will take two parameters: `tortoise`, which is the name of the turtle object, and `length`, the length of the stem.

Figure 2.7 A simple geometric "flower" with a stem.

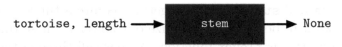

In the following function, notice all the places, highlighted in red, where the parameters are being used.

```
1 def stem(tortoise, length):
2     tortoise.pencolor('green')
3     tortoise.pensize(length / 20)
4     tortoise.up()
5     tortoise.forward(length / 2)
6     tortoise.down()
7     tortoise.right(90)
8     tortoise.forward(length)
```

For convenience, we assume that the stem length is the same as the length of a segment in the associated flower. Since the **bloom** function nicely returns the turtle to the origin, pointing east, we will assume that **tortoise** is in this state when **stem** is called. We start the function by setting the pen color to green, and thickening the turtle's tail by calling the method **pensize**. Notice that the pen size on line 3 is based on the parameter **length**, so that it scales properly with different size flowers. Next, in lines 4–6, we move halfway across the flower to start drawing the stem. So that we do not draw over the existing flower, we put the turtle's tail up with the **up** method before we move, and return it to its resting position again with **down** when we are done. Finally, in lines 7–8, we turn to the south and move the turtle forward to draw a thick green stem.

To draw a stem for our yellow flower, insert this function in your program after where the **bloom** function is defined, and then call it with

```
stem(george, 200)
```

after the call to the **bloom** function. When you run your program, the flower should look like Figure 2.7.

We now have functions—functional abstractions—that implement the two subproblems of the **flower** problem from our decomposition in Figure 2.4. So we are ready to use these to create a function (another functional abstraction) that draws a flower, as depicted below.

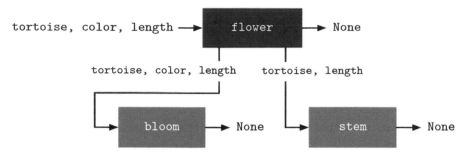

Because the **bloom** and **stem** functions together require a turtle, a fill color and a length, and we want to be able to customize our flower in these three ways, these are the parameters to our **flower** function. We pass all three of these parameters through to the **bloom** function, and then we pass two of them to the **stem** function. In Python, our function looks like this:

```
def flower(tortoise, color, length):
    bloom(tortoise, color, length)
    stem(tortoise, length)
```

A complete program incorporating these functions is shown in Figure 2.8.

Exercises 2.3.6–2.3.8 below challenge you to implement the remaining layers of the decomposition tree to create a full garden of flowers, as illustrated in Figure 2.3.

Exercises

Write a short program to answer each of the following questions. Submit each as a separate python program file with a .py extension (e.g., picture.py).

2.3.1. Modify the program in Figure 2.8 so that it calls the **flower** function three times to draw three flowers, each with a different color and size. You will want to move the turtle and reset its pen size and heading to their original values before drawing each flower so that they are drawn correctly and not on top of each other.

2.3.2* Modify the **bloom** function so that it draws 10 petals instead of 8. In each iteration of the loop, the turtle will need to turn 108 degrees instead of 135.

2.3.3. Modify the **bloom** function so that it can draw any number of petals. The revised function will need to take an additional parameter:

    bloom(tortoise, color, length, petals)

The original function with eight petals has the turtle turn 1080/8 = 135 degrees so that it travels a total of 1080 degrees, a multiple of 360. When you generalize the number of petals, the sum of all of the angles that **tortoise** turns must

```
import turtle

def bloom(tortoise, color, length):
    tortoise.pencolor('red')
    tortoise.fillcolor(color)
    tortoise.begin_fill()
    for count in range(8):
        tortoise.forward(length)
        tortoise.left(135)
    tortoise.end_fill()

def stem(tortoise, length):
    tortoise.pencolor('green')
    tortoise.pensize(length / 20)
    tortoise.up()
    tortoise.forward(length / 2)
    tortoise.down()
    tortoise.right(90)
    tortoise.forward(length)

def flower(tortoise, color, length):
    bloom(tortoise, color, length)
    stem(tortoise, length)

george = turtle.Turtle()
george.hideturtle()
george.speed(6)

flower(george, 'yellow', 200)

screen = george.getscreen()
screen.exitonclick()
```

Figure 2.8 The final flower program.

still be a multiple of 360 (like 1080). Are there any values of petals for which your function does not work? Why?

2.3.4.   Enhance the stem function so that it also draws a green leaf one third of the way up the stem, as shown to the right. One half of a pointed leaf can be drawn by repeatedly moving and turning the turtle small distances in a loop until it has turned a total of 90 degrees. The other half of the leaf can then be drawn by turning 90 degrees and repeating the same process.

2.3.5* Modify the `flower` function so that it creates a daffodil-like double bloom like the one to the right. The revised function will need two fill color parameters:

```
flower(tortoise, color1, color2, length)
```

It might help to know that the distance between any two opposite points of a bloom is about 1.08 times the segment length.

2.3.6. Write a function

```
growFlower(x, y, flowerColor, flowerLength)
```

that creates a turtle and then calls the `flower` function to draw a flower with that turtle at a particular (x,y) location. Test your new function by calling it from the flower program in Figure 2.8 in place of calling the `flower` function.

2.3.7. In this exercise, you will modify the `growFlower` function from the previous exercise so that it takes only x and y as parameters, and assigns `flowerColor` and `flowerLength` to random values in the body of the function. To do this, utilize two functions from the **random** module, which we will discuss more in Chapter 5. First, the **random.randrange** function returns a randomly chosen integer between its two arguments. To generate a random integer between 20 and 199 for the flower's size, call

```
flowerLength = random.randrange(20, 200)
```

Second, the **random.choice** function returns a randomly chosen item from a list. To generate a random color for the flower, call

```
flowerColor = random.choice(['yellow', 'pink', 'red', 'purple'])
```

Test your modified function as you did in the previous exercise. You will also need to import the random module at the top of your program.

2.3.8. In this exercise, you will implement the complete garden-drawing program from Figure 2.4 by modifying the program you wrote in the previous exercise so that it draws random flowers wherever you click in the drawing window. This will be accomplished by the following two methods of the `Screen` class:

```
screen.onclick(growFlower)
screen.mainloop()
```

Then the `mainloop` method repeatedly checks for mouse clicks and key presses, and calls designated functions when they happen. The `onclick` method indicates that `mainloop` should call `growFlower(x, y)` every time the mouse is clicked in the window at coordinates (x,y). To incorporate this functionality into your program, simply replace `screen.exitonclick()` in your program with these two statements.

2.3.9. Write a program that draws the word "CODE," as shown to the right. Use the `circle` method to draw the arcs of the "C" and "D." The `circle` method takes two arguments: the radius of the circle and the extent of the circle in degrees. For example, `george.circle(100, 180)` would draw half of a circle with radius 100. Making the extent negative draws the arc in the reverse direction.

2.3.10. Rewrite your program from Exercise 2.3.9 so that each letter is drawn by its own function. Then use your functions to draw "DECODE." (Call your "D" and "E" functions twice.)

2.3.11. Write a function

```
drawSquare(tortoise, width)
```

that uses the turtle named `tortoise` to draw a square with the given `width`. This function generalizes the code you wrote for Exercise 2.2.5 so that it can draw a square with any width. Use a `for` loop.

2.3.12. Write a function

```
drawRectangle(tortoise, length, width)
```

that uses the turtle named `tortoise` to draw a rectangle with the given `length` and `width`. This function generalizes the code you wrote for Exercise 2.2.6 so that it can draw a rectangle of any size. Use a `for` loop.

2.3.13. Write a function

```
drawPolygon(tortoise, sideLength, numSides)
```

that uses the turtle named `tortoise` to draw a regular polygon with the given number of sides and side length. This function is a generalization of your `drawSquare` function from Exercise 2.3.11. Use the value of `numSides` in your `for` loop and create a new variable for the turn angle that depends on `numSides`. The turtle will need to travel a total of 360 degrees over the course of the loop.

2.3.14. Write a function

```
drawCircle(tortoise, radius)
```

that calls your `drawPolygon` function from Exercise 2.3.13 to approximate a circle with the given radius.

2.3.15* Write a function

```
horizontalCircles(tortoise)
```

that draws ten non-overlapping circles, each with radius 50, that run horizontally across the graphics window. Use a `for` loop.

2.3.16. Write a function

```
diagonalCircles(tortoise)
```

that draws ten non-overlapping circles, each with radius 50, that run diagonally, from the top left to the bottom right, of the graphics window. Use a `for` loop.

2.3.17. Write a function

```
drawRow(tortoise)
```

that draws one row of an 8 × 8 red/black checkerboard. Use a `for` loop and the `drawSquare` function you wrote in Exercise 2.3.11.

2.3.18. Write a function

```
drawRow(tortoise, color1, color2)
```

that draws one row of an 8 × 8 checkerboard in which the colors of the squares alternate between `color1` and `color2`. The parameters `color1` and `color2` are both strings representing colors. For example, calling `drawRow(george, 'red', 'black')` should draw a row that alternates between red and black.

2.3.19. Write a function

```
checkerBoard(tortoise)
```

that draws an 8 × 8 red/black checkerboard, using a `for` loop and the function you wrote in Exercise 2.3.18.

2.3.20. Interesting flower-like shapes can also be drawn by repeatedly drawing polygons that are rotated some number of degrees each time. Write a new function

```
polyFlower(tortoise, sideLength, numSides, numPolygons)
```

that calls the **drawPolygon** function from Exercise 2.3.13 to draw an interesting flower design. The function will repeatedly call **drawPolygon** a number of times equal to the parameter **numPolygons**, rotating the turtle each time to make a flower pattern. You will need to figure out the rotation angle based on the number of polygons drawn. For example, the image to the right was drawn by calling `drawFlower(george, 40, 12, 7)`.

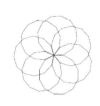

2.3.21. Rewrite your program from Exercise 2.2.8 so that all of the drawing is done inside a function

```
plotSites(sites)
```

that takes the list of sites as a parameter. In other words, modify your program so that it looks like this:

```
import turtle

def plotSites(sites):
    drawing statements here...

sites = [(1.45, 7.31), (2.99, 7.55), (7.58, 6.29), (2.17, 4.71),
         (1.07, 5.56), ... ]

plotSites(sites)
```

2.3.22. Rewrite your program from Exercise 2.2.9 so that all of the drawing is done inside a function

```
plotPopulation(population)
```

that takes the population list as a parameter. In other words, modify your program so that it looks like this:

```
import turtle

def plotPopulation(population):
    drawing statements here...

population = [(1950, 2.557), (1951, 2.594), (1952, 2.636),
             (1953, 2.681), (1954, 2.73), (1955, 2.782), ... ]

plotPopulation(population)
```

2.3.23. Write a function

```
randomWalk(steps)
```

that generalizes your random walk code from Exercise 2.2.11 so that it draws a random walk for the given number of steps.

The following additional exercises ask you to write functions that do not involve turtle graphics. Test each one by calling it with both common and boundary case arguments, as described on page 38, and document your test cases. Use a trace table on at least one test case.

2.3.24. Write a function

    basketball(fieldGoals, threePointers)

that prints your team's basketball score if the numbers of two pointers and three pointers are given in the parameters fieldgoal and threePointers.

2.3.25. Write a function

    age(birthYear)

that prints a person's age when given his or her birth year as a parameter. You can assume that this function only works this year and that the person has not had his or her birthday yet this year.

2.3.26. Write a function

    cheer(teamName)

that takes as a parameter a team name and prints "Go" followed by the team name. For example, if the function is called as cheer('Buzzards'), it should print the string 'Go Buzzards' to the screen.

2.3.27. Write a function

    sum(number1, number2)

that prints the sum of number1 and number2 to the screen.

2.3.28. Write a function

    printTwice(word)

that prints its parameter twice on two separate lines.

2.3.29. Write a function

    printMyName()

that uses a for loop to print your name 100 times.

2.4   PROGRAMMING IN STYLE

Programming style and writing style share many of the same concerns. When we write an essay, we want the reader to clearly understand our thesis and the arguments that support it. We want it to be clear and concise, and have a logical flow from beginning to end. Similarly, when we write a program, we want to help collaborators understand our program's goal, how it accomplishes that goal, and how it flows from beginning to end. Even if you are the only one to ever read your program, good style will pay dividends both while you are working through the solution, and in the future when you try to reacquaint yourself with your work. We can accomplish these goals by organizing our programs neatly and logically, using descriptive variable and function names, writing programs that accomplishes their goal in a non-obfuscated manner, and documenting our intentions within the program.

Program structure

Let's return to the program that we wrote in the previous section (Figure 2.8), and reorganize it a bit to reflect better programming habits. As shown in Figure 2.9, every program should begin with documentation that identifies the program's author and its purpose. This type of documentation, which starts and ends with three double quotes (`"""`), is called a ***docstring***; we will look more closely at docstrings and other types of documentation shortly.

We follow this with our `import` statements. Putting these at the top of our program both makes our program neater and ensures that the imported modules are available anywhere later on.

Next, we define all of our functions. Because programs are read by the interpreter from top to bottom, you need to define your functions above where you call them. For example, if we tried to call the `bloom` function at the very top of the program, before it was defined, we would generate an error message.

At the end of the flower-drawing program in Figure 2.8, there are six statements at the outermost indentation level. The first and fifth of these statements define global variable names that are visible and potentially modifiable anywhere in the program. When the value assigned to a global variable is modified in a function, it is called a ***side effect***. In large programs, where the values of global variables can be potentially modified in countless different places, errors in their use become nearly impossible to find. For this reason, we should get into the habit of never using them, unless there is a *very* good reason, and these are pretty hard to come by. See Tangent 2.2 for more information on how global names are handled in Python.

To prevent the use of global variables, and to make programs more readable, we will move statements at the global level of our programs into a function named `main`, and then call `main` as the last statement in the program, as shown at the end of the program in Figure 2.9. With this change, the call to the `main` function is where the action begins in this program. (Remember that the function definitions above only define functions; they do not execute them.) The `main` function sets up a turtle, then calls our `flower` function, which then calls the `bloom` and `stem` functions. Getting used to this style of programming has an additional benefit: it is very similar to the style of other common programming languages (e.g., C, C++, Java) so, if you go on to use one of these in the future, it should seem relatively familiar.

The functions in a program are generally determined by how the problem was decomposed during the top-down design process. Even so, identifying functions can be as much an art as a science, so here are a few guidelines to keep in mind:

1. A function should accomplish something relatively small, and make sense standing on its own.

```
"""
Purpose: Draw a flower
Author: Ima Student
Date: September 15, 2020
CS 111, Fall 2020
"""
```
program docstring

```
import turtle
```
import statements

```
def bloom(tortoise, color, length):
    """Draws a geometric flower bloom.

    Parameters:
        tortoise: a Turtle object with which to draw the bloom.
        color: a color string to use to fill the bloom.
        length: the length of each segment of the bloom.

    Return value:
        None
    """

    tortoise.pencolor('red')      # set tortoise's pen color to red
    tortoise.fillcolor(color)     # and fill color to fcolor
    tortoise.begin_fill()
    for segment in range(8):      # draw a filled 8-sided
        tortoise.forward(length)  #   geometric flower bloom
        tortoise.left(135)
    tortoise.end_fill()

# other functions omitted...
```
function
definitions

```
def main():
    """Draws a yellow flower with segment length 200, and
       waits for a mouse click to exit.
    """

    george = turtle.Turtle()
    george.hideturtle()
    george.speed(6)

    flower(george, 'yellow', 200)

    screen = george.getscreen()
    screen.exitonclick()
```
main function

```
main()
```
main function call

Figure 2.9 An overview of a program's structure.

2. Functions should be written for subproblems that are called upon frequently, perhaps with different arguments. If you find yourself duplicating some part of a program, write a function for it instead.

3. A function should generally fit on a page or, in many cases, less.

4. The `main` function should be short, generally serving only to set up the program and call other functions that carry out the work.

Documentation

Python program documentation comes in two flavors: docstrings and ***comments***. A docstring is meant to articulate everything that someone needs to know to use a program or module, or to call a function. Comments, on the other hand, are used to

Tangent 2.2: Global variables

The Python interpreter handles global names inside functions differently, depending on whether the name's value is being read or the name is being assigned a value. When the Python interpreter encounters a name that needs to be evaluated (e.g., on the righthand side of an assignment statement), it first looks to see if this name is defined inside the scope of this function. If it is, the name in the local scope is used. Otherwise, the interpreter successively looks at outer scopes until the name is found. If it reaches the global scope and the name is still not found, we see a "name error."

On the other hand, if we assign a value to a name, that name is always considered to be local, unless we have stated otherwise by using a `global` statement. For example, consider the following program:

```python
spam = 13

def func1():
    spam = 100

def func2():
    global spam
    spam = 200

func1()
print(spam)
func2()
print(spam)
```

The first `print` will display 13 because the assignment statement that is executed in `func1` defines a new local variable; it does not modify the global variable with the same name. But the second `print` will display 200 because the `global` statement in `func2` indicates that `spam` should refer to the global variable with that name, causing the subsequent assignment statement to change the value assigned to the global variable. This convention prevents accidental side effects because it forces the programmer to explicitly decide to modify a global variable. In any case, using `global` is strongly discouraged.

document individual program statements or groups of statements. In other words, a docstring explains *what* a program or function does, while comments explain *how* it works; a docstring describes an abstraction while comments describe what happens inside the black box. The Python interpreter ignores both docstrings and comments while it is executing a program; both are intended for human eyes only.

Docstrings

A docstring is enclosed in a matching pair of triple double quotes (`"""`), and may occupy several lines. We use a docstring at the beginning of every program to identify the program's author and its purpose, as shown at the top of Figure 2.9.[3] We also use a docstring to document each function that we write, to ensure that the reader understands what it does. A function docstring should articulate everything that someone needs to know to call the function: the overall purpose of the function, and descriptions of the function's parameters and return value.

The beginning of a function's docstring is indented on the line immediately following the **def** statement. Programmers prefer a variety of different styles for docstrings; we will use one that closely resembles the style in Google's official Python style guide. Docstrings for the three functions from Figure 2.8 are shown below. (The bodies of the functions are omitted.)

```python
def bloom(tortoise, color, length):
    """Draws a geometric flower bloom.

    Parameters:
        tortoise: a Turtle object with which to draw the bloom
        color:    a color string to use to fill the bloom
        length:   the length of each segment of the bloom

    Return value:
        None
    """

def stem(tortoise, length):
    """Draws a flower stem.

    Parameters:
        tortoise: a Turtle object, initially at the bloom starting
                  position
        length:   the length of the stem and each segment of the bloom

    Return value:
        None
    """

def flower(tortoise, color, length):
    """Draws a flower.

    Parameters:
        tortoise: a Turtle object with which to draw the flower
        color:    a color string to use to fill the bloom
        length:   the length of each segment of the bloom

    Return value:
        None
    """
```

---

[3]Your instructor may require a different format, so be sure to ask.

In the first line of the docstring, we succinctly explain what the function does. This is followed by a parameter section that lists each parameter with its intended purpose and the class to which it should belong. If there are any assumptions made about the value of the parameter, these should be stated also. For example, the turtle parameter of the `stem` function is assumed to start at the origin of the bloom. Finally, we describe the return value of the function. We did not have these functions return anything, so they return `None`. We will look at how to write functions that return values in Section 2.5.

Another advantage of writing docstrings is that Python can automatically produce documentation from them, in response to calling the `help` function. For example, try this short example in the Python shell:

```
>>> def printName(first, last):
        """Prints a first and last name.

        Parameters:
            first: a first name
            last:  a last name

        Return value:
            None
        """

        print(first + ' ' + last)
>>> help(printName)
Help on function printName in module __main__:

printName(first, last)
    Prints a first and last name.

    Parameters:
        first: a first name
        last:  a last name

    Return value:
        None
```

You can also use `help` with modules and built-in functions. For example, try this:

```
>>> import turtle
>>> help(turtle.color)
```

Comments

A comment is anything between a hash symbol (#) and the end of the line. As with docstrings, the Python interpreter ignores comments. Comments should generally be neatly lined up to the right of the statements they document. However, there are times when a longer comment is needed to explain a complicated section. In this case, you might want to precede that section with a comment on one or more lines by itself.

There is a fine line between under-commenting and over-commenting. As a general rule, you want to supply high-level descriptions of what your code intends to do. You do *not* want to literally repeat what each individual line does, as this is not at all helpful to someone reading your code. Doing so tends to clutter it up and make it *harder* to read! Here are examples of good comments for the body of the `bloom` function.

```
tortoise.pencolor('red')      # set tortoise's pen color
tortoise.fillcolor(color)     #   and fill color
tortoise.begin_fill()
for count in range(8):        # draw a filled 8-sided
    tortoise.forward(length)  #   geometric flower bloom
    tortoise.left(135)
tortoise.end_fill()
```

Notice that the five lines that draw the bloom are commented together, just to note the programmer's intention. In contrast, the following comments illustrate what *not* to do. The following comments are both hard to read and uninformative.

```
tortoise.pencolor('red')   # set tortoise's pen color to red
tortoise.fillcolor(color)  # set tortoise's fill color to color
tortoise.begin_fill()  # begin to fill a shape
for count in range(8):  # for count = 0, 1, 2, ..., 7
    tortoise.forward(length)  # move tortoise forward length
    tortoise.left(135)  # turn tortoise left 135 degrees
tortoise.end_fill()  # stop filling the shape
```

Notice that these comments never actually explain the purpose of the for loop; they just repeat each line. Instead, as above, you want to step back and explain the purpose of the code and, only if it is not obvious, how it is accomplished. We leave the task of commenting the other functions in this program as an exercise.

Self-documenting code

As we discussed in Section 1.3, using descriptive variable names is a very important step in making your program's intentions clear. The variable names in the flower program are already in good shape, so let's look at a different example. Consider the following statements.

```
x = 462
y = (3.95 - 1.85) * x - 140
```

Without any context, it is impossible to infer what this is supposed to represent. However, if we rename the two variables, as follows, the meaning becomes clearer.

```
cupsSold = 462
profit = (3.95 - 1.85) * cupsSold - 140
```

Now it is clear that this code is computing the profit generated from selling cups of something. But the meaning of the numbers is still a mystery. These are examples of **magic numbers**, so-called in programming parlance because they seem to appear out of nowhere. There are at least two reasons to avoid magic numbers. First, they make your code less readable and obscure its meaning. Second, they make it more difficult and error-prone to change your code, especially if you use the same value multiple times. By assigning these numbers to descriptive variable names, the code becomes even clearer.

```
cupsSold = 462
pricePerCup = 3.95
costPerCup = 1.85
fixedCost = 140
profit = (pricePerCup - costPerCup) * cupsSold - fixedCost
```

We now have **self-documenting code**. Since we have named all of our variables and values with descriptive names, just reading the code is enough to deduce its intention. These same rules, of course, apply to function names and parameters. By naming our functions with descriptive names, we make their purposes clearer and we contribute to the readability of the functions from which we call them. This practice will continue to be demonstrated in the coming chapters.

In this book, we use a naming convention that is sometimes called `camelCase`, in which the first letter is in lowercase and then the first letters of subsequent words are capitalized. But other programmers prefer different styles. For example, some programmers prefer `snake_case`, in which an underscore character is placed between words (`cupsSold` would be `cups_sold`). Unless you are working in an environment with a specific mandated style, the choice is yours, as long as it results in self-documenting code.

Exercises

2.4.1*   Incorporate all the changes we discussed in this section into your flower-drawing program, and finish commenting the bodies of the remaining functions.

2.4.2.   Reorganize the earthquake plotting program from page 63 so that it follows all of the style guidelines from this section, and the actual drawing is encapsulated in a function `plotQuakes(tortoise, earthquakes)`. A `main` function should create a turtle, assign the list of earthquakes to a variable, and then call your function with these two arguments.

2.4.3*   Rewrite this simple program so that it adheres to the guidelines in this section. All of the drawing should happen in a new function that takes the name of a turtle as its parameter. The `main` function should create a turtle and pass it into the drawing function. Be sure to include docstrings and comments.

```
import turtle
beth = turtle.Turtle()
beth.hideturtle()
beth.speed(9)
beth.fillcolor('blue')
beth.begin_fill()
beth.pencolor('red')
for count in range(8):
    beth.circle(75)
    beth.left(45)
    beth.forward(10 * 1.414)   # 10 * sqrt(2)
beth.end_fill()
```

2.4.4. Run the following program to see what it does and then edit it to make it more understandable. Give all of the variables more descriptive names and add appropriate docstrings and comments.

```python
import turtle
import math      # math module (more in the next chapter)

def doSomething(z):
    a = turtle.Turtle()
    b = turtle.Turtle()
    c = a.getscreen()
    c.setworldcoordinates(-z - 1, -z - 1, z + 1, z + 1)
    a.hideturtle()
    b.hideturtle()

    a.up()
    b.up()
    a.goto(-z, 0)
    b.goto(-z, 0)
    a.down()
    b.down()

    for d in range(-z, z + 1):
        a.goto(d, math.sqrt(z ** 2 - d ** 2)) #sqrt is square root
        b.goto(d, -math.sqrt(z ** 2  - d ** 2))

def main():
    doSomething(100)


main()
```

2.4.5* Write a program that prompts for a person's age and then prints the equivalent number of days. All of the statements should be in a `main` function.

2.4.6. Write a program that prompts for a person's favorite color and the last thing they ate. Then print the concatenation of these as their rock band name. All of the statements should be in a `main` function. For example:

```
Your favorite color? pink
Your last meal? burrito
Your band name is The pink burritos!
```

2.4.7. Write a function that implements your Mad Lib from Exercise 1.3.22, and then write a complete program (with `main` function) that calls it. Your Mad Lib function should take the words needed to fill in the blanks as parameters. Your `main` function should get these values with calls to the `input` function, and then pass them to your function. Include docstrings and comments in your program. For example, here is a new version of the example in Exercise 1.3.22 (without docstrings or comments).

```
        def party(adj1, noun1, noun2, adj2, noun3):
            print('How to Throw a Party')
            print()
            print('If you are looking for a/an', adj1, 'way to')
            print('celebrate your love of', noun1 + ', how about a')
            print(noun2 + '-themed costume party?  Start by')
            print('sending invitations encoded in', adj2, 'format')
            print('giving directions to the location of your', noun3 + '.')

        def main():
            firstAdj = input('Adjective: ')
            firstNoun = input('Noun: ')
            secondNoun = input('Noun: ')
            secondAdj = input('Adjective: ')
            thirdNoun = input('Noun: ')
            party(firstAdj, firstNoun, secondNoun, secondAdj, thirdNoun)

        main()
```

2.4.8.   Study the following program (also available on the book website), and then reorganize it with a **main** function that calls one or more other functions. Your **main** function should only create a turtle and call your functions. Document your program with appropriate docstrings and comments.

```
        import turtle
        george = turtle.Turtle()
        george.setposition(0, 100)
        george.pencolor('red')
        george.fillcolor('red')
        george.begin_fill()
        george.circle(-100, 180)
        george.right(90)
        george.forward(200)
        george.end_fill()
        george.up()
        george.right(90)
        george.forward(25)
        george.right(90)
        george.forward(50)
        george.left(90)
        george.down()
        george.pencolor('white')
        george.fillcolor('white')
        george.begin_fill()
        george.circle(-50, 180)
        george.right(90)
        george.forward(100)
        george.end_fill()
```

2.4.9. The following program (also available on the book website) draws a truck. Edit it so that it conforms to all of the guidelines discussed in this section. Include all code in appropriate functions and replace duplicate code with appropriate function calls.

```
import turtle

truck = turtle.Turtle()
truck.speed(5)
truck.hideturtle()

truck.fillcolor('red')
truck.begin_fill()
truck.forward(300)
truck.left(90)
truck.forward(75)
truck.left(45)
truck.forward(25)
truck.left(45)
truck.forward(100)
truck.right(45)
truck.forward(100)
truck.left(45)
truck.forward(75)
truck.left(90)
truck.forward(70.71)
truck.right(90)
truck.forward(200)
truck.left(90)
truck.forward(92.677)
truck.left(90)
truck.forward(167.677)
truck.end_fill()

truck.up()
truck.forward(220)
truck.right(90)
truck.forward(50)
truck.left(90)
truck.down()

truck.fillcolor('black')
truck.begin_fill()
truck.circle(50)
truck.end_fill()
truck.up()
truck.right(90)
truck.backward(25)
truck.left(90)
truck.down()
truck.fillcolor('lightgray')
truck.begin_fill()
truck.circle(25)
truck.end_fill()

truck.up()
truck.right(90)
truck.forward(25)
truck.left(90)
truck.backward(300)
truck.down()
truck.fillcolor('black')
truck.begin_fill()
truck.circle(50)
truck.end_fill()

truck.up()
truck.right(90)
truck.backward(25)
truck.left(90)
truck.down()
truck.fillcolor('lightgray')
truck.begin_fill()
truck.circle(25)
truck.end_fill()
```

2.5 A RETURN TO FUNCTIONS

We previously described a function as a computation that takes one or more inputs, called *parameters*, and produces an output, called a *return value*. But, up until now, very few of the functions we have used, and none of the functions we have written, have had return values. In this section, we will remedy that.

The math module

The `math` module contains a rich set of functions that return useful mathematical quantities. For example, to take the square root of 5, we can use `math.sqrt`:

```
>>> import math
>>> result = math.sqrt(5)
>>> result
2.23606797749979
```

Function calls with return values can also be used in longer expressions, and as arguments of other functions. In this case, it is useful to think about a function call as equivalent to the value that it returns. For example, we can use the `math.sqrt` function in the computation of the volume of a tetrahedron with edge length $h = 7.5$, using the formula $V = h^3/(6\sqrt{2})$.

```
>>> height = 7.5
>>> volume = height ** 3 / (6 * math.sqrt(2))
>>> volume
49.71844555217912
```

In the parentheses, the value of `math.sqrt(2)` is computed first, and then multiplied by 6. Finally, `height ** 3` is divided by this result, and the answer is assigned to `volume`. If we wanted the rounded volume, we could use the entire volume computation as the argument to the `round` function:

```
>>> volume = round(height ** 3 / (6 * math.sqrt(2)))
>>> volume
50
```

We illustrate below the complete sequence of events in this evaluation:

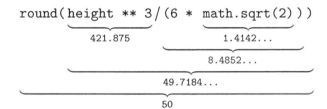

Now suppose we wanted to find the cosine of a 52° angle. We can use the `math.cos` function to compute the cosine, but the Python trigonometric functions expect their arguments to be in radians instead of degrees. (360 degrees is equivalent to 2π radians.) Fortunately, the `math` module also provides a function named `radians` that converts degrees to radians. So we can find the cosine of a 52° angle like this:

```
>>> math.cos(math.radians(52))
0.6156614753256583
```

The function call `math.radians(52)` is evaluated first, giving the equivalent of 52° in radians, and this result is used as the argument to the `math.cos` function:

```
math.cos(math.radians(52))
              0.9075...
      0.6156...
```

Other commonly used functions from the `math` module are listed in Appendix A.1. The `math` module also contains two commonly used constants: `pi` and `e`. Our sphere volume computation earlier would have been more accurately computed with:

```
>>> radius = 20
>>> volume = (4 / 3) * math.pi * (radius ** 3)
>>> volume
33510.32163829113
```

Notice that, since `pi` and `e` are variable names, not functions, there are no parentheses after their names.

Writing functions with return values

When we computed Flesch-Kincaid grade levels back in Section 1.3, they looked like this:

```
>>> averageWords = 16
>>> averageSyllables = 1.78
>>> readingLevel = 0.39 * averageWords + 11.8 * averageSyllables - 15.59
>>> print(readingLevel)
11.654
```

The problem with this approach is that, if we want the reading level of a different text, we need to type the whole thing again. For example,

```
>>> averageWords = 4.8
>>> averageSyllables = 1.9
>>> readingLevel = 0.39 * averageWords + 11.8 * averageSyllables - 15.59
>>> print(readingLevel)
8.702000000000002
```

This is obviously tedious and error-prone, analogous to building a new microwave oven from scratch every time we want to pop a bag of popcorn. Instead, we want to define a function that takes the average words per sentence and the average syllables per word as inputs and returns the reading level as output. Once we have this function in hand, we can get the reading levels of as many books as we want just by passing in different arguments. Back in Chapter 1, we visualized the problem as a black box like this:

And we wrote the algorithm in pseudocode like this:

Algorithm FLESCH KINCAID

Input: *average words, average syllables*
1   *reading level* ← 0.39 × *average words* + 11.8 × *average syllables* − 15.59
Output: *reading level*

In Python, these translate into the following function definition.

```python
def fleschKincaid(averageWords, averageSyllables):
    """Computes the reading level of a text using the Flesch-Kincaid
       reading level formula.

    Parameters:
        averageWords:     average number of words per sentence in a text
        averageSyllables: average number of syllables per word in a text

    Return value: the Flesch-Kincaid reading level score
    """

    return 0.39 * averageWords + 11.8 * averageSyllables - 15.59
```

The `return` statement defines the output of the function. Remember that the function definition by itself does not compute anything. We must call the function for it to be executed. For example, to get the two reading levels above, we can call the function twice like this:

```python
def main():
    readingLevel1 = fleschKincaid(16, 1.78)
    readingLevel2 = fleschKincaid(4.8, 1.9)

    print('The reading level of book 1 is ' + str(readingLevel1) + '.')
    print('The reading level of book 2 is ' + str(readingLevel2) + '.')
    print('The difference in reading level is ' +
                        str(readingLevel1 - readingLevel2) + '.')

main()
```

When each assignment statement is executed, the righthand side calls the function `fleschKincaid` with two arguments. Then the function `fleschKincaid` is executed with the two arguments assigned to its two parameters. Next, the value after the `return` statement is computed and returned by the function. In `main`, this return value is assigned to the variable on the left of the assignment statement. So when this program is run, it prints:

```
The reading level of book 1 is 11.654.
The reading level of book 2 is 8.702000000000002.
The difference in reading level is 2.951999999999998.
```

The return value becomes the value associated with the function call itself. For example, the first `print` statement could be changed to

```python
print('The reading level of book 1 is ' + str(fleschKincaid(6, 2.2)) + '.')
```

In addition to defining a function's return value, the `return` statement *also* causes the function to end and return this value back to the function call. So the `return` statement actually does two things:

1. defines the function's return value, *and*

2. causes the function to end.

This second point is important to remember because it means that any statements we add to a function after the `return` statement will never be executed.

Reflection 2.11 *Add the statement*

```
print('This will never, ever be printed.')
```

to the `fleschKincaid` *function after the* `return` *statement. What does it do?*

Functions can have many statements in them before the `return` statement. The following function gets characteristics about a text by prompting for them, then calls our new `fleschKincaid` function and returns the result.

```
def fleschKincaid2():
    """Prompt for characteristics about a text and then return the
        text's reading level according to the Flesch-Kincaid formula.

    Parameters: none

    Return value: the Flesch-Kincaid reading level score
    """

    averageWords = float(input('Average words per sentence: '))
    averageSyllables = float(input('Average syllables per word: '))

    readingLevel = fleschKincaid(averageWords, averageSyllables)

    return readingLevel
```

By defining functions that return values, we can also add to the existing palette of mathematical functions supplied by Python. For example, our familiar sphere volume computation looks like this as a Python function:

```
import math

def volumeSphere(radius):
    """Computes the volume of a sphere.

    Parameter:
        radius: radius of the sphere

    Return value: volume of a sphere with the given radius
    """

    return (4 / 3) * math.pi * (radius ** 3)
```

Now suppose we want to approximate the volume of the earth's mantle, which is the layer between the earth's core and its crust. This is the same as computing the difference of two volumes: the volume of the earth and the volume of the earth's core, as illustrated below.

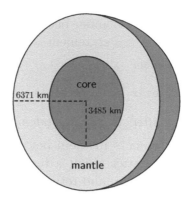

```
earthRadius = 6371 # km
coreRadius = 3485  # km
mantleVolume = volumeSphere(earthRadius) - volumeSphere(coreRadius)
print("The volume of the mantle is " + str(mantleVolume) + ' cubic km.')
```

Notice how we used two function calls in an arithmetic expression, exactly like we previously used the **int** and **math.sqrt** functions. This expression is evaluated from the inside out, just as one would expect:

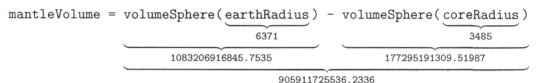

Return vs. print

A common beginner's mistake is to forget the **return** statement or end a function with a **print** instead of a **return**. For example, suppose we replaced the **return** with **print** in the **volumeSphere** function:

```
def fleschKincaid(averageWords, averageSyllables):
    """ (docstring omitted) """

    print(0.39 * averageWords + 11.8 * averageSyllables - 15.59) # WRONG!
```

> **Reflection 2.12** *Make this modification to your* fleschKincaid *function and then run your program again. Did you get the correct answer?*

When you run your program now, you will see something puzzling:

```
11.654
8.702000000000002
The reading level of book 1 is None.
The reading level of book 2 is None.
TypeError: unsupported operand type(s) for -: 'NoneType' and 'NoneType'
```

The first two lines where the reading levels are printed are coming from the **print** in the `fleschKincaid` function. Because there is no `return` in the function, the return value is `None`, which is assigned to `readingLevel1` and `readingLevel2`, and printed in the third and fourth lines. The fifth line is the error generated by trying to compute `readingLevel1` - `readingLevel2`, which is `None` - `None`, a nonsensical operation.

> **Reflection 2.13** *A similar problem will arise if you replace the last statement in* `fleschKincaid` *function with*
>
>   readingLevel = 0.39 * averageWords + 11.8 * averageSyllables - 15.59
>
> *and omit a* `return` *statement. Try it. What happens and why?*

Before continuing, be sure to fix your function so that it has a proper `return` statement.

Exercises

The following exercises ask you to write functions that `return` *(not* `print`*) values. When a program is called for, be sure to follow the guidelines in the previous section. Test each function with both common and boundary case arguments, as described on page 38, and document these test cases.*

2.5.1* The geometric mean of two numbers is the square root of their product. Write a function

    geometricMean(value1, value2)

that returns the geometric mean of the two values. Use your function to compute the geometric mean of 18 and 31.

2.5.2. If you have P (short for principal) dollars in a savings account that will pay interest rate r, compounded at a frequency of n times per year, then after t years, you will have

$$P\left(1 + \frac{r}{n}\right)^{nt}$$

dollars in your account. If the interest were compounded continuously (i.e., with n approaching infinity), you would instead have

$$Pe^{rt}$$

dollars after t years, where e is Euler's number, the base of the natural logarithm. Write a function

    compoundDiff(principal, rate, frequency, years)

that returns the difference in your savings between compounding at the given `frequency` and continuous compounding. (Use the `math.exp` function.)

Suppose you have $P = \$10,000$ in an account paying 1% interest ($r = 0.01$), compounding monthly. Use your function to determine how much more money will you have after $t = 10$ years if the interest were compounded continuously.

2.5.3. Write a program that prompts for a principal, rate, compounding frequency, and number of years, and then uses your function from Exercise 2.5.2 to display how much more money will you have if the interest were compounded continuously.

2.5.4* Write a function

    quadratic(a, b, c)

that uses the quadratic formula to return the two solutions to the equation $ax^2 + bx + c = 0$. Your function can `return` two values like this:

    return x1, x2

Show how to use your function to find the solutions to $3x^2 + 4x - 5 = 0$.

2.5.5. Write a program that prompts for values of a, b, and c using the `input` function, calls your function from Exercise 2.5.4 to find the solutions to the quadratic equation $ax^2 + bx + c = 0$, and then prints the results.

2.5.6* Suppose we have two points (x_1, y_1) and (x_2, y_2). The distance between them is equal to

$$\sqrt{(x_1 - x_2)^2 + (y_1 - y_2)^2}.$$

Write a function

    distance(x1, y1, x2, y2)

that returns the distance between points $(x1, y1)$ and $(x2, y2)$.

2.5.7. A parallelepiped is a three-dimensional box in which the six sides are parallelograms. The volume of a parallelepiped is

$$V = abc\sqrt{1 + 2\cos(x)\cos(y)\cos(z) - \cos(x)^2 - \cos(y)^2 - \cos(z)^2}$$

where a, b, and c are the edge lengths, and x, y, and z are the angles between the edges, in radians. Write a function

    ppdVolume(a, b, c, x, y, z)

that returns the volume of a parallelepiped with the given dimensions.

2.5.8. Repeat the previous exercise, but now assume that the angles passed into the function are in degrees.

2.5.9. Write a function

    total(number1, number2)

that returns the sum of `number1` and `number2`. Also write a complete program (with a `main` function) that gets these two values using the `input` function, passes them to your `total` function, and then prints the value returned by the `total` function.

2.5.10* Write a function

    power(base, exponent)

that returns the value `base`^{exponent}. Also write a complete program (with a `main` function) that gets these two values using the `input` function, passes them to your `power` function, and then prints the returned value of `base`^{exponent}.

2.5.11* Write a function

    football(touchdowns, fieldGoals, safeties)

that returns your team's football score if the number of touchdowns (worth 7 points), field goals (worth 3 points), and safeties (worth 2 points) are passed as parameters. Then write a complete program (with `main` function) that gets these three values using the `input` function, passes them to your `football` function, and then prints the score.

2.5.12. The ideal gas law states that $PV = nRT$ where

- P = pressure in atmospheres (atm)
- V = volume in liters (L)
- n = number of moles (mol) of gas
- R = gas constant = 0.08 L atm / mol K
- T = absolute temperature of the gas in Kelvin (K)

Write a function

```
moles(V, P, T)
```

that returns the number of moles of an ideal gas in V liters contained at pressure P and T degrees Celsius. (Be sure to convert Celsius to Kelvin in your function.) Also write a complete program (with a `main` function) that gets these three values using the `input` function, passes them to your `moles` function, and then prints the number of moles of ideal gas.

2.5.13. Suppose we have two containers of an ideal gas. The first contains 10 L of gas at 1.5 atm and 20 degrees Celsius. The second contains 25 L of gas at 2 atm and 30 degrees Celsius. Show how to use two calls to your function in the previous exercise to compute the total number of moles of ideal gas in the two containers.

Now replace the `return` statement in your `moles` function with a call to `print` instead. (So your function does not contain a `return` statement.) Can you still compute the total number of moles in the same way? If so, show how. If not, explain why not.

2.5.14* Most of the world is highly dependent upon groundwater for survival. Therefore, it is important to be able to monitor groundwater flow to understand potential contamination threats. Darcy's law states that the flow of a liquid (e.g., water) through a porous medium (e.g., sand, gravel) depends upon the capacity of the medium to carry the flow and the gradient of the flow:

$$Q = K\frac{dh}{dl}$$

where

- K is the hydraulic conductivity of the medium, the rate at which the liquid can move through it, measured in area/time
- dh/dl is the hydraulic gradient
- dh is the drop in elevation (negative for flow down)
- dl is the horizontal distance of the flow

Write a function

```
darcy(K, dh, dl)
```

that computes the flow with the given parameters.

Use your function to compute the amount of groundwater flow inside a hill with hydraulic conductivity of 130 m^2/day, and a 50 m drop in elevation over a distance of 1 km.

2.5.15. A person's Body Mass Index (BMI) is calculated by the following formula:

$$\text{BMI} = \frac{w}{h^2} \cdot 703$$

where w is the person's weight in pounds and h is the person's height in inches. Write a function

```
bmi(weight, height)
```

that uses this formula to return the corresponding BMI.

2.5.16* When you (or your parents) rip songs from a CD, the digital file is created by sampling the sound at some rate. Common rates are 128 kbps (128×2^{10} bits per second), 192 kbps, and 256 kbps. Write a function

```
songs(capacity, bitrate)
```

that returns the number of 4-minute songs someone can fit locally on his or her music player. The function's two parameters are the capacity of the music player in gigabytes (GB) and the sampling rate in kbps. A gigabyte is 2^{30} bytes and a byte contains 8 bits. Also write a complete program (with a `main` function) that gets these two values using the `input` function, passes them to your `songs` function, and then prints the number of songs.

2.5.17. The speed of a computer is often (simplistically) expressed in gigahertz (GHz), the number of billions of times the computer's internal clock "ticks" per second. For example, a 2 GHz computer has a clock that "ticks" 2 billion times per second. Suppose that a single computer instruction requires 3 "ticks" to execute. Write a function

```
time(instructions, gigahertz)
```

that returns the time in seconds required to execute the given number of `instructions` on a computer with clock rate `gigahertz`. For example, `time(10 ** 9, 3)` should return 1 (second).

2.5.18* Exercise 1.3.8 asked how to swap the values in two variables. Can we write a function to swap the values of two parameters? In other words, can we write a function

```
swap(a, b)
```

and call it like

```
x = 10
y = 1
swap(x, y)
```

so that after the function returns, `x` has the value 1 and `y` has the value 10? (The function should not return anything.) If so, write it. If not, explain why not.

2.5.19. Given an integer course grade from 0 to 99, we convert it to the equivalent grade point according to the following scale: 90–99: 4, 80–89: 3, 70–79: 2, 60–69: 1, < 60: 0. Write a function

```
gradePoint(score)
```

that returns the grade point (i.e., GPA) equivalent to the given score.

2.5.20. The function `time.time()` (in the `time` module) returns the current time in seconds since January 1, 1970. Write a function

    year()

that uses this function to return the current year as an integer value.

2.5.21* Write a function

    twice(text)

that uses the string concatenation operator `*` to return the string `text` repeated twice, with a space in between. For example, `twice('bah')` should return the string `'bah bah'`.

2.5.22. Write a function

    repeat(text, n)

that returns a string that is `n` copies of the string `text`. For example, `repeat('AB', 3)` should return the string `'ABABAB'`.

2.6 SCOPE AND NAMESPACES

We have been using local variables inside functions for a few sections now, relying on somewhat informal explanations for how they work. In this section, we will look more formally at scoping rules for variables so that you better understand how to use them and can hopefully prevent difficult-to-find errors in the future. As an example, let's consider the wind chill computation from Exercise 1.3.14, implemented as a function that is called from a **main** function.

```python
def windChill(temperature, windSpeed):
    """Gives the North American metric wind chill equivalent
       for the given temperature and wind speed.

    Parameters:
        temperature: temperature in degrees Celsius
        windSpeed:   wind speed at 10m in km/h

    Return value:
        equivalent wind chill in degrees Celsius, rounded to
        the nearest integer
    """

    chill = 13.12 + 0.6215 * temperature \
                + (0.3965 * temperature - 11.37) * windSpeed ** 0.16
    temperature = round(chill)
    return temperature

def main():
    temp = -3
    wind = 13
    chilly = windChill(temp, wind)
    print('The wind chill is ' + str(chilly) + ' degrees Celsius.')

main()
```

(The "backslash" (\) character above is the *line continuation character*. It indicates that the line that it ends is continued on the next line. This is sometimes handy for splitting very long lines of code.) Notice that we have introduced a variable inside the `windChill` function named `chill` to break up the computation a bit. Because we created `chill` inside the function `windChill`, its *scope* is local to the function. If we tried to refer to `chill` anywhere outside of the function `windChill` (e.g., in the `main` function), we would get the following error:

```
NameError: name 'chill' is not defined
```

Because `chill` has a local scope, it is called a *local variable*. The parameters `temperature` and `windSpeed` are also local variables and have the same local scope as `chill`.

Local namespaces

Let's look more closely at how local variable and parameter names are managed in Python. In this program, just after we call the `windChill` function, but just before the values of the arguments `temp` and `wind` are assigned to the parameters `temperature` and `windSpeed`, we can visualize the situation like this:

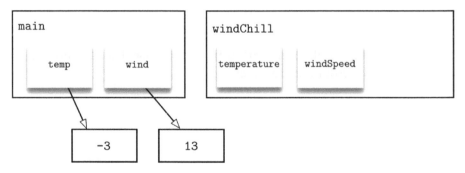

The box around `temp` and `wind` represents the scope of the `main` function, and the box around `temperature` and `windSpeed` represents the scope of the `windChill` function. In each case, the scope defines what names have been defined, or have meaning, in that function. In the picture, we are using arrows instead of affixing the "Sticky notes" directly to the values to make clear that the names, not the values, reside in their respective scopes. The names are references to the memory cells in which their values reside.

The scope corresponding to a function in Python is managed with a *namespace*. A namespace of a function is simply a list of names that are defined in that function, together with references to their values. We can view the namespace of a particular function by calling the `locals` function from within it. For example, insert the following statement into the `main` function, just before the call to `windChill`:

```
print('Local namespace in main before windChill is\n\t', locals())
```

(The `\n\t` represents a newline and tab character.) When we run the program, we will see

```
1  def windChill(temperature, windSpeed):
2      """ (docstring omitted) """
3
4      print('Local namespace at the start of windChill is\n\t', locals())
5      chill = 13.12 + 0.6215 * temperature \
6                      + (0.3965 * temperature - 11.37) * windSpeed ** 0.16
7      temperature = round(chill)
8      print('Local namespace at the end of windChill is\n\t', locals())
9      return temperature
10
11 def main():
12     temp = -3
13     wind = 13
14     print('Local namespace in main before windChill is\n\t', locals())
15     chilly = windChill(temp, wind)
16     print('Local namespace in main after windChill is\n\t', locals())
17     print('The wind chill is ' + str(chilly) + ' degrees Celsius.')
18
19 main()
```

Figure 2.10 The complete wind chill program, with calls to the `locals` function.

```
Local namespace in main before windChill is
        {'temp': -3, 'wind': 13}
The wind chill is -8 degrees Celsius.
```

This is showing us that, at that point in the program, the local namespace in the `main` function consists of two names: `temp`, which is assigned the value -3, and `wind`, which is assigned the value 13, just as we visualized above. The curly braces ({ }) around the namespace representation indicate that the namespace is a *dictionary*, another abstract data type in Python. We will explore dictionaries in more detail in Chapter 7.

Returning to the program, when `windChill` is subsequently called from `main`, it is implicitly assigning `temperature` = `temp` and `windSpeed` = `wind`, so the picture changes to this:

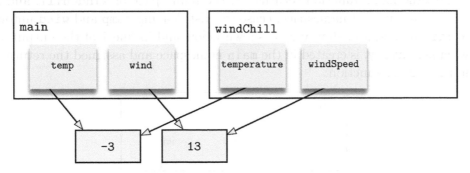

To see all of the namespace changes in the program, insert three more calls to the `locals` function, as shown in Figure 2.10. Now when we run the program, we see (line numbers added):

```
1 Local namespace in main before windChill is
          {'temp': -3, 'wind': 13}
3 Local namespace at the start of windChill is
          {'temperature': -3, 'windSpeed': 13}
5 Local namespace at the end of windChill is
          {'temperature': -8, 'windSpeed': 13, 'chill': -7.676796032159553}
7 Local namespace in main after windChill is
          {'temp': -3, 'wind': 13, 'chilly': -8}
9 The wind chill is -8 degrees Celsius.
```

Line 3 above, which corresponds to the preceding "sticky note" illustration, shows us that, at the beginning of the `windChill` function (line 4 in Figure 2.10), the only visible names are `temperature` and `windSpeed`, which have been assigned the values of `temp` and `wind`, respectively. Notice, however, that `temp` and `wind` do not exist inside `windChill`, and there is no direct connection between `temp` and `temperature`, or between `wind` and `windSpeed`; rather they are only indirectly connected through the values to which they are both assigned.

Lines 5–6 in the `windChill` function insert the new name `chill` into the local namespace, assign it the result of the wind chill computation, and reassign the local parameter `temperature` to the rounded wind chill value:

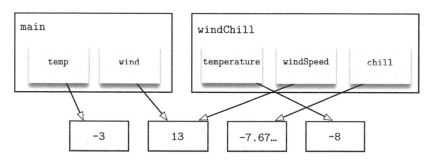

This corresponds to line 5 of the output above.

After the `windChill` function returns −8, the namespace of `windChill`, and all of the local names in that namespace, cease to exist, leaving `temp` and `wind` untouched in the `main` namespace. However, as shown below and in line 7 of the output above, a new name, `chilly`, is created in the `main` namespace and assigned the return value of the `windChill` function:

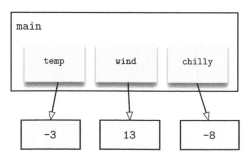

When the **main** function ends, its local namespace also disappears.

The global namespace

The namespace in which global variable names reside is called the ***global namespace***. We can view the contents of the global namespace by calling the **globals** function. For example, add the following call to **globals** to the end of **main** in our program:

```
print('The global namespace is\n\t', globals())
```

The result will be something like the following (some names are not shown):

```
The global namespace is
         {'__name__': '__main__', '__doc__': None, ...,
          '__builtins__': <module 'builtins' (built-in)>, ...,
          'windChill': <function windChill at 0x10dde8b80>,
          'main': <function main at 0x10dde8c10>}
```

Notice that the only global names that we created are the names of our two functions, **windChill** and **main**. We can think of each of these names as referring to the functions' respective namespaces, as illustrated below (references for some names are omitted):

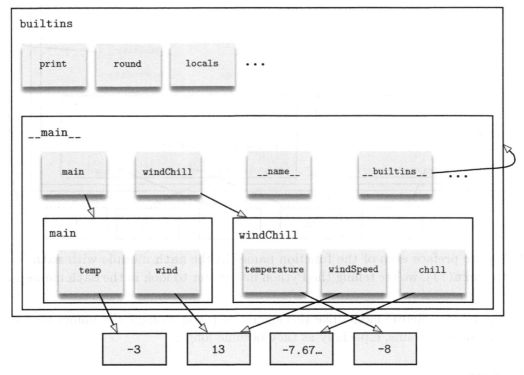

The other names defined in the global namespace are standard names defined in every Python program. The name **__name__** refers to the name of the current module, which, in this case, is '**__main__**' (not to be confused with the **main** function); **__name__** always refers to '**__main__**' when the program is executed directly by the Python interpreter (vs. being imported from another program). The name `__builtins__` refers to an implicitly imported module that contains all of Python's built-in functions.

As the illustration suggests, we can think of these namespaces as being nested inside each other because names that are not located in a local namespace are sought in enclosing namespaces. For example, when we are in the `main` function and call the function `print`, the Python interpreter first looks in the local namespace for this function name. Not finding it there, it looks in the next outermost namespace, `__main__`. Again, not finding it there, it looks in the `builtins` namespace.

Each module that we import also defines its own namespace. For example, when we import the `math` module with `import math`, a new namespace is created within `builtins`, at the same nesting level as the `__main__` namespace, as illustrated below.

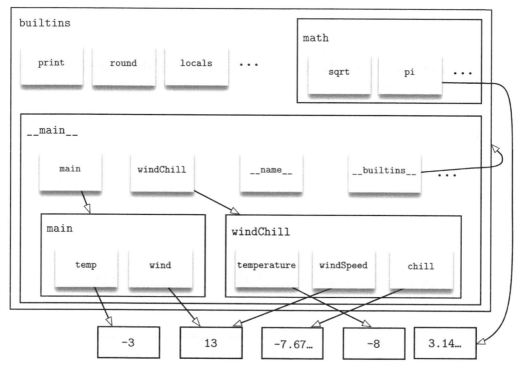

When we preface each of the function names in the `math` module with `math` (e.g., `math.sqrt(7)`), we are telling the Python interpreter to look in the `math` namespace for the function.

Maintaining a mental model like this should help you manage the names that you use in your programs, especially as they become longer.

Exercises

2.6.1* When the `windChill` function in Figure 2.10 is called from `main`, the value of the argument `temp` is assigned to the parameter named `temperature`. Then, in the function, `temperature` is assigned a new value. Does this affect the value of `temp`? Use the pictures in this section to explain your answer.

2.6.2* Exercise 2.5.6 asked you to write a `distance` function to find the distance between two points. Here is that function in a simple but complete program.

```
1   import math
2
3   def distance(x1, y1, x2, y2):
4       dist = math.sqrt((x1 - x2) ** 2 + (y1 - y2) ** 2)
5       return dist
6
7   def main():
8       theDistance = distance(3, 7.25, 9.5, 1)
9       print(theDistance)
10
11  main()
```

(a) Show how to use the `locals` function to print all of the local variable names in the `distance` function just before the function returns. What does the namespace look like?

(b) Show how to use the `globals` function to print the global namespace at the end of the `main` function. Which of the names from the program are in the global namespace?

(c) Insert a statement in the `main` function between lines 8 and 9 to print the local variable `dist`. What happens and why?

2.6.3. Look back at the program in Figure 2.8 on page 73.

(a) In what namespace is the variable `george`. Why?

(b) In the `bloom`, `stem`, and `flower` functions, we used a turtle parameter named `tortoise` instead of `george`. Would the program still work if we replaced every instance of `tortoise` with `george`? Explain your answer.

(c) If you made the changes in part (b), the name `george` would exist in two different namespaces while each of the three functions was executing. Explain why. While the `bloom` function is executing, which `george` is being used?

2.6.4. Insert a call to the `locals` function inside the `for` loop in this program. What values is the variable `line` assigned in the loop?

```
import turtle

def draw(tortoise, numLines):
    for line in range(numLines):
        tortoise.up()
        tortoise.goto(line * 10, 0)
        tortoise.down()
        tortoise.goto((numLines - line + 1) * 10, 200)

def main():
    george = turtle.Turtle()
    draw(george, 12)

main()
```

2.6.5* Sketch a picture like that on page 100 depicting the namespaces in the program in the previous exercise just before returning from the draw function. Here is a picture to get you started:

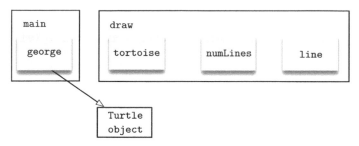

2.6.6. Consider the following program:

```python
import turtle

def drawStar(tortoise, length):
    for count in range(5):
        tortoise.forward(length)
        tortoise.left(144)

def main():
    george = turtle.Turtle()
    sideLength = 200
    drawStar(george, sideLength)

main()
```

Sketch a picture like that on page 100 depicting the namespaces in this program just before returning from the drawStar function. Here is a picture to get you started:

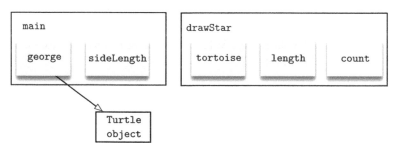

2.6.7. In economics, a demand function gives the price a consumer is willing to pay for an item, given that a particular quantity of that item is available. For example, suppose that in a coffee bean market the demand function is given by

$$D(Q) = 45 - \frac{2.3Q}{1000},$$

where Q is the quantity of available coffee, measured in kilograms, and the returned price is for 1 kg. So, for example, if there are 5000 kg of coffee beans available, the price will be $45 - (2.3)(5000)/1000 = 33.50$ dollars for 1 kg. The following program computes this value.

```
def demand(quantity):
    quantity = quantity / 1000
    return 45 - 2.3 * quantity

def main():
    coffee = 5000
    price = demand(coffee)
    print(price)

main()
```

Sketch a picture like that on page 100 depicting the namespaces in this program just before returning from the demand function and also just before returning from the main function.

2.6.8.   In the program from the previous exercise, change return 45 - 2.3 * quantity to print(45 - 2.3 * quantity). How does this change your pictures?

2.6.9.   Here is a simple program with the fleshKincaid function from the previous section.

```
def fleschKincaid(averageWords, averageSyllables):
    """ (docstring omitted) """

    readingLevel = 0.39 * averageWords \
                   + 11.8 * averageSyllables - 15.59
    return readingLevel

def main():
    theReadingLevel = fleschKincaid(4.0, 1.5)
    print('Local namespace:', locals())
    print('The reading level is ' + str(theReadingLevel) + '.')

main()
```

(a)   Run this program. What is printed by the highlighted line above? How does theReadingLevel get this value?

(b)   In the fleschKincaid function, replace return readingLevel with print(readingLevel), and run the program again. Now what is printed by the highlighted line above? Why?

2.7   SUMMARY AND FURTHER DISCOVERY

In this chapter, we made progress toward writing more sophisticated programs. The key to successfully solving larger problems is to break the problem into smaller, more manageable pieces, and then treat each of these pieces as an abstract "black box" that you can use to solve the larger problem. There are two types of "black boxes," those that represent things (i.e., data, information) and those that represent actions. A "black box" representing a thing is described by an *abstract data type* (ADT), which contains both hidden data and a set of functions that we can call to access or modify that data. In Python, an ADT is implemented with a *class*, and instances of a class are called *objects*. The class, such as `Turtle`, to which an object belongs specifies what (hidden) data the object has and what *methods* can be called to access or modify that data. Remember that a class is the "blueprint" for a category of objects, but is not actually an object. We "built" new `Turtle` objects by calling a function with the class' name:

```
george = turtle.Turtle()
```

Once the object is created, we can do things with it by calling its methods, like `george.forward(100)`, without worrying about how it actually works.

A "black box" that performs an action is called a *functional abstraction*. We implement functional abstractions in Python with functions. Earlier in the chapter, we designed functions to draw things in turtle graphics, gradually making them more general (and hence more useful) by adding parameters. We also started using `for` loops to create more interesting iterative algorithms. Later in the chapter, we also looked at how we can add return values to functions, and how to properly think about all of the names that we use in our programs. By breaking our programs up into functions, like breaking up a complex organization into divisions, we can more effectively focus on how to solve the problem at hand.

This increasing complexity becomes easier to manage if you follow the guidelines for structuring and documenting your programs that we laid out in Section 2.4.

Notes for further discovery

The chapter's first epigraph is once again from Donald Knuth, specifically his address after receiving the 1974 Turing award [32]. You can read or watch other Turing award lectures at `http://amturing.acm.org`.

The second epigraph is from Ada Lovelace, considered by many to be the first computer programmer. She was born Ada Byron in England in 1815, the daughter of the Romantic poet Lord Byron. (However, she never knew her father because he left England soon after she was born.) In marriage, Ada acquired the title "Countess of Lovelace," and is now commonly known simply as Ada Lovelace. She was educated in mathematics by several prominent tutors and worked with Charles Babbage, the inventor of two of the first computers, the Difference Engine and the Analytical Engine. Although the Analytical Engine was never actually built, Ada wrote a set of "Notes" about its design, including what many consider to be the first computer program. (The quote is from Note A, page 696.) In her "Notes" she also imagined that future computers would be able to perform tasks far more interesting than arithmetic (like make music). Ada Lovelace died in 1852, at the age of 37.

The giant tortoise named Lonesome George was, sadly, the last surviving member of his subspecies, *Chelonoidis nigra abingdonii*. The giant tortoise named Super Diego is a member of a different subspecies, *Chelonoidis nigra hoodensis*.

The commenting style we use in this book is based on Google's official Python style guide at `https://google.github.io/styleguide/pyguide.html`.

CHAPTER 3

Inside a Computer

> One day ladies will take their computers for walks in the park and tell each other, "My little computer said such a funny thing this morning."
>
> Alan Turing
> *1951*

> And now for something completely different!
>
> Monty Python's Flying Circus

> There are only 10 types of people in the world: those who understand binary, and those who don't.
>
> Unknown

A LAN Turing, the father of Computer Science, optimistically predicted that by now computers would be carrying on meaningful conversations with human beings. While this has not yet come to pass, by executing clever algorithms very fast, computers can sometimes *appear* to exhibit primitive intelligence. In a historic example, in 1997, the IBM Deep Blue computer defeated reigning world champion Garry Kasparov in a six-game match of chess. In 2011, IBM's Watson computer beat two champions in the television game show Jeopardy. Five years later, the AlphaGo program defeated the world Go champion over a five match series. And now we are on the cusp of seeing autonomous vehicles almost entirely replacing human drivers.

The intelligence that we sometimes attribute to computers, however, is actually human intelligence that was originally expressed as an algorithm, and then as a program. Contemporary computers at their cores remain dumb machines. Even the

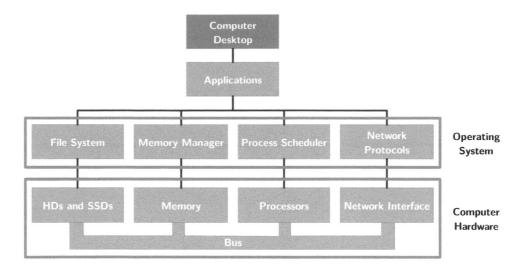

Figure 3.1 A simplified look at layers of abstraction when using a computer.

statements in a high-level programming language are themselves abstract conveniences built upon a much more rudimentary set of instructions that a computer can execute natively.

3.1 COMPUTERS ARE DUMB

When you use a computer, you are utilizing layers of functional abstractions. As illustrated in Figure 3.1, at the highest layer, you are presented with a "desktop" abstraction on which you can store files and use applications (or programs) to do work. That there appear to be many applications active simultaneously on this desktop is also an abstraction. In reality, *some* applications may be working in parallel while others are not, but the computer is alternating among them so quickly that they appear to be working in parallel. Each of these applications is a sequence of ***machine language*** instructions that can be executed by the computer hardware. Some of these instructions rely on various functional abstractions provided by the computer's ***operating system*** to save files, access the computer's memory, retrieve information from the Internet, etc. In other words, the operating system provides functional abstractions that allow us, via the applications we use, to more conveniently and efficiently use the computer's resources.

Since machine language is the only thing that a computer "understands," every statement in a Python program must be translated by the Python interpreter into a sequence of equivalent machine language instructions before it can be executed. An interpreter translates one line of a high-level program into machine language, executes it, then translates the next line and executes it, etc. Other languages (such as C++) use a ***compiler*** instead. A compiler translates a high-level language program all at once into machine language. Then the compiled machine language

---

Tangent 3.1: High performance computing

Although today's computers are extremely fast, there are some problems that are so big that additional power is necessary. These include weather forecasting, molecular modeling and drug design, aerodynamics, and deciphering encrypted data. For these problems, scientists use *supercomputers*. A supercomputer, or *high performance computer*, is made of up to tens of thousands of *nodes*, connected by a very fast data network that shuttles information between nodes. A node, essentially a standalone computer, can contain multiple processors, each with multiple cores. The fastest supercomputers today have millions of cores and a million gigabytes of memory.

To realize the power of these computers, programmers need to supply their cores with a constant stream of data and instructions. The results computed by the individual cores are then aggregated into an overall solution. The algorithm design and programming techniques, known as **parallel programming**, are beyond the scope of this book, but we provide additional resources at the end of the chapter if you would like to learn more.

---

program can be executed from start to finish without additional translation. This tends to make compiled programs faster than interpreted ones. However, interpreted languages allow us to more closely interact with a program during its execution.

The types of instructions that constitute a machine language are based on the internal design of a modern computer. As illustrated in Figure 3.1, a computer essentially consists of one or more *processors* connected to a **memory**. A computer's memory, often called *RAM* (short for *random access memory*), is conceptually organized as a long sequence of **cells**, each of which can contain one unit of information. Each cell is labeled with a unique **memory address** that allows the processor to reference it specifically. So a computer's memory is like a huge sequence of equal-sized post office boxes, each of which can hold exactly one letter. Each P.O. box number is analogous to a memory address and a letter is analogous to one unit of information. The information in each cell can represent either one instruction or one unit of data.[1] So a computer's memory stores both programs and the data on which the programs work. A variable name in Python is essentially a reference to a memory address.

A **processor**, often called a *CPU* (short for *central processing unit*) or *core*, contains both the machinery for executing instructions and a small set of memory locations called *registers* that temporarily hold data values needed by the current instruction. If a computer contains more than one core, as most modern computers do, then it is able to execute more than one instruction at a time. These instructions may be from different programs or from the same program. This means that our previous definition of an algorithm as a *sequence* of instructions is not strictly correct. In fact, an algorithm (or a program) may consist of several semi-independent sequences of steps called *threads* that cooperatively solve a problem.

---

[1]In reality, each instruction or unit of data usually occupies multiple contiguous cells.

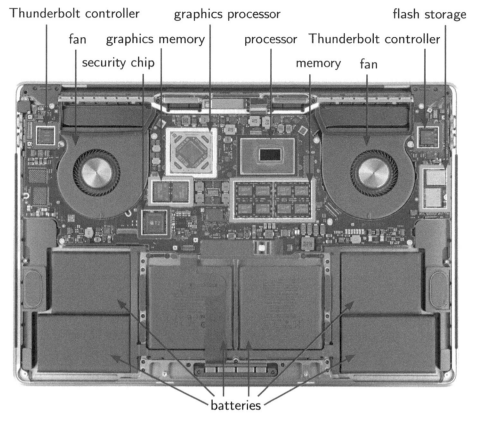

Figure 3.2   Inside an Apple MacBook Pro. Image courtesy of iFixit (`ifixit.com`).

The processors and memory are connected by a communication channel called a **bus**. When a processor needs a value in memory, it transmits the request over the bus, and then the memory returns the requested value the same way. The bus also connects the processors and memory to several other components that either improve the machine's efficiency or its convenience, like the Internet and **secondary storage** devices like hard drives (HD), solid state drives (SSD), and flash memory. As you probably know, the contents of a computer's memory are lost when the computer loses power, so we use secondary storage to preserve data for longer periods of time. We interact with these devices through a "file system" abstraction that makes it appear as if our hard drives are really filing cabinets. When you execute a program or open a file, it is first copied from secondary storage into memory where the processor can access it.

Figure 3.2 shows what these components look like inside a laptop computer. In addition to the processor, memory, and flash storage, which acts as secondary storage, a lot of real estate is occupied by the graphics processor and its dedicated memory, which are responsible for our computers' abilities to display high resolution video and fast-paced video games. The Thunderbolt controllers are responsible for transferring data between the computer and external devices (and the network) connected through Thunderbolt 3 (USB-C) ports. The security chip encrypts data in flash storage, prevents unauthorized software from running, and stores fingerprint data for securely logging in.

Reflection 3.1 *Look up the technical specifications for your computer. On a Mac, select "About This Mac" from the Apple menu. In Windows, search for "System Information" or "msinfo32."*

Machine language

The machine language instructions that a processor can execute are very limited in their abilities.[2] For example, consider something as simple as addition in Python:

```
>>> total = number1 + number2
```

Even something this simple is too complex for one machine language instruction. The machine language equivalent likely, depending on the computer, consists of four instructions that do the following.

1. Load the value in the memory cell referred to by the variable number1 into a register in the processor.

2. Load the value in the memory cell referred to by the variable number2 into another register in the processor.

3. Add the values in these two registers and store the result in a third register.

4. Store the value in the third register in the memory cell referred to by the variable total.

From the moment a computer is turned on, its processors are operating in a continuous loop called the ***fetch and execute cycle*** (or *machine cycle*). In each cycle, the processor fetches one machine language instruction from memory and executes it. This cycle repeats until the computer is turned off or loses power. This is essentially all a computer does. The rate at which a computer performs the fetch and execute cycle is related to the rate at which its internal clock "ticks" (the processor's *clock rate*). The ticks of this clock keep the machine's operations synchronized. Modern personal computers have clocks that tick a few billion times each second; a 3 gigahertz (GHz) processor ticks 3 billion times per second ("giga" means "billion" and a "hertz" is one tick per second).

So computers, at their most basic level, really are quite dumb; the processor blindly follows the fetch and execute cycle, dutifully executing whatever sequence of simple instructions we give it. The frustrating errors that we yell at computers about are, in fact, human errors. The great thing about computers is not that they are smart, but that they follow our instructions so quickly; they can accomplish an incredible amount of work in a very short amount of time. Whether that work is useful, however, is up to us.

---

[2]Python programs are actually translated into an intermediate form called byte code first. See Tangent 3.2 for details.

Tangent 3.2: Byte code

In Python, the translation process is actually a little more complicated than the more generic discussion in this section. Before they are executed, Python programs are compiled into an intermediate language called *byte code*. Then the byte code instructions are executed by a *virtual machine* that understands how to translate them into machine language. A virtual machine is a program that emulates a computer.

The Python virtual machine uses a *stack* instead of registers to store references to objects. A stack is conceptually a "pile" of values that can only be accessed from the top. The only operations on a stack are *pushing* a value onto the top of the stack and *popping* the value off the top of the stack. The following sequence of byte code instructions is what is actually produced for `total = number1 + number2` by the Python interpreter.

```
0 LOAD_FAST          0 (number1)
2 LOAD_FAST          1 (number2)
4 BINARY_ADD
6 STORE_FAST         2 (total)
```

The first two instructions push references to the variables `number1` and `number2` onto the stack. The `BINARY_ADD` instruction pops the two values off the stack, adds them together (in binary) and pushes the result onto the top of the stack. The final instruction pops the result off the stack and stores it at the memory location referred to by the variable `total`.

If you would like see byte code for yourself, you can. To see the byte code generated for a function named `myFunction`, do this:

```
import dis
dis.dis(myFunction)
```

3.2 EVERYTHING IS BITS

Our discussion so far has glossed over a very important consideration: in what form does a computer store programs and data? In addition to machine language instructions, we need to store numbers, documents, maps, images, sounds, presentations, spreadsheets, and more. Using a different storage medium for each type of information would be insanely complicated and inefficient. Instead, we need a simple storage format that can accommodate any type of data. The answer is bits. A *bit* is the simplest possible unit of information, capable of taking on one of only two values: 0 or 1 (or equivalently, off/on, no/yes, or false/true). Storing data as bits makes perfect sense because bit storage is simple, bits can represent anything, and computing with bits is almost trivial.

Bits are switches

Storing the value of a bit is absurdly simple: a bit is equivalent to an on/off switch, and the value of the bit is equivalent to the state of the switch: off = 0 and on = 1. A computer's memory is essentially composed of billions of microscopic switches, organized into memory cells. Each memory cell contains 8 switches, so each cell can store 8 bits, called a **byte**. We represent a byte simply as a sequence of 8 bits, such as 01101001. A computer with 8 gigabytes (GB) of memory contains about 8 billion memory cells, each storing one byte. (Similarly, a kilobyte (KB) is about one thousand bytes, a megabyte (MB) is about one million bytes, and a terabyte (TB) is about one trillion bytes.)

Bits can represent anything

A second advantage of storing information with bits is that, as the simplest possible unit of information, it serves as a "lowest common denominator." All information can be converted to bits in a fairly straightforward manner. Numbers, words, images, music, and machine language instructions are all encoded as sequences of bits before they are stored in memory. Information stored as bits is also said to be in **binary notation**. For example, consider the following sequence of 16 bits (or two bytes).

0100010001010101

This bit sequence can represent each of the following, depending upon how it is interpreted:

(a) the integer value 17,493;

(b) the decimal value 2.166015625;

(c) the two characters "DU";

(d) the Intel machine language instruction `inc x` ("increment" x); or

(e) the 4×4 black and white image to the right, called a **bitmap** (0 represents a white square and 1 represents a black square).

For now, let's just look more closely at how numbers are stored. Integers are represented in a computer using the *binary number system*, which is understood best by analogy to the decimal number system. In decimal, each position in a number has a value that is a power of ten: from right to left, the positional values are $10^0 = 1$, $10^1 = 10$, $10^2 = 100$, etc. The value of a decimal number comes from adding the digits, each first multiplied by the value of its position. So 1,831 represents the value

$$1 \times 10^3 + 8 \times 10^2 + 3 \times 10^1 + 1 \times 10^0 = 1000 + 800 + 30 + 1.$$

The binary number system is no different, except that each position represents a power of two, and there are only two digits instead of ten. From right to left, the binary number system positions have values $2^0 = 1$, $2^1 = 2$, $2^2 = 4$, $2^3 = 8$, etc. So, for example, the binary number 110011 represents the value

$$1 \times 2^5 + 1 \times 2^4 + 0 \times 2^3 + 0 \times 2^2 + 1 \times 2^1 + 1 \times 2^0 = 32 + 16 + 2 + 1 = 51$$

in decimal. The 16 bit number above, 0100010001010101, is equivalent to

$$2^{14} + 2^{10} + 2^6 + 2^4 + 2^2 + 2^0 = 16,384 + 1,024 + 64 + 16 + 4 + 1 = 17,493.$$

Tangent 3.3: Hexadecimal notation

Hexadecimal is base 16 notation. Just as the positional values in decimal are powers of 10 and the positional values in binary are powers of 2, the positional values in hexadecimal are powers of 16. Because of this, hexadecimal needs 16 digits, which are 0 through 9, followed by the letters `a` through `f`. The letter `a` has the value 10, `b` has the value 11, ..., `f` has the value 15. For example, the hexadecimal number `51ed` has the decimal value

$$5 \cdot 16^3 + 1 \cdot 16^2 + 14 \cdot 16^1 + 13 \cdot 16^0 = 5 \cdot 4096 + 1 \cdot 256 + 14 \cdot 16 + 13 \cdot 1 = 20{,}973.$$

Hexadecimal is used a convenient shorthand for binary. Because any 4 binary digits can represent the values 0 through 15, they can be conveniently replaced by a single hexadecimal digit. So the hexadecimal number `100522f10` is equivalent to `000100000000010100100010111100010000` in binary, as shown below:

1	0	0	5	2	2	f	1	0
0001	0000	0000	0101	0010	0010	1111	0001	0000

Instead of displaying this 36 bit binary number, it is more convenient to display the 9 digit hexadecimal equivalent.

Reflection 3.2 *To check your understanding, show why the binary number* `1001000` *is equivalent to the decimal number 72.*

This idea can be extended to numbers with a fractional part as well. In decimal, the positions to the right of the decimal point have values that are negative powers of 10: the tenths place has value $10^{-1} = 0.1$, the hundredths place has value $10^{-2} = 0.01$, etc. So the decimal number 18.31 represents the value

$$1 \times 10^1 + 8 \times 10^0 + 3 \times 10^{-1} + 1 \times 10^{-2} = 10 + 8 + 0.3 + 0.01.$$

Similarly, in binary, the positions to the right of the "binary point" have values that are negative powers of 2. For example, the binary number 11.0011 represents the value

$$1 \times 2^1 + 1 \times 2^0 + 0 \times 2^{-1} + 0 \times 2^{-2} + 1 \times 2^{-3} + 1 \times 2^{-4} = 2 + 1 + \frac{1}{8} + \frac{1}{16} = 3\frac{3}{16}$$

in decimal. This is not, however, how we derived (b) above. As we will discuss in Section 3.3, numbers with fractional components are stored in a computer using floating point notation, which converts a number to scientific notation first before storing it.

Reflection 3.3 *To check your understanding, show why the binary number* `1001.101` *is equivalent to the decimal number 9 5/8.*

Computing with bits

A third advantage of binary is that computation on binary values is exceedingly easy. In fact, there are only three fundamental operators, called **and**, **or**, and **not**.

These are known as the **Boolean operators**, after 19th century mathematician George Boole, who is credited with inventing modern mathematical logic, now called *Boolean logic* or *Boolean algebra*.

Let the variables a and b each represent a bit with a value of 0 or 1. Then a **and** b is equal to 1 only if both a and b are equal to 1; otherwise a **and** b is equal to 0.[3] This is conveniently represented by the following **truth table**:

a	b	a **and** b
0	0	0
0	1	0
1	0	0
1	1	1

Each row of the truth table represents one of the four permutations of the values of a and b. These permutations are shown in the first two columns. The last column of the truth table contains the corresponding values of a **and** b for each row. We see that a **and** b is 1 only when a and b are both 1. If we let 1 represent "true" and 0 represent "false," this conveniently matches our own intuitive meaning of "and." The statement "the barn is red *and* white" is true only if the barn both has red on it and has white on it.

The second Boolean operator, **or**, also takes two operands. The expression a **or** b is equal to 1 if at least one of a or b is equal to 1; otherwise a **or** b is equal to 0. This is represented by the following truth table:

a	b	a **or** b
0	0	0
0	1	1
1	0	1
1	1	1

Notice that a **or** b is 1 even if both a and b are 1. This is different from our normal understanding of "or." If we say that "the barn is red or white," we usually mean it is either red or white, not both. But the Boolean operator can mean both are true. (There is another Boolean operator called "exclusive or" that does mean "either/or," but we won't get into that here.)

Finally, the **not** operator only takes one operand and simply inverts a bit, changing 0 to 1, or 1 to 0. So, **not** a is equal to 1 if a is equal to 0, or 0 if a is equal to 1. The truth table for the **not** operator is simple:

a	**not** a
0	1
1	0

---

[3]In formal Boolean algebra, a **and** b is usually represented $a \wedge b$, a **or** b is represented $a \vee b$, and **not** a is represented $\neg a$.

Notice that this truth table only needs two rows because there are only two possible inputs.

With these basic operators, we can build more complicated expressions. For example, suppose we wanted to find the value of the expression **not** a **and** b. Note that here the **not** operator applies only to the variable a immediately after it, not the entire expression a **and** b. For **not** to apply to the expression, we would need parentheses: **not** $(a$ **and** $b)$. We can evaluate the Boolean expression **not** a **and** b by building a truth table for it. We start by listing all of the combinations of values for a and b, and then create a column for **not** a, since we need that value before we can evaluate the **and** in the expression.

a	b	**not** a
0	0	1
0	1	1
1	0	0
1	1	0

Then, we create a column for **not** a **and** b by **and**ing each value in the **not** a column with its corresponding value in the b column. These individual operations are shown off to the right for each row.

a	b	**not** a	**not** a **and** b	
0	0	1	0	(1 **and** 0 = 0)
0	1	1	1	(1 **and** 1 = 1)
1	0	0	0	(0 **and** 0 = 0)
1	1	0	0	(0 **and** 1 = 0)

So, referring to the first two columns of the second row, we find that **not** a **and** b is 1 only when a is 0 and b is 1. Or, equivalently, **not** a **and** b is *true* only when a is *false* and b is *true*. (Think about that for a moment; it makes sense, doesn't it?)

Python can also work with Boolean values. The Boolean value 0 is represented by False in Python and the Boolean value 1 is represented by True. (Note the capitalization.) For example, we can validate that the first row of our truth table is correct like this:

```
>>> a = False
>>> b = False
>>> not a and b
False
```

Then, by just changing b, we can validate the second row:

```
>>> b = True
>>> not a and b
True
```

Reflection 3.4 *Use Python to validate the third and fourth rows of the truth table as well.*

In Chapter 5, we will start using Boolean expressions in conditional statements and loops to control what happens in our programs.

Exercises

3.2.1* Show how to convert the binary number 1101 to decimal.

3.2.2. Show how to convert the binary number 1111101000 to decimal.

3.2.3* Show how to convert the binary number 11.0011 to decimal.

3.2.4. Show how to convert the binary number 11.110001 to decimal.

3.2.5* To convert a decimal number to binary, you can repeatedly divide the number by 2 and keep track of the remainders. The sequence of remainders in reverse order is the binary equivalent. For example, suppose we want to convert 13 to binary. First, divide 13 by 2 and get the quotient and remainder (in Python, 13 // 2 and 13 % 2), which are 6 and 1. Then do the same with 6, giving quotient 3 and remainder 0. Continue until the quotient is 0. The complete process is summarized in the table below.

	number	number // 2	number % 2
Step 1:	13	6	1
Step 2:	6	3	0
Step 3:	3	1	1
Step 4:	1	0	1

The equivalent binary number is the remainder column backwards: 1101. (Confirm that this is correct by converting this back to decimal.)

Use this process now to convert the decimal number 22 to binary.

3.2.6. Show how to convert the decimal number 222 to binary.

3.2.7* If we want to convert a decimal value less than one to binary, we need a different approach. To perform this conversion, we try to repeatedly subtract decreasing powers of 2, starting with 2^{-1}, from the decimal value. When we can subtract the power of 2, we put a 1 in that place; if we cannot subtract because the power of 2 is too large, we put a 0 in that place instead. For example, let's convert 0.3125 to binary. Since $2^{-1} = 1/2 = 0.5$ is larger than 0.3125, we place a 0 in this place:

2^{-1}	2^{-2}	2^{-3}	2^{-4}	
0.5	0.25	0.125	0.0625	...

.	0				

Next, we subtract $2^{-2} = 1/4 = 0.25$ from the remaining 0.3125, leaving 0.0625, and put a 1 in that place:

2^{-1}	2^{-2}	2^{-3}	2^{-4}	
0.5	0.25	0.125	0.0625	...

.	0	1			

The next place value, $2^{-3} = 1/8 = 0.125$ is larger than our remaining 0.0625, so we put a 0 in that place:

	2^{-1}	2^{-2}	2^{-3}	2^{-4}	
	0.5	0.25	0.125	0.0625	...

.	0	1	0		

The next place value, $2^{-4} = 1/16 = 0.0625$ fits perfectly so after subtracting, we get zero. We put a 1 in that place and we are done.

	2^{-1}	2^{-2}	2^{-3}	2^{-4}	
	0.5	0.25	0.125	0.0625	...

.	0	1	0	1	

Our work shows that 0.3125 is decimal is equivalent to 0.0101 in binary.

Use this process to convert the decimal number 3.625 to binary.

3.2.8.   Show how to convert the decimal number 25.53125 to binary.

3.2.9.   An image stored in a computer is composed of a two-dimensional grid of *pixels*. In a black and white image, each pixel is either black or white. Consider the 6×6 black and white image to the right. Describe two plausible ways to represent this image as a linear sequence of bits.

3.2.10*   Design a truth table for the Boolean expression **not** (a **and** b).

3.2.11.   Design a truth table for the Boolean expression **not** (a **or** b).

3.2.12*   Design a truth table for the Boolean expression **not** a **or not** b. Compare the result to the truth table for **not** (a **and** b). What do you notice? The relationship between these two Boolean expressions is one of *De Morgan's laws*.

3.2.13.   Design a truth table for the Boolean expression **not** a **and not** b. Compare the result to the truth table for **not** (a **or** b). What do you notice? The relationship between these two Boolean expressions is the other of *De Morgan's laws*.

3.3   COMPUTER ARITHMETIC

As we have already seen, computers store numbers in two different ways: as integers and as floats. Understanding this is important because some operators' behaviors depend upon the type they are given. There are also limitations to what is possible with computer arithmetic, meaning that it sometimes behaves differently than real arithmetic depending on which type of numbers you are using.

Limited precision

Binary representation and finite memory often mean that computer arithmetic gives us unexpected results. To illustrate, compute the following very large number:

```
>>> 2.0 ** 100
1.2676506002282294e+30
```

This result is a float because 2.0 is a float, and whenever a float is involved in a computation, the result is also a float. Very large floating point numbers like this are printed in scientific notation. The e stands for "exponent," and the number following represents a power of ten. So this number represents

$$1.2676506002282294 \times 10^{30} = 1267650600228229400000000000000.$$

(You can also use this notation in your programs, e.g., 18e6 in place of 18000000.)

Now try computing the same large number with an integer 2 in place of 2.0:

```
>>> 2 ** 100
1267650600228229401496703205376
```

▌ **Reflection 3.5** *Did* 2 ** 100 *and* 2.0 ** 100 *both give the correct answer?*

In normal arithmetic, 2.0^{100} and 2^{100} are, of course, the same number. However, in Python, the results of 2.0 ** 100 and 2 ** 100 are different. The second result is correct because Python integers have ***unlimited precision***, meaning that they can be arbitrarily long, limited only by the computer's memory. The first result is incorrect because the fixed number of bits used to represent floating point numbers leads to ***limited precision***. Although the range of numbers that can be represented in floating point notation is quite large, sometimes a value is too large or too small to even be approximated well. If we line these two numbers up and add commas, we can see that the first result is off by almost 1.5 trillion!

```
1,267,650,600,228,229,401,496,703,205,376
1,267,650,600,228,229,400,000,000,000,000
```

Some numbers cannot be represented at all. For example, try:

```
>>> 10.0 ** 500
OverflowError: (34, 'Result too large')
```

An ***overflow error*** means that the computer did not have enough space to represent the correct value. A similar fatal error will occur if we try to do something illegal, like divide by zero:

```
>>> 10.0 / 0
ZeroDivisionError: division by zero
```

You will also see the effects of limited precision when you perform more common computations. For example, try this:

```
>>> averageWords = 15
>>> averageSyllables = 1.78
>>> readingLevel = 0.39 * averageWords + 11.8 * averageSyllables - 15.59
>>> readingLevel
11.264000000000003
```

The correct answer here is 11.264, but Python didn't make an arithmetic mistake. To execute these statements, our decimal numbers are converted to binary floating point notation, the computations are performed in this format, and then the result is converted back to decimal. At each of these steps, errors may be introduced due to

> **Tangent 3.4: Floating point notation**
>
> Python floating point numbers are usually stored in 64 bits of memory, in a format known as IEEE 754 double-precision floating point. One bit is allocated to the sign of the number, 11 bits are allocated to the exponent, and 52 bits are allocated to the *mantissa*, the fractional part to the right of the point. After a number is converted to binary, the binary point and exponent are adjusted so that there is a single 1 to the left of the binary point. Then the exponent is stored in its 11 bit slot and as much of the mantissa that can fit is stored in the 52 bit slot. If the mantissa is longer than 52 bits, it is simply truncated and information is lost. This is exactly what happens when we compute 2.0 ** 100 on page 118. Since space is limited in computers' memory, tradeoffs between accuracy and space are common, and it is important to understand these limitations to avoid errors. In Chapter 4, we will see a more common situation in which this becomes quite important.

the limited precision of the floating point representation. So when we get the result, it contains a very small error. These kinds of errors are just part of the reality of computer arithmetic. In most of what we do, they won't matter. But in many real scientific computations where very small numbers are the norm, these kinds of errors can have dramatic effects that must be mitigated as a normal part of the process. If you are interested, you can learn more about floating point notation in Tangent 3.4.

Error propagation

Slight errors can become magnified in an iterative computation. To illustrate the problem, suppose we are simulating a process that is occurring continuously over time.[4] Since we cannot actually simulate a continuous process on a computer, we instead repeatedly simulate very small slices of the simulation in a loop. We will use a variable dt to represent the length of each slice of time in our simulation. The following loop shows how time would be advanced in this scenario.

```
>>> dt = 0.0001
>>> endTime = 1000000
>>> time = 0
>>> for step in range(1, endTime + 1):
>>>     time = time + dt
>>>     # one slice of the actual simulation would be here
```

| **Reflection 3.6** *What should the value of* time *be at the end of this loop?*

The loop accumulates the value 0.0001 one million times, so time should be $0.0001 \cdot 1{,}000{,}000 = 100$. However, it is actually a small fraction over.

```
>>> time
100.00000000219612
```

Since dt was very small, there was a slight error every time dt was added to time.

---

[4]We will actually develop such simulations in Section 4.4.

These errors *propagated* through the loop, making the value of `time` increasingly inaccurate. In some applications, even errors this small may be significant. And it can get even worse with more iterations. Scientific computations can often run for days or weeks, and the number of iterations involved can blow up errors significantly.

Reflection 3.7 *Run the code again but with 10 million iterations. What do you notice about the error?*

To avoid this kind of error propagation, we could have assigned `time` to be the product of `dt` and the current step number:

```
>>> for step in range(1, endTime + 1):
>>>     time = step * dt
```

In this way, the value of `time` is computed from only one arithmetic operation instead of many, reducing the potential error.

Division

When we computed `2 ** 100`, the result was an integer because both operands were integers. This is true everywhere but with division. Even when the result should be an integer, normal division, also called "true division," will give you a float.

```
>>> 100 / 2
50.0
```

Python provides another kind of division, called "floor division," that always gives an integer result. The floor division operator, represented by two slashes (`//`), rounds the quotient down to the nearest integer. (Rounding down to the nearest integer is called "taking the floor" of a number in mathematics, hence the name of the operator.)

```
>>> 14 / 3
4.6666666666666667
>>> 14 // 3
4
```

When both integers are positive, you can think of floor division as the "long division" you learned in elementary school, as it gives the whole quotient without the remainder. In this example, dividing 14 by 3 gives a quotient of 4 and a remainder of 2 because 14 is equal to $4 \cdot 3 + 2$. The operator to get the remainder is called the "modulo" operator. In mathematics, this operator is denoted mod, e.g., 14 mod 3 = 2; in Python it is denoted %.

```
>>> 14 % 3
2
```

To see why the `//` and `%` operators might be useful, think about how you would determine whether an integer is odd or even. An integer is even if it is evenly divisible by 2; i.e., when you divide it by 2, the remainder is 0. So, to decide whether an integer is even, we can "mod" the number by 2 and check the answer.

```
>>> 14 % 2
0
>>> 15 % 2
1
```

Modular arithmetic is also useful when we need a sequence of numbers to "wrap around," like minutes ticking on a clock. To simulate a clock, instead of just incrementing the minutes with `minutes = minutes + 1`, we want to increment and then "mod" by 60:

```
>>> minutes = 0
>>> minutes = (minutes + 1) % 60
>>> minutes
1
>>> minutes = (minutes + 1) % 60
>>> minutes
2
    ⋮
>>> minutes = (minutes + 1) % 60
>>> minutes
59
>>> minutes = (minutes + 1) % 60
>>> minutes
0
>>> minutes = (minutes + 1) % 60
>>> minutes
1
```

When `minutes` is between 0 and 58, `(minutes + 1) % 60` gives the same result as `minutes + 1` because `minutes + 1` is less than 60. But when `minutes` is 59, `(minutes + 1) % 60` equals `60 % 60`, which is 0.

Complex numbers

Although we will not use them in this book, it is worth pointing out that Python can also handle complex numbers. A complex number has both a real part and an imaginary part involving the imaginary unit i, which has the property that $i^2 = -1$. In Python, a complex number like $3.2 + 2i$ is represented as `3.2 + 2j`. (The letter j is used instead of i because in some fields, such as electrical engineering, i has another well-established meaning that could lead to ambiguities.) Most of the normal arithmetic operators work on complex numbers as well. For example,

```
>>> (5 + 4j) + (-4 + -3.1j)
(1+0.8999999999999999j)
>>> (23 + 6j) / (1 + 2j)
(7-8j)
>>> (1 + 2j) ** 2
(-3+4j)
>>> 1j ** 2
(-1+0j)
```

The last example illustrates the definition of i: $i^2 = -1$.

Exercises

3.3.1* The earth is estimated to be 4.54 billion years old. The oldest known fossils of anatomically modern humans are about 200,000 years old. What fraction of the earth's existence have humans been around? Use Python's scientific notation to compute this.

3.3.2. In 2012, the birth rate in the United States was 13.42 per 1,000 people and the total population was estimated to be 313.9 million. How many babies were born in 2012? Use Python's scientific notation to compute this.

3.3.3. The earth is about 4.54 billion years old. How many days are in the age of the earth, taking into account a leap year every four years? Use Python's scientific notation to compute this.

3.3.4* If you counted at an average pace of one number per second, how many years would it take you to count to 4.54 billion? Use Python's scientific notation to compute this.

3.3.5. Suppose the internal clock in a modern computer can "count" about 2.8 billion ticks per second. How long would it take such a computer to tick 4.54 billion times?

3.3.6. The floor division and modulo operators also work with negative numbers. Try some examples, and try to infer what is happening. What are the rules governing the results?

3.3.7. What is the value of each of the following Python expressions? Make sure you understand why in each case.

    (a) 15 * 3 - 2

    (b) 15 - 3 * 2

    (c) 15 * 3 // 2

    (d) 15 * 3 / 2

    (e) 15 * 3 % 2

    (f) 15 * 3 / 2e0

3.3.8* Every cell in the human body contains about 6 billion base pairs of DNA (3 billion in each set of 23 chromosomes). The distance between each base pair is about 3.4 angstroms (3.4×10^{-10} meters). Uncoiled and stretched, how long is the DNA in a single human cell? There are about 50 trillion cells in the human body. If you stretched out all of the DNA in the human body end to end, how long would it be? How many round trips to the sun is this? The distance to the sun is about 149,598,000 kilometers. Write Python statements to compute the answer to each of these three questions. Assign variables to hold each of the values so that you can reuse them to answer subsequent questions.

3.3.9* Suppose the variable **number** refers to an integer. Design a single arithmetic expression that assigns **number** to be **number - 1** if **number** is odd, or leaves **number** the same if it is even.

3.3.10. Given a variable `number` that refers to an integer value, show how to extract the individual digits in the ones, tens and hundreds places, and assign those values to three variables named `ones`, `tens`, and `hundreds`. For example, if `number = 123`, `ones`, `tens`, and `hundreds` should be assigned to 1, 2, and 3, respectively. (Use the `//` and `%` operators.)

3.3.11. Compute the very small values `2.0 ** -1074` and `2.0 ** -1075`. Explain the results.

3.3.12. Compute the very large values `2.0 ** 1023` and `2.0 ** 1024`. Explain the results.

3.3.13. Contrast and explain the results of computing `2.0 ** 1024` and `2 ** 1024`.

3.3.14* See how closely you can represent the decimal number 0.1 in binary using six places to the right of the binary point. What is the actual value of your approximation?

3.3.15. Approximate the decimal value 1/3 in binary using six places to the right of the binary point. What is the actual value of your approximation?

3.3.16. Try executing the following statements:
```
number = 1.0
for count in range(10):
    number = number - 0.1
```
What is the final value of `number`? What should it be and why is it incorrect?

*3.4 BINARY ARITHMETIC

This section is available on the book website.

3.5 THE UNIVERSAL MACHINE

The advantages of computing in binary would be useless if we could not actually use binary to compute everything we want to compute. In other words, we need binary computation to be *universal*. But is such a thing really possible? And what do we mean by *any computable problem*? Can we really perform any computation—a web browser, a chess-playing program, Mars rover software—just by converting it to binary and using the **and**, **or**, and **not** operators to get the answer?

Perhaps surprisingly, the answer is **yes**, when we combine the Boolean operators with a sufficiently large memory and a simple controller called a ***finite state machine*** (FSM) to route the correct bits through the correct operators at the correct times. A finite state machine consists of a finite set of *states*, along with *transitions* between states. A state represents the current value of some object or the degree of progress made toward some goal. For example, a simple three-level elevator can be represented by the finite state machine below.

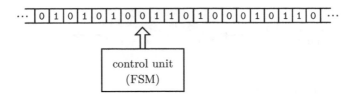

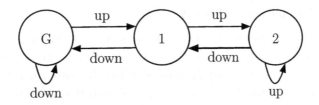

Figure 3.3 A schematic representation of a Turing machine.

The states, representing floors, are circles and the transitions, representing movement between floors, are arrows between circles. In this elevator, there are only up and down buttons (no ability to choose your destination floor when you enter). The label on each transition represents the button press event that causes that transition to occur. For example, when we are on the ground floor and the down button is pressed, we stay on the ground floor. But when the up button is pressed, we transition to the first floor. Many other simple systems, such as vending machines, subway doors, traffic lights and toll booths, can also be represented by finite state machines. A computer's finite state machine coordinates the fetch and execute cycle, as well as various intermediate steps involved in executing machine language instructions.

The question of whether a computational system is universal has its roots in the very origins of computer science itself. In 1936, Alan Turing proposed an abstract computational model, now called a **Turing machine**, that he proved could compute any problem considered to be mathematically computable. As illustrated in Figure 3.3, a Turing machine consists of a control unit containing a finite state machine that can read from and write to an infinitely long tape. The tape contains a sequence of "cells," each of which can contain a single character. The tape is initially inscribed with some sequence of input characters, and a pointer attached to the control unit is positioned at the beginning of the input. In each step, the Turing machine reads the character in the current cell. Then, based on what it reads and the current state, the finite state machine decides whether to write a character in the cell and whether to move its pointer one cell to the left or right. Not unlike the fetch and execute cycle in a modern computer, the Turing machine repeats this simple process as long as needed, until a designated final state is reached. The output is the final sequence of characters on the tape.

The Turing machine still stands as our modern definition of computability. The **Church-Turing thesis** states that a problem is computable if and only if it can be computed by a Turing machine. Any mechanism that can be shown to be equivalent

Figure 3.4 The halting problem.

in computational power to a Turing machine is considered to be computationally universal, or **Turing complete**. A modern computer, based on Boolean logic and a finite state machine, falls into this category.

Almost every problem that we would want to compute is, thankfully, computable, even if it takes an extraordinarily long time to compute. There are, however, problems that are not computable. The most famous is called the **halting problem**, illustrated in Figure 3.4. An algorithm for the halting problem, if it were to exist, would need to take another algorithm and an input for that algorithm as inputs and then decide whether that algorithm ever halts with the correct answer. But it can be proven that there are algorithms for which the halting problem cannot give an answer. Since an algorithm must be correct for every possible input, this means that there cannot exist a correct algorithm for the halting problem. This is not just an academic problem. In practice, this means that it is impossible to ever create program that can verify whether other programs are correct! So errors in programs are here to stay, unfortunately.

Exercises

3.5.1* Design a finite state machine that represents a highway toll booth controlling a single gate. First, think about what the states should be. Then design the transitions between states.

3.5.2. Design a finite state machine that represents a vending machine. Assume that the machine only takes quarters and vends only one kind of drink, for 75 cents. First, think about what the states should be. Then design the transitions between states.

3.6 SUMMARY AND FURTHER DISCOVERY

In this chapter, we took a peek under the hood to glimpse what a computer is really doing when it executes our programs. We saw that a computer system is itself a complex layering of abstractions. We are isolated from a lot of these details, thankfully, by the interpreter, which transparently translates our programs into machine language. A machine language program may yet need to request that the operating system do things on its behalf (e.g., saving a file or allocating more memory). Below that, each instruction in the resulting computation will be implemented using Boolean logic, controlled by a finite state machine. Knowing this should make you quite thankful that all of these layers of abstraction exist, and that we are able to

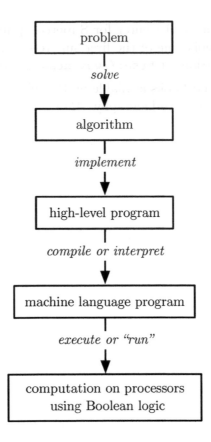

Figure 3.5 Top-to-bottom view of how an algorithm becomes a computation.

solve problems at a much higher layer! This top-to-bottom view of the process of turning an algorithm into a computation is summarized in Figure 3.5.

Notes for further discovery

There are several excellent books available that give overviews of computer science and how computers work. In particular, we recommend *The Pattern on the Stone* by Danny Hillis [23], *Algorithmics* by David Harel [22], *Digitized* by Peter Bentley [7], and *CODE: The Hidden Language of Computer Hardware and Software* by Charles Petzold [49].

A list of the world's fastest supercomputers is maintained at `http://top500.org`. You can learn more about IBM's Deep Blue supercomputer at

`http://www-03.ibm.com/ibm/history/ibm100/us/en/icons/deepblue/`

and IBM's Watson at

`https://www.ibm.com/ibm/history/ibm100/us/en/icons/watson/`.

To learn more about high performance computing in general, we recommend looking at the website of the National Center for Supercomputing Applications (NCSA) at the University of Illinois, one of the first supercomputer centers funded by the National Science Foundation, at `http://www.ncsa.illinois.edu/about/faq`.

There are also several good books available on the life of Alan Turing, the father of computer science. The definitive biography, *Alan Turing: The Enigma*, was written by Andrew Hodges [25].

CHAPTER 4

Growth and Decay

Our population and our use of the finite resources of planet Earth are growing exponentially, along with our technical ability to change the environment for good or ill.

Stephen Hawking
TED talk (2008)

L IKE the late Stephen Hawking, many natural and social scientists are concerned with the dynamic sizes of populations and other quantities over time. In addition to our growing use of natural resources, we may be interested in the size of a plant population being affected by an invasive species, the magnitude of an infection threatening a human population, the quantity of a radioactive material in a storage facility, the penetration of a product in the global marketplace, or the evolving characteristics of a dynamic social network. The possibilities are endless.

To study situations like these, scientists develop a simplified *model* that abstracts key characteristics of the actual situation so that it might be more easily understood and explored. In this sense, a model is another example of abstraction. Once we have a model that describes the problem, we can write a *simulation* that shows what happens when the model is applied over time. A simulation can provide a framework for past observations or predict future behavior. Scientists often use modeling and simulation in parallel with traditional experiments to compare their observations to a proposed theoretical framework.

These parallel scientific processes are illustrated in Figure 4.1. On the left is the computational process. In this case, we use "model" instead of "algorithm" to acknowledge the possibility that the model is mathematical rather than algorithmic. On the right side is the parallel experimental process, guided by the scientific method. The results of the computational and experimental processes can be compared, possibly leading to model adjustments or new experiments to improve the results.

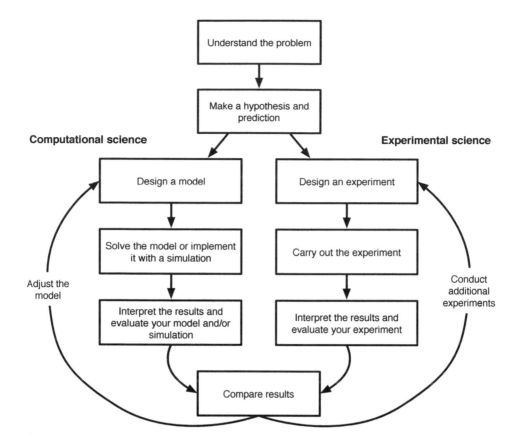

Figure 4.1 Parallel experimental and computational processes.

When we model the dynamic behavior of populations, we will assume that time ticks in discrete steps and, at any particular time step, the current population size is based on the population size at the previous time step. Depending on the problem, a time step may be anywhere from a nanosecond to a century. In general, a new time step may bring population increases, in the form of births and immigration, and population decreases, in the form of deaths and emigration. In this chapter, we will discuss a fundamental algorithmic technique, called an accumulator, that we will use to model dynamic processes like these. Accumulators crop up in all kinds of problems, and lie at the foundation of a variety of different algorithmic techniques. We will continue to see examples throughout the book.

4.1 ACCUMULATORS

Managing a fishing pond

Suppose we manage a fishing pond that contained a population of 12,000 largemouth bass on January 1 of this year. With no fishing, the bass population is expected to grow at a rate of 8% per year, which incorporates both the birth rate and the death rate of the population. The maximum annual fishing harvest allowed is 1,500 bass. Since this is a popular fishing spot, this harvest is attained every year. Is our maximum annual harvest sustainable? If not, how long until the fish population dies out? Should we reduce the maximum harvest? If so, what should it be reduced to?

We can find the projected population size for any given year by starting with the initial population size, and then repeatedly computing the population size in each successive year based on the size in the previous year. In pseudocode, if we remember the current population in a variable named *population*, then we can update the population each year with

$$\text{population} \leftarrow \text{population} + 0.08 \times \text{population} - 1500$$

Or, equivalently,

$$\text{population} \leftarrow 1.08 \times \text{population} - 1500$$

This is very similar to what we did back on page 14 in our final SPHERE VOLUME algorithm. Remember that an assignment statement evaluates the righthand side first. So the value of *population* on the righthand side of the assignment operator is the value *population* had before this assignment statement was executed. This value is used to compute the new population assigned to the variable on the lefthand side.

If we wanted to know the projected size of the fish population three years from now, we could incorporate this into the following algorithm.

Algorithm POND POPULATION

Input: the *initial population*
1 | *population* ← *initial population*
2 | repeat three times:
3 | *population* ← 1.08 × *population* − 1500
Output: the final *population*

Suppose *initial population* is 12000. Then this algorithm performs the following steps:

Trace input: *initial population* = 12000

Step	Line	*population*	Notes
1	1	12000	*population* ← *initial population*
2	2	″	no change; repeat line 3 three times
3	3	11460.0	*population* ← 1.08 × *population* − 1500 12000
4	3	10876.8	*population* ← 1.08 × *population* − 1500 11460.0
5	3	10246.944	*population* ← 1.08 × *population* − 1500 10876.8

Output: *population* = 10246.944

In the first iteration of the loop (step 3 in the trace table), *population* is assigned the previous value of *population* (12,000) times 1.08 minus 1500, which is 11,460. Then, in the second iteration, *population* is updated again after computing the previous value of *population* (now 11,460) times 1.08 minus 1500, which is 10,876.8. In the third iteration, *population* is assigned its final value of 10,246.944. The variable *population* is called an **accumulator variable** (or just an *accumulator*) because it accumulates additional value in each iteration of the loop.

So this model projects that the bass population in three years will be 10,246 (ignoring the "fractional fish" represented by the digits to the right of the decimal point).

In Python, we can implement this iterative algorithm with a `for` loop. We used the following `for` loop in Section 2.2 to draw our geometric flower with eight petals:

```
for count in range(8):
    tortoise.forward(200)
    tortoise.left(135)
```

In this case, we need a `for` loop that will iterate three times:

```
population = 12000
for year in range(3):
    population = 1.08 * population - 1500
```

Reflection 4.1 *Type in the `for` loop above and add the following statement after the assignment to* population *in the body of the `for` loop:*

```
print(year + 1, int(population))
```

Run the program. What is printed? Do you see why?

We see in this example that we can use the index variable `year` just like any other variable.

Reflection 4.2 *How would you change this loop to compute the fish population in five years? Ten years?*

Changing the number of years to compute is simple. All we have to do is change the value in the `range` to whatever we want: `range(5)`, `range(10)`, etc. If we put this computation in a function, then we can have the desired number of years passed in as a parameter. The parameter and its use are highlighted in red below.

```
1 def pond(years):
2     """Simulates a fish population in a fishing pond, and
3         prints annual population size.  The population
4         grows 8% per year with an annual harvest of 1500.
5
6     Parameter:
6         years: number of years to simulate
7
7     Return value: the final population size
8     """
```

```
 9      population = 12000
10      for year in range(years):
11          population = 1.08 * population - 1500
12          print(year + 1, int(population))

13      return population

14 def main():
15      finalPopulation = pond(10)
16      print('The final population is ' + str(finalPopulation) + '.')

17 main()
```

A trace table to show what happens when we call `pond(10)` is very similar to the one from our pseudocode algorithm, except that we now also want to trace the value of `year`, which is assigned a new value from 0 to 9 in each iteration.

Trace arguments: years = 10				
Step	Line	population	year	Notes
1	9	12000	—	population ← 12000
2	10	"	0	year ← 0
3	11	11460.0	"	population ← 1.08 * 12000 - 1500
4	12	"	"	no changes; prints 1 11460
5	10	"	1	year ← 1
6	11	10876.8	"	population ← 1.08 * 11460.0 - 1500
7	12	"	"	no changes; prints 2 10876
8	10	"	2	year ← 2
9	11	10246.944	"	population ← 1.08 * 10876.8 - 1500
10	12	"	"	no changes; prints 3 10246
⋮				
29	10	5256.718	9	year ← 9
30	11	4177.256	"	population ← 1.08 * 5256.718 - 1500
31	12	"	"	no changes; prints 10 4177
Return value: 4177.256				

Reflection 4.3 *What would happen if* `population = 12000` *was inside the body of the loop instead of before it? What would happen if we omitted the* `population = 12000` *statement altogether?*

The initialization of the accumulator variable before the loop is crucial. If `population` were not initialized before the loop, then an error would occur in the first iteration of the `for` loop because the righthand side of the assignment statement would not make any sense!

> **Reflection 4.4** *Use the* pond *function to answer the original questions: Is this maximum harvest sustainable? If not, how long until the fish population dies out? Should the pond manager reduce the maximum harvest? If so, what should it be reduced to?*

Calling this function with a large enough number of years shows that the fish population drops below zero (which, of course, can't really happen) in year 14:

```
1 11460
2 10876
3 10246
⋮
13 392
14 -1076
⋮
```

This harvesting plan is clearly not sustainable, so the pond manager should reduce it to a sustainable level. In this case, determining the sustainable level is easy: since the population grows at 8% per year and the pond initially contains 12,000 fish, we cannot allow more than $0.08 \cdot 12000 = 960$ fish to be harvested per year without the population declining.

> **Reflection 4.5** *Generalize the* pond *function with two additional parameters: the initial population size and the annual harvest. Using your modified function, compute the number of fish that will be in the pond in 15 years if we change the annual harvest to 800.*

With these modifications, your function might look like this:

```python
def pond(years, initialPopulation, harvest):
    """ (docstring omitted) """

    population = initialPopulation
    for year in range(years):
        population = 1.08 * population - harvest
        print(year + 1, int(population))

    return population
```

The value of the `initialPopulation` parameter takes the place of our previous initial population of `12000` and the parameter named `harvest` takes the place of our previous harvest of `1500`. To answer the question above, we can replace the call to the pond function from **main** with:

```python
finalPopulation = pond(15, 12000, 800)
```

The result that is printed is:

```
1 12160
2 12332
⋮
13 15439
14 15874
15 16344
The final population is 16344.338228396558.
```

Reflection 4.6 *How would you call the new version of the* pond *function to replicate its original behavior, with an annual harvest of 1500?*

Pretty printing

Before moving on, let's look at a helpful Python trick, called a ***format string***, that enables us to format our table of annual populations in a more attractive way. To illustrate the use of a format string, consider the following modified version of the previous function.

```python
def pond(years, initialPopulation, harvest):
    """ (docstring omitted) """

    population = initialPopulation
    print('Year | Population')
    print('-----|-----------')
    for year in range(years):
        population = 1.08 * population - harvest
        print('{0:^4} | {1:>9.2f}'.format(year + 1, population))

    return population
```

The first two highlighted lines print a table header to label the columns. Then, in the call to the `print` function inside the `for` loop, we utilize a format string to line up the two values in each row. The syntax of a format string is

```
'<replacement fields>'.format(<values to format>)
```

(The parts in red above are descriptive and not part of the syntax.) The period between the string and `format` indicates that `format` is a method of the string class; we will talk more about the string class in Chapter 6. The parameters of the `format` method are the values to be formatted. The format for each value is specified in a *replacement field* enclosed in curly braces (`{}`) in the format string.

In the example in the `for` loop above, the `{0:^4}` replacement field specifies that the first (really the "zero-th"; computer scientists like to start counting at 0) argument to `format`, in this case `year + 1`, should be centered (`^`) in a field of width 4. The `{1:>9.2f}` replacement field specifies that `population`, as the second argument to `format`, should be right justified (`>`) in a field of width 9 as a floating point number with two places to the right of the decimal point (`.2f`). When formatting floating point numbers (specified by the `f`), the number before the decimal point in the replacement field is the minimum width, including the decimal point. The number after the decimal point in the replacement field is the number of digits to the right of the decimal point in the number. (If we wanted to align to the left, we would use `<`.) Characters in the string that are not in replacement fields (in this case, two spaces with a vertical bar between them) are printed as-is. So, if `year` were assigned the value `11` and `population` were assigned the value `1752.35171`, the above statement would print

$$\underbrace{\llcorner 12 \llcorner \llcorner}_{\{0:^4\}} | \underbrace{\llcorner \llcorner \llcorner 1752.35}_{\{1:>9.2f\}}$$

To fill spaces with something other than a space, we can use a *fill character* immediately after the colon. For example, if we replaced the second replacement field with {1:*>9.2f}, the previous statement would print the following instead:

$$\underbrace{\llcorner 12 \llcorner \llcorner}_{\{0:^4\}} | \underbrace{\llcorner * *1752.35}_{\{1:*>9.2f\}}$$

Measuring network value

Now let's consider a different problem. Suppose we have created a new online social network (or a new group within an existing social network) that we expect to steadily grow over time. Intuitively, as new members are added, the value of the network to its members grows because new relationships and opportunities become available. The potential value of the network to advertisers also grows as new members are added. But how can we quantify this value?

We will assume that, in our social network, two members can become connected or "linked" by mutual agreement, and that connected members gain access to each other's network profile. The inherent value of the network lies in these connections, or *links*, rather than in the size of its membership. Therefore, we need to figure out how the potential number of links grows as the number of members grows. The picture below visualizes this growth. The circles, called *nodes*, represent members of the social network and lines between nodes represent links between members.

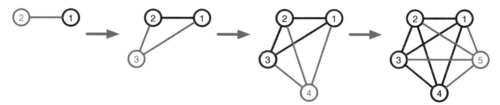

At each step, the red node is added to the network. The red links represent the potential new connections that could result from the addition of the new member.

> **Reflection 4.7** *What is the maximum number of new connections that could arise when each of nodes 2, 3, 4, and 5 are added? In general, what is the maximum number of new connections that could arise from adding node number n?*

Node 2 adds a maximum of 1 new connection, node 3 adds a maximum of 2 new connections, node 4 adds a maximum of 3 new connections, etc. In general, a maximum of $n - 1$ new connections arise from the addition of node number n. This pattern is illustrated in the table below.

node number	2	3	4	5	⋯	n
maximum increase in number of links	1	2	3	4	⋯	$n - 1$

Therefore, as shown in the last row, the maximum number of links in a network with n nodes is the sum of the numbers in the second row:

$$1 + 2 + 3 + \ldots + n - 1.$$

We will use this sum to represent the potential value of the network.

Let's write a function, similar to the previous one, that lists the maximum number of new links, and the maximum total number of links, as new nodes are added to a network. In this case, we will need an accumulator to count the total number of links. Adapting our pond function to this new purpose gives us the following:

```python
def countLinks(totalNodes):
    """Prints a table with the maximum total number of links
       in networks with 2 through totalNodes nodes.

    Parameter:
        totalNodes: the total number of nodes in the network

    Return value:
        the maximum number of links in a network with totalNodes nodes
    """

    totalLinks = 0
    for node in range(totalNodes):
        newLinks = ???
        totalLinks = totalLinks + newLinks
        print(node, newLinks, totalLinks)

    return totalLinks
```

In this function, we want our accumulator variable to count the total number of links, so we named it totalLinks instead of population, and initialized it to zero. Likewise, we named the parameter, which specifies the number of iterations, totalNodes instead of years, and we named the index variable of the for loop node instead of year because it will now be counting the number of the node that we are adding at each step. In the body of the for loop, we add to the accumulator the maximum number of new links added to the network with the current node (we will return to this in a moment) and then print a row containing the node number, the maximum number of new links, and the maximum total number of links in the network at that point. (We leave formatting this row with a format string as an exercise.)

Before we determine what the value of newLinks should be, we have to resolve one issue. In the table above, the node numbers range from 2 to the number of nodes in the network, but in our for loop, node will range from 0 to totalNodes - 1. This turns out to be easily fixed because the range function can generate a wider variety of number ranges than we have seen thus far. If we give range two arguments instead of one, like range(start, stop), the first argument is interpreted as a starting value and the second argument is interpreted as the stopping value, producing a range of values starting at **start** and going up to, *but not including*, **stop**. For example, range(-5, 10) produces the integers $-5, -4, -3, \ldots, 8, 9$.

To see this for yourself, type list(range(-5, 10)) into the Python shell (or print it in a program).

```
>>> list(range(-5, 10))
[-5, -4, -3, -2, -1, 0, 1, 2, 3, 4, 5, 6, 7, 8, 9]
```

The list function converts a range of numbers into a list that shows all of the numbers in the range.

> **Reflection 4.8** *What list of numbers does* range(1, 10) *produce? What about* range(10, 1)*? Can you explain why in each case?*

> **Reflection 4.9** *Back to our program, what do we want our* for *loop to look like?*

For **node** to start at 2 and finish at **totalNodes**, we want our for loop to be

```
for node in range(2, totalNodes + 1):
```

Now what should the value of **newLinks** be in our program? The answer is in the table we constructed above; the maximum number of new links added to the network with node number n is $n-1$. In our loop, the node number is assigned to the name **node**, so we need to add **node - 1** links in each step:

```
newLinks = node - 1
```

With these substitutions, our function looks like this:

```
1 def countLinks(totalNodes):
2     """ (docstring omitted) """

3     totalLinks = 0
4     for node in range(2, totalNodes + 1):
5         newLinks = node - 1
6         totalLinks = totalLinks + newLinks
7         print(node, newLinks, totalLinks)

8     return totalLinks

9 def main():
10    links = countLinks(10)
11    print('The total number of links is ' + str(links) + '.')

12 main()
```

As with our previous for loop, you can see more clearly what this loop does by carefully studying the following trace table.

Trace arguments: `totalNodes = 10`

Step	Line	totalLinks	node	newLinks	Notes
1	3	0	—	—	totalLinks ← 0
2	4	"	2	—	node ← 2
3	5	"	"	1	newLinks ← 2 - 1
4	6	1	"	"	totalLinks ← 0 + 1
5	7	"	"	"	no changes; prints 2 1 1
6	4	"	3	"	node ← 3
7	5	"	"	2	newLinks ← 3 - 1
8	6	3	"	"	totalLinks ← 1 + 2
9	7	"	"	"	no changes; prints 3 2 3
10	4	"	4	"	node ← 4
11	5	"	"	3	newLinks ← 4 - 1
12	6	6	"	"	totalLinks ← 3 + 3
13	7	"	"	"	no changes; prints 4 3 6
⋮					
34	4	36	10	8	node ← 10
35	5	"	"	9	newLinks ← 10 - 1
36	6	45	"	"	totalLinks ← 36 + 9
37	7	"	"	"	no changes; prints 10 9 45

Return value: 45

When we call `countLinks(10)` from the `main` function above, it prints

```
2 1 1
3 2 3
4 3 6
5 4 10
6 5 15
7 6 21
8 7 28
9 8 36
10 9 45
The total number of links is 45
```

❙ **Reflection 4.10** *What does* `countLinks(100)` *return? What does this value represent?*

Organizing a concert

Let's look at one more example. Suppose you are putting on a concert and need to figure out how much to charge per ticket. Your total expenses, for the band and the venue, are \$8,000. The venue can seat at most 2,000 and you have determined through market research that the number of tickets you are likely to sell is related to a ticket's selling price by the following relationship:

```
sales = 2500 - 80 * price
```

According to this relationship, if you give the tickets away for free, you will overfill your venue. On the other hand, if you charge too much, you won't sell any tickets at all. You would like to price the tickets somewhere in between, so as to maximize your profit. Your total income from ticket sales will be `sales * price`, so your profit will be this amount minus $8000.

To determine the most profitable ticket price, we can create a table using a `for` loop similar to that in the previous two problems. In this case, we would like to iterate over a range of ticket prices and print the profit resulting from each choice. In the following function, the `for` loop starts with a ticket price of one dollar and adds one to the price in each iteration until it reaches `maxPrice` dollars.

```
1  def profitTable(maxPrice):
2      """Prints a table of profits from a show based on ticket price.

3      Parameters:
4          maxPrice: maximum price to consider

5      Return value: None
6      """

7      print('Price      Income       Profit')
8      print('------   ---------   ---------')
9      for price in range(1, maxPrice + 1):
10         sales = 2500 - 80 * price
11         income = sales * price
12         profit = income - 8000
13         formatString = '${0:>5.2f}   ${1:>8.2f}   ${2:8.2f}'
14         print(formatString.format(price, income, profit))

15 def main():
16     profitTable(25)

17 main()
```

The number of expected sales in each iteration is computed from the value of the index variable `price`, according to the relationship above. Then we print the price and the resulting income and profit, formatted nicely with a format string. As we did previously, we can look at what happens in each iteration of the loop with a trace table:

Trace arguments: maxPrice = 25

Step	Line	price	sales	income	profit	Notes
1	7	—	—	—	—	prints header
2	8	—	—	—	—	prints underlines
3	9	1	—	—	—	price ← 1
4	10	"	2420	—	—	sales ← 2500 - 80 * 1
5	11	"	"	2420	—	income ← 2420 * 1
6	12	"	"	"	-5580	profit ← 2420 - 8000
7	13–14	"	"	"	"	prints price, income, profit
8	9	2	"	"	"	price ← 2
9	10	"	2340	"	"	sales ← 2500 - 80 * 2
10	11	"	"	4680	"	income ← 2340 * 2
11	12	"	"	"	-3320	profit ← 4680 - 8000
12	13–14	"	"	"	"	prints price, income, profit
13	9	3	"	"	"	price ← 3
⋮						

Reflection 4.11 *Complete a few more iterations in the trace table to make sure you understand how the loop works.*

Reflection 4.12 *Run the program to determine what the most profitable ticket price is.*

The program prints the following table:

```
Price      Income       Profit
------     ----------   ----------
$ 1.00     $ 2420.00    $-5580.00
$ 2.00     $ 4680.00    $-3320.00
$ 3.00     $ 6780.00    $-1220.00
$ 4.00     $ 8720.00    $   720.00
  ⋮
$15.00     $19500.00    $11500.00
$16.00     $19520.00    $11520.00
$17.00     $19380.00    $11380.00
  ⋮
$24.00     $13920.00    $ 5920.00
$25.00     $12500.00    $ 4500.00
```

The profit in the third column increases until it reaches $11,520.00 at a ticket price of $16, then it drops off. So the most profitable ticket price seems to be $16.

Reflection 4.13 *Our program only considered whole dollar ticket prices. How can we modify it to increment the ticket price by fifty cents in each iteration instead?*

The **range** function can only create ranges of integers, so we cannot ask the **range** function to increment by 0.5 instead of 1. But we can achieve our goal by doubling the range of numbers that we iterate over, and then set the price in each iteration to be the value of the index variable divided by two.

```python
def profitTable(maxPrice):
    """ (docstring omitted) """

    print('Price     Income     Profit')
    print('------  ---------  ---------')
    for price in range(1, 2 * maxPrice + 1):
        realPrice = price / 2
        sales = 2500 - 80 * realPrice
        income = sales * realPrice
        profit = income - 8000
        formatString = '${0:>5.2f}  ${1:>8.2f}  ${2:8.2f}'
        print(formatString.format(realPrice, income, profit))
```

Now when `price` is 1, the "real price" that is used to compute profit is 0.5. When `price` is 2, the "real price" is 1.0, etc.

| **Reflection 4.14** *Does our new function find a more profitable ticket price than $16?*

Our new function prints the following table.

```
Price    Income      Profit
------  ---------  ---------
$ 0.50  $ 1230.00  $-6770.00
$ 1.00  $ 2420.00  $-5580.00
$ 1.50  $ 3570.00  $-4430.00
$ 2.00  $ 4680.00  $-3320.00
   ⋮
$15.50  $19530.00  $11530.00
$16.00  $19520.00  $11520.00
$16.50  $19470.00  $11470.00
   ⋮
$24.50  $13230.00  $ 5230.00
$25.00  $12500.00  $ 4500.00
```

If we look at the ticket prices around $16, we see that $15.50 will actually make $10 more.

Just from looking at the table, the relationship between the ticket price and the profit is not as clear as it would be if we plotted the data instead. For example, does profit rise in a straight line to the maximum and then fall in a straight line? Or is it a more gradual curve? We can answer these questions by drawing a plot with turtle graphics, using the `goto` method to move the turtle from one point to the next.

```python
import turtle

def profitPlot(tortoise, maxPrice):
    """ (docstring omitted) """
```

```
    for price in range(1, 2 * maxPrice + 1):
        realPrice = price / 2
        sales = 2500 - 80 * realPrice
        income = sales * realPrice
        profit = income - 8000
        tortoise.goto(realPrice, profit)

def main():
    george = turtle.Turtle()
    screen = george.getscreen()
    screen.setworldcoordinates(0, -15000, 25, 15000)
    profitPlot(george, 25)

main()
```

Our new main function sets up a turtle and then uses the setworldcoordinates method to change the coordinate system in the drawing window to fit the points that we are likely to plot. In the for loop in the profitPlot function, since the first value of realPrice is 0.5, the first goto is

```
    george.goto(0.5, -6770)
```

which draws a line from the origin $(0,0)$ to $(0.5, -6770)$. In the next iteration, the value of realPrice is 1.0, so the loop next executes

```
    george.goto(1.0, -5580)
```

which draws a line from the previous position of $(0.5, -6770)$ to $(1.0, -5580)$. The next value of realPrice is 1.5, so the loop then executes

```
    george.goto(1.5, -4430)
```

which draws a line from from $(1.0, -5580)$ to $(1.5, -4430)$. And so on, until realPrice takes on its final value of 25 and we draw a line from the previous position of $(24.5, 5230)$ to $(25, 4500)$.

| **Reflection 4.15** *What shape is the plot? Can you see why?*

| **Reflection 4.16** *When you run this plotting program, you will notice an ugly line from the origin to the first point of the plot. How can you fix this? (We will leave the answer as an exercise.)*

Exercises

Write a function for each of the following problems. Be sure to appropriately document your functions with docstrings and comments. Test each function with both common and boundary case arguments, as described on page 38, and document your test cases. Use a trace table on at least one test case.

4.1.1*   Generalize the pond function so that it also takes the annual growth rate as a parameter.

4.1.2.   Generalize the pond function further to allow for the pond to be annually restocked with an additional quantity of fish.

4.1.3. Modify the `countLinks` function so that it prints a table like the following:

```
|       |   Links       |
| Nodes | New | Total |
| ----- | --- | ----- |
|   2   | 1   |    1  |
|   3   | 2   |    3  |
|   4   | 3   |    6  |
|   5   | 4   |   10  |
|   6   | 5   |   15  |
|   7   | 6   |   21  |
|   8   | 7   |   28  |
|   9   | 8   |   36  |
|  10   | 9   |   45  |
```

4.1.4. Modify the `profitTable` function so that it considers all ticket prices that are multiples of a quarter.

4.1.5. In the `profitPlot` function in the text, fix the problem raised by Reflection 4.16.

4.1.6. There are actually three forms of the `range` function:

- 1 parameter: range(stop)
- 2 parameters: range(start, stop)
- 3 parameters: range(start, stop, skip)

With three arguments, `range` produces a range of integers starting at the start value and ending at or before `stop - 1`, adding `skip` each time. For example,

    range(5, 15, 2)

produces the range of numbers 5, 7, 9, 11, 13 and

    range(-5, -15, -2)

produces the range of numbers -5, -7, -9, -11, -13. To print these numbers, one per line, we can use a for loop:

    for number in range(-5, -15, -2):
        print(number)

(a) Write a for loop that prints the integers from 0 to 100.

(b) Write a for loop that prints the integers from -50 to 50.

(c) Write a for loop that prints the even integers from 2 to 100, using the third form of the range function.

(d) Write a for loop that prints the odd integers from 1 to 100, using the third form of the range function.

(e) Write a for loop that prints the integers from 100 to 1 in descending order.

(f) Write a for loop that prints the values 7, 11, 15, 19.

(g) Write a for loop that prints the values 2, 1, 0, −1, −2.

(h) Write a for loop that prints the values −7, −11, −15, −19.

4.1.7* Write a function

      `triangle()`

that uses a `for` loop to print the following:

```
*
**
***
****
*****
******
*******
********
*********
**********
```

4.1.8. Write a function

      `diamond()`

that uses `for` loops to print the following:

```
***** *****
****   ****
***     ***
**       **
*         *
*         *
**       **
***     ***
****   ****
***** *****
```

4.1.9. Write a function

      `square(letter, width)`

that prints a square with the given `width` using the string `letter`. For example, `square('Q', 5)` should print:

```
QQQQQ
QQQQQ
QQQQQ
QQQQQ
QQQQQ
```

4.1.10* Write a `for` loop that uses `range(50)` to print the odd integers from 1 to 100.

4.1.11* Write a function

      `multiples(n)`

that prints all of the multiples of the parameter `n` between 0 and 100, inclusive. For example, if `n` were 4, the function should print the values 0, 4, 8, 12, ...

4.1.12. Write a function

      `countdown(n)`

that prints the integers between 0 and `n` in descending order. For example, if `n` were 5, the function should print the values 5, 4, 3, 2, 1, 0.

4.1.13. On page 122, we talked about how to simulate the minutes ticking on a digital clock using modular arithmetic. Write a function

```
clock(ticks)
```

that prints `ticks` times starting from midnight, where the clock ticks once each minute. To simplify matters, the midnight hour can be denoted 0 instead of 12. For example, `clock(100)` should print

```
0:00
0:01
0:02
```
⋮
```
0:59
1:00
1:01
```
⋮
```
1:38
1:39
```

To line up the colons in the times and force the leading zero in the minutes, use a format string like this:

```
print('{0:>2}:{1:0>2}'.format(hours, minutes))
```

4.1.14. Write a function

```
circles(tortoise)
```

that uses turtle graphics and a `for` loop to draw concentric circles with radii $10, 20, 30, \ldots, 100$. (To draw each circle, you may use the turtle graphics `circle` method or the `drawCircle` function you wrote in Exercise 2.3.14.)

4.1.15* Write a function

```
plotSine(tortoise, n)
```

that uses turtle graphics to plot $\sin x$ from $x = 0$ to $x = n$ degrees. Use `setworldcoordinates` to make the x coordinates of the window range from 0 to n and the y coordinates range from -1 to 1.

4.1.16. Python also allows us to pass function names as parameters. So we can generalize the function in Exercise 4.1.15 to plot any function we want. Write a function

```
plot(tortoise, n, f)
```

where `f` is the name of an arbitrary function that takes a single numerical argument and returns a number. Inside the `for` loop in the `plot` function, we can apply the function `f` to the index variable x with

```
tortoise.goto(x, f(x))
```

To call the `plot` function, we need to define one or more functions to pass in as arguments. For example, to plot x^2, we can define

```
def square(x):
    return x * x
```

and then call `plot` with

```
plot(george, 20, square)
```

Or, to plot an elongated $\sin x$, we could define

```
def sin(x):
    return 10 * math.sin(x)
```

and then call `plot` with

```
plot(george, 20, sin)
```

After you create your new version of `plot`, also create at least one new function to pass into `plot` for the parameter `f`. Depending on the functions you pass in, you may need to adjust the window coordinate system with `setworldcoordinates`.

4.1.17* Write a function

```
growth1(totalDays)
```

that simulates a population growing by 3 individuals each day. For each day, print the day number and the total population size.

4.1.18. Write a function

```
growth2(totalDays)
```

that simulates a population that grows by 3 individuals each day but also shrinks by, on average, 1 individual every 2 days. For each day, print the day number and the total population size.

4.1.19. Write a function

```
growth3(totalDays)
```

that simulates a population that increases by 110% every day. Assume that the initial population size is 10. For each day, print the day number and the total population size.

4.1.20. Write a function

```
growth4(totalDays)
```

that simulates a population that grows by 2 on the first day, 4 on the second day, 8 on the third day, 16 on the fourth day, etc. Assume that the initial population size is 10. For each day, print the day number and the total population size.

4.1.21* Suppose a bacteria colony grows at a rate of 10% per hour and that there are initially 100 bacteria in the colony. Write a function

```
bacteria(days)
```

that returns the number of bacteria in the colony after the given number of days. How many bacteria are in the colony after one week?

4.1.22. Generalize the function that you wrote for the previous exercise so that it also accepts parameters for the initial population size and the growth rate. How many bacteria are in the same colony after one week if it grows at 15% per hour instead?

4.1.23* Write a function

```
sumNumbers(n)
```

that returns the sum of the integers between 1 and n, inclusive. For example, `sum(4)` returns $1 + 2 + 3 + 4 = 10$. (Use a `for` loop; if you know a shortcut, don't use it.)

4.1.24. Write a function

> `sumEven(n)`

that returns the sum of the even integers between 2 and `n`, inclusive. For example, `sumEven(6)` returns $2 + 4 + 6 = 12$. (Use a `for` loop.)

4.1.25. Write a function

> `average(low, high)`

that returns the average of the integers between `low` and `high`, inclusive. For example, `average(3, 6)` returns $(3 + 4 + 5 + 6)/4 = 4.5$.

4.1.26* Write a function

> `factorial(n)`

that returns the value of $n! = 1 \times 2 \times 3 \times \cdots \times (n-1) \times n$. (Be careful; how should the accumulator be initialized?)

4.1.27. Write a function

> `power(base, exponent)`

that returns the value of `base` raised to the `exponent` power, without using the `**` operator. Assume that `exponent` is a positive integer.

4.1.28. The geometric mean of n numbers is defined to be the nth root of the product of the numbers. (The nth root is the same as the $1/n$ power.) Write a function

> `geoMean(high)`

that returns the geometric mean of the numbers between 1 and `high`, inclusive.

4.1.29. Write a function

> `sumDigits(number, numDigits)`

that returns the sum of the individual digits in a parameter `number` that has `numDigits` digits. For example, `sumDigits(1234, 4)` should return the value $1 + 2 + 3 + 4 = 10$. (Hint: use a `for` loop and integer division (`//` and `%`).)

4.1.30. Between the ages of three and thirteen, girls grow an average of about six centimeters per year. Write a function

> `growth(finalAge)`

that prints a simple height chart based on this information, with one entry for each age, assuming the average girl is 95 centimeters (37 inches) tall at age three.

4.1.31. Consider the following fun game. Pick any positive integer less than 100 and add the squares of its digits. For example, if you choose 25, the sum of the squares of its digits is $2^2 + 5^2 = 29$. Now make the answer your new number, and repeat the process. For example, if we continue this process starting with 25, we get: 25, 29, 85, 89, 145, 42, etc.

Write a function

> `fun(number, iterations)`

that prints the sequence of numbers generated by this game, starting with the two digit `number`, and continuing for the given number of `iterations`. It will be helpful to know that no number will ever have more than three digits.

Execute your function with every integer between 15 and 25, with `iterations` at least 30. What do you notice? Can you classify each of these integers into one of two groups based on the results?

4.1.32. Create trace tables that show the execution of each of the following functions.

(a)* your `growth1` function from Exercise 4.1.17 when it is called as `growth1(4)`

(b) your `growth3` function from Exercise 4.1.19 when it is called as `growth3(4)`

(c) your `bacteria` function from Exercise 4.1.21 when it is called as `bacteria(5)`

4.1.33* You have $1,000 to invest and need to decide between two savings accounts. The first account pays interest at an annual rate of 1% and is compounded daily, meaning that interest is earned daily at a rate of $(1/365)$%. The second account pays interest at an annual rate of 1.25% but is compounded monthly. Write a function

```
interest(originalAmount, rate, periods)
```

that computes the interest earned in one year on `originalAmount` dollars in an account that pays the given annual interest rate, compounded over the given number of periods. Assume the interest rate is given as a percentage, not a fraction (i.e., 1.25 vs. 0.0125). Use the function to answer the original question.

4.1.34. Suppose you want to start saving a certain amount each month in an investment account that compounds interest monthly. To determine how much money you expect to have in the future, write a function

```
invest(investment, rate, years)
```

that returns the income earned by investing `investment` dollars every month in an investment account that pays the given rate of return, compounded monthly (`rate / 12 %` each month).

4.1.35. A mortgage loan is charged some rate of interest every month based on the current balance on the loan. If the annual interest rate of the mortgage is r%, then interest equal to $r/12$ % of the current balance is added to the amount owed each month. Also each month, the borrower is expected to make a payment, which reduces the amount owed.

Write a function

```
mortgage(principal, rate, years, payment)
```

that prints a table of mortgage payments and the remaining balance every month of the loan period. The last payment should include any remaining balance. For example, paying $1,000 per month on a $200,000 loan at 4.5% for 30 years should result in the following table:

Month	Payment	Balance
1	1000.00	199750.00
2	1000.00	199499.06
3	1000.00	199247.18
⋮		
359	1000.00	11111.79
360	11153.46	0.00

4.2 DATA VISUALIZATION

Visualizing changes in population size over time will provide more insight into how population models evolve. We could plot population changes with turtle graphics, as we did in Section 4.1, but instead, we will use a dedicated plotting module called `matplotlib`, so-named because it emulates the plotting capabilities of the technical programming language MATLAB[1].

To use `matplotlib`, we first import the module using

```
import matplotlib.pyplot as pyplot
```

`matplotlib.pyplot` is the name of module; "`as pyplot`" allows us to refer to the module in our program with the abbreviation `pyplot` instead of its rather long full name. The basic plotting functions take two arguments: a list of x values and an associated list of y values. As we saw before, a list in Python is represented as a comma-separated sequence of items enclosed in square brackets, such as

```
[4, 7, 2, 3.1, 12, 2.1]
```

We will use lists much more extensively in Chapter 7. For now, we only need to know how to build a list of population sizes in our `for` loop so that we can plot them. Let's look at how to do this in the fishing pond function from page 135, reproduced below.

```
def pond(years, initialPopulation, harvest):
    """ (docstring omitted) """

    population = initialPopulation
    print('Year | Population')
    print('-----|-----------')
    for year in range(years):
        population = 1.08 * population - harvest
        print('{0:^4} | {1:>9.2f}'.format(year + 1, population))

    return population
```

To build this list, we start by creating an empty list before the loop:

```
populationList = [ ]
```

To add an annual population size to the end of the list, we will use the `append` method of the list class. We will first append the initial population size to the end of the empty list with

```
populationList.append(initialPopulation)
```

If we pass in 12000 for the initial population parameter, this will result in `populationList` becoming the single-element list `[12000]`. Inside the loop, we want to append each value of `population` to the end of the growing list with

```
populationList.append(population)
```

---

[1]MATLAB is a registered trademark of The MathWorks, Inc.

Incorporating this code into our **pond** function, and deleting the calls to **print**, yields:

```
1 def pond(years, initialPopulation, harvest):
2     """Simulates a fish population and plots annual population size.
3         The population grows 8% per year with an annual harvest.

4     Parameters:
5         years:               number of years to simulate
6         initialPopulation: the initial population size
7         harvest:             the size of the annual harvest

8     Return value: the final population size
9     """

10    population = initialPopulation
11    populationList = [ ]
12    populationList.append(initialPopulation)
13    for year in range(1, years + 1):
14        population = 1.08 * population - harvest
15        populationList.append(population)
16    return population
```

We have also changed the **for** loop range to start at 1 to reflect that the first population size computed inside the loop reflects the size at year 1 (and the population before the loop represents "year 0"). The trace table below shows how **populationList** grows with each iteration, assuming an initial population of 12,000.

Trace arguments: years = 14, initialPopulation = 12000, harvest = 1500					
Step	Line	year	population	populationList	Notes
1	11	—	12000	—	init population
2	12	—	"	[ ]	init populationList
3	13	—	"	[12000]	append 12000
4	14	1	"	"	year ← 1
5	15	"	11460.0	"	update population
6	16	"	"	[12000, 11460.0]	append 11460.0
7	14	2	"	"	year ← 2
8	15	"	10876.8	"	update population
9	16	"	"	[12000, ..., 10876.8]	append 10876.8
⋮					
43	14	14	392.539	[12000, ..., 392.539]	year ← 14
44	15	"	-1076.056	"	update population
45	16	"	"	[12000, ..., -1076.056]	append -1076.056
Return value: -1076.056					

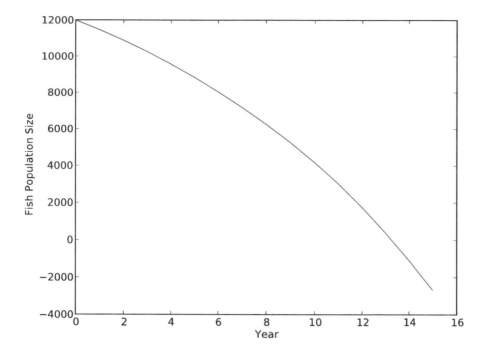

Figure 4.2 Plot of population size in our fishing pond model with `years = 15`.

In each iteration, the current value of `population` is appended to the end of `populationList`. So when the loop is finished, there are `years + 1` population sizes in the list.

> **Reflection 4.17** *Add a statement to print* `populationList` *at the end of each iteration of the loop so that you can see better how it grows.*

There is a strong similarity between the manner in which we are appending elements to a list and the accumulators that we have been talking about in this chapter. In an accumulator, we accumulate values into a sum by repeatedly adding new values to a running sum. The running sum changes (usually grows) in each iteration of the loop. With the list in the `for` loop above, we are accumulating values in a different way—by repeatedly appending them to the end of a growing list. Therefore, we call this technique a ***list accumulator***.

We now want to use this list of population sizes as the list of y values in a `matplotlib` plot. For the x values, we need a list of the corresponding years, which can be obtained with `range(years + 1)`.

> **Reflection 4.18** *Why do we need the x values to be* `range(years + 1)` *instead of* `range(1, years + 1)`*? Think about how many population values are in* `populationList`*.*

Once we have both lists, we can create a plot by calling the `plot` function and then display the plot by calling the `show` function:

```
pyplot.plot(range(years + 1), populationList)
pyplot.show()
```

The first argument to the `plot` function is the list of x values and the second parameter is the list of y values. The `matplotlib.pyplot` module includes many optional ways to customize our plots before we call `show`. Some of the simplest are functions that label the x and y axes:

```
pyplot.xlabel('Year')
pyplot.ylabel('Fish Population Size')
```

Incorporating the plotting code yields the following function, whose output is shown in Figure 4.2.

```
import matplotlib.pyplot as pyplot

def pond(years, initialPopulation, harvest):
    """ (docstring omitted) """

    population = initialPopulation
    populationList = [ ]
    populationList.append(initialPopulation)
    for year in range(1, years + 1):
        population = 1.08 * population - harvest
        populationList.append(population)

    pyplot.plot(range(years + 1), populationList)
    pyplot.xlabel('Year')
    pyplot.ylabel('Fish Population Size')
    pyplot.show()

    return population
```

For more complex plots, we can alter the scales of the axes, change the color and style of the curves, and label multiple curves on the same plot. See Appendix A.4 for a sample of what is available. Some of the options must be specified as *keyword arguments* of the form `name = value`. For example, to color a curve in a plot red and specify a label for the plot legend, you would call something like this:

```
pyplot.plot(x, y, color = 'red', label = 'Bass population')
pyplot.legend()    # creates a legend from labeled lines
```

Exercises

4.2.1* A zombie can convert two people into zombies everyday. Assuming we start with just one zombie, write a function

```
zombieApocalypse(days)
```

that plots the total number of zombies (y axis) roaming the earth over each of the given number of `days` (x axis). Appropriately label your axes. Use your function to create a plot of zombie growth over 14 days.

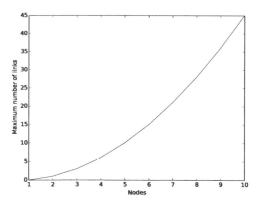

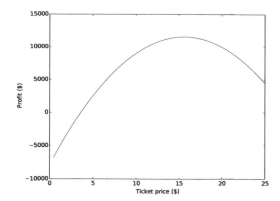

Figure 4.3 Plot for Exercise 4.2.2.   Figure 4.4 Plot for Exercise 4.2.3.

4.2.2. Modify the `countLinks` function on page 138 so that it uses `matplotlib` to plot the number of nodes on the x axis and the maximum number of links on the y axis. Create a plot that shows the maximum number of links for 1 to 10 nodes; it should look like the one in Figure 4.3.

4.2.3* Modify the `profitPlot` function on page 142 so that it uses `matplotlib` to plot ticket price on the x axis and profit on the y axis. (Remove the `tortoise` parameter.) Create a plot that shows the profit for ticket prices up to \$25; it should look like the one in Figure 4.4. To get the correct prices (in half dollar increments) on the x axis, you will need to create a second list of x values and append `realPrice` to it in each iteration.

4.2.4. Modify your `growth1` function from Exercise 4.1.17 so that it uses `matplotlib` to plot days on the x axis and the total population on the y axis. Create a plot that shows the growth of the population over 30 days.

4.2.5. Modify your `growth3` function from Exercise 4.1.19 so that it uses `matplotlib` to plot days on the x axis and the total population on the y axis. Create a plot that shows the growth of the population over 30 days.

4.2.6. Modify your `invest` function from Exercise 4.1.34 so that it uses `matplotlib` to plot months on the x axis and your total accumulated investment amount on the y axis. Create a plot that shows the growth of an investment of \$50 per month for ten years growing at an annual rate of 8%.

4.2.7* Write a function that compares the growth rates of two bacteria colonies (like in Exercise 4.1.21), one that grows 10% per hour and another that grows 15% per hour. Your function should have one `for` loop that accumulates two population variables and two lists independently. After the loop, use two `pyplot.plot` calls before `pyplot.show()`, each with its own label (as shown above), to plot the populations. Include a legend that shows which curve is which. Create a plot with your function that compares growth over a period of 3 days.

4.2.8. Vampires can each convert v people a day into vampires. However, there is a band of vampire hunters that can kill k vampires per day. Write a function

        `vampireApocalypse(v, k, vampires, people, days)`

that plots the numbers of vampires and people in a town with initial population `people` over the given number of `days`, assuming the town starts with a coven with `vampires` members. Use your function to create a plot of vampires and people over a period of 7 days. See the previous exercise for how to plot multiple lists.

4.2.9.   Write a function that compares the growth in population sizes in Exercises 4.1.17, 4.1.19, and 4.1.20 over a number of days. Create a plot with your function that compares growth over 14 days. Use three calls to `pyplot.plot` before `pyplot.show()` and include a legend. Contrast the three growth rates. What do you notice?

4.3   CONDITIONAL ITERATION

In our fishing pond model, to determine when the population size fell below zero, it was sufficient to simply print the annual population sizes for at least 14 years, and look at the results. However, if it had taken a thousand years for the population size to fall below zero, then looking at the output would be far less convenient. Instead, we would like to have a program tell us the year directly, by ceasing to iterate when `population` drops below zero, and then returning the year it happened. This is a different kind of problem because we no longer know how many iterations are required before the loop starts. In other words, we have no way of knowing what value to pass into `range` in a `for` loop.

Instead, we need a more general kind of loop that will iterate only while some condition is met. Such a loop is generally called a ***while loop***. In Python, a while loop looks like this:

```
while <condition>:
    <body>
```

The `<condition>` is replaced with a Boolean expression that evaluates to `True` or `False`, and the `<body>` is replaced with statements constituting the body of the loop. The loop checks the value of the condition before each iteration. If the condition is true, it executes the body of the loop, and then checks the condition again. If the condition is false, the body of the loop is skipped, and the loop ends.

When will the fish disappear?

To solve this problem, we want to continue to update `population` in a loop while `popluation > 0`. This Boolean expression is true if the value of `population` is positive, and false otherwise. Using this Boolean expression in the `while` loop in the following function, we can find the year that the fish population drops to 0.

```
1 def yearsUntilZero(initialPopulation, harvest):
2     """Computes the number of years until a fish population reaches zero.
3        Population grows 8% per year with an annual harvest.

4     Parameters:
5        initialPopulation: the initial population size
6        harvest:           the size of the annual harvest

7     Return value: year during which the population reaches zero
8     """

9     population = initialPopulation
10    year = 0
11    while population > 0:
12        population = 1.08 * population - harvest
13        year = year + 1
14    return year
```

The following trace table shows how the loop works when `initialPopulation` is 12000 and `harvest` is 1500, as in our original pond function in Section 4.1.

Trace arguments: initialPopulation = 12000, harvest = 1500

Step	Line	population	year	Notes
1	9	12000	—	population ← 12000
2	10	"	0	year ← 0
3	11	"	"	population > 0, so execute the body of the loop
4	12	11460.0	"	update population
5	13	"	1	increment year
6	11	"	"	population > 0, so execute the body of the loop
7	12	10876.8	"	update population
8	13	"	2	increment year
9	11	"	"	population > 0, so execute the body of the loop
⋮				
42	11	392.539	13	population > 0, so execute the body of the loop
43	12	-1076.056	"	update population
44	13	"	14	increment year
45	11	"	"	population <= 0, so exit the loop
46	14	"	"	return 14

Return value: 14

Before the loop, `population` is 12000 and `year` is 0. Since `population > 0` is true, the loop body executes in steps 4–5, causing `population` to become 11460 and `year` to become 1. We then go back to the top of the loop in step 6 to check the condition again. Since `population > 0` is still true, the loop body executes again in steps 7–8, causing `population` to become `10876.8` and `year` to become 2. Iteration continues until `year` reaches 14. In this year, `population` becomes `-1076.06`. When the condition is checked at the beginning of the next iteration, we find that `population > 0` is false, so the loop ends and the function returns 14.

Using `while` loops can be tricky for a few reasons. First, a `while` loop may not iterate at all. For example, if the initial value of `population` were zero, the condition in the `while` loop will be false before the first iteration, and the loop will be over before it starts.

> **Reflection 4.19** *What will be returned by the function if the initial value of* `population` *were zero?*

A loop that sometimes does not iterate at all is generally not a bad thing, and can even be used to our advantage. In this case, if `population` were initially zero, the function would return zero because the value of `year` would never be incremented in the loop. And this is correct; the population dropped to zero in year zero, before the clock started ticking beyond the initial population size. But it is something that one should always keep in mind when designing algorithms involving `while` loops.

Second, and related to the first point, you need to always make sure that the condition in the `while` loop makes sense before the first iteration. For example, suppose we forgot to give `population` an initial value before the loop. Then the loop condition would not make any sense because `population` was not defined.

Third, a `while` loop may become an ***infinite loop***. For example, suppose `initialPopulation` is 12000 and `harvest` is 800 instead of 1500. In this case, as we saw on page 134, the population size *increases* every year instead. So the population size will *never* reach zero and the loop condition will *never* be false, so the loop will iterate forever. For this reason, we must always make sure that the body of a `while` loop makes progress toward the loop condition becoming false.

These points can be summarized in two rules to always keep in mind when designing an algorithm with a `while` loop:

1. Initialize the condition before the loop. Always make sure that the condition makes sense and will behave in the intended way the first time it is tested.

2. In each iteration of the loop, work toward the condition eventually becoming false. Not doing so will result in an infinite loop.

When will your nest egg double?

Let's look at one more example. Suppose we have $1000 to invest and we would like to know how long it will take for our money to double in size, growing at 5% per year. To answer this question, let's start with the following incomplete loop that compounds 5% interest each year:

```
amount = 1000
while ???:
    amount = 1.05 * amount
print(amount)
```

┃ Reflection 4.20 *What should be the condition in the* while *loop?*

We want the loop to stop iterating when amount reaches 2000. Therefore, we want the loop to continue to iterate *while* amount < 2000.

```
amount = 1000
while amount < 2000:
    amount = 1.05 * amount
print(amount)
```

┃ Reflection 4.21 *What is printed by this block of code? What does this result tell us?*

Once the loop is done iterating, the final amount is printed (approximately $2078.93), but this does not answer our question.

┃ Reflection 4.22 *How do we figure out how many years it takes for the $1000 to double?*

To answer our question, we need to count the number of times the while loop iterates, which is very similar to what we did in the yearsUntilZero function. We can introduce another variable that is incremented in each iteration, and print its value after the loop, along with the final value of amount:

```
amount = 1000
while amount < 2000:
    amount = 1.05 * amount
    year = year + 1
print(year, amount)
```

┃ Reflection 4.23 *Make these changes and run the code again. Now what is printed?*

Oops, an error message is printed, telling us that the name year is undefined.

┃ Reflection 4.24 *How do we fix the error?*

The problem is that we did not initialize the value of year before the loop. Therefore, the first time year = year + 1 was executed, year was undefined on the right side of the assignment statement. Adding one statement before the loop fixes the problem:

```
amount = 1000
year = 0
while amount < 2000:
    amount = 1.05 * amount
    year = year + 1
print(year, amount)
```

┃ Reflection 4.25 *Now what is printed by this block of code? In other words, how many years until the $1000 doubles?*

We will see some more examples of while loops later in this chapter, and again in Section 5.6.

Exercises

4.3.1*   Suppose you put $1000 into the bank and you get a 3% interest rate compounded annually. How would you use a `while` loop to determine how long it will take for your account to have at least $1200 in it?

4.3.2.   Repeat the last question, but this time write a function

```
interest(amount, rate, target)
```

that takes the initial amount, the interest rate, and the target amount as parameters. The function should return the number of years it takes to reach the target amount.

4.3.3.   Since `while` loops are more general than `for` loops, we can emulate the behavior of a `for` loop with a `while` loop. For example, we can emulate the behavior of the `for` loop

```
for counter in range(10):
    print(counter)
```

with the `while` loop

```
counter = 0
while counter < 10:
    print(counter)
    counter = counter + 1
```

(a)   Create a trace table for each of the loops above to make sure you understand how they are equivalent.

(b)   What happens if we omit `counter = 0` before the `while` loop? Why does this happen?

(c)   What happens if we omit `counter = counter + 1` from the body of the `while` loop? What does the loop print?

(d)   Show how to emulate the following `for` loop with a `while` loop:

```
for counter in range(3, 12):
    print(counter)
```

(e)   Show how to emulate the following `for` loop with a `while` loop:

```
for counter in range(12, 3, -1):
    print(counter)
```

4.3.4*   In the `profitTable` function on page 142, we used a `for` loop to indirectly consider all ticket prices divisible by a half dollar. Rewrite this function so that it instead uses a `while` loop that increments `price` by $0.50 in each iteration.

4.3.5.   A zombie can convert two people into zombies everyday. Starting with just one zombie, how long would it take for the entire world population (7 billion people) to become zombies? Write a function

```
zombieApocalypse()
```

that returns the answer to this question.

4.3.6*   Tribbles increase at the rate of 50% per hour (rounding down if there are an odd number of them). How long would it take 10 tribbles to reach a population size of 1 million? Write a function

```
tribbleApocalypse()
```

that returns the answer to this question.

4.3.7.   Vampires can each convert v people a day into vampires. However, there is a band of vampire hunters that can kill k vampires per day. If a coven of vampires starts with `vampires` members, how long before a town with a population of `people` becomes a town with no humans left in it? Write a function

```
vampireApocalypse(v, k, vampires, people)
```

that returns the answer to this question.

4.3.8.   An amoeba can split itself into two once every h hours. How many hours does it take for a single amoeba to become `target` amoebae? Write a function

```
amoebaGrowth(h, target)
```

that returns the answer to this question.

4.3.9.   Write a function

```
virus(rate, target)
```

that returns the number of days until `target` people are infected by a virus, assuming one person is initially infected and the number infected grows by the given `rate` each day.

4.3.10.   Suppose each person newly infected by a virus is able to infect R additional people. R is called the *reproduction number* of the virus. (Think of this as a one-time event; the person does not infect R additional people every day.) Write a function

```
virus2(R, target)
```

that returns the number of days until `target` people are infected, assuming only one person is initially infected.

*4.4   CONTINUOUS MODELS

This section is available on the book website.

*4.5   NUMERICAL ANALYSIS

This section is available on the book website.

4.6   SUMMING UP

Although we have solved a variety of different problems in this chapter, almost all of the functions that we have designed have the same basic format:

```
def accumulator(_____):
    total = ____                    # initialize the accumulator
    for index in range(____):       # iterate some number of times
        total = total + _____    # add something to the accumulator
    return total                    # return final accumulator value
```

The functions we designed differ primarily in what is added to the accumulator (the red statement) in each iteration of the loop. Let's look at three of these functions in particular: the **pond** function from page 135, the **countLinks** function from page 138, and the solution to Exercise 4.1.30 from page 148, shown below.

```
def growth(finalAge):
    height = 95
    for age in range(4, finalAge + 1):
        height = height + 6
    return height
```

In the **growth** function, a constant value is added to the accumulator in each iteration:

```
height = height + 6
```

In the **countLinks** function, the value of the index variable, minus one, is added to the accumulator:

```
newLinks = node - 1
totalLinks = totalLinks + newLinks
```

And in the **pond** function, a factor of the accumulator itself is added in each iteration:

```
population = population + 0.08 * population  # ignoring "- 1500"
```

These three types of accumulators grow in three different ways. Adding a constant value to the accumulator in each iteration, as in the **growth** function, results in a final sum that is equal to the number of iterations times the constant value. In other words, if the initial value is a, the constant added value is c, and the number of iterations is n, then the final value of the accumulator is $a + cn$. (In the **growth** function, $a = 95$ and $c = 6$, so the final sum is $95 + 6n$.) As n increases, cn increases by a constant amount. This is called *linear growth*, and is illustrated by the blue line in Figure 4.5.

Adding the value of the index variable to the accumulator, as in the **countLinks** function, leads to faster growth. In **countLinks**, the final value of the accumulator is

$$1 + 2 + 3 + \cdots + (n - 1)$$

which is equal to

$$\frac{1}{2} \cdot n \cdot (n - 1) = \frac{n^2 - n}{2}.$$

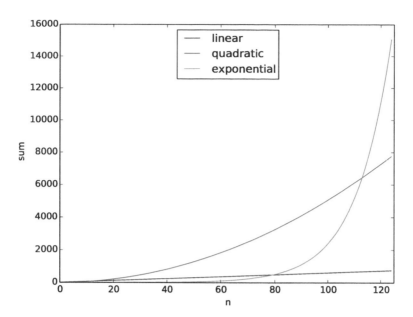

Figure 4.5 An illustration of linear, quadratic, and exponential growth. The curves are generated by accumulators adding 6, the index variable, and 1.08 times the accumulator, respectively, in each iteration.

Tangent 4.1 explains two clever ways to derive this result. Since this sum is proportional to n^2, we say that it exhibits ***quadratic growth***, as shown by the red curve in Figure 4.5. This sum is actually quite handy to know, and it will surface again in Chapter 10.

Finally, adding a factor of the accumulator to itself in each iteration, as in the `pond` function, results in even faster growth. In the `pond` function, if we add `0.08 * population` to `population` in each iteration, the accumulator variable will be equal to the initial value of `population` times 1.08^n at the end of n iterations of the loop. For this reason, we call this ***exponential growth***, which is illustrated by the green curve in Figure 4.5. Notice that, as n gets larger, exponential growth quickly outpaces the other two curves, even when the power of n is small, like 1.08.

So although all accumulator algorithms look more or less alike, the effects of the accumulators can be strikingly different. Understanding the relative rates of these different types of growth is quite important in a variety of fields, not just computer science. For example, mistaking an exponentially growing epidemic for a linearly growing one can be a life or death mistake!

These classes of growth can also be applied to the time complexity of algorithms, as we saw briefly in Section 1.2 and will see more in later chapters. When applied in this way, n represents the size of the algorithm's input and the y-axis represents the

Tangent 4.1: Triangular numbers

There are a few nice tricks to figure out the value of the sum

$$1 + 2 + 3 + \cdots + (n-2) + (n-1) + n$$

for any positive integer n. The first technique is to add the numbers in the sum from the outside in. Notice that the sum of the first and last numbers is $n+1$. Then, coming in one position from both the left and right, we find that $(n-1) + 2 = n+1$ as well. Next, $(n-2) + 3 = n+1$. This pattern will obviously continue, as we are subtracting 1 from the number on the left and adding 1 to the number on the right. In total, there is one instance of $n+1$ for every two terms in the sum, for a total of $n/2$ instances of $n+1$. Therefore, the sum is

$$1 + 2 + 3 + \cdots + (n-2) + (n-1) + n = \frac{n}{2}(n+1) = \frac{n(n+1)}{2}.$$

For example, $1+2+3+\cdots+8 = (8\cdot9)/2 = 36$ and $1+2+3+\cdots+1000 = (1000\cdot1001)/2 = 500{,}500$.

The second technique to derive this result is more visual. Depict each number in the sum as a column of circles, as shown on the left below with $n = 8$.

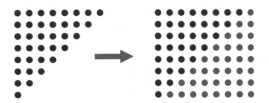

The first column has $n = 8$ circles, the second has $n - 1 = 7$, etc. So the total number of circles in this triangle is equal to the value we are seeking. Now make an exact duplicate of this triangle, and place its mirror image to the right of the original triangle, as shown on the right above. The resulting rectangle has n rows and $n + 1$ columns, so there are a total of $n(n+1)$ circles. Since the number of circles in this rectangle is exactly twice the number in the original triangle, the number of circles in the original triangle is $n(n+1)/2$. Based on this representation, numbers like 36 and 500,500 that are sums of this form are called *triangular numbers*.

number of elementary steps required by the algorithm to compute the corresponding output. Algorithms that exhibit linear or quadratic time complexity are generally considered to be acceptable algorithms, while those exhibiting exponential time complexity are essentially worthless on all but the smallest inputs.

Exercises

4.6.1.   Decide whether each of the following accumulators exhibits linear, quadratic, or exponential growth.

(a)*
```
total = 0
for count in range(n):
    total = total + count * 2
```

(b)
```
total = 10
for count in range(n):
    total = total + count / 2
```

(c)*
```
total = 1
for count in range(n):
    total = total + total
```

(d)
```
total = 0
for count in range(n):
    total = total + 1.2 * total
```

(e)
```
total = 0
for count in range(n):
    total = total + 0.01
```

(f)
```
total = 10
for count in range(n):
    total = 1.2 * total
```

4.6.2.   Look at Figure 4.5. For values of n less than about 80, the fast-growing exponential curve is actually below the other two. Explain why.

4.6.3.   Write a program to generate Figure 4.5.

4.7   FURTHER DISCOVERY

The epigraph of this chapter is from a TED talk given by Stephen Hawking in 2008. You can watch it yourself at

www.ted.com/talks/stephen_hawking_asks_big_questions_about_the_universe .

If you are interested in learning more about population dynamics models, and computational modeling in general, a great source is *Introduction to Computational Science* [61] by Angela Shiflet and George Shiflet.

*4.8   PROJECTS

This section is available on the book website.

CHAPTER 5

Forks in the Road

When you come to a fork in the road, take it.

Yogi Berra

S o far, our algorithms have been entirely *deterministic*; they have done the same thing every time we executed them with the same inputs. However, the natural world and its inhabitants (including us) are usually not so predictable. Rather, we consider many natural processes to be, to various degrees, *random*. For example, the behaviors of crowds and markets often change in unpredictable ways. The genetic "mixing" that occurs in sexual reproduction can also be considered a random process because we cannot predict the characteristics of any particular offspring. And the unpredictable movements of tiny particles in the air are often modeled as random processes, with applications to studying airborne pollutants and viruses. To model these kinds of systems, our programs need to be able to both emulate randomness and change their behavior in response to stimuli.

More generally, most run-of-the-mill programs must also be able to conditionally change course, or select from among a variety of options, in response to input. Indeed, most common desktop applications do nothing unless prompted by a key press or a mouse click. Computer games like racing simulators react to a controller several times a second. The protocols that govern data traffic on the Internet adjust transmission rates continually in response to the perceived level of congestion on the network. In this chapter, we will discover how to design algorithms that can behave differently in response to input, both random and deterministic.

5.1 RANDOM WALKS

In 1827, British Botanist Robert Brown, while observing pollen grains suspended in water under his microscope, witnessed something curious. When the pollen grains burst, they emitted much smaller particles that proceeded to wiggle around randomly. This phenomenon, now called ***Brownian motion***, was caused by the particles' collisions with the moving water molecules. Brownian motion is now used to describe the motion of any sufficiently small particle (or molecule) in a fluid.

We can model the essence of Brownian motion with a single randomly moving particle in two dimensions. This process is known as a ***random walk***. Random walks are also used to model a wide variety of other phenomena such as markets and the foraging behavior of animals, and to sample large social networks. In this section, we will develop a Monte Carlo simulation of a random walk to discover how far away a randomly moving particle is likely to get in a fixed amount of time.

You may have already modeled a simple random walk in Exercise 2.3.23 by moving a turtle around the screen and choosing a random angle to turn at each step. We will now develop a more restricted version of a random walk in which the particle is forced to move on a two-dimensional grid. At each step, we want the particle to move in one of the four cardinal directions, each with equal probability.

To simulate random processes, we need an algorithm or device that produces random numbers, called a ***random number generator*** (RNG). A conventional computer processor cannot implement a true RNG because everything it does is entirely predictable. Therefore, a computer either needs to incorporate a specialized device that can detect and transmit truly random physical events (like subatomic quantum fluctuations) or simulate randomness with a clever algorithm called a ***pseudorandom number generator*** (PRNG). A PRNG generates a sequence of numbers that *appear* to be random although, in reality, they are not.

The Python module named `random` provides a PRNG in a function named `random`. The `random` function returns a pseudorandom number between zero and one, but not including one. For example:

```
>>> import random
>>> random.random()
0.9699738944412686
```

(Your output will differ.) It is convenient to refer to the range of real numbers produced by the `random` function as [0,1). The square bracket on the left means that 0 is included in the range, and the parenthesis on the right means that 1 is not included in the range. Tangent 5.1 explains a little more about this so-called *interval notation*, if it is unfamiliar to you.

Tangent 5.1: Interval notation

It is customary to represent the interval (i.e., set or range), of *real numbers* between a and b, including a and b, with the notation $[a, b]$. In contrast, the set of *integers* between the integers a and b, including a and b, is denoted $[a..b]$. For example, $[3, 7]$ represents every real number greater than or equal to 3 and less than or equal to 7, while $[3..7]$ represents the integers $3, 4, 5, 6, 7$.

To denote an interval of real numbers between a and b that does not contain an endpoint a or b, we replace the endpoint's square bracket with a parenthesis. So $[a,b)$ is the interval of real numbers between a and b that does contain a but does not contain b. Similarly, $(a,b]$ contains b but not a, and (a,b) contains neither a nor b.

One small step

Now let's write an algorithm to take one step of a random walk. We will save the particle's (x,y) coordinates in two variables, x and y. Then we will use the `random` function to assign a random value in $[0,1)$ to a variable named `randi` (why not?).

```
x = 0                      # particle starts at (0, 0)
y = 0
randi = random.random()    # random number in the interval [0, 1)
```

To use this pseudorandom number to randomly move the particle, we need to think about the interval of possible random numbers as being divided into four equal subintervals, and associate a direction with each one:

1. If `randi` is in $[0,0.25)$, then move east.
2. If `randi` is in $[0.25,0.5)$, then move north.
3. If `randi` is in $[0.5,0.75)$, then move west.
4. If `randi` is in $[0.75,1.0)$, then move south.

We can implement this in Python with an `if` statement, which executes a particular sequence of statements only if some Boolean expression is true. The following statement increments x if `randi` is in the subinterval $[0,0.25)$:

```
if randi < 0.25:    # if randi is in [0, 0.25), then
    x = x + 1       #    move east
```

Reflection 5.1 *Why do we not need to also check whether* `randi` *is at least zero?*

An `if` statement is also called a ***conditional statement*** because, like the `while` loops we saw earlier, they make decisions that are conditioned on a Boolean expression. (Unlike `while` loops, however, an `if` statement is only executed once.) The Boolean expression in this case, `randi < 0.25`, is true if `randi` is less than 0.25 and false otherwise. If the Boolean expression is true, the statement(s) that are indented beneath the condition are executed. On the other hand, if the Boolean expression is false, the indented statement(s) are skipped, and the statement following the indented statement(s) is executed next.

Math symbol	Python symbol
<	<
≤	<=
>	>
≥	>=
=	==
≠	!=

Table 5.1   Python's six comparison operators.

Let's move now to the second case. To check whether `randi` is in $[0.25, 0.5)$, we need to check whether `randi` is greater than or equal to 0.25 *and* `randi` is less than 0.5. The meaning of "and" in the previous sentence is identical to the Boolean operator from Section 3.2. In Python, this condition is represented just as you might expect:

```
randi >= 0.25 and randi < 0.5
```

The `>=` operator is Python's representation of "greater than or equal to" (≥). It is one of six ***comparison operators*** (or *relational operators*), listed in Table 5.1, some of which have two-character representations in Python. (Note especially that `==` is used to test for equality. We will discuss these operators further in Section 5.4.) Adding this case to the first case, we now have two `if` statements:

```
if randi < 0.25:                     # if randi is in [0, 0.25), then
    x = x + 1                        #    move east
if randi >= 0.25 and randi < 0.5:    # if randi is in [0.25, 0.5), then
    y = y + 1                        #    move north
```

Let's think about how these statements will behave in two different cases. First, if `randi` is assigned a value that is less than 0.25, the condition in the first `if` statement will be true and `x = x + 1` will be executed. Next, the condition in the second `if` statement will be checked. But since this condition is false, `y` will not be incremented.

On the other hand, if `randi` is assigned a value that is between 0.25 and 0.5, then the condition in the first `if` statement will be false, so the indented statement `x = x + 1` will be skipped and execution will continue with the second `if` statement. Since the condition in the second `if` statement is true, `y = y + 1` will be executed.

To complete our four-way decision, we can add two more `if` statements:

```
1  if randi < 0.25:                     # if randi is in [0, 0.25), then
2      x = x + 1                        #    move east
3  if randi >= 0.25 and randi < 0.5:    # if randi is in [0.25, 0.5), then
4      y = y + 1                        #    move north
5  if randi >= 0.5 and randi < 0.75:    # if randi is in [0.5, 0.75), then
6      x = x - 1                        #    move west
7  if randi >= 0.75 and randi < 1.0:    # if randi is in [0.75, 1.0), then
8      y = y - 1                        #    move south
9  print(x, y)                          # executed after all 4 cases
```

There are four possible ways these statements could execute, one for each interval in which `randi` can reside. To illustrate one of these cases, suppose `randi` was randomly assigned the value 0.4.

Trace arguments: `randi` = 0.4				
Step	Line	x	y	Notes
—	—	0	0	assume x = 0 and y = 0
1	1	"	"	`randi` < 0.25 is false, so skip to line 3
2	3	"	"	`randi` >= 0.25 and `randi` < 0.5 is true, so do line 4
3	4	"	1	y ← y + 1 (move north)
4	5	"	"	`randi` >= 0.5 and `randi` < 0.75 is false, so skip to line 7
5	7	"	"	`randi` >= 0.75 and `randi` < 1.0 is false, so skip to line 9
6	9	"	"	prints 0 1

Since the condition of the first `if` statement is false, the trace table shows that the indented statement on line 2 is skipped. Next, we test the condition of the `if` statement on line 3. Since this condition is true (0.25 < 0.4 < 0.5), the indented statement on line 4, y = y + 1, is executed. We continue by testing the condition of the third `if` statement, on line 5. Since this condition is false, we skip the indented statement on line 6. Next, we continue to the fourth `if` statement on line 7, and test its condition, which is false. So line 8 is skipped and execution continues on line 9, which prints the values of x and y. Notice that, for any possible value of `randi`, only one of the four indented statements will be executed.

Reflection 5.2 *Is this sequence of steps efficient? If not, what steps could be skipped and in what circumstances?*

The code behaves correctly, but it seems unnecessary to test subsequent conditions after we have already found the correct case. If there were many more than four cases, this extra work could be substantial. Here is a much more efficient structure:

```
1  if randi < 0.25:      # if randi is in [0, 0.25), then
2      x = x + 1         #    move east and finish
3  elif randi < 0.5:     # otherwise, if randi is in [0.25, 0.5), then
4      y = y + 1         #    move north and finish
5  elif randi < 0.75:    # otherwise, if randi is in [0.5, 0.75), then
6      x = x - 1         #    move west and finish
7  elif randi < 1.0:     # otherwise, if randi is in [0.75, 1.0), then
8      y = y - 1         #    move south and finish
9  print(x, y)           # executed after all 4 cases
```

The keyword `elif` is short for "else if," meaning that the condition that follows is checked *only* if no preceding condition was true. In other words, as we sequentially check each of the four conditions, if we find that one is true, then the associated indented statement(s) are executed, and we *skip* the remaining conditions in the group. We also eliminated the unnecessary `>=` checks from each condition (e.g., `randi >= 0.25`). These are redundant because, if we encounter an `elif` condition, we know that the previous condition must have been false, i.e., we know that `randi` must be greater than all of the previously tested intervals.

The next trace table, with `randi` again randomly assigned 0.4, illustrates the advantage of this alternative structure.

Step	Line	x	y	Notes
—	—	0	0	assume x = 0 and y = 0
1	1	"	"	randi < 0.25 is false, so skip to line 3
2	3	"	"	randi < 0.5 is true, so do line 4
3	4	"	1	y ← y + 1 (move north) and skip to line 9
4	9	"	"	prints 1 0

Trace arguments: `randi = 0.4`

Everything up through step 3 is identical, but now, after the condition on line 3 is found to be true and line 4 is executed, the remaining `elif` statements are skipped, and execution continues on line 9, after the last `elif`.

> **Reflection 5.3** *For each of the four possible intervals to which* `randi` *could belong, how many* `elif` *conditions are checked?*

> **Reflection 5.4** *Suppose you replace every* `elif` *with* `if` *in the most recent version above. What would then happen if* `randi` *had the value* 0.4?

This code can be streamlined a bit more. Since `randi` must be in [0,1), there is no point in checking the last condition, `randi < 1.0`. If execution has proceeded that far, `randi` *must* be in [0.75,1). So we can safely execute the last statement, `y = y - 1`, without checking anything. This is accomplished by replacing the last `elif` with an `else` statement:

```
1  if randi < 0.25:      # if randi is in [0, 0.25), then
2      x = x + 1         #    move east and finish
3  elif randi < 0.5:     # otherwise, if randi is in [0.25, 0.5), then
4      y = y + 1         #    move north and finish
5  elif randi < 0.75:    # otherwise, if randi is in [0.5, 0.75), then
6      x = x - 1         #    move west and finish
7  else:                 # otherwise,
8      y = y - 1         #    move south and finish
9  print(x, y)           # executed after all 4 cases
```

The `else` signals that, if no previous condition is true, the statement(s) indented under the `else` should be executed.

> **Reflection 5.5** *Again, suppose you replace every* `elif` *with* `if` *in this newest version. What would happen now if* `randi` *had the value* 0.4?

If we (erroneously) replaced the two instances of `elif` above with `if`, then the final `else` would be associated *only* with the last `if`. So if `randi` had the value 0.4, the second and third `if` conditions would both be true and the second and third indented statements would both be executed. The last indented statement would not be executed because the last `if` condition was true.

In situations where there are only two choices, an `else` can just accompany an `if`. For example, if wanted to randomly move a particle on a line instead of in two dimensions, our conditional would look like:

```
1 if randi < 0.5:    # if randi is in [0, 0.5), then
2     x = x + 1       #   move east and finish
3 else:              # otherwise,
4     x = x - 1       #   move west and finish
5 print(x)           # executed after the if/else
```

Monte Carlo simulation

The `randomWalk` function below uses our `if/elif/else` conditional structure in a loop to simulate a random walk, and then returns the distance the particle has moved from the origin. To make the grid movement easier to see, we multiply the turtle's movement by a variable `moveLength`. Figure 5.1 shows an example of what you will see when you call `randomWalk` from a `main` function.

```
def randomWalk(steps, tortoise):
    """Displays a random walk on a grid.

    Parameters:
        steps:    the number of steps in the random walk
        tortoise: a Turtle object

    Return value: the final distance from the origin
    """

    x = 0                        # initialize (x, y) = (0, 0)
    y = 0
    moveLength = 10              # length of a turtle step
    for step in range(steps):
        randi = random.random()    # randomly choose a direction
        if randi < 0.25:      # if randi is in [0, 0.25), then
            x = x + 1          #   move east and finish
        elif randi < 0.5:    # otherwise, if randi is in [0.25, 0.5), then
            y = y + 1          #   move north and finish
        elif randi < 0.75:   # otherwise, if randi is in [0.5, 0.75), then
            x = x - 1          #   move west and finish
        else:                 # otherwise,
            y = y - 1          #   move south and finish
        tortoise.goto(x * moveLength, y * moveLength)  # draw one step

    return math.sqrt(x * x + y * y)  # return distance from (0, 0)
```

How far, on average, does a randomly walking particle move from its origin in a given number of steps? The answer to this question can, for example, provide insight into the rate at which a fluid spreads or the extent of an animal's foraging territory.

The distance traveled in any one particular random walk is meaningless; the particle

Figure 5.1 A 1000-step random walk produced by the `randomWalk` function.

may return the origin, walk away from the origin at every step, or do something in between. None of these outcomes tells us anything about the *expected*, or average, behavior of the system. To model the expected behavior, we need to compute the average distance over many, many random walks. This kind of simulation is called a **Monte Carlo simulation**, after the famous casino in Monaco.

As we will be calling `randomWalk` many times, we would like to speed things up by skipping the turtle visualization of the random walks. We can prevent drawing by incorporating a **flag variable** as a parameter to `randomWalk`. A flag variable has a Boolean value, and is used to switch some behavior on or off. In Python, the two possible Boolean values are named `True` and `False` (note the capitalization). In the `randomWalk` function, we will call the flag variable `draw`, and cause its value to influence the drawing behavior with another `if` statement:

```
def randomWalk(steps, tortoise, draw):
    """Displays a random walk on a grid.

    Parameters:
        steps:    the number of steps in the random walk
        tortoise: a Turtle object
        draw:     a Boolean indicating whether to draw the random walk

    Return value: the final distance from the origin
    """

    ⋮

    if draw:
        tortoise.goto(x * moveLength, y * moveLength)

    ⋮
```

Now, when we call `randomWalk`, we pass in either `True` or `False` for our third argument. If `draw` is `True`, then `tortoise.goto(···)` will be executed but, if `draw` is `False`, it will be skipped.

Reflection 5.6 *Incorporate* `draw` *into your* `randomWalk` *function and try calling it with both* `True` *and* `False` *passed in for the third parameter.*

To find the average over many trials, we will call our `randomWalk` function repeatedly in a loop, and use an accumulator variable to sum up all the distances.

```
def rwMonteCarlo(steps, trials):
    """A Monte Carlo simulation to find the expected distance
       that a random walk finishes from the origin.

    Parameters:
        steps:  the number of steps in the random walk
        trials: the number of random walks

    Return value: the average distance from the origin
    """

    totalDistance = 0
    for trial in range(trials):
        distance = randomWalk(steps, None, False)
        totalDistance = totalDistance + distance
    return totalDistance / trials
```

The parameters `steps` and `trials` are the number of steps in each random walk and the number of times to call the `randomWalk` function, respectively. Notice that we have passed in `None` as the argument for the second parameter (`tortoise`) of `randomWalk`. With `False` being passed in for the parameter `draw`, the value assigned to `tortoise` is never used, so we pass in `None` as a placeholder.

Reflection 5.7 *Call* `rwMonteCarlo(500, 5)` *ten times in a loop, printing the result each time. What do you notice? Do you think five trials is enough? Now perform the same experiment with 10, 100, 1000, and 10000 trials. How many trials do you think are sufficient to get a reliable result?*

As we increase the number of trials in a Monte Carlo simulation, our average results become more consistent, but what do the individual trials look like? To find out, we can generate a *histogram* of the individual random walk distances. A histogram for a data set is a bar graph that shows how the items in the data set are distributed across some number of intervals, which are usually called "bins" or "buckets." To make a histogram of the distances, we need to create a list of these values in the loop, and then call the `pyplot.hist` function to display them as a histogram. A modified version of `rwMonteCarlo` that also displays a histogram is shown below.

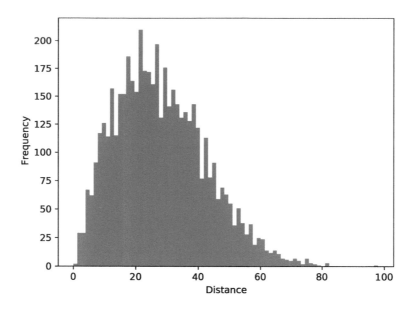

Figure 5.2 A histogram showing the distribution of distances in 5000 trials of a 1000-step random walk.

```python
def rwMonteCarlo(steps, trials):
    """ (docstring omitted) """

    totalDistance = 0
    distances = [ ]
    for trial in range(trials):
        distance = randomWalk(steps, None, False)
        totalDistance = totalDistance + distance
        distances.append(distance)

    pyplot.hist(distances, 75)
    pyplot.xlabel('Distance')
    pyplot.ylabel('Frequency')
    pyplot.show()

    return totalDistance / trials
```

The first argument to `pyplot.hist` is the list of values, and the second is the number of bins to use. A histogram produced by calling the modified function with `rwMonteCarlo(1000, 5000)` is shown in Figure 5.2. The x-axis represents the distance moved from the origin in the random walks, grouped into 75 bins, and the y-axis is the number of times each bin of distances appeared among the 5000 trials. The mean distance returned by the function was about 28, and you can see that the histogram shows that most of the trials were near that value. The overall shape of the histogram resembles a "bell curve," more formally known as a normal distribution. (To learn more about why this phenomenon occurs, see Section 5.3.)

Ultimately, we want to understand the distance traveled as a function of the number of steps. In other words, if the particle moves n steps, does it travel an average distance of $n/2$ or $n/25$ or $\sqrt{n}$ or $\log_2 n$ or ...? To empirically discover the answer, we need to run the Monte Carlo simulation for many different numbers of steps, and try to infer a pattern from a plot of the results. We leave this as an exercise.

Exercises

5.1.1*   What is printed by the following sequence of statements in each of the cases below? Explain your answers.

```
if votes1 >= votes2:
    print('Candidate one wins!')
elif votes1 <= votes2:
    print('Candidate two wins!')
else:
    print('There was a tie.')
```

(a)   votes1 = 184 and votes2 = 206

(b)   votes1 = 255 and votes2 = 135

(c)   votes1 = 195 and votes2 = 195

5.1.2*   There is a problem with the statements in the previous exercise. Fix them so that they correctly fulfill their intended purpose.

5.1.3.   What is printed by the following sequence of statements in each of the cases below? Explain your answers.

```
majority = (votes1 + votes2 + votes3) / 2
if votes1 > majority:
    print('Candidate one wins!')
if votes2 > majority:
    print('Candidate two wins!')
if votes3 > majority:
    print('Candidate three wins!')
else:
    print('A runoff is required.')
```

(a)   votes1 = 5 and votes2 = 5 and votes3 = 5

(b)   votes1 = 9 and votes2 = 2 and votes3 = 4

(c)   votes1 = 0 and votes2 = 15 and votes3 = 0

5.1.4.   Make the statements in the previous problem more efficient and fix them so that they fulfill their intended purpose.

5.1.5. What is syntactically wrong with the following sequence of statements?

```
if x < 1:
    print('Something.')
else:
    print('Something else.')
elif x > 3:
    print('Another something.')
```

5.1.6. What is the final value assigned to `result` after each of the following code segments?

(a)
```
n = 13
result = n
if n > 12:
    result = result + 12
if n < 5:
    result = result + 5
else:
    result = result + 2
```

(b)
```
n = 13
result = n
if n > 12:
    result = result + 12
elif n < 5:
    result = result + 5
else:
    result = result + 2
```

5.1.7* Suppose the weather forecast calls for a 70% chance of rain. Write a function

```
weather()
```

that prints `'RAIN'` with probability 0.7, and `'SUN!'` otherwise. Then write another version that snows with probability 0.66, produces a sunny day with probability 0.33, and rains cats and dogs with probability 0.01.

5.1.8* Write a function

```
roll()
```

that simulates the rolling of a single fair die by returning each of the integers 1 through 6 with equal probability. Use `random.random()`.

5.1.9. Write a function

```
loaded()
```

that simulates the rolling of a single "loaded die" that rolls more 1's and 6's than it should. The probability of rolling each of 1 or 6 should be 0.25. The function should use the `random.random` function and an `if/elif/else` conditional construct to assign a roll value to a variable named `roll`, and then return the value of `roll`.

5.1.10* Write a function that chooses a random number between 1 and 100, prompts for a guess, and prints whether the guess is correct, too high, or too low. Use the function `random.randrange(1, 101)` to get your random number. For example, your function might display:

```
Guess my number: 50
Your guess was too high.  My number was 5.
```

5.1.11.   Write a function to implement a simple calculator. The function should prompt for an operation (addition, subtraction, multiplication, or division), the two numbers to operate on, and then print the result. If an unknown operation is entered, the program should say so. For example, your function might display:

```
Operation: *
First number: 67
Second number: 34.1
The answer is 2284.7.
```

or

```
Operation: &
First number: 5
Second number: 3.2
I don't know how to do that!
```

5.1.12.   Write a function

```
factors(number)
```

that prints all of the factors of the given number. For example, `factors(66)` should print 2 3 6 11 22 33 66 (one per line).

5.1.13*   Write a function

```
countVotes(votes)
```

that implements the algorithm from Exercise 1.2.7, but also accounts for the possibility of a tie. The parameter is a list of strings like `['John', 'Laura', 'Laura', 'John', 'Laura']`. If Laura receives the most votes, return the string `'Laura'`; if John receives the most votes, return `'John'`; if it is a tie, return `'Tie'`.

5.1.14.   Write a function

```
assignGrades(scores)
```

that returns a list of letter grades corresponding to the numerical scores in the list `scores`. For example, `assignGrades([78, 91, 85])` should return the list `['C', 'A', 'B']`.

5.1.15.   Sometimes we want a random walk to reflect circumstances that bias the probability of a particle moving in some direction (i.e., gravity, water current, or wind). For example, suppose that we need to incorporate gravity, so a movement to the north is modeling a real movement up, away from the force of gravity. Then we might want to decrease the probability of moving north to 0.15, increase the probability of moving south to 0.35, and leave the other directions as they were. Show how to modify the `randomWalk` function to implement this situation.

5.1.16*   To discover the distance traveled by a randomly walking particle as a function of the number of its steps, we can call the `rwMonteCarlo` function for many different numbers of steps, and try to infer a pattern from a plot of the results.

   (a)   Write a function

```
plotDistances(maxSteps, trials)
```

that does this with `steps` equal to 100, 200, ..., `maxSteps`, and then plots the results with `matplotlib.pyplot`. Include properly labeled axes and a legend.

(b) Call `plotDistances(1000, 5000)` to view the relationship between the number of steps taken and the distance moved from the origin. What is your hypothesis for the function approximated by the plot?

(c) The function we are seeking has actually been mathematically determined, and is approximately $\sqrt{n}$. Confirm this empirically by plotting this function alongside the simulated results. To do so, initialize a new list of y values before your loop, and append `math.sqrt(steps)` to this list inside your loop (`steps` is your `for` loop index variable). This creates a list of values of the $\sqrt{n}$ function. Plot these values alongside your random walk results.

(d) As you discovered in Reflection 5.7, the quality of any Monte Carlo approximation depends on the number of trials. Call `plotDistances` a few more times with smaller and larger numbers of trials. What do you notice in your plot?

5.1.17. Determining the number of bins to use in a histogram is part science, part art. If you use too few bins, you might miss the shape of the distribution. If you use too many bins, there may be many empty bins and the shape of the distribution will be too jagged. Experiment with the correct number of bins for 10,000 trials in the `rwHistogram` function you wrote in the previous exercise. At the extremes, create a histogram with only 3 bins and another with 1,000 bins. Then try numbers in between. What seems to be a good number of bins? (You may also want to do some research on this question.)

5.1.18. The Monty Hall problem is a famous puzzle based on the game show "Let's Make a Deal," hosted, in its heyday, by Monty Hall. You are given the choice of three doors. Behind one is a car, and behind the other two are goats. You pick a door, and then Monty, who knows what's behind all three doors, opens a different one, which always reveals a goat. You can then stick with your original door or switch. What do you do (assuming you would prefer a car)?

We can write a Monte Carlo simulation to find out. First, write a function

    `montyHall(choice, switch)`

that decides whether we win or lose, based on our original door choice and whether we decide to switch doors. Assume that the doors are numbered 0, 1, and 2, and that the car is always behind door number 2. If we originally chose the car, then we lose if we switch but we win if we don't. Otherwise, if we did not originally choose the car, then we win if we switch and lose if we don't. The function should return `True` if we win and `False` if we lose.

Now write a function

    `monteMonty(trials)`

that performs a Monte Carlo simulation with the given number of trials to find the probability of winning if we decide to switch doors. For each trial, choose a random door number (between 0 and 2), and call the `montyHall` function with your choice and `switch = True`. Count the number of times we win, and return this number divided by the number of trials. Can you explain the result?

5.1.19. The value of π can be estimated with Monte Carlo simulation. Suppose you draw a circle on the wall with radius 1, inscribed inside a square with side length 2, as shown to the right. You then close your eyes and throw darts at the circle. Assuming every dart lands inside the square, the fraction of the darts that land in the circle estimates the ratio between the area of the circle and the area of the square. We know that the area of the circle is $C = \pi r^2 = \pi 1^2 = \pi$ and the area of the square is $S = 2^2 = 4$. So the exact ratio is $\pi/4$. With enough darts, f, the fraction (between 0 and 1) that lands in the circle will approximate this ratio: $f \approx \pi/4$, which means that $\pi \approx 4f$.

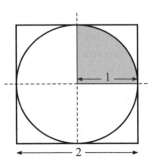

To make matters a little simpler, we can just throw darts in the upper right quarter of the circle (shaded above). The ratio here is the same: $(\pi/4)/1 = \pi/4$. If we place this quarter circle on x and y axes, with the center of the circle at $(0,0)$, our darts will now all land at points with x and y coordinates between 0 and 1. Use this idea to write a function

    `montePi(darts)`

that approximates the value π by repeatedly throwing random virtual darts that land at points with x and y coordinates in [0,1). Count the number that land at points within distance 1 of the origin, and return this fraction.

5.1.20. The Good, The Bad, and The Ugly are in a three-way gun fight (sometimes called a "truel"). The Good always hits his target with probability 0.8, The Bad always hits his target with probability 0.7, and The Ugly always hits his target with probability 0.6. Initially, The Good aims at The Bad, The Bad aims at The Good, and The Ugly aims at The Bad. The gunmen shoot simultaneously. In the next round, each gunman, if he is still standing, aims at his same target, if that target is alive, or at the other gunman, if there is one, otherwise. This continues until only one gunman is standing or all are dead. What is the probability that they all die? What is the probability that The Good survives? What about The Bad? The Ugly? On average, how many rounds are there? Write a function

    `goodBadUgly()`

that simulates one instance of this three-way gun fight. Your function should return 1, 2, 3, or 0 depending upon whether The Good, The Bad, The Ugly, or nobody is left standing, respectively. Next, write a function

    `monteGBU(trials)`

that calls your `goodBadUgly` function repeatedly in a Monte Carlo simulation to answer the questions above.

*5.2 PSEUDORANDOM NUMBER GENERATORS

This section is available on the book website.

*5.3 SIMULATING PROBABILITY DISTRIBUTIONS

This section is available on the book website.

5.4   BACK TO BOOLEANS

In this section, we will further develop your facility with conditional expressions and Boolean logic. (If your Boolean logic is rusty, you may want to review Section 3.2 first.)

In Python, Boolean expressions evaluate to either the value `True` or the value `False`, which correspond to the binary values 1 and 0, respectively, that we worked with in Section 3.2. The values `True` and `False` can be printed, assigned to variable names, and manipulated just like numeric values. For example, try the following examples and make sure you understand each result.

```
>>> print(0 < 1)
True
>>> result = 0 > 1
>>> print(result)
False
>>> name = 'Kermit'
>>> print(name == 'Gonzo')
False
```

The "double equals" (`==`) operator tests for equality; it has nothing to do with assignment. The Python interpreter will remind you if you mistakenly use a single equals in an `if` statement. For example, try this:

```
>>> if value = 0:
    if value = 0:
            ^
SyntaxError: invalid syntax
```

However, the interpreter will *not* catch the error if you mistakenly use `==` in an assignment statement. For example, try this:

```
>>> value = 1
>>> value == value + 1    # increment value?
False
```

In a program, nothing will be printed as a result of the second statement, and `value` will not be incremented as expected. So be careful!

As we saw in Section 3.2, Boolean expressions can be combined with the ***Boolean operators*** (or *logical operators*) **and**, **or**, and **not**. As a reminder, Figure 5.3 contains the truth tables for the three Boolean operators, expressed in Python notation. In the tables, the variable names `a` and `b` represent arbitrary Boolean variables or expressions.

For example, suppose we wanted to determine whether a household has an annual income within some range, say $40,000 to $65,000. We can use an `and` operator, as we initially did to check if `randi` was within an interval earlier.

a	b	a and b	a or b	not a
False	False	False	False	True
False	True	False	True	True
True	False	False	True	False
True	True	True	True	False

Figure 5.3 Combined truth table for the three Python Boolean operators.

```
>>> pay = 53000
>>> (pay >= 40000) and (pay <= 65000)
True
>>> pay = 12000
>>> (pay >= 40000) and (pay <= 65000)
False
>>> pay = 78000
>>> (pay >= 40000) and (pay <= 65000)
False
```

When 53000 is assigned to pay, the two Boolean expressions pay >= 40000 and pay <= 65000 are both True, so (pay >= 40000) and (pay <= 65000) is also True, as summarized in the table below.

pay	pay >= 40000	pay <= 65000	(pay >= 40000) and (pay <= 65000)
53000	True	True	True
12000	False	True	False
78000	True	False	False

However, as shown in the second and third rows, when 12000 or 78000 is assigned to pay, one of the components in the and expression is False, so the entire and expression is also False.

Using an or operator in this situation would be incorrect, as you can see below.

pay	pay >= 40000	pay <= 65000	(pay >= 40000) or (pay <= 65000)
53000	True	True	True
12000	False	True	True
78000	True	False	True

Since an or expression is True if at least one of its operands is True, the expression (pay >= 40000) or (pay <= 65000) will be True for *every* possible value of pay! (Think about it.)

Predicate functions

We can incorporate this income test into a function like this:

```python
def middleClass(pay):
    """Decide whether an income is classified as "middle class."

    Parameter:
        pay: annual household income

    Return: Boolean value indicating whether pay is a middle class income
    """

    if (pay >= 40000) and (pay <= 65000):
        result = True
    else:
        result = False
    return result
```

Functions that return Boolean values are called ***predicate functions***. Calling `middleClass(53000)` will return the value True while `middleClass(12000)` will return False. But this function is equivalent to one that just returns the value of the Boolean expression:

```python
def middleClass(pay):
    """ (docstring omitted) """

    return (pay >= 40000) and (pay <= 65000)
```

To see that these two functions return identical values, notice that the return value in the first version is always the same as the value of the expression `(pay >= 40000) and (pay <= 65000)`. If the expression is True, the function returns True. If the expression is False, the function returns False. So simply returning the value of the expression, as in the second version, accomplishes the same thing.

As another example, suppose we wanted to write a function to decide, in some for-profit company, whether the CEO's compensation divided by the average employees' is at most some "fair" ratio. A simple function that returns the result of this test looks like this:

```python
def fair(employee, ceo, ratio):
    """Decide whether the ratio of CEO to employee pay is fair.

    Parameters:
        employee: average employee pay
        ceo:      CEO pay
        ratio:    the fair ratio

    Return:
        a Boolean indicating whether ceo / employee is fair
    """

    return (ceo / employee) <= ratio
```

Reflection 5.8 *There is a subtle problem though with this function. What is it?*

This function will not always work properly because, if the average employees'
compensation equals zero (or zero is mistakenly passed in), the division operation
will result in an error. Therefore, we have to test whether `employee == 0` before
attempting the division and, if so, return `False` (because not paying employees is
obviously not fair). Otherwise, we want to return the result of the fairness test. The
following function implements this algorithm.

```python
def fair(employee, ceo, ratio):
    """ (docstring omitted) """

    if employee == 0:
        result = False
    else:
        result = (ceo / employee) <= ratio
    return result
```

Short circuit evaluation

The `fair` function can be simplified by making use of a feature that Python applies
to both the `and` and `or` operators called *short circuit evaluation*. Since only
one operand of an `and` expression must be `False` for the expression to be `False`,
the Python interpreter does not bother to evaluate the second operand in an `and`
expression if the first is `False`. Likewise, since only one operand of an `or` expression
must be `True` for the expression to be `True`, the Python interpreter does not bother
to evaluate the second operand in an `or` expression if the first is `True`.

This means that our `fair` function can be simplified to:

```python
def fair(employee, ceo, ratio):
    """ (docstring omitted) """

    return (employee != 0) and ((ceo / employee) <= ratio)
```

If `employee` is 0, then `(employee != 0)` is `False`, and the function returns
`False` *without* evaluating `(ceo / employee <= ratio)`. On the other hand, if
`(employee != 0)` is `True`, then `(ceo / employee <= ratio)` is evaluated, and
the return value depends on this outcome. Notice that this would not work if the
`and` operator did not use short circuit evaluation because, if `(employee != 0)` were
`False` and then `(ceo / employee <= ratio)` was evaluated, the division would
result in a "divide by zero" error!

To illustrate the analogous mechanism with the `or` operator, suppose we wanted to
write the function in the opposite way, instead returning `True` if the ratio is unfair.
The first version of the function would look like this:

```
def unfair(employee, ceo, ratio):
    """ (docstring omitted) """

    if employee == 0:
        result = True
    else:
        result = (ceo / employee) > ratio
    return result
```

However, taking advantage of short circuit evaluation with the **or** operator, we can simplify the whole function to:

```
def unfair(employee, ceo, ratio):
    """ (docstring omitted) """

    return (employee == 0) or ((ceo / employee) > ratio)
```

In this case, if (`employee == 0`) is True, the whole expression returns True *without* evaluating the division test, thus avoiding an error. On the other hand, if (`employee == 0`) is False, the division test is evaluated, and the final result is equal to the outcome of this test.

DeMorgan's laws

Let's now create a new function that uses a **while** loop to repeatedly prompt for employee and CEO salaries, and decide whether the ratio is fair. The function will ask at the end of each iteration whether it should continue.

```
def fairnessChecker():
    """ (docstring omitted) """

    ratio = float(input('Maximum fair ceo:employee pay ratio: '))
    answer = 'y'
    while answer != 'n':
        employee = float(input('Employee pay: '))
        ceo = float(input('CEO pay: '))
        if fair(employee, ceo, ratio):
            print("That's fair.")
        else:
            print("That's not fair.")
        answer = input('Continue (y/n)? ')
```

| **Reflection 5.9** *Why is* answer *initialized to* 'y' *before the loop?*

The function repeatedly prompts for salaries while **answer**, which is obtained at the end of the loop body, is not **'n'**. If **answer** is not initialized before the loop, then the **while** loop condition will not make sense before the first iteration. If it is not initialized to something other than `'n'`, then the loop will not iterate the first time. It could be intialized to anything other than `'n'`, but `'y'` makes the most sense. Notice also that, because `fair` is a predicate function, we simply use its return value as the Boolean condition in the `if` statement.

How can we modify the `while` loop condition to also allow an uppercase `'N'` to exit the loop? Should the `while` loop condition be changed to

    (answer != 'n') and (answer != 'N')

or to

    (answer != 'n') or (answer != 'N') ?

To make the correct choice, it sometimes helps to think about the opposite situation: when we want the loop to *stop*. This is rather easy in this case: when `answer` is either `'n'` or `'N'`. In other words, we want the loop to stop when `(answer == 'n') or (answer == 'N')`. So the `while` loop condition needs to be the negation of this, or:

    not((answer == 'n') or (answer == 'N')) .

We can use *De Morgan's laws*, named after 19th century British mathematician Augustus De Morgan, to express this condition in a different way. They are:

1. **not** (a **and** b) is equivalent to **not** a **or not** b.

2. **not** (a **or** b) is equivalent to **not** a **and not** b.

You may recognize these from Exercises 3.2.12 and 3.2.13, which asked you to construct the following truth tables to prove the laws' veracity!

a	b	a **and** b	**not**(a **and** b)	**not** a	**not** b	**not** a **or not** b
0	0	0	1	1	1	1
0	1	0	1	1	0	1
1	0	0	1	0	1	1
1	1	1	0	0	0	0

a	b	a **or** b	**not**(a **or** b)	**not** a	**not** b	**not** a **and not** b
0	0	0	1	1	1	1
0	1	1	0	1	0	0
1	0	1	0	0	1	0
1	1	1	0	0	0	0

The first law says that a **and** b is false if either a is false or b is false. The second law says that a **or** b is false if both a is false and b is false. Applying the first law to our condition, we find that `not((answer == 'n') or (answer == 'N'))` is equivalent to

    not (answer == 'n') and not (answer == 'N')

or

    (answer != 'n') and (answer != 'N') .

	Operators	Description
1.	**	exponentiation (power)
2.	+, -	unary positive and negative
3.	*, /, //, %	multiplication and division
4.	+, -	addition and subtraction
5.	<, <=, >, >=, !=, ==, in, not in	comparison operators
6.	not	Boolean **not**
7.	and	Boolean **and**
8.	or	Boolean **or**

Table 5.2 Operator precedence, listed from highest to lowest. This is an expanded version of Table 1.1.

Incorporating this new condition into the `while` loop in `fairnessChecker` is easy.

Let's take the complexity one step further by changing two things. First, let's stop the loop when a fair pay ratio is obtained. Second, instead of iterating while **answer** is anything but `'n'` or `'N'`, let's iterate only while **answer** is either `'y'` or `'Y'`. These changes are incorporated into the following revised function.

```
 1 def fairnessChecker():
 2     """ (docstring omitted) """

 3     ratio = float(input('Maximum fair ceo:employee pay ratio: '))
 4     answer = 'y'
 5     isFair = False
 6     while (answer == 'y' or answer == 'Y') and not isFair:
 7         employee = float(input('Employee pay: '))
 8         ceo = float(input('CEO pay: '))
 9         isFair = fair(employee, ceo, ratio)
10         if isFair:
11             print("That's fair.")
12         else:
13             print("That's not fair.")
14             answer = input('Continue (y/n)? ')
```

We have changed the test involving **answer** on line 6 and introduced a new Boolean flag variable **isFair** to keep track of whether the current pay ratio is fair. Notice that, to keep the `while` loop going, we need *both* **answer** to be `'y'` or `'Y'` *and* for the pay ratio to be unfair, that is, `not isFair`. We have been using parentheses around certain expressions in this section mostly for clarity, but the parentheses in this `while` loop condition are actually necessary. As shown in Table 5.2, the **and** operator has precedence over the **or** operator. Therefore, without the parentheses, the expression `answer == 'Y' and not isFair` would be evaluated first, and that would not make sense.

The variable `isFair` is initialized to `False` before the loop so that it iterates at least once, and assigned within the loop on line 9 to be the value returned by the `fair` function. To avoid unnecessarily calling `fair` twice, we also use `isFair` as the `if` condition. We also now only prompt to continue if the pay ratio is not fair.

Thinking inside the box

Let's next use a random walk simulation to analyze how long it takes for a particle (or a person) to escape an enclosed space. This sort of scenario can also simulate how likely it is for a virus to escape quarantine if there is a slight chance of a break out. We will use turtle graphics to visualize a simple square room with a door, as shown below:

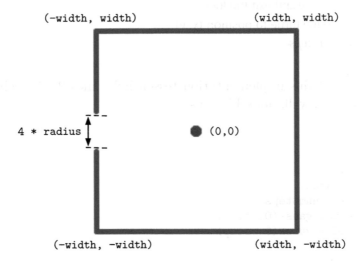

The variables `width` and `radius` will be set to half the width of the room and the radius of the particle, respectively. We want to move the particle randomly in the room while also respecting the walls. For the particle movement, we will use a slightly different random walk in which the amount added to the particle's position is dictated by a normal probability distribution with mean zero. (Also see Exercise 5.3.1.) Here is the overall idea of the algorithm in pseudocode.

Algorithm ESCAPE

Input: *width* of the room

```
 1  draw the room with the given width and create a turtle
 2  x ← 0
 3  y ← 0
 4  number of steps ← 0
 5  repeat while the particle has not escaped:
 6      number of steps ← number of steps + 1
 7      make one normally distributed step, modifying x and y
 8      if the particle hits a wall, then:
 9          bounce back to the previous position
10      else if the particle finds the door, then:
11          escape and exit the loop
12      move the turtle to position (x, y)
```

Output: *number of steps*

The easier parts of this implementation (essentially lines 2–7), including how to perform the random walk, look like this:

```
x = 0       # position of the particle
y = 0
escaped = False
numSteps = 0
while not escaped:
    numSteps = numSteps + 1
    dx = random.gauss(0, step)  # normal with mean 0 and std dev step
    dy = random.gauss(0, step)
    x = x + dx
    y = y + dy

    # bounce off the walls and set escaped to True if
    # the particle finds the door

    particle.goto(x, y)
```

Since the normal (i.e., Gaussian) distribution is centered at zero, `dx` and `dy` can be either positive or negative, meaning that the particle can move in any direction. The random walk will continue until the Boolean variable `escaped` is set to `True`, which we will implement next.

When the particle hits a wall, we want it to "bounce" back to its previous position. We can tell that the left edge of the particle is touching the west wall if (`x - radius <= -width`) is true. Similarly, if (`x + radius >= width`) is true, then the right edge of the particle must be touching the east wall. By combining these with analogous expressions for the north and south walls, we can make the particle bounce back like this:

```
if (x - radius <= -width) or (x + radius >= width) \
   or (y - radius <= -width) or (y + radius >= width):
    x = x - dx    # return to previous position
    y = y - dy
```

Reflection 5.10 *Why is* or *the correct Boolean operator here? When would the expression be true if we used* and *instead?*

To incorporate the door, we need to modify the condition so that it excludes the opening in the west wall. The door opening extends from y coordinate `-2 * radius` at the bottom to `2 * radius` at the top. So we will know if the particle is in the doorway if it is touching the west wall and

$$\text{(y - radius >= -2 * radius) and (y + radius <= 2 * radius),}$$

or equivalently, `(y >= -radius) and (y <= radius)`. But we need the negation of this expression so we can *exclude* the opening in the "bounce" condition.

Reflection 5.11 *What is the negation of* `(y >= -radius) and (y <= radius)`*?*

Using DeMorgan's laws, the negation of this expression is

$$\text{not(y >= -radius) or not(y <= radius).}$$

Or equivalently,

$$\text{(y < -radius) or (y > radius).}$$

Therefore, the modified `if` condition, causing the particle to bounce back when it touches a wall, is:

```
if ((x <= -width + radius) and ((y < -radius) or (y > radius))) \
   or (x >= width - radius) or (y <= -width + radius) \
   or (y >= width - radius):
    x = x - dx
    y = y - dy
elif (x <= -width + radius) and ((y >= -radius) and (y <= radius)):
    escaped = True
```

Note that the outer parentheses around `((y < -radius) or (y > radius))` are necessary to ensure that the expression is evaluated correctly. We added an `elif` clause to catch when the particle has found the open doorway and set the flag variable to `True` to end the `while` loop. The finished function, with drawing statements omitted, follows. The complete function can be found on the book website.

```
import random
import turtle

def escape(width):
    """Compute the number of steps required for a randomly moving
       particle to escape a square room with a door.

    Parameter:
        width: the width of the room

    Return value: the number of steps needed to escape
    """

    step = 15        # standard deviation of one particle step
    radius = 10      # radius of the particle

    # draw the room and create a turtle named particle here (omitted)

    x = 0            # position of the particle
    y = 0
    escaped = False
    numSteps = 0
    while not escaped:
        numSteps = numSteps + 1
        dx = random.gauss(0, step)   # normal with mean 0 and std dev step
        dy = random.gauss(0, step)
        x = x + dx
        y = y + dy

        if ((x <= -width + radius) and ((y < -radius) or (y > radius))) \
           or (x >= width - radius) or (y <= -width + radius) \
           or (y >= width - radius):
            x = x - dx
            y = y - dy
        elif (x <= -width + radius) and ((y >= -radius) and (y <= radius)):
            escaped = True

        particle.goto(x, y)

    return numSteps
```

▌ Reflection 5.12 *How can we confirm that this expression is really correct?*

To confirm that any Boolean expression is correct, we can create a truth table for it, and then confirm that every case matches what we intended. This is often not really necessary in practice but, at times, with really complex situations, it can reassuring. We will illustrate by just considering the expression testing whether the particle is touching the west wall but is not in the doorway:

```
(x <= -width + radius) and ((y < -radius) or (y > radius))
```

In this expression, there are three separate Boolean "inputs," one for each expression containing a comparison operator. In the truth table, we will represent each of these with a letter to save space:

- `(x <= -width + radius)` will be represented by a,
- `(y < -radius)` will be represented by b, and
- `(y > radius)` will be represented by c.

So the final expression we want to evaluate is a and $(b$ or $c)$.

In the truth table below, the first three columns represent our three inputs. With three inputs, we need $2^3 = 8$ rows, one for each possible assignment of truth values. There is a trick to quickly writing down all the truth value combinations; see if you can spot it in the first three columns. (We are using T and F as abbreviations for True and False.)

a	b	c	b or c	a and $(b$ or $c)$
F	F	F	F	F
F	F	T	T	F
F	T	F	T	F
F	T	T	T	F
T	F	F	F	F
T	F	T	T	T
T	T	F	T	T
T	T	T	T	T

We need to first evaluate `(y < -radius)` or `(y > radius)`. The result, shown in the fourth column, is the **or** of the second and third columns. Then, in the fifth column, we **and** the first column with the fourth to get our final result. This column says that the expression is true in the three highlighted cases. For our expression to be correct, these need to be exactly the situations in which we want the particle to bounce off the west wall. (We can assume that the particle is also within the proper y bounds because that is checked elsewhere in the original expression.) Let's examine each highlighted row to make sure that this result is correct:

- row 6: a is true, b is false, and c is true

  In this case, `(x <= -width + radius)` is true, `(y < -radius)` is false, and `(y > radius)` is true. So the particle is touching the wall and is not below the door and is above the door. Check.

- row 7: a is true, b is true, and c is false

  In the second case, `(x <= -width + radius)` is true, `(y < -radius)` is true, and `(y > radius)` is false. So the particle is touching the wall and is below the door and is not above the door. Check.

- row 8: *a* is true, *b* is true, and *c* is true

  Finally, this case is when all three are true. So the particle is touching the wall and is below the door and is above the door. This cannot possibly happen, so it doesn't matter that the expression is (oddly) true. Check.

Many happy returns

We often come across situations in which we want a function to return different values depending on the outcome of a condition. The simplest example is finding the maximum of two numbers `a` and `b`. If `a` is at least as large as `b`, we want to return `a`; otherwise, `b` must be larger, so we return `b`.

```
def max(a, b):
    """ (docstring omitted) """

    if a >= b:
        result = a
    else:
        result = b
    return result
```

We can simplify this function a bit by returning the appropriate value right in the `if/else` statement:

```
def max(a, b):
    """ (docstring omitted) """

    if a >= b:
        return a
    else:
        return b
```

It may look strange at first to see two **return** statements in one function, but it all makes perfect sense. Recall from Section 2.5 that **return** *both* ends the function *and* assigns the function's return value. So this means that at most one **return** statement can ever be executed in a function. In this case, if `a >= b` is True, the function ends and returns the value of `a`. Otherwise, the function executes the `else` clause, which returns the value of `b`.

The fact that the function ends if `a >= b` is True means that we can simplify it even further: if execution continues past the `if` part of the `if/else`, it *must* be the case that `a >= b` is False. So the `else` is extraneous; the function can be simplified to:

```
def max(a, b):
    """ (docstring omitted) """

    if a >= b:
        return a
    return b
```

This same principle can be applied to situations with more than two cases. Suppose we wanted to use `if` statements to convert a percentage grade to a grade point (i.e., GPA) on a 0–4 scale. A natural implementation of this might look like the following:

```
def assignGP(score):
    """Returns the grade point equivalent of score.

    Parameter:
        score: a score between 0 and 100

    Return value: the equivalent grade point value
    """

    if score >= 90:
        return 4
    elif score >= 80:
        return 3
    elif score >= 70:
        return 2
    elif score >= 60:
        return 1
    else:
        return 0
```

Reflection 5.13 *Why do we not need to check upper bounds on the scores in each case? In other words, why does the second condition not need to be* `score >= 80 and score < 90`*?*

Suppose `score` was 92. Then the first condition is `True`, so the function returns the value 4 and ends. Execution never proceeds past the statement `return 4`. For this reason, the "el" in the next `elif` is extraneous. In other words, because execution would never have made it there if the previous condition was `True`, there is no need to tell the interpreter to skip testing this condition if that was the case.

Now suppose `score` was 82. In this case, the first condition would be `False`, so we continue on to the first `elif` condition. Because we got to this point, we already know that `score < 90` (hence the omission of that check). The first `elif` condition is `True`, so we immediately return the value 3. So there is no need for the "el" in the second `elif` either because there is no need to skip testing this condition if either of the previous conditions were `True`. In fact, we can remove the "el"s from all of the `elif`s, and the final `else`, with no loss in efficiency at all.

```
def assignGP(score):
    """ (docstring omitted) """

    if score >= 90:
        return 4
    if score >= 80:
        return 3
    if score >= 70:
        return 2
    if score >= 60:
        return 1
    return 0
```

Some programmers find it clearer to leave the elif statements in, and that is fine too. We will do it both ways in the coming chapters. But, as you begin to see more algorithms, you will probably see code like this, and so it is important to understand why it is correct.

Exercises

Write a function for each of the following exercises. Test each one with both common and boundary case arguments, as described on page 38, and document your test cases.

5.4.1*   Write a function

   password()

   that asks for a username and a password. It should return True if the username is entered as **alan.turing** and the password is entered as **notTouring**, and return False otherwise.

5.4.2.   Suppose that in a game that you are making, the player wins if her score is at least 100. Write a function

   hasWon(score)

   that returns True if she has won, and False otherwise.

5.4.3.   Suppose you have designed a sensor that people can wear to monitor their health. One task of this sensor is to monitor body temperature: if it falls outside the range 97.9° F to 99.3° F, the person may be getting sick. Write a function

   monitor(temperature)

   that takes a temperature (in Fahrenheit) as a parameter, and returns True if **temperature** falls in the healthy range and False otherwise.

5.4.4*   A year is a leap year if it is divisible by four, unless it is a century year in which case it must be divisible by 400. For example, 2028 and 1600 are leap years, but 2027 and 1800 are not. Write a function

   leapYear(year)

   that returns the value of a single Boolean expression to indicate whether the year is a leap year. Also write a function

   leapYears(beginYear, endYear)

that uses your `leapYear` function to return a list of all the leap years between (and including) the two years given as parameters.

5.4.5* Write a function

```
nextLeapYear(afterYear)
```

that uses your `leapYear` function from the previous exercise to return the closest leap year after the year given as a parameter.

5.4.6. Write a function

```
even(number)
```

that returns `True` if `number` is even, and `False` otherwise.

5.4.7* Write a function

```
between(number, low, high)
```

that returns `True` if `number` is in the interval [`low`,`high`] (between `low` and `high`, including both `low` and `high`), and `False` otherwise.

5.4.8. Write a function

```
justOne(a, b)
```

that returns `True` if exactly one (but not both) of the numbers a or b is 10, and `False` otherwise.

5.4.9. Write a function

```
roll()
```

that simulates rolling two of the loaded dice implemented in Exercise 5.1.9 (by calling the function `loaded`), and returns `True` if the sum of the dice is 7 or 11, or `False` otherwise.

5.4.10. The following function returns a Boolean value indicating whether an integer `number` is a perfect square. Rewrite the function in one line, taking advantage of the short-circuit evaluation of `and` expressions.

```
def perfectSquare(number):
    if number < 0:
        return False
    else:
        return math.sqrt(number) == int(math.sqrt(number))
```

5.4.11. Write a function

```
previousSquare(before)
```

that uses your `perfectSquare` function from the previous exercise to return the maximum perfect square smaller than the number given as a parameter. If the parameter is not positive, return 0.

5.4.12* Write a function

```
winner(score1, score2)
```

that returns 1 or 2, indicating whether the winner of a game is Player 1 or Player 2. The higher score wins and you can assume that there are no ties.

5.4.13. Repeat the previous exercise, but also return 0 to indicate a tie.

5.4.14* Your firm is looking to buy computers from a distributor for $1500 per machine. The distributor will give you a 5% discount if you purchase more than 20 computers. Write a function

`cost(quantity)`

that takes as a parameter the `quantity` of computers you wish to buy, and returns the cost of buying them from this distributor.

5.4.15. Repeat the previous exercise, but add three more parameters: the cost per machine, the number of computers necessary to get a discount, and the discount.

5.4.16. The speeding ticket fine in a nearby town is $50 plus $5 for each mph over the posted speed limit. In addition, there is an extra penalty of $200 for all speeds above 90 mph. Write a function

`fine(speedLimit, clockedSpeed)`

that returns the fine amount (or 0 if `clockedSpeed` ≤ `speedLimit`).

5.4.17. Write a function

`gradeRemark()`

that prompts for a grade, and then returns the corresponding remark (as a string) from the table to the right.

Grade	Remark
96–100	Outstanding
90–95	Exceeds expectations
80–89	Acceptable
1–79	Trollish

5.4.18. Write a function that takes two integer values as parameters and returns their sum if they are not equal and their product if they are.

5.4.19. Write a function

`amIRich(amount, rate, years)`

that accumulates interest on `amount` dollars at an annual rate of `rate` percent for a number of `years`. If your final investment is at least double your original amount, return `True`; otherwise, return `False`.

5.4.20* Write a function

`maxOfThree(a, b, c)`

the returns the maximum value of the parameters a, b, and c. Be sure to test it with many different numbers, including some that are equal.

5.4.21. Write a function

`shipping(amount)`

that returns the shipping charge for an online retailer based on a purchase of `amount` dollars. The company charges a flat rate of $6.95 for purchases up to $100, plus 5% of the amount over $100.

5.4.22* Write a function

`oddFactors(number)`

that returns a list of all of the odd factors of the given number. For example, `oddFactors(66)` should return the list `[3, 11, 33]`.

5.4.23. Write a function

> commonFactors(number1, number2)

that returns a list containing all of the common factors of two numbers. For example, commonFactors(18, 36) should return the list [2, 3, 6, 9, 18].

5.4.24. Write a function

> isPrime(number)

that checks whether a given number is prime. The function should return True if the number is prime and False otherwise. (Use a for loop.) Then write a function

> primes(begin, end)

that uses your isPrime function to return a list of all prime numbers between (and including) the two numbers given as parameters.

5.4.25. Write a function

> nextPrime(after)

that uses your isPrime function from the previous exercise to return the smallest prime number after the number given as a parameter.

5.4.26. Starting with two positive integers a and b, consider the sequence in which the next number is the digit in the ones place of the sum of the previous two numbers. For example, if $a = 1$ and $b = 1$, the sequence is $1, 1, 2, 3, 5, 8, 3, 1, 4, 5, 9, 4, 3, 7, 0, \ldots$ Write a function

> mystery(a, b)

that returns the length of the sequence when the last two numbers repeat the values of a and b for the first time. (When $a = 1$ and $b = 1$, the function should return 62.)

5.4.27. The Chinese zodiac relates each year to an animal in a twelve-year cycle. The animals for one particular cycle are given in the table to the right. Write a function

> zodiac(year)

that takes as a parameter a year (this could be any year in the past or future) and returns the corresponding animal as a string. Then write another function

Year	Animal	Year	Animal
2004	monkey	2010	tiger
2005	rooster	2011	rabbit
2006	dog	2012	dragon
2007	pig	2013	snake
2008	rat	2014	horse
2009	ox	2015	goat

> zodiacTable(beginYear, endYear)

that uses your zodiac function to print a table of the zodiac animals for all years between (and including) the two parameters.

5.4.28. Consider the rwMonteCarlo function on page 173. What will the function return if trials equals 0? What if trials is negative? Propose a way to deal with these issues by adding statements to the function.

5.4.29. Write a Boolean expression that is true if a point (x,y) resides in either of the shaded boxes below (including their boundaries), and false otherwise. Assume that the particle is not able to ever roam outside the outermost square. The shaded rectangle on the right represents all points with x coordinates at least d.

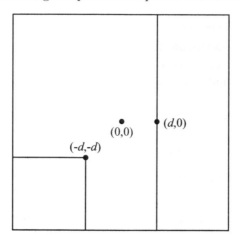

5.4.30. Use a truth table to show that the expression you derived in the previous exercise is correct.

5.4.31. Use a truth table to show that the Boolean expressions

```
(x > d and y > d) or (x < -d and y > d)
```

and

```
(y > d) and (x > d or x < -d)
```

are equivalent.

5.4.32. Write a function

```
drawRow(tortoise, row)
```

that uses turtle graphics to draw one row of an 8×8 red/black checkerboard. If the value of **row** is even, the row should start with a red square; otherwise, it should start with a black square. You may want to use the **drawSquare** function you wrote in Exercise 2.3.11. Your function should only need one **for** loop and only need to draw one square in each iteration.

5.4.33. Write a function

```
checkerBoard(tortoise)
```

that draws an 8×8 red/black checkerboard, using the function you wrote in Exercise 5.4.32.

5.5 DEFENSIVE PROGRAMMING

At the end of the first chapter, we previewed the coming attractions by pointing out that once your toolbox contained the four types of statements you now know—assignments, arithmetic, loops, and conditionals—the possibilities were endless. But with great power comes great responsibility.[1] On the one hand, you can let your creativity flourish; on the other hand, you know enough to get yourself into convoluted situations that are harder to debug. So it is time to start taking a more deliberate approach to writing correct programs. Our strategy will be twofold. First, we will think more carefully and rigorously about what the inputs to a problem should look like and anticipate what might go awry if they don't. Second, we will start testing each function more formally with carefully chosen inputs to make sure it really does what we think it does.

Checking parameters

When we are identifying the input to a problem, we need to also think about constraints on the input. What class(es) should the input belong to? What range of values make sense for the problem? How should the algorithm or function behave if it receives input that doesn't make sense? Thinking about these issues proactively in advance, *defensively*, tends to result in more robust and correct programs. This is especially important if other people are going to use your programs because you cannot control what (foolish) things they might do. Taken further, defensive programming is a key component of **computer security**. A security analyst's job is to anticipate how a criminal might exploit errors in a program to gain access to files and resources that should be off-limits.

To illustrate these strategies, we will revisit the `leapYear` and `nextLeapYear` functions from Exercises 5.4.4–5.4.5. Here are possible implementations of these functions.

```python
def leapYear(year):
    """Determine whether a year is a leap year.

    Parameter:
        year: an integer year

    Return value: a Boolean value indicating whether year is a leap year
    """

    if year % 100 != 0:          # if year is not a century year
        return year % 4 == 0     #   it is a leap year if divisible by 4
    else:                        # else if year is a century year
        return year % 400 == 0   #   it is a leap year if divisible by 400
```

---

[1] Also known as the Peter Parker principle.

```
def nextLeapYear(afterYear):
    """Determine the next leap year after a given year.

    Parameter:
        afterYear: an integer year

    Return value: the next leap year
    """

    year = afterYear + 1        # start looking in the next year
    while not leapYear(year):    # while we haven't found a leap year
        year = year + 1          #   keep looking ...
    return year
```

Reflection 5.14 *In the* `leapYear` *function, are there any values of* `year` *that should be disallowed?*

To answer this question, it helps to know something about the Gregorian calendar, which is divided into two eras: the Common Era (CE) and Before the Common Era (BCE) (or AD and BC in the Christian tradition). Both CE and BCE start at year one; there is no year zero. Therefore, since the function does not allow a way to specify CE or BCE, we should assume that only CE years, starting at year one, are allowed. If any value of `year` less than one is given, we will simply return `False` by inserting an `if` statement at the beginning of the function.

```
def leapYear(year):
    """Determine whether a year is a leap year.

    Parameter:
        year: an integer year greater than zero in the Common Era

    Return value: a Boolean value indicating whether year is a leap year
    """

    if year < 1:
        return False

    if year % 100 != 0:          # if year is not a century year
        return year % 4 == 0     #   it is a leap year if divisible by 4
    else:                        # else if year is a century year
        return year % 400 == 0   #   it is a leap year if divisible by 400
```

The highlighted requirement that `year` must be an integer greater than zero is called a **precondition**. A precondition for a function is something that must be true when the function is called for the function to behave correctly. But our `leapYear` function currently only enforces part of the stated precondition.

Reflection 5.15 *What happens if the argument passed in for* `year` *is not an integer? For example, try calling* `leapYear('cookies')`.

Calling `leapYear('cookies')` results in the following error:

`TypeError: not all arguments converted during string formatting`

This happens when the `%` operator is applied to the value of `year`, which is `'cookies'`, and 100 in the first `if` statement. Because `year` is a string, Python is interpreting this expression as an old kind of string formatting operation that we don't cover. To avoid this rather opaque error message, we need to make sure that `year` is an integer at the beginning of the function. We can do this with the `isinstance` function, which takes two arguments: a value and the name of a class. The function returns `True` if the variable or value refers to an object (i.e., instance) of the class, and `False` otherwise. For example,

```
>>> isinstance(5.0, int)
False
>>> isinstance(5.0, float)
True
>>> word = 'cookies'
>>> isinstance(word, str)
True
>>> isinstance(word, int)
False
```

To use this in the `leapYear` function, we replace the first `if` statement with

```
if not isinstance(year, int) or (year < 1):
    return False
```

▌ Reflection 5.16 *The order of the two conditions in the* or *expression is important. Why?*

Similar to a precondition, the **postcondition** for a function is a statement of what must be true when the function finishes. A postcondition usually specifies what the function returns and what, if any, side effects it has. Recall that a side effect occurs when a global variable is modified or some other event in a function modifies a global resource. For example, calls to `print` and modifications of files are considered to be side effects because they have impacts outside of the function itself.

▌ Reflection 5.17 *What is the postcondition of the* `leapYear` *function?*

The postcondition for the `leapYear` function is that the function returns a Boolean indicating whether `year` is a leap year, which is already stated in the docstring. Because they describe the input and output of a function, and therefore how the function can be used, preconditions and postconditions are often included explicitly in the docstring. For now, we will retain our docstring format and just make sure that preconditions and postconditions are implicitly stated in our parameter and return value sections.

The use of preconditions and postconditions is called **design by contract** because the precondition and postcondition establish a contract between the function designer and the function caller. The function caller understands that the precondition must be met before the function is called and the function designer guarantees that, if the precondition is met, the postcondition will also be met.

Now let's look at the `nextLeapYear` function.

Reflection 5.18 *In the* `nextLeapYear` *function, what happens if* `afterYear` *is a float? Or something else? Or a negative integer?*

The precondition for the `nextLeapYear` function should be the same as the `leapYear` function since the parameter is also a year in CE. Indeed, if `afterYear` is anything but an `int`, then the `while` loop will be infinite because we modified `leapYear` to always return `False` in these cases! So we definitely need to check that `afterYear` is an `int` but making sure it is positive is a judgment call. If `afterYear` is a negative integer, one could argue that the function behaves correctly because it will eventually return 4, the smallest leap year in CE. On the other hand, passing in any year less than one is technically an error because there are no valid years less than one in CE. When in doubt, it is best to take the more cautious approach to prevent the most errors.

Reflection 5.19 *What should the* `nextLeapYear` *function return if the precondition is not met?*

Knowing what to return in this case is trickier. One option would be to return `None`. But this could be inconvenient for a calling function to handle because the possible return values are of two different types. An alternative would be to return the same type as the normal return value (an `int`) but a value that the function would not otherwise return, like zero in this case. This behavior needs to be clearly stated in the docstring as part of the function's postcondition.

```
def nextLeapYear(afterYear):
    """Determine the next leap year after a given year.

    Parameter:
        afterYear: an integer year greater than zero in the Common Era

    Return value: the next leap year or zero if afterYear is not
                  a positive integer
    """

    if not isinstance(afterYear, int) or (afterYear < 1):
        return 0

    year = afterYear + 1        # start looking in the next year
    while not leapYear(year):    # while we haven't found a leap year
        year = year + 1          #    keep looking ...
    return year
```

Assertions

An alternative way to enforce preconditions is to raise an ***exception*** in lieu of letting the function return normally. This is precisely what happens when the Python interpreter displays a `TypeError` or a `ValueError` and aborts a program. A built-in function raises an exception when something goes wrong and the function cannot continue. When a function raises an exception, it does not return normally. Instead, execution of the function ends at the moment the exception is raised and execution instead continues in part of the Python interpreter called an *exception handler*. By default, the exception handler prints an error message and aborts the entire program.

It is possible for our functions to also raise `TypeError` and `ValueError` exceptions, but we will not address this option until Chapter 12. We will instead consider just one particularly simple type of exception called an `AssertionError`, which may be raised by an `assert` statement. An `assert` statement tests a Boolean condition, and raises an `AssertionError` if the condition is `False`. If the condition is `True`, the `assert` statement does nothing. For example,

```
>>> year = 2021
>>> assert year > 0   # does nothing
>>> year = -1
>>> assert year > 0
AssertionError
>>> assert year > 0, 'year must be a positive'
AssertionError: year must be a positive
```

The first `assert` statement above does nothing because the condition being asserted is `True`. But the condition in the second `assert` statement is `False`, so an `AssertionError` exception is raised. The third `assert` statement demonstrates that we can also include an informative message to accompany an `AssertionError`.

We can replace the first `if` statement in our `leapYear` function with one or more assertions to catch both types of errors that we discussed previously:

```
assert isinstance(year, int), 'year must be an integer'
assert year > 0, 'year must be positive'
```

Or, we could combine them into one `assert` statement:

```
assert isinstance(year, int) and (year > 0),
        'year must be a positive integer'
```

This statement is saying that `year` must both be an integer and positive. If either of these conditions is `False`, then the `assert` statement will display

```
AssertionError: year must be a positive integer
```

and abort the program.

Reflection 5.20 *Call this modified version of* `leapYear` *from the* `nextLeapYear` *function. What happens now when you call* `nextLeapYear(2020.4)`*?*

Note that, since the `assert` statement aborts the entire program, it should only be used in circumstances in which there is no other reasonable course of action. But the definition of "reasonable" usually depends on the circumstances.

Unit testing

The only way to really ensure that a function is correct is to either mathematically prove it is correct or test it with every possible input. But since both of these strategies are virtually impossible in all but the most trivial situations, the best we can do is to test our functions with a variety of carefully chosen inputs that are representative of the entire range of possibilities. In large software companies, there are dedicated teams whose sole jobs are to design and carry out tests of individual functions, the interplay between functions, and the overall software project.

In the context of a program with many functions, it is very important to test each function *before* you move on to other functions. The process of writing a program consists of multiple iterations of Polya's four-step process, as we outlined in Chapter 1.

1. Understand the problem.
2. Design an algorithm.
3. Write a program.
4. Look back.

Once you come up with an overall design and identify what functions you need in your program, you should follow the "Design–Program–Test" process in steps 2–4 for *each function individually.* If you do not follow this advice and instead test everything for the first time when you think you are done, it will be very hard to discern where your errors are and you are guaranteed to waste all sorts of time. As you test each function, you are likely to discover situations that you had not thought of previously, sending you back to the drawing board, so to speak. If you discover these issues too late, they may have adverse effects on everything else and throw your whole project into disarray.

We will group our tests for each function in what is known as a ***unit test***. The "unit" in our case will be an individual function, but in general it may be any block of code with a specific purpose. Each unit test will itself be a function, named `test_` followed by the name of the function that we are testing. For example, our unit test function for the `leapYear` function will be named `test_leapYear`. Each unit test function will contain several individual tests, each of which will `assert` that calling the function with a particular set of parameters returns the correct answer.

Let's design a unit test for the `leapYear` function. We will assume that the functions we are testing are checking preconditions with `if` statements rather than assertions. We will start with a few easy tests:

```
def test_leapYear():
    assert leapYear(2024) == True
    assert leapYear(2025) == False

    print('Passed all tests of leapYear!')
```

(Since `leapYear` returns a Boolean value, these could also be written as

> **Tangent 5.2: Unit testing frameworks**
>
> Python also provides two modules to specifically facilitate unit testing. The `doctest` module provides a way to incorporate tests directly into function docstrings. The `unittest` module provides a fully featured unit testing framework that automates the unit and regression testing process, and is more similar to the approach we are taking in this section. If you would like to learn more about these tools, visit
>
> $$\text{http://docs.python.org/3/library/development.html}$$

`assert leapYear(2024)` and `assert not leapYear(2025)`.) Add this function to the same file as your `leapYear` and `nextLeapYear` functions. Also include another function that will call all of your unit tests:

```
def test():
    test_leapYear()
```

Reflection 5.21 *What is printed by the* `assert` *statements in the* `test_leapYear` *function when you call the* `test` *function?*

If the `leapYear` function is working correctly, *nothing* should be printed by the `assert` statements. On the other hand, if the `leapYear` function were to fail one of the tests, the program would abort at that point with an `AssertionError` exception. To see this, change the first assertion to (incorrectly) read `assert leapYear(2024) == False`. Then rerun the program. You should see

```
Traceback (most recent call last):
    ⋮ (order of function calls displayed here)
    assert leapYear(2024) == False
AssertionError
```

This error tells you which assertion failed so that you can track down the problem. (In this case, there is no problem; change the `assert` statement back to the correct version.)

On their own, the results of these two tests do not provide enough evidence to show that the `leapYear` function is correct. As we first discussed back in Section 1.4, we need to choose a variety of tests that are representative of the entire range of possibilities. The input that we use for a particular test is called a **test case**. As we first saw back on page 38, we can generally divide test cases into *common case*, *boundary cases*, and *corner cases*.

Common cases

First, test the function on several straightforward inputs to make sure that its basic functionality is intact, as we started to do above. Be sure to choose test cases that cover the range of possible inputs and possible outputs.

```
assert leapYear(2024) == True
assert leapYear(2025) == False
assert leapYear(1969) == False
assert leapYear(1900) == False
assert leapYear(40) == True
assert leapYear(11111) == False
```

Boundary and corner cases

A ***boundary case*** is an input that rests on a boundary of the range of legal inputs or on the boundary between different outputs. In the case of the `leapYear` function, we want to test the function on the smallest allowable years. (If there were a maximum year, we would want to test that too.) We also want to test on inputs that are next to each other but result in different answers.

```
assert leapYear(1) == False
assert leapYear(0) == False
assert leapYear(-1) == False
assert leapYear(4) == True

assert leapYear(2019) == False
assert leapYear(2020) == True
assert leapYear(2021) == False
```

| **Reflection 5.22** *Does the* `leapYear` *function pass these tests?*

A ***corner case*** is any other kind of rare input that might cause the function to break. For the `leapYear` function, our boundary cases took care of most of these. Thinking up pathological corner cases is an acquired skill that comes with experience. Many companies pay top dollar for programmers whose sole job is to discover corner cases that break their software!

After adding test cases for the `nextLeapYear` function, our program looks like this:

```
# test_leapyear.py

def test_leapYear():
    # omitted here...

def test_nextLeapYear():
    assert nextLeapYear(2020) == 2024      # common cases
    assert nextLeapYear(2025) == 2028
    assert nextLeapYear(1899) == 1904
    assert nextLeapYear(100) == 104
    assert nextLeapYear(11111) == 11112

    assert nextLeapYear(1) == 4            # boundary cases
    assert nextLeapYear(0) == 0
    assert nextLeapYear(-100) == 0
    assert nextLeapYear(2023) == 2024
    assert nextLeapYear(2024) == 2028
```

```
    print('Passed all tests of nextLeapYear!')

def test():
    test_leapYear()
    test_nextLeapYear()

test()
```

Notice that we always call all of the individual test functions from `test()`. This is called *regression testing*; we will revisit this in the next chapter.

Testing floats

Special care must be taken when testing functions that return floating point numbers. To see why, consider the following small function.

```
def addFloats(steps):
    total = 0
    for count in range(steps):
        total = total + 0.0001
    return total
```

If we call this function with `addFloats(1000000)`, the loop adds one ten-thousandth one million times, so the answer should be one hundred. However, if we try to test this with `assert addFloats(1000000) == 100.0`, the `assert` will fail because rounding errors caused the value of `total` to be slightly greater than 100. To deal with this inconvenience, we need to always test floating point values within a range instead. In this case, the following `assert` statement is much more appropriate:

```
assert (addFloats(1000000) > 99.9999) and (addFloats(1000000) < 100.0001)
```

The size of the range that you test will depend on the accuracy that is necessary in your particular application.

Catching exceptions

As you know, when exceptions like `ValueError` or `TypeError` are raised, the default behavior is for the program to abort. However, it is possible to change this behavior by "catching" exceptions. A good application of this is testing whether numeric values are received by `input` functions. For example, consider the first prompt in the `fairnessChecker` function on page 186.

```
ratio = float(input('Maximum fair ceo:employee pay ratio: '))
```

If one mistakenly enters a non-numeric value at this prompt, the `float` function will generate a `ValueError` exception like this:

```
Maximum fair ceo:employee pay ratio: cookies

ValueError: could not convert string to float: 'cookies'
```

To avoid this behavior and print a more helpful error message, we can use a `try/except` statement:

```
try:
    ratio = float(input('Maximum fair ceo:employee pay ratio: '))
except ValueError:
    print('The ratio must be a number.')
    return
```

If an exception is raised while executing the statement(s) in the try clause, execution immediately jumps to an except clause for that exception. In this case, if a value is entered that cannot be converted by the float function, triggering a **ValueError** exception, the print statement in the except clause will be executed followed by a return to end the function since it cannot go forward without a value for ratio. If an exception is generated but no matching except clause is found, the default behavior (usually aborting the program) is followed. After executing the except clause, execution continues normally. If no exception occurs in the try clause, then the except clause is skipped.

An even nicer solution would be to place the input function in a loop to prompt again if an exception is raised.

```
good = False
while not good:
    try:
        ratio = float(input('Maximum fair ceo:employee pay ratio: '))
    except ValueError:
        print('Please enter a number.')
    else:                                   # no exception was raised
        good = True                         # so end the loop
```

The optional else clause is executed if no exception is raised in the try clause. In this case, if a **ValueError** exception is raised, the print in the except clause is executed and the prompt is issued again. If no exception is raised, **good** is set to True, causing the loop to end.

Exercises

For each of the following functions from earlier chapters, (a) write a suitable precondition and postcondition, and (b) add assert *statement(s) to enforce your precondition.*

5.5.1*   import math

```
def volumeSphere(radius):
    return (4 / 3) * math.pi * (radius ** 3)
```

5.5.2.   def fair(employee, ceo, ratio):
```
    return (ceo / employee <= ratio)
```

5.5.3.   def middleClass(pay):
```
    return (pay >= 40000) and (pay <= 65000)
```

5.5.4.
```
def windChill(temperature, windSpeed):
    # Note: only valid for temperatures <= 10 degrees Celsius
    #       and wind speeds above 4.8 km/h.
    chill = 13.12 + 0.6215 * temperature \
                  + (0.3965 * temperature - 11.37) \
                  * windSpeed ** 0.16
    temperature = round(chill)
    return temperature
```

5.5.5*
```
import turtle

def plot(tortoise, n):
    for x in range(-n, n + 1):
        tortoise.goto(x, x * x)
```

5.5.6.
```
def pond(years):
    population = 12000
    for year in range(1, years + 1):
        population = 1.08 * population - 1500
    return population
```

5.5.7.
```
def decayC14(originalAmount, years, dt):
    amount = originalAmount
    k = -0.00012096809434
    numIterations = int(years / dt) + 1
    for i in range(1, numIterations):
        amount = amount + k * amount * dt
    return amount
```

5.5.8.
```
def argh(n):
    return 'A' + ('r' * n) + 'gh!'
```

Design a thorough unit test for each of the following functions. If you discover errors during your testing, identify and fix them.

5.5.9*
```
def assignGP(score):
    """Assign a grade point to a score between 0 and 100."""

    if score >= 90:
        return 4
    if score >= 80:
        return 3
    if score >= 70:
        return 2
    if score >= 60:
        return 1
    return 0
```

5.5.10.
```
def power(base, exponent):
    """Compute base ** exponent."""

    count = 0
    result = 1
    while count <= exponent:
        result = result * base
        count = count + 1
    return result
```

5.5.11.
```
def factorial(n):
    """Compute n! = 1 * 2 * 3 * ... * n."""

    result = 1
    for number in range(n):
        result = result * number
    return result
```

5.5.12* Design a thorough unit test for the `volumeSphere` function in Exercise 5.5.1.

5.5.13. Design a thorough unit test for the `windChill` function in Exercise 5.5.4.

5.5.14. Design a thorough unit test for the `decayC14` function in Exercise 5.5.7.

Add a `try/except` clause within a loop to each of the two following functions to re-prompt for input if converting it to a number causes an exception.

5.5.15*
```
def daysAlive():
    text = input('How old are you? ')
    age = int(text)
    print('You have been alive for', round(age * 365.25), 'days!')
```

5.5.16.
```
def guessMyNumber():
    myNumber = random.randrange(1, 11)
    guess = int(input('Guess a number from 1 to 10: '))
    if guess == myNumber:
        print('Nice guess!')
    else:
        print('Nope.')
```

5.5.17. An alternative way to deal with a possible division by zero error in the `fair` function on page 182 is to let the division happen and catch the `ZeroDivisionError` exception if it occurs. Modify the function, shown below, in this way. The function should return 0 if division by zero is detected.
```
def fair(employee, ceo, ratio):
    return (ceo / employee) <= ratio
```

5.6 GUESS MY NUMBER

In this section, we will design a function to play the classic "I'm thinking of a number" game to practice a bit more with complex conditionals and `while` loops. Here is a first attempt at a function to play the game.

```
import random

def guessingGame(maxGuesses):
    """Plays a guessing game.  The human player tries to guess
       the computer's number from 1 to 100.

    Parameter:
        maxGuesses: the maximum number of guesses allowed

    Return value: None
    """

    secretNumber = random.randrange(1, 101)
    for guesses in range(maxGuesses):
        myGuess = input('Please guess my number: ')
        try:
            myGuess = int(myGuess)
        except ValueError:
            myGuess = 0                     # count this as a miss

        if myGuess == secretNumber:     # win
            print('You got it!')
        else:                           # try again
            print('Nope.  Try again.')
```

The **randrange** function returns a random integer that is at least the value of its first argument, but less than its second argument (similar to the way the **range** function interprets its arguments). After the function chooses a random integer between 1 and 100, it enters a **for** loop that will allow us to guess up to **maxGuesses** times. The function prompts us for our guess with the **input** function, and then assigns the response to **myGuess** as a string. Because we want to interpret the response as an integer, we use the **int** function to convert the string. If **myGuess** cannot be converted to an **int**, we catch the exception and assign **myGuess** to 0 so it will count as a missed guess. Once it has **myGuess**, the function uses the **if/else** statement to tell us whether we have guessed correctly. After this, the loop will give us another guess, until we have used them all up.

Reflection 5.23 *Try playing the game by calling* **guessingGame(20)**. *Does it work? Is there anything we need to improve?*

You may have noticed three issues:

1. After we guess correctly, unless we have used up all of our guesses, the loop iterates again and gives us another guess. Instead, we want the game to end.

2. It would be much friendlier for the game to tell us whether an incorrect guess is too high or too low.

3. If we do not guess correctly in at most **maxGuesses** guesses, the last thing we see

is 'Nope. Try again.' before the function ends. But there is no opportunity to try again; instead, it should tell us that we have lost.

We will address these issues in order.

Ending the game nicely

Our current `for` loop, like all `for` loops, iterates a prescribed number of times. Instead, we want the loop to only iterate for as long as we need another guess. So this is another instance that calls for a `while` loop. In this case, we need the loop to iterate while we have not guessed the secret number, in other words, while `myGuess != secretNumber`. But we also need to stop when we have used up all of our guesses, as counted by the index variable `guesses`. So we also want our `while` loop to iterate while `guesses < maxGuesses`. Since both of these conditions must be `True` for us to keep iterating, our desired `while` loop condition is:

```
while (myGuess != secretNumber) and (guesses < maxGuesses):
```

Because we are replacing our `for` loop with this `while` loop, we will now need to manage the index variable manually. We do this by initializing `guesses = 0` before the loop and incrementing `guesses` in the body of the loop. Here is the updated function with these changes highlighted:

```
def guessingGame(maxGuesses):
    """ (docstring omitted) """

    secretNumber = random.randrange(1, 101)
    myGuess = 0
    guesses = 0
    while (myGuess != secretNumber) and (guesses < maxGuesses):
        myGuess = input('Please guess my number: ')
        try:
            myGuess = int(myGuess)
        except ValueError:
            myGuess = 0
        guesses = guesses + 1            # increment # of guesses
        if myGuess == secretNumber:      # win
            print('You got it!')
        else:                            # try again
            print('Nope.  Try again.')
```

Reflection 5.24 *Notice that we have also included* `myGuess = 0` *before the loop. Why do we bother to assign a value to* `myGuess` *before the loop? Is there anything special about the value 0? (Hint: try commenting it out.)*

If we comment out `myGuess = 0`, we will see the following error on the line containing the `while` loop:

```
UnboundLocalError: local variable 'myGuess' referenced before assignment
```

This error means that we have referred to an unknown variable named `myGuess`. The name is unknown to the Python interpreter because we had not defined it before it was first referenced in the `while` loop condition. Therefore, we need to initialize `myGuess` before the `while` loop, so that the condition makes sense the first time it is tested. Recall from Section 4.3 that this was one of the two important things to remember about `while` loops. We initialize `myGuess` to 0, a value that cannot be the secret number, to make sure the loop iterates at least once.

The second important consideration for `while` loops is to ensure that the condition will eventually become false. For the `and` expression in this `while` loop to become false, either `(myGuess != secretNumber)` must be false or `(guesses < maxGuesses)` must be false. This reasoning is the same as De Morgan's first law that we discussed in the previous section.

Reflection 5.25 *How do the statements in the body of the loop ensure that eventually* `(myGuess != secretNumber)` *or* `(guesses < maxGuesses)` *will be* `False`?

Prompting for a new guess creates the opportunity for the first part to become `False`, while incrementing `guesses` ensures that the second part will eventually become `False`. Therefore, we cannot have an infinite loop.

Friendly hints

Inside the loop, we currently handle two cases: (1) we win, and (2) we do not win but get another guess. To be friendlier, we should split the second case into two subcases: (2a) our guess was too low, and (2b) our guess was too high. We can accomplish this by replacing the not-so-friendly `print('Nope. Try again.')` with another `if/else` that decides between the two new subcases:

```
if myGuess == secretNumber:            # win
    print('You got it!')
else:                                  # try again
    if myGuess < secretNumber:         # too low
        print('Too low.  Try again.')
    else:                              # too high
        print('Too high.  Try again.')
```

Now, if `myGuess == secretNumber` is false, we execute the first `else` clause, the body of which is the new `if/else` construct. If `myGuess < secretNumber` is true, we print that the number is too low; otherwise, we print that the number is too high.

Reflection 5.26 *Do you see a way in which the conditional construct above can be simplified?*

The conditional construct above is really just equivalent to a decision between three disjoint possibilities: (a) the guess is equal to the secret number, (b) the guess is less than the secret number, or (c) the guess is greater than the secret number. In other words, it is equivalent to:

```
if myGuess == secretNumber:          # win
    print('You got it!')
elif myGuess < secretNumber:         # too low
    print('Too low.  Try again.')
else:                                # too high
    print('Too high.  Try again.')
```

A proper win/lose message

Now inside the loop, we currently handle three cases: (a) we win, and (b) our guess is too low and we get another guess, and (c) our guess is too high and we get another guess. But we are missing the case in which we run out of guesses. In this situation, we want to print something like `'Too bad. You lose.'` instead of one of the "try again" messages.

> **Reflection 5.27** *How can we augment the* `if/elif/else` *statement so that it correctly handles all four cases?*

In the game, if we incorrectly use our last guess, then two things must be true just before the `if` condition is tested: `myGuess` is not equal to `secretNumber` and `guesses` is equal to `maxGuesses`. So we can incorporate this condition into the `if/elif/else` too:

```
if (myGuess != secretNumber) and (guesses == maxGuesses):   # lose
    print('Too bad.  You lose.')
elif myGuess == secretNumber:        # win
    print('You got it!')
elif myGuess < secretNumber:         # too low
    print('Too low.  Try again.')
else:                                # too high
    print('Too high.  Try again.')
```

Notice that we have made the previous first `if` statement into an `elif` statement because we only want one of the four messages to be printed. However, here is an alternative structure that is more elegant:

```
if myGuess == secretNumber:          # win
    print('You got it!')
elif guesses == maxGuesses:          # lose
    print('Too bad.  You lose.')
elif myGuess < secretNumber:         # too low
    print('Too low.  Try again.')
else:                                # too high
    print('Too high.  Try again.')
```

By placing the new condition second, we can leverage the fact that, if we get to the first `elif`, we already know that `myGuess != secretNumber`. Therefore, we do not need to include it explicitly.

There is a third way to handle this situation that is perhaps even more elegant. Notice that both of the first two conditions are going to happen at most once, and at the end of the program. So it might make more sense to put them *after* the loop.

Doing so also exhibits a nice parallel between these two events and the two parts of the `while` loop condition. As we discussed earlier, the negation of the `while` loop condition is

```
(myGuess == secretNumber) or (guesses >= maxGuesses)
```

So when the loop ends, at least one of these two things is true. Notice that these two events are exactly the events that define a win or a loss: if the first part is true, then we won; if the second part is true, we lost. So we can move the win/loss statements after the loop, and decide which to print based on which part of the `while` loop condition became false:

```
if myGuess == secretNumber:          # win
    print('You got it!')
else:                                # lose
    print('Too bad.  You lose.')
```

In the body of the loop, with these two cases gone, we will now need to check if we still get another guess (mirroring the `while` loop condition) before we print one of the "try again" messages:

```
if (myGuess != secretNumber) and (guesses < maxGuesses):
    if myGuess < secretNumber:          # too low
        print('Too low.  Try again.')
    else:                               # too high
        print('Too high.  Try again.')
```

Reflection 5.28 *Why is it not correct to combine the two `if` statements above into a single statement like the following?*

```
if (myGuess != secretNumber) and (guesses < maxGuesses) \
                        and (myGuess < secretNumber):
    print('Too low.  Try again.')
else:
    print('Too high.  Try again.')
```

Hint: what does the function print when `guesses < maxGuesses` *is false and* `myGuess < secretNumber` *is true?*

All of these changes are incorporated into the final game shown below. As you play it, think about what the best strategy is. Exercise 5.6.7 asks you to write a Monte Carlo simulation to compare three different strategies for playing the game.

```
import random

def guessingGame(maxGuesses):
    """ (docstring omitted) """

    secretNumber = random.randrange(1, 101)
    myGuess = 0
    guesses = 0
    while (myGuess != secretNumber) and (guesses < maxGuesses):
        myGuess = input('Please guess my number: ')
        try:
            myGuess = int(myGuess)
        except ValueError:
            myGuess = 0
        guesses = guesses + 1          # increment # of guesses used

        if (myGuess != secretNumber) and (guesses < maxGuesses):
            if myGuess < secretNumber:          # guess is too low
                print('Too low.  Try again.')   #    give a hint
            else:                               # guess is too high
                print('Too high.  Try again.')  #    give a hint

    if myGuess == secretNumber:        # win
        print('You got it!')
    else:                              # lose
        print('Too bad.  You lose.')

def main():
    guessingGame(10)

main()
```

Exercises

5.6.1*   Write a function

    ABC()

that prompts for a choice of A, B, or C and keeps prompting until it receives one of those strings. Your function should return the final choice.

5.6.2.   Write a function

    numberPlease()

that prompts for an integer between 1 and 100 (inclusive) and continues to prompt until it receives a number within this range. Your function should return the final number.

5.6.3.   Write a function

    differentNumbers()

that prompts for two different numbers. The function should use a while loop to keep prompting for a pair of numbers until the two numbers are different, and then print the final numbers.

5.6.4. Write a function

```
rockPaperScissorsLizardSpock(player1, player2)
```

that decides who wins in a game of rock-paper-scissors-lizard-Spock.[2] Each of player1 and player2 is a string with value 'rock', 'paper', 'scissors', 'lizard', or 'Spock'. The function should return 1 if player 1 wins, -1 if player 2 wins, or 0 if they tie. Test your function by playing the game with the following main program:

```
def main():
    player1 = input('Player1: ')
    player2 = input('Player2: ')
    outcome = rockPaperScissorsLizardSpock(player1, player2)
    if outcome == 1:
        print('Player 1 wins!')
    elif outcome == -1:
        print('Player 2 wins!')
    else:
        print('Player 1 and player 2 tied.')
```

5.6.5* Write a function

```
yearsUntilDoubled(amount, rate)
```

that returns the number of years until amount is doubled when it earns the given rate of interest, compounded annually. Use a while loop.

5.6.6. The *hailstone numbers* are a sequence of numbers generated by the following simple algorithm. First, choose any positive integer. Then, repeatedly follow this rule: if the current number is even, divide it by two; otherwise, multiply it by three and add one. For example, suppose we choose the initial integer to be 3. Then this algorithm produces the following sequence: $3, 10, 5, 16, 8, 4, 2, 1, 4, 2, 1, 4, 2, 1, \ldots$ For every initial integer ever tried, the sequence always reaches one and then repeats the sequence 4,2,1 forever after. Interestingly, however, no one has ever *proven* that this pattern holds for every integer! Write a function

```
hailstone(start)
```

that prints the hailstone number sequence starting from the parameter start, until the value reaches one. Your function should return the number of integers in your sequence. For example, if start were 3, the function should return 8. (Use a while loop.)

5.6.7. In this exercise, you will design a Monte Carlo simulation to compare the effectiveness of three strategies for playing the guessing game. Each of these strategies will be incorporated into the guessing game function we designed in this chapter, but instead of checking whether the player wins or loses, the function will continue until the number is guessed, and then return the number of guesses used. We will also make the maximum possible secret number a parameter, so that we can compare the results for different ranges of secret numbers.

---

[2]See http://en.wikipedia.org/wiki/Rock-paper-scissors-lizard-Spock for the rules.

The first strategy is to make a random guess each time, ignoring any previous guesses:

```python
def guessingGame1(maxNumber):
    """Play the guessing game by making random guesses."""

    secretNumber = random.randrange(1, maxNumber + 1)
    myGuess = 0
    guesses = 0
    while (myGuess != secretNumber):
        myGuess = random.randrange(1, maxNumber + 1)
        guesses = guesses + 1
    return guesses
```

The second strategy is to avoid duplicate guesses by trying every number from 1 to 100. This function is identical, except it replaces the red statement above as follows:

```python
def guessingGame2(maxNumber):
    """Play the guessing game by making incremental guesses."""
    ⋮
        myGuess = myGuess + 1
    ⋮
```

Finally, the third strategy uses previous outcomes to narrow in on the secret number:

```python
def guessingGame3(maxNumber):
    """Play the guessing game intelligently by narrowing in
       on the secret number."""

    secretNumber = random.randrange(1, maxNumber + 1)
    myGuess = 0
    low = 1
    high = maxNumber
    guesses = 0
    while (myGuess != secretNumber):
        myGuess = (low + high) // 2
        guesses = guesses + 1
        if myGuess < secretNumber:
            low = myGuess + 1
        elif myGuess > secretNumber:
            high = myGuess - 1
    return guesses
```

Write a Monte Carlo simulation to compare the expected (i.e., average) behavior of these three strategies. Use a sufficiently high number of trials to get consistent results. Similarly to what we did in Section 5.1, run your simulation for a range of maximum secret numbers, specifically $5, 10, 15, \ldots, 100$, and plot the average number of guesses required by each strategy for each maximum secret number. (The x-axis of your plot will be the maximum secret number and the y-axis will be the average number of guesses.) Explain the results. In general, how many guesses on average do you think each strategy requires to guess a secret number between 1 and n?

5.7 SUMMARY AND FURTHER DISCOVERY

In previous chapters, we designed deterministic algorithms that did the same thing every time we executed them, if we gave them the same inputs. Giving those algorithms different arguments, of course, could change their behavior, whether it be drawing a different size shape, modeling a different population, or experimenting with a different investment scenario. In this chapter, we started to investigate a new class of algorithms that can change their behavior "on the fly," so to speak. These algorithms all make choices using *Boolean logic*, the same Boolean logic on which computers are fundamentally based. By combining *comparison operators* and *Boolean operators*, we can characterize any decision. By incorporating these Boolean expressions into *conditional statements* (`if/elif/else`) and *conditional loops* (`while`), we vastly increase the diversity of algorithms that we can design. These are fundamental techniques that we will continue to use and develop over the next several chapters, as we start to work with textual and numerical data that we read from files and download from the web.

Notes for further discovery

This chapter's epigraph is a famous "Yogiism," from Hall of Fame catcher, coach, and manager Yogi Berra [8].

If you would like to learn more about Robert Brown's experiments, and the history and science behind them, visit the following website, titled "What Brown Saw and You Can Too."

`http://physerver.hamilton.edu/Research/Brownian/index.html`

The Drunkard's Walk by Leonard Mlodinow [41] is a very accessible book about how randomness and chance affect our lives. For more information about generating random numbers, and the differences between PRNGs and true random number generators, visit

`https://www.random.org/randomness/` .

The Park-Miller random number generator is due to Keith Miller and the late Steve Park [46].

The Roper Center for Public Opinion Research, at Cornell University, maintains some helpful educational resources about random sampling and errors in the context of public opinion polling at

`https://ropercenter.cornell.edu/learn/polling-and-public-opinion` .

*5.8 PROJECTS

This section is available on the book website.

CHAPTER 6

Text, Documents, and DNA

So, here's what I can say: the Library of Congress has more than 3 petabytes of digital collections. What else I can say with all certainty is that by the time you read this, all the numbers—counts and amount of storage—will have changed.

Leslie Johnston, former Chief of Repository Development, Library of Congress
Blog post (2012)

The roughly 2000 sequencing instruments in labs and hospitals around the world can collectively sequence 15 quadrillion nucleotides per year, which equals about 15 petabytes of compressed genetic data. A petabyte is 2^{50} bytes, or in round numbers, 1000 terabytes. To put this into perspective, if you were to write this data onto standard DVDs, the resulting stack would be more than 2 miles tall. And with sequencing capacity increasing at a rate of around three- to fivefold per year, next year the stack would be around 6 to 10 miles tall. At this rate, within the next five years the stack of DVDs could reach higher than the orbit of the International Space Station.

Michael C. Schatz and Ben Langmead
The DNA Data Deluge (2013)

DATA has become a disruptive force not only in business but also in a broad swath of academic inquiry. Some literary scholars have embraced a new research mode known as "distant reading" in which they seek new insights through computational analyses of entire corpora from growing digital libraries. Similarly, many historians and political scientists are now conducting research in vast digital archives maintained by governments, universities, and nonprofits. In the biological and medical sciences, major advances are being driven by computational analyses of genomic data. The list could go on and on. Despite the variety of application areas however, much of this data shares a common underlying format. In this chapter, we will look at how this textual data are represented in a computer, how to access them from both files and the web, and how to algorithmically process and analyze them to extract useful information.

6.1 FIRST STEPS

In this section, we will finish the reading level problem that we started in Chapter 1 and, in the process, introduce some first steps in text analyses. You may recall that, in Figure 1.4, we decomposed the reading level problem into three main subproblems, and then decomposed those subproblems further until we arrived at four unique leaves: computing the Flesch-Kincaid formula, computing the number of syllables in a word, and counting the number of words and sentences in a text. We were able to write a function pretty easily for the first of these subproblems and we wrote an algorithm in pseudocode for the second. We will focus in this section on the last two subproblems.

Counting words and sentences are special cases of a problem called ***tokenization***. A ***token*** is defined to be the basic unit of interest in a text, and tokenization is the problem of producing a list of all of the tokens in the text. Usually tokens are words or sentences, but they could also be numbers in a data file or individual characters in a DNA sequence; it depends on the context. Tokenization is also the first step in interpreting or compiling a program. In Python, tokens are names, keywords, literals, operators, delimiters, the newline character, and indentation characters.

Defining what words and sentences are is thornier than it seems. Normally, we can identify words in an English language text because they are separated by spaces or punctuation. But there are always exceptions. For example, what are the rules delimiting words and sentences in the following?

"It's-a me—Mario!"

It's 8:43 a.m. and I am typing from 140.141.132.1.

To keep things manageable, we will get words by simply splitting the text at runs of one or more whitespace characters (spaces, tabs, and newlines). When we tokenize sentences, we will split at runs of end punctuation marks (., ?, !).

Before text is analyzed, it is often simplified by removing superficial differences between words that should be considered equivalent (e.g., *The* and *the*, *10a.m.* and *10AM*), a process called ***normalization***. Before we perform word tokenization, we will normalize the text by making it all lowercase and removing punctuation. (When we tokenize sentences, we will not want to remove end punctuation marks.) Normalization can also involve spelling correction, removing plurals and other suffixes (called *stemming*), standardizing verb tense (called *lemmatization*), and removing common words (called *stop words*).

The texts that we analyze will be stored as strings. You'll recall that a string is a sequence of characters, and a string constant (also called a *string literal*) is enclosed

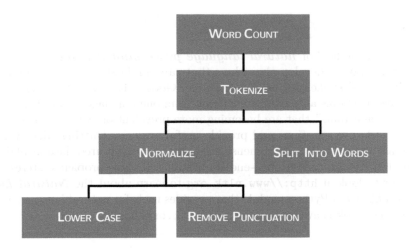

Figure 6.1 Functional decomposition tree for the **Word Count** problem.

in either single quotes (') or double quotes ("). For example, consider the following string, with spaces (␣) shown explicitly:

```
>>> shortText = "This␣isn't␣long.␣␣But␣it'll␣do.␣␣\nJust␣a␣few␣sentences..."
```

Reflection 6.1 *Why must this string be enclosed in double quotes rather than single quotes?*

According to our rules, the lists of word and sentence tokens in this text, after normalization, should be:

```
['this', 'isnt', 'long', 'but', 'itll', 'do', 'just', 'a', 'few', 'sentences']
```

and

```
["This isn't long.", "But it'll do.", 'Just a few sentences.']
```

Recall that lists are delimited by square brackets ([ ]) and items are separated by commas. So these lists contain ten and three string items, respectively. Once we have lists of tokens like these, the lengths of the lists will give us the outputs for the word count and sentence count algorithms.

This discussion suggests the functional decomposition of the **Word Count** problem shown in Figure 6.1. As usual, we will start at the bottom of the decomposition tree and work our way up.

Normalization

Strings, like turtles, are objects. So the string class, called `str`, is another example of an abstract data type. Recall that an abstract data type hides the details of how its data is stored, allowing a programmer to interact with it at a higher level through methods. (As we will discuss in Section 6.3, strings are actually stored as sequences of bytes.) One of many methods available for the `str` class[1] will solve the

---

[1]For a list, see Appendix A.6.

Tangent 6.1: Natural language processing

Researchers in the field of **_natural language processing_** seek to not only search and organize text, but to develop algorithms that can "understand" and respond to it, in both written and spoken forms. For example, Google Translate (`http://translate.google.com`) performs automatic translation from one language to another in real time. The "virtual assistants" that are becoming more prevalent on commercial websites seek to understand your questions and provide useful answers. Cutting edge systems seek to derive an understanding of immense amounts of unstructured data available on the web and elsewhere to answer open-ended questions. If these problems interest you, you might want to look at `http://www.nltk.org` to learn about the **_Natural Language Toolkit (NLTK)_**, a Python module that provides tools for natural language processing. An associated book is available at `http://nltk.org/book` .

---

subproblem in the leftmost leaf in our decomposition tree. As we did with `Turtle` methods, we preface the name of the method with the name of the object to which we want the method to apply:

```
>>> shortText.lower()
"this isn't long.  but it'll do. \njust a few sentences..."
```

The `lower` method returns a new string in which all characters in a string are made lowercase.

To remove punctuation characters, we could use the `replace` method. The following example removes all periods from `shortText`.

```
>>> shortText.replace('.', '')
"This isn't long  But it'll do \nJust a few sentences"
```

The `replace` method returns a new string in which all instances of its first argument are replaced with its second argument. In this case, we passed in the **_empty string_** `''`, consisting of zero characters, for the second argument, which in effect deletes all instances of the first argument.

Notice that neither of these methods changed the value of `shortText`. Indeed, none of the string methods do because strings are **_immutable_**, meaning that they cannot be changed. Instead, string methods always create a new string with the desired changes, leaving the original untouched.

To remove multiple punctuation characters from a text, we could call the `replace` method repeatedly, each time overwriting the previous string:

```
>>> newText = shortText
>>> newText = newText.replace('.', '')
>>> newText = newText.replace("'", '')
>>> newText
'This isnt long  But itll do \nJust a few sentences'
```

In a function to remove all punctuation, we would need to repeatedly call the `replace` method for *every* punctuation character, which is both tedious and inefficient.

> **Reflection 6.2** *Why is this inefficient? Think about how the `replace` method must work and how many times each character in the text must be examined.*

The `replace` method must examine each character in the string, compare it to the first argument, and then replace it with the second argument. So each time we call `replace` we are performing another pass across the characters in the string. Instead, we would like to make only one pass through the string and remove every punctuation character during that one pass.

To do this, we iterate over the characters in a string with a `for` loop, just like we iterated over integers in a `range`. For example, the following `for` loop iterates over the characters in the string `shortText` and prints each one.

```
>>> for character in shortText:
        print(character)
```

In each iteration of this loop, the next character in the string is assigned to the index variable `character`. If we wanted to omit characters from being printed, we would put the call to `print` inside an `if` statement:

```
>>> for character in shortText:
        if character != '.' and character != "'":
            print(character)
```

To adapt this technique to remove punctuation, we need to create a new, modified string in the body of the loop. In general, to create a modified string (remember that we cannot modify the original string), we need to iterate over each character of the original string and, in each iteration, create a new string that is the concatenation of the growing string from the previous iteration and the current character or something else based on the current character. The following function implements the simplest example of this idea, in which every character is concatenated to the end of the new string, creating an exact duplicate of the original.

```
def copy(text):
    """Return a copy of text.

    Parameter:
        text: a string object

    Return value: a copy of text
    """
1   newText = ''
2   for character in text:
3       newText = newText + character
4   return newText
```

This technique is really just another version of an accumulator, called a ***string accumulator***, conceptually similar to the list accumulators that we have been using for plotting. The trace table below illustrates how this works when `text` is `'abcd'`. Changes in values are highlighted in red.

Trace arguments: text = 'abcd'				
Step	Line	newText	character	Notes
1	1	' '	—	newText is initialized to the empty string
2	2	' '	'a'	character ← 'a'
3	3	'a'	'a'	newText ← '' + 'a'
4	2	'a'	'b'	character ← 'b'
5	3	'ab'	'b'	newText ← 'a' + 'b'
6	2	'ab'	'c'	character ← 'c'
7	3	'abc'	'c'	newText ← 'ab' + 'c'
8	2	'abc'	'd'	character ← 'd'
9	3	'abcd'	'd'	newText ← 'abc' + 'd'
Return value: 'abcd'				

In the first iteration, the first character in `text`, which is `'a'`, is assigned to `character`. Then `newText` is assigned the concatenation of the current value of `newText` and `character`, which is `'' + 'a'`, or `'a'`. In the second iteration, `character` is assigned `'b'`, and `newText` is assigned the concatenation of `newText` and `character`, which is `'a' + 'b'`, or `'ab'`. This continues for two more iterations, resulting in a value of `newText` that is identical to the original `text`.

To apply this technique to remove punctuation from a string, we simply prevent the concatenation from taking place if `character` is a punctuation mark:

```
for character in text:
    if character != '.' and character != "'":   # and ... etc.
        newText = newText + character
```

Reflection 6.3 *What happens if we replace the* and *operator with* or?

Adding in another test for every remaining punctuation character would be tedious at best, but we can simplify `if` conditions like this using the `in` operator, which evaluates to `True` if one string is contained inside another string. There is also a `not in` operator that has the opposite effect. For example:

```
>>> 'b' in 'abcd'
True
>>> 'bg' in 'abcd'
False
>>> 'b' not in 'abcd'
False
```

To make this even more convenient, there are string literals in the **string** module that contain all of the punctuation and whitespace characters:

```
>>> import string
>>> string.punctuation
'!"#$%&\'()*+,-./:;<=>?@[\\]^_`{|}~'
>>> string.whitespace
' \t\n\r\x0b\x0c'
```

Notice that two of the characters in `string.punctuation`—\' and \\—are preceded by a backslash. The backslash (\) character, called the *escape character*, causes the following character to be interpreted literally by the interpreter rather than as a meaningful character in the Python language. Escaping the single quote character allows it to be contained inside a string delimited by single quotes. The backslash character is also escaped because of its special meaning as the escape character! In `string.whitespace`, the first three characters are space, tab, and newline; the others are less common forms of whitespace that will likely not concern us.

Combining these two simplifications, we have the following function:

```
import string

def removePunctuation(text):
    """Remove punctuation from a text.

    Parameter:
        text: a string object

    Return value: a copy of text with punctuation removed
    """

    newText = ''
    for character in text:
        if character not in string.punctuation:
            newText = newText + character
    return newText
```

Now we can use this function and the `lower` method to write `normalize`:

```
def normalize(text):
    """Normalize a text by making it lowercase and removing punctuation.

    Parameter:
        text: a string object

    Return value: a normalized copy of text
    """

    newText = text.lower()
    newText = removePunctuation(newText)
    return newText
```

```
>>> normalize(shortText)
'this isnt long  but itll do \njust a few sentences'
```

Tokenization

The next step, as we work our way up the decomposition tree in Figure 6.1, is to write an algorithm to split a string into words at runs of whitespace characters. There is actually a string method named `split` that can do this for us. When `split` is given a string argument, it returns a list of strings that are separated by that argument. But with no arguments, `split` returns a list of strings that are separated by runs of whitespace:

```
>>> drSeuss = 'one fish two fish red fish blue fish'
>>> drSeuss.split('fish')
['one ', ' two ', ' red ', ' blue ', '']
>>> drSeuss.split()
['one', 'fish', 'two', 'fish', 'red', 'fish', 'blue', 'fish']
```

Although we could use this existing method, we are going to implement the function from scratch instead. There are two reasons for this. First, the general technique will be useful in similar situations that the `split` method cannot handle (e.g., splitting sentences at runs of end punctuation). Second, it will be another good example of how to use string accumulators, and of how to use string and list accumulators together.

The idea in the algorithm is to use a string accumulator to build up a string containing a word, as long as the character we are looking at is not whitespace. When we encounter whitespace, marking the end of the word, we want to append the word to a list of words and then reset the word to be an empty string to capture the next word. In pseudocode, a first draft of this algorithm can be expressed as follows.

Algorithm SPLIT INTO WORDS − DRAFT

Input: *text*
1.   *word list* ← an empty list
2.   *word* ← an empty string
3.   repeat for each *character* in *text*:
4.   if *character* is not whitespace:
5.   *word* ← *word* + *character*
6.   else:
7.   append *word* to the end of *word list*
8.   *word* ← an empty string
Output: *word list*

Notice how, in each iteration of the loop, we are either adding a character to the word or adding a word to the list. The equivalent Python function is very similar:

```
0   def splitIntoWords_Draft(text):
1       wordList = []
2       word = ''
3       for character in text:
4           if character not in string.whitespace:
5               word = word + character
6           else:
7               wordList.append(word)
8               word = ''
9       return wordList
```

Let's test our function by tracing its execution on the simple string `'i am'`.

Trace arguments: text = `'i am'`

Step	Line	wordList	word	character	Notes
1	1	[ ]	—	—	wordList ← an empty list
2	2	[ ]	`' '`	—	word ← an empty string
3	3	[ ]	`' '`	`'i'`	character ← `'i'`
4	4	[ ]	`' '`	`'i'`	condition is true; execute line 5
5	5	[ ]	`'i'`	`'i'`	word ← `''` + `'i'`
6	3	[ ]	`'i'`	`' '`	character ← `' '`
7	4	[ ]	`'i'`	`' '`	condition is false; execute line 7
8	7	`['i']`	`'i'`	`' '`	append `'i'` to wordList
9	8	`['i']`	`' '`	`' '`	word ← an empty string
10	3	`['i']`	`' '`	`'a'`	character ← `'a'`
11	4	`['i']`	`' '`	`'a'`	condition is true; execute line 5
12	5	`['i']`	`'a'`	`'a'`	word ← `''` + `'a'`
13	3	`['i']`	`'a'`	`'m'`	character ← `'m'`
14	4	`['i']`	`'a'`	`'m'`	condition is true; execute line 5
15	5	`['i']`	`'am'`	`'m'`	word ← `'a'` + `'m'`

Return value: `['i']`

Reflection 6.4 *Why wasn't the last word appended to the list? How do we fix the algorithm so that it is?*

If there had happened to be another space at the end of **text**, this would have prompted the algorithm to append `'am'`. But there wasn't, so it didn't. To fix this, we need to check after the loop if there is a final word remaining to be appended and, if so, append it:

```
if word != '':
    wordList.append(word)
```

There is also a more subtle issue with our algorithm. If there happen to be consecutive whitespace characters in **text**, then lines 7–8 will be executed in consecutive iterations, causing empty strings to be appended to **wordList**. For example, calling the function with

```
splitIntoWords_Draft('i am   it ')
```

will return the list `['i', '', 'am', '', '', 'it']`. To prevent this, we only want to execute the `else` clause for the first whitespace character in a run of whitespace.

Reflection 6.5 *If the value of* `character` *is whitespace, how can we tell if it is the first in a sequence of whitespace characters? (Hint: if it is the first whitespace, what must the previous character not be?)*

If the value of `character` is a whitespace character, we know it is the first in a sequence if the previous character was *not* whitespace. So we need to replace the `else` with an `elif` statement that allows lines 7–8 to execute only if the previous character was not whitespace.

These two fixes are reflected in our updated algorithm below.

Algorithm SPLIT INTO WORDS

Input: *text*

1	*word list* ← an empty list
2	*word* ← an empty string
3	repeat for each *character* in *text*:
4	if *character* is not whitespace:
5	*word* ← *word* + *character*
6	else if the previous *character* was not also whitespace:
7	append *word* to the end of *word list*
8	*word* ← an empty string
9	if *word* is not an empty string:
10	append *word* to the end of *word list*

Output: *word list*

In our Python function, there isn't a way to refer to the "previous character" without explicitly keeping track of it. So we need to save the current value of `character` in a new variable `prevCharacter` at the end of each iteration so it is available when `character` is updated in the next iteration. The final function, with new parts highlighted, looks like this:

```python
def splitIntoWords(text):
    """Split a text into words.

    Parameter:
        text: a string object

    Return value: the list of words in the text
    """
```

```
wordList = []
prevCharacter = ' '
word = ''
for character in text:
    if character not in string.whitespace:
        word = word + character
    elif prevCharacter not in string.whitespace:
        wordList.append(word)
        word = ''
    prevCharacter = character

if word != '':
    wordList.append(word)

return wordList
```

Reflection 6.6 *What happens if we do not initialize* `prevCharacter` *before the loop? Why did we initialize* `prevCharacter` *to a space? Does its initial value matter?*

To answer this question, let's consider two possibilities for the value assigned to `character` in the first iteration of the loop. First, suppose `character` is not a whitespace character. Then the `if` condition will be true and the `elif` condition will not be tested, so the initial value of `prevCharacter` does not matter. On the other hand, if the first value assigned to `character` *is* a whitespace character, then the `if` condition will be false and the `elif` condition will be checked. But we want to make sure that the `elif` condition is false so that an empty string is not inappropriately appended to the list of words. Setting `prevCharacter` to a space initially will prevent this from happening.

Now that we have both the `normalize` and `splitIntoWords` functions, we can easily write a tokenization function:

```
def wordTokens(text):
    """Break a text into words with punctuation removed.

    Parameter:
        text: a string object

    Return value: a list of word tokens
    """

    newText = normalize(text)
    tokens = splitIntoWords(newText)

    return tokens
```

And now the `wordCount` function is even easier. The only new thing we need is the `len` function, which returns the length of its argument. When applied to lists, it returns the number of items in the list. When applied to strings, it returns the number of characters in the string:

```
>>> len('i am it')
7
>>> len(['i', 'am', 'it'])
3
```

So the `wordCount` function simply gets a list of words from `wordTokens` and then returns the length of that list.

```
def wordCount(text):
    """Count the number of words in a string.

    Parameter:
        text: a string object

    Return value: the number of words in text
    """

    words = wordTokens(text)
    return len(words)
```

Creating your own module

The five functions that we wrote in this section will be very useful in the future, so let's package them into our own module that we can `import`. A module is just a Python program that is ready to be imported. First, if you haven't already, create a new file that contains the five functions that we wrote in this section and name it `textlib.py`.[2] It should look like this (with the function bodies present, of course):

```
import string

def removePunctuation(text):
    # body omitted

def normalize(text):
    # body omitted

def splitIntoWords(text):
    # body omitted

def wordTokens(text):
    # body omitted

def wordCount(text):
    # body omitted

def main():
    # body omitted

if __name__ == '__main__':
    main()
```

---

[2]`lib` is short for "library." This is a common naming convention for modules (e.g., `matplotlib`).

When a module is imported, all of the code in the module is executed, so we generally only want a module to contain function definitions, and perhaps some assignments of values to constants, but no function calls. To make a module dual-purpose— to be able to be executed on its own and be imported—we need to be able to differentiate between the two situations and only call `main` if the module is not being imported. This is accomplished by checking the value of `__name__` in the `if` statement before calling `main`. As we saw back in Section 2.6, `__name__` is assigned the value `'__main__'` if the module is executed directly by the Python interpreter. (If our module `textlib.py` is imported instead, then `__name__` will be assigned the value `'textlib'`.) So now if we run our module directly in IDLE, `main` will be executed, but if we import it instead, it won't.

Testing your module

Finally, let's test the module more completely using the techniques from the previous chapter. We will implement our tests in a new file named `test_textlib.py` with the following structure:

```python
from textlib import *

def test_removePunctuation():
    # tests of removePunctuation here

    print('Passed all tests of removePunctuation!')

def test_normalize():
    # tests of normalize here

    print('Passed all tests of normalize!')

def test_splitIntoWords():
    # tests of splitIntoWords here

    print('Passed all tests of splitIntoWords!')

def test_wordTokens():
    # tests of wordTokens here

    print('Passed all tests of wordTokens!')

def test_wordCount():
    # tests of wordCount here

    print('Passed all tests of wordCount!')

def test():
    test_removePunctuation()
    test_normalize()
    test_splitIntoWords()
    test_wordTokens()
    test_wordCount()

test()
```

Save this program in the same folder as `textlib.py` so that the `import` statement can find the module.

The first line of the test program imports all of the functions from `textlib.py` into the global namespace of the test program. Recall from Section 2.6 that a normal `import` statement creates a new namespace containing all of the functions from an imported module. Instead, this form of the `import` statement imports functions into the *current* namespace. The advantage is that we do not have to preface every function call with the name of the module. If we wanted to only import some functions, we could replace the * with a list of those to import.

Notice that the test program calls `test()` instead of individual unit test functions. Besides being convenient, this technique has the advantage that, when we test new functions, we also re-test previously tested functions. If we make changes to any one function in a program, we want to *both* make sure that this change worked *and* make sure that we have not inadvertently broken something that was working earlier. This idea is called **regression testing** because we are making sure that our program has not *regressed* to an earlier error state.

Exercise 6.1.19 below asks you to complete these unit tests. Then exercises 6.1.20–6.1.26 challenge you to write functions for the remaining subproblems in Figure 1.4 and add them to your `textlib.py` module. With this complete module, you will be able to compute the Flesch-Kincaid reading level of any text!

In the next section, we will see how to read an entire text file or web page into a string so that you can use your module to compute the reading levels of actual books. In the next chapter, we will use your module to, among other things, analyze the relative frequencies of all the words and word bigrams in a text.

Exercises

Write a function for each of the following problems. Test each function with both common and boundary case arguments, and document your test cases.

6.1.1* The string method `count` returns the number of occurrences of a string in another string. For example, `shortText.count('is')` would return 2. Write a function

```
vowels(word)
```

that uses the `count` method to return the number of vowels in the string `word`. (Note that `word` may contain upper and lowercase letters.)

6.1.2. Write a function

```
whitespace(text)
```

that uses the `count` method to return the number of whitespace characters (spaces, tabs, and newlines) in the string `text`.

6.1.3*   Write a function

      `underscore(sentence)`

that uses the `replace` string method to return a version of the string `sentence` in which all the spaces have been replaced by the underscore (`_`) character.

6.1.4.   Write a function

      `nospaces(sentence)`

that uses the `replace` string method to return a version of the string `sentence` in which all the spaces have been removed.

6.1.5.   Write a function

      `txtHelp(txt)`

that returns an expanded version of the string `txt`, which may contain texting abbreviations like "brb" and "lol." Your function should expand at least four different texting abbreviations. For example, `txtHelp('imo u r lol brb')` might return the string `'in my opinion you are laugh out loud be right back'`.

6.1.6*   Write a function

      `letters(text)`

that prints the characters of the string `text`, one per line. For example `letters('abc')` should print

    a
    b
    c

6.1.7*   Write a function

      `countCharacter(text, letter)`

that returns the number of occurrences of the one-character string named `letter` in the string `text`, *without* using the `count` method. (Use a `for` loop and an accumulator instead.)

6.1.8.   Write a function

      `vowels(word)`

that returns the same result as Exercise 6.1.1 *without* using the `count` method. (Use a `for` loop instead.)

6.1.9.   Write a function

      `replacePunctuation(text)`

that uses a `for` loop to return a modified version of the string `text` in which all punctuation characters are replaced by spaces.

6.1.10* Write a function

      `underscore(sentence)`

that returns the same result as Exercise 6.1.3 *without* using the `replace` method.

6.1.11. Write a function

      `nospaces(sentence)`

that returns the same result as Exercise 6.1.4 *without* using the `replace` method.

6.1.12.   Write a function

   noVowels(text)

that returns a version of the string `text` with all the vowels removed. For example, `noVowels('this is an example.')` should return the string `'ths s n xmpl.'`.

6.1.13.   Write a function

   daffy(word)

that returns a string that has Daffy Duck's lisp added to it (Daffy would pronounce the 's' sound as though there was a 'th' after it). For example, `daffy("That's despicable!")` should return the string `"That'sth desthpicable!"`.

6.1.14.   Write a function

   reverse(text)

that returns a copy of the string `text` in reverse order.

6.1.15.   Create a modified version of the `splitIntoWords` function that just counts the words instead of appending them to a list. Your function should return the word count and should not use a list variable.

6.1.16.   Write a function

   split(text, splitCharacters)

that generalizes the `splitIntoWords` function so that it splits `text` at any of the characters, or runs of any of the characters, in the string `splitCharacters`. For example, `split('the best of times', 'sei')` should return the list `['th', ' b', 't of t', 'm']`.

6.1.17* Show how the `wordCount` function can be shortened to a single line by composing functions.

6.1.18.   Show how the `wordTokens` function can be shortened to a single line by composing functions.

6.1.19.   Test the five functions we developed in this section by completing the `test_textlib.py` program.

The following seven exercises ask you to write the remaining functions in the reading level problem. To guide you, Figure 6.2 shows how data flows between algorithms for the subproblems in Figure 1.4. Consistent with prior diagrams, problem inputs are shown entering on the left and outputs are shown exiting on the right. Values exiting nodes from the bottom are being sent to subproblems a level below as inputs, and the outputs of subproblems are shown returning to the caller. Add each function that you write to your `textlib` module, and design a unit test for the function in `test_textlib.py`.

6.1.20.   Write a function that implements the final SYLLABLE COUNT algorithm from page 16. Lines 1–3 of the algorithm can together be implemented in a manner very similar to the `splitIntoWords` function. The idea is to only increment the count if a vowel is the first in a run of vowels. Here is a modified algorithm showing this idea.

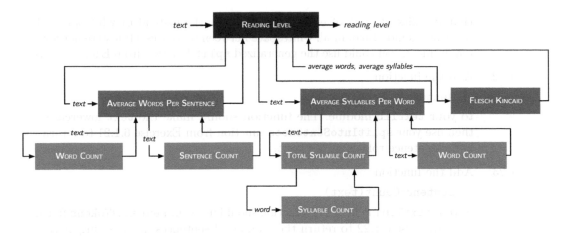

Figure 6.2 Flows of inputs and outputs in the reading level problem from Figure 1.4.

Algorithm SYLLABLE COUNT (VERSION 3)

Input: a *word*

1. *count* ← 0
2. repeat for each *letter* in *word*:
3.   if *letter* is a vowel and the previous letter is not a vowel, then:
4.   *count* ← *count* + 1
5. if *word* ends in *e*, then:
6.   *count* ← *count* − 1

Output: *count*

The last character in the word can be examined with the string method endswith:

```
if word.endswith('e'):
    count = count - 1
```

Once you have written the syllableCount function, you can get the total number of syllables in a text with the following function.

```
def totalSyllableCount(text):
    wordList = wordTokens(text)
    count = 0
    for word in wordList:    # iterate over each word in wordList
        count = count + syllableCount(word)
    return count
```

Add these two functions to textlib.py and test them thoroughly in test_textlib.py.

6.1.21. Add the function

splitIntoSentences(text)

to your textlib module. The function should return the number of sentences in the string text. This is very similar to the splitIntoWords function except that it splits at runs of end punctuation marks instead of whitespace. The function should also omit all whitespace between sentences. (If it were not for this requirement, you could use the generalized `split` function from Exercise 6.1.16.)

6.1.22. Add the function

```
sentenceTokens(text)
```

to your `textlib` module. The function should make the `text` lowercase and then use your `splitIntoSentences` function from Exercise 6.1.21 to return the list of sentence tokens in the `text`.

6.1.23. Add the function

```
sentenceCount(text)
```

to your `textlib` module. The function should use your `sentenceTokens` function from Exercise 6.1.22 to return the number of sentences in the string `text`.

6.1.24. Add the function

```
averageWords(text)
```

to your `textlib` module. The function should use the `wordCount` function and your `sentenceCount` function from Exercise 6.1.23 to return the average number of words per sentence in the string `text`.

6.1.25. Add the function

```
averageSyllables(text)
```

to your `textlib` module. The function should use your `totalSyllableCount` function from Exercise 6.1.20 and the `wordCount` function to return the average number of syllables per word in the string `text`.

6.1.26. Finally, add the function

```
readingLevel(text)
```

to your `textlib` module. The function should use your `averageWords` and `averageSyllables` functions from Exercises 6.1.24 and 6.1.25, and the `fleschKincaid` function from page 90 to return the Flesch-Kincaid reading level of the string `text`.

6.2 TEXT DOCUMENTS

To apply our text analysis functions to full-size texts, we need to be able to read them from *files* stored on a hard drive or flash drive. Like everything else in a computer system, files are stored as sequences of bits. But we interact with files as electronic documents containing information such as text, spreadsheets, or images. These abstractions are mediated by a part of the operating system called the *file system*. The file system organizes files in folders in a hierarchical tree, such as in the simplified view of a macOS file system in Figure 6.3.

The root of the tree is denoted by a forward slash / symbol. Below the root in this figure is a folder named Users where every user of the computer has a *home folder* labeled with his or her name, say **george**. This home folder contains several subfolders, one of which is Documents. The two subfolders in Documents are named

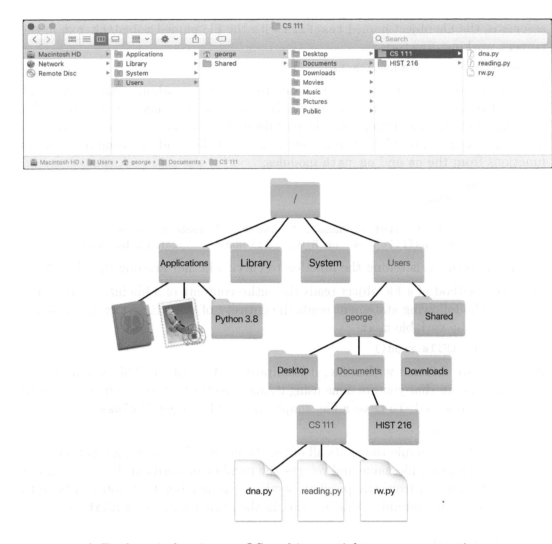

Figure 6.3 A Finder window in macOS and its partial tree representation.

CS 111 and HIST 216. We can represent the location of a file with the *path* one must follow to get there from the root. For example, the path to **reading.py**, colored blue, is /Users/george/Documents/CS\ 111/reading.py. Notice the backslash before the space in CS\ 111; this is because spaces usually need to be escaped in pathnames. Any path without the first forward slash is considered to be a *relative path*, relative to the current *working directory* set by the operating system. For example, if the current working directory were /Users/george/Documents, then **reading.py** could be specified with the relative path CS\ 111/reading.py.

Reading from text files

In Python, we access files through an abstraction called a ***file object***, which we associate with a file with the open function. For example, the following statement associates the file object named `textFile` with the file named `mobydick.txt` in the current working directory.[3]

```
textFile = open('mobydick.txt', 'r')
```

The second argument to `open` is the *mode* to use when working with the file; `'r'` means that we want to read from the file. If a file with that filename does not exist, a `FileNotFoundError` exception will be raised. If necessary, you can proactively determine in advance whether a file exists and can be read by using a couple of functions from the `os` and `os.path` modules:

```
import os
import os.path

assert os.path.isfile(fileName), fileName + ' does not exist'
assert os.access(fileName, os.R_OK), fileName + ' cannot be read'
```

The value `os.R_OK` is telling the function to check whether <u>R</u>eading the file is <u>OK</u>.

The `read` method of a file object reads the entire contents of a file into a string. For example, the following statement reads the entirety of `mobydick.txt` into a string assigned to the variable `text`.

```
text = textFile.read()
```

When you are finished with a file, it is important to close it. This signals to the operating system that you are done using it, and ensures that any memory allocated to the file is released. To close a file, simply use the file object's `close` method:

```
textFile.close()
```

Let's look at an example that puts all of this together. The following function reads a file with the given file name and returns the number of words in the file using our `wordCount` function from the previous section. (Remember that you will have to save the program containing this function in the same folder as `textlib.py`.)

```
import textlib

def wordCountFile(fileName):
    """Return the number of words in the file with the given name.

    Parameter:
        fileName: the name of a text file

    Return value: the number of words in the file
    """

    textFile = open(fileName, 'r', encoding = 'utf-8')
    text = textFile.read()
    textFile.close()

    return textlib.wordCount(text)
```

---

[3]Download from the book website or `http://www.gutenberg.org/files/2701/2701-0.txt`.

The optional **encoding** parameter to the **open** function indicates how the bits in the file should be interpreted (we will discuss what UTF-8 is in Section 6.3).

| **Reflection 6.7** *How many words are there in the file* **mobydick.txt**?

Now suppose we want to print a text file, formatted with line numbers to the left of each line. A "line" is defined to be a sequence of characters that end with a newline character. To make this easier, rather than read the whole file in at once, we can read it one line at a time. In the same way that we can iterate over a range of integers or the characters of a string, we can iterate over the lines in a file. When we use a file object as the sequence in a **for** loop, the index variable is assigned a string containing each line in the file, one line per iteration. For example, the following loop prints each line in the file object named **textFile**:

```
for line in textFile:
    print(line)
```

In each iteration of this loop, **line** is assigned the next line in the file, which is then printed in the body of the loop. We can easily extend this idea to a line-numbering function:

```
def lineNumbers(fileName):
    """Print the contents of a file with line numbers added.

    Parameter:
        fileName: the name of a text file

    Return value: None
    """

    textFile = open(fileName, 'r', encoding = 'utf-8')
    count = 1
    for line in textFile:
        print('{0:<5} {1}'.format(count, line.rstrip()))
        count = count + 1
    textFile.close()
```

The **lineNumbers** function combines an accumulator with a **for** loop that reads the text file line by line. After the file is opened, the accumulator variable **count** is initialized to one. Inside the loop, each line is printed using a format string that precedes the line with the current value of **count**. The **rstrip()** method removes whitespace from the right end of the string. (There are also **lstrip()** and **strip()** methods. See Appendix A.6.) At the end of the loop, the accumulator is incremented and the loop repeats.

| **Reflection 6.8** *What effect does the* **rstrip** *method have? What happens if you replace* **line.rstrip()** *with just* **line***?*

| **Reflection 6.9** *How would the output change if* **count** *was incremented before calling* **print** *instead?*

| **Reflection 6.10** *How many lines are there in the file* `mobydick.txt`?

Writing to text files

We can also create new files or write to existing ones. To write text to a new file, we first have to open it using `'w'` ("write") mode:

```
newTextFile = open('newfile.txt', 'w')
```

Opening a file in this way will create a new file named `newfile.txt`, if a file by that name does not exist, or overwrite the file by that name if it does exist. (So be careful!) To append to the end of an existing file, use the `'a'` ("append") mode instead. Once the file is open, we can write text to it using the `write` method:

```
newTextFile.write('Hello.\n')
```

The `write` method does not write a newline character at the end of the string by default, so we have to include one explicitly, as desired.

Remember to always close the new file when you are done.

```
newTextFile.close()
```

Closing a file to which we have written ensures that the changes have actually been written to the drive. To improve efficiency, an operating system does not necessarily write text out to the drive immediately. Instead, it usually waits until a sufficient amount builds up, and then writes it all at once. Therefore, if you forget to close a file and your computer crashes, your program's last writes may not have actually been written. (This is one reason why we sometimes have trouble with corrupted files after a computer crash.)

The following function highlights how to modify the `lineNumbers` function so that it writes the file with line numbers directly to another file instead of printing it.

```
def lineNumbersFile(fileName, newFileName):
    """Write the contents of a file to a new file with line numbers added.

    Parameters:
        fileName:    the name of a text file
        newFileName: the name of the output text file

    Return value: None
    """

    textFile = open(fileName, 'r', encoding = 'utf-8')
    newTextFile = open(newFileName, 'w')
    count = 1
    for line in textFile:
        newTextFile.write('{0:<5} {1}\n'.format(count, line.rstrip()))
        count = count + 1
    textFile.close()
    newTextFile.close()
```

Reading from the web

We can also read text directly from the web using the `urllib.request` module. The function `urlopen` returns a file object abstraction for a web page that is similar to the one returned by `open`. The `urlopen` function takes a web page address, formally known as a *URL*, or *uniform resource locator*, as a parameter. URLs normally begin with the prefix `http://` (http is short for hypertext transfer protocol).

Let's download a book from Project Gutenberg (`www.gutenberg.org`), a vast repository of free classic literature. Mary Shelley's *Frankenstein*, for example, can be downloaded like this:

```
>>> import urllib.request as web
>>> webPage = web.urlopen('http://www.gutenberg.org/files/84/84-0.txt')
>>> rawBytes = webPage.read()
>>> webPage.close()
```

Behind the scenes, the Python interpreter communicates with a web server over the Internet to read this web page. But thanks to the magic of abstraction, we did not have to worry about any of those details. To find the URL for a different book, search for it on Project Gutenberg's web page and then find the link for the "Plain Text UTF-8" version. After you click on the link, copy the URL and use it as the argument to the `urlopen` function.

Because the `urlopen` function does not accept an encoding parameter, the `read` function cannot tell how the text of the web page is encoded. Therefore, `read` returns a `bytes` object instead of a string. A `bytes` object contains a sequence of raw bytes that are not interpreted in any particular way. To convert the `bytes` object to a string before we print it, we can use the `decode` method, as follows:

```
>>> text = rawBytes.decode('utf-8')
```

(Again, we will see what UTF-8 is in Section 6.3.) Now `text` refers to the entire 440 KB text of *Frankenstein* and can be used like any other string.

> **Reflection 6.11** *Write a short program with these statements that uses your* `wordCount` *function to find the number of words in* Frankenstein. *(You should get about 78,000.)*

It's worth noting that the vast majority of content on the web is not plain text like this. Rather it is written in HTML (short for hypertext markup language), which is the language that web browsers "understand." To see what HTML looks like, try this:

```
>>> webPage = web.urlopen('http://stibitz.denison.edu')
>>> rawBytes = webPage.read()
>>> rawBytes.decode('utf-8')
```

What you see printed is the HTML code for the main web page at this address.

Exercises

6.2.1.   If you implemented the `readingLevel` function in Exercise 6.1.26, write a function

   `readingLevelFile(fileName)`

   that returns the Flesch-Kincaid reading level of the file with the given `fileName`.

6.2.2.   Modify the `lineNumbers` function so that it only prints a line number on every tenth line (for lines $1, 11, 21, \ldots$).

6.2.3*   Write a function

   `lowerCaseFile(fileName)`

   that prints the contents of a file with every character converted to lowercase. Read the file one line at a time in a loop.

6.2.4.   Write a function

   `wordCountLines(fileName)`

   that uses the `wordCount` function from your `textlib` module to print the number of words in each line of the file with the given `fileName`.

6.2.5.   Write a function

   `paragraphCount(fileName)`

   that returns the number of paragraphs in the file with the given `fileName`. Assume that paragraphs are separated by one or more blank lines.

6.2.6*   Write a function

   `plotWordsPerParagraph(fileName)`

   that uses `matplotlib.pyplot` and the `wordCount` function from your `textlib` module to plot the number of words in the paragraphs of the file with the given `fileName`. Assume that paragraphs are separated by one or more blank lines.

6.2.7.   Write a function

   `plotIsPerParagraph(fileName)`

   that plots the *fraction* of words that are the word "I" in the paragraphs of `fileName`. You may find the string method `count` helpful. Assume that paragraphs are separated by one or more blank lines. Use `matplotlib.pyplot` and the `wordCount` function from your `textlib` module.

6.2.8.   Write a function

   `plotWordsPerChapter(fileName, chapterOneStart)`

   that uses `matplotlib.pyplot` and the `wordCount` function from your `textlib` module to plot the number of words in the chapters of the book with the given `fileName`. Assume that new chapters begin when the word "chapter" is the first non-whitespace word on a line and the previous line is blank. (See the string method `startswith` in Appendix A.6.) The parameter `chapterOneStart` is the line number of the first chapter in the book. Your function should begin by skipping this many lines to get past the table of contents and any other front matter in the text. Remember to include the last chapter (marked by the end of the file) in your plot. You can test your function with the files `mobydick.txt` and `frankenstein.txt` on the book website. The first chapters in these books start on lines 489 and 684, respectively.

6.2.9.   Write a function

        `strip(fileName, newFileName)`

that creates a new version of the file with the given `fileName` in which all whitespace has been removed. The second parameter is the name of the new file.

6.2.10*   Write a function

        `writeLineLengths(fileName, outputFile)`

that writes the lengths of all the lines in `fileName` (not counting newline characters) to a new file named `outputFile`. Each line in the output file should simply be the length of one line.

6.2.11.   Write a function

        `writeWordsPerParagraph(fileName, outputFile)`

that writes the number of words in each paragraph in `fileName` to a new file named `outputFile`. Each line in the output file should contain a paragraph number and the number of words in that paragraph, like this:

    1: 9
    2: 44
    3: 6
    ⋮

6.2.12.   Write a function that makes a new copy of a file in which every sentence begins on a new line. You may assume that every period, question mark, and exclamation point in the file end a sentence. Before you process each line, use the string method `strip` to remove whitespace (including the newline) from both ends of the line. Then add a space at the end of the line (after the last word). For an extra challenge, also prevent whitespace from appearing at the beginning of each line before a sentence. Your function should take two parameters: the name of the original file and the name of the new file.

6.2.13*   Write a function

        `wordCountWeb(url)`

that reads the text file from the given URL and returns the number of words in the file using the `wordCount` function from your `textlib` module. Test your function on books from Project Gutenberg. Alternatively, you can access mirrored copies of books from the book website.

6.2.14.   According to the HTML standard specification, every HTML web page should begin with the declaration

        `<!DOCTYPE html>`

This declaration is not case sensitive and may contain additional elements such as

        `<!DOCTYPE HTML PUBLIC "-//W3C//DTD HTML 4.01//EN"`
        `"http://www.w3.org/TR/html4/strict.dtd">`

Write a function

        `isHTML(url)`

that uses this information to detect whether a web page is an HTML document or not. The function should return `True` if it is HTML and `False` otherwise.

6.3 ENCODING STRINGS

As web pages travel across the Internet to your browser, the transmissions can be corrupted by faulty equipment or electromagnetic interference. Errors can be as small as a single bit being "flipped" or as large as an entire chunk of data being lost. In this section, we will discuss how knowing something about how text is stored at a lower level enables us to detect these kinds of errors. This knowledge will also prove essential for some of the more interesting text analysis we will do in the following sections.

Computing checksums

Network protocols detect errors by sending additional information, called a **checksum**, along with the data.

In a nutshell, a checksum is used to tell whether what is received is the same as what was sent. When the transmission is received at the destination, a checksum is computed for the data and compared to the transmitted checksum. If they match, all is well. If they don't match, then the receiver asks the sender to retransmit.

The following algorithm represents the simplest way to compute a checksum for a raw sequence of bytes. It just adds the bytes together, each time taking the remainder mod 256 so that the checksum value will fit in one byte. (Recall that one byte is 8 bits, so a byte can store values between 0 and $2^8 - 1 = 255$.)

Algorithm SIMPLE CHECKSUM

Input: a *byte sequence*

1 | *checksum* ← 0
2 | repeat for each *byte* in the *byte sequence*:
3 | *checksum* ← (*checksum* + *byte*) mod 256

Output: *checksum*

For example, suppose we wanted to send the following byte sequence:

| 42 | 207 | 111 | 199 |

The algorithm will compute a checksum like this:

Control characters	Space	Punctuation characters	Digits	Punctuation characters	Upper case letters	Punctuation characters	Lower case letters	Punctuation characters	Delete
0 31	32	33 47	48 57	58 64	65 90	91 96	97 122	123 126	127

Figure 6.4 A not-to-scale overview of the organization of the ASCII character set (and the Basic Latin segment of Unicode) with decimal code ranges.

Trace input: *byte sequence* = [42, 207, 111, 199]

Step	Line	*byte*	*checksum*	Notes
1	1	—	0	*checksum* ← 0
2	2	42	"	*byte* ← 42
3	3	"	42	*checksum* ← (0 + 42) mod 256 = 42
4	2	207	"	*byte* ← 207
5	3	"	249	*checksum* ← (42 + 207) mod 256 = 249
6	2	111	"	*byte* ← 111
7	3	"	104	*checksum* ← (249 + 111) mod 256 = 104
8	2	199	"	*byte* ← 199
9	3	"	47	*checksum* ← (104 + 199) mod 256 = 47

Return value: 47

The computed checksum is 47, so we append this to the transmitted message:

	data			checksum
42	207	111	199	47

Unicode

To apply this algorithm to text, we need to look more closely at how strings are encoded in binary in a computer's memory. English language text has historically been encoded in a format known as **ASCII** (pronounced "ASS-key").[4] ASCII assigns each character a 7-bit binary code. In memory, each ASCII character is stored in one byte, with the leftmost bit of the byte being a 0. So a string is stored as a sequence of bytes. For example, the first six letters of the quote

If you don't like something, change it. If you can't change it, change your attitude.

—Maya Angelou

are encoded in ASCII as

I	f	␣	y	o	u
01001001	01100110	00100000	01111001	01101111	01110101
73	102	32	121	111	117

---

[4]ASCII is an acronym for American Standard Code for Information Interchange.

The values underneath are the decimal equivalents of the binary codes. Figure 6.4 uses these decimal values to illustrate the organization of the ASCII character set. Notice that different types of characters are grouped together. Digits are in the range 48–57, uppercase letters are in 65–90, lowercase letters are in 97–122, etc. Python uses this encoding to define "alphabetical order" when comparing strings.

Reflection 6.12 *Consult Figure 6.4 to explain each of the following results.*

```
>>> '3.14159' < 'pi'
True
>>> 'pi' == 'Pi'
False
>>> 'Zebra' < 'antelope'
True
>>> '314159' < '32'
True
```

The ASCII character set has been largely supplanted, including in Python, by an international standard known as ***Unicode***. Whereas ASCII only provides codes for Latin characters, Unicode encodes over 100,000 different characters from more than 100 languages, using up to 4 bytes per character. A Unicode string can be encoded in one of three ways, but is most commonly encoded using a variable-length system called UTF-8 (that we used in the previous section). Conveniently, UTF-8 is backwards-compatible with ASCII, so each character in the ASCII character set is encoded in the same 1-byte format in UTF-8.

In Python, we can view the Unicode (in decimal) for any character using the `ord` function (short for "ordinal"). For example,

```
>>> ord('I')
73
```

The `chr` function is the inverse of `ord`; given a Unicode value, `chr` returns the corresponding character.

```
>>> chr(73)
'I'
```

Reflection 6.13 *Use `ord` on the first characters of the strings in Reflection 6.12 to explain the results of the comparisons.*

The following Python function uses `ord` to apply our SIMPLE CHECKSUM algorithm to strings. Once the one-byte checksum is computed, we convert it to a character using `chr` so that we can concatenate it to the string before sending it.

```
def simpleChecksum(text):
    """Compute a simple one-character checksum for a string.

    Parameter:
        text: a string

    Return value: a character representing the one-byte checksum
    """
```

```
    checksum = 0
    for character in text:
        checksum = (checksum + ord(character)) % 256

    return chr(checksum)
```

Let's use this function to create a checksum for our Maya Angelou quote.

```
>>> quote = "If you don't like something, change it.  If you can't
            change it, change your attitude."
>>> checksum = simpleChecksum(quote)
>>> checksum
'ç'
```

The computed checksum value was 231, which corresponds to a lowercase c with a cedilla in Unicode. (The character representation of the checksum doesn't really matter since it is not really part of the text.) To create a message to send across a network, we would next concatenate the string and the checksum.

```
>>> message = quote + checksum
>>> message
"If you don't like something, change it.  If you can't change it,
 change your attitude.ç"
```

This simple checksum algorithm is actually too weak to be used in practice. Most notably, it cannot detect when two bytes are sent out of order.

Reflection 6.14 *Why does the simple checksum algorithm have this problem?*

Fletcher's checksum algorithm fixes this by adding a second checksum that incrementally sums the values of the first checksum.

```
def fletcherChecksum(text):
    """Compute a two character checksum for a string using the
       Fletcher-16 algorithm.

    Parameter:
        text: a string

    Return value: a two-character string representing the checksum
    """

    checksum1 = 0
    checksum2 = 0
    for character in text:
        checksum1 = (checksum1 + ord(character)) % 255
        checksum2 = (checksum2 + checksum1) % 255

    return chr(checksum2) + chr(checksum1)
```

Note that this algorithm also differs in that it mods by 255 instead of 256. The return value is a two-character string created by concatenating the characters corresponding to the two checksum values.

Tangent 6.2: Compressing text files

If a text file is stored in UTF-8 format, then each character is represented by an eight-bit code, requiring one byte of storage per character. For example, the file mobydick.txt contains about 1.2 million characters, so it requires about 1.2 MB of disk space. But text files can usually be modified to use far less space, without losing any information. Suppose that a text file contains upper and lowercase letters, plus whitespace and punctuation, for a total of sixty unique characters. Since $2^6 = 64$, we can adopt an alternative encoding scheme in which each of these sixty unique characters is represented by a six-bit code instead. By doing so, the text file will use only 6/8 = 75% of the space.

The **Huffman coding** algorithm can do even better by using variable-length codes that are shorter for more frequent characters. As a simple example, suppose a 23,000-character text file contains only five unique characters: A, C, G, N, and T with frequencies of 5, 6, 4, 3, and 5 thousand, respectively. Using the previous fixed-length scheme, we could devise a three-bit code for these characters and use only $3 \cdot 23,000 = 69,000$ bits instead of the original $8 \cdot 23,000 = 184,000$ bits. But, by using a prefix code that assigns the more frequent characters A, C, and T to shorter two-bit codes (A = 10, C = 00, and T = 11) and the less frequent characters G and N to three-bit codes (G = 010 and N = 011), we can store the file in

$$2 \cdot 5,000 + 2 \cdot 6,000 + 3 \cdot 4,000 + 3 \cdot 3,000 + 2 \cdot 5,000 = 53,000$$

bits instead. This is called a *prefix code* because no code is a prefix of another code, which is essential for decoding the file.

An alternative compression technique, used by the **Lempel-Ziv-Welch algorithm**, replaces repeated strings of characters with fixed-length codes. For example, in the string CANTNAGATANCANCANNAGANT, the repeated sequences CAN and NAG might each be represented with its own code.

Reflection 6.15 *Show how to compute the Fletcher checksums by hand for the string* 'abc'. *(You should get 39 and 76 for* checksum1 *and* checksum2, *respectively, corresponding to the string* "L'".*)*

We can now apply the Fletcher checksum algorithm to our quote like this:

```
>>> checksum = fletcherChecksum(quote)
>>> checksum
'\r\x05'
>>> message2 = quote + checksum
>>> message2
"If you don't like something, change it.  If you can't
 change it, change your attitude.\r\x05"
```

(The character '\r' is the "carriage return" character and '\x05' represents the symbol with ASCII code 5, which is an antiquated non-printable control character that was once used to request a response from computer terminals and teletype machines. But their meanings are irrelevant here.)

Indexing and slicing

To confirm that a message is error-free, the receiver needs to remove the two-character checksum and compare it to a checksum that it computes itself on the remaining text. To implement this, we need to be able to directly access those last few characters. Conceptually, we already know that a string is stored as a sequence of bytes, where each byte represents one character. These bytes are stored in contiguous memory cells. So the first sentence of the Maya Angelou quote, `"If you don't like something, change it."`, can be represented like this:

```
                                          · · · -8 -7 -6 -5 -4 -3 -2 -1
┌─┬─┬─┬─┬─┬─┬─┬─┬─┬─┬─┬─┬─┬─┬─┬─┬─┬─┬─┬─┬─┬─┬─┬─┬─┬─┬─┬─┬─┬─┬─┬─┐
│I│f│ │y│o│u│ │d│o│n│'│t│ │l│i│k│e│ │s│o│m│e│t│h│i│n│g│,│ │c│h│a│n│g│e│ │i│t│.│
└─┴─┴─┴─┴─┴─┴─┴─┴─┴─┴─┴─┴─┴─┴─┴─┴─┴─┴─┴─┴─┴─┴─┴─┴─┴─┴─┴─┴─┴─┴─┴─┘
 0 1 2 3 4 5 6 7 8 9 10 · · ·                            · · · 37 38
```

Each character in the string is identified by an *index* that indicates its position. Indices always start from the left at 0, as shown below the characters above. We can also use *negative indexing*, which starts from the right end of the string, as shown above the characters. We can use these indices to access a character directly by referring to the index in square brackets following the name of the string. For example,

```
>>> shortQuote = "If you don't like something, change it."
>>> shortQuote[0]
'I'
>>> shortQuote[9]
'n'
>>> shortQuote[-30]
'n'
>>> shortQuote[-1]
'.'
```

Notice that each character is itself represented as a single-character string in quotes, and that `quote[9]` and `quote[-30]` refer to the same character. The last character in a string can always be accessed with index `-1`, regardless of the string's length. We can use this to access the checksum character in the first `message`.

```
>>> message[-1]
'ç'
```

To get a string's length, we use the `len` function:

```
>>> len(shortQuote)
39
>>> shortQuote[38]
'.'
>>> shortQuote[39]
IndexError: string index out of range
```

▎ Reflection 6.16 *Why does the last statement above result in an error?*

Notice that `len` returns the number of characters in the string, *not* the index of the last character. The positive index of the last character in a string is always the length of the string minus one. As shown above, referring to an index that does not exist will give an ***index error*** exception.

To access a substring consisting of multiple characters, like the two-character Fletcher checksum, we use *slicing*. Slice notation uses two indices separated by a colon. The first index is the position of the first character in the slice and the second is the index of the character *just past* the last character in the slice (analogous to how `range` stops just shy of its argument). So we can get the Fletcher checksum from `message2` like this:

```
>>> message2[len(message2)-2:len(message2)]
'\r\x05'
```

or, much more simply,

```
>>> message2[-2:]
'\r\x05'
```

Here we used a negative index for the beginning of the slice and omitted the second index, which means that we want the slice to go to the end of the string. Similarly, if we want a slice from the beginning of a string, we can omit the first index. So `message[:-1]` will give us the "data" portion of the first message and `message2[:-2]` will give us the "data" portion of the second message.

```
>>> message[:-1]
"If you don't like something, change it.  If you can't change it, ..."
>>> message2[:-2]
"If you don't like something, change it.  If you can't change it, ..."
```

The following function uses slicing to verify whether a message with a Fletcher checksum was "received" correctly. If the checksum is correct, it returns the data portion of the message. Otherwise, it returns an empty string.

```
def verifyMessage(message):
    """Verify a message with a Fletcher-16 checksum.

    Parameter:
        message: a string containing data + checksum

    Return value: the data if verified or '' if not
    """

    data = message[:-2]
    checksum = message[-2:]
    if fletcher(data) == checksum:
        return data
    else:
        return ''
```

We will continue to use indexing and slicing in the next sections, as we explore more sophisticated techniques to analyze large texts.

Exercises

When an exercise asks you to write a function, test it with both common and boundary case arguments, and document your test cases.

6.3.1. Suppose you have a string stored in a variable named **word**. Show how you would print

  (a)* the string's length

  (b)* the first character in the string

  (c)* the third character in the string

  (d)* the last character in the string

  (e) the last three characters in the string

  (f) the string consisting of the second, third, and fourth characters

  (g) the string consisting of the fifth, fourth, and third to last characters

  (h) the string consisting of all but the last character

6.3.2. The following string is a quote by Benjamin Franklin.

  quote = 'Well done is better than well said.'

  Use slicing notation to answer each of the following questions.

  (a)* What slice of **quote** is equal to 'done'?

  (b)* What slice of **quote** is equal to 'well said.'?

  (c) What slice of **quote** is equal to 'one is bet'?

  (d) What slice of **quote** is equal to 'Well do'?

6.3.3. What are the values of each of the following expressions? Explain why in each case.

  (a)* 'cat' < 'dog'

  (b)* 'cat' < 'catastrophe'

  (c)* 'cat' == 'Cat'

  (d) '1' > 'one'

  (e) '8188' < '82'

  (f) 'many' > 'One'

6.3.4* When we print a numeric value using the print function, each digit in the number must be converted to its corresponding character to be displayed. In other words, the value 0 must be converted to the character '0', the value 1 must be converted to the character '1', etc. The Unicode codes for the digit characters are conveniently sequential, so the code for any digit character is equal to ord('0') plus the value of the digit. For example, ord('2') is the same as ord('0') + 2 and chr(ord('0') + 2) is '2'. Write a function

  digit2String(digit)

that generalizes this example to return the string equivalent of the number `digit`. For example, `digit2String(4)` should return `'4'`. If `digit` is not the value of a decimal digit, return `None`.

6.3.5. Suppose we want to convert a letter to an integer representing its position in the alphabet. In other words, we want to convert `'A'` or `'a'` to 1, `'B'` or `'b'` to 2, etc. Like the characters for the digits, the codes for the uppercase and lowercase letters are in consecutive order. Therefore, for an uppercase letter, we can subtract the code for `'A'` from the code for the letter to get the letter's offset relative to `'A'`. Similarly, we can subtract the code for `'a'` from the code for a lowercase letter. For example, `ord('D') - ord('A')` is 3. Write a function

```
letter2Position(letter)
```

that uses this idea to return the position in the alphabet (1–26) of the upper or lowercase `letter`. If `letter` is not a letter, return `None`.

6.3.6. Write a function

```
position2Letter(n)
```

that returns the nth uppercase letter in the alphabet, using the `chr` and `ord` functions.

6.3.7. Write a function

```
string2Digit(digitString)
```

that returns the integer value corresponding to the string `digitString`. The parameter will contain a single character `'0'`, `'1'`, ..., `'9'`. Use the `ord` function. For example, `string2Digit('5')` should return the integer value 5.

6.3.8. Any exam score between 60 and 99 can be converted to a letter grade with a single expression using `chr` and `ord`. Demonstrate this by replacing `SOMETHING` in the function below.

```
def letterGrade(score):
    if grade >= 100:
        return 'A'
    if grade > 59:
        return SOMETHING
    return 'F'
```

6.3.9. Write a function

```
capitalize(word)
```

that uses `ord` and `chr` to return a version of the string `word` with the first letter capitalized. (Note that the word may already be capitalized!)

6.3.10. Write a function

```
int2String(number)
```

that converts any positive integer value **number** to its string equivalent, *without* using the `str` function. For example, `int2String(1234)` should return the string `'1234'`. (Use the `digit2String` function from Exercise 6.3.4.)

6.3.11. Suppose you work for a state in which all vehicle license plates consist of a string of letters followed by a string of numbers, such as `'ABC 123'`. Write a function

<dl>
<dd>

```
randomPlate(length)
```

that returns a string representing a randomly generated license plate consisting of `length` uppercase letters followed by a space followed by `length` digits. Use the `random.randrange` function.

</dd>
</dl>

6.3.12. Write a function

```
username(first, last)
```

that constructs and returns a username, specified as the last name followed by an underscore and the first initial. For example, `username('martin', 'freeman')` should return the string `'freeman_m'`.

6.3.13. Write a function

```
piglatin(word)
```

that returns the Pig Latin equivalent of the string `word`. If the first character is a consonant, Pig Latin moves it to the end, and follows it with `'ay'`. If the first character is a vowel, nothing is moved and `'way'` is added to the end. For example, Pig Latin translations of `'python'` and `'asp'` are `'ythonpay'` and `'aspway'`.

6.3.14. Write a function

```
pigLatinDict(fileName)
```

that prints the Pig Latin equivalent of every word in the dictionary file with the given file name. (See Exercise 6.3.13.) Assume there is exactly one word on each line of the file. Start by testing your function on small files that you create. An actual dictionary file can be found on most Mac OS X and Linux computers at `/usr/share/dict/words`. There is also a dictionary file available on the book website.

6.3.15. Repeat the previous exercise, but have your function write the results to a new file instead, one Pig Latin word per line. Add a second parameter for the name of the new file.

6.3.16* When some people get married, they choose to take the last name of their spouse or hyphenate their last name with the last name of their spouse. Write a function

```
marriedName(fullName, spouseLastName, hyphenate)
```

that returns the person's new full name with hyphenated last name if `hyphenate` is `True` or the person's new full name with the spouse's last name if `hyphenate` is `False`. The parameter `fullName` is the person's current full name in the form `'Firstname Lastname'` and the parameter `spouseLastName` is the spouse's last name. For example, `marriedName('Jane Doe', 'Deer', True)` should return the string `'Jane Doe-Deer'` and `marriedName('Jane Doe', 'Deer', False)` should return the string `'Jane Deer'`.

6.3.17. *Parity checking* is an even simpler error detection algorithm that is used directly on sequences of bits (often called *bit strings*). A bit string has *even parity* if it has an even number of ones, and *odd parity* otherwise. In an even parity scheme, the sender adds a single bit to the end of the bit string so that the final bit string has an even number of ones. For example, if we wished to send the data 1101011, we would actually send 11010111 instead so that the bit string has an even number of ones. If we wished to send 1101001 instead, we would actually send 11010010. The receiver checks whether the received bit string has even parity; if it does not, the receiver requests a retransmission.

(a) Parity can only detect very simple errors. Give an example of an error that cannot be detected by an even parity scheme.

(b) Propose a solution that would detect the example error you gave above.

(c) In the next two problems, we will pretend that bits are sent as strings (they are not; this would be terribly inefficient). Write a function

```
evenParity(bits)
```

that uses the `count` method to return True if the string `bits` has even parity and False otherwise. For example, `evenParity('110101')` should return True and `evenParity('110001')` should return False.

(d) Now write the `evenParity` function without using the `count` method.

(e) Write a function

```
makeEvenParity(bits)
```

that returns a string consisting of `bits` with one additional bit concatenated so that the returned string has even parity. Your function should call your `evenParity` function. For example, `makeEvenParity('110101')` should return `'1101010'` and `makeEvenParity('110001')` should return `'1100011'`.

6.3.18. Julius Caesar is said to have sent secret correspondence using a simple encryption scheme that is now known as the Caesar cipher. In the Caesar cipher, each letter in a text is replaced by the letter some fixed distance, called the *shift*, away. For example, with a shift of 3, A is replaced by D, B is replaced by E, etc. At the end of the alphabet, the encoding wraps around so that X is replaced by A, Y is replaced by B, and Z is replaced by C. Write a function

```
encipher(text, shift)
```

that returns the result of encrypting `text` with a Caesar cypher with the given `shift`. Assume that `text` contains only uppercase letters.

6.3.19. Modify the `encipher` function from the previous problem so that it either encrypts or decrypts `text`, based on the value of an additional Boolean parameter.

6.4   A CONCORDANCE

A *concordance* is an alphabetical listing of all the words in a text, with their contexts. The context is usually one or more lines in which the target word appears. Suppose we want to know where "lash" appears in the text of *Moby Dick*. If we searched, we would find matches on 60 lines, the first 6 of which are:

```
things not properly belonging to the room, there was a hammock lashed
ship was gliding by, like a flash he darted out; gained her side; with
which to manage the barrow--Queequeg puts his chest upon it; lashes it
blow her homeward; seeks all the lashed sea's landlessness again;
sailed with. How he flashed at me!--his eyes like powder-pans! is he
I was so taken all aback with his brow, somehow. It flashed like a
```

Note that we are not necessarily looking for complete words. When we search for the root of a word like "lash," we might also be interested in derivatives like "lashes" and "lashed." But we might also get other words that contain "lash," like "flash" and "flashed." (We will leave finding only complete words as an exercise.)

To make viewing this information easier, we will line up the words and note the line on which each appears in the text:

```
1188 ... properly belonging to the room, there was a hammock lashed
2458                         ship was gliding by, like a flash he ...
2551 ... manage the barrow--Queequeg puts his chest upon it; lashes it
4396                         blow her homeward; seeks all the lashed ...
5103                         sailed with. How he flashed at ...
5127     I was so taken all aback with his brow, somehow. It flashed like a
```

We will focus here on creating a concordance entry for just one word. Once we have written a function to do this, it will actually be quite easy to create an entire concordance, but the result could be quite large (e.g., *Moby Dick* contains over 20,000 unique words) and we have not yet discussed how we could quickly search through such a large file for a desired entry.

To create a concordance entry, we will iterate over the lines of the text file, and search for the target word in each line. For each line in which the target word is found, we will print the line, prefaced by a line number, lining up the words in a column for easy reading. Here is the algorithm in pseudocode:

Algorithm CONCORDANCE ENTRY

Input: a *text file*, a *target word*
1 | *line number* ← 1
2 | repeat for each *line* in the *text file*:
3 | *index* ← FIND (*line*, *target word*)
4 | if the *target word* was found in *line*, then:
5 | print the *line number* and the *line*, using *index* to line up the *target words*
6 | *line number* ← *line number* + 1
Output: none

Finding a word

The FIND algorithm, which we will write next, will search through a line and return the index of the first occurrence of the target word in that line, if it exists. There is an existing string method to do just this.[5]

```
>>> benFranklin = 'Diligence is the mother of good luck.'
>>> benFranklin.find('good')
27
```

---

[5]This quote is from *The Way to Wealth* (1758) by Benjamin Franklin.

But we will implement a `find` function from scratch because, as with `splitIntoWords`, the technique involved is important and useful for other problems down the road. The idea is to make a pass across the text, comparing the target string to slices of the text with the same length as the target. When a matching slice is found, we want to return the index in the text where that slice begins. In pseudocode, the algorithm looks like this:

Algorithm FIND

Input: *text, target*

   1 | *target index* ← −1
   2 | repeat for each *slice* of *text* with the same length as *target*:
   3 | if *slice* = *target*, then:
   4 | *target index* ← starting position of the *slice* in *text*
   5 | break out of the loop

Output: *target index*

The variable *target index* will store the index of the matching slice when it is found. It is initialized to −1 at the beginning of the algorithm to signify that a match has not been found yet. We chose the value −1 because this is not a value that could possibly be returned by the algorithm if the target is found. Notice that the value of *target index* remains −1 if a matching slice is never found in the loop. If a matching slice is found, then *target index* is assigned to the index of that slice and we exit the loop immediately so that a possible later match does not overwrite this value.

To see how to implement this in Python, let's first consider the simpler problem of searching for a single character in a string. If we iterate over the characters in the string to search for the target character, as we have done in all of our string algorithms to this point, it would look like this:

```
for character in text:
    if character == targetCharacter:   # target character is found
        targetIndex = ???              # get the index where it was found?
```

But when we find the target character, we are left without a satisfactory return value because we do not know the index of `character`!

Instead, we need to iterate over the *indices* of `text` so that, when we find the target character, we know where it is located in the string. In other words, for all values of `index` equal to 0, 1, 2, ..., we need to test whether `text[index]` is equal to `targetCharacter`. If this condition is true, then we know that `targetCharacter` exists at position `index`!

| **Reflection 6.17** *How can we get a list of every index in a string to use in a `for` loop?*

The list of indices in a string named `text` is 0, 1, 2, ..., `len(text) - 1`. This is precisely the list of integers given by `range(len(text))`. So our desired `for` loop looks like the following:

```
for index in range(len(text)):
    if text[index] == targetCharacter: # target character is found
        targetIndex = index             # get the index where it was found
```

Now when we find that `text[index] == targetCharacter`, we know that the desired character is at position `index`.

> **Reflection 6.18** *Although it isn't always necessary, we can use this kind of loop any time we need to iterate over a string. Use the examples above to show how to accomplish exactly the same thing as the following* for *loop by iterating over the indices of* **text** *instead:*
>
> ```
> for character in text:
>     print(character)
> ```

The following function uses the new loop above to find a target character in a string.

```
1 def findCharacter(text, targetCharacter):
2     """Find the index of first occurrence of a target character in text.
3
4     Parameters:
5         text:            a string object to search in
6         targetCharacter: a character to search for
7
8     Return value: index of the first occurrence of targetCharacter in text
9     """
10
11    targetIndex = -1                        # assume it won't be found
12    for index in range(len(text)):
13        if text[index] == targetCharacter:  # if found, then
14            targetIndex = index             #    remember where
15            break                           #    and exit the loop early
16    return targetIndex
```

The `break` statement on line 12 exits the loop immediately, even if it is not yet done.

> **Reflection 6.19** *What do you get when you call this function with* `findCharacter('Diligence is the mother of good luck.', 'g')`*? If you remove the* break *statement from the loop, what do you get? Why?*

We need to exit the loop when the first occurrence of `targetCharacter` is found because, if we don't and `targetCharacter` occurs again later in `text`, then `targetIndex` will be overwritten, and the index of the *last* occurrence will be returned instead. The following trace table shows this more explicitly, along with how the changing value of `index` affects the value of `text[index]` in the `if` condition.

Trace arguments: text = 'Diligence is the mother of good luck.',
targetCharacter = 'g'

Step	Line	targetIndex	index	text[index]	Notes
1	8	-1	—	—	targetCharacter ← -1
2	9	"	0	'D'	index ← 0
3	10	"	"	"	'D' != 'g'; skip lines 11-12
4	9	"	1	'i'	index ← 1
5	10	"	"	"	'i' != 'g'; skip lines 11-12
6	9	"	2	'l'	index ← 2
7	10	"	"	"	'l' != 'g'; skip lines 11-12
8	9	"	3	'i'	index ← 3
9	10	"	"	"	'i' != 'g'; skip lines 11-12
10	9	"	4	'g'	index ← 4
11	10	"	"	"	'g' == 'g'; do lines 11-12
12	11	4	"	"	targetIndex ← index
13	12	"	"	"	break from loop; go to line 13
14	13	"	"	"	return 4

Return value: 4

To generalize this function to find a target string of any length, we need to compare the target string to all *slices* with the same length as the target in text. For example, suppose we want to search for the target string 'good' in text. We would need to check whether text[0:4] is equal to 'good', then whether text[1:5] is equal to 'good', then whether text[2:6] is equal to 'good', etc. More concisely, for all values of index equal to 0, 1, 2, ..., we need to test whether text[index:index + 4] is equal to 'good'. In general, to find a target string named target, we need to test whether text[index:index + len(target)] is equal to target, as in the following function.

```
 1 def find(text, target):
 2     """Find the index of the first occurrence of a target string in text.
 3
 4     Parameters:
 5         text:   a string object to search in
 6         target: a string object to search for
 7
 8     Return value: the index of the first occurrence of target in text
 9     """
 8     targetIndex = -1
 9     for index in range(len(text) - len(target) + 1):
10         if text[index:index + len(target)] == target:
11             targetIndex = index
12             break
13     return targetIndex
```

Notice how similar this is to `findCharacter` and that, if `len(target)` equals 1, the `find` function does exactly the same thing as `findCharacter`.

> **Reflection 6.20** *Why is the last index in the* `for` *loop equal to* `len(text) - len(target)` *instead of* `len(text) - 1`*?*

Suppose `text` is `'Diligence is the mother of good luck.'` and `target` is `'good'`. Then `len(text)` is 37 and `len(target)` is 4. If we had the loop iterate until `index` was `len(text) - 1 = 36`, then the last three slices to be examined would be the strings corresponding to `text[34:38]`, `text[35:39]`, and `text[36:40]`, which are `'ck.'`, `'k.'`, and `'.'`, respectively. But these strings are too short to possibly be equal to this `target`. In general, we never need to look at a slice that starts after `len(text) - len(target)`, hence we use `range(len(text) - len(target) + 1)`.

> **Reflection 6.21** *Is what we just said really true? What is returned by a slice that extends beyond the last character (e.g.,* `'good'[2:10]`*)? What is returned by a slice that starts beyond the last character in the string (e.g.,* `'good'[4:8]`*)?*

Let's look more closely at how `find` works when we call it with these arguments. We will omit `targetIndex` from the trace table this time to save space and instead show `text[index:index+len(target)]`.

Trace arguments: text = 'Diligence is the mother of good luck.',
target = 'good'

Step	Line	index	text[index:index+4]	Notes
1	8	—	—	initialize `targetIndex` ← −1
2	9	0	'Dili'	index ← 0
3	10	"	"	'Dili' != 'good'; skip lines 11-12
4	9	1	'ilig'	index ← 1
5	10	"	"	'ilig' != 'good'; skip lines 11-12
6	9	2	'lige'	index ← 2
7	10	"	"	'lige' != 'good'; skip lines 11-12
⋮				
54	9	26	' goo'	index ← 26
55	10	"	"	' goo' != 'good'; skip lines 11-12
56	9	27	'good'	index ← 27
57	10	"	"	'good' == 'good'; do lines 11-12
58	11	"	"	targetIndex ← index
59	12	"	"	break out of the loop; go to line 13
60	13	"	"	return 27

Return value: 27

A concordance entry

We are finally ready to use our **find** function to print a concordance entry. Here is an outline of a function that follows our pseudocode algorithm.

```
def concordanceEntry_Draft(textFile, targetWord):
    """Print all lines in a text file containing the target word.

    Parameters:
        textFile:   a file object
        targetWord: the word to search for

    Return value: None
    """

    lineNumber = 1
    for line in textFile:
        index = find(line.lower(), targetWord)
        # if targetWord is found in line (using the find function):
            print(lineNumber, line)   # not formatted nicely yet
        lineNumber = lineNumber + 1
```

Reflection 6.22 *When we call the* **find** *function to search for* **targetWord**, *how do we know if it was found?*

Because **find** returns **-1** if the target string is not found, any nonnegative value of **index** means that it was found. So the comment above will be replaced with

```
index = find(line.lower(), targetWord)
if index >= 0:
```

To line up the printed lines nicely, we will use a format string to ensure that the line number always takes up the same amount of space and the rightmost ends of the target words line up. We can do this by splitting the line at the end of the **targetWord**, right justifying the first half, and left justifying the second half.

```
align = index + len(targetWord)  # index of the end of targetWord in line
print('{0:<6}{1:>80}{2}'.format(lineNumber, line[:align], line[align:-1]))
```

Incorporating these changes, here is the complete function to print a single concordance entry:

```
def concordanceEntry(textFile, targetWord):
    """ (docstring omitted) """

    lineNumber = 1
    for line in textFile:
        index = find(line.lower(), targetWord)
        if index >= 0:    # targetWord is found in line
            align = index + len(targetWord)
            print('{0:<6}{1:>80}{2}'.format(lineNumber, line[:align],
                                            line[align:-1]))
        lineNumber = lineNumber + 1
```

There are many more enhancements we can make to this function, some of which we leave as exercises.

A complete concordance

Now we could, if we wanted to, print an entire concordance for a book! The `concordance` function below does just that. Because a full concordance can be very long indeed, we have added a parameter `numEntries` to limit the number of entries to print. There are also a couple of new things in this function that we encourage you to explore more on your own.

```python
import textlib
import string

def concordance(fileName, numEntries):
    """Print entries in the concordance for a text file.

    Parameters:
        fileName:   name of the text file
        targetWord: number of entries to print

    Return value: None
    """

    textFile = open(fileName, 'r', encoding = 'utf-8')
    text = textFile.read()
    words = textlib.wordTokens(text) # get all the words in textFile
    vocabulary = list(set(words))    # get the set of unique words
    vocabulary.sort()                # sort the words

    count = 0
    for word in vocabulary:                    # iterate over the sorted words
        if word[0] not in string.digits:       # omit if starts with a digit
            textFile.seek(0)                    # reset file pointer
            print('\n' + word.upper() + '\n')
            concordanceEntry(textFile, word)
            count = count + 1
        if count >= numEntries:                 # break when enough entries
            break
    textFile.close()

def main():
    concordance('mobydick.txt', 10)

main()
```

Exercises

6.4.1.   For each of the following `for` loops, write an equivalent loop that iterates over the indices of the string `text` instead of the characters.

(a)*
```
for character in text:
    print(character)
```

(b)*
```
newText = ''
for character in text:
    if character != ' ':
        newText = newText + character
```

(c)
```
for character in text[2:10]:
    if character >= 'a' and character <= 'z':
        print(character)
```

(d)
```
for character in text[1:-1]:
    print(text.count(character))
```

6.4.2* Show how to rewrite each of the `for` loops in the previous exercise as `while` loops that increment an index variable in each iteration.

6.4.3.   Describe what is wrong with each the following blocks of code, and show how to fix it.

(a)*
```
veggie = 'carrots'
for character in veggie:
    bigVeggie = bigVeggie + character.upper()
```

(b)*
```
while answer != 'q':
    answer = input('Word? ')
    print(len(answer))
```

(c)*
```
veggie = 'peas'
for index in range(veggie):
    if veggie[index] != ' ':
        print(index)
```

(d)
```
veggie = 'sweet potatoes'
for index in len(veggie):
    if veggie[index] != ' ':
        print(veggie[index])
```

(e)
```
for index in range(len(okra)):
    print(okra[len(okra) - index - 1])
```

(f)
```
text = 'I love veggies!'
for character in range(len(text)):
    if character != ' ':
        print(character)  # print a character in text?
```

(g)
```
text = 'Veggies rule!'
for index in text:
    print(text[index])
```

```
(h)    veggies = 'pepperoni'  # not
       for index in range(len(veggies)):
           if index == len(veggies) - 1:
               realVeggies = realVeggies + 'cin'
           realVeggies = realVeggies + index
       print(realVeggies)
```

6.4.4.   Write a function

```
prefixes(word)
```

that prints all of the prefixes of the given word. For example, `prefixes('cart')` should print

```
c
ca
car
cart
```

6.4.5.   Write a function

```
replace(text, target, replacement)
```

that returns a new version of `text` in which all occurrences of the substring `target` are replaced with the string `replacement`. For example, `replace('I am cool, very cool.', 'cool', 'very vain'))` should return `'I am very vain, very very vain.'`. Use a `while` loop; do not use the string method `replace`.

6.4.6.   An annoying trick used by some simple chatbots is to reply to a statement by reframing it as a question. For some statements, like those starting with "This is" and "There are," this is very easy: just reverse the first two words. For example, "This is a cool sentence." becomes "Is this a cool sentence?" Write a function

```
makeQuestion(sentence)
```

that carries out this transformation on a sentence by finding and swapping the first two words, correcting the capitalization, and ending the sentence with a question mark.

6.4.7*   Suppose you develop a secret code that replaces a string with a new string that consists of all the even indexed characters of the original followed by all the odd indexed characters. For example, the string `'computers'` would be encoded as `'cmuesoptr'`. Write a function

```
encode(word)
```

that returns the encoded version of the string named `word`.

6.4.8.   Write a function

```
decode(codeword)
```

that reverses the process from the `encode` function in the previous exercise.

6.4.9*   Write a function

```
palindrome(text)
```

that returns `True` if `text` is a palindrome and `False` otherwise. Your function should ignore spaces and capitalization. For example,

```
palindrome('Lisa Bonet ate no basil')
```

should return `True`.

6.4.10. Write an interactive program that uses the `find` function from this section to find the first occurrence of any desired word in *Moby Dick*.

6.4.11. The `find` function from this section can also be written like this:

```
def find(text, target):
    for index in range(len(text) - len(target) + 1):
        if text[index:index + len(target)] == target:
            return index
    return -1
```

(a) Explain why this version is also correct.

(b) Why is the following version of the `for` loop incorrect?

```
for index in range(len(text) - len(target) + 1):
    if text[index:index + len(target)] == target:
        return index
    else:
        return -1
```

6.4.12. Write a modified version of the `find` function named `findWord` that only finds an instance of `target` that is a whole word.

6.4.13. Write a modified version of the `find` function named `findAll` that returns a list containing the indices of all matches for the target.

6.4.14. Enhance the `concordanceEntry` function in each of the following ways:

(a) In the line that is printed for each match, display `targetWord` in all caps. For example:

```
... any whale could so SMITE his stout sloop-of-war
...     vessel, so as to SMITE down some of the spars and
```

(b) Use the modified `findWord` function from Exercise 6.4.12 so that each target word is matched only if it is a complete word.

(c) The current version of `concordanceEntry` will only identify the first instance of a word on each line. Modify it so that it will display a new context line for every instance of the target word in every line of the text. For example, "ship" appears twice on line 14673 of *Moby Dick*:

upon the ship, than to rejoice that the ship had so victoriously gained

In this case, the function should print:

```
14673                                upon the SHIP, than...
        upon the ship, than to rejoice that the SHIP had so...
```

The `findAll` function from Exercise 6.4.13 will be useful here.

6.5 WORD FREQUENCY TRENDS

One common way to gain a little insight into the arc of a particular theme in a text is to visualize the relative frequencies of related terms over the course of the text. Figure 6.5 shows an example that visualizes the usage of masculine and feminine

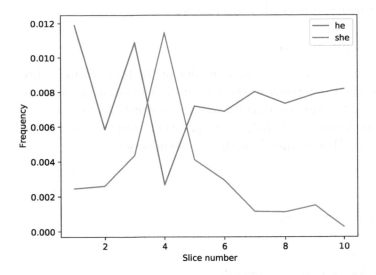

Figure 6.5 A sample plot of word frequencies across ten slices of *Frankenstein*.

pronouns over the course of *Frankenstein*. In this plot, the frequencies of the two words are shown as fractions of the total number of words in each of ten equal-sized slices of the text.

Since writing a program for this problem is a bit more involved, let's explicitly decompose it into subproblems first.

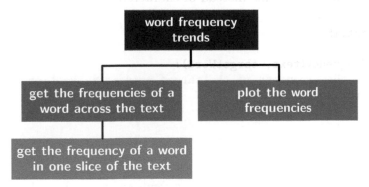

In the first subproblem, we need to compute the frequencies of a word over all of the slices of the text. As a part of this subproblem we will need a function that computes the frequency of a word in just one slice. In the second subproblem, we actually plot the frequencies computed in the first subproblem.

The first subproblem will take three inputs—the text, the desired number of slices, and one of the words—and return a list of the frequencies of the word in the slices of the text. (The main program will need to call this function twice, once for each word.)

To solve this subproblem, we will start at the bottom leaf in the decomposition tree: finding the frequency of a word in a single slice.

Finding the frequency of a word

Computing the frequency of a word in a slice of the text requires three steps. First, we get a list of all of the words in the slice using the `wordTokens` function from our `textlib` module. Second, we iterate over these words and count how many times the target word shows up. Third, we return that count divided by the number of words in the slice. Here is the algorithm in pseudocode.

Algorithm WORD FREQUENCY

Input: a *text* and a *target word*
1 | *word list* ← WORD TOKENS (*text*)
2 | *count* ← 0
3 | repeat for each *word* in *word list*:
4 | if *word* = *target word*, then:
5 | *count* ← *count* + 1
6 | *frequency* ← *count* / length of *word list*
Output: *frequency*

We already know how to perform all of these steps in Python. Iterating over a list of items looks and works just like iterating over a string, except the index variable is assigned consecutive list items instead of characters.

```
1 import textlib

2 def wordFrequency(text, targetWord):
3     """Get the frequency of the target word as a fraction of all
4        words in the text.

5     Parameters:
6         text:       a string object
7         targetWord: a word to count

8     Return value: frequency of the target word
9     """

10     wordList = textlib.wordTokens(text)
11     count = 0
12     for word in wordList:
13         if word == targetWord:
14             count = count + 1
15     return count / len(wordList)
```

In each iteration of this loop, `word` is a assigned a word in `wordList`, and then `word` is compared to the target word. If they are the same, `count` is incremented. We return the final value of `count` divided by the length of `wordList`, which is the total number of words in `text`. The following trace table illustrates this loop more concretely with a fun input.

Trace arguments: `text = 'one fish two fish'`, `targetWord = 'fish'`					
Step	Line	wordList	count	word	Notes
1	10	['one', 'fish', 'two', 'fish']	—	—	get words from wordTokens
2	11	"	0	—	initialize count ← 0
3	12	"	"	'one'	word ← first item in wordList
4	13	"	"	"	'one' != 'fish'; skip line 14
5	12	"	"	'fish'	word ← second item in wordList
6	13	"	"	"	'fish' == 'fish'; do line 14
7	14	"	1	"	increment count
8	12	"	"	'two'	word ← third item in wordList
9	13	"	"	"	'two' != 'fish'; skip line 14
10	12	"	"	'fish'	word ← fourth item in wordList
11	13	"	"	"	'fish' == 'fish'; do line 14
12	14	"	2	"	increment count
13	15	"	"	"	return 2/4 = 0.5

Return value: 0.5

Getting the frequencies in slices

Now, to get the frequencies of a word across the entire text, we need to divide the text into slices and call `wordFrequency` with each slice. The algorithm will return a list of these slice frequencies.

Algorithm SLICE FREQUENCIES

Input: a *text*, a *word*, and a *number of slices*
1.   *slice length* ← length of *text* / *number of slices*
2.   *word frequencies* ← empty list
3.   repeat for each *slice* of *slice length* characters in the *text*:
4.   *frequency* ← WORD FREQUENCY (*slice*, *word*)
5.   append *frequency* to *word frequencies*
Output: *word frequencies*

Implementing this in Python is not quite as straightforward as the pseudocode.

```
def sliceFrequencies(text, word, numSlices):
    """Find the frequency of the word in each slice of the text.

    Parameters:
        text:      a string containing a text
        word:      a word to analyze
        numSlices: the integer number of text slices

    Return values: list of slice frequencies
    """

    sliceLength = (len(text) // numSlices) + 1     # round up
    wordFreqs = [ ]
    for index in range(0, len(text), sliceLength):  # for each slice...
        textSlice = text[index:index + sliceLength]
        frequency = wordFrequency(textSlice, word)
        wordFreqs.append(frequency)
    return wordFreqs
```

To get the slices of the text, we iterate over the indices of `text`, skipping the length of a slice each time. So, in each iteration, the value of `index` is the beginning of a slice. Each slice is located between indices `index` and `index + sliceLength`. This slice of `text` is passed into our `wordFrequency` function along with the `word`, and the returned `frequency` is appended to the list of frequencies.

Plotting the frequencies

Finally, we combine this function with a simple function to plot the frequencies (our second subproblem) to tie it all together.

```
def plotWordFreqs(word1, word2, wordFreqs1, wordFreqs2):
    """Plot 2 lists of word frequencies.

    Parameters:
        word1, word2:           2 words being analyzed
        wordFreqs1, wordFreqs2: lists of 2 words' frequencies

    Return value: None
    """

    numSlices = len(wordFreqs1)
    pyplot.plot(range(1, numSlices + 1), wordFreqs1, label = word1)
    pyplot.plot(range(1, numSlices + 1), wordFreqs2, label = word2)
    pyplot.legend()
    pyplot.xlabel('Slice number')
    pyplot.ylabel('Frequency')
    pyplot.show()
```

```
def wordTrends(fileName, word1, word2, numSlices):
    """Plot frequencies of 2 words across a text.

    Parameters:
        fileName:      name of a text file
        word1, word2:  2 words being analyzed
        numSlices:     the integer number of text slices

    Return value: None
    """

    # open and read the file
    textFile = open(fileName, 'r', encoding = 'utf-8')
    text = textFile.read()
    textFile.close()

    wordFreqs1 = sliceFrequencies(text, word1, numSlices)
    wordFreqs2 = sliceFrequencies(text, word2, numSlices)

    plotWordFreqs(word1, word2, wordFreqs1, wordFreqs2)
```

Exercise 6.5.5 asks you to combine the four functions from this section into a program that you can use to experiment with plotting frequencies of different words in books from Project Gutenberg or the book website.

Exercises

6.5.1*   Repeat Exercise 6.1.7 but use a `for` loop that iterates over the indices of the string instead of the characters.

6.5.2*   Write a function

           count(text, target)

         that returns the number of occurrences of the string `target` in the string `text`. Use a `for` loop; do not use the string method `count`.

6.5.3.   Write a function

           countAll(text, targets)

         that returns the number of occurrences in the string `text` of any of the strings in the list of strings named `targets`. You can use the in operator to determine whether an item is in a list.

6.5.4.   Draw a diagram like the one in Figure 6.2 on page 237 that shows how the inputs and outputs flow among the four functions from this section. Use the functional decomposition tree on page 267 as a starting point.

6.5.5.   Combine the four functions from this section into a program that prompts for a filename, two words to analyze, and a number of slices, and then calls `wordTrends`. Experiment with plotting frequencies of different words in books from `http://www.gutenberg.org` or the book website.

6.5.6.   Modify the `sliceFrequencies` function so that the slices overlap by a given amount. Substitute the `numSlices` parameter with two parameters:

`sliceLength` and `sliceStep`, the length of each slice and the amount that each slice should shift right in each step, respectively. In the words, the first slice will be from index 0 to `sliceLength`, the second slice will be from `sliceStep` to `sliceStep + sliceLength`, the third slice will be from `2 * sliceStep` to `2 * sliceStep + sliceLength`, etc.

6.5.7. Modify the word frequency trends program you wrote for Exercise 6.5.5 so that it prompts for two *lists* of words instead. Each list might represent a particular theme; an example from *Frankenstein* is shown below. The `wordFrequency` function will need some minor modifications. You can use the `in` operator to determine whether an item is in a list.

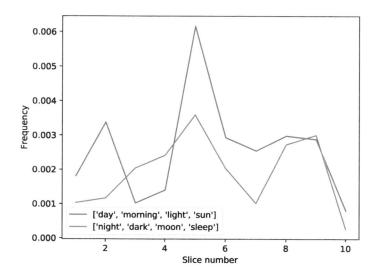

6.6 COMPARING TEXTS

There have been many methods developed to measure similarity between texts, most of which are beyond the scope of this book. But one particular method, called a *dot plot* is both accessible and quite powerful. In a dot plot, we associate one text with the x-axis of a plot and another text with the y-axis. We place a dot at position (x,y) if the character or slice of text at index x in the first text is the same as the character or slice at index y in the second text. In this way, a dot plot visually illustrates the similarity between the two texts.

Let's begin by writing an algorithm that only compares individual characters at the same indices in the two texts. Consider the following two sentences:

Text 1: `Peter Piper picked a peck of pickled peppers.`
Text 2: `Peter Pepper picked a peck of pickled capers.`

We will compare the first character in text 1 to the first character in text 2, then the second character in text 1 to the second character in text 2, etc. Although this algorithm, shown below, must iterate over both strings at the same time, and compare the two strings at each position, it requires only one loop because we always compare the strings at the same index.

```
import matplotlib.pyplot as pyplot

def dotplot1(text1, text2):
    """Display a simplified dot plot comparing two equal-length strings.

    Parameters:
        text1: a string object
        text2: a string object

    Return value: None
    """

    text1 = text1.lower()
    text2 = text2.lower()
    x = []
    y = []
    for index in range(len(text1)):
        if text1[index] == text2[index]:
            x.append(index)
            y.append(index)
    pyplot.scatter(x, y)              # scatter plot
    pyplot.xlim(0, len(text1))        # x axis covers entire text1
    pyplot.ylim(0, len(text2))        # y axis covers entire text2
    pyplot.xlabel(text1)
    pyplot.ylabel(text2)
    pyplot.show()
```

Reflection 6.23 *What is the purpose of the calls to the* `lower` *method?*

Reflection 6.24 *Why must we iterate over the indices of the strings rather than the characters in the strings?*

Every time two characters are found to be equal in the loop, the index of the matching characters is added to both a list of x-coordinates and a list of y-coordinates. These lists are then plotted with the `scatter` function from `matplotlib.pyplot`, which plots points without lines attaching them. Figure 6.6 shows the result for the two strings above.

Reflection 6.25 *Look at Figure 6.6. Which dots correspond to which characters? Why are there only dots on the diagonal?*

We can see that, because this function only recognizes matches at the same index and most of the identical characters in the two sentences do not line up perfectly, this function does not reveal their true degree of similarity. If we were to insert two gaps into the strings, the character-by-character comparison would be quite different:

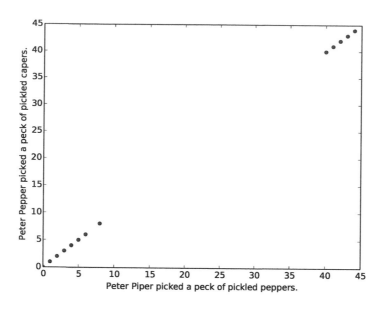

Figure 6.6 Output from the `dotplot1` function.

Text 1: `Peter Pip er picked a peck of pickled peppers.`
Text 2: `Peter Pepper picked a peck of pickled ca pers.`

Dot plots

A real dot plot compares every character in one sequence to every character in the other sequence. This means that we want to compare `text1[0]` to `text2[0]`, then `text1[0]` to `text2[1]`, then `text1[0]` to `text2[2]`, etc., as illustrated below:

```
            0 1 2 3 4 5 6 7 8 9 ...
    text1: Peter  Piper  picked  a  peck  of  pickled  peppers.
                  ...
    text2: Peter  Pepper  picked  a  peck  of  pickled  capers.
            0 1 2 3 4 5 6 7 8 9 ...
```

After we have compared `text1[0]` to all of the characters in `text2`, we need to repeat this process with `text1[1]`, comparing `text1[1]` to `text2[0]`, then `text1[1]` to `text2[1]`, then `text1[1]` to `text2[2]`, etc., as illustrated below:

```
            0 1 2 3 4 5 6 7 8 9 ...
    text1: Peter  Piper  picked  a  peck  of  pickled  peppers.
                  ...
    text2: Peter  Pepper  picked  a  peck  of  pickled  capers.
            0 1 2 3 4 5 6 7 8 9 ...
```

In other words, for each value of `index`, we want to compare `text1[index]` to every character in `text2`, not just to `text2[index]`. To accomplish this, we need to replace the `if` statement in `dotplot1` with another `for` loop:

```
1 import matplotlib.pyplot as pyplot

2 def dotplot(text1, text2):
3     """Display a dot plot comparing two strings.

4     Parameters:
5         text1: a string object
6         text2: a string object

7     Return value: None
8     """

9     text1 = text1.lower()
10     text2 = text2.lower()
11     x = []
12     y = []
13     for index1 in range(len(text1)):
14         for index2 in range(len(text2)):
15             if text1[index1] == text2[index2]:
16                 x.append(index1)
17                 y.append(index2)
18     pyplot.scatter(x, y)
19     pyplot.xlim(0, len(text1))
20     pyplot.ylim(0, len(text2))
21     pyplot.xlabel(text1)
22     pyplot.ylabel(text2)
23     pyplot.show()
```

With this change inside the first `for` loop (we also renamed `index` to `index1`), each character `text1[index1]` is compared to every character in `text2`, indexed by the index variable `index2`, just like the illustrations above. If a match is found, we append `index1` to the `x` list and `index2` to the `y` list because we want to draw a dot at coordinates (`index1, index2`).

The following trace table shows how this works in more detail, with much smaller inputs. The iterations of the outer `for` loop are separated by thicker black lines and set apart with the curly braces on the left side, annotated with values of `index1`. The iterations of the inner `for` loop are separated by thinner red lines.

Trace arguments: `text1 = 'spam', text2 = 'pea'`

Step	Line	x	y	index1	index2	Notes
1–4	9–12	[ ]	[ ]	—	—	initialize variables
5	13	"	"	0	—	index1 ← 0
6	14	"	"	"	0	index2 ← 0
7	15	"	"	"	"	's' != 'p'; skip lines 16–17
8	14	"	"	"	1	index2 ← 1
9	15	"	"	"	"	's' != 'e'; skip lines 16–17
10	14	"	"	"	2	index2 ← 2
11	15	"	"	"	"	's' != 'a'; skip lines 16–17
12	13	"	"	1	"	index1 ← 1
13	14	"	"	"	0	index2 ← 0
14	15	"	"	"	"	'p' == 'p'; do lines 16–17
15–16	16–17	[1]	[0]	"	"	we want a dot at (1,0)
17	14	"	"	"	1	index2 ← 1
18	15	"	"	"	"	'p' != 'e'; skip lines 16–17
19	14	"	"	"	2	index2 ← 2
20	15	"	"	"	"	'p' != 'a'; skip lines 16–17
21	13	"	"	2	"	index1 ← 2
22	14	"	"	"	0	index2 ← 0
23	15	"	"	"	"	'a' != 'p'; skip lines 16–17
24	14	"	"	"	1	index2 ← 1
25	15	"	"	"	"	'a' != 'e'; skip lines 16–17
26	14	"	"	"	2	index2 ← 2
27	15	"	"	"	"	'a' == 'a'; do lines 16–17
28–29	16–17	[1, 2]	[0, 2]	"	"	we want a dot at (2,2)
30	13	"	"	3	"	index1 ← 3
31	14	"	"	"	0	index2 ← 0
⋮						⋮
37–42	18–23	[1, 2]	[0, 2]	3	2	draw the plot

Notice that when `index1` is 0, the inner `for` loop runs through all the values of `index2`. The inner loop finishes in step 11, also finishing the body of the outer `for` loop. Therefore, in step 12, the outer loop begins its second iteration, with `index1 = 1`. The inner loop then runs through all of its values again, and so on. There are `len(text1) · len(text2)` = 4 · 3 = 12 total comparisons because each of the four characters in `'spam'` is compared to each of the three characters in `'pea'`. These kinds of loops are called ***nested loops***. They will become very important in the next few chapters.

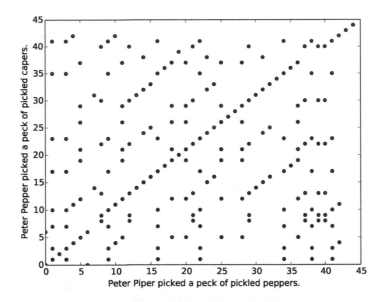

Figure 6.7 Output from the revised `dotplot` function.

Figure 6.7 shows the dot plot from the revised version of the function with the longer strings. Because the two strings share many characters, there are quite a few matches, contributing to a "noisy" plot. But the plot now does pick up the similarity in the strings, illustrated by the dots along the main diagonal.

We can reduce the "noise" in a dot plot by comparing substrings instead of individual characters. In textual analysis applications and computational linguistics, substrings with length n are known as n-grams.[6] When $n = 2$ and $n = 3$, they are also called bigrams and trigrams, respectively. When $n > 1$, there are many more possible substrings, so fewer matches tend to exist. Exercise 6.6.14 asks you to generalize this dot plot function so that it compares n-grams instead of single characters. Figure 6.8 shows the result of this function with $n = 3$.

Dot plots can be helpful in detecting potential plagiarism. Consider the controversy that erupted at the 2016 Republican National Convention, when portions of Melania Trump's speech seemed to closely resemble portions of Michelle Obama's convention speech from eight years prior. The offending portions of these two speeches are compared with a dot plot in Figure 6.9.

Reflection 6.26 *Just by looking at Figure 6.9, would you conclude that portions had been plagiarized? (Think about what a dot plot comparing two random passages would look like.)*

---

[6]n-grams can also refer to sequences of n words, as we will see in the next chapter.

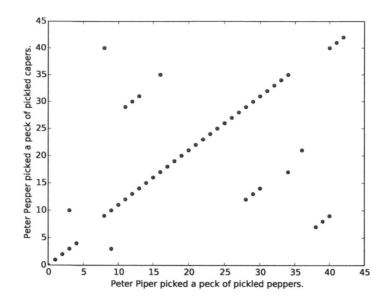

Figure 6.8 Output from the `dotplot` function from Exercise 6.6.14 (trigrams).

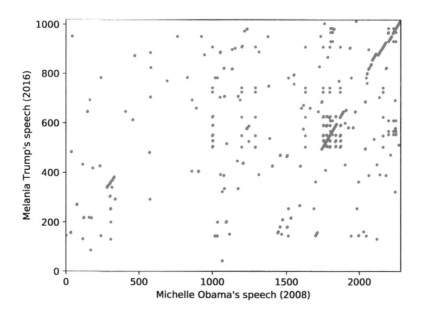

Figure 6.9 A dot plot comparing 6-grams from segments of Michelle Obama's and Melania Trump's convention speeches in 2008 and 2016.

Exercises

6.6.1.   What is printed by the following loop? Explain why.

```
text1 = 'tbontb'
text2 = 'oerooe'
for index in range(len(text1)):
    print(text1[index] + text2[index])
```

6.6.2*   Consider the following nested loop.

```
text1 = 'abcd'
text2 = 'xyz'
for index1 in range(len(text1)):
    for index2 in range(len(text2)):
        if text1[index1] == text2[index2]:
            print(index1, index2)
```

List the pairs of characters that are compared by the if statement, in the order they are compared. How many comparisons are there in total?

6.6.3.   Repeat the previous exercise, but with the for statements swapped, as shown below.

```
text1 = 'abcd'
text2 = 'xyz'
for index2 in range(len(text2)):
    for index1 in range(len(text1)):
        if text1[index1] == text2[index2]:
            print(index1, index2)
```

6.6.4.   What is printed by the following nested loop? Explain why.

```
text = 'imho'
for index1 in range(len(text)):
    for index2 in range(index1, len(text)):
        print(text[index1:index2 + 1])
```

6.6.5.   Write a function

```
difference(word1, word2)
```

that returns the first index at which the strings word1 and word2 differ. If the words have different lengths, and the shorter word is a prefix of the longer word, the function should return the length of the shorter word. If the two words are the same, the function should return −1. Do this without directly testing whether word1 and word2 are equal.

6.6.6*   Hamming distance, defined to be the number of bit positions that are different between two bit strings, is used to measure the error that is introduced when data is sent over a network. For example, suppose we sent the bit sequence 011100110001 over a network, but the destination received 011000110101 instead. To measure the transmission error, we can find the Hamming distance between the two sequences by lining them up as follows:

Sent: 011100110001
Received: 011000110101

Since the bit sequences are different in two positions, the Hamming distance is 2. Write a function

```
hamming(bits1, bits2)
```

that returns the Hamming distance between the two given bit strings. Assume that the two strings have the same length.

6.6.7. Repeat Exercise 6.6.6, but make it work correctly even if the two strings have different lengths. In this case, each "missing" bit at the end of the shorter string counts as one toward the Hamming distance. For example, `hamming('000', '10011')` should return 3.

6.6.8* The following nested `for` loop is intended to print information about characters that are repeated in the string `text`.

```
text = 'two words'
for index1 in range(len(text)):
    for index2 in range(len(text)):
        if text[index1] == text[index2]:
            print(text[index1], index1, index2)
```

There are only two repeated characters in this short string—`'w'` at indices 1 and 4 and `'o'` at indices 2 and 5—but this loop prints more than that. Fix the nested loop so that it correctly prints only two lines. Explain why your solution is correct.

6.6.9. Write a function

```
longestRun(text)
```

that returns the length of the longest run of the same character in the string `text`. For example, `longestRun('aabbbbcccd')` should return 4.

6.6.10. Write a function

```
uniqueCharacters(text)
```

that returns the number of characters that only appear once in the string `text`.

6.6.11* Write a function

```
findRepeats(text, length)
```

that locates all words with the given `length` that are repeated consecutively in the string `text`. For each found repeat, your function should print the word and the index of the first occurrence of the word. Assume that words do not start with a space and that there will be a space between repeats. For example, `findRepeats('the the repeats are are repeating', 3)` should print

```
0 the
16 are
```

6.6.12. Write a function

```
findRepeats(text)
```

that locates words with any length from 2–10 that are repeated consecutively in the string `text`. See the previous problem for assumptions and what to print.

6.6.13. Write a function

```
findDuplicates(text, length)
```

that locates all pairs of identical substrings with the given `length` anywhere in the string `text`. The function should print the substring and a pair of indices representing the first index in each match. For example, `findDuplicates('the the repeats are are repeating', 4)` should print

```
 the  0  4
 e re  6 22
  rep  7 23
 repe  8 24
 epea  9 25
 peat 10 26
  are 15 19
  are 16 20
```

6.6.14. Generalize the `dotplot` function so that it compares n-grams instead of individual characters. The third parameter of the function should be n.

*6.7 TIME COMPLEXITY

This section is available on the book website.

*6.8 COMPUTATIONAL GENOMICS

This section is available on the book website.

6.9 SUMMARY AND FURTHER DISCOVERY

Text is stored as a sequence of bytes, which we can read into one or more strings. The most fundamental string algorithms have one of the following structures:

```
for character in text:
    # process character

for index in range(len(text)):
    # process text[index]
```

In the first case, consecutive characters in the string are assigned to the `for` loop index variable `character`. In the body of the loop, each character can then be examined individually. In the second case, consecutive integers from the list `[0, 1, 2, ..., len(text) - 1]`, which are precisely the indices of the characters in `text`, are assigned to the `for` loop index variable `index`. In this case, the algorithm has more information because, not only can it access the character at `text[index]`, it also knows where that character resides in the string. The first choice tends to be more elegant, but the second choice is necessary when the algorithm needs to know the index of each character, or if it needs to process slices of the string, which can only be accessed with indices.

We called one special case of these loops a ***string accumulator***:

```
newText = ''
for character in text:
    newText = newText + _____
```

Like an integer accumulator and a list accumulator, a string accumulator builds its result cumulatively in each iteration of the loop. Because strings are immutable, a string accumulator must create a new string in each iteration that is composed of the old string with a new character concatenated.

Algorithms like these that perform one pass over their string parameters and execute a constant number of elementary steps per character are called *linear-time algorithms* because their number of elementary steps is proportional to the length of the input string.

In some cases, we need to compare every character in one string to every character in a second string, so we need a nested loop like the following:

```
for index1 in range(len(text1)):
    for index2 in range(len(text2)):
        # process text1[index1] and text2[index2]
```

If both strings have length n, then a nested loop like this constitutes a *quadratic-time algorithm* with time complexity $\mathcal{O}(n^2)$ (as long as the body of the loop is constant-time) because every one of n characters in the first string is compared to every one of n characters in the second string. We will see more loops like this in later chapters.

Notes for further discovery

The first of the two epigraphs at the beginning of this chapter is from the following blog post by Leslie Johnston, the former Chief of the Repository Development Center at the Library of Congress. She is currently Director of Digital Preservation at The National Archives.

```
http://blogs.loc.gov/digitalpreservation/2012/04/
a-library-of-congress-worth-of-data-its-all-in-how-you-define-it/
```

The second epigraph is from an article titled "The DNA Data Deluge" by Michael C. Schatz and Ben Langmead [55], which can be found at

```
http://spectrum.ieee.org/biomedical/devices/the-dna-data-deluge .
```

To learn more about how tokenization is performed in the Python interpreter, look here: `https://docs.python.org/3/reference/lexical_analysis.html`.

For the complete Unicode character set, refer to `http://unicode.org`.

The Fletcher checksum algorithm was invented by John Fletcher at the Lawrence Livermore National Laboratory and published in 1982 [18].

A concordance for the works of William Shakespeare can be found at

```
http://www.opensourceshakespeare.org/concordance/.
```

The Keyword in Context (KWIC) indexing system, also known as a permuted index, is similar to a concordance. In a KWIC index, every word in the title of an article appears in the index in the context in which it appears.

To learn more about text analysis in the digital humanities, we recommend *Macro-*

analysis [26] by Matthew Jockers and *Exploring Big Historical Data* [20] by Shawn Graham, Ian Milligan, and Scott Weingart.

If you are interested in learning more about computational biology, two good places to start are *The Mathematics of Life* [62] by Ian Stewart and *Natural Computing* [60] by Dennis Shasha and Cathy Lazere. The latter book has a wider focus than just computational biology.

*6.10 PROJECTS

This section is available on the book website.

CHAPTER 7

Data Analysis

"Data! Data! Data!" he cried impatiently. "I can't make bricks without clay."

Sherlock Holmes
The Adventure of the Copper Beeches (1892)

I N this chapter, we will focus on analyzing and manipulating numerical data: earthquake measurements, SAT scores, isotope ratios, unemployment rates, meteorite locations, consumer demand, river flow, and more. Data sets such as these have become a (if not, *the*) vital component of many scientific, nonprofit, and commercial ventures. Many of these sectors now employ experts in *data science* who use advanced techniques to transform data into valuable information to guide the organization.

To solve these problems, we need an abstract data type (ADT) in which to store a collection of data. The simplest and most intuitive such abstraction is a *list*, which is simply a sequence of items. In previous chapters, we discovered how to generate Python `list` objects with the `range` function and how to accumulate lists of coordinates to visualize in plots. To solve the problems in this chapter, we will also grow and shrink lists, and modify and rearrange their contents, without having to worry about where or how they are stored in memory. Later in the chapter, we will develop algorithms to compute the frequencies of all the words and bigrams in a book, perform linear regression analyses, and cluster data into groups of similar items.

7.1 SUMMARY STATISTICS

Suppose we are running a small business, and we need to get some basic descriptive statistics about last week's daily sales. We can store these sales numbers in a list like this:

```
>>> sales = [32, 42, 11, 15, 58, 44, 16]
```

You'll recall that a list is represented as a sequence of items, separated by commas, and enclosed in square brackets ([ ]). Lists can contain any kind of data we want, even items with different types. For example, these are all valid lists:

```
>>> unemployment = [0.082, 0.092, 0.091, 0.063, 0.068, 0.052]
>>> votes = ['yea', 'yea', 'nay', 'yea', 'nay']
>>> points = [[2, 1], [12, 3], [6, 5], [3, 14]]
>>> crazyTown = [15, 'gtaaca', [1, 2, 3], max(4.1, 1.4), 'cookies']
```

Mean and variance

Let's start by computing the mean (or average) daily sales for the week. To find the mean of a list of numbers, we need to first find their sum by iterating over the list. As we saw a few times before, iterating over the values in a list is essentially identical to iterating over the characters in a string.

```
total = 0
for item in sales:
    total = total + item
return total / len(sales)
```

In each iteration of the for loop, item is assigned the next value in the list named sales, and then added to the running sum. After the loop, we divide the sum by the length of the list, which is retrieved with the same len function we used on strings.

| **Reflection 7.1** *Does this work when the list is empty?*

If sales is the empty list ([ ]), then the value of len(sales) is zero, resulting in a "division by zero" error in the return statement. We have several options to deal with this. First, we could just let the error happen. Second, we could use an assert statement to print an error message and abort. Third, we could catch the error with a try/except statement. Fourth, we could detect this error before it happens with an if statement and return something that indicates that an error occurred. We adopt the last option in the following function by returning None and indicating this possibility in the docstring.

```
1 def mean(data):
2     """Compute the mean of a non-empty list of numbers.

3     Parameter:
4         data: a list of numbers

5     Return value: the mean of numbers in data or None if data is empty
6     """

7     if len(data) == 0:
8         return None

9     total = 0
10    for item in data:
11        total = total + item
12    return total / len(data)
```

This `for` loop is yet another example of an accumulator. To illustrate what is happening, let's trace through the function with one week of sales data.

Trace arguments: data = [32, 42, 11, 15, 58, 44, 16]				
Step	Line	total	item	Notes
1	7	—	—	len(data) is 7 > 0; skip line 8
2	9	0	—	total ← 0
3	10	"	32	item ← data[0]
4	11	32	"	total ← total + item = 0 + 32
5	10	"	42	item ← data[1]
6	11	74	"	total ← total + item = 32 + 42
⋮				
15	10	202	16	item ← data[6]
16	11	218	"	total ← total + item = 202 + 16
17	12	"	"	return 218 / 7
Return value: 31.142857142857142				

> **Reflection 7.2** *Fill in the missing steps above to show how the function arrives at a* `total` *of* 218.

The mean of a data set does not adequately describe it if there is a lot of variability in the data, i.e., if there is no "typical" value. In these cases, we need to accompany the mean with the ***variance***, which is measure of how much the data varies from the mean. Computing the variance is left as Exercise 7.1.10.

Minimum and maximum

Now let's think about how to find the minimum and maximum sales in the list. Of course, it is easy for us to just look at a short list like the one above and pick out the minimum and maximum. But a computer does not have this ability. Therefore, as you think about these problems, it may be better to think about a very long list instead, one in which the minimum and maximum are not so obvious.

Reflection 7.3 *Think about how you would write an algorithm to find the minimum value in a long list. (Similar to a running sum, keep track of the current minimum.)*

As the hint suggests, we want to maintain the current minimum while we iterate over the list with a `for` loop. When we examine each item, we need to test whether it is smaller than the current minimum. If it is, we assign the current item to be the new minimum. The following function implements this algorithm.

```python
def min(data):
    """Compute the minimum value in a non-empty list of numbers.

    Parameter:
        data: a list of numbers

    Return value: the minimum value in data or None if data is empty
    """

    if len(data) == 0:
        return None

    minimum = data[0]
    for item in data[1:]:
        if item < minimum:
            minimum = item
    return minimum
```

Since lists are sequences like strings, they can also be indexed and sliced. But now indices refer to list elements instead of characters and slices are sublists instead of substrings. We use indexing before the loop to initialize `minimum` to be the first value in the list. Then we iterate over the slice of remaining values in the list. In each iteration, we compare the current value of `item` to `minimum` and, if `item` is smaller, update `minimum` to be the value of `item`. At the end of the loop, `minimum` has been assigned the smallest value in the list.

Reflection 7.4 *If the list* [32, 42, 11, 15, 58, 44, 16] *is assigned to* data, *then what are the values of* data[0] *and* data[1:]?

Let's look at a small example of how this function works when we call it with the list containing only the first four numbers from the list above: [32, 42, 11, 15]. The function begins by assigning the value 32 to `minimum`. The first value of `item` is 42. Since 42 is not less than 32, `minimum` remains unchanged. In the next iteration of the loop, the third value in the list, 11, is assigned to `item`. In this case, since 11 is less than 32, the value of `minimum` is updated to 11. Finally, in the last iteration of the loop, `item` is assigned the value 15. Since 15 is greater than 11, `minimum` is unchanged. At the end, the function returns the final value of `minimum`, which is 11. A function to compute the maximum is very similar, so we leave it as an exercise.

Reflection 7.5 *What would happen if we iterated over* `data` *instead of* `data[1:]`*? Would the function still work?*

If we iterated over the entire list instead, the first comparison would be useless (because `item` and `minimum` would be the same) so it would be a little less efficient, but the function would still work fine.

Now what if we also wanted to know on which day of the week the minimum sales occurred? To answer this question, assuming we know how indices correspond to days of the week, we need to find the index of the minimum value in the list. As we learned in Chapter 6, we need to iterate over the indices in situations like this:

```python
def minDay(data):
    """Find the index of the minimum value in a non-empty list.

    Parameter:
        data: a list of numbers

    Return value: index of the minimum value in data or -1 if data == [ ]
    """

    if len(data) == 0:
        return -1

    minIndex = 0
    for index in range(1, len(data)):
        if data[index] < data[minIndex]:
            minIndex = index
    return minIndex
```

This function performs almost exactly the same algorithm as our `min` function, but now each value in the list is identified by `data[index]` instead of `item`, and we remember the index of current minimum in the loop instead of its value.

Reflection 7.6 *How can we modify the* `minDay` *function to return a day of the week instead of an index, assuming the sales data starts on a Sunday?*

One option would be to replace `return minIndex` with `if/elif/else` statements, like the following:

```python
if minIndex == 0:
    return 'Sunday'
elif minIndex == 1:
    return 'Monday'
    ⋮
else:
    return 'Saturday'
```

But a more clever solution is to create a list of the days of the week that are in the same order as the sales data. Then we can simply use the value of `minIndex` as an index into this list to return the correct string.

```
days = ['Sunday', 'Monday', 'Tuesday', 'Wednesday', 'Thursday',
        'Friday', 'Saturday']
return days[minIndex]
```

There are many other descriptive statistics that we can use to summarize the contents of a list. The following exercises challenge you to implement some of them.

Exercises

When an exercise asks you to write a function, test it with both common and boundary case arguments, and document your test cases. Also use a trace table to show the execution of the function with at least one of the test cases.

7.1.1. Suppose a list is assigned to the variable name `data`. Show how you would

(a)* print the length of `data`

(b)* print the third element in `data`

(c)* print the last three elements in `data`

(d) print the last element in `data`

(e) print the first four elements in `data`

(f) print the list consisting of the second, third, and fourth elements in `data`

7.1.2. In the `mean` function, we returned `None` if `data` was empty. Show how to modify the following `main` function so that it properly tests for this possibility and prints an appropriate message.

```
def main():
    someData = getInputFromSomewhere()
    average = mean(someData)
    print('The mean value is ' + str(average) + '.')
```

7.1.3. Write a function

```
sumList(data)
```

that returns the sum of all of the numbers in the list `data`. For example, `sumList([1, 2, 3])` should return 6.

7.1.4* Write a function

```
sumOdds(data)
```

that returns the sum of only the odd integers in the list `data`. For example, `sumOdds([1, 2, 3])` should return 4.

7.1.5. Write a function

```
countOdds(data)
```

that returns the number of odd integers in the list `data`. For example, `countOdds([1, 2, 3])` should return 2.

7.1.6.   Write a function

      `multiples5(data)`

that returns the number of multiples of 5 in a list of integers. For example, `multiples5([5, 7, 2, 10])` should return 2.

7.1.7.   Write a function

      `countNames(words)`

that returns the number of capitalized names in the list of strings named `words`. For example,

      `countNames(['Fili', 'Oin', 'Thorin', 'and', 'Bilbo', 'are',`
                 `'characters', 'in', 'a', 'book', 'by', 'Tolkien'])`

should return 5.

7.1.8.   The percentile associated with a particular value in a data set is the number of values that are less than or equal to it, divided by the total number of values, times 100. Write a function

      `percentile(data, value)`

that returns the percentile of `value` in the list named `data`.

7.1.9.   Write a function

      `meanSquares(data)`

that returns the mean of the squares of the numbers in a list named `data`.

7.1.10.   Write a function

      `variance(data)`

that returns the variance of a list of numbers named `data`. The variance is defined to be the mean of the squares of the numbers in the list minus the square of the mean of the numbers in the list. In your implementation, call your function from Exercise 7.1.9 and the `mean` function from this section.

7.1.11.   Write a function

      `max(data)`

that returns the maximum value in the list of numbers named `data`. Do not use the built-in `max` function.

7.1.12*   Write a function

      `shortest(words)`

that returns the shortest string in a list of strings named `words`. In case of ties, return the first shortest string. For example,

      `shortest(['spider', 'ant', 'beetle', 'bug'])`

should return the string `'ant'`.

7.1.13.   Write a function

      `span(data)`

that returns the difference between the largest and smallest numbers in the list named `data`. Do not use the built-in `min` and `max` functions. (But you may use your own functions.) For example, `span([9, 4, 1, 7, 7])` should return 8.

7.1.14. Write a function

    `maxIndex(data)`

that returns the *index* of the maximum item in the list of numbers named `data`. Do not use any built-in functions.

7.1.15. Write a function

    `secondLargest(data)`

that returns the second largest number in `data`. Do not use the built-in `max` function. (But you may use your `maxIndex` function from Exercise 7.1.14.)

7.1.16* Write a function

    `linearSearch(data, target)`

that returns True if `target` is in the list named `data`, and False otherwise. Do not use the `in` operator to test whether an item is in the list. For example,

    `linearSearch(['Tris', 'Tobias', 'Caleb'], 'Tris')`

should return True, but

    `linearSearch(['Tris', 'Tobias', 'Caleb'], 'Peter')`

should return False.

7.1.17* Write a function

    `linearSearch(data, target)`

that returns the index of `target` if it is found in `data`, and -1 otherwise. Do not use the `in` operator or the `index` method to test whether items are in the list. For example,

    `linearSearch(['Tris', 'Tobias', 'Caleb'], 'Tris')`

should return 0, but

    `linearSearch(['Tris', 'Tobias', 'Caleb'], 'Peter')`

should return -1.

7.1.18* Write a function

    `intersect(data1, data2)`

that returns True if the two lists named `data1` and `data2` have any common elements, and False otherwise. (You may use your `linearSearch` function from Exercise 7.1.16.) For example,

    `intersect(['Katniss', 'Peeta', 'Gale'], ['Foxface', 'Marvel'])`

should return False, but

    `intersect(['Katniss', 'Peeta', 'Gale'], ['Gale', 'Haymitch'])`

should return True.

7.1.19. Write a function

    `differ(data1, data2)`

that returns the first index at which the two lists `data1` and `data2` differ. If the two lists are the same, your function should return -1. You may assume that the lists have the same length. For example,

    `differ(['CS', 'rules', '!'], ['CS', 'totally', 'rules!'])`

should return the index 1.

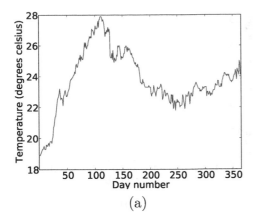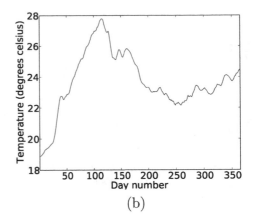

Figure 7.1 Plots of (a) daily temperatures and (b) the same temperatures smoothed over a five-day window.

7.1.20. The Luhn algorithm is the standard algorithm used to validate credit card numbers and protect against accidental errors. Read about the algorithm online, and then write a function

        validateLuhn(number)

that returns True if the number if valid and False otherwise. The number parameter will be a list of digits. For example, to determine if the credit card number 4563 9601 2200 1999 is valid, one would call the function with the parameter [4, 5, 6, 3, 9, 6, 0, 1, 2, 2, 0, 0, 1, 9, 9, 9]. (Hint: use a for loop that iterates in reverse over the indices of the list.)

7.2 WRANGLING DATA

Suppose, as part of an ongoing climate study, we are tracking daily surface seawater temperatures recorded by a drifting buoy in the Atlantic Ocean.[1] Our list of daily temperature readings (in degrees Celsius) starts like this:

        [18.9, 18.9, 19.0, 19.2, 19.3, 19.3, 19.2, 19.1, 19.4, 19.3, ...]

Often, when we are dealing with data sets like this, anomalies can arise due to errors in the sensing equipment, human fallibility, or corruption in the network used to send results to a lab or another collection point. We can mask these erroneous measurements by "smoothing" the data, replacing each value with the mean of the values in a "window" of values containing it. This technique is also useful for extracting general patterns in data by eliminating distracting "bumpy" areas. For example, Figure 7.1 shows a year's worth of raw temperature data from an actual ocean buoy, next to the same data smoothed over a five day window. Smoothing data like this is sometimes also called computing *moving averages*, as in "the 5-day moving average price of the stock is $27.13."

---

[1]For example, see http://www.coriolis.eu.org.

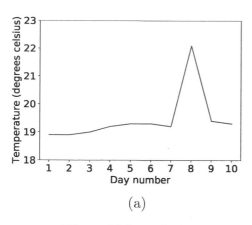 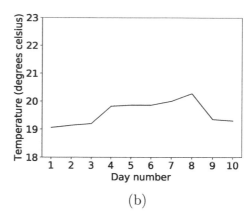

(a)   (b)

Figure 7.2 Plots of (a) ten daily temperatures and (b) the same temperatures smoothed over a five-day window.

Smoothing data

Let's design an algorithm for this problem. We will begin by looking at a small example consisting of the ten temperature readings above, with an anomalous reading inserted, marked in red:

    [18.9, 18.9, 19.0, 19.2, 19.3, 19.3, 19.2, 22.1, 19.4, 19.3]

The plot of this data in Figure 7.2(a) illustrates this erroneous "bump."

Now let's smooth the data by averaging over windows of size five. For each value in the original list, its window will include itself and the four values that come after it. (The last four values do not have four values after them, so their windows will be smaller.) Our algorithm will need to compute the mean of each of these windows, and then add each of these means to a new smoothed list. The first window looks like this:

    [18.9, 18.9, 19.0, 19.2, 19.3, 19.3, 19.2, 22.1, 19.4, 19.3]
         mean = 95.3 / 5 = 19.06

To find the mean temperature for the window, we sum the five values and divide by 5. The result, 19.06, will represent this window in the smoothed list. The remaining windows are computed in the same way:

    [18.9, 18.9, 19.0, 19.2, 19.3, 19.3, 19.2, 22.1, 19.4, 19.3]
              mean = 95.7 / 5 = 19.14

                            ⋮

    [18.9, 18.9, 19.0, 19.2, 19.3, 19.3, 19.2, 22.1, 19.4, 19.3]
                        mean = 99.3 / 5 = 19.86

$$[18.9, \ 18.9, \ 19.0, \ 19.2, \ 19.3, \ 19.3, \ \boxed{19.2, \ 22.1, \ 19.4, \ 19.3}]$$
$$\text{mean} = 80.0 \ / \ 4 = 20.00$$

$$[18.9, \ 18.9, \ 19.0, \ 19.2, \ 19.3, \ 19.3, \ 19.2, \ \boxed{22.1, \ 19.4, \ 19.3}]$$
$$\text{mean} = 60.8 \ / \ 3 = 20.27$$

$$[18.9, \ 18.9, \ 19.0, \ 19.2, \ 19.3, \ 19.3, \ 19.2, \ 22.1, \ \boxed{19.4, \ 19.3}]$$
$$\text{mean} = 38.7 \ / \ 2 = 19.35$$

$$[18.9, \ 18.9, \ 19.0, \ 19.2, \ 19.3, \ 19.3, \ 19.2, \ 22.1, \ 19.4, \ \boxed{19.3}]$$
$$\text{mean} = 19.3 \ / \ 1 = 19.3$$

In the end, our list of smoothed temperature readings is:

[19.06, 19.14, 19.20, 19.82, 19.86, 19.86, 20.0, 20.27, 19.35, 19.3]

We can see from the plot of this smoothed list in Figure 7.2(b) that the "bump" has indeed been smoothed (although, due to the small window size, it still causes the window means to increase more than we would probably like).

Suppose that our list of values is named **data** and our desired window size is assigned to variable named **width**. Then we can realize this algorithm with a *list accumulator* just like the ones we have been using to plot data since Chapter 4.

```
smoothedData = [ ]                          # initialize list
for index in range(len(data)):
    window = data[index:index + width]
    smoothedData.append(mean(window))       # append the next mean
```

Before the loop, the list **smoothedData** is initialized to be an empty list. In each iteration, we call our **mean** function from the previous section on one window, and append the result to the list of smoothed data. After the loop, we have "acccumulated" the means for all of the windows.

A more efficient algorithm

Reflection 7.7 *Can you think of a way to solve the smoothing problem with fewer arithmetic operations?*

We can design a more efficient algorithm by exploiting the simple observation that, while finding the sums of neighboring windows in the **mean** function, we unnecessarily performed some addition operations multiple times. For example, we added the fourth and fifth temperature readings four different times, once in each of the first four windows. We can eliminate this extra work by taking advantage of the relationship between the sums of two contiguous windows. For example, consider the first window:

$$\boxed{18.9, \ 18.9, \ 19.0, \ 19.2, \ 19.3} \ 19.3, \ 19.2, \ 22.1, \ 19.4, \ 19.3$$
$$\text{sum} = 95.3$$

The sum for the second window must be almost the same as the first window, since they have four numbers in common. The only difference in the second window is that it loses the first 18.9 and gains 19.3. So once we have the sum for the first window (95.3), we can get the sum of the second window with only two additional arithmetic operations: 95.3 – 18.9 + 19.3 = 95.7.

$$18.9, \boxed{18.9,\ 19.0,\ 19.2,\ 19.3,\ 19.3,}\ 19.2,\ 22.1,\ 19.4,\ 19.3$$

$$\text{sum} = 95.7$$

We can apply this process to every subsequent window as well, as demonstrated by the following improved algorithm.

```
1 def smooth(data, width):
2     """Return a new list of data, smoothed over windows of the given width.
3
4     Parameters:
5         data:  a list of numbers
6         width: the width of each window
7
8     Return value: a list of smoothed data values
9     """
10
11    smoothedData = []
12    total = 0                               # get sum for the first window
13    for index in range(width):
14        total = total + data[index]
15
16    for index in range(len(data)):
17        width = min(width, len(data) - index) # adjust width near the end
          smoothedData.append(total / width)    # append the window mean
          total = total - data[index]           # subtract leftmost value
          if index + width < len(data):         # if possible,
              total = total + data[index + width] #   add rightmost value

      return smoothedData
```

At the beginning of the function, in lines 8–11, we initialize a new list and get the sum of the values in the first window. Then, in the `for` loop, in lines 13–14, the mean for the window is appended to the new list. Before the mean is computed, if necessary, the `width` of the window is reduced to the number of remaining values in `data`. In lines 15–17, the sum is adjusted for the next iteration by subtracting the leftmost value in the current window and, if possible, adding the next value after the current window.

> **Reflection 7.8** *To make sure you understand the algorithm, use a trace table to execute the* `smooth` *function on the list above with a window size of 5. You should get the same smoothed list that we derived previously.*

To see how much better this algorithm is than our original, let's compare the number of arithmetic operations that are performed by each algorithm, since this is the vast majority of the work taking place. In the first algorithm, if each window has size 5, then we perform five addition operations and one division operation each time we call the mean function, for a total of six arithmetic operations per full-size window. Therefore, the total number of arithmetic operations is at most six times the number of windows. In general, if the window width is denoted w, the algorithm performs at most w additions and one division per window, for a total of $n(w + 1)$ arithmetic operations.

The new algorithm is performing w additions in the first for loop. In each iteration of the second for loop, it is performing a division and at most two additions, for a total of at most $3n$ arithmetic operations. In total then, the new algorithm performs at most $3n + w$ arithmetic operations. Therefore, our old algorithm requires

$$\frac{n(w + 1)}{3n + w}$$

times as many operations as the new one. It may be hard to tell from this ratio, but our new algorithm is doing about $w/3$ times less work. To see this more concretely, suppose our list contains ten years (about 3,652 days) worth of temperature readings, so the speedup ratio is

$$\frac{3652(w + 1)}{3 \cdot 3652 + w}.$$

The following table shows the value of this fraction for increasing window sizes w.

w	Speedup
5	2.0
10	3.7
20	7.0
100	33.4

When w is small, our new algorithm does not make much difference, but the speedup becomes quite pronounced when w gets larger. In real applications of smoothing on extremely large data sets containing billions or trillions of items, such as statistics on DNA sequences, window sizes can be as high as $w = 100,000$. So our refined algorithm can have a marked impact!

Modifying lists in place

We can modify existing lists with append because, unlike strings, lists are *mutable*. In other words, the items in a list can be changed directly. This means that we could smooth the data in a list by overwriting each individual item in the list itself instead of creating a new list. This is often referred to as modifying the list *in place*.

Before we tackle that problem, let's look at a simpler problem to illustrate the mechanics involved. Suppose we have a list of monthly unemployment rates like those below.

```
>>> unemployment = [0.082, 0.092, 0.091, 0.063, 0.068, 0.052]
```

If we need to change the second value in the list, we can do so like this:

```
>>> unemployment[1] = 0.062
>>> unemployment
[0.082, 0.062, 0.091, 0.063, 0.068, 0.052]
```

We can change individual elements in a list because each of the elements is an independent reference to a value, like any other variable name. We can visualize the original **unemployment** list like this:

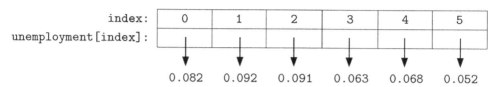

The value 0.082 is assigned to the name **unemployment[0]**, the value 0.092 is assigned to the name **unemployment[1]**, etc. When we assigned a new value to **unemployment[1]**, we were simply assigning a new value to the name **unemployment[1]**, like any other assignment statement:

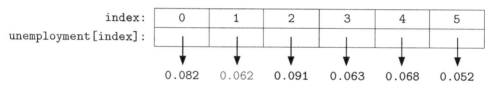

Suppose we wanted to adjust all of the unemployment rates in this list by subtracting one percent from each of them. We can do this with a **for** loop that iterates over the indices of the list.

```
>>> for index in range(len(unemployment)):
        unemployment[index] = unemployment[index] - 0.01
>>> unemployment
[0.072, 0.052, 0.081, 0.053, 0.058, 0.042]
```

This **for** loop is equivalent to the following six assignment statements:

```
unemployment[0] = unemployment[0] - 0.01
unemployment[1] = unemployment[1] - 0.01
unemployment[2] = unemployment[2] - 0.01
unemployment[3] = unemployment[3] - 0.01
unemployment[4] = unemployment[4] - 0.01
unemployment[5] = unemployment[5] - 0.01
```

Reflection 7.9 *Is it possible to modify a list in place by iterating over the values in the list instead? In other words, does the following* for *loop accomplish the same thing? (Try it.) Why or why not?*

```
for rate in unemployment:
    rate = rate - 0.01
```

This loop does *not* modify the list because **rate**, which is being modified, is not actually a name in the list. Instead, it is being assigned the same value as an item in the list. So, although the value assigned to `rate` is being modified, the list itself is not. As illustrated below, at the beginning of the first iteration, 0.082 is assigned to `rate`.

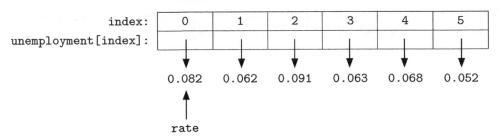

Then, when the modified value `rate - 0.01` is assigned to `rate`, this only affects `rate`, not the original list, as illustrated below.

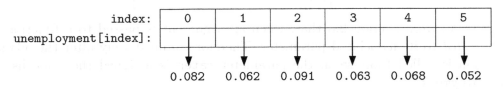

Now let's put the correct loop above in a function named `adjust` that takes a list of unemployment rates as a parameter.

```
def adjust(rates):
    """Subtract one percent (0.01) from each rate in a list.

    Parameter:
        rates: a list of numbers representing rates (percentages)

    Return value: None
    """

    for index in range(len(rates)):
        rates[index] = rates[index] - 0.01
```

In the following `main` function, the list named `unemployment` is passed into the `adjust` function for the parameter `rates`.

```
def main():
    unemployment = [0.053, 0.071, 0.065, 0.074]
    adjust(unemployment)
    print(unemployment)

main()
```

Inside the `adjust` function, every value in `rates` is decremented by 0.01. What effect, if any, does this have on the list assigned to `unemployment`? To find out, we need to look carefully at what happens when the function is called.

Right after the assignment statement in the `main` function, the situation looks like the following, with the variable named `unemployment` in the `main` namespace assigned the list [0.053, 0.071, 0.065, 0.074].

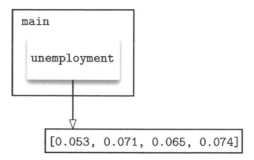

Now recall from Section 2.5 that, when an argument is passed to a function, it is *assigned* to its associated parameter. Therefore, immediately after the `adjust` function is called from `main`, the parameter `rates` is assigned the same list as `unemployment`:

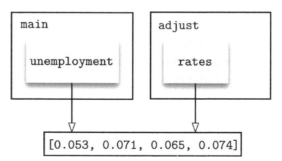

After `adjust` executes, 0.01 has been subtracted from each value in `rates`, as the following picture illustrates.

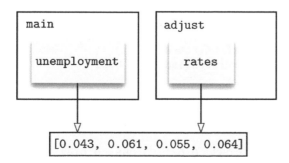

Notice that, since the same list is assigned to `unemployment`, these changes will also be reflected in the value of `unemployment` back in the `main` function. In other words, after the `adjust` function returns, the picture looks like this:

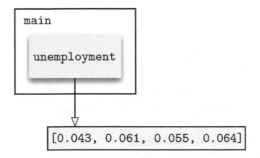

So when **unemployment** is printed at the end of **main**, the adjusted list [0.043, 0.061, 0.055, 0.064] will be displayed.

Reflection 7.10 *Why does the argument's value change in this case when it did not in the parameter passing examples in Section 2.5? What is different?*

The difference here is that lists are mutable. When you pass a mutable type as an argument, any changes to the associated formal parameter inside the function will be reflected in the value of the argument. Therefore, when we pass a list as an argument to a function, the values in the list can be changed inside the function.

What if we did *not* want to change **unemployment** when we passed it to the **adjust** function, and instead return a *new* adjusted list? One alternative, illustrated in the function below, would be to make a copy of **rates**, using the list method **copy**, and then modify this copy instead.

```
def adjust(rates):
    """ (docstring omitted) """

    ratesCopy = rates.copy()
    for index in range(len(ratesCopy)):
        ratesCopy[index] = ratesCopy[index] - 0.01
    return ratesCopy
```

The **copy** method creates an independent copy of the list in memory, and returns a reference to this new list so that it can be assigned to a variable name (in this case, **ratesCopy**). There are other solutions to this problem as well, which we leave as exercises.

With this knowledge in hand, we can return to the problem of smoothing data in place. The following modified function does this by replacing each value of **data[index]** with the mean of the window starting at position **index**.

```
1 def smoothInPlace(data, width):
2     """Smooth data in place over windows with the given width.
3
4     Parameters:
5         data: a list of numbers
6         width: the width of each window
7
8     Return value: None
9     """
```

```
 8    total = 0                            # get the sum for the first window
 9    for index in range(width):
10        total = total + data[index]

11    for index in range(len(data)):
12        width = min(width, len(data) - index) # adjust width near the end
13        mean = total / width                   # compute the window mean
14        total = total - data[index]            # subtract leftmost value
15        if index + width < len(data):            # if possible,
16            total = total + data[index + width] #    add rightmost value
17        data[index] = mean                     # replace with window mean
```

The first things to notice are that the function has no **smoothedData** list and it does not return anything because smoothing will be reflected directly in **data**. The only two other changes are highlighted. In the first highlighted line, the mean value is computed for the window, but not yet changed in the list. The mean is assigned to **data[index]** in the second highlighted line, at the bottom of the loop. The reason for the separation between these two steps is subtle but important.

| **Reflection 7.11** *Why can we not change the first highlighted line to* **data[index] = total / width***?*

If we assigned the window mean to **data[index]** on line 13, then we would be overwriting the original value of **data[index]** that we need in line 14! The ordering of events here is crucial: computing the mean of the current window in line 13 must come before **total** is modified for the next window in lines 14–16, and subtracting **data[index]** from **total** on line 14 must come before updating **data[index]** on line 17.

List operators and methods

In addition to **append**, there are several more ways to create and modify lists. These will be especially helpful in the projects at the end of this chapter.

List operators

First, the two operators that we used to create new strings can also be used to create new lists. The repetition operator * creates a new list that is built from repeats of the contents of a smaller list. For example:

```
>>> empty = [0] * 5
>>> empty
[0, 0, 0, 0, 0]
>>> ['up', 'down'] * 4
['up', 'down', 'up', 'down', 'up', 'down', 'up', 'down']
```

The concatenation operator + creates a new list that is the result of "sticking together" two lists. For example:

```
>>> unemployment = [0.082, 0.092, 0.091, 0.063, 0.068, 0.052]
```

```
>>> unemployment = unemployment + [0.087, 0.101]
>>> unemployment
[0.082, 0.092, 0.091, 0.063, 0.068, 0.052, 0.087, 0.101]
```

Notice that the concatenation operator combines two lists to create a new list, whereas the **append** method *inserts* a new element into the end of an existing list. In other words,

```
unemployment = unemployment + [0.087, 0.101]
```

accomplishes the same thing as the two statements

```
unemployment.append(0.087)
unemployment.append(0.101)
```

However, using concatenation actually creates a new list that is then assigned to **unemployment**, whereas using **append** modifies an existing list. So using **append** is usually more efficient than concatenation if you are just adding to the end of an existing list.

Sorting a list

The **sort** method sorts the items in a list in increasing order. For example, suppose we have a list of SAT scores that we would like to sort:

```
>>> scores = [620, 710, 520, 550, 640, 730, 600]
>>> scores.sort()
>>> scores
[520, 550, 600, 620, 640, 710, 730]
```

It is worth emphasizing that none of these list methods return new lists; instead they modify the lists in place. In other words, the following is a mistake:

```
>>> scores = [620, 710, 520, 550, 640, 730, 600]
>>> newScores = scores.sort()   # MISTAKE
```

❚ **Reflection 7.12** *What is the value of* **newScores** *after we execute the statements above?*

Printing the value of **newScores** reveals that it refers to the value **None** because **sort** does not return anything. However, **scores** was modified as we expected:

```
>>> newScores
>>> scores
[520, 550, 600, 620, 640, 710, 730]
```

The **sort** method will sort any list that contains comparable items, including strings. For example, suppose we have a list of names that we want to be in alphabetical order:

```
>>> names = ['Eric', 'Michael', 'Connie', 'Graham']
>>> names.sort()
>>> names
['Connie', 'Eric', 'Graham', 'Michael']
```

❚ **Reflection 7.13** *What happens if you try to sort a list containing items that cannot be compared to each other? For example, try sorting the list* [3, 'one', 4, 'two'].

Inserting and deleting items

The `insert` method inserts an item into a list at a particular index. For example, suppose we want to insert new names into the sorted list above to maintain alphabetical order:

```
>>> names.insert(3, 'John')
>>> names
['Connie', 'Eric', 'Graham', 'John', 'Michael']
>>> names.insert(0, 'Carol')
>>> names
['Carol', 'Connie', 'Eric', 'Graham', 'John', 'Michael']
```

The first parameter of the `insert` method is the index where the inserted item will reside *after* the insertion.

The `pop` method is the inverse of `insert`; `pop` deletes the list item at a given index and returns the deleted value. For example,

```
>>> inMemoriam = names.pop(3)
>>> names
['Carol', 'Connie', 'Eric', 'John', 'Michael']
>>> inMemoriam
'Graham'
```

If the argument to `pop` is omitted, `pop` deletes and returns the last item in the list.

Using `pop` in a loop can be tricky. To see why, try this loop, which is meant to delete all of the items in **names** that start with a *C*.

```
>>> for index in range(len(names)):
        name = names[index]
        if name[0] == 'C':
            names.pop(index)


'Carol'
IndexError: list index out of range
```

Reflection 7.14 *Where and why does the* `IndexError` *occur in this loop? Were both* `'Carol'` *and* `'Connie'` *deleted as intended?*

The error occurs because, after each call to `pop` is executed, the **names** list becomes shorter. But the loop is still going to iterate through the length of the original list because `len(names)` was evaluated before the loop started. So, in the latter iterations, the value of **index** will be beyond the end of the modified list, triggering an `IndexError` exception. There is also a more subtle issue. The condition in the `if` statement is first true when the value of **index** is 0, causing `'Carol'` to be popped. After this happens, the list looks like this: `['Connie', 'Eric', 'John', 'Michael']`. In the next iteration of the loop, **index** will be 1, so `names[index]` will be `'Eric'`. But `'Connie'`, which is now at index 0, was skipped! To avoid this mistake, the loop needs to not increment **index** when an item is popped.

To fix these errors, we need to use a `while` loop. In a `while` loop, we can make sure that the value of `len(names)` will be re-evaluated before each iteration and that `index` is only incremented when an item is not popped:

```
>>> index = 0
>>> while index < len(names):
        name = names[index]
        if name[0] == 'C':
            names.pop(index)
        else:
            index = index + 1
```

Reflection 7.15 *Reset* names *to be* `['Carol', 'Connie', 'Eric', 'John', 'Michael']` *and try this new loop. How does it fix the problems in the* `for` *loop above?*

The `remove` method also deletes an item from a list, but takes the *value* of an item as its parameter rather than its index. If there are multiple items in the list with the given value, the `remove` method only deletes the first one. For example,

```
>>> names.remove('John')
>>> names
['Carol', 'Connie', 'Eric', 'Michael']
```

Reflection 7.16 *What happens if you try to remove* `'Graham'` *from* names?

As you saw, the `remove` method raises a `ValueError` exception if its argument is not found. It is usually a good idea to catch this exception rather than have your program abort. If it doesn't matter whether the argument is found, you can catch the exception but do nothing:

```
try:
    names.remove('Graham')
except ValueError:
    pass
```

*List comprehensions

The list accumulator pattern is so common that there is a shorthand for it in Python called a ***list comprehension***. A list comprehension allows us to build up a list in a single statement. For example, suppose we wanted to create a list of the first 15 even numbers. Using a `for` loop, we can construct the desired list with:

```
evens = [ ]
for i in range(15):
    evens.append(2 * i)
```

An equivalent list comprehension looks like this:

```
evens = [2 * i for i in range(15)]
```

The first part of the list comprehension is an expression representing the items we want in the list. This is the same as the expression that would be passed to the `append` method if we constructed the list the "long way" with a `for` loop. This expression is followed by a `for` loop clause that specifies the values of an index variable for which the expression should be evaluated. The `for` loop clause is also

---

Tangent 7.1: NumPy arrays

NumPy is a Python module that provides a different list-like class named `array`. (Because the `numpy` module is required by the `matplotlib` module, you should already have it installed.) Unlike a list, a NumPy `array` is treated as a mathematical *vector*. There are several different ways to create a new array. We will only illustrate two:

```
>>> import numpy
>>> a = numpy.array([1, 2, 3, 4, 5])
>>> print(a)
[1 2 3 4 5]
>>> b = numpy.zeros(5)
>>> print(b)
[ 0.  0.  0.  0.  0.]
```

In the first case, a was assigned an `array` created from a list of numbers. In the second, b was assigned an `array` consisting of 5 zeros. One advantage of an `array` over a `list` is that arithmetic operations and functions are applied to each of an `array` object's elements individually. For example:

```
>>> print(a * 3)
[ 3  6  9 12 15]
>>> c = numpy.array([3, 4, 5, 6, 7])
>>> print(a + c)
[ 4  6  8 10 12]
```

There are also many functions and methods available to `array` objects. For example:

```
>>> print(c.sum())
25
>>> print(numpy.sqrt(c))
[ 1.73205081  2.          2.23606798  2.44948974  2.64575131]
```

An `array` object can also have more than one dimension, as we will discuss in Chapter 8. If you are interested in learning more about NumPy, visit `http://www.numpy.org`.

---

identical to the `for` loop that we would use to construct the list the "long way." This correspondence is illustrated below:

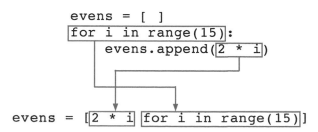

List comprehensions can also incorporate `if` statements. For example, suppose we wanted a list of the first 15 even numbers that are not divisible by 6. A `for` loop to create this list would look just like the previous example, with an additional `if` statement that checks that `2 * i` is not divisible by 6 before appending it:

```
evens = [ ]
for i in range(15):
    if 2 * i % 6 != 0:
        evens.append(2 * i)
```

This can be reproduced with a list comprehension that looks like this:

```
evens = [2 * i for i in range(15) if 2 * i % 6 != 0]
```

The corresponding parts of this loop and list comprehension are illustrated below:

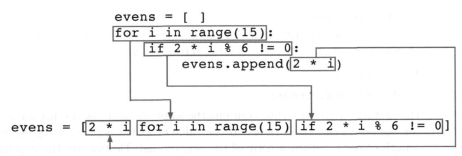

In general, the initial expression in a list comprehension can be followed by any sequence of `for` and `if` clauses that specify the values for which the expression should be evaluated.

Exercises

When an exercise asks you to write a function, test it with both common and boundary case arguments, and document your test cases.

7.2.1* Show how to add the string `'grapes'` to the end of the following list using both concatenation and the **append** method.

```
fruit = ['apples', 'pears', 'kiwi']
```

7.2.2* Write a function

```
squares(n)
```

that returns a list containing the squares of the integers 1 through n. Use a `for` loop.

7.2.3. Write a function

```
getCodons(dna)
```

that returns a list containing the codons in the string **dna**. Your algorithm should use a `for` loop. (This exercise assumes that you have read Section 6.8.)

7.2.4* Write a function

```
square(data)
```

that takes a list of numbers named **data** and squares each number in **data** in place. The function should not return anything. For example, if the list `[4, 2, 5]` is assigned to a variable named **numbers** then, after calling `square(numbers)`, **numbers** should have the value `[16, 4, 25]`.

7.2.5* Write a function

      `swap(data, i, j)`

that swaps the positions of the items with indices `i` and `j` in the list named `data`.

7.2.6. Write a function

      `reverse(data)`

that reverses the list `data` in place. Your function should not return anything. (Hint: use the `swap` function you wrote above.)

7.2.7. Suppose you are given a list of `'yea'` and `'nay'` votes. Write a function

      `winner(votes)`

that returns the majority vote. For example, `winner(['yea', 'nay', 'yea'])` should return `'yea'`. If there is a tie, return `'tie'`.

7.2.8* Write a function

      `delete(data, index)`

that returns a new list that contains the same elements as the list `data` except for the one at the given `index`. If the value of `index` is negative or exceeds the length of `data`, return a copy of the original list. Do not use the `pop` method. For example, `delete([3, 1, 5, 9], 2)` should return the list `[3, 1, 9]`.

7.2.9. Write a function

      `removeAll(data, value)`

that returns a new list that contains the same elements as the list `data` except for those that equal `value`. Do not use the builit-in `remove` method. Note that, unlike the built-in `remove` method, your function should remove *all* items equal to `value`. For example, `remove([3, 1, 5, 3, 9], 3)` should return the list `[1, 5, 9]`.

7.2.10. Write a function

      `centeredMean(data)`

that returns the average of the numbers in `data` with the largest and smallest numbers removed. You may assume that there are at least three numbers in the list. For example, `centeredMean([2, 10, 3, 5])` should return 4.

7.2.11. On page 301, we showed one way to write the `adjust` function so that it returned an adjusted list rather than modifying the original list. Give another way to accomplish the same thing.

7.2.12. Write a function

      `shuffle(data)`

that shuffles the items in the list named `data` in place, without using the `shuffle` function from the `random` module. Instead, use the `swap` function you wrote in Exercise 7.2.5 to swap 100 pairs of randomly chosen items. For each swap, choose a random index for the first item and then choose a greater random index for the second item.

7.2.13. Write a function

      `median(data)`

that returns the median number in a list of numbers named `data`.

7.2.14.   Consider the following alphabetized grocery list:

            groceries = ['cookies', 'gum', 'ham', 'ice cream', 'soap']

Show a sequence of calls to list methods that insert each of the following into their correct alphabetical positions, so that the final list containing nine items is alphabetized:

(a)* 'jelly beans'

(b)* 'donuts'

(c)   'bananas'

(d)   'watermelon'

Next, show a sequence of calls to the `pop` method that delete all of the following items from the final list above.

(e)* 'soap'

(f)* 'watermelon'

(g)   'bananas'

(h)   'ham'

7.2.15* *Stop words* are common words that are often ignored when a text is analyzed.

(a)   Write a function

            getStopWords(fileName)

that reads stop words from the file with the given `fileName` and returns them in a list. The file will contain one word per line; some stop word files are available on the book website. Remove all punctuation from the words using the `removePunctuation` function from Section 6.1.

(b)   Write a function

            removeStopWords(wordList, stopWordList)

that uses `pop` to delete all of the stop words in `stopWordList` from the list of words named `wordList`.

7.2.16.   Write a function

            removeNumbers(wordList)

that uses `pop` to delete all of the words that begin with a digit from the list of words named `wordList`.

7.2.17.   The string method `join` takes a list of strings as an argument and creates a new string that is the concatenation of the strings in the list, separated by the string object on which the method is operating. For example, `', '.join('cookies', 'gum', 'ham')` returns the string `'cookies, gum, ham'` and `'/'.join('either', 'or')` returns the string `'either/or'`.

Rewrite your `makeQuestion` function from Exercise 6.4.6 by using `textlib.wordTokens` from Section 6.1 to split the `sentence` into a list words, and then using `join` to create the question from this list.

7.2.18. Given n people in a room, what is the probability that at least one pair of people shares a birthday? To answer this question, first write a function

```
sameBirthday(numPeople)
```

that creates a list of `numPeople` random birthdays and returns `True` if two birthdays are the same, and `False` otherwise. Use the numbers 0 to 364 to represent 365 different birthdays. Next, write a function

```
birthdayProblem(numPeople, trials)
```

that performs a Monte Carlo simulation with the given number of `trials` to approximate the probability that, in a room with `numPeople` people, two people share a birthday.

7.2.19. Write a function

```
birthdayProblem2(trials)
```

that uses your `birthdayProblem` function from the previous problem to return the smallest number of people for which the probability of a pair sharing a birthday is at least 0.5.

7.2.20* Rewrite the `squares` function from Exercise 7.2.2 using a list comprehension.

7.2.21. Rewrite the `remove` function from Exercise 7.2.9 using a list comprehension.

7.2.22. Rewrite the `getCodons` function from Exercise 7.2.3 using a list comprehension. (This exercise assumes that you have read Section 6.8.)

7.3 TALLYING FREQUENCIES

In Section 6.5, we designed an algorithm to track the frequency of specific words across a text. In this section, we will use a new kind of abstract data type to record the frequencies of *every* word in a text. Word frequencies are the most basic building blocks of algorithms used to discover patterns and themes in raw texts.

Word frequencies

To find the number of times that each word appears in a text, we can iterate over the list of words, keeping track of how many times we see each word. We can imagine using a simple table for this purpose. To illustrate, suppose we have the following very short text and associated list of words, obtained by calling the **wordTokens** function from Section 6.1:

```
>>> import textlib
>>> drSeuss = 'one fish two fish red fish blue fish'
>>> wordList = textlib.wordTokens(drSeuss)
>>> wordList
['one', 'fish', 'two', 'fish', 'red', 'fish', 'blue', 'fish']
```

Upon seeing the first word in the list, `'one'`, we create an entry in the table for it and add a tally mark.

Word:	'one'
Frequency:	I

The second word in the list is `'fish'`, so we create another entry and tally mark.

Word:	'one'	'fish'
Frequency:	I	I

The third word is `'two'`, so we create a third entry and tally mark.

Word:	'one'	'fish'	'two'
Frequency:	I	I	I

The fourth word is `'fish'` again, so we add a tally mark to that entry.

Word:	'one'	'fish'	'two'
Frequency:	I	II	I

Continuing in this way with the rest of the list, we get the following final table.

Word:	'one'	'fish'	'two'	'red'	'blue'
Frequency:	I	IIII	I	I	I

Or, equivalently:

Word:	'one'	'fish'	'two'	'red'	'blue'
Frequency:	1	4	1	1	1

Dictionaries

Notice how the frequency table resembles the picture of a list on page 298, except that the indices are replaced by words. In other words, the frequency table looks like a generalized list in which the indices are replaced by values that we choose. This kind of abstract data type is called a ***dictionary***. In a dictionary, each index is replaced with a unique ***key***. Unlike a list, in which the indices are implicit, a dictionary in Python (called a `dict` object) must define the correspondence between a key and its value explicitly with a `key:value` pair. To differentiate it from a list, a dictionary is enclosed in curly braces (`{ }`). For example, the frequency table above would be represented in Python like this:

```
>>> wordFreqs = {'one': 1, 'fish': 4, 'two': 1, 'red': 1, 'blue': 1}
```

The first pair in `wordFreqs` has key `'one'` and value 1, the second pair has key `'fish'` and value 4, etc.

Each entry in a dictionary object can be referenced using the familiar indexing notation, but using a key in the square brackets instead of an index. For example:

```
>>> wordFreqs['blue']
1
>>> wordFreqs['fish']
4
```

The model of a dictionary in memory is similar to a list:

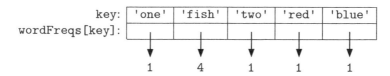

Each entry in a dictionary is a reference to a value in the same way that each entry in a list is a reference to a value. So, as with a list, we can change values in a dictionary. For example, we can increment the value associated with the key `'two'`:

```
>>> wordFreqs['two'] = wordFreqs['two'] + 1
>>> wordFreqs
{'one': 1, 'fish': 4, 'two': 2, 'red': 1, 'blue': 1}
```

To insert a new pair into the dictionary, we assign a value to the new key just like we would assign a value to an item in a list:

```
>>> wordFreqs['whale'] = 5
>>> wordFreqs
{'one': 1, 'fish': 4, 'two': 2, 'red': 1, 'blue': 1, 'whale': 5}
```

Now let's use a dictionary to implement the algorithm that we developed above to find the frequencies of words. To begin, we will create an empty dictionary named wordFreqs in which to record our tally marks:

```
wordFreqs = { }
```

Each entry in this dictionary will have its key equal to a unique word and its value equal to the word's frequency count. To tally the frequencies, we need to iterate over the words in wordList. As in our tallying algorithm, if there is already an entry in wordFreqs with a key equal to the word, we will increment the word's associated value; otherwise, we will create a new entry with wordFreqs[word] = 1. To differentiate between the two cases, we can use the in operator: word in wordFreqs evaluates to True if there is a key equal to word in the dictionary named wordFreqs.

The following function puts all of this together to create a word frequency dictionary for all of the words in a given text.

```
 1 import textlib

 2 def wordFrequencies(text):
 3     """ (docstring omitted) """

 4     wordList = textlib.wordTokens(text)  # get the list of words in text
 5     wordFreqs = { }
 6     for word in wordList:
 7         if word in wordFreqs:      # if word is already a key in wordFreqs,
 8             wordFreqs[word] = wordFreqs[word] + 1    # count the word
 9         else:                      # otherwise,
10             wordFreqs[word] = 1    #    create a new entry word:1

11     return wordFreqs
```

Carefully study the following trace table for the function, which assumes that wordList and wordFreqs have already been assigned in lines 4–5.

Step	Line	wordFreqs	word	Notes
Trace arguments: wordList = ['one', 'fish', 'two', 'fish', 'red', 'fish', 'blue', 'fish']				
3	6	{ }	'one'	word ← wordList[0]
4	7	"	"	'one' not a key; skip to line 10
5	10	{'one': 1}	"	insert 'one': 1
6	6	"	'fish'	word ← wordList[1]
7	7	"	"	'fish' not a key; skip to line 10
8	10	{'one': 1, 'fish': 1}	"	insert 'fish': 1
9	6	"	'two'	word ← wordList[2]
10	7	"	"	'two' not a key; skip to line 10
11	10	{'one': 1, 'fish': 1, 'two': 1}	"	insert 'two': 1
12	6	"	'fish'	word ← wordList[3]
13	7	"	"	'fish' is a key; do line 8
14	8	{'one': 1, 'fish': 2, 'two': 1}	"	increment wordFreqs['fish']
⋮				
24	6	{'one': 1, 'fish': 3, 'two': 1, 'red': 1, 'blue': 1}	'fish'	word ← wordList[7]
25	7	"	"	'fish' is a key; do line 8
26	8	{'one': 1, 'fish': 4, 'two': 1, 'red': 1, 'blue': 1}	"	increment wordFreqs['fish']
27	11	"	"	return wordFreqs
Return value: {'one': 1, 'fish': 4, 'two': 1, 'red': 1, 'blue': 1}				

If we are to apply this function to a larger text, we will need a nice way to display the results. The following function prints an alphabetized table of words with their frequencies.

```
def printFrequencies(frequencies, number):
    """Print an alphabetized table of keys and frequencies.

    Parameters:
        frequencies: a dictionary containing key:count pairs
        number:      the number of entries to print

    Return value: None
    """
```

```
keyList = list(frequencies.keys())    # get a list of the keys
keyList.sort()                         # and sort them

print('{0:<20} {1}'.format('Key', 'Frequency'))
print('{0:<20} {1}'.format('---', '---------'))
for key in keyList[:number]:           # iterate over the sorted list
    print('{0:<20} {1:>5}'.format(str(key), frequencies[key]))
```

We have designed the function to refer to generic keys, rather than words, to make it more general. To print the keys in alphabetical order, we first get a list of the keys in the dictionary using the **keys** method. Since **keys** returns an object from the specialized **dict_keys** class, we need to convert it to a list before we sort it. Then we iterate over the desired **number** of words in this sorted list instead of the **frequencies** dictionary.

We can find the frequencies of the first five words (alphabetically) in *Frankenstein* with the following program:

```
def main():
    textFile = open('frankenstein.txt', 'r')
    text = textFile.read()
    textFile.close()

    freqs = wordFrequencies(text)
    printFrequencies(freqs, 5)

main()
```

The result is the following table.

Key	Frequency
1	4
10	2
11	2
11th	2
12	2

| **Reflection 7.17** *Why are the first "words" in the table numbers?*

If you remove the numbers from **keyList** before printing, using the **removeNumbers** function from Exercise 7.2.16, you will see this instead:

Key	Frequency
a	1384
abandon	2
abandoned	3
abbey	1
abhor	5

Tangent 7.2: Hash tables

A Python dictionary can be implemented with a structure called a *hash table*. A hash table contains a fixed number of indexed *slots* in which the key:value pairs are stored. The slot assigned to a particular key:value pair is determined by a *hash function* that "translates" the key to a slot index. The picture below shows how some items in the wordFreqs dictionary might be placed in an underlying hash table.

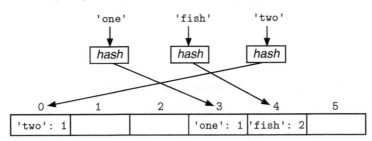

In this illustration, the hash function associates the key 'one' with slot 3, 'fish' with slot 4, and 'two' with slot 0.

The underlying hash table allows us to access a value in a dictionary (e.g., wordFreqs['fish']) or test for inclusion (e.g., key in wordFreqs) in a constant amount of time because each operation only involves a hash computation and then a direct access (like indexing in a string or a list). In contrast, if the pairs were stored in a list, then the list would need to be searched (in linear time) to perform these operations.

Unfortunately, this constant-time access could be foiled if a key is mapped to an occupied slot, an event called a *collision*. Collisions can be resolved by using adjacent slots, using a second hash function, or associating a list of items with each slot. A good hash function tries to prevent collisions by assigning slots in a seemingly random manner, so that keys are evenly distributed in the table and similar keys are not mapped to the same slot. Because hash functions tend to be so good, we can still consider an average dictionary access to be a constant-time operation, or one elementary step, even with collisions.

Finding the most frequent word

To find the highest frequency word(s) in a text, we first need to find the maximum frequency. To do this, we first extract a list of the values from the frequency dictionary using the **values** method.

```
frequencyValues = list(frequencies.values())
```

Because the **values** method returns an object from another special class called **dict_values**, we convert the result to a list. Then we can find the maximum frequency in that list:

```
maxFrequency = max(frequencyValues)
```

To find the word(s) (there could be more than one) with the highest frequencies, we need to iterate over all the keys in the frequency dictionary, checking if the frequency of each is equal to **maxFrequency**. To iterate over the keys in a dictionary, we simply iterate over the dictionary itself with a familiar `for` loop. The following function uses a loop like this to append every key with the maximum frequency to a list.

```
def mostFrequent(frequencies):
    """Find the key(s) with the highest frequency.

    Parameter:
        frequencies: a dictionary containing key:count pairs

    Return value: a list of the most frequent keys in frequencies
    """

    frequencyValues = list(frequencies.values())
    maxFrequency = max(frequencyValues)

    mostFrequentKeys = [ ]
    for key in frequencies:
        if frequencies[key] == maxFrequency:
            mostFrequentKeys.append(key)

    return mostFrequentKeys
```

Reflection 7.18 *Use this function to find the most frequent word in Frankenstein.*

Not surprisingly, the word in *Frankenstein* with the highest frequency is *the*. Because results like this are not very interesting, common words, called *stop words*, are often removed from word lists. (You may have already written a function to do this in Exercise 7.2.15.)

Let's go one step further and write a function to print a table of words, sorted by frequency, from highest to lowest. We did something similar in the `printFrequencies` function by sorting the keys and then iterating over this sorted list. But this function is a little trickier because, once we have a sorted list of dictionary values, there is no way to recover the associated keys. In a dictionary, we can get the value of a pair given the key, but not vice versa.

But here is a trick we can use. We will create a list of (value, key) pairs, and then sort this list. When the `sort` method is given a list of tuples, it sorts the list by the first item in the tuple, so this will give us a list sorted by frequency, and each frequency will be accompanied by its key. Then we can iterate over this sorted list. The following function demonstrates this technique.

```
def printMostFrequent(frequencies, number):
    """Print a table of the highest frequency keys.

    Parameters:
        frequencies: a dictionary containing key:count pairs
        number:      the number of entries to print

    Return value: None
    """
```

```
sortedValues = []                    # create list of (value, key) tuples
for key in frequencies:
    sortedValues.append((frequencies[key], key))
sortedValues.sort(reverse = True)        # sort in descending order

print('{0:<20} {1}'.format('Key', 'Frequency'))
print('{0:<20} {1}'.format('---', '---------'))
for pair in sortedValues[:number]:    # iterate over the sorted list
    key = pair[1]
    print('{0:<20} {1:>5}'.format(str(key), frequencies[key]))
```

| Reflection 7.19 *Use this function to find the five most frequent words in Frankenstein.*

The five most frequent words are again not terribly surprising:

Key	Frequency
the	4187
and	2970
i	2842
of	2639
to	2092

But after removing stop words, they are more meaningful. (Producing this list is left as an exercise.)

Key	Frequency
man	131
life	114
father	112
eyes	104
time	98

Bigram frequencies

In the field of natural language processing (NLP), word frequencies by themselves are known as a "bag of words" language model. More insight into a text can be had by computing the frequencies of pairs of adjacent words, called *bigrams*. For example, in the **drSeuss** text, there are seven bigrams:

```
[('one', 'fish'), ('fish', 'two'), ('two', 'fish'), ('fish', 'red'),
 ('red', 'fish'), ('fish', 'blue'), ('blue', 'fish')]
```

Bigram frequencies, and *n*-gram frequencies more generally, are one of the basic measures used in speech recognition algorithms; knowing which words are most likely to follow other words can dramatically reduce the number of possibilities the algorithm must consider. More generally, distributions of bigram frequencies serve as the basis of language models in many NLP classification algorithms. Bigram frequencies can also serve as a simple "digital signature" of an author's writing style.

> ## Tangent 7.3: Sentiment analysis
>
> Sentiment analysis is the problem of determining whether some text is expressing a positive or negative opinion (or possibly something in between). It is frequently applied to movie and product reviews, as well as social media posts, by those wishing to study how a product or topic is being viewed by some constituency.
>
> Word and bigram probabilities are the building blocks of *machine learning* algorithms for this and other classification problems in the field of natural language processing (NLP). The probability that a word appears in a text is simply the word's frequency divided by the total number of words in the text.
>
> A machine learning algorithm first goes through a training phase in which probabilistic models of the classes are built from large corpora that have been previously classified by human beings. The algorithm classifies a new text by computing the probability that the text is in each class, and outputting the class with the highest probability.
>
> A naive Bayes classifier is the simplest machine learning algorithm used for sentiment analysis. It is "naive" because it assumes that word probabilities are independent of both their positions in the text and their relationships to other words in the text. The algorithm is trained by computing two sets of probabilities. First, it computes the probability that each word appears in a set of pre-classified documents with positive sentiment. Then it computes the probability that each word appears in a different set of pre-classified documents with negative sentiment. To classify an unknown text, the algorithm computes the probability that the text belongs to each class, defined to be the product of the prior probability of the class (usually 1/2) and the probabilities that every word in the new text appears in that class. The output is the class giving the highest probability.

Computing bigram frequencies is similar to computing word frequencies, with two main differences. First, as we iterate over the list of words, since we are interested in consecutive pairs of words, we need to also keep track of the previous word. (This is similar to keeping track of the previous character in the `splitIntoWords` function from Section 6.1.)

```
prevWord = wordList[0]
for index in range(1, len(wordList)):
    word = wordList[index]

    # count the bigram (prevWord, word)

    prevWord = word
```

Before the loop, we initialize `prevWord` to be the first word in the list of words, and then start the `for` loop at the second word in the list. In each iteration of the loop, the bigram we are counting is the pair `(prevWord, word)`. At the bottom of the loop, we update `prevWord` in preparation for the next iteration.

The second difference is that a bigram is a pair of strings. We could store bigrams as two-item lists, but dictionaries only allow immutable objects as keys. Instead, we will use **tuples**, which are like lists, except they are enclosed in parentheses and are immutable. In general, tuples are used in place of lists when the objects being represented have a fixed length, and individual components are not likely to change. For example, tuples are often used to represent the (red, green, blue) components of colors and the (x,y) coordinates of points. Tuples are also more memory efficient because extra memory is set aside in a list for a few future appends.

With the exception of these two differences, highlighted below, the following `bigramFrequencies` function is very similar to `wordFrequencies`.

```
import textlib

def bigramFrequencies(text):
    """Find the frequencies of all bigrams in a text.

    Parameter:
        text: a string object

    Return value: a dictionary containing the bigram frequencies
    """

    wordList = textlib.wordTokens(text)
    bigramFreqs = { }
    prevWord = wordList[0]
    for index in range(1, len(wordList)):
        word = wordList[index]
        bigram = (prevWord, word)
        if bigram not in bigramFreqs:
            bigramFreqs[bigram] = 1
        else:
            bigramFreqs[bigram] = bigramFreqs[bigram] + 1
        prevWord = word

    return bigramFreqs
```

Reflection 7.20 *Use this function and* `printMostFrequent` *to find the five most frequent bigrams in* Frankenstein.

The five most frequent bigrams in *Frankenstein* are:

Key	Frequency
('of', 'the')	526
('of', 'my')	272
('in', 'the')	262
('i', 'was')	226
('i', 'had')	219

The following exercises ask you to apply and modify these functions, and explore some additional uses for dictionaries. In Chapter 11, we will also use dictionaries to model social networks and other types of highly connected phenomena, and show

how computer algorithms applied to these networks can help diffuse pandemics, market new products, and make infrastructures more resilient.

Exercises

7.3.1. Write a function

```
wordFrequenciesFile(fileName)
```

that uses the `wordFrequencies` function to return a dictionary containing the frequencies of the words in the file with the given `fileName`.

7.3.2* Show how to find the five words in Jane Austen's *Sense and Sensibility* (available on the book website) with the highest frequencies. What are they? Similarly, what are the five bigrams with the highest frequencies?

7.3.3* Use the functions from Exercise 7.2.15 to modify the `wordFrequencies` function so that it does not include stop words. With your changes, what are the five most frequent words in *Sense and Sensibility*?

7.3.4. Write a new version of the `printMostFrequent` function that prints a desired number of most frequent words, but does not include stop words. Use the `getStopWords` function from Exercise 7.2.15.

7.3.5* Write a function

```
firstLetterCounts(wordList)
```

that takes as a parameter a list of strings named `words` and returns a dictionary with lowercase letters as keys and the number of words in `words` that begin with that letter (lower or uppercase) as values. For example, if the list is `['ant', 'bee', 'armadillo', 'dog', 'cat']`, then your function should return the dictionary `{'a': 2, 'b': 1, 'c': 1, 'd': 1}`.

7.3.6. Similar to the Exercise 7.3.5, write a function

```
firstLetterWords(wordList)
```

that takes as a parameter a list of strings named `words` and returns a dictionary with lowercase letters as keys. But now associate with each key the *list of the words* in `words` that begin with that letter. For example, if the list is `['ant', 'bee', 'armadillo', 'dog', 'cat']`, then your function should return the following dictionary:

```
{'a': ['ant', 'armadillo'], 'b': ['bee'], 'c': ['cat'],
 'd': ['dog']}
```

7.3.7. The *probability mass function* (PMF) of a data set gives the probability of each value in the set. A dictionary representing the PMF is a frequency dictionary with each frequency value divided by the total number of values in the original data set. For example, the (rounded) probabilities for the values in the dictionary `{18.9: 2, 19.0: 1, 19.2: 1, 19.3: 2}` are

```
{18.9: 0.286, 19.0: 0.143, 19.2: 0.143, 19.3: 0.286}
```

Write a function

```
pmf(frequency)
```

that returns a dictionary containing the PMF of the frequency dictionary passed as a parameter.

7.3.8. The probability that a word appears in a text can be found by dividing the frequency of the word by the total number of words in the text. These probabilities form the basis of many machine learning algorithms like those described in Tangent 7.3. Write a function

```
wordProbabilities(text)
```

that returns a dictionary containing the probabilities of all words in `text`. Your function should call the `wordFrequencies` function.

7.3.9. Write a function

```
histogram(data, numBins)
```

that displays a histogram of the values in the list `data` using `numBins` bins. The bins correspond to equal sized intervals between the minimum and maximum values in `data`. Each bin will count the number of values that fall in its corresponding interval. For example, if `data = [4, 7, 2, 8, 3]` and `numBins = 3`, then the bins will correspond to the intervals $[2, 4)$, $[4, 6)$, and $[6, 8]$, and the counts in these bins will be 2, 1, and 3. The histogram can be displayed using the `bar` function from `matplotlib.pyplot`:

```
pyplot.bar(range(1, numBins + 1), binCounts, align = 'center')
pyplot.xticks(range(1, numBins + 1))  # label the bins
```

Test your function with both small and large lists of randomly generated values in a variety of ranges. Also test it with a list of sums of random values such as

```
data = []
for count in range(10000):
    data.append(random.randrange(20, 80) + random.randrange(50))
```

What do you notice?

7.3.10* Write a function

```
bonus(salaries)
```

that takes as a parameter a dictionary named `salaries`, with names as keys and salaries as values, and increases the salary of everyone in the dictionary by 5%.

7.3.11. Write a function

```
updateAges(names, ages)
```

that takes as parameters a list of `names` of people whose birthday is today and a dictionary named `ages`, with names as keys and ages as values, and increments the age of each person in the dictionary whose birthday is today.

7.3.12. Write a function

```
seniorList(students, year)
```

that takes as a parameter a dictionary named `students`, with names as keys and class years as values, and returns a list of names of students who are graduating in `year`.

7.3.13* Dictionaries are also well-suited for handling translations. For example, the following dictionary associates a meaning with each of three texting abbreviations.

```
translations = {'lol': 'laugh out loud', 'u': 'you', 'r': 'are'}
```

With this, we can find the meaning of `lol` with

```
translations['lol']
```

Write a function

```
txtTranslate(txtWord)
```

that uses a dictionary to return the English meaning of the texting abbreviation `txtWord`. Incorporate translations for at least ten texting abbreviations. If the abbreviation is not in the dictionary, your function should return a suitable string message instead. For example, `txtTranslate('lol')` should return `'laugh out loud'`.

7.3.14. Write a function

```
createDictionary()
```

that creates a dictionary, inserts several English words as keys and the Pig Latin (or any other language) translations as values, and then returns the completed dictionary.

Next write a function

```
translate()
```

that calls your `createDictionary` function to create a dictionary, and then repeatedly asks for a word to translate. For each entered word, it should print the translation using the dictionary. If a word does not exist in the dictionary, the function should say so. The function should end when the word `quit` is typed.

7.3.15. Write a function

```
login(passwords)
```

that takes as a parameter a dictionary named `passwords`, with usernames as keys and passwords as values, and repeatedly prompts for a username and password until a valid pair is entered. Your function should continue to prompt even if an invalid username is entered.

7.3.16. Write a function

```
union(dict1, dict2)
```

that returns a new dictionary that contains all of the entries of the two dictionaries `dict1` and `dict2`. If the dictionaries share a key, use the value in the first dictionary. For example, `union({'pies': 3, 'cakes': 5},` `{'cakes': 4, 'tarts': 2})` should return the dictionary `{'pies': 3,}` `{ 'cakes': 5, 'tarts': 2}`.

7.3.17. The *Mohs hardness scale* rates the hardness of a rock or mineral on a 10-point scale, where 1 is very soft (like talc) and 10 is very hard (like diamond). Suppose we have a list such as

```
rocks = [('talc', 1), ('lead', 1.5), ('copper', 3),
         ('nickel', 4), ('silicon', 6.5), ('emerald', 7.5),
         ('boron', 9.5), ('diamond', 10)]
```

where the first element of each tuple is the name of a rock or mineral, and the second element is its hardness. Write a function

```
hardness(rocks)
```

that returns a dictionary organizing the rocks and minerals in such a list into four categories: soft (1–3), medium (3.1–5), hard (5.1–8), and very hard (8.1–10). For example, given the list above, the function would return the dictionary

```
{'soft': ['talc', 'lead', 'copper'],
 'medium': ['nickel'],
 'hard': ['silicon', 'emerald'],
 'very hard': ['boron', 'diamond']}
```

7.3.18. Write a function

   `getBigramProbabilities(bigramFreqs)`

that returns a new dictionary containing, for each bigram in `bigramFreqs`, the probability that the second word in the bigram follows the first word in the bigram. This is defined as the bigram's frequency divided by the sum of the frequencies of all bigrams with the same first word.

7.3.19. Write a function

   `printNextWords(bigramFreqs, word)`

that prints a table containing all of the words that come after `word` according to the dictionary `bigramFreqs`. Each word in the table should be accompanied by its frequency and the probability that it follows `word`, defined as its frequency divided by the sum of the frequencies of all bigrams with `word` as their first word. For example, in *Sense and Sensibility*, passing `'twisted'` in for `word` should print

```
Next Word        Frequency Probability
---------        --------- -----------
in                       1  0.250
tree                     1  0.250
blasted                  1  0.250
his                      1  0.250
```

7.3.20* Write a function

   `wordPredictor(bigramFreqs)`

that mimics the predictive text function of phones using the given dictionary of bigram frequencies. The function should prompt for a first word, then suggest the top three highest frequency words that follow that word. The chosen word will serve as the next word in a loop. The loop should continue until either no next word is found or a word is entered that is not among the choices offered. For example, a possible session based on bigram frequencies from *Sense and Sensibility* might look like the following.

```
First word: she
Choose among ['was', 'had', 'could']: could
she could
Choose among ['not', 'be', 'have']: be
she could be
Choose among ['a', 'the', 'in']: the
she could be the
Choose among ['same', 'world', 'house']: world
she could be the world
Choose among ['to', 'and', 'of']: quit
```

7.3.21. Bigram frequencies can be used to create fun, computer-generated "poetry." Write a function

    writer(bigramFreqs, firstWord, length)

that returns a string containing a sequence of words in which the next word is randomly chosen from among the most likely words to follow the previous word, based on the given bigram frequencies. When choosing the next word, if there are n bigrams starting with the previous word, the list of candidates should be created from the $n/2$ with the highest frequencies. The second and third parameters are the starting word and the desired number of words in the "poem." For example, one particular 15-word output, based on the bigram frequencies in *Sense and Sensibility*, is

    she read and unaffected sincerity that what say it by him such
    behaviour in many particulars

This exercise is very similar to the previous exercise, but with no human intervention.

7.3.22. (This exercise assumes that you have read Section 6.8.) Rewrite the complement function on page O6.8-5 using a dictionary. (Do not use any if statements.)

7.3.23. (This exercise assumes that you have read Section 6.8.) Suppose we have a set of homologous DNA sequences with the same length. A *profile* for these sequences contains the frequency of each base in each position. For example, suppose we have the following five sequences, lined up in a table:

```
         G  G  T  T  C
         G  A  T  T  A
         G  C  A  T  A
         C  A  A  T  C
         G  C  A  T  A
     A:  0  2  3  0  3
     C:  1  2  0  0  2
     G:  4  1  0  0  0
     T:  0  0  2  5  0
         G  A  A  T  A  ⟵ consensus sequence
```

Their profile is shown below the sequences. The first column of the profile indicates that there is one sequence with a C in its first position and four sequences with a G in their first position. The second column of the profile shows that there are two sequences with A in their second position, two sequences with C in their second position, and one sequence with G in its second position. And so on. The *consensus sequence* for a set of sequences has in each position the most common base in the profile. The consensus for this list of sequences is shown below the profile.

A profile can be implemented as a list of 4-element dictionaries, one for each column. A consensus sequence can then be constructed by finding the base with the maximum frequency in each position. In this exercise, you will build up a function to find a consensus sequence in four parts.

(a) Write a function

   `profile1(sequences, index)`

   that returns a dictionary containing the frequency of each base in position `index` in the list of DNA sequences named `sequences`. For example, if we pass in `['GGTTC', 'GATTA', 'GCATA', 'CAATC', 'GCATA']` for `sequences` (the sequences from the example above) and 2 for `index`, then the function should return the dictionary `{'A': 3, 'C': 0, 'G': 0, 'T': 2}`, equivalent to the third column in the profile above.

(b) Write a function

   `profile(sequences)`

   that returns a list of dictionaries representing the profile for the list of DNA sequences named `sequences`. For example, given the list of sequences above, the function should return the list

   ```
   [{'A': 0, 'C': 1, 'G': 4, 'T': 0},
    {'A': 2, 'C': 2, 'G': 1, 'T': 0},
    {'A': 3, 'C': 0, 'G': 0, 'T': 2},
    {'A': 0, 'C': 0, 'G': 0, 'T': 5},
    {'A': 3, 'C': 2, 'G': 0, 'T': 0}]
   ```

   Your `profile` function should call your `profile1` function in a loop.

(c) Write a function

   `maxBase(freqs)`

   that returns the base with the maximum frequency in a dictionary of base frequencies named `freqs`. For example,

   `maxBase({'A': 0, 'C': 1, 'G': 4, 'T': 0})`

   should return `'G'`.

(d) Write a function

   `consensus(sequences)`

   that returns the consensus sequence for the list of DNA sequences named `sequences`. Your `consensus` function should call your `profile` function and also call your `maxBase` function in a loop.

7.4   READING TABULAR DATA

The earthquake locations that we plotted back in Section 2.2 came from the U.S. Geological Survey (USGS), which maintains up-to-the-minute data about earthquakes happening around the world.[2] In this section, we will read this data directly from the USGS and plot it with `matplotlib.pyplot`, incorporating other characteristics such as the magnitudes and depths of the earthquakes, to visualize our planet's major tectonic plates and how they interact.

---

[2]`http://earthquake.usgs.gov/earthquakes/feed/v1.0/csv.php`

Earthquakes

USGS earthquake data is available in many formats, the simplest of which is a tabular format called CSV, short for "comma-separated values." The first few rows and columns of a USGS CSV file look like the following.

```
time,latitude,longitude,depth,mag,...
2020-04-19T16:34:38.090Z,19.361166,-155.0753326,6.08,1.84,...
2020-04-19T16:34:03.110Z,35.7088333,-117.5816667,10.66,1.02,...
2020-04-19T16:32:18.020Z,61.3918,-150.1225,30.5,1.4,...
2020-04-19T16:27:34.030Z,35.768,-117.603,3.41,1,...
2020-04-19T16:24:50.590Z,38.0505,-118.6257,7.2,1.1,...
2020-04-19T16:16:42.700Z,38.1872,-118.7235,0.1,1.4,...
```

CSV files contain one row of text per line, with columns separated by commas. The first row is a header row containing the names of the fifteen columns in the file, only the first five of which are shown here. Each additional row consists of data from one earthquake. If you were to view these first five columns in a spreadsheet program, it would like something like this:

time	latitude	longitude	depth	mag
2020-04-19T16:34:38.090Z	19.361166	-155.0753326	6.08	1.84
2020-04-19T16:34:03.110Z	35.7088333	-117.5816667	10.66	1.02
2020-04-19T16:32:18.020Z	61.3918	-150.1225	30.5	1.4
2020-04-19T16:27:34.030Z	35.768	-117.603	3.41	1
2020-04-19T16:24:50.590Z	38.0505	-118.6257	7.2	1.1
2020-04-19T16:16:42.700Z	38.1872	-118.7235	0.1	1.4

The first earthquake in this file was detected at 16:34 UTC (Coordinated Universal Time) on 2020-04-19 at 19.361166 degrees latitude and −155.0753326 degrees longitude. The earthquake occurred at a depth of 6.08 km and had magnitude 1.84.

A CSV file containing data about all of the earthquakes in the past 30 days is available on the web at the URL

```
http://earthquake.usgs.gov/earthquakes/feed/v1.0/summary/all_month.csv
```

(If you have trouble with this file, you can try smaller files by replacing `all_month` with `2.5_month` or `4.5_month`. The numbers indicate the minimum magnitude of the earthquakes included in the file.)

> **Reflection 7.21** *Enter the URL above into a web browser to see the data file for yourself. About how many earthquakes were recorded in the past 30 days?*

We can read the contents of this CSV file in Python using the same techniques you learned in Section 6.2. We can either download and save the file manually (and then read the file from our program), or we can download it directly in our program using the `urllib.request` module. We use the latter method in the following function.

```
1 import urllib.request as web
2 import matplotlib.pyplot as pyplot

3 def plotQuakes():
4     """Plot the locations of all earthquakes in the past 30 days.

5     Parameters: None

6     Return value: None
7     """

8     url = 'http://earthquake.usgs.gov/...' # see above for full URL
9     quakeFile = web.urlopen(url)
10    header = quakeFile.readline()            # get past the header row

11    longitudes = []
12    latitudes = []
13    for rawLine in quakeFile:
14        line = rawLine.decode('utf-8')     # interpret the line as text
15        row = line.split(',')              # split columns at commas
16        latitudes.append(float(row[1]))    # append latitude
17        longitudes.append(float(row[2]))   # append longitude
18    quakeFile.close()

19    pyplot.scatter(longitudes, latitudes, 10)  # 10 = area of each point
20    pyplot.show()
```

To begin our function, in lines 8–10, we open the URL, and read the header row containing the column names. We do not actually use the header row; we just need to get past it to get to the data.

To visualize fault boundaries with `matplotlib.pyplot`, we need all the longitude (x) values in one list and all the latitude (y) values in another list. These lists are initialized before the loop in lines 11–12. To maintain an association between the latitude and longitude of a particular earthquake, we need these lists to be ***parallel lists***, in the sense that the longitude and latitude at any particular index belong to the same earthquake.

The `for` loop in lines 13–17 iterates over the lines in the file. Remember that data from the web is read as a raw `bytes` object that needs to be converted to text before we can use it. To extract the necessary information from each line, we use the `split` method from the string class. Recall that `split` splits a string at every instance of a given character, and returns the list of strings that result. In this case, in line 15, we want to split `line` at every comma. The resulting list named `row` will have the time of the earthquake at index 0, the latitude at index 1, the longitude at index 2, etc. Note that each of these values is a string, so we need to convert the latitude and longitude to numbers using `float`. After converting each value, we append it to its respective list in lines 16–17.

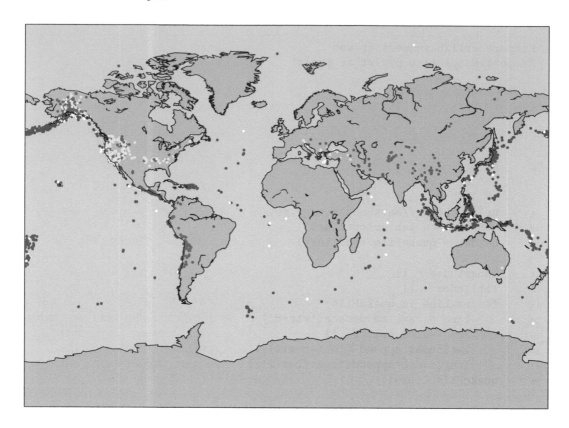

Figure 7.3 Plotted earthquake locations with colors representing depths (yellow are shallower, red are medium depth, and blue are deeper).

The plotted earthquakes are shown in Figure 7.3 over a map background. (Your plot will not show the map, but if you would like to add it, look into the `Basemap` class from the `mpl_toolkits.basemap` module.) The colors of the points in this plot reflect the earthquakes' depths. To incorporate these colors into our function, we will also need to extract the depths of the earthquakes in a third list.

> **Reflection 7.22** *What do we need to add to our function to also get a list of earthquake depths?*

Between lines 12 and 13, we will need to initialize a third parallel list named `depths` and then, after line 17, append the value in column 3 to this list with

```
depths.append(float(row[3]))
```

We can color each point according to its depth by passing the `scatter` function a list of colors, one for each point. Shallow (less than 10 km deep) earthquakes will be yellow, medium depth (between 10 and 50 km) earthquakes will be red, and deep earthquakes (greater than 50 km deep) will be blue. To create this list, we will iterate over the final `depths` list and, for each depth, append the appropriate color string to another list named `colors`:

```
colors = []
for depth in depths:
    if depth < 10:
        colors.append('yellow')
    elif depth < 50:
        colors.append('red')
    else:
        colors.append('blue')
```

To assign colors to points, we pass this `colors` list into `scatter` as a *keyword argument*:

```
pyplot.scatter(longitudes, latitudes, 10, color = colors)
```

We also saw keyword arguments briefly in Section 4.1. The name `color` is the name of a parameter of the `scatter` function for which we are passing the argument `colors`. (We will only use keyword arguments with `matplotlib.pyplot` functions, although we could also use them in our functions if we wished to do so.)

> **Reflection 7.23** *Make these modifications to the* `plotQuakes` *function, and look at the resulting figure. Try to identify the different tectonic plates. Can you infer anything about the way neighboring plates interact from the depth colors?*

Looking at Figure 7.3, the ring of red and yellow dots around Africa encloses the African plate, and the dense line of blue and red dots northeast of Australia delineates the boundary between the Pacific and Australian plates. The depth information gives geologists information about the types of the boundaries and the directions in which the plates are moving. For example, the shallow earthquakes on the west coast of North America mark a transform boundary in which the plates are sliding past from each other, while the deeper earthquakes in the Aleutian islands in Alaska mark a subduction zone at a convergent boundary where the Pacific plate to the south is diving underneath the North American plate to the north.

Exercises

7.4.1*   Modify `plotQuakes` so that it also reads earthquake magnitudes into a list, and draws larger circles for higher magnitude earthquakes. The sizes of the points can be changed by passing a list of sizes, similar to the list of colors, as the third argument to the `scatter` function. The size of each point should be the square of the magnitude of the corresponding earthquake.

7.4.2.   Modify the `firstLetterCounts` function from Exercise 7.3.5 so that it takes a file name as a parameter and uses the words from this file instead. Test your function using the SCRABBLE dictionary on the book website.[3]

7.4.3*   Modify the `login` function from Exercise 7.3.15 so that it takes a file name as a parameter and creates a username/password dictionary with the usernames and passwords in that file before it starts prompting for a username and password. Assume that the file contains one username and password per line, separated by a space. There is an example file on the book website.

---

[3]SCRABBLE is a registered trademark of Hasbro Inc.

7.4.4.   Write a function

      `plotPopulation()`

that plots the world population over time from the tab-separated data file on the book website named `worldpopulation.txt`. To read a tab-separated file, split each line with `line.split('\t')`. These figures are U.S. Census Bureau midyear population estimates from 1950–2050. Your function should create two plots. The first shows the years on the x-axis and the populations on the y-axis. The second shows the years on the x-axis and the annual growth rate on the y-axis. The growth rate is the difference between this year's population and last year's population, divided by last year's population. Be sure to label your axes in both plots with the `xlabel` and `ylabel` functions.

What is the overall trend in world population growth? Do you have any hypotheses regarding the most significant spikes and dips?

7.4.5.   Write a function

      `plotMeteorites()`

that plots the location (longitude and latitude) of every known meteorite that has fallen to earth, using a tab-separated data file from the book website named `meteoritessize.txt`. Split each line of a tab-separated file with `line.split('\t')`. There are large areas where no meteorites have apparently fallen. Is this accurate? Why do you think no meteorites show up in these areas?

7.4.6*   Write a function

      `plotTemps()`

that reads a CSV data file from the book website named `madison_temp.csv` to plot several years of monthly minimum temperature readings from Madison, Wisconsin. The temperature readings in the file are integers in tenths of a degree Celsius and each date is expressed in a `YYYYMMDD` format. Rather than putting every date in a list for the x-axis, just make a list of the years that are represented in the file. Then plot the data and put a year label at each January tick with

```
pyplot.plot(range(len(minTemps)), minTemps)
pyplot.xticks(range(0, len(minTemps), 12), years)
```

The first argument to the `xticks` function says to only put a tick at every twelfth x value, and the second argument supplies the list of years to use to label those ticks. It will be helpful to know that the data file starts with a January 1 reading.

7.4.7.   Write a function

      `plotZebras()`

that plots the migration of seven Burchell's zebra in northern Botswana. (The very interesting story behind this data can be found at `https://www.movebank.org/node/11921`.) The function should read a CSV data file from the book website named `zebra.csv`. Each line in the data file is a record of the location of an individual zebra at a particular time. Each individual has a unique identifier. There are over 50,000 records in the file. For each record, your function should extract the individual identifier (column index 9), longitude (column index 3), and latitude (column index 4). Store the data in two dictionaries, each with identifiers as keys. In one dictionary, the value associated with each identifier should be a list of the longitudes of all tracking events for the zebra with that identifier. Similarly, the second dictionary should contain the corresponding latitude values. Plot the locations of the seven zebras in seven different colors to visualize their migration patterns.

How can you determine from the data which direction the zebras are migrating?

7.4.8. On the book website, there is a tab-separated data file named `education.txt` that contains information about the maximum educational attainment of U.S. citizens, as of 2013. Each non-header row contains the number of people in a particular category (in thousands) that have attained each of fifteen different educational levels. Look at the file in a text editor (*not* a spreadsheet program) to view its contents. Write a function

> `plotEducation()`

that reads this data and then plots separately (but in one figure) the educational attainment of all males, females, and both sexes together over 18 years of age. The x-axis should be the fifteen different educational attainment levels and the y axis should be the *percentage* of each group that has attained that level. Notice that you will only need to extract three lines of the data file, skipping over the rest. To label the ticks on the x-axis, use the following:

> `pyplot.xticks(range(15), titles[2:], rotation = 270)`
> `pyplot.subplots_adjust(bottom = 0.45)`

The first statement labels the x ticks with the educational attainment categories, rotated 270 degrees. The second statement reserves 45% of the vertical space for these x tick labels. Can you draw any conclusions from the plot about relative numbers of men and women who pursue various educational degrees?

7.4.9. The ocean temperature data that we used in Section 7.2 is based on data acquired from *Coriolis*[4], a French organization that monitors the characteristics of the oceans from satellites, ships, and floating monitoring stations. These data are used to better understand and predict climate change. A CSV file containing data from one floating station in the eastern Mediterranean Sea can be downloaded on the book website as `float.csv`. Each row in the file contains one measurement of temperature and practical salinity of the seawater at a particular depth. The depth is recorded in terms of decibars of water pressure. This file contains the records of 45 profiles, where each profile consists of 39–164 measurements at varying depths. Each profile is designated by a date and time. Look at the data file carefully to understand its format.

(a) Write a function

> `getData()`

that reads the data from the file into a dictionary in which each key is a date (a string) representing a profile. The value corresponding to each date will be a list of (pressure, salinity, temperature) tuples representing the measurements made in that profile. To simplify matters, use the first ten characters of the values in the DATE column as your keys. Your function should return the data dictionary for use by the functions that follow.

---

[4]`http://www.coriolis.eu.org`

(b) Write a function

    `plotDateTemp(dataDict)`

that plots the surface seawater temperature recorded for each date in the dictionary named `dataDict`. You may assume that the maximum recorded temperature represents the surface temperature. Label your axes appropriately. Since there are too many dates to display on the x-axis neatly, you can display every tenth date with `pyplot.xticks(range(0, len(dates), 10), dates[::10])`.

(c) Write a function

    `plotTempPressure(dataDict)`

that plots temperature (x-axis) vs. water pressure (y-axis) readings for November 17, 2019 (`'2019/11/17'`). Sort the list of triples for that day (by pressure) to ensure a clean plot. You can reverse the y axis so that the pressure reading decreases to mimic ocean depth with `pyplot.ylim(maxPressure, 0)`, where `maxPressure` is the maximum pressure reading on that day.

(d) Write a function

    `plotSalinityTemp(dataDict)`

that plots salinity (x-axis) vs. temperature (y-axis) readings from all 45 profiles on a single plot. To differentiate the different curves, you can use a colormap that gradually changes color as the days progress. Doing this is much more arcane than usual, so here is an outline of the function that includes the colormap implementation:

```python
def plotSalinityTemp(dataDict):
    numberDays = len(dataDict)     # set up the color map
    colorMap = cm.get_cmap('plasma', numberDays)
    normalizer = pyplot.Normalize(0, numberDays)
    pyplot.colorbar(cm.ScalarMappable(norm = normalizer,
                            cmap = colorMap),
                            label = 'Profile Number')
    count = 0
    for date in dataDict:
        readings = dataDict[date]
        readings.sort()

        # get the lists of salinity and temperature
        # measurements for this date

        pyplot.plot(salinities, temperatures,
                    linewidth = 0.25,
                    color = colorMap(count / numberDays))
        count = count + 1

    pyplot.xlabel('Practical Salinity')
    pyplot.ylabel('Temperature (degrees Celsius)')
    pyplot.show()
```

*7.5 DESIGNING EFFICIENT ALGORITHMS

This section is available on the book website.

*7.6 LINEAR REGRESSION

This section is available on the book website.

*7.7 DATA CLUSTERING

This section is available on the book website.

7.8 SUMMARY AND FURTHER DISCOVERY

It is often said that those who know how to manipulate and extract meaning from data will be the decision makers of the future.

In this chapter, we developed algorithms to summarize the contents of a list with various descriptive statistics, modify the contents of lists, and use dictionaries to describe the frequency of values in a list. The beauty of these techniques is that they can be used with a wide variety of data types and applications. But before any of them can be used on real data, the data must be read from its source and wrangled into a usable form. To this end, we also discussed basic methods for reading and formatting tabular data both from local files and from the web.

In later sections, we went beyond simply describing data sets to *data mining* techniques that can make predictions from them. *Linear regression* seeks a linear pattern in data and then uses this pattern to predict missing data points. The *k-means clustering* algorithm partitions data into clusters of like items to elicit hidden relationships.

Algorithms that manipulate lists can quickly become much more complicated than what we have seen previously, and therefore paying attention to their time complexity is important. To illustrate, we worked through a sequence of increasingly more elegant and more efficient algorithms for removing duplicates from a list. In the end, we saw that the additional time taken to think through a problem carefully and reduce its time complexity can pay dividends.

Notes for further discovery

Sherlock Holmes was an early (fictional) data scientist, always insisting on fact-based theories (and not vice versa). The chapter epigraph is from Sir Arthur Conan Doyle's short story, *The Adventure of the Copper Beeches* [14].

A good resource for current data-related news is the "data journalism" website *FiveThirtyEight* at http://fivethirtyeight.com . If you are interested in learning more about the emerging field of data science, one resource is *Doing Data Science* by Rachel Schutt and Cathy O'Neil [58].

Tangent 7.4: Privacy in the age of big data

Companies collect (and buy) a lot of data about their customers, including demographics (age, address, marital status), education, financial and credit history, buying habits, and web browsing behavior. They then mine this data, using techniques like clustering, to learn more about customers so they can target them with advertising that is more likely to lead to sales. But when does this practice lead to unacceptable breaches of privacy? For example, a recent article explained how a major retailer is able to figure out when a woman is pregnant before her family does.

When companies store this data online, it also becomes vulnerable to unauthorized access by hackers. In recent years, there have been several high-profile incidents of retail, government, and financial data breaches. As our medical records also begin to migrate online, more people are taking notice of the risks involved in storing "big data."

So as you continue to work with data, remember to always balance the reward with the inherent risk. Just because we *can* do something doesn't mean that we *should* do it.

There really are drifting buoys (called profiling floats) in the world's oceans that are constantly taking temperature readings to monitor climate change. For example, see

http://www.coriolis.eu.org .

The article referenced in Tangent 7.4 is from *The New York Times* [15]. The nonprofit Electronic Frontier Foundation (EFF), founded in 1990, works at the forefront of issues of digital privacy and free speech. To learn more about contemporary privacy issues, visit its website at http://www.eff.org. For more about ethical issues in computing in general, we recommend *Computer Ethics* by Deborah Johnson and Keith Miller [27].

*7.9 PROJECTS

This section is available on the book website.

CHAPTER 8

Flatland

Suffice it that I am the completion of your incomplete self. You are a Line, but I am a Line of
Lines, called in my country a Square: and even I, infinitely superior though I am to you, am
of little account among the great nobles of Flatland, whence I have come to visit you, in the
hope of enlightening your ignorance.

Edwin A. Abbott
Flatland: A Romance of Many Dimensions (1884)

I N Edwin Abbott's eponymous novel, a square who lives in the two-dimensional
world of Flatland grapples with comprehending the three-dimensional world of
Spaceland, while simultaneously recognizing the profound advantages he enjoys over
those living in the zero- and one-dimensional worlds of Pointland and Lineland.

Analogously, we have discovered the advantages of one-dimensional data (strings
and lists) over zero-dimensional numbers and characters. In this chapter, we will
discover the further possibilities afforded us by understanding how to work with two-
dimensional data. We will begin by looking at how we can create a two-dimensional
table of data read in from a file. Then we will explore a powerful two-dimensional
simulation technique called *cellular automata*. At the end of the chapter are several
projects that illustrate how simulations similar to cellular automata can be used to
model a variety of problems. We will also explore how digital photos are stored, and
write some image filters to enhance them.

8.1 TABULAR DATA

There are a few different ways to store two-dimensional data as a table. To illustrate
the most straightforward technique, let's revisit the simple tabular data set from
Exercise 7.4.6. This CSV file (`madison_temp.csv`, available on the book website)

contains over forty years worth of monthly extreme temperature readings from Madison, Wisconsin. The first few rows look like this:

```
STATION,STATION_NAME,DATE,EMXT,EMNT
GHCND:USW00014837,MADISON DANE CO REGIONAL AIRPORT WI US,19700101,33,-294
GHCND:USW00014837,MADISON DANE CO REGIONAL AIRPORT WI US,19700201,83,-261
GHCND:USW00014837,MADISON DANE CO REGIONAL AIRPORT WI US,19700301,122,-139
⋮
```

Because all of the data in this file is based on conditions at the same site, the first two columns are identical in every data row. The third column contains the dates, in YYYYMMDD format, on which data was collected. The fourth and fifth columns contain the maximum and minimum monthly temperatures, respectively, which are in tenths of a degree Celsius (i.e., 33 represents $3.3°$ C). Previously, we would have extracted these data into three parallel lists containing dates, maximum temperatures, and minimum temperatures, like this:

```python
def readDataLists():
    """Read monthly extreme temperature data into 3 parallel lists.

    Parameters: none

    Return value: 3 lists containing dates, and min and max temperatures
    """

    dataFile = open('madison_temp.csv', 'r')
    header = dataFile.readline()

    dates = []
    maxTemps = []
    minTemps = []
    for line in dataFile:
        row = line.split(',')
        dates.append(row[2])
        maxTemps.append(int(row[3]))
        minTemps.append(int(row[4]))
    dataFile.close()

    return dates, maxTemps, minTemps
```

Reading a table of temperatures

Alternatively, we may wish to extract the data into a single table. For example, the last three columns could be stored in a unified tabular structure like the following:

DATE	EMXT	EMNT
19700101	33	-294
19700201	83	-261
19700301	122	-139
⋮	⋮	⋮

We can represent this structure in Python as a list of rows, where each row is a list of values in that row. In other words, the table above can be stored like this:

```
[['19700101', 33, -294], ['19700201', 83, -261], ['19700301', 122, -139], ...]
```

To better visualize this list as a table, we can reformat its presentation a bit:

```
[
  [ '19700101',  33, -294 ],  # row 0
  [ '19700201',  83, -261 ],  # row 1
  [ '19700301', 122, -139 ],  # row 2
  ⋮
]
```

In the `readDataLists` function, `row` is already assigned to each of these row lists in the `for` loop. Therefore, to create this structure, we can simply append each value of `row`, with the temperature values converted to integers and the first two redundant columns removed, to a growing list of rows named `table`. These changes are highlighted below.

```python
def readDataTable():
    """Read monthly extreme temperature data into a table.

    Parameters: none

    Return value: list of lists containing dates and extreme temperatures
    """

    dataFile = open('madison_temp.csv', 'r')
    header = dataFile.readline()

    table = []
    for line in dataFile:
        row = line.split(',')
        row[3] = int(row[3])
        row[4] = int(row[4])
        table.append(row[2:])  # add a new row to the table
    dataFile.close()

    return table
```

Since each element of `table` is a list containing one row, the first row is assigned to `table[0]`, the second row is assigned to `table[1]`, and the third row is assigned to `table[2]`, as illustrated below.

$$[\underbrace{['19700101', 33, -294]}_{table[0]}, \underbrace{['19700201', 83, \overbrace{-261}^{table[1][2]}]}_{table[1]}, \underbrace{['19700301', \overbrace{122}^{table[2][1]}, -139]}_{table[2]}, \ldots]$$

> **Reflection 8.1** *How would you access the minimum temperature in February, 1970* (*'19700201'*) *from this list?*

The minimum temperature in February, 1970 is the third value in `table[1]`. Since `table[1]` is a list, we can use indexing to access individual items contained in it. Therefore, the third value in `table[1]` is `table[1][2]`, which equals -261 (−26.1°C), as indicated above. Likewise, `table[2][1]` is the maximum temperature in March, 1970: 122 (12.2°C).

> **Reflection 8.2** *In general, how can you access the value in row* `r` *and column* `c`?

Notice that, for a particular value `table[r][c]`, `r` is the index of the row and `c` is the index of the column. So if we know the row and column of any desired value, it is easy to retrieve that value with this convenient notation.

Now suppose we want to search this table for the minimum temperature in a particular month. To access this value in the table, we will need both its row and column indices. We already know that the column index must be 2, since the minimum temperatures are in the third column. To find the correct row index, we need to search all of the values in the first column until we find the row that contains the desired string. Once we have the correct row index `r`, we can simply return the value of `table[r][2]`. The following function does exactly this.

```
def getMinTemp(table, date):
    """Return the minimum temperature for the given date string.

    Parameters:
        table: a table containing extreme temperature data
        date:  a date string

    Return value: the minimum temperature for the given date
                  or None if the date does not exist
    """

    numRows = len(table)
    for r in range(numRows):
        if table[r][0] == date:
            return table[r][2]
    return None
```

The `for` loop iterates over the the indices of the rows in the table. For each row with index `r`, we check if the first value in that row, `table[r][0]`, is equal to the date we are looking for. If it is, we return the value in column 2 of that row. If we

---

Tangent 8.1: Pandas

The Python module `pandas` is used by many data scientists to analyze tabular data. It allows one to easily read a CSV file into a tabular object called a *data frame*, and then perform a variety of analyses on it. Here's how you could read the Madison temperature data using `pandas`:

```
>>> import pandas as pd
>>> temps = pd.read_csv('madison_temp.csv',
                        usecols = ['DATE', 'EMXT', 'EMNT'],
                        index_col = 'DATE')
```

The variable `temps` is now a data frame containing the data from the file `madison_temp.csv`. Since we noticed that the first two columns in this file are redundant, we elected to create the data frame with only the last three columns, and we selected the `DATE` column as the index, allowing us to use the dates as unique row identifiers. The first few rows of the data frame look like this:

```
>>> temps.head(3)   # display first 3 rows
           EMXT  EMNT
DATE
19700101    33  -294
19700201    83  -261
19700301   122  -139
```

Now if we want the minimum temperature in February, 1970, we can select the desired row and column:

```
>>> temps.at[19700201, 'EMNT']
-261
```

This just barely scratches the surface of what `pandas` can do. If you find yourself working with a lot of CSV data in the future, you might want to learn more by visiting `https://pandas.pydata.org`.

---

get all the way through the loop without returning a value, the desired date must not exist, so we return `None`.

Reflection 8.3 *We see in the* `getMinTemp` *function that the number of rows in the table can be found with* `len(table)`. *How could we get the number of columns in the table?*

The number of columns in a table is the length of any row, for example `len(table[0])`.

If a tabular data set contains a unique key that is frequently searched, we can alternatively store it as a dictionary. We leave an exploration of this alternative as an exercise.

Exercises

From this point on, we will generally not specify what the name and parameters of a function should be. Instead, we would like you to design the function(s).

8.1.1* Show how the following table can be stored in a list named `scores`.

Student ID	SAT MATH	SAT EBRW
10305	700	610
11304	680	590
10254	710	730
12007	650	690
10089	780	760

8.1.2. In the list you created above, how do you refer to each of the following?

(a)* the `SAT M` value for student 10089

(b)* the `SAT EBRW` value for student 11304

(c) the `SAT M` value for student 10305

(d) the `SAT EBRW` value for student 12007

8.1.3. Alternatively, a table could be stored as a list of columns.

(a) Show how to store the table in Exercise 8.1.1 in this way.

(b) Redo Exercise 8.1.2 using this new list.

(c) Why is this method less convenient when reading data in from a file?

(d) Why might this method be more convenient if you are plotting the data in the table?

8.1.4. Write a program that calls the `readDataTable` function to read the Madison temperatures into a table, and then repeatedly asks for a date string to search for in the table. For each date string entered, your function should call the `getMinTemp` function to get the corresponding minimum temperature. For example, your function should print something like the following:

```
Minimum temperature for which date (q to quit)? 20050501
The minimum temperature for 20050501 was -2.2 degrees Celsius.

Minimum temperature for which date (q to quit)? 20050801
The minimum temperature for 20050801 was 8.3 degrees Celsius.

Minimum temperature for which date (q to quit)? q
```

8.1.5. Write a function that does the same thing as the `getMinTemp` function above, but returns the maximum temperature for a particular date instead.

8.1.6* As mentioned previously, a table can alternatively be stored as a dictionary. In this representation, one column acts as the key and the remaining columns are stored in a list as the corresponding value. For example, the temperature table

```
[
  [ '19700101',  33, -294 ],
  [ '19700201',  83, -261 ],
  [ '19700301', 122, -139 ]
]
```

could be stored in a dictionary as

```
{
  '19700101': [33, -294],
  '19700201': [83, -261],
  '19700301': [122, -139]
}
```

This implementation makes searching for a particular row very efficient.

Rewrite the `readDataTable` and `getMinTemp` functions so that the temperature data is stored in this way instead. Then incorporate these new functions into your program from Exercise 8.1.4.

8.1.7. Write a function that reads the earthquake data from the CSV file at `http://earthquake.usgs.gov/earthquakes/feed/v1.0/summary/2.5_month.csv` into a table with four columns containing the latitude, longitude, depth, and magnitude of each earthquake. All four values should be stored as floating point numbers.

8.1.8. Write a function that takes the table returned by Exercise 8.1.7 as its parameter and plots the earthquake locations in that table.

8.1.9. Write a function that takes as a parameter a table returned by your function from Exercise 8.1.7 and prints a formatted table of the data. Your table should look similar to this:

```
Latitude  Longitude  Depth  Magnitude
--------  ---------  -----  ---------
   33.49    -116.46   19.8     1.1
   33.14    -115.65    2.1     1.8
   -2.52     146.12   10.0     4.6
   ⋮
```

8.1.10. Write a function that takes as a parameter a table returned by your function from Exercise 8.1.7, and repeatedly prompts for a minimum earthquake magnitude. With each response, the function should create a new table containing the rows corresponding to earthquakes with at least that magnitude, and then print this table using your function from Exercise 8.1.9. The output from your function should look similar to this:

```
Minimum magnitude (q to quit)? 6.2

Latitude  Longitude  Depth  Magnitude
--------  ---------  -----  ---------
  -46.36      33.77   10.0     6.2
  -37.68     179.69   22.0     6.7
    1.93     126.55   35.0     7.1
   -6.04     148.21   43.2     6.6
```

```
Minimum magnitude (q to quit)? 7

Latitude  Longitude  Depth  Magnitude
--------  ---------  -----  ---------
    1.93     126.55   35.0       7.1

Minimum magnitude (q to quit)? 8
There were no earthquakes with magnitude at least 8.0.

Minimum magnitude (q to quit)? q
```

8.1.11. On the book website is a CSV file named `rents.csv` that contains the average monthly rents for studio through four-bedroom apartments in every state.

(a) Write a function that reads this data into a list of lists.

(b) Write a function that repeatedly prompts for a state and an apartment type, and uses the list of lists from part (a) to print the corresponding rent. For example, your program output might look like the following:

```
State (or quit): Ohio
Apartment type (0-4): 1
The average rent is $667.
State (or quit): Delaware
Apartment type (0-4): 3
The average rent is $1653.
State (or quit): Albuquerque
That is not a state.
State (or quit): quit
```

(c) Write a function that computes the average rent for each apartment type using the list of lists from part (a).

8.1.12. Redo Exercise 8.1.11 but read the data into a dictionary like that in Exercise 8.1.6 instead.

8.2 THE GAME OF LIFE

A *cellular automaton* is a rectangular grid of discrete cells, each of which has an associated state or value. Each cell represents an individual entity, such as an organism or a particle. At each time step, every cell can simultaneously change its state according to some *rule* that depends only on the states of its neighbors. Depending upon on the rules used, cellular automata may evolve *global, emergent* behaviors based only on these *local* interactions.

The most famous example of a cellular automaton is the *Game of Life*, invented by mathematician John Conway in 1970. In the Game of Life, each cell can be in one of two states: alive or dead. At each time step, the makeup of a cell's neighborhood dictates whether it will pass into the next generation alive (or be reborn if it is dead). Depending upon the initial configuration of cells (which cells are initially alive and which are dead), the Game of Life can produce amazing patterns.

Each cell in the Game of Life has the eight neighbors illustrated below:

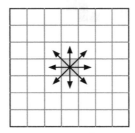

In each step, every cell simultaneously observes the states of its neighbors, and changes its state according to the following rules:

1. If a live cell has fewer than two live neighbors, it dies from loneliness.
2. If a live cell has two or three live neighbors, it remains alive.
3. If a live cell has more than three live neighbors, it dies due to overcrowding.
4. If a dead cell has exactly three live neighbors, it is reborn.

To see how these rules affect the cells in the Game of Life, consider the initial configuration in the top left of Figure 8.1. Dead cells are represented by white squares and live cells are represented by black squares. To apply rule 1 to the initial configuration, we need to check whether there are any live cells with fewer than two live neighbors. As illustrated below, there are two such cells, each marked with D.

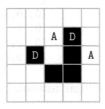

According to rule 1, these two cells will die in the next generation. To apply rule 2, we need to check whether there are any live cells that have two or three live neighbors. Since this rule applies to the other three live cells, they will remain alive into the next generation. There are no cells that satisfy rule 3, so we move on to rule 4. There are two dead cells with exactly three live neighbors, marked with A. According to rule 4, these two cells will come alive in the next generation.

❚ Reflection 8.4 *Show what the second generation looks like, after applying these rules.*

The figure in the top center of Figure 8.1 shows the resulting second generation, followed by generations three, four, and five. After five generations, as illustrated in the bottom center of Figure 8.1, the grid has returned to its initial state, but it has moved one cell down and to the right of its initial position. If we continued computing generations, we would find that it would continue in this way indefinitely, or until it collides with a border. For this reason, this initial configuration generates what is known as a "glider."

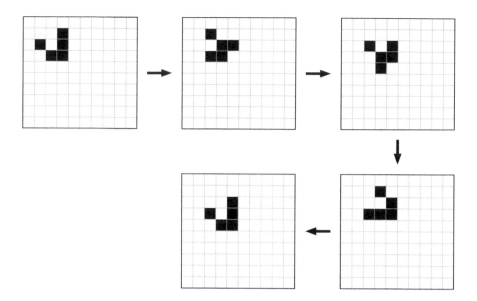

Figure 8.1 The first five generations of a "glider" in the Game of Life.

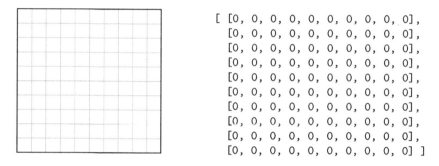

```
[ [0, 0, 0, 0, 0, 0, 0, 0, 0, 0],
  [0, 0, 0, 0, 0, 0, 0, 0, 0, 0],
  [0, 0, 0, 0, 0, 0, 0, 0, 0, 0],
  [0, 0, 0, 0, 0, 0, 0, 0, 0, 0],
  [0, 0, 0, 0, 0, 0, 0, 0, 0, 0],
  [0, 0, 0, 0, 0, 0, 0, 0, 0, 0],
  [0, 0, 0, 0, 0, 0, 0, 0, 0, 0],
  [0, 0, 0, 0, 0, 0, 0, 0, 0, 0],
  [0, 0, 0, 0, 0, 0, 0, 0, 0, 0],
  [0, 0, 0, 0, 0, 0, 0, 0, 0, 0] ]
```

Figure 8.2 Views of the "empty" cellular automaton as a grid and as a list.

Creating a grid

To implement this cellular automaton, we first need to create an empty grid of cells. For simplicity, we will keep it relatively small, with 10 rows and 10 columns. We will represent each live cell with a 1 and each dead cell with a 0. For clarity, it is best to assign these values to meaningful names:

```
ALIVE = 1
DEAD = 0
```

An initially empty grid, like the one on the left side of Figure 8.2, will be represented by a list of row lists, each of which contains a zero for every column. For example, the list on the right side of Figure 8.2 represents the grid to its left.

❙ **Reflection 8.5** *How can we easily create a list of many zeros?*

If the number of columns in the grid is assigned to **columns**, then each of these rows can be created with the list repetition operator:

```
row = [DEAD] * columns
```

We can then create the entire grid by simply appending copies of row to a list named grid:

```
def makeGrid(rows, columns):
    """Create a rows x columns grid of zeros.

    Parameters:
        rows:    the number of rows in the grid
        columns: the number of columns in the grid

    Return value: a list of ROWS lists of COLUMNS zeros
    """

    grid = []
    for r in range(rows):
        row = [DEAD] * columns
        grid.append(row)
    return grid
```

Initial configurations

The cellular automaton will evolve differently depending upon the initial configuration of alive and dead cells. We will assume that all cells are dead initially, except for those we explicitly specify. Each cell can be conveniently represented by a (row, column) tuple. The coordinates of the initially live cells can be stored in a list of tuples, and passed into the following function to initialize the grid.

```
def initialize(grid, coordinates):
    """Set a given list of coordinates to be ALIVE in the grid.

    Parameters:
        grid:        a grid of values for a cellular automaton
        coordinates: a list of coordinates

    Return value: None
    """

    for (r, c) in coordinates:
        grid[r][c] = ALIVE
```

The function iterates over the list of tuples and sets the cell at each position to be alive. For example, to match the initial configuration in the upper left of Figure 8.1, we would pass in the list

```
[(1, 3), (2, 3), (3, 3), (3, 2), (2, 1)]
```

Notice that by using a generic tuple as the index variable, we can conveniently assign the two values in each tuple to r and c.

Surveying the neighborhood

To algorithmically carry out the rules in the Game of Life, we will need a function that returns the number of live neighbors of any particular cell.

> **Reflection 8.6** *Consider a cell at position* (r, c). *What are the coordinates of the eight neighbors of this cell?*

The coordinates of the eight neighbors are visualized in the following grid with coordinates (r, c) in the center.

$(r-1, c-1)$	$(r-1, c)$	$(r-1, c+1)$
$(r, c-1)$	(r, c)	$(r, c+1)$
$(r+1, c-1)$	$(r+1, c)$	$(r+1, c+1)$

We could use an eight-part `if/elif/else` statement to check whether each neighbor is alive. However, an easier approach is illustrated below.

```
def neighborhood(grid, row, column):
    """Finds the number of live neighbors of the cell at (row, column).

    Parameters:
        grid:   a two-dimensional grid of cells
        row:    the row index of a cell
        column: the column index of a cell

    Return value: the number of live neighbors of (row, column)
    """

    offsets = [(-1, -1),(-1, 0), (-1, 1), (0, -1),
               (0, 1), (1, -1), (1, 0), (1, 1)]
    rows = len(grid)
    columns = len(grid[0])
    count = 0
    for offset in offsets:
        r = row + offset[0]
        c = column + offset[1]
        if (r >= 0 and r < rows) and (c >= 0 and c < columns):
            if grid[r][c] == ALIVE:
                count = count + 1
    return count
```

The list `offsets` contains tuples with the offsets of all eight neighbors. We iterate over these offsets, adding each one to the given row and column to get the coordinates of each neighbor. Then, if the neighbor is on the grid and is alive, we increment a counter.

Performing one pass

Once we can count the number of live neighbors, we can simulate one generation of Life by iterating over all of the cells and updating them appropriately. But before we look at how to iterate over every cell in the grid, let's consider how we can iterate over just the first row.

| **Reflection 8.7** *What is the name of the first row of* grid?

The first row of grid is named grid[0]. Since grid[0] is a list, we already know how to iterate over it, either by value or by index.

| **Reflection 8.8** *Should we iterate over the indices of* grid[0] *or over its values? Does it matter?*

As we saw above, we need to access a cell's neighbors by specifying their relative row and column indices. So we are going to need to know the indices of the row and column of each cell as we iterate over them. This means that we need to iterate over the indices of grid[0], which are also its column indices, rather than over its values. Therefore, the for loop looks like this, assuming the number of columns is assigned to the variable name columns:

```
for c in range(columns):
    # update grid[0][c] here
```

Notice that, in this loop, the row number stays the same while the column number (c) increases. We can generalize this idea to iterate over any row with index r by simply replacing the row index with r:

```
for c in range(columns):
    # update grid[r][c] here
```

Now, to iterate over the entire grid, we need to repeat the loop above with values of r ranging from 0 to rows - 1, where rows is assigned the number of rows in the grid. We can do this by nesting the loop above in the body of another for loop that iterates over the rows:

```
for r in range(rows):
    for c in range(columns):
        # update grid[r][c] here
```

| **Reflection 8.9** *In what order will the cells of the grid be visited in this nested loop? In other words, what sequence of* r,c *values does the nested loop generate?*

The value of r is initially set to 0. While r is 0, the inner for loop iterates over values of c from 0 to columns - 1. So the first cells that will be visited are

grid[0][0], grid[0][1], grid[0][2], ..., grid[0][9]

Once the inner for loop finishes, we go back up to the top of the outer for loop. The value of r is incremented to 1, and the inner for loop executes again. So the next cells that will be visited are

grid[1][0], grid[1][1], grid[1][2], ..., grid[1][9]

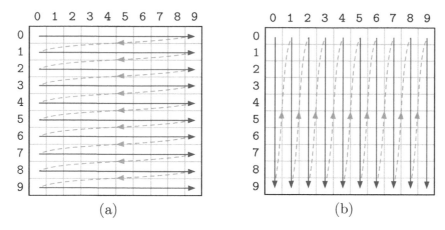

Figure 8.3 Passing over a grid (a) row by row and (b) column by column.

This process repeats with r assigned to 2, 3, ..., 9, until finally the cells in the last row are visited:

grid[9][0], grid[9][1], grid[9][2], ..., grid[9][9]

Therefore, the cells in the grid are being visited row by row, as illustrated in Figure 8.3(a).

Reflection 8.10 *How would we change the nested loop so that the cells in the grid are visited column by column instead?*

To visit the cells column by column, we can simply swap the positions of the loops:

```
for c in range(columns):
    for r in range(rows):
        # update grid[r][c] here
```

In this new nested loop, for each value of c, the inner for loop iterates all of the values of r, visiting all of the cells in that column. So the first cells that will be visited are

grid[0][0], grid[1][0], grid[2][0], ..., grid[9][0]

Then the value of c is incremented to 1 in the outer for loop, and the inner for loop executes again. So the next cells that will be visited are

grid[0][1], grid[1][1], grid[2][1], ..., grid[9][1]

This process repeats with consecutive values of c, until finally the cells in the last column are visited:

grid[0][9], grid[1][9], grid[2][9], ..., grid[9][9]

This is illustrated in Figure 8.3(b).

In some two-dimensional simulations, the order in which cells are visited is important but, in the Game of Life, it isn't. We will choose to update the cells row by row.

Tangent 8.2: NumPy arrays in two dimensions

Two-dimensional (and higher) data can also be represented with a NumPy `array` object. (See Tangent 7.1.) As in one dimension, we can initialize an `array` by either passing in a list, or passing a size to one of several functions that fill the array with particular values. Here are some examples.

```
>>> import numpy
>>> temps = numpy.array([[3.3, -29.4, 8.3], [-26.1, 12.2, -13.9]])
>>> temps
array([[  3.3, -29.4,   8.3],
       [-26.1,  12.2, -13.9]])
>>> grid = numpy.zeros((2, 4))    # zero-filled with 2 rows, 4 cols
>>> grid
array([[ 0.,  0.,  0.,  0.],
       [ 0.,  0.,  0.,  0.]])
```

In the second case, the tuple (2, 4) specifies the "shape" of the array: two rows and four columns. We can modify individual `array` elements with indexing by simply specifying the comma-separated row and column in a single pair of square brackets:

```
>>> grid[1, 3] = 1
>>> grid
array([[ 0.,  0.,  0.,  0.],
       [ 0.,  0.,  0.,  1.]])
```

As we saw in Tangent 7.1, the real power of NumPy arrays lies in the ability to change every element in a single statement. For example, the following statement adds one to every element of the `temps` array.

```
>>> temps = temps + 1
>>> temps
array([[  4.3, -28.4,   9.3],
       [-25.1,  13.2, -12.9]])
```

For more details, see `http://numpy.org` .

Updating the grid

Now we are ready to implement one generation of the Game of Life by iterating over all of the cells and applying the rules to each one. For each cell in position (r,c), we first need to find the number of neighbors by calling the `neighborhood` function that we wrote above. Then we set the cell's new value, if it changes, according to the four rules, as follows.

```
for r in range(rows):
    for c in range(columns):
        neighbors = neighborhood(grid, r, c)
        if grid[r][c] == ALIVE and neighbors < 2:      # rule 1
            grid[r][c] = DEAD
        elif grid[r][c] == ALIVE and neighbors > 3:    # rule 3
            grid[r][c] = DEAD
        elif grid[r][c] == DEAD and neighbors == 3:    # rule 4
            grid[r][c] = ALIVE
```

| **Reflection 8.11** *Why is rule 2 not represented in the code above?*

Since rule 2 does not change the state of any cells, there is no reason to check for it.

Reflection 8.12 *There is one problem with the algorithm we have developed to update cells. What is it? (Think about the values referenced by the* **neighborhood** *function when it is applied to neighboring cells. Are the values from the previous generation or the current one?)*

To see the subtle problem, suppose that we change cell (r,c) from alive to dead. Then, when the live neighbors of the next cell in position $(r+1,c)$ are being counted, the cell at (r,c) will not be counted. But it should have been because it was alive in the previous generation. To fix this problem, we cannot modify the grid directly while we are updating it. Instead, we need to make a copy of the grid before each generation. When we count live neighbors, we will look at the original grid, but make modifications in the copy. Then, after we have looked at all of the cells, we can update the grid by assigning the updated copy to the main grid. These changes are shown below in red.

```
newGrid = copy.deepcopy(grid)
for r in range(rows):
    for c in range(columns):
        neighbors = neighborhood(grid, r, c)
        if grid[r][c] == ALIVE and neighbors < 2:     # rule 1
            newGrid[r][c] = DEAD
        elif grid[r][c] == ALIVE and neighbors > 3:   # rule 3
            newGrid[r][c] = DEAD
        elif grid[r][c] == DEAD and neighbors == 3:   # rule 4
            newGrid[r][c] = ALIVE
grid = newGrid
```

The **deepcopy** function from the **copy** module creates a completely independent copy of the grid.

Now that we can simulate one generation, we can simply repeat this process to simulate many generations. The complete function is shown below. The grid is initialized with our **makeGrid** and **initialize** functions, then the nested loop that updates the grid is further nested in a loop that iterates for the number of generations.

```
def life(rows, columns, generations, initialCells):
    """Simulates the Game of Life for the given number of
       generations, starting with the given live cells.

    Parameters:
        rows:          the number of rows in the grid
        columns:       the number of columns in the grid
        generations:   the number of generations to simulate
        initialCells:  a list of (row, column) tuples indicating
                       the positions of the initially alive cells

    Return value: the final configuration of cells in a grid
    """
```

```
    grid = makeGrid(rows, columns)
    initialize(grid, initialCells)

    for g in range(generations):
        newGrid = copy.deepcopy(grid)
        for r in range(rows):
            for c in range(columns):
                neighbors = neighborhood(grid, r, c)
                if grid[r][c] == ALIVE and neighbors < 2:      # rule 1
                    newGrid[r][c] = DEAD
                elif grid[r][c] == ALIVE and neighbors > 3:    # rule 3
                    newGrid[r][c] = DEAD
                elif grid[r][c] == DEAD and neighbors == 3:    # rule 4
                    newGrid[r][c] = ALIVE
        grid = newGrid

    return grid
```

On the book website, you can find an enhanced version of this function that uses turtle graphics to display the evolution of the system with a variety of initial configurations. Two projects at the end of this chapter use similar algorithms to simulate two very different scenarios: the evolution of segregated urban neighborhoods and ferromagnetic materials.

Exercises

8.2.1* Download the enhanced Game of Life program from the book website and run it with each of the following lists of coordinates set to be alive in the initial configuration. Use at least a 50×50 grid. Describe what happens in each case.

(a) `[(1, 3), (2, 3), (3, 3), (3, 2), (2, 1)]`

(b) `[(9, 10), (10, 10), (11, 10)]`

(c) `[(18, 5), (18, 6), (18, 7), (19, 5), (19, 7), (20, 5),`
`(20, 7), (21, 6), (22, 3), (22, 5), (22, 6), (22, 7),`
`(23, 4), (23, 6), (23, 8), (24, 6), (24, 9), (25, 5),`
`(25, 7), (26, 5), (26, 7)]`

(d) `[(10, c + 1), (10, c + 4), (11, c), (12, c), (12, c + 4),`
`(13, c), (13, c + 1), (13, c + 2), (13, c + 3)]`
with `c = columns - 5`

(e) `[(r + 1, c + 2), (r + 2, c + 4), (r + 3, c + 1),`
`(r + 3, c + 2), (r + 3, c + 5), (r + 3, c + 6),`
`(r + 3, c + 7)]`
with `r = rows // 2` and `c = columns // 2`

8.2.2. Modify the **neighborhood** function so that it treats the grid as if all four sides "wrap around." For example, in the first 7×7 grid to the right, the neighbors of (4,6) include (3,0), (4,0), and (5,0). In the rightmost grid, the neighbors of the corner cell (6,6) include (0,0), (0,5), (0,6), (5,0), and (6,0).

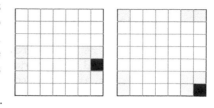

8.2.3* Write a function that prints the contents of a parameter named **grid**, which is a list of lists. The contents of each row should be printed on one line with spaces in between. Each row should be printed on a separate line.

8.2.4. Write a function that takes an integer n as a parameter, and returns an $n \times n$ multiplication table as a list of lists. The value in row r and column c should be the product of r and c.

8.2.5* Write a function that takes an integer n as a parameter, and returns an $n \times n$ grid (list of lists) in which all cells on the main diagonal contain a 1 and the rest of the cells contain a 0. For example, if $n = 5$, your function should return the grid

```
[[1, 0, 0, 0, 0],
 [0, 1, 0, 0, 0],
 [0, 0, 1, 0, 0],
 [0, 0, 0, 1, 0],
 [0, 0, 0, 0, 1]]
```

8.2.6. Write a function that takes an integer n as a parameter, and returns an $n \times n$ grid (list of lists) in which all cells on *and below* the main diagonal contain a 1 and the rest of the cells contain a 0. For example, if $n = 5$, your function should return

```
[[1, 0, 0, 0, 0],
 [1, 1, 0, 0, 0],
 [1, 1, 1, 0, 0],
 [1, 1, 1, 1, 0],
 [1, 1, 1, 1, 1]]
```

8.2.7. Write a function that takes as a parameter a two-dimensional grid (list of lists) of numbers, and prints (a) the sum of each row, (b) the sum of each column, and (c) the sum of all the entries.

8.2.8* Write a function that takes as parameters a two-dimensional grid (list of lists) and a value to search for, and returns the (row, column) where the value first appears, if it appears anywhere in the grid, and $(-1, -1)$ otherwise.

8.2.9. Write a function that returns a two-dimensional grid (list of lists) representation of an 8×8 checkerboard in which the squares in both directions alternate between the values **'B'** and **'R'**.

8.2.10. A magic square is a grid of numbers for which the sum of all the columns and all the rows is the same. For example, in the magic square to the right, all rows and columns add up to 15. The following algorithm generates magic squares with odd-length sides, using the consecutive numbers $1, 2, 3, \ldots$

5	7	3
1	6	8
9	2	4

(a)   Put 1 in a randomly chosen cell in your square.

(b)   Look in the cell diagonally to the lower right of the previous cell, wrapping around if you go off the right or bottom edge.

    i. If this cell is unoccupied, put the next number there.

    ii. Otherwise, put the next number directly above the previous number (again wrapping to the bottom if you are on the top row).

(c)   Continue step (b) until all the positions are filled.

Write a function that takes an odd integer n as a parameter and returns an $n \times n$ magic square.

8.2.11.   A two-dimensional grid can also be stored as a dictionary in which the keys are tuples representing grid positions. For example, the small grid

```
[ [0, 1],
  [1, 1] ]
```

would be stored as the following dictionary:

```
{ (0, 0): 0,
  (0, 1): 1,
  (1, 0): 1,
  (1, 1): 1 }
```

Rewrite the Game of Life program on the book website so that it stores the grid in this way instead. The following four functions will need to change: `emptyGrid`, `initialize`, `neighborhood`, and `life`.

8.3   DIGITAL IMAGES

Digital photographs and other images are also "flat" two-dimensional objects that can be manipulated with the same techniques that we discussed in previous sections. A digital image is a two-dimensional grid (sometimes called a **bitmap**) in which each cell, called a *pixel* (short for "picture element"), contains a value representing its color.

Colors

In a grayscale image, colors are limited to shades of gray. These shades are more commonly referred to as levels of *brightness* or *luminance*, and in theory are represented by values between 0 and 1, 0 being black and 1 being white. As we briefly explained in Tangent 2.1, each pixel in a color image can be represented by a (red, green, blue), or *RGB*, tuple. Each component, or *channel*, of the tuple represents the brightness of the respective color. The value (0,0,0) is black and (1, 1, 1) is white. Values between these can represent any color in the spectrum. For example, $(0, 0.5, 0)$ is a medium green and $(1, 0.5, 0)$ is orange. In practice, each channel is represented by eight bits (one byte) or, equivalently, a value between 0 and 255. So black is represented by $(0, 0, 0)$ or

```
00000000 00000000 00000000,
```

Tangent 8.3: Additive vs. subtractive color models

Colors in digital images are usually represented in one of two ways. In the text, we focus on the RGB color model because it is the most common, especially for digital cameras and displays. RGB is called an *additive* color model because the default "no color" $(0,0,0)$ is black, and adding all of the colors, represented by $(255,255,255)$, is white. In contrast, printers use a *subtractive* color model that "subtracts" from the brightness of a white paper background by applying color. The most common subtractive color model is CMY (short for "Cyan Magenta Yellow"). In CMY, the "no color" $(0,0,0)$ is white, and $(255,255,255)$ combines cyan, magenta, and yellow at full intensities to produce black. In practice, a black channel is added to the CMY color model because black is so common in print, and combining cyan, magenta, and yellow to produce black tends to be both imperfect and expensive in practice. The resulting four-color model is called CMYK where K stands for "Key" or "blacK," depending on who you ask.

Some color models also allow an *alpha channel* to specify transparency. An alpha value of 0 means the color is completely transparent (i.e., invisible), 255 means it is opaque, and values in between correspond to degrees of translucency. Translucency effects are implemented by combining the translucent color in the foreground with the background color to an extent specified by the alpha channel. In other words,

$$\text{displayed color} = \alpha \cdot \text{foreground color} + (1 - \alpha) \cdot \text{background color}.$$

white is $(255,255,255)$ or

    11111111 11111111 11111111,

and orange is $(255,127,0)$ or

    11111111 01111111 00000000.

RGB is generally used for images produced by digital cameras and viewed on a screen. Another encoding, called *CMYK* is used for print. See Tangent 8.3 for details.

Reflection 8.13 *If we use eight bits to represent the intensity of each channel, can we still represent any color in the spectrum? If not, how many different colors can we represent?*

Using eight bits per channel, we cannot represent the continuous range of values between 0 and 1 that would be necessary to represent any color in the spectrum. In effect, we are only able to represent 254 values between 0 and 1: $1/255$, $2/255$, ..., $254/255$. This is another example of how some objects represented in a computer are limited versions of those existing in nature. Looking at it another way, by using 8 bits per channel, or 24 bits total, we can represent $2^{24} = 16,777,216$ distinct colors. The good news is that, while this does not include all the colors in the spectrum, it is greater than the number of colors distinguishable by the human eye.

Reflection 8.14 *Assuming eight bits are used for each channel, what RGB tuple represents pure blue? What tuple represents purple? What color is $(0,128,128)$?*

Bright blue is $(0,0,255)$ and any tuple with equal parts red and blue, for example

$(128, 0, 128)$ is a shade of purple. The tuple $(0, 128, 128)$, equal parts medium green and medium blue, is teal.

The digital images produced by digital cameras can be quite large. For example, some high end cameras can produce an image that is 6720 pixels wide and 4480 pixels high, and therefore contains a total of $6720 \times 4480 = 30{,}105{,}600$ pixels. At one byte per pixel, a grayscale image of this size would require about 28.7 MB of storage. A 6720 by 4480 color image requires $6720 \times 4480 \times 3 = 90{,}316{,}800$ bytes, or about 86.1 MB, of storage. In practice, color image files are *compressed* to take up much less space. (See Tangent 8.4.)

Image filters

To illustrate some basic image processing techniques, let's consider how we can produce a grayscale version of a color image. An operation such as this is known as an *image filter* algorithm. Photo-editing software typically includes several different image filters for enhancing digital photographs.

To change an image to grayscale, we need to convert every color pixel (an RGB tuple) to a gray pixel with similar brightness. A white pixel (RGB color $(255, 255, 255)$) is the brightest, so we would map this to a grayscale brightness of 255 while a black pixel (RGB color $(0, 0, 0)$) is the least bright, so we would map this to a grayscale brightness of 0.

‖ Reflection 8.15 *How can we compute the brightness of a color pixel in general?*

Consider the RGB color $(250, 50, 200)$. The red and blue channels of this color contribute a lot of brightness to the color while the green channel does not. To estimate the overall brightness, we can simply average the three values. In this case, $(250 + 50 + 200)/3 \approx 167$. In RGB, any tuple with equal parts red, green, and blue will be a shade of gray. Therefore, we can encode this shade of gray in RGB with the tuple $(167, 167, 167)$. A function to perform this conversion is straightforward:

```python
def color2gray(color):
    """Convert a color to a shade of gray.

    Parameter:
        color: a tuple representing an RGB color

    Return value: a tuple representing an equivalent gray
    """

    brightness = (color[0] + color[1] + color[2]) // 3
    return (brightness, brightness, brightness)
```

The parameter `color` is a three-element tuple of integers between 0 and 255. The function computes the average of the three channels and returns a tuple representing a shade of gray with that brightness.

Tangent 8.4: Image storage and compression

Digital images are stored in a variety of file formats. Three of the most common are BMP, GIF, and JPEG. The technical details of each format can be quite complex, so we will just highlight the key differences, advantages, and disadvantages.

All image files begin with a short header that contains information about the dimensions of the image, the number of bits that are used to encode the color of each pixel (usually 24), and other format-specific characteristics. The header is followed by information about the actual pixels. In a BMP (short for "BitMaP") file, the pixels are simply stored row by row, starting from the bottom left corner (upside down). Assuming 24-bit color, the size of a BMP file is roughly three bytes per pixel. For example, the 300×200 pixel color image in Figure 8.4 requires about $300 \cdot 200 \cdot 3 = 180,000$ bytes ≈ 180 KB in BMP format.

GIF (short for "Graphics Interchange Format") files try to cut down on the amount of memory required to store an image in two ways. First, rather than store the actual color of each pixel individually, GIF files encode each pixel with an 8-bit index into a table of $2^8 = 256$ image-dependent colors. Second, GIF files compress the resulting pixel data using the Lempel-Ziv-Welch (LZW) data compression algorithm (see Tangent 6.2). This compression algorithm is *lossless*, meaning that the original data can be completely recovered from the compressed data, resulting in no loss of image quality. So the size of a GIF file is typically less than one byte per pixel. The color image in Figure 8.4 requires about 46 KB in GIF format.

JPEG (short for "Joint Photographic Experts Group," the name of the group that created it) files use a *lossy compression* algorithm to further cut down on their size. "Lossy" means that information is lost from the original image. However, the lossy compression algorithm used in JPEG files selectively removes characteristics that are less noticeable to the naked eye, resulting in very little noticeable difference in quality. The color image in Figure 8.4 requires about 36 KB in JPEG format.

To apply this transformation to an entire image, we need to iterate over the positions of all of the pixels. Since an image is a two-dimensional object, we can process its pixels row by row as we did in the previous section:

```
for r in range(rows):
    for c in range(columns):
        # process the pixel at position (r, c)
```

To be consistent with the language typically used in image processing, we will use different names for the variables, however. Rather than referring to the size of an image in terms of rows and columns, we will use height and width. And we will use x and y (with $(0,0)$ in the top left corner) to denote the horizontal and vertical positions of a pixel instead of the row and column numbers. So the following is equivalent to the nested loop above:

```
for y in range(height):
    for x in range(width):
        # process the pixel at coordinates (x, y)
```

The standard Python module for displaying images (and creating graphical interface elements like windows and buttons) is called **tkinter** (This name is short for "Tk interface." Tk is a widely used graphical programming package that predates Python; **tkinter** provides an "interface" to Tk.) Because simple image manipulation in **tkinter** is slightly more complicated than we would like, we will interact with **tkinter** indirectly through a simple class named **Image**. The **Image** class is available in the module **image.py** on the book website. Download this file and copy it into the same folder as your programs for this section.

The following program illustrates how to use the **Image** class to read a digital image file, iterate over its pixels, and produce a new image that is a grayscale version of the original. Each of the methods and functions below is described in Appendix A.8.

```python
import image

def grayscale(photo):
    """Convert a color image to grayscale.

    Parameter:
        photo: an Image object

    Return value: a new grayscale Image object
    """

    width = photo.width()
    height = photo.height()
    newPhoto = image.Image(width, height, title = 'Grayscale image')
    for y in range(height):
        for x in range(width):
            color = photo.get(x, y)
            newPhoto.set(x, y, color2gray(color))
    return newPhoto

def main():
    penguin = image.Image(file = 'penguin.gif', title = 'Penguin')
    penguinGray = grayscale(penguin)
    penguin.show()
    penguinGray.show()
    image.mainloop()

main()
```

Let's look at the **grayscale** function first. The lone parameter named **photo** is the **Image** object that we want to turn to grayscale. The first two statements in the function call the **width** and **height** methods of **photo** to get the image's dimensions. Then the third statement creates a new, empty **Image** object with the same dimensions. This will be our grayscale image. Next, we iterate over all of the pixels in **photo**. Inside the nested loop, we call the **get** method to get the color of the pixel at each position (x,y) in **photo**. The color is returned as a three-element

Figure 8.4 The original image of a penguin and the grayscale version.

tuple of integers between 0 and 255. Next, we **set** the pixel at the same position in **newPhoto** to the color returned by the **color2gray** function that we wrote above. Once the nested loop has finished, we return the grayscale photo.

In the **main** function, we create an **Image** object named **penguin** from a GIF file named **penguin.gif** that can be found on the book website. (GIF is a common image file format; see Tangent 8.4 for more about image files.) We then call the **grayscale** function with **penguin**, and assign the resulting grayscale image to **penguinGray**. Finally, we display both images in their own windows by calling the **show** method of each one. The **mainloop** function at the end causes the program to wait until all of the windows have been closed before it quits the program. The results are shown in Figure 8.4.

This simple filter is just the beginning; we leave several other fun image filters as exercises. If you would like to save any of your creations, you can do so with the **save** method. For example, to save the final **penguinGray** image above, call

```
penguinGray.save('gray penguin.gif')
```

Transforming images

There are, of course, many other ways we might want to transform an image. For example, we commonly need to rotate landscape images 90 degrees clockwise. This is illustrated in Figure 8.5. From the figure, we notice that the pixel in the corner at $(0,0)$ in the original image needs to be in position $(h-1,0)$ after rotation. Similarly, the pixel in the corner at $(w-1,0)$ needs to be in position $(h-1,w-1)$ after rotation. The transformations for all four corners are shown below.

Before		After
$(0,0)$	$\Rightarrow$	$(h-1,0)$
$(w-1,0)$	$\Rightarrow$	$(h-1,w-1)$
$(w-1,h-1)$	$\Rightarrow$	$(0,w-1)$
$(0,h-1)$	$\Rightarrow$	$(0,0)$

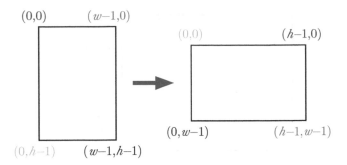

Figure 8.5 Rotating an image 90 degrees clockwise. After rotation, the corners with the same colors should line up. The width and height of the image are represented by w and h, respectively.

Reflection 8.16 *Do you see a pattern in these transformations? Use this pattern to infer a general rule about where each pixel at coordinates (x,y) should be in the rotated image.*

The first thing to notice is that the width and height of the image are swapped, so the x and y coordinates in the original image need to be swapped in the rotated image. However, just swapping the coordinates leads to the mirror image of what we want. Notice that the y coordinate of each rotated corner is the same as the x coordinate of the corresponding original corner. But the x coordinate of each rotated corner is $h-1$ minus the y coordinate of the corresponding corner in the original image. So we want to draw each pixel at (x,y) in the original image at position $(h-1-y, x)$ in the rotated image. The following function does this. Notice that it is identical to the **grayscale** function, with the exceptions of parts of two statements in red.

```
def rotate90(photo):
    """Rotate an image 90 degrees clockwise.

    Parameter:
        photo: an Image object

    Return value: a new rotated Image object
    """

    width = photo.width()
    height = photo.height()
    newPhoto = image.Image(height, width, title = 'Rotated image')
    for y in range(height):
        for x in range(width):
            color = photo.get(x, y)
            newPhoto.set(height - y - 1, x, color)
    return newPhoto
```

Let's look at one more example, and then we will leave several more as exercises.

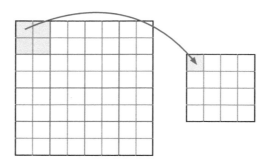

Figure 8.6 Reducing an image by one quarter.

Suppose we want to reduce the size of an image to one quarter of its original size. In other words, we want to reduce both the width and height by half. In the process, we are obviously going to lose three quarters of the pixels. Which ones do we throw away? One option would be to group the pixels of the original image into 2×2 blocks and choose the color of one of these four pixels for the corresponding pixel in the reduced image, as illustrated in Figure 8.6. This is accomplished by the following function. Again, it is very similar to the previous functions.

```python
def reduce(photo):
    """Reduce an image to one quarter of its size.

    Parameter:
        photo: an Image object

    Return value: a new reduced Image object
    """

    width = photo.width()
    height = photo.height()
    newPhoto = image.Image(width // 2, height // 2, title = 'Reduced')
    for y in range(0, height, 2):
        for x in range(0, width, 2):
            color = photo.get(x, y)
            newPhoto.set(x // 2, y // 2, color)
    return newPhoto
```

Although this works, a better option would be to average the three channels of the four pixels in the block, and use this average color in the reduced image. This is left as an exercise.

Once we have filters like this, we can combine them in any way we like. For example, we can create an image of a small, upside down, grayscale penguin:

```
def main():
    penguin = image.Image(file = 'penguin.gif', title = 'Penguin')
    penguinSmall = reduce(penguin)
    penguinGray = grayscale(penguinSmall)
    penguinRotate1 = rotate90(penguinGray)
    penguinRotate2 = rotate90(penguinRotate1)
    penguinRotate2.show()
    image.mainloop()
```

By implementing some of the additional filters in the exercises below, you can devise many more fun creations.

Exercises

8.3.1. Real grayscale filters take into account how different colors are perceived by the human eye. Human sight is most sensitive to green and least sensitive to blue. Therefore, for a grayscale filter to look more realistic, the intensity of the green channel should contribute the most to the grayscale luminance and the intensity of the blue channel should contribute the least. The following formula is a common way to weigh these intensities:

$$\text{luminance} = 0.2126 \cdot \text{red} + 0.7152 \cdot \text{green} + 0.0722 \cdot \text{blue}$$

Modify the `color2gray` function in the text so that it uses this formula instead.

8.3.2* The colors in an image can be made "warmer" by increasing the yellow tone. In the RGB color model, this is accomplished by increasing the intensities of both the red and green channels. Write a function that returns an `Image` object that is warmer than the original by some factor between -1 and 1 that is passed as a parameter. If the factor is positive, the image should be made warmer; if the factor is negative, it should be made less warm.

8.3.3. The colors in an image can be made "cooler" by increasing the intensity of the blue channel. Write a function that returns an `Image` object that is cooler than the original by some factor between -1 and 1 that is passed as a parameter. If the factor is positive, the image should be made cooler; if the factor is negative, it should be made less cool.

8.3.4. The overall brightness in an image can be adjusted by increasing the intensity of all three channels. Write a function that returns an `Image` object that is brighter than the original by some factor between -1 and 1 that is passed as a parameter. If the factor is positive, the image should be made brighter; if the factor is negative, it should be made less bright.

8.3.5. A negative image is one in which the colors are the opposite of the original. In other words, the intensity of each channel is 255 minus the original intensity. Write a function that returns an `Image` object that is the negative of the original.

8.3.6* Write a function that returns an `Image` object that is a horizontally flipped version of the original. Put another way, the image should be reflected along an imaginary vertical line drawn down the center. See the example on the left of Figure 8.7.

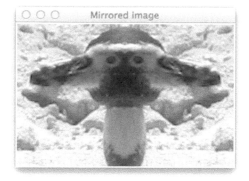

Figure 8.7 Horizontally flipped and mirrored versions of the original penguin image from Figure 8.4.

8.3.7. Write a function that returns an `Image` object with left half the same as the original but with right half that is a mirror image of the original. (Imagine placing a mirror along a vertical line down the center of an image, facing the left side.) See the example on the right of Figure 8.7.

8.3.8* In the text, we wrote a function that reduced the size of an image to one quarter of its original size by replacing each 2 × 2 block of pixels with the pixel in the top left corner of the block. Now write a function that reduces an image by the same amount by instead replacing each 2 × 2 block with a pixel that has the average color of the pixels in the block.

8.3.9. An image can be blurred by replacing each pixel with the average color of its eight neighbors. Write a function that returns a blurred version of the original.

8.3.10. An item can be further blurred by repeatedly applying the blur filter you wrote above. Write a function that returns a version of the original that has been blurred any number of times.

8.3.11. Write a function that returns an image that is a cropped version of the original. The portion of the original image to return will be specified by a rectangle, as illustrated below.

The function should take in four additional parameters that specify the (x,y) coordinates of the top left and bottom right corners (shown above) of the crop rectangle.

8.4   SUMMARY AND FURTHER DISCOVERY

As we saw in the previous chapter, a lot of data is naturally stored in two-dimensional tables. So it makes sense that we would also want to store this data in a two-dimensional structure in a program. We discussed two ways to do this. First, we can store the data in a *list of lists* in which each inner list contains one row of data. Second, in Exercises 8.1.6 and 8.2.11, we looked at how two-dimensional data can be stored in a *dictionary*. The latter representation has the advantage that it can be searched efficiently, if the data has an appropriate key.

Aside from storing data, two-dimensional structures have many other applications. Two-dimensional *cellular automata* are widely used to model a great variety of phenomena. The *Game of Life* is probably the most famous, but cellular automata can also be used to model actual cellular systems, pigmentation patterns on sea shells, climate change, racial segregation (Project 8.1), ferromagnetism (Project 8.2), and to generate pseudorandom numbers. Digital images are also stored as two-dimensional structures, and *image filters* are simply algorithms that manipulate these structures.

Notes for further discovery

The chapter epigraph is from *Flatland: A Romance of Many Dimensions*, written by Edwin A. Abbott in 1884 [1].

If you are interested in learning more about cellular automata, or emergent systems in general, we recommend *Turtles, Termites, and Traffic Jams* by Mitchell Resnick [53] and *Emergence* by Steven Johnson [28] as good places to start. Also, we recommend *Agent-Based Models* by Nigel Gilbert [19] if you would like to learn more about using cellular automata in the social sciences. *Biological Computation* by Ehud Lamm and Ron Unger [34] is about using biologically-inspired computational techniques, such as cellular automata, genetic algorithms and artificial neural networks, to solve hard problems.

*8.5   PROJECTS

This section is available on the book website.

CHAPTER 9

Self-similarity and Recursion

Clouds are not spheres, mountains are not cones, coastlines are not circles, and bark is not smooth, nor does lightning travel in a straight line.

Benoît Mandelbrot
The Fractal Geometry of Nature (1983)

Though this be madness, yet there is method in't.

William Shakespeare
Hamlet (Act II, Scene II)

H AVE you ever noticed, while laying on your back under a tree, that each branch of the tree resembles the tree itself? If you could take any branch, from the smallest to the largest, and place it upright in the ground, it could probably be mistaken for a smaller tree. This phenomenon, called ***self-similarity***, is widespread in nature. There are also computational problems that, in a more abstract way, exhibit self-similarity. In this chapter, we will discuss a computational technique, called *recursion*, that we can use to elegantly solve problems that exhibit this property. As the second quotation above suggests, recursion may seem foreign at first, but it really is quite natural and just takes some practice to master.

9.1 FRACTALS

Nature is not geometric, at least not in a traditional sense. Instead, natural structures are complex and not easily described. But many natural phenomena do share a common characteristic: if you zoom in on any part, that part resembles the whole. For example, consider the images in Figure 9.1. In the bottom two images, we can

Figure 9.1 Fractal patterns in nature. Clockwise from top left: a nautilus shell [69], the coastline of Norway [70], a closeup of a leaf [71], branches of a tree, a rock outcropping, and lightning [72]. The insets in the bottom two images show how smaller parts resemble the whole.

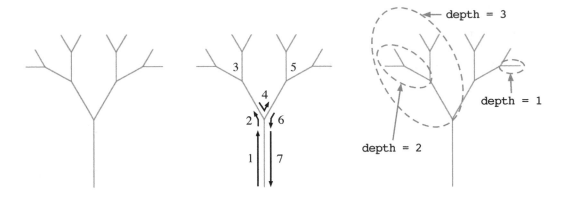

Figure 9.2 A tree produced by tree(george, 100, 4). The center figure illustrates what is drawn by each numbered step of the function. The figure on the right illustrates the self-similarity in the tree.

see that if we zoom in on parts of the rock face and tree, these parts resemble the whole. (In nature, the resemblance is not always exact, of course.) These kinds of structures are called ***fractals***, a term coined by mathematician Benojt Mandelbrot, who developed the first theory of fractal geometry.

Trees

An algorithm for creating a fractal shape is *recursive*, meaning that it invokes itself on smaller and smaller scales. Let's consider the example of the simple tree shown on the left side of Figure 9.2. Notice that each of the two main branches of the tree is a smaller tree with the same structure as the whole. As illustrated in the center of Figure 9.2, to create this fractal tree, we first draw a trunk and then, for each branch, we draw two smaller trees at 30-degree angles using the same algorithm. Each of these smaller trees is composed of a trunk and two yet smaller trees, again drawn with the same tree-drawing algorithm. This process could theoretically continue forever, producing a tree with infinite complexity. In reality, however, the process eventually stops by invoking a non-recursive ***base case***. The base case in Figure 9.2 is a "tree" that consists of only a single line segment.

This recursive structure is shown more precisely on the right side of Figure 9.2. The *depth* of the tree is a measure of its distance from the base case. The overall tree in Figure 9.2 has depth 4 and each of its two main branches is a tree with depth 3. Each of the two depth 3 trees is composed of two depth 2 trees. Finally, each of the four depth 2 trees is composed of two depth 1 trees, each of which is only a line segment.

The following tree function uses turtle graphics to draw this tree.

```
import turtle

def tree(tortoise, length, depth):
    """Recursively draw a tree.

    Parameters:
        tortoise: a Turtle object
        length:   the length of the trunk
        depth:    the desired depth of recursion

    Return value: None
    """

    if depth <= 1:                      # the base case
        tortoise.forward(length)
        tortoise.backward(length)
    else:                               # the recursive case
1       tortoise.forward(length)
2       tortoise.left(30)
3       tree(tortoise, length * (2 / 3), depth - 1)
4       tortoise.right(60)
5       tree(tortoise, length * (2 / 3), depth - 1)
6       tortoise.left(30)
7       tortoise.backward(length)

def main():
    george = turtle.Turtle()
    george.left(90)             # point north

    tree(george, 100, 4)        # draw the tree

main()
```

The initial statements in the main function initialize the turtle and orient it to the north. Then the tree function is called with tree(george, 100, 4). On lines 1–2, the turtle moves forward length units to draw the trunk, and then turns 30 degrees to the left. This is illustrated in the center of Figure 9.2; the numbers correspond to the line numbers in the function. Next, to draw the smaller tree, we call the tree function *recursively* on line 3 with two-thirds of the length, and a value of depth that is one less than what was passed in. The depth parameter controls how long we continue to draw smaller trees recursively. After the call to tree returns, the turtle turns 60 degrees to the right on line 4 to orient itself to draw the right tree. On line 5, we recursively call the tree function again with arguments that are identical to those on line 3. When that call returns, the turtle retraces its steps in lines 6–7 to return to the origin.

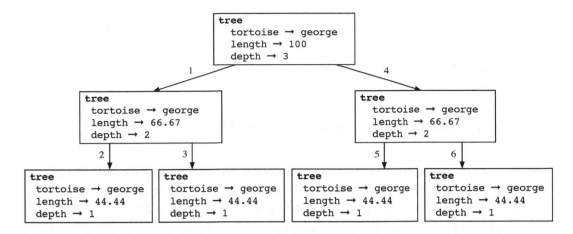

Figure 9.3 An illustration of the recursive calls in `tree(george, 100, 4)`.

The case when `depth` is at most 1 is called the *base case* because it does not make a recursive call to the function; this is where the recursion stops.

> **Reflection 9.1** *Try running the tree-growing function with a variety of parameters. Also, try changing the turn angles and the amount `length` is shortened. Do you understand the results you observe?*

Figure 9.3 illustrates the recursive function calls that are made by the `tree` function when `length` is 100 and `depth` is 3. The top box represents a call to the `tree` function with parameters `tortoise = george`, `length = 100`, and `depth = 3`. This function calls two instances of `tree` with `length = 100 * (2 / 3) = 66.67` and `depth = 2`. Then, each of these instances of `tree` calls two instances of `tree` with `length = 66.67 * (2 / 3) = 44.44` and `depth = 1`. When `depth` is 1, `tree` simply draws a line segment and returns.

> **Reflection 9.2** *The numbers on the lines in Figure 9.3 represent the order in which the recursive calls are made. Can you see why that is?*

> **Reflection 9.3** *What would happen if we removed the base case from the algorithm by deleting the first four statements, so that the line numbered 1 was always the first statement executed?*

Without the base case, the function would continue to make recursive calls forever! Therefore, the base case is extremely important to the correctness of the algorithm.

Snowflakes

One of the most famous fractal shapes is the *Koch curve*, named after Swedish mathematician Helge von Koch. A Koch curve begins with a single line segment with length ℓ. Then, as shown in Figure 9.4(b), that line segment is divided into three equal parts, each with length $\ell/3$. The middle part of this divided segment is replaced by two sides of an equilateral triangle (with side length $\ell/3$). Next, each of the four line segments of length $\ell/3$ is divided in the same way, with the middle

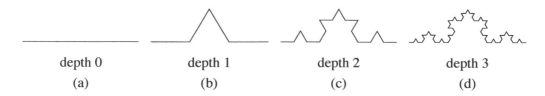

depth 0   depth 1   depth 2   depth 3

(a)   (b)   (c)   (d)

Figure 9.4 The Koch curve at depths 0, 1, 2, and 3.

segment again replaced by two sides of an equilateral triangle with side length $\ell/9$, etc., as shown in Figures 9.4(c)–(d). As with the tree above, this process could theoretically go on forever, producing an infinitely intricate pattern.

Notice that, like the tree, this shape exhibits self-similarity; each "side" of the Koch curve is itself a Koch curve with smaller depth. The Koch curve in Figure 9.4(b) with depth 1 consists of four smaller Koch curves with depth 0 and length $\ell/3$. Likewise, the Koch curve with depth 2 in Figure 9.4(c) consists of four smaller Koch curves with depth 1, and the Koch curve with depth 3 in Figure 9.4(d) consists of four smaller Koch curves with depth 2.

We can use our understanding of this self-similarity to write an algorithm to produce a Koch curve with any desired overall length and depth:

Algorithm KOCH CURVE

Input: overall *length* and the *depth*

1	if *depth* is 0:
2	draw a line with length equal to *length*
3	else:
4	draw a Koch curve with length = *length* / 3 and depth = *depth* – 1
5	turn left 60 degrees
6	draw another Koch curve with length = *length* / 3 and depth = *depth* – 1
7	turn right 120 degrees
8	draw another Koch curve with length = *length* / 3 and depth = *depth* – 1
9	turn left 60 degrees
10	draw another Koch curve with length = *length* / 3 and depth = *depth* – 1

The base case occurs when the depth is zero, in which case we simply draw a line. Otherwise, the algorithm runs through the steps we followed above. But notice that steps 4, 6, 8, and 10 are actually recursively calling upon the algorithm itself to draw smaller Koch curves. So the algorithm is more correctly written as follows.

Algorithm KOCH CURVE

Input: overall *length* and the *depth*

1	if *depth* is 0:
2	draw a line with length equal to *length*
3	else:
4	KOCH CURVE (*length* / 3, *depth* − 1)
5	turn left 60 degrees
6	KOCH CURVE (*length* / 3, *depth* − 1)
7	turn right 120 degrees
8	KOCH CURVE (*length* / 3, *depth* − 1)
9	turn left 60 degrees
10	KOCH CURVE (*length* / 3, *depth* − 1)

Reflection 9.4 *Follow the algorithm above to draw (on paper) a Koch curve with depth 1. Then follow the algorithm again to draw one with depth 2.*

This algorithm can be directly translated into Python. The only additional thing we need is a turtle to do the drawing.

```python
def koch(tortoise, length, depth):
    """Recursively draw a Koch curve.

    Parameters:
        tortoise: a Turtle object
        length:   the length of a line segment
        depth:    the desired depth of recursion

    Return value: None
    """

    if depth == 0:                              # base case
        tortoise.forward(length)
    else:                                       # recursive case
        koch(tortoise, length / 3, depth - 1)
        tortoise.left(60)
        koch(tortoise, length / 3, depth - 1)
        tortoise.right(120)
        koch(tortoise, length / 3, depth - 1)
        tortoise.left(60)
        koch(tortoise, length / 3, depth - 1)
```

Reflection 9.5 *Write a* main *function that creates a* Turtle *object and calls this function. Experiment by calling* koch *with different values of* length *and* depth.

We can attach three Koch curves at 120-degree angles to produce an intricate snowflake shape like that in Figure 9.5.

Figure 9.5 A three-sided Koch snowflake.

Reflection 9.6 *Look carefully at Figure 9.5. Can you see where the three individual Koch curves are connected?*

The following function draws this Koch snowflake.

```
def kochSnowFlake(tortoise, length, depth):
    """Recursively draw a Koch snowflake.

    Parameters:
        tortoise: a Turtle object
        length:   the length of a line segment
        depth:    the desired depth of recursion

    Return value: None
    """

    for side in range(3):
        koch(tortoise, length, depth)
        tortoise.right(120)
```

Reflection 9.7 *Insert this function into the previous program and call it from* main. *Try making different snowflakes by increasing the number of sides (and decreasing the right turn angle).*

Imagine a Koch snowflake made from *infinitely* recursive Koch curves. Paradoxically, while the area inside any Koch snowflake is clearly finite (because it is bounded), the length of its border is infinite! In fact, the distance between any two points on its border is infinite! To see this, notice that, at every stage in its construction, each line segment is replaced with four line segments that are one-third the length of the original. Therefore, the total length of that "side" increases by one-third. Since this happens infinitely often, the perimeter of the snowflake continues to grow forever.

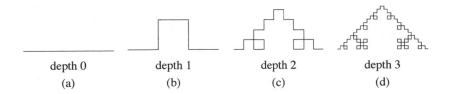

Figure 9.6 Depths 0, 1, 2, and 3 of a quadratic Koch curve.

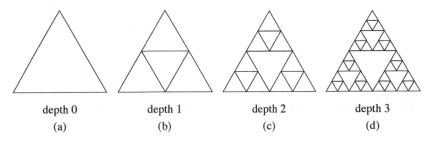

Figure 9.7 Depths 0, 1, 2, and 3 of a Sierpinski triangle.

Exercises

9.1.1* Modify the recursive tree-growing function so that it branches at random angles between 10 and 60 degrees (instead of 30 degrees) and it shrinks the trunk/branch length by a random fraction between 0.5 and 0.75. Do your new trees now look more "natural"?

9.1.2. The *quadratic Koch curve* is similar to the Koch curve, but it replaces the middle segment of each side with three sides of a square instead, as illustrated in Figure 9.6. Write a recursive function

```
quadkoch(tortoise, length, depth)
```

that draws the quadratic Koch curve with the given segment length and depth.

9.1.3. The following activities are recursive in the sense that each step can be considered a smaller version of the original activity. Describe how this is the case and how the "input" gets smaller each time. What is the base case of each operation below?

(a) evaluating an arithmetic expression like $7 + (15 - 3)/4$

(b) the chain rule in calculus (if you have taken calculus)

(c) one hole of golf

(d) driving directions to some destination

9.1.4* Generalize the Koch snowflake function with an additional parameter so that it can be used to draw a snowflake with any number of sides.

9.1.5. The Sierpinski triangle, depicted in Figure 9.7, is another famous fractal. The fractal at depth 0 is simply an equilateral triangle. The triangle at depth 1 is composed of three smaller triangles, as shown in Figure 9.7(b). (The larger outer triangle and the inner "upside down" triangle are indirect effects of the

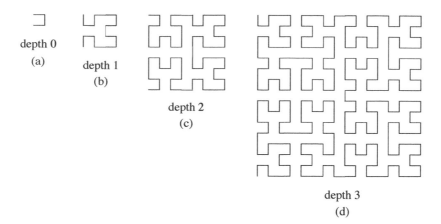

Figure 9.8 Hilbert space-filling curves with depths 0, 1, 2, and 3.

positions of these three triangles.) At depth 2, each of these three triangles is replaced by three smaller triangles. And so on. Write a recursive function

    sierpinski(tortoise, p1, p2, p3, depth)

that draws a Sierpinski triangle with the given depth. The triangle's three corners should be at coordinates p1, p2, and p3 (all tuples). It will be helpful to also write two smaller functions that you can call from sierpinski: one to draw a simple triangle, given the coordinates of its three corners, and one to compute the midpoint of a line segment.

9.1.6.   The Hilbert space-filling curve, shown in Figure 9.8, is a fractal path that visits all of the cells in a square grid in such a way that close cells are visited close together in time. For example, the figure to the right shows how a depth 2 Hilbert curve visits the cells in an 8 × 8 grid.

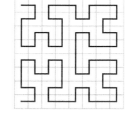

The following high-level algorithm draws a Hilbert curve.

Algorithm HILBERT CURVE

Input: *depth* and *mode*

1	if *depth* > 0:
2	turn 90 degrees to the right [left]
3	HILBERT CURVE (*depth* – 1, opposite *mode*)
4	draw a line segment
5	turn 90 degrees to the left [right]
6	HILBERT CURVE (*depth* – 1, same *mode*)
7	draw a line segment
8	HILBERT CURVE (*depth* – 1, same *mode*)
9	turn 90 degrees to the left [right]
10	draw a line segment
11	HILBERT CURVE (*depth* – 1, opposite *mode*)
12	turn 90 degrees to the right [left]

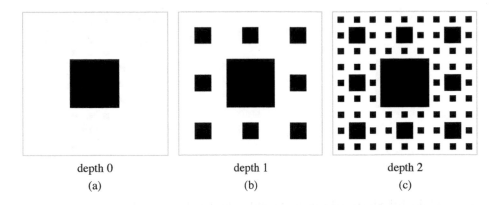

depth 0

(a)

depth 1

(b)

depth 2

(c)

Figure 9.9 Sierpinski carpets with depths 0, 1, and 2. (The gray bounding box shows the extent of the drawing area; it is not actually part of the fractal.)

In the base case, when the depth is 0, the algorithm draws nothing. In the recursive case, the algorithm can be in one of two different modes. In the first mode, lines 2 and 12 turn right, and lines 5 and 9 turn left. In the other mode, these directions are reversed (indicated in square brackets). Lines 3 and 11 make recursive calls that switch the mode. The algorithm assumes the turtle is initially pointing north. Each of the line segments is the same length (say 10).

Write a recursive function

```
hilbert(tortoise, mode, depth)
```

that draws a Hilbert space-filling curve with the given depth. The Boolean parameter mode indicates which mode the algorithm should draw in. (Think about how you can accommodate both drawing modes by changing the angle of the turns.)

9.1.7. A fractal pattern called the Sierpinski carpet is shown in Figure 9.9. At depth 0, it is simply a filled square one-third the width of the overall square space containing the fractal. At depth 1, this center square is surrounded by eight one-third size Sierpinski carpets with depth 0. At depth 2, the center square is surrounded by eight one-third size Sierpinski carpets with depth 1. Write a function

```
carpet(tortoise, upperLeft, width, depth)
```

that draws a Sierpinski carpet with the given depth. The parameter upperLeft refers to the coordinates of the upper left corner of the fractal and width refers to the overall width of the fractal.

9.1.8. Modify your Sierpinski carpet function from the last exercise so that it displays the color pattern shown in Figure 9.10.

9.2 RECURSION AND ITERATION

We typically only solve problems recursively when they obviously exhibit self-similarity or seem "naturally recursive," as with fractals. But recursion is not some obscure problem-solving technique. Although recursive algorithms may seem quite

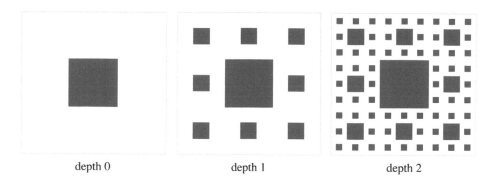

depth 0   depth 1   depth 2

Figure 9.10   Colorful Sierpinski carpets with depths 0, 1, and 2.

different from iterative algorithms, recursion and iteration are actually just two sides of the same coin. Every iterative algorithm can be written recursively, and vice versa. This realization may help take some of the mystery out of the technique.

Consider the problem of summing the numbers in a list. Of course, this is easily achieved iteratively with a `for` loop:

```python
def sumList(data):
    """Compute the sum of the values in a list.

    Parameter:
        data: a list of numbers

    Return value: the sum of the values in the list
    """

    total = 0
    for value in data:
        total = total + value
    return total
```

Let's think about how we could achieve the same thing recursively. To solve a problem recursively, we need to think about how we could solve it if we had a solution to a smaller *subproblem*. A subproblem is the same as the original problem, but with only part of the original input.

In the case of summing the numbers in a list named `data`, a subproblem would be summing the numbers in a *slice* of `data`. Consider the following example:

$$\text{data} \longrightarrow [1, \underbrace{7, 3, 6}_{\text{data[1:]}}]$$

If we had the sum of the numbers in `data[1:]`, i.e., `sumList(data[1:])`, then we could compute the value of `sumList(data)` by simply adding this sum to `data[0]`. In other words, `sumList(data)` is equal to `data[0]` plus the solution to the subproblem `sumList(data[1:])`. In terms of the example above, if

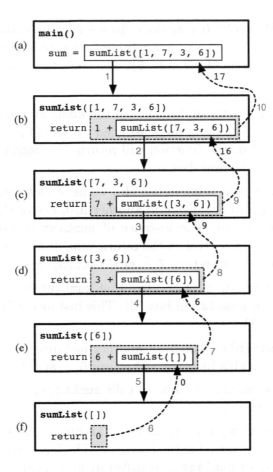

Figure 9.11 A representation of the function calls in the recursive sumList function. The red numbers indicate the order in which the events occur. The black numbers next to the dashed arrows are return values.

we knew that sumList([7, 3, 6]) returned 16, then we could easily find that sumList([1, 7, 3, 6]) is 1 + 16 = 17.

∎ Reflection 9.8 *Will this work if* data *is empty?*

Since there is no data[0] or data[1:] when data is empty, the method above will not work. But we can easily check for this case and return 0; this is the base case of the function. Putting these two parts together, we have the following recursive version of the function:

```python
def sumList(data):
    """ (docstring omitted) """

    if len(data) == 0:              # base case
        return 0
    return data[0] + sumList(data[1:])  # recursive case
```

But does this actually work? It sure does. To see why, let's look at Figure 9.11. At the top of the diagram, in box (a), is a representation of a main function that calls sumList with the argument [1, 7, 3, 6]. The steps that follow are marked in red in the figure.

1. Calling sumList creates an instance of the sumList function, represented in box (b), with the parameter data assigned the list [1, 7, 3, 6]. Since data is not an empty list, the function will return 1 + sumList([7, 3, 6]), the value enclosed in the gray box.

2. To evaluate the return value in box (b), we must call sumList again with the argument [7, 3, 6], resulting in another instance of the sumList function, represented in box (c). The instance of sumList in box (b) must wait to return its value until it receives the return value from box (c). The instance of sumList in box (c) will return 7 + sumList([3, 6]).

3. Evaluating this return value requires that sumList be called again, resulting in the instance of sumList in box (d). This instance will return the result of 3 + sumList([6]).

4. Calling sumList([6]) creates yet another instance of the sumList function, shown in box (e). This instance will return 6 + sumList([]).

5. The instance of sumList in box (e) calls sumList([]), creating the instance of sumList in box (f).

6. The value of the data parameter in box (f) is an empty list, so the if condition in sumList is True, invoking the base case. The base case immediately returns 0 to the instance of sumList that called it, in box (e).

7. Once the instance of sumList in box (e) receives 0 from sumList([]), it returns 6 + 0 = 6 to the instance of sumList in box (d).

8. Since the instance of sumList in box (d) now has a value for sumList([6]), it can return 3 + 6 = 9 to the instance of sumList in box (c).

9. Now that the instance of sumList in box (c) has a value for sumList([3, 6]), it returns 7 + 9 = 16 to the instance of sumList in box (b).

10. Finally, the instance of sumList in box (b) can return 1 + 16 = 17 to main.

Notice that the sequence of function calls, moving down the figure from (a) to (f), only ended because we eventually reached the *base case* in step 6, which caused the function to return without making another recursive call. This step initiated a process of moving back up through the previous function calls, allowing each one in turn to return their value to the instance of the function that called it.

Every recursive function must have a non-recursive base case, and each recursive call must get one step closer to the base case. This may sound familiar; it is very similar to the way we must think about while loops. Each iteration of a while loop must move one step closer to the loop condition becoming false.

Solving a problem recursively

The following five questions generalize the process we followed to design the recursive `sumList` function. We will illustrate each question by summarizing how we answered it in the design of the `sumList`.

1. *What does a subproblem look like?*

   A subproblem is to compute the sum of a slice of the list.

2. *Suppose you could ask an all-knowing oracle for the solution to any subproblem (but not for the problem itself). Which subproblem solution would be the most useful for solving the original problem?*

   The most useful subproblem solution would be the solution for the slice of the list that contains all but one element of the original, e.g., `sumList(data[1:])`.

3. *How do you find the solution to the original problem using this subproblem solution? Implement this as the recursive step of your recursive function.*

   The solution to `sumList(data)` is `data[0] + sumList(data[1:])`. Therefore, the recursive step in the function should be

   ```
   return data[0] + sumList(data[1:])
   ```

4. *What are the simplest subproblems that you can solve non-recursively, and what are their solutions? Implement your answer as the base case of the recursive function.*

   The simplest subproblem would be to compute the sum of an empty list, which is 0, of course. So the base case should be

   ```
   if len(data) == 0:
       return 0
   ```

5. *For any possible parameter value, will the recursive calls eventually reach the base case?*

   Yes, since an empty list will obviously reach the base case and passing any other list as an argument will result in a sequence of recursive calls, each of which involves a list that is one element shorter than in the previous call.

Reflection 9.9 *How could we have answered question 2 differently? What is another subproblem that involves all but one element of the original list? Using this subproblem instead, answer the rest of the questions to write an alternative recursive* `sumList` *function.*

An alternative subproblem would be `sumList(data[:-1])` (all but the last element). In this version of the function, the base case is the same, but the recursive case would be

```
return sumList(data[:-1]) + data[-1]    # recursive case
```

Palindromes

Let's look at another example. A *palindrome* is any sequence of characters that reads the same forward and backward. For example, radar, star rats, and now I won are all palindromes. An iterative function that determines whether a string is a palindrome is shown below.

```
def palindrome(text):
    """Determine whether a string is a palindrome.

    Parameter: a string text

    Return value: a Boolean value indicating whether text is a palindrome
    """

    for index in range(len(text) // 2):
        if text[index] != text[-(index + 1)]:
            return False
    return True
```

Let's answer the five questions above to develop an equivalent recursive algorithm for this problem.

| **Reflection 9.10** *First, what does a subproblem look like?*

A subproblem would be to determine whether a slice of the string (i.e., a substring) is a palindrome.

| **Reflection 9.11** *Second, if you could know whether any slice is a palindrome, which would be the most helpful?*

It is often helpful to look at an example. Consider the following:

$$\text{text} \longrightarrow \text{'n} \underbrace{\text{o w I w o}}_{\texttt{text[1:-1]}} \text{n'}$$

If we begin by looking at the first and last characters and determine that they are *not* the same, then we know that the string is not a palindrome. But if they *are* the same, then the question of whether the string is a palindrome is decided by whether the slice that omits the first and last characters, i.e., `text[1:-1]`, is a palindrome. So it would be helpful to know the result of `palindrome(text[1:-1])`.

| **Reflection 9.12** *Third, how could we use this information to determine whether the whole string is a palindrome?*

If the first and last characters are the same and `text[1:-1]` is a palindrome, then `text` is a palindrome. Otherwise, `text` is not a palindrome. In other words, our desired return value is the value of the following Boolean expression.

```
    return (text[0] == text[-1]) and palindrome(text[1:-1])
```

If the first part is true, then the answer depends on whether the slice is a palindrome (`palindrome(text[1:-1])`). Otherwise, if the first part is false, then the entire

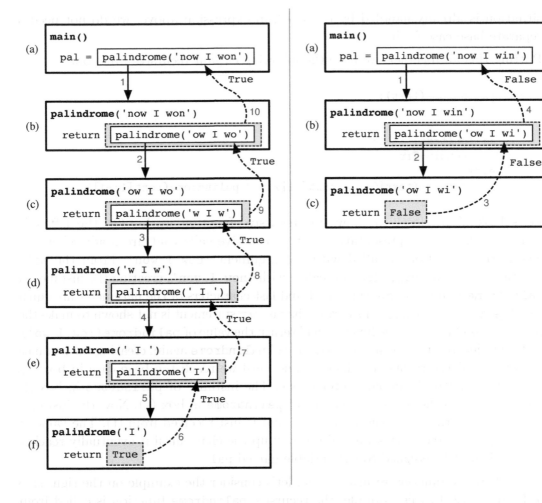

Figure 9.12 A representation of the function calls in the recursive `palindrome` function. The red numbers indicate the order in which the events happen. On the left is an instance in which the function reaches the base case and returns `True`. On the right is an instance in which the function returns `False`.

and expression is false. Furthermore, due to the short circuit evaluation of the `and` operator, the recursive call to `palindrome` will be skipped.

Reflection 9.13 *What are the simplest subproblems that we can solve non-recursively, and what are their solutions? Implement your answer as the base case.*

The simplest string is, of course, the empty string, which we can consider a palindrome. But strings containing a single character are also palindromes, since they read the same forward and backward. So we know that any string with length at most one is a palindrome. But we also need to think about strings that are obviously *not* palindromes. Our discussion above already touched on this; when the first and last characters are different, we know that the string cannot be a palindrome. Since this situation is already handled by the Boolean expression above, we do not need a separate base case for it.

Putting this all together, we have the following elegant recursive function:

```
def palindrome(text):
    """ (docstring omitted) """

    if len(text) <= 1:     # base case
        return True
    else:
        return (text[0] == text[-1]) and palindrome(text[1:-1])
```

Let's look more closely at how this recursive function works. On the left side of Figure 9.12 is a representation of the recursive calls that are made when the `palindrome` function is called with the argument `'now I won'`. From the `main` function in box (a), `palindrome` is called with `'now I won'`, creating the instance of `palindrome` in box (b). Since the first and last characters of the parameter are equal (the (`text[0] == text[-1]`) part of the `return` statement is not shown to make the pictures less cluttered), the function will return the value of `palindrome('ow I wo')`. But, in order to get this value, it needs to call `palindrome` again, creating the instance in box (c). These recursive calls continue until we reach the base case in box (f), where the length of the parameter is one. The instance of `palindrome` in box (f) returns `True` to the previous instance of `palindrome` in box (e). Now the instance in box (e) returns to (d) the value `True` that it just received from (f). The value of `True` is propagated in this way all the way up the chain until it eventually reaches `main`, where it is assigned to the variable named `pal`.

To see how the function returns `False`, let's consider the example on the right side of Figure 9.12. In this example, the recursive `palindrome` function is called from `main` in box (a) with the non-palindromic argument `'now I win'`, which creates the instance of `palindrome` in box (b). As before, since the first and last characters of the parameter are equal, the function will return the value of `palindrome('ow I wi')`. Calling `palindrome` with this parameter creates the instance in box (c). But now, since (`text[0] == text[-1]`) is `False`, the instance of `palindrome` in box (c) returns `False`, and this value is propagated up to the `main` function.

Guessing passwords

One technique that hackers use to compromise computer systems is to rapidly try all possible passwords up to some given length.

Reflection 9.14 *How many possible passwords are there with length n, if there are c possible characters to choose from?*

The number of different passwords with length n is

$$\underbrace{c \cdot c \cdot c \cdot \cdots \cdot c}_{n \text{ times}} = c^n.$$

For example, there are

$$26^8 = 208{,}827{,}064{,}576 \approx 208 \text{ billion}$$

different eight-character passwords that use only lowercase letters. But there are

$$67^{12} = 8{,}182{,}718{,}904{,}632{,}857{,}144{,}561 \approx 8 \text{ sextillion}$$

different twelve-character passwords that draw from the lower and uppercase letters, digits, and the five special characters \$, &, #, ?, and !, which is why websites make you use long passwords with all of these characters! When you use a long enough password and enough different characters, the "guess and check" method is useless.

Let's think about how we could generate a list of possible passwords by first considering the simpler problem of generating all binary strings (or "bit strings") of a given length. This is the same problem, but using only two characters: '0' and '1'. For example, the list of all binary strings with length three is ['000', '001', '010', '011', '100', '101', '110', '111'].

Thinking about this problem iteratively can be daunting. However, it becomes *easier* if we think about it recursively, in terms of smaller versions of itself. As shown below, a list of binary strings with a particular length can be created easily if we already have a list of binary strings that are one bit shorter. We simply make two copies of the list of shorter binary strings, and then precede all of the strings in the first copy with a 0 and all of the strings in the second copy with a 1.

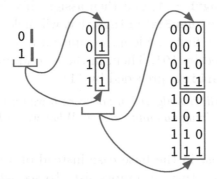

In the illustration above, the list of binary strings with length 2 is created from two copies of the list of binary strings with length 1. Then the list of binary strings with length 3 is created from two copies of the list of binary strings with length 2. In general, the list of all binary strings with a given length is the concatenation of

(a) the list of all binary strings that are one bit shorter and preceded by zero and

(b) the list of all binary strings that are one bit shorter and preceded by one.

▌ **Reflection 9.15** *What is the base case of this algorithm?*

The base case occurs when the length is 0, and there are no binary strings. However, the problem says that the return value should be a list of strings, so we will return a list containing an empty string in this case. The following function implements this recursive algorithm.

```python
def bitStrings(length):
    """Return a list of all binary strings with the given length.

    Parameter:
        length: the length of the binary strings

    Return value: the list of binary strings
    """

    if length == 0:                                 # base case
        return ['']

    shorterList = bitStrings(length - 1)  # recursively get shorter
                                          #   bit strings
    newBitStrings = []                              # create a list
    for shorterString in shorterList:               #   of bit strings
        newBitStrings.append('0' + shorterString) #   with prefix 0
    for shorterString in shorterList:               # append bit strings
        newBitStrings.append('1' + shorterString) #   with prefix 1

    return newBitStrings                            # return all bit strings
```

In the recursive step, we call `bitStrings(length - 1)` to get a list of all bit strings with length equal to `length - 1`, and then assign this list to `shorterList`. Next we create a new list named `newBitStrings` that will hold all of the bit strings with the desired `length`. In the first `for` loop, we append to this list all of the bit strings in `shorterList`, preceded by `'0'`. Then, in the second `for` loop, we append all of the bit strings in `shorterList`, preceded by `'1'`.

Reflection 9.16 *Why will this algorithm not work if we return an empty list in the base case instead of a list containing an empty string? What would be returned if we did return an empty list instead?*

If we return an empty list in the base case instead of a list containing an empty string, the function will return an empty list. To see why, consider what would happen if we called `bitStrings(1)`. Then `shorterList = bitStrings(0)` will be assigned an empty list. This would mean that there is nothing to iterate over in the two `for` loops, and nothing is appended to `newBitStrings`. Since `bitStrings(2)` calls `bitStrings(1)`, this means that `bitStrings(2)` will also return the empty list, and so on for any value of `length`!

Reflection 9.17 *The `bitStrings` function above contains two nearly identical `for` loops, one for the `'0'` prefix and one for the `'1'` prefix. How can we combine these two loops?*

We can combine the two loops by repeating a more generic version of the loop for each of the characters `'0'` and `'1'`:

```
def bitStrings(length):
    """ (docstring omitted) """

    if length == 0:
        return ['']

    shorterList = bitStrings(length - 1)

    newBitStrings = []
    for character in ['0', '1']:
        for shorterString in shorterList:
            newBitStrings.append(character + shorterString)

    return newBitStrings
```

We can use a very similar algorithm to generate a list of possible passwords. The only difference is that, instead of preceding each shorter string with 0 and 1, we need to precede each shorter string with every character in the set of allowable characters. The following function, with a string of allowable characters assigned to an additional parameter, is a simple generalization of our bitStrings function.

```
def passwords(length, characters):
    """Return a list of all possible passwords with the given length,
       using the given characters.

    Parameters:
        length:     the length of the passwords
        characters: a string containing the characters to use

    Return value: the list of passwords
    """

    if length == 0:
        return ['']

    shorterList = passwords(length - 1, characters)

    passwordList = []
    for character in characters:
        for shorterPassword in shorterList:
            passwordList.append(character + shorterPassword)

    return passwordList
```

Reflection 9.18 *How would we call the* passwords *function to generate a list of all bit strings with length 5? What about all passwords with length 4 containing the characters* 'abc123'*? What about all passwords with length 8 containing lowercase letters? (Do not actually try this last one!)*

Exercises

*Write a **recursive** function for each of the following problems. Test your functions with both common and boundary case arguments, and document your test cases.*

9.2.1* Write a recursive function

   sumIt(n)

   that returns the sum of the integers from 1 to n.

9.2.2. Write a recursive function

   factorial(n)

   that returns the value of $n! = 1 \cdot 2 \cdot 3 \cdots n$.

9.2.3. Write a recursive function

   power(a, n)

   that returns the value of a^n without using the ** operator.

9.2.4. Euclid's greatest common divisor (GCD) algorithm uses the fact that the GCD of m and n is the same as the GCD of n and m mod n. Write a recursive function

   gcd(m, n)

   that implements Euclid's algorithm. In the base case, gcd(m, 0) is m.

9.2.5* Write a recursive function

   length(data)

   that returns the length of the list data without using the len function.

9.2.6* Write a recursive function

   minList(data)

   that returns the minimum of the items in the list of numbers named data. You may use the built-in min function for finding the minimum of (only) two numbers.

9.2.7* Write a recursive function

   reverse(text)

   that returns the reverse of the string named text.

9.2.8. Write a recursive function

   underscore(text)

   that returns a version of the string named text with all spaces replaced by underscore (_) characters.

9.2.9. Write a recursive function

   noSpaces(text)

   that returns a version of the string named text with all spaces removed.

9.2.10. Write a recursive function

   increment(data)

   that returns a new list containing all of the values in the list of numbers named data incremented by one.

9.2.11. Write a recursive function

      `int2string(n)`

that converts an integer value `n` to its string equivalent, *without* using the `str` function. For example, `int2string(1234)` should return the string `'1234'`.

9.2.12* Write a recursive function

      `countUpper(text)`

that returns the number of uppercase letters in the string `text`.

9.2.13. Write a recursive function

      `count(text, target)`

that returns the number of occurrences of the string `target` in the string `text`.

9.2.14. Write a recursive function

      `evenLength(data)`

that returns `True` if `data` contains an even number of items, and `False` otherwise. Do not use the `len` function.

9.2.15. Write a recursive function

      `search(data, target)`

that returns `True` if `target` is contained in the list `data`, and `False` otherwise.

9.2.16. Write a recursive function

      `equal(list1, list2)`

that returns a Boolean value indicating whether the two lists are equal without testing whether `list1 == list2`. Only compare the lengths of the lists and test whether individual list elements are equal.

9.2.17. Write a recursive function

      `powerSet(n)`

that returns a list of all subsets of the integers $1, 2, \ldots, n$. A subset is a list of zero or more unique items from a set. The set of all subsets of a set is also called the *power set*. For example, `subsets(n)` should return the list `[[], [1], [2], [2, 1], [3], [3, 1], [3, 2], [3, 2, 1]]`. (Hint: this is similar to the `bitStrings` function.)

9.2.18. Suppose you work for a state in which all vehicle license plates consist of a string of letters followed by a string of numbers, such as `'ABC 123'`. Write a recursive function

      `licensePlates(length, letters, numbers)`

that returns a list of strings representing all possible license plates of this form, with `length` letters and `length` numbers chosen from the given strings. For example, `licensePlates(2, 'XY', '12')` should return the following list of 16 possible license plates consisting of two letters drawn from `'XY'` followed by two digits drawn from `'12'`:

```
['XX 11', 'XX 21', 'XY 11', 'XY 21', 'XX 12', 'XX 22',
 'XY 12', 'XY 22', 'YX 11', 'YX 21', 'YY 11', 'YY 21',
 'YX 12', 'YX 22', 'YY 12', 'YY 22']
```

(Hint: this is similar to the `passwords` function.)

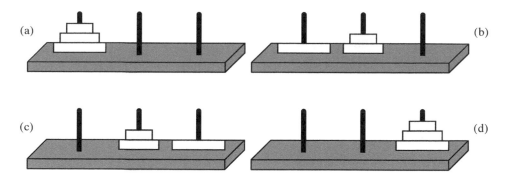

Figure 9.13 Illustration of the recursive algorithm for Tower of Hanoi with three disks.

9.3 THE MYTHICAL TOWER OF HANOI

The **Tower of Hanoi** is a game that was first marketed in 1883 by French mathematician Édouard Lucas. As illustrated in Figure 9.13(a), the game is played on a board with three pegs. One peg holds some number of disks with unique diameters, ordered smallest to largest. The objective of the game is to move this "tower" of disks from their original peg to another peg, one at a time, without ever placing a larger disk on top of a smaller one. The game was purported to have originated in an ancient legend. In part, the game's instruction sheet reads:

> According to an old Indian legend, the Brahmins have been following each other for a very long time on the steps of the altar in the Temple of Benares, carrying out the moving of the Sacred Tower of Brahma with sixty-four levels in fine gold, trimmed with diamonds from Golconde. When all is finished, the Tower and the Brahmins will fall, and that will be the end of the world![1]

This game is interesting because it is naturally solved using the following recursive insight. To move n disks from the first peg to the third peg, we must first be able to move the bottom (largest) disk on the first peg to the bottom position on the third peg. The only way to do this is to somehow move the top $n-1$ disks from the first peg to the second peg, to get them out of the way, as illustrated in Figure 9.13(b). But notice that moving $n-1$ disks is a subproblem of moving n disks because it is the same problem but with only part of the input. The source and destination pegs are different in the original problem and the subproblem, but this can be handled by making the source, destination, and intermediate pegs additional inputs to the problem. Because this step is a subproblem, we can perform it recursively! Once this is accomplished, we are free to move the largest disk from the first peg to the third peg, as in Figure 9.13(c). Finally, we can once again recursively move the $n-1$ disks from the second peg to the third peg, shown in Figure 9.13(d). In summary, we have the following recursive algorithm:

---

[1] http://www.cs.wm.edu/~pkstoc/toh.html

1. Recursively move the top $n - 1$ disks from the source peg to the intermediate peg, as in Figure 9.13(b).

2. Move one disk from the source peg to the destination peg, as in Figure 9.13(c).

3. Recursively move the $n - 1$ disks from the intermediate peg to the destination peg, as in Figure 9.13(d).

Reflection 9.19 *What is the base case in this recursive algorithm? In other words, what is the simplest subproblem that will be reached by these recursive calls?*

The simplest case would involve having no disks at all, in which case, we do nothing.

We cannot actually write a Python function to move the disks for us, but we can write a function that gives us instructions on how to do so. The following `hanoi` function does this, following exactly the algorithm described above.

```python
def move(source, destination):   # just print an instruction
    print('Move a disk from peg ' + str(source) + ' to peg '
                            + str(destination) + '.')

def hanoi(n, source, destination, intermediate):
    """Print instructions for solving the Tower of Hanoi puzzle.

    Parameters:
        n:            the number of disks
        source:       the source peg
        destination:  the destination peg
        intermediate: the other peg

    Return value: None
    """

    if n >= 1:
        hanoi(n - 1, source, intermediate, destination)
        move(source, destination)
        hanoi(n - 1, intermediate, destination, source)
```

The parameters `n`, `source`, `destination`, and `intermediate` represent the number of disks, the source peg, the destination peg, and the remaining peg that can be used as a temporary resting place for disks that we need to get out of the way. In our examples, the left peg was the source, the right peg was the destination, and the middle peg was the intermediate. Notice that the base case is implicit: if n is less than one, the function simply returns.

When we execute this function, we can name our pegs anything we want. For example, if we name our pegs A, B, and C, then

```python
hanoi(8, 'A', 'C', 'B')
```

will print instructions for moving eight disks from A to C, using B as the intermediate.

Reflection 9.20 *Execute the function with three disks. Does it work? How many steps are necessary? What about with four and five disks? Do you see a pattern?*

*Is the end of the world nigh?

The original game's instructions claimed that the world would end when the monks finished moving 64 disks. So how long does this take? To derive a general answer, let's start by looking at small numbers of disks. When there is one disk, only one move is necessary: move the disk from the source peg to the destination peg. When there are two disks, the algorithm moves the smaller disk to the intermediate peg, then the larger disk to the destination peg, and finally the smaller disk to the destination peg, for a total of three moves.

When n is three, we need to first move the top two disks to the intermediate peg which, we just deduced, requires three moves. Then we move the largest disk to the destination peg, for a total of four moves so far. Finally, we move the two disks from the intermediate peg to the destination peg, which requires another three moves, for a total of seven moves.

In general, notice that the number of moves required for n disks is the number of moves required for $n-1$ disks, plus one move for the bottom disk, plus the number of moves required for $n-1$ disks again. In other words, if the function $M(n)$ represents the number of moves required for n disks, then

$$M(n) = M(n-1) + 1 + M(n-1) = 2M(n-1) + 1.$$

Does this look familiar? This is a *difference equation*, just like those in Chapter 4. In this context, a function that is defined in terms of itself is also called a **recurrence relation**. The sequence produced by this recurrence relation is shown in the following table.

n	$M(n)$
1	1
2	3
3	7
4	15
5	31
⋮	⋮

Reflection 9.21 *Do you see the pattern in the table? What is the formula for $M(n)$ in terms of n?*

$M(n)$ is always one less than 2^n. In other words, the algorithm requires

$$M(n) = 2^n - 1$$

moves to solve the game when there are n disks. This expression is called a *closed form* for the recurrence relation because it is defined only in terms of n, not $M(n-1)$. According to this formula, moving 64 disks would require

$$2^{64} - 1 = 18{,}446{,}744{,}073{,}709{,}551{,}615$$

moves. The end of the world is apparently not coming any time soon!

Exercises

9.3.1.   Design a recursive algorithm for a version of the Tower of Hanoi puzzle in which you can only move disks between adjacent pegs, in either direction. In other words, you cannot move a disk directly from A to C or from C to A. Implement your algorithm as a recursive function in Python.

9.3.2.   How many moves does your algorithm from Exercise 9.3.1 make when there are n disks? (Think about $n = 1$, 2, and 3 disks first. Then derive a general formula.)

9.3.3*   In another variation of the Tower of Hanoi puzzle, there are four pegs, labeled A, B, C, and D, and two stacks of disks. A white stack of n disks starts on peg A and a black stack starts on peg C. The goal is to exchange the two stacks, i.e., move the white stack to peg C and the black stack to peg A, without ever placing a larger disk on top of a smaller one. This problem can be solved by using the classical Tower of Hanoi algorithm three times.

    (a)   Explain how with a pseudocode algorithm.

    (b)   Implement your algorithm in Python. You will first need to create slightly modified versions of the `move` and `hanoi` functions that incorporate the color of the disk(s) that are being moved. Then write a new function `solveTower4` that calls your modified `hanoi` function appropriately to solve this problem.

    (c)   How many moves does your algorithm make with n disks?

9.3.4.   The four-peg problem in Exercise 9.3.3 can be solved in fewer moves with the following algorithm:

1.	Use the classical Tower of Hanoi algorithm to move the top $n-1$ white disks from peg A to peg B, using peg D as the intermediate peg.
2.	Move the largest white disk from peg A to peg D.
3.	Use the classical algorithm to move all n black disks from peg C to peg A, using peg D as the intermediate.
4.	Move the largest white disk from peg D to peg C.
5.	Use the classical algorithm to move the top $n-1$ white disks from peg B to peg C, using peg D as the intermediate.

    (a)   When all n black disks are moved in step 3 of the algorithm, using peg D as the intermediate peg, the largest white disk is still on peg D. Why does this not violate the rules of the puzzle?

    (b)   Implement this algorithm in Python.

    (c)   How many moves does this algorithm make with n disks?

9.4   RECURSIVE LINEAR SEARCH

As we have already seen, linear search is a workhorse of an algorithm, used in a variety of settings. In this section, we will develop a recursive version of this algorithm and then show that it has the same time complexity as the iterative version. Later, in Section 10.1, we will develop a more efficient algorithm for searching in a sorted list.

> **Reflection 9.22** *What does a subproblem look like in the search problem? What would be the most useful subproblem to have an answer for?*

In the search problem, a subproblem is to search for the target item in a smaller list. Since we can only "look at" one item at a time, the most useful subproblem will be to search for the target item in a sublist that contains all but one item, say the first one. This way, we can break the original problem into two parts: (a) determine if the target is the first item and (b) determine if the target is in the rest of the list. Of course, if the first item is the one we are searching for, we can avoid the recursive call altogether. Otherwise, we return the index that is returned by the search of the rest of the list.

> **Reflection 9.23** *What is the base case for this problem?*

We have already discussed one base case: if the target item is the first item in the list, we simply return its index. Another base case would be when the list is empty. In this case, the item for which we are searching is not in the list, so we return −1. The following function (almost) implements the recursive algorithm we have described.

```
def linearSearch_Draft1(data, target):
    """Recursively find the first occurrence of target in data.

    Parameters:
        data:   a list object to search in
        target: an object to search for

    Return value: index of the first occurrence of target in data
    """

    if len(data) == 0:                              # base case 1: not found
        return -1
    if target == data[0]:                           # base case 2: found
        return ??
    return linearSearch_Draft1(data[1:], target)    # recursive case
```

However, as indicated by the red question marks above, we have a problem.

> **Reflection 9.24** *What is the problem indicated by the red question marks? Why can we not just return 0 in that case?*

When we find the target at the beginning of the list and are ready to return its index in the original list, we do not know what it was! We know that it is at index 0 in the current sublist being searched, but we have no way of knowing where this sublist starts in the original list. Therefore, we need to add a third parameter to the function that keeps track of the original index of the first item in the sublist `data`. In each recursive call, we add one to this argument since the index of the new front item in the list will be one more than that of the current front item.

```
def linearSearch_Draft2(data, target, first):
    """ (docstring omitted) """

    if len(data) == 0:                      # base case 1: not found
        return -1
    if target == data[0]:                   # base case 2: found
        return first
    return linearSearch_Draft2(data[1:], target, first + 1)  # recursive
```

Creating a new slice of the list in each recursive call, which is a relatively costly operation, can also now be eliminated. We can pass in the entire list instead, and use the value of `first` to identify the "first" item we are considering in the second base case.

```
def linearSearch(data, target, first):
    """ (docstring omitted) """

    if (first < 0) or (first >= len(data)):    # base case 1: not found
        return -1
    if target == data[first]:                  # base case 2: found
        return first
    return linearSearch(data, target, first + 1)  # recursive case
```

As shown above, this change also necessitates a change in our first base case because the length of the list is no longer decreasing to zero. Since the intent of the function is to search in the list between indices `first` and `len(data) - 1`, we will consider the list under consideration to be empty if the value of `first` is greater than the last index in the list. Just to be safe, we also make sure that `first` is at least zero.

Reflection 9.25 *Use the recursive* `linearSearch` *function to search for* `'keys'` *in the list* `['sock', 'keys', 'phone', 'remote']`. *What do you pass in for the third parameter?*

When calling the recursive `linearSearch` function, we need to initially pass 0 in as the third parameter since that is the index of the first item that we wish to search.

```
position = linearSearch(['sock', 'keys', 'phone', 'remote'], 'keys', 0)
```

*Efficiency of recursive linear search

Like the iterative linear search, this algorithm has linear time complexity. But we cannot derive this result in the same way we did for the iterative version. Instead, we need to use a recurrence relation, as we did to find the number of moves required in the Tower of Hanoi algorithm.

Let $T(n)$ represent the worst case number of comparisons required by a linear search when the length of the list is n. When we look at the algorithm above, we see that there are two comparisons that the algorithm must make before reaching a recursive function call. But since it only matters asymptotically that this number is a constant, we will simply represent the number of comparisons before the recursive call as a constant value c. Therefore, the number of comparisons necessary in the base case in which the list is empty $(n = 0)$ is $T(0) = c$. In recursive cases, there are additional comparisons to be made in the recursive call.

| **Reflection 9.26** *How many more comparisons are made in the recursive call to* `linearSearch`*?*

The size of the sublist yet to be considered in each recursive call is $n - 1$, one less than in the current instance of the function. Therefore, the number of comparisons in each recursive call must be the number of comparisons required by a linear search on a list with length $n - 1$, which is $T(n - 1)$. So the total number of comparisons is

$$T(n) = T(n - 1) + c.$$

But this is not very helpful in determining what the time complexity of the linear search is. To get this recurrence relation into a more useful form, we can think about the recurrence relation as saying that the value of $T(n)$ is equal to, or can be replaced by, the value of $T(n - 1) + c$, as illustrated below:

$$T(n - 1) + c$$

| **Reflection 9.27** *Now what can we replace $T(n - 1)$ with?*

$T(n - 1)$ is just $T(n)$ with $n - 1$ substituted for n. Therefore, using the definition of $T(n)$ above,
$$T(n - 1) = T(n - 1 - 1) + c = T(n - 2) + c.$$

So we can also substitute $T(n - 2) + c$ for $T(n - 1)$, as shown in the third row of Figure 9.14. Similarly, Figure 9.14 uses the equivalences

$$T(n - 2) = T(n - 2 - 1) + c = T(n - 3) + c$$

and

$$T(n - 3) = T(n - 3 - 1) + c = T(n - 4) + c$$

to continue these substitutions until we reach $T(0)$.

The right side of the figure illustrates the accumulation of c's (which are not substituted) as we proceed downward. Since c is the number of comparisons in each recursive call, these values on the right represent the total number of comparisons made so far. Notice that the number subtracted from n in the argument of T at

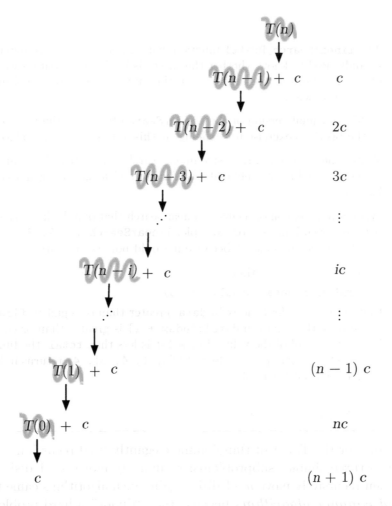

Figure 9.14 An illustration of how to derive a closed form for the recurrence relation $T(n) = T(n - 1) + c$.

each step is equal to the multiplier in front of the accumulated c's at that step. In other words, to the right of each $T(n - i)$, the accumulated value of c's is $i \cdot c$. When we finally reach $T(0)$, which is the same as $T(n - n)$, the total on the right must be nc. Finally, we showed above that $T(0) = c$, so the total number of comparisons is $(n+1)c$. This expression is called the *closed form* of the recurrence relation because it does not involve any values of $T(n)$. Since $(n + 1)c$ is $\mathcal{O}(n)$ asymptotically, recursive linear search is a linear-time algorithm, just like the iterative linear search. Intuitively, this should make sense because the two algorithms essentially do the same thing: they both look at every item in the list until the target is found.

Exercises

9.4.1* The `linearSearch_Draft1` function, without the `first` parameter, can work if we only need to know whether the target is in the list. Write a working version of this function that returns `True` if the target item is contained in the list and `False` otherwise.

9.4.2* Unlike our final version of the `linearSearch` function, the function you wrote in the previous exercise uses slicing. Is this still a linear-time algorithm?

9.4.3. Write a new version of recursive linear search that instead looks at the last item in the list, and recursively calls the function with the sublist not containing the last item.

9.4.4. Write a new version of recursive linear search that only looks at the items in the list with even indices. For example, `linearSearch([1, 2, 3, 4, 2], 2, 0)` should return the index 4 because it would not see the target, 2, at index 1.

9.4.5. Write a recursive function

      sumSearch(data, total, first)

   that returns the first index in `data`, greater than or equal to `first`, for which the sum of the values in `data[:index + 1]` is greater than or equal to `total`. If the sum of all of the values in the list is less than `total`, the function should return –1. For example, `sumSearch([2, 1, 4, 3], 4)` returns index 2 because $2 + 1 + 4 \geq 4$ but $2 + 1 < 4$.

9.5 DIVIDE AND CONQUER

The algorithm for the Tower of Hanoi game elegantly used recursion to divide the problem into three simpler subproblems: recursively move $n - 1$ disks, move one disk, and then recursively move $n - 1$ disks again. Such algorithms came to be called **divide and conquer algorithms** because they "divide" a hard problem into two or more subproblems, and then "conquer" each subproblem recursively. The divide and conquer technique has been found to yield similarly elegant, and often quite efficient, algorithms for a wide variety of problems.

It is actually useful to think of divide and conquer algorithms as comprising three steps instead of two:

1. *Divide* the problem into two or more subproblems.

2. *Conquer* each subproblem recursively.

3. *Combine* the solutions to the subproblems into a solution for the original problem.

In the Tower of Hanoi algorithm, the "combine" step was essentially non-existent. Once the subproblems had been "conquered," we were done. But other problems do require this step at the end.

In this section, we will design elegant divide and conquer algorithms that choose optimal buy and sell dates on the stock market and navigate a rover through a maze.

Buy low, sell high

Suppose that you have created a model to predict the future daily closing prices of a particular stock. With this list of prices, you would like to determine when to buy and sell the stock to maximize your profit. For example, when should you buy and sell if your model predicts the following prices for the next ten days?

Day	1	2	3	4	5	6	7	8	9	10
Price	3.90	3.60	3.65	3.71	3.78	4.95	3.21	4.50	3.18	3.53

It is tempting to look for the minimum price ($3.18) and then look for the maximum price after that day. But this clearly does not work with this example. Even choosing the second smallest price ($3.21) does not give the optimal answer. The most profitable choice is to buy on day 2 at $3.60 and sell on day 6 at $4.95, for a profit of $1.35 per share.

One way to find this answer is to look at all possible pairs of buy and sell dates, and pick the pair with the maximum profit. (You may actually have already done this in Exercise 7.5.7.) Since there are $n(n-1)/2$ such pairs, this yields an algorithm with time complexity $\mathcal{O}(n^2)$.

However, divide and conquer yields a more efficient algorithm. Notice that if we divide the list of prices in half, then the optimal pair of dates must either be in the left half, the right half, or straddle the two halves, with the buy date in the left half and sell date in the right half. This observation can be used to design the following divide and conquer algorithm:

1. *Divide* the problem into two subproblems: (a) finding the optimal buy and sell dates in the left half of the list and (b) finding the optimal buy and sell dates in the right half of the list.

2. *Conquer* the two subproblems by executing the algorithm recursively on these two smaller lists of prices.

3. *Combine* the solutions by choosing the most profitable buy and sell dates from among (a) the best dates in the left half, (b) the best dates in the right half, and (c) the best dates that straddle the two halves.

Reflection 9.28 *Is there an easy way to find the best buy and sell dates that straddle the two halves, with the buy date in the left half and sell date in the right half?*

At first glance, it might look like the "combine" step would require another recursive call to the algorithm. But finding the optimal buy and sell dates with this particular restriction is actually quite easy. The best buy date in the left half must be the one with the minimum price, and the best sell date in the right half must be the one with the maximum price. So finding these buy and sell dates simply amounts to finding the minimum price in the left half of the list and the maximum price in the right half, which we already know how to do.

Before we implement this algorithm, let's apply it to the example above:

[3.90, 3.60, 3.65, 3.71, 3.78, 4.95, 3.21, 4.50, 3.18, 3.53]

1. First, we divide the list into two halves: [3.90, 3.60, 3.65, 3.71, 3.78] and [4.95, 3.21, 4.50, 3.18, 3.53].

2. Next, we recursively find the maximum profits in the left half and the right half. In the left half, the maximum profit is attained by buying on day 2 for 3.60 and selling on day 5 at 3.78, for a profit of $3.78 - 3.60 = 0.18$. In the right half, we maximize our profit by buying on day 7 for 3.21 and selling on day 8 at 4.50, for a profit of $4.50 - 3.21 = 1.29$. In the actual algorithm, these results will be derived from a sequence of several more recursive calls, but we will pretend for now that this has already happened.

3. Finally, we find the maximum profit possible by holding the stock from the first half to the second half. Since the minimum price in the first half is 3.60 on day 2 and the maximum price in the second half is 4.95 on day 6, this profit is $4.95 - 3.60 = 1.35$. We return the maximum of 0.18, 1.29, and 1.35, which is 1.35. We achieved this by buying on day 2 and selling on day 6.

> **Reflection 9.29** *Since this is a recursive algorithm, we also need a base case. What is the simplest list in which to find the optimal buy and sell dates?*

The easiest case would be a list with less than two prices; then we never buy at all (or, equivalently, buy and sell on the same day), for zero profit. The following function implements the divide and conquer algorithm in a very straightforward way, but it just finds the optimal profit, not the actual buy and sell days. Finding these days requires just a little more work, which we leave for you as an exercise.

```
1 def profit(prices):
2     """Find the maximum profit from a list of daily stock prices.

3     Parameter:
4         prices: a list of daily stock prices

5     Return value: the maximum profit
6     """

7     if len(prices) <= 1:                      # base case
8         return 0

9     midIndex = len(prices) // 2               # divide in half
10    leftProfit = profit(prices[:midIndex])    # conquer 2 halves
11    rightProfit = profit(prices[midIndex:])

12    buy = min(prices[:midIndex])              # min price on left
13    sell = max(prices[midIndex:])             # max price on right
14    midProfit = sell - buy                    # max left -> right profit

15    return max(leftProfit, rightProfit, midProfit) # combine 3 cases
```

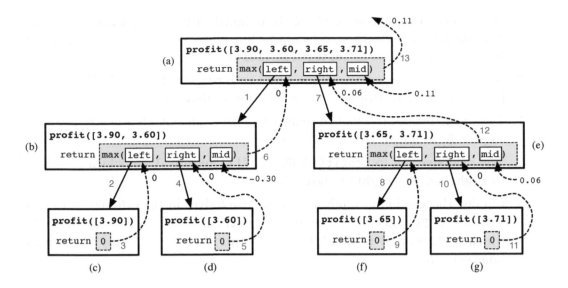

Figure 9.15 A representation of the function calls in the recursive `profit` function. The red numbers indicate the order in which the events happen.

> **Reflection 9.30** *Call this function with the list of prices that we used in the example above.*

That this algorithm actually works may seem like magic at this point. But rest assured that, like all recursive algorithms, there is a perfectly good reason why it works. The process is sketched out in Figure 9.15 for a small list containing just the first four prices in our example. Each bold rectangle represents an instance of a function call. The smaller gray boxes represent how the return value is computed in each one. In all but the base cases, the return value is the maximum of `leftProfit` (represented by `left`), `rightProfit` (represented by `right`), and `midProfit` (represented by `mid`).

At the top of Figure 9.15, the `profit` function is called with a list of four prices. The `profit` function then recursively calls itself with the first two prices and the last two prices (lines 10–11 in the function). The red numbers on the arrows in the figure show the order of the subsequent events.

1. The first recursive call (on line 10) to `profit([3.90, 3.60])` is represented by box (b). This call to `profit` results in two more recursive calls, labeled (c) and (d).

2–3. The call to `profit([3.90])` in box (c) is a base case which returns 0. This value is assigned to `leftProfit` (`left`) in box (b).

4–5. The second recursive call from box (b) to `profit([3.60])`, shown in box (d), is also a base case which returns 0. This value is assigned to `rightProfit` (`right`) in box (b).

6. Back in box (b), after the two recursive calls return, the profit from holding the

stock in the combine step, -0.30, is assigned in line 14 to `midProfit` (`mid`). The maximum of the three values, which in this case is 0, is returned back to box (a) and assigned to `leftProfit` (`left`).

7. Now the second recursive call (on line 11) to `profit([3.65, 3.71])` is made from box (a). This instance of the function is shown in box (e).

8-11. This recursive call results in a sequence of function calls that is very similar to steps 2–5, as illustrated in boxes (e)–(g).

12. The recursive call to `profit([3.65, 3.71])` returns 0.06, which is assigned to `rightProfit` (`right`) in box (a).

13. Finally, the maximum profit across the two halves in (a) is found to be 3.71 – 3.60 = 0.11. Then the maximum of `leftProfit`, which is 0, `rightProfit`, which is 0.06, and `midProfit`, which is 0.11, is returned by the original function call.

Navigating a maze

Suppose we want to navigate a robotic rover through an unknown, obstacle-filled terrain. For simplicity, we will assume that the landscape is laid out on a grid and the rover is only able to "see" and move to the four grid cells to its east, south, west, and north in each step, as long as they do not contain obstacles.

To navigate the rover to its destination on the grid (or determine that the destination cannot be reached), we can use a technique called ***depth-first search***. The depth-first search algorithm explores a grid by first exploring in one direction as far as it can from the source. Then it *backtracks* to follow paths that branch off in each of the other three directions.

Put another way, a depth-first search divides the problem of searching for a path to the destination into four subproblems: searching for a path starting from the cell to the east, from the cell to the south, from the cell to the west, and from the cell to the north. To solve each of these subproblems, the algorithm follows this identical procedure again, just from a different starting point. In terms of the three divide and conquer steps, the depth-first search algorithm looks like this:

1. *Divide* the problem into four subproblems. Each subproblem searches for a path that starts from one of the four neighboring cells.

2. *Conquer* the subproblems by recursively executing the algorithm from each of the neighboring cells.

3. *Combine* the solutions to the subproblems by returning success if any of the subproblems were successful. Otherwise, return failure.

To illustrate, consider the grid in Figure 9.16(a). In this example, we are attempting to find a path from the green cell in position (1,1) to the red cell in position (3,0). The black cells represent obstacles that the rover cannot move through. The depth-

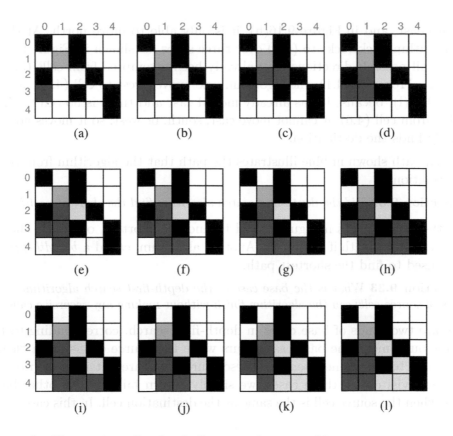

Figure 9.16 An illustration of a depth-first search on a grid.

first search algorithm will visit neighboring cells in clockwise order: east, south, west, north. The algorithm starts at cell $(1,1)$ and looks east to $(1,2)$, but cannot move in that direction due to an obstacle. Therefore, it next explores the cell to the south in position $(2,1)$, colored blue in Figure 9.16(b). From this cell, it recursively executes the same algorithm, first looking east to $(2,2)$. Since this cell is not blocked, it is the next one visited, as represented in Figure 9.16(c). The depth-first search algorithm is recursively called again from cell $(2,2)$, but the cells to the east, south, and north are blocked; and the cell to the west has already been visited. Therefore, the depth-first search algorithm returns failure to the cell at $(2,1)$. We color cell $(2,2)$ light blue to indicate that it has been visited, but is no longer on the path to the destination. From cell $(2,1)$, the algorithm has already looked east, so it now moves south to $(3,1)$, as shown in Figure 9.16(d). In the next step, shown in Figure 9.16(e), the algorithm moves south again to $(4,1)$ because the cell to the east is blocked.

Reflection 9.31 *When it is at cell $(3,1)$, why does the algorithm not "see" the destination in cell $(3,0)$?*

It does not yet "see" the destination because it looks east and south before it looks west. Since there is an open cell to the south, the algorithm will follow that possibility first. In the next steps, shown in Figure 9.16(f)–(g), the algorithm is able to move east, and in Figure 9.16(h), it is only able to move north. At this point, the algorithm backtracks to (4,1) over three steps, as shown in Figure 9.16(i)–(k), because all possible directions have already been attempted from cells (3,3), (4,3), and (4,2). From cell (4,1), the algorithm next moves west to cell (4,0), as shown in Figure 9.16(l), because it has already moved east and there is no cell to the south. Finally, from cell (4,0), it cannot move east, south, or west; so it moves north where it finally finds the destination.

The final path shown in blue illustrates the path that the algorithm from the source to destination.

Reflection 9.32 *Did the depth-first search algorithm find the shortest path?*

A depth-first search is not guaranteed to find the shortest, or even a short, path. But it will find *a* path if one exists. Another algorithm, called a *breadth-first search*, can be used to find the shortest path.

Reflection 9.33 *What is the base case of the depth-first search algorithm? For what types of source cells can the algorithm finish without making any recursive calls?*

There are two kinds of base cases in depth-first search, corresponding to the two possible outcomes. One base case occurs when the source cell is not a "legal" cell from which to start a new search. These source cells are outside the grid, blocked, or already visited. In these cases, we simply return failure. The other base case occurs when the source cell is the same as the destination cell. In this case, we return success.

The depth-first search algorithm is implemented by the following function. The function returns `True` (success) if the destination was reached by a path and `False` (failure) if the destination could not be found.

```python
BLOCKED = 0  # site is blocked
OPEN = 1     # site is open and not visited
VISITED = 2  # site is open and already visited

def dfs(grid, source, dest):
    """Perform a depth-first search on a grid to determine if there
       is a path between a source and destination.

    Parameters:
        grid:   a two-dimensional grid (list of lists)
        source: a (row, column) tuple to start from
        dest:   a (row, column) tuple to reach

    Return value: Boolean indicating whether destination was reached
    """

    (row, col) = source
    rows = len(grid)
    columns = len(grid[0])
```

```
    if (row < 0) or (row >= rows) or (col < 0) or (col >= columns) \
        or (grid[row][col] == BLOCKED) or (grid[row][col] == VISITED):
        return False                    # dead end (base case 1)

    if source == dest:                  # dest found (base case 2)
        return True

    grid[row][col] = VISITED            # visit this cell

    if dfs(grid, (row, col + 1), dest): # search east
        return True                     #   and return if dest found
    if dfs(grid, (row + 1, col), dest): # else search south
        return True                     #   and return if dest found
    if dfs(grid, (row, col - 1), dest): # else search west
        return True                     #   and return if dest found
    if dfs(grid, (row - 1, col), dest): # else search north
        return True                     #   and return if dest found

    return False                        # destination was not found
```

The variable names BLOCKED, VISITED, and OPEN represent the possible status of each cell. For example, the grid in Figure 9.16 is represented by

```
grid = [[BLOCKED, OPEN, BLOCKED, OPEN,    OPEN],
        [OPEN,    OPEN, BLOCKED, OPEN,    OPEN],
        [BLOCKED, OPEN, OPEN,    BLOCKED, OPEN],
        [OPEN,    OPEN, BLOCKED, OPEN,    BLOCKED],
        [OPEN,    OPEN, OPEN,    OPEN,    BLOCKED]]
```

When a cell is visited, its value is changed from OPEN to VISITED by the dfs function. There is a program available on the book website that includes additional turtle graphics code to visualize how the cells are visited in this depth-first search. Download this program and run it on several random grids.

> **Reflection 9.34** *Our dfs function returns a Boolean value indicating whether the destination was reached, but it does not actually give us the path (as marked in blue in Figure 9.16). How can we modify the function to do this?*

This modification is actually quite simple, although it may take some time to understand how it works. The idea is to add another parameter, a list named path, to which we append each cell after we mark it as visited. The values in this list contain the sequence of cells visited in the recursive calls. However, we remove the cell from path if we get to the end of the function where we return False because getting this far means that this cell is not part of a successful path after all. In our example in Figure 9.16, initially coloring a cell blue is analogous to appending that cell to the path, while recoloring a cell light blue when backtracking is analogous to removing the cell from the path. We leave an implementation of this change as an exercise. Two projects at the end of this chapter demonstrate how depth-first search can be used to solve other problems as well.

Exercises

*Write a **recursive** divide and conquer function for each of the following problems. Each of your functions should contain at least two recursive calls.*

9.5.1*   Write a recursive divide and conquer function

    power(a, n)

that returns the value of a^n, utilizing the fact that $a^n = (a^{n/2})^2$ when n is even and $a^n = (a^{(n-1)/2})^2 \cdot a$ when n is odd. Assume that n is a non-negative integer.

9.5.2.   The Fibonacci sequence is a sequence of integers in which each number is the sum of the previous two. The first two Fibonacci numbers are 1,1, so the sequence begins $1, 1, 2, 3, 5, 8, 13, \ldots$. Write a function

    fibonacci(n)

that returns the nth Fibonacci number.

9.5.3.   In the profit function, we defined the left half as ending at index midIndex − 1 and the right half starting at index midIndex. Would it also work to have the left half end at index midIndex and the right half start at index midIndex + 1? Why or why not?

9.5.4*   The profit function in the text takes a single list as the parameter and calls the function recursively with slices of this list. In this exercise, you will write a more efficient version of this function

    profit(prices, first, last)

that does not use slicing in the arguments to the recursive calls. Instead, the function will pass in the entire list in each recursive call, with the two additional parameters assigned the first and last indices of the sublist that we want to consider. In the divide step, the function will need to assign midIndex the index that is midway between first and last (which is usually not last // 2). To find the maximum profit achievable with a list of prices, the function must initially be called with profit(prices, 0, len(prices) - 1).

9.5.5.   Modify the version of the function that you wrote in Exercise 9.5.4 so that it returns the most profitable buy and sell days instead of the maximum profit.

9.5.6.   Write a divide and conquer version of the recursive linear search from Section 9.4 that checks if the middle item is equal to the target in each recursive call and then recursively calls the function with the first half and second half of the list, as needed. Your function should return the index in the list where the target value was found, or −1 if it was not found. If there are multiple instances of the target in the list, your function will not necessarily return the minimum index at which the target can be found. (This function is quite similar to Exercise 9.5.4.)

9.5.7.   Write a new version of the depth-first search function

    dfs(grid, source, dest, path)

in which the parameter path contains the sequence of cell coordinates that comprise a path from source to dest in the grid when the function returns. The initial value of path will be an empty list. In other words, to find the path in Figure 9.16, your function will be called like this:

```
        path = []
        if dfs(grid, (1, 1), (3, 0), path):
            print('A path was found: ' + str(path))
        else:
            print('A path was not found.')
```

In this example, the final value of `path` should be

```
        [(1, 1), (2, 1), (3, 1), (4, 1), (4, 0)]
```

9.5.8*   Write a recursive function

    `numPaths(n, row, column)`

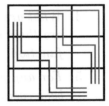

that returns the number of distinct paths in an empty $n \times n$ grid from the cell in the given row and column to the cell in position $(n-1, n-1)$. For example, if $n = 3$, then the number of paths from $(0,0)$ to $(2,2)$ is six, as illustrated to the right.

9.5.9.   In Section 9.2, we developed a recursive function named `bitStrings` that returned a list of all binary strings with a given length. We can design an alternative divide and conquer algorithm for the same problem by using the following insight. The list of n-bit binary strings with the common prefix p (with length less than n) is the concatenation of

(a)   the list of n-bit binary strings with the common prefix p + '0' and

(b)   the list of n-bit binary strings with the common prefix p + '1'.

For example, the list of all 4-bit binary strings with the common prefix 01 is the list of 4-bit binary strings with the common prefix 010 (namely, 0100 and 0101) plus the list of 4-bit binary strings with the common prefix 011 (namely, 0110 and 0111).

Write a recursive divide and conquer function

    `binary(prefix, n)`

that uses this insight to return a list of all n-bit binary strings with the given prefix. To compute the list of 4-bit binary strings, you would call the function initially with `binary('', 4)`.

*9.6   LINDENMAYER SYSTEMS

This section is available on the book website.

9.7   SUMMARY AND FURTHER DISCOVERY

Some problems, like many natural objects, "naturally" exhibit self-similarity. In other words, a problem solution is simply stated in terms of solutions to smaller versions of itself. It is often easier to see how to solve such problems recursively than it is iteratively. An algorithm that utilizes this technique is called *recursive*.

We suggested answering five questions to solve a problem recursively:

1. *What does a subproblem look like?*

2. *Which subproblem solution would be the most useful for solving the original problem?*

3. *How do we find the solution to the original problem using this subproblem solution? Implement this as the recursive step of our recursive function.*

4. *What are the simplest subproblems that we can solve non-recursively, and what are their solutions? Implement your answer as the base case of the recursive function.*

5. *For any possible parameter value, will the recursive calls eventually reach the base case?*

We designed recursive algorithms for about a dozen different problems in this chapter to illustrate how widely recursion can be applied. But learning how to solve problems recursively definitely takes time and practice. The more problems you solve, the more comfortable you will become!

Notes for further discovery

The first epigraph at the beginning of this chapter is from the first page of Benojt Mandelbrot's *The Fractal Geometry of Nature* [38]. The second is from Shakespeare's *Hamlet*, Act II, Scene II.

Aristid Lindenmayer's work was described in a now freely available book titled, *The Algorithmic Beauty of Plants* [52], published in 1990.

*9.8   PROJECTS

This section is available on the book website.

CHAPTER 10

Organizing Data

> Search is an unsolved problem. We have a good 90 to 95% of the solution, but there is a lot to go in the remaining 10%.
>
> Marissa Mayer, President and CEO of Yahoo!
> *Los Angeles Times interview (2008)*

I N this age of "big data," we take search algorithms for granted. Without web search algorithms that sift through billions of pages in a fraction of a second, the web would be practically useless. Similarly, large data repositories, such as those maintained by the U.S. Geological Survey (USGS) and the National Institutes of Health (NIH), would be useless without the ability to search for specific information. Even the operating systems on our personal computers now supply integrated search capabilities to help us navigate our increasingly large collections of files.

To enable fast access to these data, they must be organized in an efficient *data structure*. Hidden data structures in the implementations of the list and dictionary abstract data types enable their methods to access and modify their contents quickly. (The data structure behind a dictionary was briefly explained in Tangent 7.2.) In this chapter, we will explore one of the simplest ways to organize data—maintaining it in a sorted list—and the benefits this can provide. We will begin by developing a significantly faster search algorithm that can take advantage of knowing that the data is sorted. Then we will design three algorithms to sort data in a list, effectively creating a sorted list data structure. If you continue to study computer science, you can look forward to seeing many more sophisticated data structures in the future that enable a wide variety of efficient algorithms.

10.1 BINARY SEARCH

The spelling checkers that are built into most word processing programs work by searching through a list of English words, seeking a match. If the word is found, it is considered to be spelled correctly. Otherwise, it is assumed to be a misspelling. These word lists usually contain about a quarter million entries. If the words in the list are in no particular order, then we have no choice but to search through it one item at a time from the beginning, until either we happen to find the word we seek or we reach the end. We previously encountered this algorithm, called a *linear search* (or *sequential search*) because it searches in a linear fashion from beginning to end, and has linear time complexity.

Now let's consider the improvements we can make if the word list has been sorted in alphabetical order, as they always are. If we use a linear search on a sorted list, we know that we can abandon the search if we reach a word that is alphabetically after the word we seek. But we can do even better. Think about how we would search a physical, bound dictionary for the word "espresso." Since "E" is in the first half of the alphabet, we might begin by opening the book to a point about 1/4 of the way through. Suppose that, upon doing so, we find ourselves on a page containing words beginning with the letter "G." We would then flip backwards several pages, perhaps finding ourselves on a page on which the last word is "eagle." Next, we would flip a few pages forward, and so on, continuing to hone in on "espresso" until we find it.

❙ **Reflection 10.1** *How can we apply this idea to searching a sorted list?*

We can search a sorted list in a similar way, except that we usually do not know much about the distribution of the list's contents, so it is hard to make that first guess about where to start. In this case, the best strategy is to start in the middle. After comparing the target item to the middle item, we continue searching in the half of the list that must contain the target alphabetically. Because we are effectively dividing the list into two halves in each step, this algorithm is called *binary search*.

For example, suppose we wanted to search for the number 70 in the following sorted list of numbers. (We will use numbers instead of words in our example to save space.)

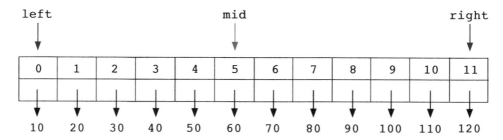

As we hone in on our target, we will update two variables named `left` and `right` to keep track of the first and last indices of the sublist that we are still considering. In addition, we will maintain a variable named `mid` that is assigned to the index of the middle value of this sublist. (When there are two middle values, we choose the

---

Tangent 10.1: Databases

A database is a structured file (or set of files) that contains a large amount of searchable data. The most common type of database, called a *relational database*, stores its data in tables. Each row in a table has a unique *key* that can be used to search for that row. For example, the tables below represent a small portion of the earthquake data that we worked with in Section 7.4. The key in each table is underlined.

Earthquakes

QuakeID	Latitude	Longitude	Mag	NetID
nc72076126	40.1333	-123.863	1.8	NC
ak10812068	59.8905	-151.2392	2.5	AK
nc72076101	37.3242	-122.1015	1.8	NC
ci11369570	34.3278	-116.4663	1.2	CI
ci11369562	35.0418	-118.3227	1.4	CI
ci11369546	32.0487	-115.0075	3.2	CI

Networks

NetID	NetName
AK	Alaska Regional
CI	Southern California
NC	Northern California
US	US National
UW	Pacific Northwest

The table on the left contains information about individual earthquakes, each of which is identified with a `QuakeID`. The last column in the left table contains a two-letter `NetID` that identifies the preferred source of information about that earthquake. The table on the right contains the names associated with each `NetID`.

Relational databases are queried using a programming language called SQL. A simple SQL query looks like this:

```
select Mag from Earthquakes where QuakeID = 'nc72076101'
```

This query is asking for the magnitude (`Mag`), from the `Earthquakes` table, of the earthquake with `QuakeID` nc72076101. The response to this query would be the value `1.8`. Searching a table quickly for a particular key is facilitated by an *index*. An index is data structure that maps keys to rows in a table (similar to a Python dictionary). The keys in the index can be maintained in sorted order so that any key, and hence any row, can be found quickly using a binary search. (But database indices are more commonly maintained in a hash table or a specialized data structure called a B-tree.)

---

leftmost one.) In each step, we will compare the target item to the item at index `mid`. If the target is equal to this middle item, we return `mid`. Otherwise, we either set `right` to be `mid - 1` (to hone in on the left sublist) or we set `left` to be `mid + 1` (to hone in on the right sublist).

In the list above, we start by comparing the item at index `mid` (60) to our target item (70). Then, because 70 > 60, we decide to narrow our search to the second half of the list. To do this, we assign `left` to `mid + 1`, which is the index of the item immediately after the middle item. In this case, we assign `left` to 5 + 1 = 6, as shown below.

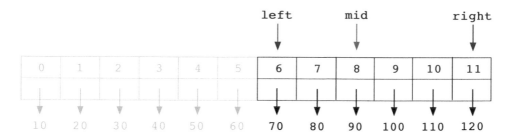

Then we update `mid` to be the index of the middle item in this sublist between `left` and `right`, in this case, 8. Next, since 70 is less than the new middle value, 90, we discard the second half of the sublist by assigning `right` to `mid - 1`, in this case, 8 - 1 = 7, as shown below.

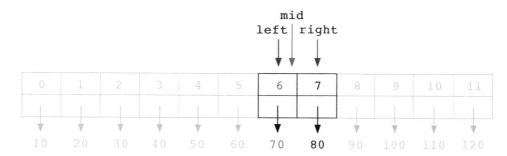

Then we update `mid` to be 6, the index of the "middle" item in this short sublist. Finally, since the item at index `mid` is the one we seek, we return the value of `mid`.

Reflection 10.2 *What would have happened if we were looking for a non-existent number like 72 instead?*

If we were looking for 72 instead of 70, all of the steps up to this point would have been the same, except that when we looked at the middle item in the last step, it would not have been equal to our target. Therefore, picking up from where we left off, we would notice that 72 is greater than our middle item 70, so we update `left` to be the index after `mid`, as shown below.

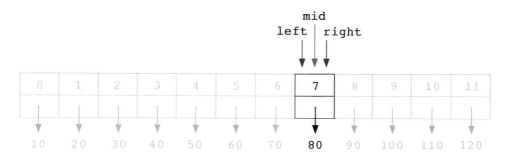

Now, since `left` and `right` are both equal to 7, `mid` must be assigned to 7 as well. Then, since 72 is less than the middle item, 80, we continue to blindly follow the algorithm by assigning `right` to be one less than `mid`.

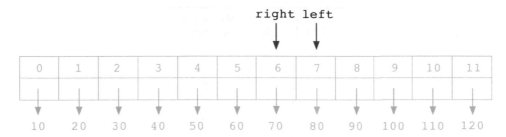

At this point, since `right` is to the left of `left` (i.e., `left > right`), the sublist framed by `left` and `right` is empty! Therefore, 72 must not be in the list, and we return −1.

This description of the binary search algorithm can be translated into a Python function in a very straightforward way:

```python
def binarySearch(keys, target):
    """Find the index of target in a sorted list of keys.

    Parameters:
        keys:   a sorted list of keys
        target: a key for which to search

    Return value: an index of target in keys or -1 if not found
    """

    left = 0
    right = len(keys) - 1
    while left <= right:
        mid = (left + right) // 2
        if target < keys[mid]:
            right = mid - 1
        elif target > keys[mid]:
            left = mid + 1
        else:
            return mid
    return -1
```

Notice that we have named our list parameter `keys` (instead of the usual `data`) because, in real databases (see Tangent 10.1), we typically try to match a unique *key* associated with the item we are seeking. For example, if we search for "Cumberbatch" in a phone directory, we are looking for a directory entry in which the last name (the key) matches "Cumberbatch;" we are not expecting the entire directory entry to match "Cumberbatch." When the search term is found, we return the entire directory entry that corresponds to this key. In our function, we return the index at which the key was found which, if we had data associated with the key, might provide us with enough information to find it in an associated data structure. We will look at an example of this in Section 10.2.

List length n	Worst case comparisons c
1	1
2	2
4	3
8	4
16	5
$\vdots$	$\vdots$
$2^{10} = 1{,}024$	11
$\vdots$	$\vdots$
$2^{20} \approx 1$ million	21
$\vdots$	$\vdots$
$2^{30} \approx 1$ billion	31

Table 10.1 The worst case number of comparisons in a binary search.

Reflection 10.3 *Write a* `main` *function that calls* `binarySearch` *with the list that we used in our example. Search for 70 and 72.*

Reflection 10.4 *Insert a statement in the* `binarySearch` *function, after* `mid` *is assigned its value, that prints the values of* `left`, `right`, *and* `mid`. *Then search for more target values. Do you see why* `mid` *is assigned to the printed values?*

Efficiency of iterative binary search

How much better is binary search than linear search? When we analyzed the linear search in Section 6.7, we counted the worst case number of comparisons between the target and a list item, so let's perform the same analysis for binary search. Since the binary search contains a `while` loop, we will need to think more carefully this time about when the worst case happens.

Reflection 10.5 *Under what circumstances will the binary search algorithm perform the most comparisons between the target and a list item?*

In the worst case, the `while` loop will never execute `return mid`, instead iterating until `left > right`, rendering the `while` loop condition `False`. This happens when `target` is not found in the list.

Suppose we have a very short list with length $n = 4$. In the worst case, we first look at the item in the middle of this list, and then are faced with searching a sublist with length 2. Next, we look at the middle item of this sublist and, upon not finding the item, search a sublist of length 1. After one final comparison to this single item, the algorithm will return `-1`. So we needed a total of 3 comparisons for a list of length 4.

Reflection 10.6 *Now what happens if we double the size of the list to* $n = 8$*?*

After we compare the middle item in a list with length $n = 8$ to our target, we

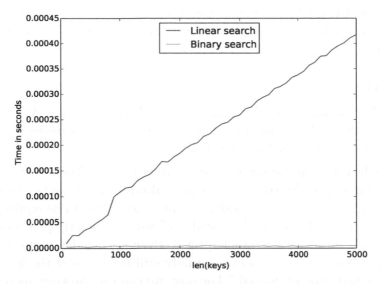

Figure 10.1   Execution times of linear search and binary search on small sorted lists.

are left with a sublist with length 4. We already know that a list with length 4 requires 3 comparisons in the worst case, so a list with length 8 must require $3 + 1 = 4$ comparisons in the worst case. Similarly, a list with length 16 must require only one more comparison than a list with length 8, for a total of 5. And so on. This pattern is summarized in Table 10.1. Notice that a list with over a billion items requires at most 31 comparisons!

Reflection 10.7 *In general, for list of length n, how many comparisons are necessary in the worst case?*

In each row of the table, the length of the list (n) is 2 raised to the power of 1 less than the number of comparisons (c), or

$$n = 2^{c-1}.$$

Therefore, for a list of size n, the binary search requires

$$c = \log_2 n + 1$$

comparisons in the worst case. So binary search is a ***logarithmic-time algorithm*** or, equivalently, an algorithm with $\mathcal{O}(\log n)$ time complexity. Since the time complexity of linear search is $\mathcal{O}(n)$, this means that linear search is *exponentially* slower than binary search.

This is a degree of speed-up that is *only* possible through algorithmic refinement; a faster computer simply cannot have this kind of impact. Figure 10.1 shows a comparison of actual running times of both search algorithms on some small lists. The time required by binary search is barely discernible as the red line parallel to the x-axis. But the real power of binary search becomes evident on very long lists.

As suggested by Table 10.1, a binary search takes almost no time at all, even on huge lists, whereas a linear search, which must potentially examine every item, can take a very long time.

A spelling checker

Now let's apply our binary search to the spelling checker problem. We will write a program that reads an alphabetized word list, and then allows someone to repeatedly enter a word to see if it is spelled correctly.

A list of English words can be found on computers running Mac OS X or Linux in the file /usr/share/dict/words, or one can be downloaded from the book website. This list is already sorted if you consider an uppercase letter to be equivalent to its lowercase counterpart. (For example, "academy" usually directly precedes "Acadia" in this file.) However, as we saw in Chapter 6, Python considers uppercase letters to come before lowercase letters, so we actually still need to sort the list to have it match Python's definition of "sorted." For now, we can use the **sort** method; in the coming sections, we will develop our own sorting algorithms.

The following function implements our spelling checker, using the **binarySearch** function (highlighted).

```python
def spellcheck():
    """Repeatedly ask for a word to spell-check and print the result.

    Parameters: none

    Return value: None
    """

    dictFile = open('/usr/share/dict/words', 'r', encoding = 'utf-8')
    dictionaryWords = [ ]
    for word in dictFile:
        dictionaryWords.append(word[:-1])   # remove newline before append
    dictFile.close()
    dictionaryWords.sort()

    word = input('Enter a word to spell-check (q to quit): ')
    while word != 'q':
        index = binarySearch(dictionaryWords, word) # search for word
        if index != -1:                             # word was found
            print(word, 'is spelled correctly.')
        else:                                       # word was not found
            print(word, 'is not spelled correctly.')
        print()

        word = input('Enter a word to spell-check (q to quit): ')
```

The function begins by opening the word list file and reading each word (one word per line) into a list. After all of the words have been read, we sort the list. Then a while loop repeatedly prompts for a word until the letter q is entered. Notice that we ask for a word before the while loop to initialize the value of word, and then again at the bottom of the loop to set up for the next iteration. In each iteration, we call the binary search function to check if the word is contained in the list. If the word is found (index != -1), we assume it is spelled correctly.

Reflection 10.8 *Combine the* spellcheck *function with the* binarySearch *function in a program. Run the program to try it out.*

Recursive binary search

You may have noticed that the binary search algorithm displays a high degree of self-similarity. In each step, the problem is reduced to solving a subproblem involving half of the original list. In particular, the problem of searching for a key between indices left and right is reduced to the subproblem of searching between left and mid - 1, or the subproblem of searching between mid + 1 and right. Therefore, binary search is a natural candidate for a recursive algorithm. In the following function, we add left and right as parameters because they define the subproblem that is being solved.

```
def binarySearch(keys, target, left, right):
    """Recursively find the index of target in a sorted list of keys.

    Parameters:
        keys:   a sorted list of keys
        target: a value for which to search

    Return value: an index of target in keys or -1 if not found
    """

    if left > right:              # base case 1: not found
        return -1

    mid = (left + right) // 2
    if target == keys[mid]:       # base case 2: found
        return mid

    if target < keys[mid]:        # recursive cases
        return binarySearch(keys, target, left, mid - 1)  # left half
    else:
        return binarySearch(keys, target, mid + 1, right) # right half
```

Like the recursive linear search from Section 9.4, this function needs two base cases. In the first base case, when the list is empty (left > right), we return -1. In the second base case, if target == keys[mid], we return mid. If neither of these cases holds, we solve one of the two subproblems recursively. If the target is less than the middle item, we recursively call the binary search with right set to mid - 1. Or, if the `target` is greater than the middle item, we recursively call the binary search with `left` set to `mid + 1`.

> **Reflection 10.9** *Repeat Reflections 10.3 and 10.4 with the recursive binary search function. Does the recursive version "look at" the same values of* `mid`*?*

*Efficiency of recursive binary search

Like the iterative binary search, this algorithm has logarithmic, or $\mathcal{O}(\log n)$, time complexity. But, as with the recursive linear search, we have to derive this result differently using a recurrence relation. Let $T(n)$ denote the worst case number of comparisons between the target and a list item in a binary search when the length of the list is n. In the recursive `binarySearch` function, there are two such comparisons before reaching a recursive function call. As we did in Section 9.4, we will simply represent the number of comparisons before each recursive call with the constant c. When $n = 0$, we reach a base case with no recursive calls, so $T(0) = c$.

> **Reflection 10.10** *How many more comparisons are there in a recursive call to* `binarySearch`*?*

Since each recursive call divides the size of the list under consideration by (about) half, the size of the list we are passing into each recursive call is (about) $n/2$. Therefore, the number of comparisons in each recursive call must be $T(n/2)$. The total number of comparisons is then

$$T(n) = T(n/2) + c.$$

Now we can use the same substitution method that we used with recursive linear search to arrive at a closed form expression in terms of n. First, since $T(n) = T(n/2) + c$, we can substitute $T(n)$ with $T(n/2) + c$:

$$T(n/2) + c$$

Now we need to replace $T(n/2)$ with something. Notice that $T(n/2)$ is just $T(n)$ with $n/2$ substituted for n. Therefore, using the definition of $T(n)$ above,

$$T(n/2) = T(n/2/2) + c = T(n/4) + c.$$

Similarly,

$$T(n/4) = T(n/4/2) + c = T(n/8) + c$$

and

$$T(n/8) = T(n/8/2) + c = T(n/16) + c.$$

This sequence of substitutions is illustrated in Figure 10.2. Notice that the denominator under the n at each step is a power of 2 whose exponent is the multiplier in

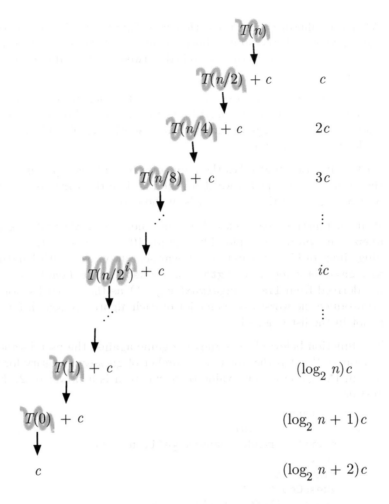

Figure 10.2 An illustration of how to derive a closed form for the recurrence relation $T(n) = T(n/2) + c$.

front of the accumulated c's at that step. In other words, for each denominator 2^i, the accumulated value on the right is $i \cdot c$. When we finally reach $T(1) = T(n/n)$, the denominator has become $n = 2^{\log_2 n}$, so $i = \log_2 n$ and the total on the right must be $(\log_2 n)c$. Finally, we know that $T(0) = c$, so the total number of comparisons is

$$T(n) = (\log_2 n + 2)\, c.$$

Therefore, as expected, the recursive binary search is a $\mathcal{O}(\log n)$ algorithm.

Exercises

10.1.1*   Modify both of the binary search functions so that, when the target is not found, the functions also print the values in keys that would have been on either side of the target if it were in the list.

10.1.2* When the value of `target` is less than `keys[mid]` in the binary search algorithms, they next search the sublist between indices `left` and `mid - 1`. Would the algorithms still work if they searched between `left` and `mid` instead? Why or why not?

10.1.3. Similar to the previous exercise, suppose the binary search algorithms next searched the sublist between `mid` and `right` (instead of between `mid + 1` and `right`) when the `target` is greater than `keys[mid]`. Would the algorithms still work? Why or why not?

10.1.4. Write a function that takes the name of a text file as a parameter and returns the number of misspelled words in the file. Use the `wordTokens` function from Section 6.1 to get the list of words in the text file.

10.1.5. Write a function that takes three parameters—`minLength`, `maxLength`, and `step`—and produces a plot like Figure 10.1 comparing the worst case running times of binary search and linear search on lists with length `minLength`, `minLength + step, minLength + 2 * step, ..., maxLength`. Use a slice of the list derived from `list(range(maxLength))` as the sorted list for each length. To produce the worst case behavior of each algorithm, search for an item that is not in the list (e.g., -1).

10.1.6. The function below plays a guessing game against the pseudorandom number generator. What is the worst case number of guesses necessary for the function to win the game for any value of `n`, where `n` is a power of 2? Explain your answer.

```
import random
def guessingGame(n):
    secret = random.randrange(1, n + 1)
    left = 1
    right = n
    guessCount = 1
    guess = (left + right) // 2
    while guess != secret:
        if guess > secret:
            right = guess - 1
        else:
            left = guess + 1
        guessCount = guessCount + 1
        guess = (left + right) // 2
    return guessCount
```

10.2 SELECTION SORT

Sorting is a well-studied problem, and a wide variety of sorting algorithms have been designed, including the one used by the familiar `sort` method of the `list` class. In this section and the two that follow, we will develop and compare three other common algorithms, named *selection sort*, *insertion sort*, and *merge sort*.

Reflection 10.11 *Before you read further, think about how you would sort a list of items (names, numbers, books, socks, etc.) in some desired order. Write down your algorithm in pseudocode.*

The **selection sort** algorithm is so called because, in each step, it selects the next smallest value in the list and places it in its proper sorted position by swapping it with whatever is currently there. For example, consider the list of numbers [50, 30, 40, 20, 10, 70, 60]. To sort this list in ascending order, the selection sort algorithm first finds the smallest number, 10. We want to place 10 in the first position in the list, so we swap it with the number that is currently in that position, 50, resulting in the modified list

[10, 30, 40, 20, 50, 70, 60]

Next, we find the second smallest number, 20, and swap it with the number in the second position, 30:

[10, 20, 40, 30, 50, 70, 60]

Then we find the third smallest number, 30, and swap it with the number in the third position, 40:

[10, 20, 30, 40, 50, 70, 60]

Next, we find the fourth smallest number, 40. But since 40 is already in the fourth position, no swap is necessary. This process continues until we reach the end of the list.

Reflection 10.12 *Work through the remaining steps in the selection sort algorithm. What numbers are swapped in each step?*

Implementing selection sort

Let's look at how we can implement this algorithm, using a more detailed representation of this list which, as before, we will name `keys`:

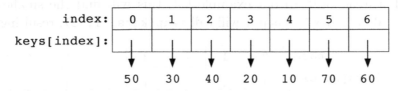

To begin, we want to search for the smallest value in the list, and swap it with the value at index 0. We have actually already implemented both parts of this step. In Exercise 7.2.5, you may have written a function

    swap(data, i, j)

that swaps the two values with indices `i` and `j` in the list `data`. To use this function to swap items, we will need the index of the smallest value. We already did this back on page 289 in the `minDay` function:

```
minIndex = 0
for index in range(1, len(keys)):
    if keys[index] < keys[minIndex]:
        minIndex = index
```

Once we have the index of the minimum value in `minIndex`, we can swap it with the item at index 0 with:

```
if minIndex != 0:
    swap(keys, 0, minIndex)
```

▌Reflection 10.13 *Why do we check if* `minIndex != 0` *before calling the* `swap` *function?*

In our example, these steps will find the smallest value, 10, at index 4, and then call `swap(keys, 0, 4)`. We first check if `minIndex != 0` so we do not needlessly swap the value in position 0 with itself. This swap results in the following modified list:

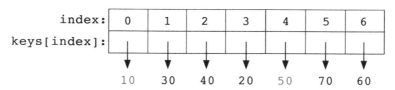

In the next step, we need to do the same thing, but for the second smallest value.

▌Reflection 10.14 *How we do we find the second smallest value in the list?*

Notice that, now that the smallest value is "out of the way" at the front of the list, the second smallest value in `keys` must be the smallest value in `keys[1:]`. Therefore, we can use exactly the same process as above, but on `keys[1:]` instead. This requires only four small changes in the code, marked in red below.

```
minIndex = 1
for index in range(2, n):
    if keys[index] < keys[minIndex]:
        minIndex = index
if minIndex != 1:
    swap(keys, 1, minIndex)
```

Instead of initializing `minIndex` to 0 and starting the `for` loop at 1, we initialize `minIndex` to 1 and start the `for` loop at 2. Then we swap the smallest value into position 1 instead of 0. In our example list, this will find the smallest value in `keys[1:]`, 20, at index 3. Then it will call `swap(keys, 1, 3)`, resulting in:

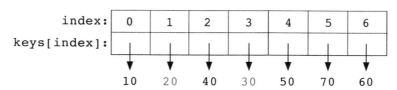

Similarly, the next step is to find the index of the smallest value starting at index 2, and then swap it with the value in index 2:

```
minIndex = 2
for index in range(3, n):
    if keys[index] < keys[minIndex]:
        minIndex = index
if minIndex != 2:
    swap(keys, 2, minIndex)
```

In our example list, this will find the smallest value in keys[2:], 30, at index 3. Then it will call swap(keys, 2, 3), resulting in:

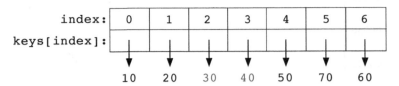

We continue by repeating this sequence of steps, with increasing values of the numbers in red, until we reach the end of the list.

To implement this algorithm, we need to situate the loop above in another loop that iterates over the increasing values in red. We can do this by replacing the initial value assigned to minIndex in red with a variable named start:

```
minIndex = start
for index in range(start + 1, n):
    if keys[index] < keys[minIndex]:
        minIndex = index
if minIndex != start:
    swap(keys, start, minIndex)
```

Then we place these steps inside a for loop that has start take on all of the integers from 0 to len(keys) - 2:

```
1 def selectionSort(keys):
2     """Sort a list in ascending order using the selection sort algorithm.

3     Parameter:
4         keys: a list of keys

5     Return value: None
6     """

7     n = len(keys)
8     for start in range(n - 1):
9         minIndex = start
10        for index in range(start + 1, n):
11            if keys[index] < keys[minIndex]:
12                minIndex = index
13        if minIndex != start:
14            swap(keys, start, minIndex)
```

Reflection 10.15 *In the outer* for *loop of the* selectionSort *function, why is the last value of* start *equal to* n - 2 *instead of* n - 1*? Think about what steps would be executed if* start *were assigned the value* n - 1 *in the last iteration of the loop.*

Reflection 10.16 *What would happen if we called* selectionSort *with the list* ['dog', 'cat', 'Monkey', 'Zebra', 'platypus', 'armadillo']*? Would it work? If so, in what order would the words be sorted?*

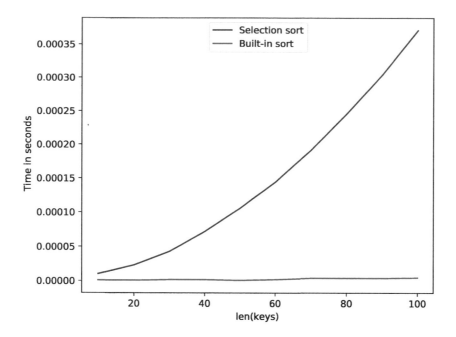

Figure 10.3 Execution times of selection sort and the list **sort** method on small randomly shuffled lists.

Because the comparison operators are defined for both numbers and strings, we can use our **selectionSort** function to sort either kind of data. For example, call **selectionSort** on each of the following lists, and then print the results. (Remember to incorporate the **swap** function from Exercise 7.2.5.)

```
numbers = [50, 30, 40, 20, 10, 70, 60]
animals = ['dog', 'cat', 'Monkey', 'Zebra', 'platypus', 'armadillo']
heights = [7.80, 6.42, 8.64, 7.83, 7.75, 8.99, 9.25, 8.95]
```

Efficiency of selection sort

Next, let's look at the time complexity of the selection sort algorithm. We can derive the asymptotic time complexity by counting the number of times the most frequently executed elementary step executes. In the **selectionSort** function, this is the comparison in the **if** statement on line 11. Since line 11 is in the body of the inner **for** loop that starts on line 10, it will be executed in every iteration of that loop. When **start** is 0, the inner **for** loop on line 10 runs from 1 to $n-1$, for a total of $n-1$ iterations. So line 11 is also executed $n-1$ times. Next, when **start** is 1, the inner **for** loop runs from 2 to $n-1$, a total of $n-2$ iterations, so line 11 is executed $n-2$ times. With each new value of **start**, there is one less iteration of the inner **for** loop. Therefore, the total number of times that line 11 is executed is

$$(n-1) + (n-2) + (n-3) + \cdots$$

Where does this sum stop? To find out, we look at the last iteration of the outer for loop, when start is n - 2. In this case, the inner for loop runs from n - 1 to n - 1, for only one iteration. So the total number of steps is

$$(n - 1) + (n - 2) + (n - 3) + \cdots + 3 + 2 + 1.$$

We have encountered this sum a few times before (see Tangent 4.1):

$$(n - 1) + (n - 2) + (n - 3) + \cdots + 3 + 2 + 1 = \frac{n(n - 1)}{2} = \frac{1}{2}n^2 - \frac{1}{2}n.$$

Ignoring the 1/2 in front of n^2 and the low order term $(1/2)n$, we find that this expression is asymptotically $\mathcal{O}(n^2)$. So selection sort has quadratic time complexity.

Figure 10.3 shows the results of an experiment comparing the running time of selection sort to the sort method of the list class. (Exercise 10.3.3 asks you to replicate this experiment.) The parabolic blue curve in Figure 10.3 represents the quadratic time complexity of the selection sort algorithm. The red curve at the bottom of Figure 10.3 represents the running time of the sort method. Although this plot compares the algorithms with very small lists, on which both algorithms are very fast, we see a marked difference in the growth rates of the execution times. We will see why the sort method is so much faster in Section 10.4.

Querying data

Suppose we want to write a program that allows someone to query the USGS earthquake data that we worked with in Section 7.4. Although we did not use them then, each earthquake was identified by a unique key such as ak10811825. The first two characters identify the monitoring network (ak represents the Alaska Regional Network) and the last eight digits are a unique ID assigned by the network. Our program will search for a given key, and return the associated latitude, longitude, magnitude, and depth. This associated data is sometimes called *satellite data* because it revolves around the key.

To use the efficient binary search algorithm in our program, we need to first sort the data by its keys. When we read this data into memory, we can either read it into parallel lists, as we did in Section 7.4, or we can read it into a table (i.e., a list of lists), as we did in Section 8.1. In this section, we will modify our selection sort algorithm to handle the first option. We will leave the second option as an exercise.

We will read the data into two lists named ids and data, which are a list of keys and a list of tuples, respectively. Each tuple in the second list will contain the satellite data for one earthquake. By design, these two lists will be *parallel* in the sense that the satellite data in data[index] belongs to the earthquake with the key in ids[index]. When we sort the earthquakes' keys, we will need to make sure that their associations with the satellite data are maintained. In other words, if, during the sort of the list ids, we swap the values in ids[9] and ids[4], we also need to swap data[9] and data[4].

Modifying our selection sort algorithm in this way is actually quite simple. First, we will add a second parameter named `data` that contains the satellite data corresponding to `keys`. The function will still make all of its sorting decisions based on the list of `keys`. But when we swap two values in `keys`, we also swap the corresponding values in `data`. The modified function looks like this (with changes in red):

```python
def selectionSort2(keys, data):
    """Sort parallel lists of keys and data values in ascending
       order using the selection sort algorithm.

    Parameters:
        keys: a list of keys
        data: a list of data values corresponding to the keys

    Return value: None
    """

    n = len(keys)
    for start in range(n - 1):
        minIndex = start
        for index in range(start + 1, n):
            if keys[index] < keys[minIndex]:
                minIndex = index
        swap(keys, start, minIndex)
        swap(data, start, minIndex)
```

Once we have the sorted parallel lists `ids` and `data`, we can use binary search to retrieve the index of a particular ID in the list `ids`, and then use that index to retrieve the corresponding satellite data from the list `data`. The following function implements this idea by repeatedly prompting for an earthquake ID.

```python
def queryQuakes(ids, data):
    """ (docstring omitted) """

    key = input('Earthquake ID (q to quit): ')
    while key != 'q':
        index = binarySearch(ids, key, 0, len(ids) - 1)
        if index >= 0:
            print('Location: ' + str(data[index][:2]) + '\n' +
                    'Magnitude: ' + str(data[index][3]) + '\n' +
                    'Depth: ' + str(data[index][2]) + '\n')
        else:
            print('An earthquake with that ID was not found.')
        key = input('Earthquake ID (q to quit): ')
```

The `main` function below reads the earthquakes from the file (left as an exercise), sorts the data with our selection sort algorithm for parallel lists, and then calls `queryQuakes`.

```
def main():
    ids, data = readQuakes()      # left as an exercise
    selectionSort2(ids, data)
    queryQuakes(ids, data)
```

Exercises

10.2.1. Can you find a list of length 5 that requires more comparisons in `selectionSort` (on line 11) than another list of length 5? In general, with lists of length n, is there a worst case list and a best case list with respect to comparisons? How many comparisons do the best case and worst case lists require?

10.2.2. Now consider the number of swaps. Can you find a list of length 5 that requires more swaps (on line 14) than another list of length 5? In general, with lists of length n, is there a worst case list and a best case list with respect to swaps? How many swaps do the best case and worst case lists require?

10.2.3* The inner `for` loop of the selection sort function can be eliminated by using two built-in Python functions instead, as shown in the following alternative selection sort implementation.

```
def selectionSortAlt(keys):
    n = len(keys)
    for start in range(n - 1):
        minimum = min(keys[start:])
        minIndex = start + keys[start:].index(minimum)
        if minIndex != start:
            swap(keys, start, minIndex)
```

Is this function more or less efficient than the `selectionSort` function we developed? Explain.

10.2.4. Suppose we already have a list that is sorted in ascending order, and want to insert new values into it. Write a function that inserts an item into a sorted list, maintaining the sorted order, without re-sorting the list.

10.2.5* Write the function

`readQuakes()`

that is needed by the program at the end of this section. The function should read earthquake IDs and earthquake satellite data, consisting of latitude, longitude, depth and magnitude, from the data file on the web at

`http://earthquake.usgs.gov/earthquakes/feed/v1.0/summary/2.5_month.csv`

and return two parallel lists, as described on page 423. The satellite data for each earthquake should be stored as a tuple of floating point values. For example, the satellite data for a earthquake that occurred at 19.5223 degrees latitude and -155.5753 degrees longitude with magnitude 1.1 and depth 13.6 km should be stored in the tuple (19.5223, -155.5753, 1.1, 13.6).

Use this function to complete a working version of the program on page 425. (Remember to incorporate the recursive binary search and the `swap` function from Exercise 7.2.5.) Look at the above URL in a web browser to find some earthquake IDs for which to search, or do the next exercise to have your program print a list.

10.2.6. Add to the `queryQuakes` function on page 424 the option to print an alphabetical list of all earthquakes, in response to typing `list` for the earthquake ID. The output should look something like this:

```
Earthquake ID (q to quit): ci37281696
Location: (33.4436667, -116.6743333)
Magnitude: 0.54
Depth: 13.69

Earthquake ID (q to quit): list
    ID              Location          Magnitude  Depth
---------- ----------------------- --------- -----
ak11406701  (63.2397, -151.4564)           5.5    1.3
ak11406705  (58.9801, -152.9252)          69.2    2.3
ak11406708  (59.7555, -152.6543)          80.0    1.9
    . . .


uw60913561  (41.8655, -119.6957)           0.2    2.4
uw60913616  (44.2917, -122.6705)           0.0    1.3
```

10.2.7. An alternative to storing the earthquake data in two parallel lists is to store it in one table (a list of lists). For example, the beginning of a table containing the earthquakes shown in the previous exercise would look like this:

```
[['ak11406701', 63.2397, -151.4564, 5.5, 1.3],
 ['ak11406705', 58.9801, -152.9252, 69.2, 2.3],
 . . .
]
```

Rewrite the `readQuakes`, `selectionSort`, `binarySearch`, and `queryQuakes` functions so that they work with the earthquake data stored in this way instead. Your functions should assume that the key for each earthquake is in column 0. Combine your functions into a working program that is driven by a `main` function like the one on page 425.

10.2.8. The Sieve of Eratosthenes is a simple algorithm for generating prime numbers that has a structure that is similar to the nested loops in selection sort. The algorithm begins by initializing a list of n Boolean values named `prime` as follows. (In this case, $n = 12$.)

```
prime:  F | F | T | T | T | T | T | T | T | T | T | T
        0   1   2   3   4   5   6   7   8   9  10  11
```

At the end of the algorithm, we want `prime[index]` to be False if `index` is not prime and True if `index` is prime. The algorithm continues by initializing a loop `index` variable to 2 (indicated by the arrow below) and then setting the list value of every multiple of 2 to be False.

```
        F | F | T | T | F | T | F | T | F | T | F | T
        0   1   2   3   4   5   6   7   8   9  10  11
                ↑
```

Next, the loop index variable is incremented to 3 and, since `prime[3]` is True, the list value of every multiple of 3 is set to be False.

F	F	T	T	F	T	F	T	F	F	F	T
0	1	2	3	4	5	6	7	8	9	10	11

↑ (at index 3)

Next, the loop index variable is incremented to 4. Since `prime[4]` is `False`, we do not need to set any of its multiples to `False`, so we do not do anything.

F	F	T	T	F	T	F	T	F	F	F	T
0	1	2	3	4	5	6	7	8	9	10	11

↑ (at index 4)

This process continues with the loop index variable set to 5:

F	F	T	T	F	T	F	T	F	F	F	T
0	1	2	3	4	5	6	7	8	9	10	11

↑ (at index 5)

And so on. How long must the algorithm continue to increment `index` before it has marked all non-prime numbers? Once it is done filling in the list, the algorithm iterates over it one more time to build the list of prime numbers, in this case, [2, 3, 5, 7, 11]. Write a function that implements this algorithm to return a list of all prime numbers less than or equal to a parameter `n`.

10.3   INSERTION SORT

Our second sorting algorithm, named *insertion sort*, is familiar to anyone who has sorted a hand of playing cards. Working left to right through our hand, the insertion sort algorithm inserts each card into its proper place with respect to the previously arranged cards. For example, consider our previous list, arranged as a hand of cards:

We start with the second card from the left, 30, and decide whether it should stay where it is or be inserted to the left of the first card. In this case, it should be inserted to the left of 50, resulting in the following slightly modified ordering:

Then we consider the third card from the left, 40. We see that 40 should be inserted between 30 and 50, resulting in the following order.

Next, we consider 20, and see that it should be inserted all the way to the left, before 30.

This process continues with 10, 70, and 60, at which time the hand will be sorted.

Implementing insertion sort

To implement this algorithm, we need to repeatedly find the correct location to insert an item among the items to the left, assuming that the items to the left are already sorted. Let's name the index of the item that we wish to insert `insertIndex` and the item itself `itemToInsert`. In other words, we assign

```
itemToInsert = keys[insertIndex]
```

To illustrate, suppose that `insertIndex` is 4 (and `itemToInsert` is 10), as shown below:

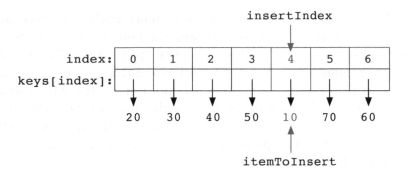

We need to compare `itemToInsert` to each of the items to the left, first at index `insertIndex - 1`, then at `insertIndex - 2`, `insertIndex - 3`, etc. When we come to an item that is less than or equal to `itemToInsert` or we reach the beginning of the list, we know that we have found the proper location for the item. This process can be expressed with a `while` loop:

```
index = insertIndex - 1
while index >= 0 and keys[index] > itemToInsert:
    index = index - 1
```

The variable `index` tracks which item we are currently comparing to `itemToInsert`. The value of `index` is decremented while it is still at least zero and the item at position `index` is still greater than `itemToInsert`. When the `while` loop ends, it is because either `index` has reached `-1` or `keys[index] <= itemToInsert`. In either case, we want to insert `itemToInsert` into position `index + 1`. In the example above, we would reach the beginning of the list, so we want to insert `itemToInsert` into position `index + 1 = 0`.

To actually insert `itemToInsert` in its correct position, we need to delete `itemToInsert` from its current position, and insert it into position `index + 1`. One option is to use `pop` and `insert`:

```
keys.pop(insertIndex)
keys.insert(index + 1, itemToInsert)
```

In the insertion sort algorithm, we want to repeat this process for each value of `insertIndex`, starting at 1, so we enclose these steps in a `for` loop:

```
def insertionSort_Draft(keys):
    """ (docstring omitted) """

    n = len(keys)
    for insertIndex in range(1, n):
        itemToInsert = keys[insertIndex]
        index = insertIndex - 1
        while index >= 0 and keys[index] > itemToInsert:
            index = index - 1
        keys.pop(insertIndex)
        keys.insert(index + 1, itemToInsert)
```

Although this function is correct, it performs more work than necessary. To see why, think about how the `pop` and `insert` methods must work, based on the picture of the list on page 429. First, to delete (`pop`) `itemToInsert`, which is at position `insertIndex`, all of the items to the right, from position `insertIndex + 1` to position `n - 1`, must be shifted one position to the left. Then, to insert `itemToInsert` into position `index + 1`, all of the items to the right, from position `index + 2` to `n - 1`, must be shifted one position to the right. So the items from position `insertIndex + 1` to position `n - 1` are shifted twice, only to end up back where they started.

A more efficient algorithm only shifts those items that need to be shifted, and does so while we are already iterating over them. The following modified algorithm does just that.

```
1  def insertionSort(keys):
2      """ Sort a list in ascending order using the insertion sort algorithm.

3      Parameter:
4          keys: a list of keys to sort

5      Return value: None
6      """

7      n = len(keys)
8      for insertIndex in range(1, n):
9          itemToInsert = keys[insertIndex]
10         index = insertIndex - 1
11         while index >= 0 and keys[index] > itemToInsert:
12             keys[index + 1] = keys[index]
13             index = index - 1
14         keys[index + 1] = itemToInsert
```

The highlighted assignment statement on line 8 copies each item at position `index` one position to the right. Therefore, when we get to the end of the loop, position `index + 1` is available to store `itemToInsert`.

Reflection 10.17 *To get a better sense of how this works, carefully work through the steps with the three remaining items to be inserted in the illustration on page 429.*

Reflection 10.18 *Write a* `main` *function that calls the* `insertionSort` *function to sort the list from the beginning of this section:* [50, 30, 40, 20, 10, 70, 60].

Efficiency of insertion sort

Is the insertion sort algorithm any more efficient than selection sort? To discover its time complexity, we first need to identify the most frequently executed elementary step(s). In this case, these appear to be the two assignment statements on lines 8–9 in the body of the `while` loop. However, the most frequently executed step is *actually* the test of the `while` loop condition on line 7 because the condition of a

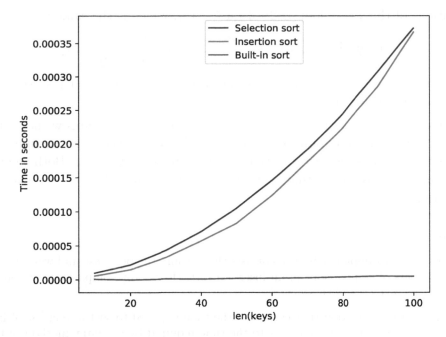

Figure 10.4 Execution times of selection sort, insertion sort, and the **sort** method on small randomly shuffled lists.

while loop is always tested when the loop is first reached, and again after each iteration. Therefore, a **while** loop condition is always tested once more than the body of the loop.

> **Reflection 10.19** *What are the minimum and maximum numbers of times the* **while** *loop condition is tested, for any particular value of* **insertIndex** *in the outer* **for** *loop?*

In the best case, it is possible that the condition is only tested once. This will happen if the item immediately to the left of **itemToInsert** is less than or equal to **itemToInsert**. Since there are $n - 1$ iterations of the outer **for** loop, this means that the **while** loop condition could be tested only $n - 1$ times in total for the entire algorithm. So, in the best case, insertion sort has linear-time, or $\mathcal{O}(n)$, time complexity.

In the worst case, the **while** loop will always iterate until **index >= 0** is **False**, i.e., until **index == -1**. This will happen if **keys** is initially in reverse order, meaning that **itemToInsert** is always less than every item to its left. Since **index** starts at **insertIndex - 1**, this will cause the **while** loop condition to be tested **insertIndex + 1** times. So in the first iteration of the outer **for** loop, when **insertIndex** is 1, the **while** loop condition is tested **insertIndex + 1 = 2** times. When **insertIndex** is 2, it is tested 3 times. This continues until **insertIndex** is **n - 1**, at which time, the **while** loop condition is tested **n** times. So the total number of iterations of the while loop is $2 + 3 + 4 + \cdots + n$, which is the same as

$$(1 + 2 + 3 + \cdots + n) - 1 = \frac{n(n+1)}{2} - 1 = \frac{1}{2}n^2 + \frac{1}{2}n - 1.$$

Ignoring the constants and slower growing terms, this means that insertion sort is also a quadratic-time, or $\mathcal{O}(n^2)$, algorithm in the worst case.

Figure 10.4 shows the actual running times of the sorting algorithms we have studied so far on very small, randomly shuffled lists. We can see that the running time of insertion sort is almost identical to that of selection sort in practice. Both algorithms are still significantly slower than the built-in sort method. We will see why in the next section.

Exercises

10.3.1. Give examples of 10-element lists that require the best case and worst case numbers of comparisons in an insertion sort. How many comparisons are necessary to sort each of these lists?

10.3.2* Write a function that compares the time required to sort a long list of English words using insertion sort to the time required by the sort method of the list class. You can use the function time.time() function, which returns the number of seconds that have elapsed since January 1, 1970, to record the time required to execute each function. A list of English words can be found on computers running Mac OS X or Linux in the file /usr/share/dict/words, or one can be downloaded from the book website. This list is already sorted if you consider an uppercase letter to be equivalent to its lowercase counterpart. However, since Python considers uppercase letters to come before lowercase letters, the list is not really sorted for our purposes. But it is "almost" sorted, which means that insertion sort should perform relatively well. Be sure to make a separate copy of the original list for each sorting algorithm.

How many seconds did each sort require? (Be patient; insertion sort could take several minutes!) If you can be *really* patient, try timing selection sort as well.

10.3.3. Write a function

    sortPlot(minLength, maxLength, step)

that produces a plot like Figure 10.4 comparing the running times of insertion sort, selection sort, and the sort method of the list class on shuffled lists with length minLength, minLength + step, minLength + 2 * step, ..., maxLength. At the beginning of your function, produce a shuffled list with length maxLength with

    data = list(range(maxLength))
    random.shuffle(data)

Then time each function for each list length using a new, unsorted slice of this list.

10.3.4* A sorting algorithm is called *stable* if two items with the same value always appear in the sorted list in the same order as they appeared in the original list. Are selection sort and insertion sort stable sorts? Explain your answer in each case.

10.3.5. A third simple quadratic-time sorting algorithm is called *bubble sort* because it repeatedly "bubbles" large items toward the end of the list by swapping each item repeatedly with its neighbor to the right if it is larger than this neighbor.

For example, consider the short list [3, 2, 4, 1]. In the first pass over the list, bubble sort compares pairs of items, starting from the left, and swaps them if they are out of order. The illustration below depicts in red the items that are compared in the first pass, and the arrows depict which of those pairs are swapped because they are out of order.

At the end of the first pass, the largest item (in blue) is in its correct location. We repeat the process, but stop before the last item.

$$\boxed{2 \quad 3 \quad 1 \quad 4} \quad \boxed{2 \quad 3 \quad 1 \quad 4} \quad \boxed{2 \quad 1 \quad 3 \quad 4}$$

After the second pass, we know that the two largest items (in blue) are in their correct locations. On this short list, we make just one more pass.

$$\boxed{2 \quad 1 \quad 3 \quad 4} \quad \boxed{1 \quad 2 \quad 3 \quad 4} \quad \boxed{1 \quad 2 \quad 3 \quad 4}$$

After $n-1$ passes, we know that the last $n-1$ items are in their correct locations. Therefore, the first item must be also, and we are done. Write a function that implements this algorithm.

10.3.6. In the bubble sort algorithm, if no items are swapped during a pass over the list, the list must be in sorted order. The bubble sort algorithm can be made somewhat more efficient by detecting when this happens, and returning early if it does. Write a function that implements this modified bubble sort algorithm. (Hint: replace the outer `for` loop with a `while` loop and introduce a Boolean variable that controls the `while` loop.)

10.3.7. Write a modified version of the insertion sort function that sorts two parallel lists named `keys` and `data`, based on the values in `keys`, like the parallel list version of selection sort on page 424.

10.4 EFFICIENT SORTING

In the preceding sections, we developed two sorting algorithms, but discovered that they were both significantly less efficient than the built-in `sort` method. The `sort` method is based on a recursive sorting algorithm called ***merge sort***.[1]

Merge sort

As illustrated in Figure 10.5(a), merge sort is a *divide and conquer* algorithm, like those from Section 9.5. Divide and conquer algorithms generally consist of three steps:

---

[1]The Python sorting algorithm, called ***Timsort***, has elements of both merge sort and insertion sort. If you would like to learn more, visit `http://bugs.python.org/file4451/timsort.txt`.

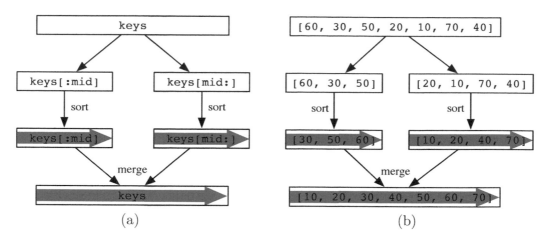

Figure 10.5 Illustrations of merge sort (a) in general and (b) on an example.

1. *Divide* the problem into two or more subproblems.

2. *Conquer* each subproblem recursively.

3. *Combine* the solutions to the subproblems into a solution for the original problem.

| **Reflection 10.20** *Based on Figure 10.5(a), what are the divide, conquer, and combine steps in the merge sort algorithm?*

The *divide* step of merge sort is very simple: just divide the list in half. The *conquer* step recursively calls the merge sort algorithm on the two halves. The *combine* step merges the two sorted halves into the final sorted list. This elegant algorithm is implemented by the following function:

```
def mergeSort(keys):
    """Sort a list in ascending order using the merge sort algorithm.

    Parameter:
        keys: a list of keys to sort

    Return value: None
    """

    n = len(keys)
    if n > 1:
        mid = n // 2                # divide list in half
        left = keys[:mid]
        right = keys[mid:]

        mergeSort(left)             # recursively sort the left half
        mergeSort(right)            # recursively sort the right half
        merge(left, right, keys)    # merge sorted halves into keys
```

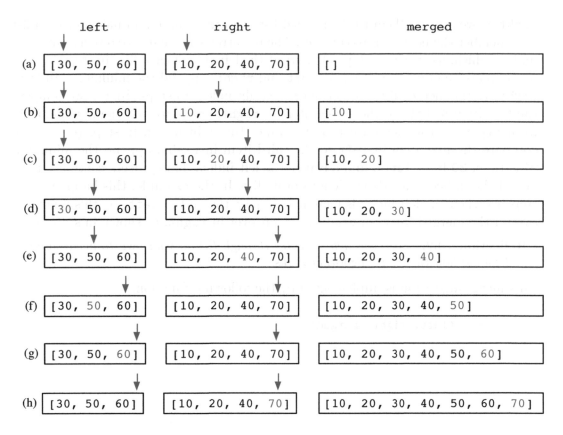

Figure 10.6 An illustration of the merge algorithm with example sublists.

❙ Reflection 10.21 *Where is the base case in this function?*

The base case in this function is implicit; when n <= 1, the function just returns because a list containing zero or one values is, of course, already sorted.

To flesh out **mergeSort**, we need to implement the **merge** function. Suppose we want to sort the list [60, 30, 50, 20, 10, 70, 40]. As illustrated in Figure 10.5(b), the merge sort algorithm first divides this list into the two sublists **left** = [60, 30, 50] and **right** = [20, 10, 70, 40]. After recursively sorting each of these lists, we have **left** = [30, 50, 60] and **right** = [10, 20, 40, 70]. Now we want to efficiently merge these two sorted lists into one final sorted list. We could, of course, concatenate the two lists and then call merge sort with them. But that would be far too much work; we can do much better!

Because **left** and **right** are sorted, the first item in the merged list must be the minimum of the first item in **left** and the first item in **right**. So we place this minimum item into the first position in the merged list, and remove it from **left** or **right**. The next item in the merged list must again be at the front of **left** or **right**. This process continues until we run out of items in one of the lists.

This algorithm is illustrated in Figure 10.6. Rather than delete items from **left** and `right` as we append them to the merged list, we will maintain an index for each list to remember the next item to consider. The red arrows in Figure 10.6 represent these indices which, as shown in step (a), start at the left side of each list. In steps (a)–(b), we compare the two front items in `left` and `right`, append the minimum (10 from `right`) to the merged list, and advance the right index. In steps (b)–(c), we compare the first item in `left` to the second item in `right`, again append the minimum (20 from `right`) to the merged list, and advance the right index. In steps (c)–(d), we compare the first item in `left` to the third item in `right`, append the minimum (this time, 30 from `left`), and advance the left index. This process continues until one of the indices exceeds the length of its list. In the example, this happens after step (g) when the left index is incremented past the end of `left`. At this point, we extend the merged list with whatever is left over in `right`, as shown in step (h).

Reflection 10.22 *Work through steps (a) through (h) on your own to make sure you understand how the merge algorithm works.*

This merge algorithm is implemented by the following function.

```
1 def merge(left, right, merged):
2     """Merge two sorted lists, left and right, into one sorted list
3        named merged.
4
5     Parameters:
6         left:    a sorted list
7         right:   another sorted list
8         merged:  the merged sorted list
9
10    Return value: None
11    """
12
13    merged.clear()    # clear contents of merged
14    leftIndex = 0     # index in left
15    rightIndex = 0    # index in right
16
17    while leftIndex < len(left) and rightIndex < len(right):
18        if left[leftIndex] <= right[rightIndex]: # left value is smaller
19            merged.append(left[leftIndex])
20            leftIndex = leftIndex + 1
21        else:                                    # right value is smaller
22            merged.append(right[rightIndex])
23            rightIndex = rightIndex + 1

    if leftIndex >= len(left):                   # remaining items are in right
        merged.extend(right[rightIndex:])
    else:                                        # remaining items are in left
        merged.extend(left[leftIndex:])
```

The `merge` function begins by clearing out the contents of the merged list and initializing the indices for the left and right lists to zero. The `while` loop starting on line 13 constitutes the main part of the algorithm. The loop iterates while both `leftIndex` and `rightIndex` are valid indices in their respective lists. In lines 14–19, the algorithm compares the items at the two indices and appends the smallest to `merged`. When the loop finishes, we know that either `leftIndex >= len(left)` or `rightIndex >= len(right)`. In the first case (lines 20–21), there are still items remaining in `right` to append to `merged`. In the second case (lines 22–23), there are still items remaining in `left` to append to `merged`.

Reflection 10.23 *Write a program that uses the merge sort algorithm to sort the list in Figure 10.5(b).*

Internal vs. external sorting

We have been assuming all along that the data that we want to sort is small enough to fit in a list in a computer's memory. The selection and insertion sort algorithms must have the entire list in memory at once because they potentially pass over the entire list in each iteration of their outer loops. For this reason, they are called *internal sorting algorithms*.

But what if the data is larger than the few gigabytes that can fit in memory all at once? This is routinely the situation with real databases. In these cases, we need an ***external sorting algorithm***, one that can sort data in secondary storage by bringing smaller pieces of it into memory at a time.

The merge sort algorithm can be implemented as an external sorting algorithm. In the `merge` function, each of the sorted halves could reside in a file on disk and the algorithm could just bring the current front items into memory when it needs them. The merged list can also reside in a file on disk; when a new item is added to end of the merged result, it just needs to be written to the merged file after the previous item. Exercise 10.4.7 asks you to write a version of the `merge` function that merges two sorted files in this way.

Efficiency of merge sort

To formally derive the time complexity of merge sort, we would need to set up a recurrence relation like the one for the recursive binary search. But doing so for merge sort is a little more complicated, so let's look at it in a different way. Figure 10.7 illustrates the work that is done through the recursive calls in the algorithm. These recursive calls divide the list into smaller and smaller lists until they reach the base case, as illustrated in the top half of the diagram. The number of elementary steps performed when dividing each list through slicing is proportional to the length of the list, since every element is copied. In each of these "divide" levels, all n items are being copied once in a slicing operation. The number of slices gets larger as we work down toward the base case, and each one is smaller, but the total number of items remains constant at n. So there are $\mathcal{O}(n)$ elementary steps being done in each "divide" level.

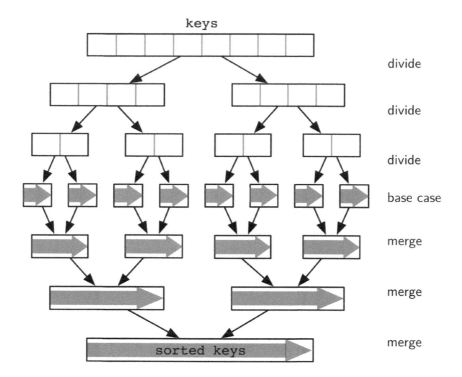

Figure 10.7 An illustration of the work performed by the merge sort algorithm.

Reflection 10.24 *How many "divide" levels are there until the base case is reached when $n = 8$? When $n = 16$? For n in general?*

When $n = 8$, as in the diagram, there are three "divide" levels. If n were doubled to 16, there would be just one more level needed. In general, because the lists are being halved at each level, until each list contains just one item, there must be $\log_2 n$ levels until the base case is reached. Therefore, the total number of elementary steps in the top half of the diagram is proportional to $n \cdot \log_2 n$, or $\mathcal{O}(n \log n)$.

Now let's analyze the number of elementary steps in the bottom half of the diagram. In the base case, each list contains at most one item, so they are sorted, as depicted by the red arrows. Then those short lists are merged into lists that are about twice as long. This merging continues until all of the original items are merged into the final sorted list. The number of "merge" levels in the diagram is the same as the number of "divide" levels because the same process is performed in reverse order. So the total number of elementary steps in the bottom half of the diagram is proportional to $\log_2 n$ times the number of elementary steps performed in each "merge" level.

Reflection 10.25 *About how many elementary steps does the* merge *function contain when* merged *contains 8 items? 16 items? n items?*

Since all of the items in the **left** and **right** lists are copied to the **merged** list exactly once, the total number of elementary steps in **merge** is proportional to the

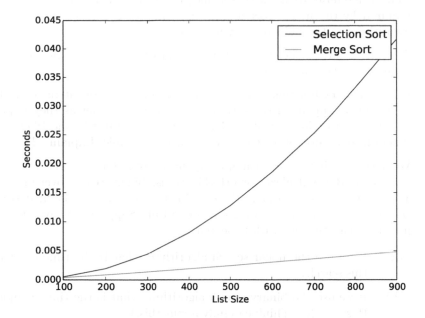

Figure 10.8 A comparison of the execution times of selection sort and merge sort on small randomly shuffled lists.

length of the **merged** list. In each "merge" level of the diagram, since all n items are involved in one merge operation, the combined lengths of the **merged** lists is n. So the total number of elementary steps in each "merge" level must be proportional to n. Therefore, the total number of elementary steps in the bottom half of the diagram is also proportional to $n \cdot \log_2 n$, or $\mathcal{O}(n \log n)$.

Adding the $\mathcal{O}(n \log n)$ from the top half of the diagram to the $\mathcal{O}(n \log n)$ from the bottom half gives us $\mathcal{O}(n \log n)$ elementary steps in total because the "big-oh" notation hides the constant coefficient that comes from this addition. So the time complexity of merge sort is $\mathcal{O}(n \log n)$.

How much faster is this than the quadratic-time selection and insertion sorts? Figure 10.8 illustrates the difference by comparing the merge sort and selection sort functions on small randomly shuffled lists. The merge sort algorithm is *much* faster. Recall that the algorithm behind the built-in **sort** method is based on merge sort, which explains why it was so much faster than our previous sorts. Exercise 10.4.1 asks you to compare the algorithms on much longer lists as well.

Exercises

10.4.1. Suppose the selection sort algorithm requires exactly n^2 steps and the merge sort algorithm requires exactly $n \log_2 n$ steps. About how many times slower is selection sort than merge sort when $n = 100$? $n = 1000$? $n = 1$ million?

10.4.2. Repeat Exercise 10.3.2 with the merge sort algorithm. How does the time required by the merge sort algorithm compare to that of the insertion sort algorithm and the built-in `sort` method?

10.4.3. Add merge sort to the running time plot in Exercise 10.3.3. How does its time compare to the other sorts?

10.4.4. Our `mergeSort` function is a stable sort, meaning that two items with the same value always appear in the sorted list in the same order as they appeared in the original list. However, if we changed the `<=` operator in line 18 of the `merge` function to a `<` operator, it would no longer be stable. Explain why.

10.4.5* We have seen that binary search is exponentially faster than linear search in the worst case. But is it always worthwhile to use binary search over linear search? The answer, as is commonly the case in the "real world," is "it depends." In this exercise, you will investigate this question. Suppose we have an *unordered* list of n items that we wish to search.

    (a) If we use the linear search algorithm, what is the time complexity of this search?

    (b) If we use the binary search algorithm, what is the time complexity of this search? (Think carefully about this.)

    (c) If we perform n (where n is also the length of the list) individual searches of the list, what is the time complexity of the n searches together if we use the linear search algorithm?

    (d) If we perform n individual searches with the binary search algorithm, what is the time complexity of the n searches together?

    (e) What can you conclude about when it is best to use binary search vs. linear search?

10.4.6. Suppose we have a list of n keys that we anticipate needing to search k times. We have two options: either we sort the keys once and then perform all of the searches using a binary search algorithm or we forgo the sort and simply perform all of the searches using a linear search algorithm. Suppose the sorting algorithm requires exactly $n^2/2$ steps, the binary search algorithm requires $\log_2 n$ steps, and the linear search requires n steps. Assume each step takes the same amount of time.

    (a) If the length of the list is $n = 1024$ and we perform $k = 100$ searches, which alternative is better?

    (b) If the length of the list is $n = 1024$ and we perform $k = 500$ searches, which alternative is better?

    (c) If the length of the list is $n = 1024$ and we perform $k = 1000$ searches, which alternative is better?

10.4.7. Write a function that merges two sorted files into one sorted file. Your function should take the names of the three files as parameters. Assume that all three files contain one string value per line. Your function should not use any lists, instead reading only one item at a time from each input file and writing one item at a time to the output file. In other words, at any particular time, there should be at most one item from each file assigned to any variable in your function. You will know when you have reached the end of one of the input files when a call to `readline` returns an empty string. There are two files on the book website named `left.txt` and `right.txt` that you can use to test your function.

*10.5 TRACTABLE AND INTRACTABLE ALGORITHMS

This section is available on the book website.

10.6 SUMMARY AND FURTHER DISCOVERY

Sorting and searching are perhaps the most fundamental problems in computer science for good reason. We have seen how simply sorting a list can *exponentially* decrease the time it takes to search it, using the *binary search algorithm*. Since binary search is one of those algorithms that "naturally" exhibits self-similarity, we designed both iterative and recursive algorithms that implement the same idea. We also designed two basic sorting algorithms named *selection sort* and *insertion sort*. Each of these algorithms can sort a short list relatively quickly, but they are both very inefficient when it comes to larger lists. By comparison, the recursive *merge sort* algorithm is very fast. Merge sort has the added advantage of being an *external sorting algorithm*, meaning we can adapt it to sort very large data sets that cannot be brought into a computer's memory all at once.

Although the selection and insertion sort algorithms are quite inefficient compared to merge sort, they are still *tractable*, meaning that they will finish in a "reasonable" amount of time. In fact, all algorithms with time complexities that are polynomial functions of their input sizes are considered to be tractable. On the other hand, exponential-time algorithms are called *intractable* because even when their input sizes are relatively small, they require eons to finish.

Notes for further discovery

This chapter's epigraph is from an interview given by Marissa Mayer to the *Los Angeles Times* in 2008 [21].

The subjects of this chapter are fundamental topics in second-semester computer science courses, and there are many books available that cover them in more detail. A higher-level overview of some of the tricks used to make searching fast can be found in John MacCormick's *Nine Algorithms that Changed the Future* [37].

*10.7 PROJECTS

This section is available on the book website.

CHAPTER 11

Networks

Fred Jones of Peoria, sitting in a sidewalk cafe in Tunis and needing a light for his cigarette, asks the man at the next table for a match. They fall into conversation; the stranger is an Englishman who, it turns out, spent several months in Detroit studying the operation of an interchangeable-bottlecap factory. "I know it's a foolish question," says Jones, "but did you ever by any chance run into a fellow named Ben Arkadian? He's an old friend of mine, manages a chain of supermarkets in Detroit. . . "

"Arkadian, Arkadian," the Englishman mutters. "Why, upon my soul, I believe I do! Small chap, very energetic, raised merry hell with the factory over a shipment of defective bottlecaps."

"No kidding!" Jones exclaims in amazement.

"Good lord, it's a small world, isn't it?"

Stanley Milgram
The Small-World Problem (1967)

W HAT do Instagram, food webs, the banking system, and our brains all have in common? They are all *networks*: systems of interconnected units that exchange information over the links between them. There are networks all around us: social networks, road networks, protein interaction networks, electrical transmission networks, the Internet, networks of seismic faults, terrorist networks, networks of political influence, transportation networks, and semantic networks, to name a few.

The continuous and dynamic local interactions in large networks such as these make them extraordinarily complex and hard to predict. Learning more about networks can help us combat disease, terrorism, and power outages. Realizations that some networks are *emergent* systems that develop global behaviors based on local interactions have improved our understanding of insect colonies, urban planning, and even our brains. Too little understanding of networks has had unfortunate

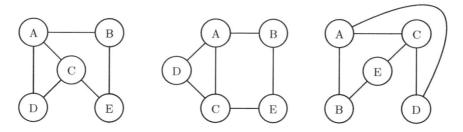

Figure 11.1 Three representations of the same graph.

consequences, such as when invasive species have been introduced into poorly understood ecological networks.

As with the other types of "big data," we need computer algorithms to understand large and complex networks. In this chapter, we will begin by discussing how we can represent networks in algorithms so that we can analyze them. Then we will develop an algorithm to find the distance between any two nodes in a network. Recent discoveries have shown that many real networks exhibit a "small-world property," meaning that the average distance between nodes is relatively small. In later sections, we will investigate the characteristics of small-world networks and their ramifications for solving real problems.

11.1 MODELING WITH GRAPHS

Networks are modeled with a mathematical structure called a *graph*. A graph consists of a set of *nodes* (or *vertices*) and a set of *links* (or *edges*) that connect pairs of nodes. If two nodes are connected by a link, we say they are *adjacent*. Nodes are usually drawn as circles (or another shape) and links are drawn as lines between them, but the placement of the nodes and links on the page is arbitrary. For example, all three of the graphs in Figure 11.1 are equivalent.

A social network (like Facebook or LinkedIn) can be represented by a graph in which the nodes are people and the links represent relationships (e.g., friends, connections, circles, followers). For example, in the social network in Figure 11.2, Caroline has three friends: Amelia, Lillian, and Nick. In a neural network, the nodes represent neurons and the links represent axons that transmit nerve impulses between the neurons. Figure 11.3 represents the interconnections between neurons in one of the simple neural networks that control digestion in the guts of arthropods. In a graph representing a power grid, like that in Figure 11.4, the nodes represent power stations and the links represent high-voltage transmission lines connecting them.

In an algorithm, a graph is usually represented in one of two ways. The first is called an *adjacency matrix*. An adjacency matrix contains a row and a column for every node in the network. A one in a matrix entry represents a link between the nodes in

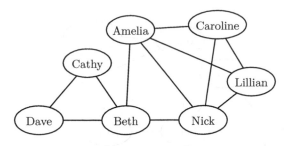

Figure 11.2 A small social network.

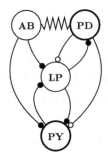

Figure 11.3 A model of the pyloric central pattern generator that controls stomach motion in lobsters.

Figure 11.4 The electrical transmission network in New Zealand. [67]

the corresponding row and column. A zero means that there is no link. The following table represents an adjacency matrix for the network in Figure 11.2.

	Amelia	Beth	Caroline	Cathy	Dave	Lillian	Nick
Amelia	0	1	1	0	0	1	1
Beth	1	0	0	1	1	0	1
Caroline	1	0	0	0	0	1	1
Cathy	0	1	0	0	1	0	0
Dave	0	1	0	1	0	0	0
Lillian	1	0	1	0	0	0	1
Nick	1	1	1	0	0	1	0

The first row indicates that Amelia is connected to Beth, Caroline, Lillian, and Nick. The second row shows that Beth is connected to Amelia, Cathy, Dave, and Nick. In Python, we would represent this matrix with the following nested list.

```
graph = [[0, 1, 1, 0, 0, 1, 1],
         [1, 0, 0, 1, 1, 0, 1],
         [1, 0, 0, 0, 0, 1, 1],
         [0, 1, 0, 0, 1, 0, 0],
         [0, 1, 0, 1, 0, 0, 0],
         [1, 0, 1, 0, 0, 0, 1],
         [1, 1, 1, 0, 0, 1, 0]]
```

Although the nodes' labels are not stored in the adjacency matrix itself, they could

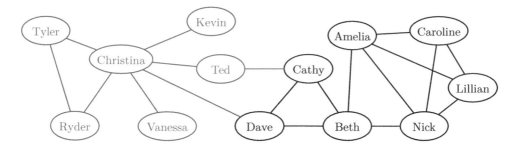

Figure 11.5 An expanded social network. The nodes and links in red are additions to the graph in Figure 11.2.

be stored separately as strings in a list. The index of each string in the list should equal the row/column of the corresponding node in the adjacency matrix.

Reflection 11.1 *Create an adjacency matrix for the graph in Figure 11.1. (Remember that all three pictures depict the same graph.)*

The alternative representation, which we will use in this chapter, is an *adjacency list*. An adjacency list, which is actually a collection of lists, contains, for each node, a list of nodes to which it is connected. In Python, an adjacency list can be stored as a dictionary. The following dictionary represents the network in Figure 11.2.

```
graph = { 'Amelia':   ['Beth', 'Caroline', 'Lillian', 'Nick'],
          'Beth':     ['Amelia', 'Cathy', 'Dave', 'Nick'],
          'Caroline': ['Amelia', 'Lillian', 'Nick'],
          'Cathy':    ['Beth', 'Dave'],
          'Dave':     ['Beth', 'Cathy'],
          'Lillian':  ['Amelia', 'Caroline', 'Nick'],
          'Nick':     ['Amelia', 'Beth', 'Caroline', 'Lillian'] }
```

Each key in this dictionary, a string, represents a node, and each corresponding value is a list of strings representing the nodes to which the key node is connected. Notice that, if two nodes are connected, that information is stored in both nodes' lists. For example, there is a link connecting Amelia and Beth, so Beth is in Amelia's list and Amelia is in Beth's list.

Reflection 11.2 *Create an adjacency list for the graph in Figure 11.1.*

Making friends

Social networking sites often have an eerie ability to make good suggestions about who you should add to your list of "connections" or "friends." One way they do this is by examining the connections of your connections (or "friends-of-friends"). For example, consider the expanded social network graph in Figure 11.5. Dave currently has only three friends. But his friends have an additional seven friends that an algorithm could suggest to Dave.

Reflection 11.3 *Who are the seven friends-of-friends of Dave in Figure 11.5?*

In graph terminology, the connections of a node are called the node's *neighborhood*, and the size of a node's neighborhood is called its *degree*. In the graph in Figure 11.5, Dave's neighborhood contains Beth, Cathy and Christina, and therefore his degree is three.

Reflection 11.4 *How can you compute the degree of a node from the graph's adjacency matrix? What about from the graph's adjacency list?*

Once we have a network in an adjacency list, writing an algorithm to collect new friend suggestions is relatively easy. The function below iterates over the neighbors of the node for which we would like suggestions and then, for each of these neighbors, iterates over the neighbors' neighbors.

```
1 def friendsOfFriends(network, node):
2     """Find new neighbors-of-neighbors of a node in a network.
3     Parameters:
4         network: a graph represented by a dictionary
5         node:    a node in the network
6     Return value: a list of new neighbors-of-neighbors of node
7     """
8     suggestions = [ ]
9     neighbors = network[node]
10    for neighbor in neighbors:                  # neighbors of node
11        for neighbor2 in network[neighbor]:     # neighbors of neighbors
12            if neighbor2 != node and \
13                neighbor2 not in neighbors and \
14                neighbor2 not in suggestions:
15                suggestions.append(neighbor2)
16    return suggestions
```

On line 9, `network[node]` is the list of nodes to which `node` is connected in the adjacency list named `network`. We assign this list to `neighbors`, and then iterate over it on line 10. On line 11, in the inner `for` loop, we then iterate over the list of each neighbors' neighbors. In the `if` statement, we choose `suggestions` to be a list of unique neighbors-of-neighbors that are not the `node` itself or neighbors of the `node`.

Reflection 11.5 *Look carefully at the three-part if statement in the function above. How does each part contribute to the desired characteristics of `suggestions` listed above?*

Reflection 11.6 *Insert the additional nodes and links from Figure 11.5 (in red) into the dictionary on page 446. Then call the `friendsOfFriends` function with this graph to find new friend suggestions for Dave.*

In the next section, we will design an algorithm to find paths to nodes that are farther away. The ability to compute the distance between nodes will also allow us to better characterize and understand large networks.

Exercises

11.1.1. Besides those presented in this section, describe three more examples of networks.

11.1.2. Draw the networks represented by the following adjacency matrices.

(a)*

	A	B	C	D	E
A	0	1	0	1	0
B	1	0	1	1	1
C	0	1	0	1	0
D	1	1	1	0	1
E	0	1	0	1	0

(b)

	A	B	C	D	E
A	0	1	1	0	0
B	1	0	0	1	1
C	1	0	0	0	1
D	0	1	0	0	1
E	0	1	1	1	0

11.1.3. Draw the networks represented by each of the following adjacency lists.

(a)*
```
graph = {'A': ['C', 'D', 'F'],
         'B': ['C', 'E'],
         'C': ['A', 'B', 'D'],
         'D': ['A', 'C'],
         'E': ['B', 'F'],
         'F': ['A', 'E']}
```

(b)
```
graph = {'A': ['C', 'D'],
         'B': ['C', 'D'],
         'C': ['A', 'B', 'D'],
         'D': ['A', 'B'],
         'E': ['F'],
         'F': ['E']}
```

11.1.4* Consider the following network.

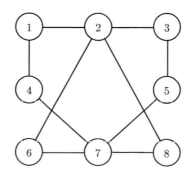

(a) Show how to represent this network in Python as an adjacency matrix.

(b)　Show how to represent this network in Python as an adjacency list.

(c)　What is the neighborhood of each of the nodes in the network?

(d)　What is the degree of each node? Which node(s) have the maximum degree?

11.1.5.　Consider the following network.

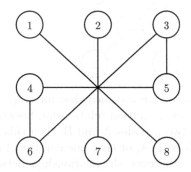

(a)　Show how to represent this network in Python as an adjacency matrix.

(b)　Show how to represent this network in Python as an adjacency list.

(c)　What is the neighborhood of each of the nodes in the network?

(d)　What is the degree of each node? Which node(s) have the maximum degree?

11.1.6.　Are the networks in each of the following pairs the same or different? Why?

(a)*

(b)

(c)

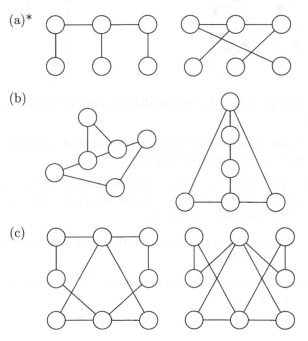

11.1.7*　A graph can be represented in a file by listing one link per line, with each link represented by a pair of nodes. For example, the graph below is represented by the file on the right. Write a function that reads such a file and returns an adjacency list (as a dictionary) for the graph. Notice that, for each line A B in the file, your function will need to insert node B into the list of neighbors of A *and* insert node A into the list of neighbors of B.

```
graph.txt
A B
A C
A D
B E
C D
C E
```

11.1.8. In this chapter, we assumed that all graphs are *undirected*, meaning that each link represents a mutual relationship between two nodes. For example, if there is a link between nodes A and B, then this means that A is friends with B *and* B is friends with A, or that one can travel from city A to city B *and* from city B to city A. However, the relationships between nodes in some networks are not mutual or do not exist in both directions. Such a network is more accurately represented by a *directed graph* (or *digraph*), in which links are directed from one node to another. In a picture, the directions are indicated arrows. For example, in the directed graph below, one can go directly from node A to node B, but not vice versa. However, one can go in both directions between nodes B and E.

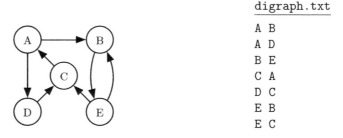

```
digraph.txt
A B
A D
B E
C A
D C
E B
E C
```

(a) Give three examples of networks that are better represented by a directed graph.

(b) How would an adjacency list representation of a directed graph differ from that of an undirected graph?

(c) Write a function that reads a file representing a directed graph (see the example above), and returns an adjacency list (as a dictionary) representing that directed graph.

11.1.9. Write a function that returns the maximum degree in a network represented by an adjacency list (dictionary).

11.1.10. Write a function that returns the average degree in a network represented by an adjacency list (dictionary).

11.2   SHORTEST PATHS

A sequence of links (or equivalently, linked nodes) between two nodes is called a *path*. A path with the minimum number of links is called a *shortest path*. For example, in Figure 11.5, a shortest path from Dave to Lillian starts with Dave, then visits Beth, then Nick, then Lillian. The *distance* between two nodes is the number of links on a shortest path between them. Because three links were crossed along the shortest path from Dave to Lillian, the distance between them is 3.

$$\text{Dave} \xrightarrow{1} \text{Beth} \xrightarrow{2} \text{Nick} \xrightarrow{3} \text{Lillian}$$

Computing the distance between two nodes is a fundamental problem in network analysis. In a transportation network, the distance between a source and destination gives the number of stops along the route. In an ecological network, the distance between two organisms may be a measure of how directly dependent one organism is upon the other. In a social network, the distance between two people is the number of introductions by friends that would be necessary for one person to meet the other.

Reflection 11.7 *Are shortest paths always unique? Is there another shortest path between Dave and Lillian?*

Yes, there is:

$$\text{Dave} \xrightarrow{1} \text{Beth} \xrightarrow{2} \text{Amelia} \xrightarrow{3} \text{Lillian}$$

There may be many shortest paths between two nodes in a network, but in most applications we are concerned with just finding one.

Breadth-first search

Shortest paths can be computed using an algorithm called **breadth-first search** (BFS). A breadth-first search explores outward from a source node, first visiting all nodes with distance one from the source, then all nodes with distance two, etc., until it has visited every reachable node in the network. In other words, the BFS algorithm incrementally pushes its "frontier" of visited nodes outward from the source. When the algorithm finishes, it has computed the distances between the source node and every other node.

For example, suppose we wanted to discover the distance from Beth to every other person in the social network in Figure 11.5, reproduced below.

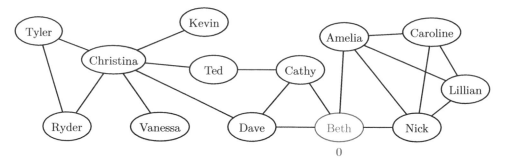

As indicated above, we begin by labeling Beth's node with distance 0, signifying that there are zero links between the node and itself. Then, in the first round of the algorithm, we explore all neighbors of Beth, colored red below.

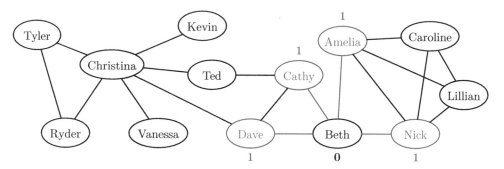

Since these nodes are one hop away from the source, we label them with distance 1. These nodes now comprise the "frontier" being explored by the algorithm. In the next round, we explore all unvisited neighbors of the nodes on this frontier, as shown below.

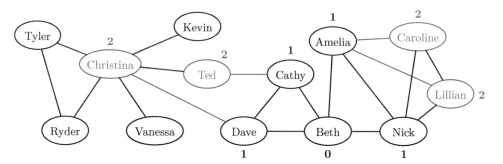

As indicated by the red links, Christina is visited from Dave, Ted is visited from Cathy, and both Caroline and Lillian are visited from Amelia. Notice that Caroline and Lillian could have been visited from Nick as well. The decision is arbitrary, depending, as we will see, on the order in which nodes are considered by the algorithm. Since all four of these nodes are neighbors of a node with distance 1, we label them with distance 2. Finally, in the third round, we visit all unvisited neighbors of the new frontier of nodes, as shown below.

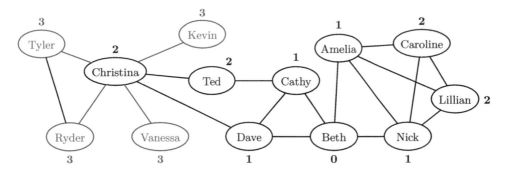

Since these newly visited nodes are all neighbors of a node labeled with distance 2, we label all of them with distance 3. At this point, all of the nodes have been visited, and the final label of each node gives its distance from the source.

Reflection 11.8 *If you also studied the depth-first search algorithm in Section 9.5, compare and contrast that approach with breadth-first search.*

In an algorithm, keeping track of the nodes on the current frontier could get complicated. The trick is to use a *queue*. A queue is a list in which items are always inserted at the end and deleted from the front. The insertion operation is called *enqueue* and the deletion operation is called *dequeue*.

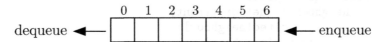

Reflection 11.9 *In Python, if we use a list named* queue *to implement a queue, how do we perform the enqueue and dequeue operations?*

An enqueue operation is simply an append:

```
queue.append(item)   # enqueue an item
```

And then a dequeue can be implemented by "popping" the front item from the list:

```
item = queue.pop(0)   # dequeue an item
```

In the breadth-first search algorithm, we use a queue to remember those nodes on the "frontier" that have been visited, but from which the algorithm has not yet visited new nodes. When we are ready to visit the unvisited neighbors of a node on the frontier, we dequeue that node, and then enqueue the newly visited neighbors so that we can remember to explore outward from them later.

Reflection 11.10 *Why can we not explore outward from these newly visited neighbors right away? Why do they need to be stored in the queue for later?*

We need to wait because there may be nodes further ahead in the queue that have smaller distances from the source. For the algorithm to work correctly, we have to explore outward from these nodes first.

The Python function implements the breadth-first search algorithm.

```
1 import math

2 def bfs(network, source):
3     """Perform a breadth-first search on network, starting from source.

4     Parameters:
5         network: a graph represented by a dictionary
6         source:  the node in network from which to start the BFS

7     Return value: a dictionary with distances from source to all nodes
8     """

9     visited = { }                      # initialize all nodes
10    distance = { }                     #    to be unvisited
11    for node in network:
12        visited[node] = False
13        distance[node] = math.inf
14    visited[source] = True             # mark source visited
15    distance[source] = 0

16    queue = [source]                   # start with the source
17    while queue != [ ]:
18        front = queue.pop(0)           # dequeue front node
19        for neighbor in network[front]:  # visit every neighbor
20            if not visited[neighbor]:
21                visited[neighbor] = True
22                distance[neighbor] = distance[front] + 1
23                queue.append(neighbor)   # enqueue visited node

24    return distance
```

The function maintains two dictionaries: **visited** keeps track of whether each node has been visited and **distance** keeps track of the distance from the **source** to each node. Lines 8–14 initialize the dictionaries. Every node, except the source, is marked as unvisited and assigned an initial distance of infinity (∞), represented by **math.inf**, because we do not yet know which nodes can be reached from the source. The source is marked as visited and assigned distance zero. On line 16, the queue is initialized to contain just the source node. Then, while the queue is not empty, the algorithm repeatedly dequeues the front node (line 18), and explores all neighbors of this node (lines 19–23). If a neighbor has not yet been visited (line 20), it is marked as visited (line 21), assigned a distance that is one greater than the node from which it is being visited (line 22), and then enqueued (line 23). Once the queue is empty, we know that all reachable nodes have been visited, so we return the **distance** dictionary, which now contains the distance to each node.

Reflection 11.11 *Call the* **bfs** *function with the* **graph** *that you created in the previous section to find the distances from Beth to all other nodes.*

Reflection 11.12 *What does it mean if the* `bfs` *function returns a distance of* ∞ *for a node?*

If the final distance is ∞, then the node must not have been visited by the algorithm, which means that there is no path to it from the source.

Reflection 11.13 *If you just want the distance between two particular nodes, named* `source` *and* `dest`*, how can you use the* `bfs` *function to find it?*

The `bfs` function finds the distance from a source node to every node, so you just need to call `bfs` and then pick out the particular distance you are interested in:

```
allDistances = bfs(graph, source)
distance = allDistances[dest]
```

Finding the actual paths

In some applications, just finding the distance between two nodes is not enough; we actually need a path between the nodes. For example, just knowing that you are only three hops away from that potential employer in your social network is not very helpful. You want to know who to ask to introduce you! And in a road network, we want to know the actual directions, not just the distance.

Fortunately, the breadth-first search algorithm is already finding the shortest paths; we just need make some modifications to remember them. Consider how the distance from Beth to Tyler was computed in the previous example. As depicted below, from Beth, we visited Dave; from Dave, we visited Christina; and from Christina, we visited Tyler.

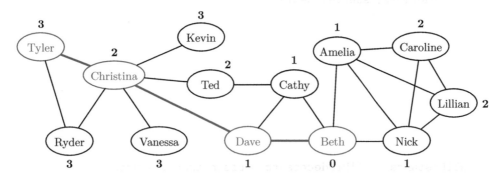

This sequence of nodes is the shortest path on which we based the distance to Tyler. Therefore, all we have to do is remember this order of nodes, as we visit them.

We implement this by adding another dictionary, named `predecessor`, to the `bfs` function. The `predecessor` dictionary remembers the node that comes before each node on the shortest path to it from the source. The dictionary needs to be initially assigned a value of `None` for every node in the `for` loop on lines 11–13. In the `while` loop, after line 22, when each `neighbor` is visited, we set `predecessor[neighbor]` to be `front`.

> **Reflection 11.14** *Modify the* bfs *function to incorporate the* predecessor *dictionary. At the end of the function, return* predecessor *in addition to* distance. *Test the function with your* graph *dictionary by calling it with:*
>
> ```
> distances, predecessors = bfs(graph, 'Beth')
> ```
>
> *What are the predecessors of* 'Beth', 'Dave', 'Christina', *and* 'Tyler'*?*

> **Reflection 11.15** *How can we use the final values in the* predecessor *dictionary to construct a shortest path between the source node and another node?*

To construct the path to any particular node, we need to follow the predecessors *backward* from the destination. As we follow them, we will insert each one into the *front* of a list so they are in the correct order when we are done. To find the shortest path from Beth to Tyler, we start at Tyler.

```
path = ['Tyler']
```

Tyler's predecessor was Christina, so we insert Christina into the front of the list:

```
path = ['Christina', 'Tyler']
```

Christina's predecessor was Dave, so we next insert Dave into the front of the list:

```
path = ['Dave', 'Christina', 'Tyler']
```

Finally, Dave's predecessor was Beth:

```
path = ['Beth', 'Dave', 'Christina', 'Tyler']
```

Since Beth was the source, we stop. The following function implements this algorithm.

```
def path(network, source, dest):
    """Find a shortest path in network from source to dest.

    Parameters:
        network: a graph represented by a dictionary
        source:  the source node in network
        dest:    the destination node in network

    Return value: a list containing a path from source to dest
    """

    allDistances, allPredecessors = bfs(network, source)

    path = [ ]
    current = dest
    while current != source:
        path.insert(0, current)
        current = allPredecessors[current]
    path.insert(0, source)

    return path
```

Starting with **current = dest**, in each iteration, the **while** loop moves **current** one step closer to the source by assigning it to its predecessor. As this is happening, each value of `current` is inserted into the front of `path`. When `current` reaches the `source`, the loop ends and we insert the `source` as the first node in the `path`.

Reflection 11.16 *Find the shortest path between Beth and Tyler with* `print(path(graph, 'Beth', 'Tyler'))`.

In the next section, we will use information about shortest paths to investigate a special kind of network called a *small-world* network.

Exercises

11.2.1* List the order in which nodes are visited by `bfs` when it is called to find the distance from Ted to every node in the graph in Figure 11.5. (There is more than one correct answer.)

11.2.2. List the order in which nodes are visited by `bfs` when it is called to find the distance between Caroline and every node in the graph in Figure 11.5. (There is more than one correct answer.)

11.2.3. By modifying one line, the `visited` dictionary can be completely removed from the `bfs` function. Show how.

11.2.4. Write a function that uses `bfs` to return the distance in a graph between two particular nodes. The function should take three parameters: the graph, the source node, and the destination node.

11.2.5. We say that a graph is *connected* if there is a path between any pair of nodes. Show how to modify `bfs` so that it returns a Boolean value indicating whether a graph is connected.

11.2.6. A depth-first search algorithm (see Section 9.5) can also be used to determine whether a graph is connected. Recall that a depth-first search recursively searches as far from the source as it can, and then backtracks when it reaches a dead end. Writing a depth-first search algorithm for a graph is actually much easier than writing the one in Section 9.5 because there are fewer base cases to deal with.

(a)* Write a function

```
dfs(network, source, visited)
```

that performs a depth-first search on the given `network`, starting from the given `source` node. The third parameter, `visited`, is a list of nodes that have been visited by the depth-first search. The initial list argument passed in for `visited` should be empty, but when the function returns, `visited` should contain all of the visited nodes. In other words, you should call the function initially like this:

```
visited = []
dfs(network, source, visited)
```

(b) Write another function

```
connected(network)
```

that calls your `dfs` function to determine whether `network` is connected. (The source node can be any node in the network.)

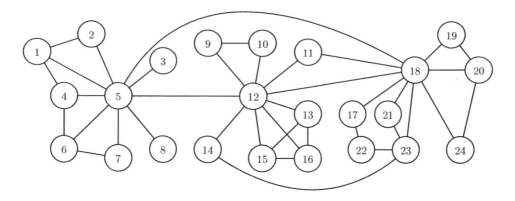

Figure 11.6 A very small small-world network.

11.3 IT'S A SMALL WORLD...

In a famous 1967 experiment, sociologist Stanley Milgram asked several individuals in the midwestern United States to forward a postcard to a particular person in Boston, Massachusetts. If they did not know this person on a first-name basis, they were asked instead to forward it to someone they thought might have a better chance of knowing the person. Each intermediate person was asked to follow the same instructions. Of the postcards that made it to the destination (many were simply not forwarded), the average number of hops was about six.

Small world networks

From this experiment later came the suggestion that there are only "six degrees of separation" between any two people on Earth, and that the human race must constitute a ***small-world network***. In the late 1990s, using computers, researchers began to discover that networks representing a wide range of unrelated phenomena, from social networks to neural networks to the Internet, all exhibit the same small-world property: for most nodes in the network, there is a very short path connecting them. Put another way, in a small-world network, the average distance between any two nodes is small.

Intuitively, it seems as though a small-world network must have a lot of links to facilitate so many short paths. However, it has been shown that small-world networks can actually be quite ***sparse***, meaning that the number of links is quite small relative to the number possible. The keys to a small-world network are a high degree of *clustering* and a few long-range shortcuts that facilitate short paths between clusters. A cluster is a set of nodes that are highly connected among themselves. In your social network, you probably participate in several clusters: family, friends at school, friends at home, co-workers, teammates, etc. Many of the members of each of these clusters are probably also connected to one another, but members of different clusters might be far apart if you did not act as a shortcut link between them.

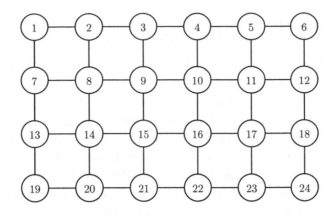

Figure 11.7 A grid network.

Although it is too small to really be called a small-world network, the network in Figure 11.6 illustrates these ideas. The graph contains three clusters of nodes, centered around nodes 5, 12 and 18, that are connected by a few shortcut links (e.g., the links between nodes 5 and 18 and between nodes 14 and 23). These two characteristics together give an average distance between nodes of about 2.42. On the other hand, the highly structured grid network in Figure 11.7 has an average node distance of about 3.33. Both of these graphs have 24 nodes and 38 links, so they are both sparse relative to their $(24 \cdot 23)/2 = 276$ maximum possible links.

Clustering coefficients

The extent to which the neighborhood of a node is clustered is measured by its *local clustering coefficient*. The local clustering coefficient of a node is the number of links between its neighbors, divided by the maximum number of possible links between its neighbors. For example, consider the cluster on the left below surrounding the blue node in the center.

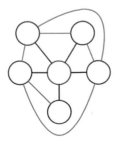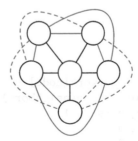

The blue node has five neighbors, with six links between them (in red). Notice that each of these links, together with two black links, forms a closed cycle, called a *triangle*. So we can also think about the local clustering coefficient as counting these triangles. As shown on the right, there are four dashed links between neighbors of the blue node (i.e., four additional triangles) that are not present on the left, for a total of ten possible links altogether. So the local clustering coefficient of the blue node is 6/10 = 0.6. (The clustering coefficient will always be between 0 and 1.)

Reflection 11.17 *In general, if a node has k neighbors, how many possible links are there between pairs of these neighbors?*

Each of the k neighbors could be connected to $k - 1$ other neighbors, for a total of $k(k - 1)$ links. However, this counts each link twice, so the total number of unique links is actually $k(k - 1)/2$. Therefore, the local clustering coefficient of a node with k neighbors is the number of pairs of neighbors that are connected to each other, divided by $k(k - 1)/2$. The clustering coefficient for a network is the average local clustering coefficient of its nodes. The highly structured grid or mesh graph in Figure 11.7 does not have any triangles at all, so its clustering coefficient is 0. On the other hand, the graph in Figure 11.6 has a clustering coefficient of about 0.59.

Reflection 11.18 *If you had a small local clustering coefficient in your social network (i.e., if your friends are not friends with each other), what implications might this have?*

It has been suggested that situations like this breed instability. Imagine that, instead of a social network, we are talking about a network of nations and links represent the existence of diplomatic relations. A nation with diplomatic relations with many other nations that are enemies of each other is likely in a stressful situation. It might be helpful to detect such situations in advance to curtail potential conflicts.

To compute the local clustering coefficient for a node, we iterate over each of the node's neighbors and count the number of links between it and the other neighbors of the node. Then we divide this number by the maximum possible number of links between the node's neighbors. This is accomplished by the following function.

```python
def clusteringCoefficient_Draft(network, node):
    """Compute the local clustering coefficient for a node.

    Parameters:
        network: a graph represented by a dictionary
        node:    a node in the network

    Return value: the local clustering coefficient of node
    """

    neighbors = network[node]
    numNeighbors = len(neighbors)
    if numNeighbors <= 1:
        return 0
    numLinks = 0
    for neighbor1 in neighbors:
        for neighbor2 in neighbors:
            if neighbor1 != neighbor2 and neighbor1 in network[neighbor2]:
                numLinks = numLinks + 1
    return numLinks / (numNeighbors * (numNeighbors - 1))
```

This function is relatively straightforward. The nested `for` loops iterate over every possible pair of neighbors, and the `if` statement checks for a link between unique neighbors. However, this process effectively counts every link twice, so at the end we divide by `numNeighbors * (numNeighbors - 1)` (i.e., $k(k-1)$), which is twice what we discussed previously.

Reflection 11.19 *Do you see why the function counts every link twice? How can we fix this?*

The function effectively counts every link twice because it checks whether each neighbor is in every other neighbor's list of adjacent nodes. Therefore, for any two connected neighbors, call them A and B, we are counting the link once when we see A in the list of adjacent nodes of B and again when we see B in the list of adjacent nodes of A.

To count each link just once, we can use the following trick. In the list of `neighbors`, we first check whether the node at index 0 is connected to nodes at indices $1, 2, \ldots, k-1$. Then, to prevent counting a link twice, we never want to check whether any node is connected to node 0 again. So we next check whether node 1 is connected to nodes $2, 3, \ldots, k-1$. Now, to prevent double counting, we never want to check whether any node is connected to nodes 0 or 1. So we next check whether node 2 is connected to nodes $3, 4, \ldots, k-1$. Do you see the pattern? In general, we only want to check whether node i is connected to nodes $i+1, i+2, \ldots, k-1$. (This is the same trick you may have seen in Exercise 7.5.6.) This is implemented in the following improved version of the function, with changes highlighted.

```python
def clusteringCoefficient(network, node):
    """ (docstring omitted) """

    neighbors = network[node]
    numNeighbors = len(neighbors)
    if numNeighbors <= 1:
        return 0
    numLinks = 0
    for index1 in range(len(neighbors) - 1):
        for index2 in range(index1 + 1, len(neighbors)):
            neighbor1 = neighbors[index1]
            neighbor2 = neighbors[index2]
            if neighbor1 != neighbor2 and neighbor1 in network[neighbor2]:
                numLinks = numLinks + 1
    return numLinks / (numNeighbors * (numNeighbors - 1) / 2)
```

Once we have this function, to compute the clustering coefficient for the network, we just have to call it for every node, and compute the average. We leave this, and writing a function to compute the average distance, as exercises.

Scale-free networks

In addition to having short paths and high clustering, researchers soon discovered that most small-world networks also contain a few highly connected (i.e., high degree)

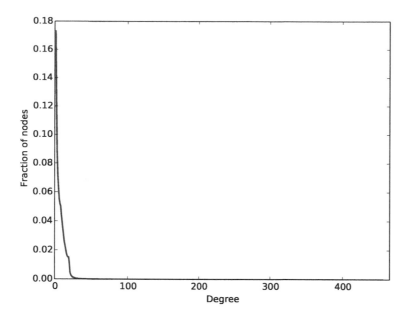

Figure 11.8 The degree distribution of 875,713 nodes in the web network.

nodes called *hubs* that facilitate even shorter paths. In Figure 11.6, nodes 5, 12, and 18 are hubs because their degrees are large relative to the other nodes.

❘ **Reflection 11.20** *How do connected hubs facilitate short paths?*

The existence of hubs in a large network can be seen by plotting, for each degree in the network, the fraction of the nodes that have that degree. This is called the *degree distribution* of the network. The degree distribution for a network with a few hubs will show the vast majority of nodes having relatively small degree and just a few nodes having very large degrees. For example, Figure 11.8 shows such a plot for a small portion of the (world wide) web. In the web graph, each node represents a web page and a directed link from one node to another represents a hyperlink from the first page to the second page.[1] In this network, 99% of the nodes have degree at most 25, while just a few have degrees that are much higher. (In fact, 98% of the nodes have degrees at most 20 and 90% have degrees at most 15.) These few hubs with high degree enable a small average distance and a clustering coefficient of about 0.37.

❘ **Reflection 11.21** *In the web network from Figure 11.8, the degree of a node is the number of hyperlinks from that page. How do you think the degree distribution might change if we instead counted the number of hyperlinks to each page?*

Networks with this characteristic shape to their degree distributions are called *scale-free networks*. The name comes from the observation that the fraction of nodes

---

[1] Web network data obtained from `http://snap.stanford.edu/data/web-Google.html`

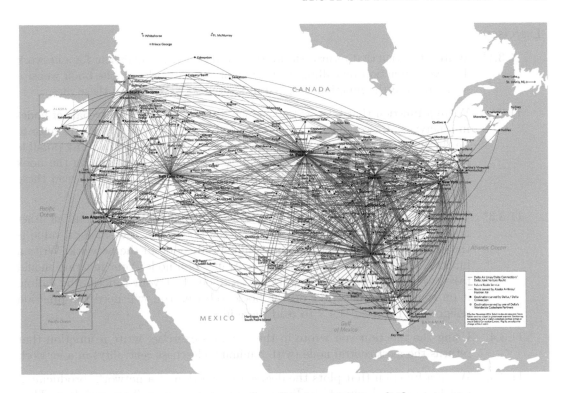

Figure 11.9 The North American routes of Delta Airlines. [12]

with degree d is roughly $(1/d)^a$, for some small value of a. Such functions are called "scale-free" because their plots have the same shape regardless of the scale at which you view them. A scale-free degree distribution is very different from the normal distribution that seems to describe most natural phenomena, which is why this discovery was so interesting.

Reflection 11.22 *How could recognizing that a network is scale-free and then identifying the hubs have practical importance?*

The presence of hubs in a network is a double-edged sword. On the one hand, hubs enable efficient communication and transportation. For this reason, the Internet is structured in this way, as are airline networks (see Figure 11.9). Also, because so many of the nodes in a scale-free network are relatively unimportant, scale-free networks tend to be very robust when subjected to random attacks or damage. Some have speculated that, because some natural networks are scale-free, they may represent an evolutionary advantage. On the other hand, because the few hubs are so important, a directed attack on a hub can cause the network to fail. (Have you ever noticed the havoc that ensues when an airline hub is closed due to weather?) A directed attack on a hub can also be advantageous if we *want* the network to fail. For example, if we suspect that the network through which an epidemic is traveling is scale-free, we may have a better chance of stopping it if we vaccinate the hubs.

Exercises

11.3.1*   Write a function that returns the average local clustering coefficient for a network. Test your function by calling it on some of the networks on the book website. You will need the function assigned in Exercise 11.1.7 to read these files.

11.3.2.   Write a function that returns the average distance between every pair of nodes in a network. If two nodes are not connected by a path, assign their distance to be the number of nodes in the network (since this is longer than any possible path). Test your function by calling it on some of the networks on the book website. You will need the function assigned in Exercise 11.1.7 to read these files.

11.3.3*   The *closeness centrality* of a node is the total distance between it and all other nodes in the network. By this measure, the node with the smallest value is the most central (and perhaps most influential) node in the network. Write a function that computes the closeness centrality of a node. Your function should take two parameters: the network and a node. Test your function by calling it on some of the networks on the book website. You will need the function assigned in Exercise 11.1.7 to read these files.

11.3.4.   Using the function you wrote in the previous exercise, write a function that returns the most central node (with minimum closeness centrality) in a network.

11.3.5.   Write a function that plots the degree distribution of a network, producing a plot like that in Figure 11.8. Test your function on a small network first. Then call your function on the large Facebook network (with 4,039 nodes and 88,234 links) that is available on the book website. (You will need the function assigned in Exercise 11.1.7 to read these files.) Is the network scale-free?

11.4   RANDOM GRAPHS

Since small-world and scale-free networks seem to be so common, it is natural to ask whether such networks just happen randomly. To answer this question, we can compare the characteristics of these networks to a class of randomly generated graphs. In particular, we will look at the class of *uniform random graphs*, which are created by adding each possible edge with some probability p.

Creating a uniform random graph is straightforward. We first create an adjacency list with the desired number of nodes, then iterate over all possible pairs of nodes. For each pair of nodes, we link them with probability p, as shown below.

```
import random

def randomGraph(n, p):
    """Return a uniform random graph with n vertices.

    Parameters:
        n: the number of nodes
        p: the probability that two nodes are connected

    Return value: a random graph
    """
```

```
graph = { }
for node in range(n):              # label nodes 0, 1, ..., n-1
    graph[node] = [ ]              # graph has n nodes, 0 links

for node1 in range(n - 1):
    for node2 in range(node1 + 1, n):
        if random.random() < p:
            graph[node1].append(node2)   # add edge between
            graph[node2].append(node1)   #    node1 and node2
return graph
```

Because we will get a different random graph every time we call this function, any characteristics that we want to measure will have to be averages over many random graphs with the same values of n and p. To illustrate, let's compute the average distance, clustering coefficient, and degree distribution for uniform random graphs with the same number of nodes and links as the graphs in Figures 11.6 and 11.7. Recall that those graphs had 24 nodes and 38 links.

Reflection 11.23 *What parameters should we use to create a uniform random graph with 24 nodes and 38 links?*

We cannot specify the number of links specifically in a uniform random graph, but we can set the probability so that we are likely to get a particular number, on average, over many trials. In particular, we want 38 out of a possible $(24 \cdot 23)/2$ links, so we set

$$p = \frac{38}{(24 \cdot 23)/2} = \frac{38}{276} \approx 0.14.$$

Averaging over 20,000 uniform random graphs, each generated by calling `randomGraph(24, 0.14)`, we find that the average distance between nodes is about 4.32 and the average clustering coefficient is about 0.12. The table below compares these results to what we computed previously for the other two graphs.

Graph	Average distance	Clustering coefficient
Figure 11.6 (clusters)	2.42	0.59
Figure 11.7 (grid)	3.33	0
Uniform random	4.32	0.12

The random graph with the same number of nodes and edges has a slightly longer average distance and a markedly smaller clustering coefficient than the graph in Figure 11.6 with the three clusters. Because these graphs are so small, these numbers alone, while suggestive, are not very strong evidence that random graphs do not have the small-world or scale-free properties. So let's also look at the average degree distribution of the random graphs, shown in Figure 11.10. The shape of the degree distribution is quite different from that of a scale-free network, and is much closer to a normal distribution. Because the probability of adding an edge was relatively low, the average degree was only about 3 and there were a number of nodes with degree

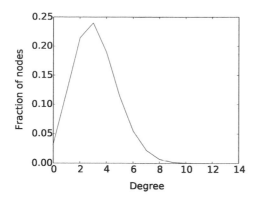
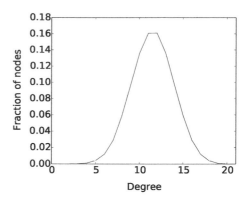

Figure 11.10 The degree distribution of random graphs with $n = 24$ and $p = 38/276$.

Figure 11.11 The degree distribution of random graphs with $n = 24$ and $p = 1/2$.

0, causing the plot to "run into" the y-axis. If we perform the same experiment with $p = 0.5$, as shown in Figure 11.11, we get a much clearer bell curve. These distributions show that random graphs do not have hubs; instead, the nodes all tend to have about the same degree. So there is definitely something non-random happening to generate scale-free networks.

Reflection 11.24 *What kind of process do you think might create a scale-free network with a few high-degree nodes?*

The presumed process at play has been dubbed *preferential attachment* or, colloquially the "rich get richer" phenomenon. The idea is relatively intuitive: popular people, destinations, and web pages tend to get more popular over time as word of them moves through the network.

Exercises

11.4.1* Show how to call `randomGraph` to create a uniform random graph with 30 nodes and 50 links, on average.

11.4.2* Exercise 11.3.1 asked you to write a function that returns the clustering coefficient for a graph. Use this function to write another function

    avgCCRandom(n, p, trials)

that returns the average clustering coefficient, over the given number of trials, of random graphs with the given values of n and p.

11.4.3. Exercise 11.3.2 asked you to write a function that returns the average distance between any two nodes in a graph. Use this function to write another function

    avgDistanceRandom(n, p, trials)

that returns the average of this value, over the given number of trials, for random graphs with the given values of n and p.

11.4.4. Exercise 11.3.5 asked you to write a function to plot the degree distribution of a graph and then call the function on the large Facebook network on the book website. This network has 4,039 nodes and 88,234 links. To compare the degree distribution of this network to a random graph of the same size, write a function

    `degreeDistributionRandom(n, p, trials)`

that plots the average degree distribution, over the given number of trials, of random graphs with the given values of n and p. Then use this function to plot the degree distribution of random graphs with 4,039 nodes and an average of 88,234 links. What do you notice?

11.4.5. We say that a graph is *connected* if there is a path between any pair of nodes. Random graphs that are generated with a low probability p are unlikely to be connected, while random graphs generated with a high probability p are very likely to be connected. But for what value of p does this transition between disconnected and connected graphs occur?

To determine whether a graph is connected, we can use either a breadth-first search (as in Exercise 11.2.5) or a depth-first search (as in Exercise 11.2.6). In either case, we start from any node in the network, and try to visit all of the other nodes. If the search is successful, then the graph must be connected. Otherwise, it must not be connected.

(a) Write a function

    `connectedRandom(n, minp, maxp, stepp, trials)`

that plots the fraction of random graphs with n nodes that are connected for values of p ranging from `minp` to `maxp`, in increments of `stepp`. To compute the fraction that are connected for each value of p, generate `trials` random graphs and count how many of those are connected using your `connected` function from either Exercise 11.2.5 or Exercise 11.2.6.

(b) For $n = 24$, what do you find? For what value of p is there a 50% chance that the graph will be connected? Does the transition from disconnected graphs to connected graphs happen gradually or is change abrupt?

11.5   SUMMARY AND FURTHER DISCOVERY

In this chapter, we took a peek at one of the more exciting interdisciplinary areas in which computer scientists have become engaged. Networks are all around us, some obvious and some not so obvious. But they can all be described using the language of *graphs*. The shortest path and distance between any two nodes in a graph can be found with the *breadth-first search* algorithm. Graphs in which the distance between any two nodes is relatively short and the *clustering coefficient* is relatively high are called *small-world networks*. Networks that are also characterized by a few high-degree hubs are called *scale-free* networks. Scientists have discovered over the last two decades that virtually all large-scale natural and human-made networks are scale-free. Knowing this about a network can give a lot of information about how the network works and about its vulnerabilities.

Notes for further discovery

This chapter's epigraph is from a 1967 article by Stanley Milgram titled, *The Small-World Problem* [40]. Dr. Milgram was an influential American social psychologist. Besides his small world experiment, he is best known for experiments in which he demonstrated that ordinary people are capable of disregarding their consciences when instructed to do so by those in authority.

There are several excellent books for a general audience about the emerging field of network science. Three of these are *Six Degrees* by Duncan Watts [66], *Sync* by Steven Strogatz [63], and *Linked* by Albert-László Barabási [3]. *Think Complexity* by Allen Downey [13] introduces slightly more advanced material on implementing algorithms on graphs, small-world networks, and scale-free networks in Python.

*11.6 PROJECTS

This section is available on the book website.

CHAPTER 12

Object-oriented Design

> What we desire from an abstraction is a mechanism which permits the expression of relevant details and the suppression of irrelevant details. In the case of programming, the use which may be made of an abstraction is relevant; the way in which the abstraction is implemented is irrelevant.
>
> Barbara Liskov
> *Programming with Abstract Data Types (1974)*

O UR problem solving strategy to this point has focused on the decomposition of a problem into smaller subproblems, each viewed as a functional abstraction. We design algorithms, and then write functions, for these subproblems, and combine them to solve our overall problem.

An alternative design strategy, called object-oriented design, instead focuses on the data, or objects, in a problem. To solve a problem, we identify the objects involved, design *abstract data types* for them, and then implement them as *classes*.

Recall that an ADT is defined by the information it can store, called *attributes*, and a set of *operations* that can access that information. We have used a variety of ADTs, such as turtles, strings, lists, and dictionaries, each implemented as a class in Python. A class serves as a blueprint for a category of data. An *object* is a particular instance of a class. In Section 2.1, we described this difference by analogy to a species and the organisms that belong to that species. The species description is like a class; it describes a category of organisms but is not an organism itself. The individual organisms belonging to a species are like objects from the same class.

The attributes of a class are assigned to a set of variables called *instance variables*. The operations of a class are special functions called *methods*. Instance variables remain hidden to a programmer using the class, and are only accessed or modified indirectly through methods. For example, the `Turtle` class contains several hidden instance variables that store each `Turtle` object's position, color, heading, and whether its tail is up or down. The `Turtle` class also defines several familiar methods, such as `forward/backward`, `left/right`, `speed`, and `up/down` that we can call to indirectly interact with these instance variables. When we create the two new `Turtle` objects named `george` and `diego` below, although they belong to the same class, they maintain independent identities because each instance (object) has its own copies of the `Turtle` instance variables.

```
george = turtle.Turtle()
diego = turtle.Turtle()
```

In this chapter, we will use object-oriented design to solve problems with new custom classes that behave the same way the built-in classes do. We will start by designing an object-oriented simulation of an epidemic virus. Then we will implement a more utilitarian class to illustrate all of the ways in which a class can be made to behave like the standard classes that you have been using all along. Then we will explore a more advanced simulation of flocking birds and the design of two new ADTs.

12.1 SIMULATING AN EPIDEMIC

Simulations are widely used to facilitate planning for large-scale epidemics, or a pandemic like COVID-19. These simulations can generally take one of two forms: a population model or an agent-based model. A population model treats a population as a group of identical individuals and is only concerned with the populations' sizes. The SIR model that you may have seen in Section 4.4 is the basis of most population models for viral epidemics like COVID-19. In contrast, an **agent-based simulation** contains a set of independent individuals (the agents) that interact with each other in some way over time. Schelling's model of racial segregation from Project 8.1 is a simple example of an agent-based simulation.

In this section, we will write an agent-based simulation of a viral epidemic using an object-oriented design. The main objects in the simulation are the agents (in our case, people) and a two-dimensional "world" in which the agents move. The world will also act as the glue that binds the agents together and drives the simulation by repeating the following simple algorithm for some length of time:

Algorithm EPIDEMIC SIMULATION STEP
1   repeat for each *person* in the world:
2   move the *person* one step forward
3   if the *person* is infected, then:
4   probabilistically infect every non-infected person within some distance

Object design

The first step in writing this simulation is to design the two objects as abstract data types, analogous to how we start a functional design by writing algorithms in pseudocode. When we design an ADT or write an algorithm, we are free to focus on the problem at hand, unencumbered by the requirements of the programming language. After this design phase, we will implement each of the ADTs as a class.

Reflection 12.1 *Based on the simulation algorithm above, what attributes and operations does a person object need?*

You can probably think of many possible attributes for a person in this simulation, but we will keep it simple at first. Every **Person** object will at least need a world to live in, a position and heading as they move in the world, and a variable that tracks whether they are infected with the virus.

Instance Variable	Description
world	the world inhabited by the person
position, heading	the person's current position and heading in the **world**
infected	whether the person is currently infected (Boolean)

Based on the simulation algorithm, every person will need the ability to move around (randomly) in the world and become infected if they come too close to an infected person. We will also need to be able to access attributes of people, such as their position, whether they are infected, and whether they are too close to another infected person. The following six operations will handle these basic needs.

Method	Arguments	Description
create	world, infected	create a new person with random **position** and **heading** in **world** and infect if **infected** is true
get position	—	return the person's **position** as a tuple
is infected	—	return whether the person is **infected**
within	person, distance	return true if a given **person** is within **distance** of my **position**, false otherwise
infect	infection probability	set **infected** to true with the given probability
step	—	take one step in the simulation

You may notice that these methods fall into three categories:

1. A *constructor* creates a new instance of an ADT.

2. An *accessor* reads the attributes of an instance and returns information derived from them, but does not modify the attributes' values.

3. A *mutator* modifies the values of the attributes of an instance.

| **Reflection 12.2** *To which category does each of the six* Person *methods belong?*

The first operation we defined is the constructor because it creates a new **Person** instance. The next three operations are accessors because they give information derived from the attributes of an instance without modifying it. Finally, **infect** and **step** are mutators because they may change the attributes of an instance.

Before we implement the **Person** class, let's also lay out the structure of the **World** ADT. The world will need dimentions, a list of the people in the world, the probability that a person becomes infected if they come into contact with an infected person, and the number of people infected. These are maintained in the following five attributes.

Instance Variable	Description
width, height	the width and height of the world
infection probability	the probability that a person becomes infected if they come into contact with an infected person
people	a list of people in the world
number infected	the number of infected people

In addition, based on the simulation algorithm, we know that the **World** will need to able to infect people who come too close to an already-infected person, and run one step of the main simulation loop, which we call **step all**. We will also need some accessor methods to get attributes of the world when needed.

Method	Arguments	Description
create	**width, height, infection probability, population size**	create a new world with the given dimensions and **infection probability**, and populate it with one infected person and **population size** – 1 uninfected people
get width, get height	—	return the **width** and **height**
get number infected	—	return **number infected**
infect neighbors	person	infect neighbors of an infected **person** with probability = **infection probability**
step all	—	move all inhabitants one step and spread the infection

Person class

Let's begin our implementation by designing a class that implements a simplified version of the **Person** ADT, one that is not tied to any **World**. This will allow us to experiment and get a better feel for how classes work, before we dive into the complete simulation.

The constructor

The definition of a new class begins with the keyword `class` followed by the name of the class and, of course, a colon. The class' methods are indented below.

The constructor of a class is named `__init__` (with two underscore characters at both the beginning and the end). The beginning of the `SimplePerson` class, with its constructor, is shown below.

```python
class SimplePerson:
    """A simple person class."""

    _STEP = 5    # class variable (constant)

    def __init__(self, infected):
        """Create a new, possibly infected, person with random heading."""

        self._infected = infected
        self._turtle = turtle.Turtle()
        self._turtle.setheading(random.randrange(360))

        if self._infected:
            self._turtle.color('red')
        else:
            self._turtle.color('blue')
```

The constructor is *implicitly* called when we create a new object by calling the function bearing the name of the class. For example, when we created the two `Turtle` objects above, we implicitly invoked the `Turtle` constructor twice. To invoke the constructor of the `SimplePerson` class to create a new, uninfected `SimplePerson` object, we could call

```python
someone = SimplePerson(False)
```

The first parameter of the `__init__` method, named `self`, is an *implicit* reference to the object on which the method is being called. In the assignment statement above, `self` is assigned to the new object being created. This same object is returned by the constructor and assigned to `someone`. We never *explicitly* pass anything in for `self`. The additional constructor parameter `infected` is a Boolean value used to initialize the object's infection status.

The `SimplePerson` class has two instance variables named `self._infected` and `self._turtle`. The former is a Boolean value indicating whether the person is currently infected with the virus and the latter is a visual representation of the person in the simulation. We will also use `self._turtle` to implicitly store each person's position and heading (since it will do that anyway).

Every instance variable name is preceded by `self` to signify that it belongs to the particular instance (object) of the class assigned to `self`. For example, since `self` is assigned to the new object created by the constructor, the assignment statement

```python
someone = SimplePerson(False)
```

is creating a new `SimplePerson` object named `someone` and assigning values to `someone._infected` and `someone._turtle`.

The underscore (`_`) character before each instance variable name is a Python convention that indicates that the instance variables should be *private*, i.e., never accessed from outside the class.[1] We want instance variables to be private so they can only be changed by methods of the class, and not in unintended ways outside the class. For example, we do not want a simulation using our class to incorrectly move a person's turtle or change their infection status in ways that might mess up the simulation. This idea, which is a key characteristic of object-oriented programming, is called ***encapsulation***. Encapsulation also refers more generally to the practice of bundling instance variables and methods together in a class.

The scope of an instance variable is the *entire object*. This means that we can access and change the value of any instance variable in any method of the class. In contrast, variable names defined inside a method that are not preceded by `self`, such as the `infected` parameter in the constructor, are just normal local variables with scope limited to the method.

Just before the constructor above is a ***class variable*** named `_STEP`, which will act as a constant move distance for all people turtles. A class variable is shared by all objects in a class. Since `_STEP` is a constant, it doesn't make sense to have a separate copy for every object; instead, all objects will share this one copy.

Accessor methods

Now let's add the three accessor methods to the `SimplePerson` class.

```
def getPosition(self):
    """Return the person's position as a tuple.

    Parameter:
        self: the Person object

    Return value: position of self as a tuple
    """

    return self._turtle.position()

def isInfected(self):
    """Return whether the person is infected.

    Parameter:
        self: the Person object

    Return value: Boolean indicating whether self is infected
    """

    return self._infected
```

---

[1] Python does not actually enforce this, but some other languages do.

```
    def within(self, otherPerson, distance):
        """Return True if otherPerson is within distance
           of my position, False otherwise.

        Parameters:
            self:       the Person object
            otherPerson: another Person object
            distance:   a number

        Return value: Boolean indicating whether otherPerson's position
                      is within distance of self's position
        """

        myPosition = self.getPosition()
        otherPosition = otherPerson.getPosition()
        diffX = myPosition[0] - otherPosition[0]
        diffY = myPosition[1] - otherPosition[1]
        return math.sqrt(diffX ** 2 + diffY ** 2) <= distance
```

The `getPosition` method uses the `position` method of `self._turtle` to return a tuple containing the current position. The only parameter to this method is `self`. If we called `someone.getPosition()`, the object `someone` is implicitly passed in for the parameter `self`, even though it is not passed in the parentheses following the name of the method. Similarly, the `isInfected` method simply returns the value of `self._infected`. The `within` method computes the distance between `self` and another `SimplePerson` object and returns a Boolean value indicating whether they are within the given `distance` of each other. Notice that the method calls the `getPosition` method of both `self` and `otherPerson` to get tuples of their positions. When we call a method of the class from within another method, we still need to preface the name of the method with `self` or another object, just as we do with instance variables.

Mutator methods

To round out the class, we will add the following two mutator methods.

```
    def infect(self, infectionProbability):
        """Infect self with the given probability.

        Parameters:
            self:                  the Person object
            infectionProbability: probability of infection

        Return value: Boolean indicating whether infection happened
        """

        if not self._infected and random.random() < infectionProbability:
            self._infected = True
            self._turtle.color('red')
            return True

        return False
```

```
    def step(self):
        """Advance self one step in the simulation.

        Parameter:
            self: the Person object

        Return value: None
        """

        if random.random() < 0.1:
            self._turtle.left(random.randrange(-90, 90))
        self._turtle.forward(self._STEP)
```

The `infect` method infects the person, if they are not already infected, with the given probability. If the person is infected, the method returns `True` to signify "success." If the object is not infected, it returns `False`. In the `step` method, we simulate a person's movement by normally (90% of the time) moving forward along their current heading, and occasionally (10% of the time) turning to the left or right by some random angle.

When we write classes, we will store each one in its own file. By convention, the names of our classes will be capitalized, but the filenames will be in lowercase.

Reflection 12.3 *Create a new file named* `simpleperson.py` *containing the* `SimplePerson` *class. (You will also need to* `import` *some modules at the top.)*

After saving the `SimplePerson` class in `simpleperson.py`, we can create a new, uninfected `SimplePerson` object with

```
>>> import simpleperson
>>> someone = simpleperson.SimplePerson(False)
```

or

```
>>> from simpleperson import *
>>> someone = SimplePerson(False)
```

Reflection 12.4 *Create a new* `SimplePerson` *object in a Python shell with one of the options above. Or you can write a short program in the same directory as* `simpleperson.py` *if you have trouble importing from the shell. What happens when create the object?*

When you create a new `SimplePerson` object, a turtle graphics window should open and display a blue turtle facing in a random direction in the center of the screen. This is `someone._turtle`, the `Turtle` object inside the `someone` object. Now call the `getPosition` method, followed by a few calls to `step`.

```
>>> someone.getPosition()
(0.00,0.00)
>>> someone.step()
>>> someone.step()
>>> someone.getPosition()
(9.21,-3.91)  # your result will differ
```

Each time you call **step**, you are invoking the **step** method on the **SimplePerson** object named **someone**, which moves **someone**'s turtle a little. You can see how this has changed **someone**'s **_turtle** instance variable when you call **getPosition** again. Since **step** moves the turtle so little, try calling it in a loop:

```
>>> for count in range(50):
        someone.step()
```

Initially, **someone** is not infected with the virus (because we passed **False** into the constructor), which you can verify by calling the **isInfected** method.

```
>>> someone.isInfected()
False
```

Now try infecting **someone** with probability 0.5. You may have to try a few times until it is successful. Then verify that it worked by calling **isInfected** again.

```
>>> someone.infect(0.5)
False
>>> someone.infect(0.5)
True
>>> someone.isInfected()
True
```

After **someone** becomes infected, you should notice that the turtle turns red. Next create another, uninfected **SimplePerson** object and move them a bit.

```
>>> someoneElse = SimplePerson(False)
>>> someoneElse.isInfected()
False
>>> for count in range(50):
        someoneElse.step()
```

If we want to know if this new person is within some distance of the infected **someone**, we can call the **within** method.

```
>>> someoneElse.within(someone, 10)
False
>>> someoneElse.within(someone, 500)
True
```

When you call the **within** method in this way, **someoneElse** is passed in for **self** and **someone** is passed in for **otherPerson**. Chances are, they are not very close to each other but if you keep trying larger distances, the method should eventually return True.

Reflection 12.5 *Does calling* someone.within(someoneElse, 500) *do the same thing? In this case, which object is assigned to* self *and which is assigned to* otherPerson*?*

Augmenting the Person class

Now that you are a more comfortable with the mechanics of classes, let's flesh out the full **Person** class that we will use in our simulation. The **Person** class will be identical to the **SimplePerson** class, except for edits and additions to two methods. The first changes are to the constructor, highlighted below.

```
class Person:
    """A person in an epidemic simulation."""

    _STEP = 5   # class variable (constant)

    def __init__(self, myWorld, infected):
        """Create a person with random position/heading in myWorld."""

        self._world = myWorld
        self._infected = infected

        self._turtle = turtle.RawTurtle(self._world._screen)
        self._turtle.speed(0)
        self._turtle.up()
        self._turtle.resizemode('user')
        self._turtle.shape('circle')
        self._turtle.shapesize(0.5)

        self._turtle.setheading(random.randrange(360))
        x = random.randrange(self._world.getWidth())
        y = random.randrange(self._world.getHeight())
        self._turtle.goto(x, y)

        if self._infected:
            self._turtle.color('red')
        else:
            self._turtle.color('blue')
```

First, we added a `myWorld` parameter that will serve as the `World` object to which the `Person` belongs. (We will implement `World` next.) We have also assigned `_turtle` to a `RawTurtle` object instead of a normal `Turtle` object. `RawTurtle` is just like `Turtle`, but it will allow us to do some fancier graphical interface things later. The `TurtleScreen` object named `self._world._screen` that we pass into the `RawTurtle` constructor is an instance variable of the `World` class. Its purpose is to make sure that every `Person` turtle draws in the same window. We also added some turtle formatting that will make each person a small circle. Finally, we give each person a random starting position, using the soon-to-be-implemented `getWidth` and `getHeight` methods of the `World` class to set the bounds of the position.

The second edit is to the **step** method as highlighted below.

```
    def step(self):
        """ (docstring omitted) """

        if random.random() < 0.1:
            self._turtle.left(random.randrange(-90, 90))
        self._turtle.forward(self._STEP)

        # wrap around to the other side of the world if necessary
        newX = self._turtle.xcor() % self._world.getWidth()
        newY = self._turtle.ycor() % self._world.getHeight()
        if self._turtle.position() != (newX, newY):
            self._turtle.goto(newX, newY)
```

This addition guards against a person stepping off the edge of the world. When this happens, rather than have them "bounce" back, we wrap them around to the other side by using modular arithmetic. In this way, the world is treated like a torus.

Reflection 12.6 *Create a new file named* person.py *containing the* Person *class. Start from the* SimplePerson *class and make the highlighted changes.*

World class

The constructor of the World class will take five parameters, in addition to self.

```
from person import *

class World:
    """A two-dimensional world class."""

    _INFECT_DISTANCE = 6    # class variable (constant)

    def __init__(self, width, height, infectProb, popSize, screen):
        """Create a new world with the given dimensions and infection
            probability, and populate it with one infected person and
            popSize - 1 uninfected people."""

        self._width = width
        self._height = height
        self._infectionProbability = infectProb
        self._screen = screen

        self._numberInfected = 1
        self._people = [Person(self, True)]  # one infected person

        for index in range(popSize - 1):       # uninfected people
            person = Person(self, False)
            self._people.append(person)
```

At the top of the file, we need to import the Person class so that we can create new people in the constructor. Just before the constructor is a class variable named _INFECT_DISTANCE which is how close someone needs to be to an infected person to become infected themselves.

Reflection 12.7 *How many instance variables does the* World *class have?*

The class has six instance variables. The first four, self._width, self._height, self._infectionProbability and self._screen, are initialized by parameters. The _screen instance variable is the name of the TurtleScreen object on which all of the Person turtles will be drawn. It will be created by the main program. The remainder of the constructor populates the world by creating a list named self._people containing one infected person and popSize - 1 uninfected people. The Person constructor is called to create each person.

In addition to the constructor, the `World` class will have the following three accessor methods.

```
def getWidth(self):
    """ (docstring omitted) """

    return self._width

def getHeight(self):
    """ (docstring omitted) """

    return self._height

def getNumberInfected(self):
    """ (docstring omitted) """

    return self._numberInfected
```

As in the `Person` class, these methods simply return the values of instance variables so that the instance variables are never accessed directly from outside the class. The `getWidth` and `getHeight` methods are used in the `step` method of the `Person` class, and the `getNumberInfected` method will be used by our main program to plot the number of infected individuals over the course of the simulation.

Finally, the `World` class is rounded out by two mutator methods.

```
def infectNeighbors(self, infectedPerson):
    """ (docstring omitted) """

    for otherPerson in self._people:
        if not otherPerson.isInfected() and \
          otherPerson.within(infectedPerson, self._INFECT_DISTANCE):
            if otherPerson.infect(self._infectionProbability):
                self._numberInfected = self._numberInfected + 1

def stepAll(self):
    """ (docstring omitted) """

    for person in self._people:
        person.step()
        if person.isInfected():
            self.infectNeighbors(person)
```

The `infectNeighbors` method takes an infected person as a parameter and then iterates over everyone in the world, infecting anyone within `self._INFECT_DISTANCE` with probability `self._infectionProbability`. If a person is successfully infected, the value of `self._numberInfected` is incremented. The `stepAll` method implements each step of the simulation, as we laid out at the beginning of the section.

| Reflection 12.8 *Create another new file named* `world.py` *containing the* World *class.*

The simulation

With our classes created, the following program will drive the simulation.

```
import turtle
from world import *

WIDTH = 600           # width of the world
HEIGHT = 600          # height of the world
NUM_PEOPLE = 200      # number of people to simulate
INFECTION_PROB = 0.5  # probability that someone gets infected

def main():
    worldScreen = turtle.Screen()      # a screen for the turtles
    worldScreen.setup(WIDTH, HEIGHT)   # set window size
    worldScreen.setworldcoordinates(0, 0, WIDTH - 1, HEIGHT - 1)
    worldScreen.tracer(0)              # turn off screen updates

    world = World(WIDTH, HEIGHT, INFECTION_PROB, NUM_PEOPLE, worldScreen)

    while world.getNumberInfected() < NUM_PEOPLE:  # until all infected
        world.stepAll()          # advance all people one step
        worldScreen.update()     # manually update screen after each step

    worldScreen.exitonclick()

main()
```

The `main` function creates a `Screen` object named `worldScreen` on which the turtles representing people can live. This is passed in as the last parameter of the `World` constructor. Then the program iterates until the number of infected people is equal to the total number of people. In each iteration, the simulation is advanced one step by calling `world.stepAll()`. A screenshot of the finished simulation is shown on the lefthand side of Figure 12.1.

> **Reflection 12.9** *Augment the* `main` *function so that it plots the number of infected people over the course of the simulation. Display your plot just before* `worldScreen.exitonclick()`. *It should look similar to the plot on the righthand side of Figure 12.1.*

On the book website you can find an augmented version of this program that incorporates sliders for the number of people and infection probability, and plots the number infected as the simulation is running. A screenshot is shown in Figure 12.2. This program also demonstrates how to use the graphics framework underlying turtle graphics, called `Tkinter`, to add graphical user interface elements to programs. Later in this chapter, we will design a more sophisticated agent-based simulation of flying birds in which each bird interacts with other birds in the flock, resulting in emergent flocking behavior.

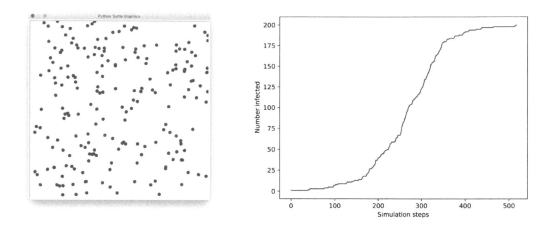

Figure 12.1 On the left is a screenshot midway through the epidemic simulation with 200 people and infection probability 0.5. On the right is a plot of the number infected.

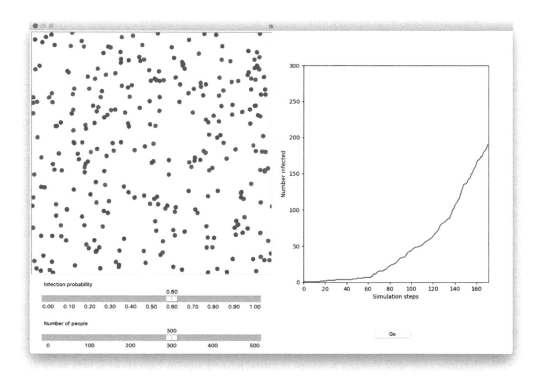

Figure 12.2 A screenshot midway through the augmented epidemic simulation.

Exercises

12.1.1* Name two accessor methods and two mutator methods in the `Turtle` class.

12.1.2. Name two accessor methods and two mutator methods in the `list` class.

12.1.3. Add a new method

```
allInfected(self)
```

to the `World` class that returns True if everyone in the world is infected, and False otherwise. Show how to use this new method in the `while` loop of the main simulation.

12.1.4* Add a new method

```
add(self, person)
```

to the `World` class that adds a new `Person` object named `person` to the world. If the person is infected, increment the value of `self._numberInfected`.

12.1.5. Add a new method

```
distance(self, otherPerson)
```

to the `Person` class that returns the distance between the `Person` objects `self` and `otherPerson`. Show how to use your new method to simplify the `within` method.

12.1.6. In this exercise, you will modify the epidemic simulation so that some people stay at home during the epidemic.

(a) Add a new instance variable to the `Person` class named `self._home`, initialized to False, which will indicate whether the person is sheltered at home.

(b) Add a method named `stayHome` to the `Person` class that sets `self._home` to True.

(c) Modify the `infect` method of the `Person` class so that a person at home cannot become infected.

(d) Modify the `step` method of the `Person` class so that the person does not move if they are at home.

(e) Add a parameter to the constructor of the `World` class that defines the probability that a person will stay home. In the loop that populates the world, call `person.stayHome()` with that probability.

(f) Run the simulation with these modifications. You will need to modify the loop in the `main` function so that it runs for a particular number of iterations (say, 1000) since now the entire population is unlikely to get infected all at once. What do you notice from the plot? (This assumes you have completed Reflection 12.9.)

12.1.7. In this exercise, you will modify the epidemic simulation so that infected people can recover and become immune after a specified number of simulation steps.

(a) Add two new instance variables to the `Person` class named `self._infectedSteps` and `self._immune`. The former counts the number of simulation steps that have elapsed since the person has been infected. The second is a Boolean value indicating whether the person is immune to the virus.

(b)   Add a method named `isImmune` to the `Person` class that returns the value of `self._immune`.

(c)   Modify the `infect` method of the `Person` class so that a person cannot become infected if they are immune.

(d)   Add a method named `isRecovered` to the `Person` class that checks if the person is infected and, if so, checks whether `self._infectedSteps` is equal to a constant class variable named `_INFECTION_PERIOD`. If this is the case, the person becomes infected so set the person's `self._infected` and `self._immune` instance variables appropriately and their turtle's color to yellow. If the person is infected but has not yet been so for `self._INFECTION_PERIOD` steps, the method should increment the value of `self._infectedSteps`. The method should return `True` if the person becomes newly immune or `False` otherwise.

(e)   Modify the `stepAll` method of the `World` class so that it calls `isRecovered` for every infected person in each iteration of the loop. If `isRecovered` returns `True`, then decrement the value of `self._numberInfected`.

(f)   Run the simulation with your modifications and the class variable `_INFECTION_PERIOD` set to 100. You will need to modify the loop as specified in part (f) of the previous exercise. What do you notice from the plot? (This assumes you have completed Reflection 12.9.)

12.1.8.   Design a research question you would like to investigate using the original epidemic simulation or the modified simulations from the previous two exercises. Run the simulation with various parameters to answer your question.

12.1.9*   (a)   Write a `BankAccount` class that has a single instance variable (the available balance), a constructor that takes the initial balance as a parameter, and methods `getBalance` (which should return the amount left in the account), `deposit` (which should deposit a given amount into the account), and `withdraw` (which should remove a given amount from the account).

(b)   Using your `BankAccount` class from part (a), write a program that prompts for an initial balance, creates a `BankAccount` object with this balance, and then repeatedly prompts for deposits or withdrawals. After each transaction, it should update the `BankAccount` object and print the current balance. For example:

```
Initial balance? 100
(D)eposit, (W)ithdraw, or (Q)uit? d
Amount = 50
Your balance is now $150.00
(D)eposit, (W)ithdraw, or (Q)uit? w
Amount = 25
Your balance is now $125.00
(D)eposit, (W)ithdraw, or (Q)uit? q
```

12.1.10. (a) Write a class that represents a U.S. president. The class should include instance variables for the president's name, party, home state, religion, and age when he or she took office. The constructor should initialize the president's name to a parameter value, but initialize all other instance variables to default values (empty strings or zero). Write accessor and mutator methods for all five instance variables.

(b) On the book website is a tab-separated file containing a list of all U.S. presidents with the five instance variables from part (a). Write a function that reads this information and returns a list of president objects representing all of the presidents in the file. Also, write a function that, given a list of president objects and an age, prints a table with all presidents who where at least that old when they took office, along with their ages when they took office.

12.1.11. Write a `Movie` class that has as instance variables the movie title, the movie year, and a list of actors (all of which are initialized in the constructor). Write accessor and modifier functions for all the instance variables and an `addActor` method that adds an actor to the list of actors in the movie. Finally, write a method that takes as a parameter *another* movie object and checks whether the two movies have any common actors.

There is a program on the book website with which to test your class. The program reads actors from a movie file (like those used in Project 11.3), and then prompts for movie titles. For each movie, you can print the actors, add an actor, and check whether the movie has actors in common with another movie.

12.1.12. (a) Write a class representing a U.S. senator. The `Senator` class should contain instance variables for the senator's name, political party, home state, and a list of committees on which they serve. The constructor should initialize all of the instance variables to parameter values, except for the list of committees, which should be initialized to an empty list. Add accessor methods for all four instance variables, plus a mutator method that adds a committee to a senator's list of committees.

(b) On the book website is a function that reads a list of senators from a file and returns a list of senator objects, using the `Senator` class that you wrote in the previous exercise. Write a program that uses this function to create a list of `Senator` objects, and then iterates over the list of `Senator` objects, printing each senator's name, party, and committees. Then your program should prompt repeatedly for the name of a committee, and print the names and parties of all senators who are on that committee.

12.1.13. Write a class named `Student` that has the following instance variables: student name, exam grades, quiz grades, lab grades, and paper grades. The constructor should only take the student name as a parameter, but initialize all the other instance variables (to empty lists). Write an accessor method for the name and methods to add grades to the lists of exam, quiz, paper, and lab grades. Next, write methods for returning the exam, quiz, paper, and lab averages. Finally, write a method to compute the final grade for the course, assuming the average exam grade is worth 50%, the average quiz grade is worth 10%, and the average lab and paper grades are worth 20% each.

12.1.14* Write a class that represents a set of numerical data from which simple descriptive statistics can be computed. The class should contain five methods, in addition to the constructor: add a new value to the data set, return the minimum and maximum values in the data set, return the average of the values in the data set, and return the size of the data set. Think carefully about the instance variables needed for this class. It is not actually necessary for the class to include a list of all of the values that have been added to it.

12.1.15. This exercise assumes you read Section 6.8. Write a `Sequence` class to represent a DNA, RNA, or amino acid sequence. The class should store the type of sequence, a sequence identifier (or accession number), and the sequence itself. Identify and implement at least three useful methods, in addition to the constructor.

12.2 OPERATORS AND POLYMORPHISM

Suppose you are on the planning commission for your local town, and are evaluating possible locations for a new high school. One consideration is how central the new school will be with respect to homes within the district. If you know the location of each home, then you can compute the most central location, called the *centroid*, with respect to the homes. The centroid is the point whose x and y coordinates are the average of the x and y coordinates of the homes. (You may recall centroids from Section 7.7.)

For example, the five black points below might represent five houses, each with (x, y) coordinates representing the east-west and north-south distances (in km), respectively, from the point $(0,0)$. The centroid of these points is shown in blue.

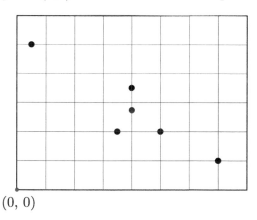

$(0, 0)$

If the points are represented by a list of tuples like

    homes = [(0.5, 5), (3.5, 2), (4, 3.5), (5, 2), (7, 1)]

then the following function can be used to return the centroid. (We will use abbreviated docstrings to save space.)

```
def centroid(points):
    """Compute the centroid of a list of points stored as tuples."""

    n = len(points)
    if n == 0:
        return None

    sumX = 0
    sumY = 0
    for point in points:
        sumX = sumX + point[0]
        sumY = sumY + point[1]
    return (sumX / n, sumY / n)
```

Calling `centroid(homes)` returns the tuple `(4, 2.7)`.

We can simplify working with points by designing a new, general-purpose *ordered pair* class. In addition to a geographic location, we could use this class to represent the (x,y) position of a particle, a (row, column) position in a grid, or a vector in two dimensions. The goal of this design will be to create a new utility class that behaves as if it was one of the standard Python classes. To that end, we want to be able to do arithmetic with pairs, print them, compare them, and even using indexing to access the individual elements.

Designing a Pair ADT

Let's begin by designing an ADT for this class. The obvious attributes are the two numbers, which we will simply name a and b.

Instance Variable	Description
a	the pair's first value
b	the pair's second value

> **Reflection 12.10** *What methods do we need for our pair ADT if we want to use it to compute centroids?*

The `centroid` function added points and divided by a scalar value, so we at least need those two operations. We will also need a constructor, and we should include methods to access and change the numbers in the pair. These operations are summarized in the table below.

Method	Arguments	Description
create	a and b	create a new pair instance (a, b)
getFirst	—	return the first value of the pair
getSecond	—	return the second value of the pair
get	—	return a tuple (a, b) representing the pair
add	pair 2	return a new pair that is the sum of this pair and pair 2
set	a and b	set new a and b values of the pair
scale	a number	multiply the values of a and b in the pair by number

Pair class

Let's now implement the **Pair** abstract data type as a class. We will start with the constructor and four other straightforward methods.

```python
class Pair:
    """An ordered pair class."""

    def __init__(self, a = 0, b = 0):
        """Create a new Pair object initialized to (a, b)."""

        self._a = a    # the pair's first value
        self._b = b    # the pair's second value

    def getFirst(self):
        """ (docstring omitted) """

        return self._a

    def getSecond(self):
        """ (docstring omitted) """

        return self._b

    def get(self):
        """ (docstring omitted) """

        return (self._a, self._b)

    def set(self, a, b):
        """ (docstring omitted) """

        self._a = a
        self._b = b
```

❙ **Reflection 12.11** *Create a new file* `pair.py` *containing this class.*

The = 0 following each of the a and b parameters in the constructor is specifying a *default argument*. This allows us to call the constructor with either no arguments, in which case 0 will be assigned to a and b, or with explicit arguments for a and b that will override the default arguments. If we supply only one argument, then a will be assigned to it, and 0 will be assigned to b. For example:

```
pair1 = Pair()         # pair1 will represent (0, 0)
pair2 = Pair(3)        # pair2 will represent (3, 0)
pair3 = Pair(3, 14)    # pair3 will represent (3, 14)
```

Reflection 12.12 *How would you create a new* Pair *object with value* $(0, 18)$*?*

Arithmetic methods

We define the sum of two pairs (a, b) and (c, d) as the pair $(a + c, b + d)$. For example, $(3, 8) + (4, 5) = (7, 13)$. If we represented pairs as tuples, then an addition function would look like this:

```
def add(pair1, pair2):
    """Return a tuple representing the sum of tuples pair1 and pair2."""

    return (pair1[0] + pair2[0], pair1[1] + pair2[1])
```

To use this function to find (3, 8) + (4, 5), we could do the following:

```
duo1 = (3, 8)
duo2 = (4, 5)
sumPair = add(duo1, duo2)     # sumPair is assigned (7, 13)
print(sumPair)                # prints "(7, 13)"
```

In an analogous **add** *method* for the **Pair** class, one of the points will be assigned to **self** and the other will be assigned to a parameter, as shown below.

```
def add(self, pair2):
    """Return a new Pair that is the sum of Pairs self and pair2."""

    sumA = self._a + pair2._a
    sumB = self._b + pair2._b
    return Pair(sumA, sumB)
```

Notice that the method creates and returns a *new* **Pair** object. To find the sum of two **Pair** objects named **duo1** and **duo2**, we could call this method as follows:

```
duo1 = Pair(3, 8)
duo2 = Pair(4, 5)
sumPair = duo1.add(duo2)      # sumPair is assigned Pair(7, 13)
print(sumPair.get())          # prints "(7, 13)"
```

When the **add** method is called, **duo1** is assigned to **self** and **duo2** is assigned to **pair2**.

Reflection 12.13 *Add the* **add** *method to your* **Pair** *class. Then, define two new* **Pair** *objects in a* **main** *function and compute their sum. Because you may wish to import this module in the future, be sure to call* **main** *like this:*

```
    if __name__ == '__main__':
        main()
```

Reflection 12.14 *Using the* add *method as a template, write a* subtract *method that subtracts another* Pair *object from* self.

In contrast to add, the **scale** method, as we defined it above, will modify the existing object rather than create a new one:

```
        def scale(self, scalar):
            """Multiply the values in self by a scalar value."""

            self.set(self._a * scalar, self._b * scalar)
```

The scale method takes a numerical value (called a *scalar* in mathematics) as a parameter and uses the set method to multiply it by the values of self._a and self._b.

Reflection 12.15 *How could you write the* scale *method without calling* self.set?

Reflection 12.16 *Add the* scale *method to your class and use it on some* Pair *objects in your* main *function.*

Let's now revisit the **centroid** function, but modify it to handle a list of **Pair** objects instead of a list of tuples. The changes are highlighted below in red.

```
def centroid(points):
    """Compute the centroid of a list of Pair objects."""

    n = len(points)
    if n == 0:
        return None

    sumPair = Pair()                        # sumPair is the Pair (0, 0)
    for point in points:
        sumPair = sumPair.add(point)        # sumPair = sumPair + point
    sumPair.scale(1 / n)                     # divide sumPair by n
    return sumPair
```

We have replaced the two sumX and sumY variables with a single sumPair variable, initialized to the pair $(0,0)$. Inside the for loop, each value of point, which is now a Pair object, is added to sumPair using the add method. After the loop, we use the scale method to multiply the point by 1 / n which, of course, is the same as dividing by n.

To use this function on the homes list from earlier, we would need to assign homes to be a list of Pair objects instead of tuples.

```
homes = [Pair(0.5, 5), Pair(3.5, 2), Pair(4, 3.5), Pair(5, 2), Pair(7, 1)]
central = centroid(homes)   # central is a Pair object
print(central.get())
```

Printing the value of the centroid is slightly more cumbersome because we have to convert it to a tuple first with the get method, but we will fix that shortly.

Reflection 12.17 *Add the code above to your* main *function. What is the value of the centroid?*

Special methods

The centroid method would be even more elegant if we could simply add Pair objects with the + operator. We have already seen how the + operator can be used with a variety of different classes, including numbers, strings and lists, so why not Pair objects too? The ability to define operators differently for different classes is called ***operator overloading***. Operator overloading is an example of ***polymorphism***, a feature of object-oriented programming languages in which methods and operators respond differently to objects of different classes. For example, consider the following list of different objects:

```
>>> things = [42, 'eggs ', [1, 2, 3], 3.14]
```

If we multiply every item in this list by 2, the multiplication operator will act differently for each item, appropriate to its class:

```
>>> for item in things:
        print(item * 2)
84
eggs eggs
[1, 2, 3, 1, 2, 3]
6.28
```

When the + operator is used, a *special method* named __add__ is implicitly called (like how __init__ is implicitly called by the constructor). In other words, an assignment statement like

```
name = first + last
```

is identical to

```
name = first.__add__(last)
```

The ability to define this special method for each class is what allows us to use the + operator in different ways on different objects. We can implement the + operator on Pair objects by simply changing the name of our add method to __add__:

```
def __add__(self, pair2):
    """ (docstring omitted) """

    sumA = self._a + pair2._a
    sumB = self._b + pair2._b
    return Pair(sumA, sumB)
```

With this special method defined, we can carry out our previous example as follows:

```
duo1 = Pair(3, 8)
duo2 = Pair(4, 5)
sumPair = duo1 + duo2    # sumPair is assigned Pair(7, 13)
print(sumPair.get())     # prints "(7, 13)"
```

Reflection 12.18 *Incorporate the __add__ method into your* Pair *class and experiment with adding* Pair *objects.*

Reflection 12.19 *The behavior of the - operator is similarly defined by the __sub__ method. Modify your* subtract *method so that it is called when the - operator is used with* Pair *objects.*

Similarly, we can define the * and / operators to implement multiplication and division with Pair objects. The methods corresponding to these operators are named __mul__ and __truediv__, respectively. (Recall that / is called true division in Python while // is called floor division. The // operator is defined by the __floordiv__ method.) Defining multiplication of a Pair object by a scalar quantity is similar to the scale method, but we return a new Pair instead.

```
def __mul__(self, scalar):
    """Return a new Pair representing self multiplied by scalar."""

    return Pair(self._a * scalar, self._b * scalar)
```

Reflection 12.20 *How is the __mul__ method different from* scale? *What does each return?*

With this new method, we can easily scale pairs of numbers in one statement:

```
bets = Pair(150, 100)
double = bets * 2      # double is assigned Pair(300, 200)
```

This assignment statement is equivalent to

```
double = bets.__mul__(2)
```

(but we would never call it that way).

Reflection 12.21 *Why would typing* double = 2 * bets *instead give an error?*

Reflection 12.22 *Using the __mul__ operator as a template, write the __truediv__ method to divide a* Pair *object by a scalar value.*

Applying the new addition and (true) division operators to our **centroid** function makes the code much more elegant!

```
def centroid(points):
    """Compute the centroid of a list of Pair objects."""

    n = len(points)
    if n == 0:
        return None

    sumPair = Pair()
    for point in points:
        sumPair = sumPair + point
    return sumPair / n
```

You may have already noticed that printing a Pair object is not very helpful:

```
>>> myPair = Pair(5, 7)
>>> print(myPair)
<__main__.Pair object at 0x1063551d0>
```

This is a default string representation of an object; it tells us that `myPair` is a `Pair` object in the `__main__` namespace, located in memory at address `1063551d0` (in hexadecimal notation). To override the default printing behavior for a `Pair`, we need to define another special method named `__str__`. The `__str__` method is called implicitly whenever we call the `str` function on an object. In other words, calling

```
str(myPair)
```

is identical to calling

```
myPair.__str__()
```

Since the `print` function implicitly calls `str` on an object, defining the `__str__` method also dictates how `print` behaves. The following `__str__` method for the `Pair` class returns a string representing the pair in parentheses (like a tuple).

```
def __str__(self):
    """Return an '(a, b)' string representation of self."""

    return '(' + str(self._a) + ', ' + str(self._b) + ')'
```

With this method added to the class, if we want to include a string representation of a `Pair` object in a larger string, we can do something like this:

```
print('The current values are ' + str(myPair) + '.')
```

Also, just calling `print(myPair)` will now print `(5, 7)`.

> **Reflection 12.23** *Add the* `__str__` *method to your* `Pair` *class. Then print some of the* `Pair` *objects in your* `main` *function.*

Comparison operators

We can also overload the comparison operators `==`, `<`, `<=`, etc. using the following special methods.

Operator	==	!=	<	<=	>	>=
Method	__eq__	__ne__	__lt__	__le__	__gt__	__ge__

We will start by defining how the `==` operator behaves by defining the special method `__eq__`. It is natural to say that two pairs are equal if their corresponding values are equal, as the following method implements.

```
def __eq__(self, pair2):
    """Return whether self and pair2 have the same values."""

    return (self._a == pair2._a) and (self._b == pair2._b)
```

Let's also override the < operator. If duo1 and duo2 are two Pair objects, then duo1 < duo2 should return True if duo1._a < duo2._a, or if duo1._a == duo2._a and duo1._b < duo2._b. Otherwise, it should return False.

```
    def __lt__(self, pair2):
        """Return whether self < pair2."""

        return (self._a < pair2._a) or \
               ((self._a == pair2._a) and (self._b < pair2._b))
```

Suppose we store the number of wins and ties in a Pair object for each of three teams. If a team is ranked higher when it has more wins, and the number of ties is used to rank teams with the same number of wins, then the comparison operators we defined can be used to decide rankings.

```
wins1 = Pair(6, 2)      # 6 wins, 2 ties
wins2 = Pair(6, 4)      # 6 wins, 4 ties
wins3 = Pair(6, 2)      # 6 wins, 2 ties

print(wins1 < wins2)    # prints "True"
print(wins2 < wins3)    # prints "False"
print(wins1 == wins3)   # prints "True"
```

With the __eq__ and __lt__ methods defined, Python will automatically deduce the outcomes of the other four comparison operators. However, we will still leave their implementations to you as practice exercises.

> **Reflection 12.24** *Add these two new methods to your* Pair *class. Experiment with some comparisons, including those we did not implement, in your* main *function.*

Indexing

When an element in a string, list, tuple, or dictionary is accessed with indexing, a special method named __getitem__ is implicitly called. For example, if **maxPrices** and **minPrices** are lists, then

```
priceRange = maxPrices[0] - minPrices[0]
```

is equivalent to

```
priceRange = maxPrices.__getitem__(0) - minPrices.__getitem__(0)
```

Similarly, when we use indexing to change the value of an element in a sequence, a method named __setitem__ is implicitly called. For example,

```
temperatures[1] = 18.9
```

is equivalent to

```
temperatures.__setitem__(1, 18.9)
```

In the Pair class, we can use indexing with __getitem__ as an alternative to the getFirst and getSecond methods to access the individual values in a Pair object.

```
def __getitem__(self, index):
    """Return the first (index 0) or second (index 1) value in self.
       For other index values, return None."""

    if index == 0:
        return self._a
    if index == 1:
        return self._b
    return None
```

The `__getitem__` method returns the value of `self._a` or `self._b` if index is 0 or 1, respectively. If index is anything else, it returns `None`.

Reflection 12.25 *Is this behavior consistent with what happens when you use an erroneous index with a list?*

When we use an erroneous index with an object from one of the built-in classes, we get a `IndexError`. We will look at how to implement this alternative behavior in Sections 12.4 and 12.5.

As an example, suppose we have a `Pair` object defined as follows:

```
counts = Pair(12, 15)
```

With the new `__getitem__` method, we can retrieve the individual values in `counts` with

```
first = counts[0]
second = counts[1]
```

as these statements are equivalent to

```
first = counts.__getitem__(0)
second = counts.__getitem__(1)
```

Next, we can implement the `__setitem__` method as follows.

```
def __setitem__(self, index, value):
    """Set the first (index 0) or second (index 1) item to value."""

    if index == 0:
        self._a = value
    elif index == 1:
        self._b = value
```

The `__setitem__` method assigns `self._a` or `self._b` to the given `value` if `index` is 0 or 1, respectively.

Reflection 12.26 *What does the `__setitem__` method do if index is not 0 or 1?*

With the new `__setitem__` method, we can assign a new value to `counts` with

```
counts[0] = 14
counts[1] = 16
print(counts)    # prints "(14, 16)"
```

With these indexing methods defined, we can now also use indexing within other methods, as convenient. For example, we can use indexing in the `__add__` method to get the individual values and in the `set` method to assign new values.

```
    def __add__(self, pair2):
        """ (docstring omitted) """

        sumA = self[0] + pair2[0]
        sumB = self[1] + pair2[1]
        return Pair(sumA, sumB)

    def set(self, a, b):
        """ (docstring omitted) """

        self[0] = a
        self[1] = b
```

Reflection 12.27 *Add the two indexing methods to your* Pair *class. Then modify the* __lt__ *method so that it uses indexing to access values of* self._a *and* self._b *instead.*

You can find a summary of these and other special methods in Appendix A.9.

Exercises

12.2.1* Add a method to the Pair class named **round** that rounds the two values to the nearest integers.

12.2.2* Suppose you are tallying the votes in an election between two candidates. Write a program that repeatedly prompts for additional votes for both candidates, stores these votes in a Pair object, and then adds this Pair object to a running sum of votes, also stored in Pair object. For example, your program output may look like this:

```
Enter votes (q to quit): 1 2
Enter votes (q to quit): 2 4
Enter votes (q to quit): q

Candidate 1: 3 votes
Candidate 2: 6 votes
```

12.2.3* Suppose you are writing code for a runner's watch that keeps track of a list of split times and total elapsed times. While the timer is running, and the split button is pressed, the time elapsed since the last split is recorded in a Pair object along with the total elapsed time so far. For example, if the split button were pressed at 65, 67, and 62 second intervals, the list of (split, elapsed) pairs would be [(65, 65), (67, 132), (62, 194)] (where a tuple represents a Pair object). Write a function that is meant to be called when the split button is pressed to update this list of Pair objects. Your function should take two parameters: the current list of Pair objects and the current split time.

12.2.4. A data logging program for a jetliner periodically records the time along with the current altitude in a Pair object. Write a function that takes such a list of Pair objects as a parameter and plots the data using **matplotlib**.

12.2.5. Write a function that returns the distance between two two-dimensional points, each represented as a Pair object.

12.2.6. Write a function that returns the average distance between a list of points, each represented by a Pair object, and a given site, also represented as a Pair object.

12.2.7. The file `africa.txt`, available on the book website, contains (longitude, latitude) locations for cities on the African continent. The following program reads this file into a list of `Pair` objects, find the closest and farthest pairs of points in the list, and then plot all of the points using turtle graphics, coloring the closest pair blue and farthest pair red. Finish this program by adding a method named `draw(self, tortoise, color)` to the `Pair` class that plots a `Pair` object as an (x,y) point, and writing the functions named `closestPairs` and `farthestPairs`.

```python
import turtle

class Pair:
    FILL IN THE CLASS HERE FROM THE TEXT

    def draw(self, tortoise, color):
        pass

def closestPairs(points):
    pass

def farthestPairs(points):
    pass

def main():
    points = []
    inputFile = open('africa.txt', 'r', encoding = 'utf-8')
    for line in inputFile:
        values = line.split()
        longitude = float(values[0])
        latitude = float(values[1])
        p = Pair(longitude, latitude)
        points.append(p)

    cpoint1, cpoint2 = closestPairs(points)
    fpoint1, fpoint2 = farthestPairs(points)

    george = turtle.Turtle()
    screen = george.getscreen()
    screen.setworldcoordinates(-37, -23, 37, 58)
    george.hideturtle()
    george.speed(0)
    screen.tracer(10)
    for point in points:
        point.draw(george, 'black')
    cpoint1.draw(george, 'blue')
    cpoint2.draw(george, 'blue')
    fpoint1.draw(george, 'red')
    fpoint2.draw(george, 'red')
    screen.update()
    screen.exitonclick()

main()
```

12.2.8. Rewrite the `Pair` class so that it stores its two values in a two-element list instead. The way in which the class' methods are called should remain exactly the same. In other words, the way someone uses the class (the ADT specification) must remain the same even though the implementation changes.

12.2.9* Implement alternative `__mul__` and `__truediv__` methods for the `Pair` class that multiply two `Pair` objects. The product of two `Pair` objects `pair1` and `pair2` is a `Pair` object in which the first value is the product of the first values of `pair1` and `pair2`, and the second value is the product of the second values of `pair1` and `pair2`. Division is defined similarly.

12.2.10. Implement the remaining four comparison operators (`!=`, `<=`, `>`, `>=`) for the `Pair` class.

12.2.11. Rewrite your `linearRegression` function from Exercise 7.6.1 so that it takes a list of `Pair` objects as a parameter.

12.2.12. Add a `__str__` method to the president class that you wrote in Exercise 12.1.10. The method should return a string containing the president's name and political party, for example, `'Kennedy (D)'`. Also, write a function that, given a list of president objects and a state abbreviation, prints the presidents in this list (indirectly using the new `__str__` method) that are from that state.

12.2.13. Add a `__lt__` method to the president class that you wrote in Exercise 12.1.10. The method should base its results on a comparison of the presidents' ages.

12.2.14. Add a `__str__` method to the `Senator` class from Exercise 12.1.12 that prints the name of the senator followed by their party, for example, `'Brown, Sherrod (D)'`. Also modify your program from part (b) so that it uses the new `__str__` method.

12.2.15. Rewrite the distance function from Exercise 12.2.5 so that it uses indexing to get the first and second values from each pair.

12.2.16. Write a class that represents a rational number (i.e., a number that can be represented as a fraction). The constructor for your class should take a numerator and denominator as parameters. In addition, implement the following methods for your class:

- arithmetic: `__add__`, `__sub__`, `__mul__`, `__truediv__`
- comparison: `__lt__`, `__eq__`, `__le__`
- `__str__`

When you are done, you should be able to perform calculations like the following:

```
a = Rational(3, 2)    # 3/2
b = Rational(1, 3)    # 1/3
total = a + b
print(total)          # should print 11/6
print(a < b)          # should print False
```

*12.3 A FLOCKING SIMULATION

This section is available on the book website.

*12.4 A STACK ADT

This section is available on the book website.

*12.5 A DICTIONARY ADT

This section is available on the book website.

12.6 SUMMARY AND FURTHER DISCOVERY

When we design an algorithm using an object-oriented approach, we begin by identifying the main objects in our problem, and then define abstract data types for them. When we design a new ADT, we need to identify the data that the ADT will contain and the operations that will be allowed on that data. These operations are generally organized into three categories: *constructors*, *accessors*, and *mutators*.

In an *object-oriented programming language* like Python, abstract data types are implemented as *classes*. A Python class contains a set of functions called *methods* and a set of *instance variables* whose names are preceded by self within the class. The name self always refers to the object on which a method is called. Bundling instance variables and methods together in a class, and restricting public access to the instance variables, is known as *encapsulation*, a key feature of object-oriented programming.

A class can also define the meaning of several *special methods* that dictate how operators and built-in functions behave on the class. These special methods partially implement another feature of object-oriented languages called *polymorphism*, which refers to the ability of a programming language to do different things when the same method is called on objects from different classes.

The manner in which a class implements the specification given by the abstract data type is called a *data structure*. There may be many different data structures that one can use to implement a particular abstract data type. For example, the **Pair** ADT from the beginning of this chapter may be implemented with two individual variables, a list of length two, a two-element tuple, or a dictionary with two entries.

To illustrate how classes are used in larger programs, we designed an *agent-based simulation* that simulates a viral epidemic in the first section and then a more complex simulation of flocking birds or schooling fish later on. These simulations consist of two main classes that interact with each other: an agent class and a class for the world that the agents inhabit. Agent-based simulations can be used in a variety of disciplines including sociology, biology, economics, and the physical sciences.

Finally, we designed two *collection* classes, a **Stack** and a **Dictionary**, to demonstrate how more complex classes can be implemented in Python.

Notes for further discovery

This chapter's epigraph is from one of the first papers written by Barbara Liskov, in 1974 [35]. In 1968, Dr. Liskov was one of the first women to earn a Ph.D. in computer science in the United States. She has taught computer science at MIT since 1972, and was honored with the Turing Award in 2008.

The boids model was created by Craig Reynolds [54]. For more information on agent-based simulations, we suggest looking at *The Computational Beauty of Nature* by Gary Flake [17], *Think Complexity* by Allen Downey [13], *Agent-based Models* by Nigel Gilbert [19], and *Introduction to Computational Science* by Angela Shiflet and George Shiflet [61].

*12.7 PROJECTS

This section is available on the book website.

Bibliography

[1] Edwin A. Abbott. Flatland: A Romance of Many Dimensions. Dover Publications, 1992.

[2] Kevin A. Agatstein. Oscillating Systems II: Sustained Oscillation. *MIT System Dynamics in Education Project*, `http://ocw.mit.edu/courses/` `sloan-school-of-management/15-988-system-dynamics-self-study` `-fall-1998-spring-1999/readings/oscillating2.pdf`, 2001.

[3] Albert-László Barabási. Linked: How Everything is Connected to Everything Else and What It Means for Business, Science, and Everyday Life. Plume, 2003.

[4] Al-Khwārizmī, Muḥammad ibn Mūsā. The Compendious Book on Calculation by Completion and Balancing. Translated by Frederic Rosen as *The Algebra of Mohammed ben Musa*, 1831. `https://www.wilbourhall.org/pdfs/The_Algebra_of_Mohammed_` `Ben_Musa2.pdf`

[5] Frank Bass. A new product growth model for consumer durables. *Management Science* 15(5):215–227, 1969.

[6] Ruha Benjamin. Race after Technology: Abolitionist Tools for the New Jim Code. Polity Press, 2019.

[7] Peter J. Bentley. Digitized: The Science of Computers and How It Shapes Our World. Oxford University Press, 2012.

[8] Yogi Berra with Dave Kaplan. When you Come to a Fork in the Road, Take it! Inspiration and Wisdom from One of Baseball's Greatest Heroes. Hyperion, 2001.

[9] Carey Caginalp. Analytical and Numerical Results on Escape of Brownian Particles. B. Phil. thesis, University of Pittsburgh, 2011.

[10] William J. Cook. In Pursuit of the Traveling Salesman: Mathematics at the Limits of Computation. Princeton University Press, 2012.

[11] Kord Davis. Ethics of Big Data: Balancing Risk and Innovation. O'Reilly Media, 2012.

[12] Delta Airlines North American route map. `https://www.delta.com/content/dam/` `delta-www/pdfs/route-maps/us-route-map.pdf`

[13] Allen B. Downey. Think Complexity. O'Reilly Media, 2012.

[14] Sir Arthur Conan Doyle. The Adventures of Sherlock Holmes. Harper, 1892.

[15] Charles Duhigg. How Companies Learn Your Secrets. *The New York Times*, `http://www.` `nytimes.com/2012/02/19/magazine/shopping-habits.html`, published February 16, 2012.

[16] Michael R. Fellows and Ian Parberry. SIGACT trying to get children excited about CS. *Computing Research News*, p. 7, January 1993.

[17] Gary W. Flake. The Computational Beauty of Nature. MIT Press, 2000.

[18] J. Fletcher. An Arithmetic Checksum for Serial Transmissions. *IEEE Transactions on Communications* 30(1):247–252, 1982.

[19] Nigel Gilbert. Agent-Based Models. SAGE Publications, 2008.

[20] Shawn Graham, Ian Milligan, and Scott Weingart. Exploring Big Historical Data: the Historian's Macroscope. Imperial College Press, 2016.

[21] Jessica Guynn. Marissa Mayer talks about Google at 10 — and 20. *Los Angeles Times*, http://latimesblogs.latimes.com/technology/2008/09/marissa-mayer-t.html, September 7, 2008.

[22] David Harel. Algorithmics: The Spirit of Computing, third edition. Addison-Wesley, 2004.

[23] W. Daniel Hillis. The Pattern On The Stone: The Simple Ideas That Make Computers Work. Basic Books, 1998.

[24] Eric Hobsbawm. The Age of Extremes: A History of the World, 1914-1991. Vintage Books, 1994.

[25] Andrew Hodges. Alan Turing: The Enigma. Princeton University Press, 1983.

[26] Matthew L. Jockers. Macroanalysis: Digital Methods & Literary History. University of Illinois Press, 2013.

[27] Deborah G. Johnson with Keith W. Miller. Computer Ethics: Analyzing Information Technology, fourth edition. Prentice Hall, 2009.

[28] Steven Johnson. Emergence: The Connected Lives of Ants, Brains, Cities, and Software. Scribner, 2001.

[29] William O. Kermack and Anderson G. McKendrick. A Contribution to the Mathematical Theory of Epidemics. *Proceedings of the Royal Society A* 115: 700–721, 1927.

[30] Joseph Migga Kizza. Ethical and Secure Computing: A Concise Module, Second Edition. Springer Nature, 2019.

[31] Donald E. Knuth. The Art of Computer Programming, volumes 1–4A. Addison-Wesley, 1968–2011.

[32] Donald E. Knuth. Computer Programming as an Art. *Communications of the ACM* 17(12):667–673, 1974.

[33] Donald E. Knuth. Computer Science and Mathematics. *American Scientist* 61(6), 1973.

[34] Ehud Lamm and Ron Unger. Biological Computation. Chapman & Hall/CRC Press, 2011.

[35] Barbara Liskov and Stephen Zilles. Programming with Abstract Data Types. In *Proceedings of the ACM Conference on Very High Level Languages*, SIGPLAN Notices 9(4):50–59, 1974.

[36] Mark Lutz. Programming Python. O'Reilly Media, 1996.

[37] John MacCormick. Nine Algorithms that Changed the Future. Princeton University Press, 2013.

[38] Benoit B. Mandelbrot. The Fractal Geometry of Nature. Macmillan, 1983.

[39] Steve McConnell. Software Project Survival Guide: How to Be Sure Your First Important Project Isn't Your Last. Microsoft Press, 1998.

[40] Stanley Milgram. The Small-World Problem. *Psychology Today* 1(1):61–67, May 1967.

[41] Leonard Mlodinow. The Drunkard's Walk: How Randomness Rules Our Lives. Vintage Books, 2009.

[42] Philip Morrison and Phylis Morrison. 100 or so Books that shaped a Century of Science. *American Scientist* 87(6), November—December 1999.

[43] Alexander J. Nicholson and Victor A. Bailey. The Balance of Animal Populations—Part I. *Proceedings of the Zoological Society of London* 105:551—598, 1935.

[44] Safiya Umoja Noble. Algorithms of Oppression: How Search Engines Reinforce Racism. New York University Press, 2018.

[45] Cathy O'Neil. Weapons of Math Destruction: How Big Data Increases Inequality and Threatens Democracy. Broadway Books, 2016.

[46] Stephen K. Park and Keith W. Miller. Random Number Generators: Good Ones Are Hard to Find. *Communications of the ACM* 31(10):1192–1201, 1988.

[47] William R. Pearson and David J. Lipman. Improved Tools for Biological Sequence Comparison. *Proceedings of the National Academy of Science* 85(8):2444–2448, 1988.

[48] Jean R. Petit, *et al.* Climate and Atmospheric History of the Past 420,000 years from the Vostok Ice Core, Antarctica. *Nature* 399:429–436.

[49] Charles Petzold. CODE: The Hidden Language of Computer Hardware and Software. Microsoft Press, 2000.

[50] George Polya. How to Solve It: A New Aspect of Mathematical Method. Princeton University Press, 1945.

[51] Jean-Yves1 Potvin. Genetic algorithms for the traveling salesman problem. *Annals of Operations Research* 63(3):337–370, 1996.

[52] Przemyslaw Prusinkiewicz and Aristid Lindenmayer. The Algorithmic Beauty of Plants. `http://algorithmicbotany.org/papers/abop/abop.pdf`, 1990.

[53] Mitchell Resnick. Turtles, Termites, and Traffic Jams: Explorations in Massively Parallel Microworlds. MIT Press, 1994.

[54] Craig W. Reynolds. Flocks, Herds, and Schools: A Distributed Behavioral Model. *Computer Graphics, SIGGRAPH '87* 21(4):25–34, 1987.

[55] Michael C. Schatz and Ben Langmead. The DNA Data Deluge. *IEEE Spectrum* 50(7):28–33, 2013.

[56] Thomas C. Schelling. Dynamic Models of Segregation. *Journal of Mathematical Sociology* 1:143–186, 1971.

[57] Thomas C. Schelling. Micromotives and Macrobehavior. W. W. Norton & Company, 1978.

[58] Rachel Schutt and Cathy O'Neil. Doing Data Science. O'Reilly Media, 2014.

[59] Dr. Seuss. The Sneetches and Other Stories. Random House, 1961.

[60] Dennis Shasha and Cathy Lazere. Natural Computing: DNA, Quantum Bits, and the Future of Smart Machines. W. W. Norton & Company, 2010.

[61] Angela B. Shiflet and George W. Shiflet. Introduction to Computational Science: Modeling and Simulation for the Sciences, second edition. Princeton University Press, 2014.

[62] Ian Stewart. The Mathematics of Life. Basic Books, 2011.

[63] Steven Strogatz. Sync: How Order Emerges from Chaos in the Universe, Nature, and Daily Life. Hyperion, 2003.

[64] Alexander L. Taylor III, Peter Stoler, and Michael Moritz. The Wizard inside the Machine *Time* 123(6):64–73, April 1984.

[65] Christophe Van den Bulte and Yogesh V. Joshi. New Product Diffusion with Influentials and Imitators. *Marketing Science* 26(3):400–421, 2007.

[66] Duncan J. Watts. Six Degrees: The Science of a Connected Age. W. W. Norton & Company, 2004.

[67] Wikipedia. Electricity sector in New Zealand. `http://en.wikipedia.org/w/index.php?title=Electricity_sector_in_New_Zealand`, 2014.

[68] James Zachos, *et al.* Trends, Rhythms, and Aberrations in Global Climate 65 Ma to Present. *Science* 292: 686–692, 2001.

[69] `http://www.pd4pic.com/nautilus-cephalopods-sea-holiday-memory-housing-2.html`, 2015.

[70] `http://photojournal.jpl.nasa.gov/jpeg/PIA03424.jpg`, 2015.

[71] `http://www.pd4pic.com/leaf-green-veins-radiating-patterned.html`, 2015.

[72] `http://www.pd4pic.com/strait-of-malacca-sky-clouds-lightning-storm.html`, 2015.

Index

Page numbers of the form O⟨section⟩-⟨page⟩ and P⟨project⟩-⟨page⟩ refer to page numbers in sections and projects, respectively, that are available on the book website.